The Mans' Digest

Copyright © 2009 Raymond Claude Perdue

Cover and Text Design by: Vince Pannullo
Editor by: Richelle

Published by:
Dudley Publications
P.O. Box 1392
Steubenville, OH 43952

All rights reserved. No part of this publication may be reproduced, stored in a retrieval system or transmitted, in any form, or by any means, electronic, mechanical, recorded, photocopied, or otherwise, without the prior permission of the copyright owner, except by a reviewer who may quote brief passages in a review.

Printed in the United States of America

ISBN # 978-0-578-01110-3

The Mans' Digest

A story of love toward & from women, & respect toward and from men.

by

Raymond Claude Perdue

DEDICATION

THIS book is dedicated to the memory of Ms. E.R. Minor and fond memories at Edward Waters College. Ms. Eleanor Minor was a black lady, with a law degree in the south, and disallowed to practice law during the early and mid-sixties, because of her sex and race. This writer is fortunate in having been taught the course "Shakespeare" by her at the oldest black college in the state of Florida.

She also became director of the public relations department during the mentioned time period at the small, private, church related school. This writer, through the lady's aid and assistance, replaced her as that department's head, during his senior year, and carried through until he graduated from the institution in Jacksonville. She did not live through the following decade; never having been married and having no children, it is doubtful she is regularly thought of, except by this one.

This entire composition (cover & contents) is dedicated to the memory of the person mentioned above.

Question:

If a tiger was tamed would it still be a tiger?. . .

Disclaimer

THIS is a work of fiction, conceived through the imagination of the writer. Any similarities pertaining to facts related to this story or its characters are coincidental.

– Facts about the Author –

IN completing his initial book "The Toe", and while working on "The Mans' Digest" Raymond Claude Perdue found his way to Tampa, Florida after an extensive amount of traveling. Other than having been a boy scout, a U.S. Army soldier, and a registered voter, his only professional ties are with NATRA – National Association for Television and Radio Announcers. The Tampa Bay vicinity is now hailed as "The City of Champions" due to the Lightnings' (Hockey Team) winning the Stanley Cup and The Buccaneers' (NFL Football Team) winning the Vince Lombardi Trophy.

Too, Portland, Oregon is the home of the University of Portland and the Trailblazers Basketball Team. The School sits in a glade, on a bluff overlooking the Willamette River, which is the seaport of the industrious city. While in attendance, the school was second to MIT in engineering and second to Villanova in nursing. The small school is the only sister school to Notre Dame, and affords one of the top 10 "Most Beautiful" campuses in America. It was No.1 in Communications, which was Perdues' graduate major; during his stay, the Trail Blazers won their only NBA Championship.

"Ray" Claude Perdue looks forward in sharing with you "The Mans' Digest" Part II – An evening with Cindy. Perhaps his future writings of romance and adventure will lead him through the streets of your city, or the roads in your town, in his travels in America.

Raymond Claude Perdue, *The Mans' Digest. Book Synopsis*

What began as a road trip for two friends, who had not seen each other in more than a decade, turns out to be a roller coaster ride of adventure in pursuit of sex and fun. Soame and Frank bill this as a romantic-adventure novel of intense exploration and keen on the spot wit. The ingenuity and know how of the story's main character lead to the revitalization of a small Midwestern town and its inhabitants.

At a random motel stop en route to Los Angeles Frank, Soame's partner decides to have fun and tap into the phone in the next room. After discovering a drun and drop-off exchange, they decide to seize the opportunity to get rich quick. A successful plan, despite the death of Frank, leads Soame out of New Orleans, with DD. After meeting her, and on the lam, they pick up and adolescent runaway, Charily. Their undecided destination from this point takes a trip up to the mid-west. Each of them share a common dream of a comfortable life and being free of their past.

Moving about from state to state, the trio decides to plant roots in a farming township in Montana, just outside of Rapid City, South Dakota. It is there that Soame ultimately makes his niche, and begins his journey to legal financial success and obtains the status of the town hero. He befriends the locals and enjoys the joyful follies with various females he encounters. Though the country town was impoverished and displayed a previous drug scene, Soame discovers the instrumental tact in bringing the community back to life after the area and states had been ravaged by the Reagan and Bush administrations.

Successful efforts are made to open a jewelry box factory. The set up comes through the hiring of a crew of carpenters, loans to local farmers and cultivating the minds of his household which has expanded far beyond the three of them. It is fascinating to observe his interest in each of his constituents which now include a local realtor and her two daughters, who now live with him. The accommodations shift from a farm to a large home formally owned by the town's physician, to an eight-bedroom mansion. All of this is inspired with the use of drug money form the hotel heist and the scene left behind the story's main character---Soasme Hudson---in New Orleans.

It is worthwhile to note Fifi and Mutt, a miniature poodle and a huge calico which reside with the adopted family, taken in by the trio. The antics and adventuresome frolicking of the pets add another dimension to the writings of "Ray" Claude.

Scenic routes and description of each mountain state is also weaved in a panoramic view, as well as contributions each state has made in our nations history.

Soame was instrumental in the reapplication for a federal loan as well as a government grant for the further existence of the town settled in. With the carpenters he put to work, he established a corporation and motivated local farmers to setup a co-op, which coincided with his corporation.

The book ends with cliffhanger that makes way for a sequel to this thrilling and adventure-romance filled urban-Midwestern quest for an American dream.

Acknowledgements

Editor – "The Great Hank"

Type Set - Derrick D. McNealy & Teresa Abney who typed Perdue's previous work "The Toe" and was not acknowledged.

Production – This work was produced at Fedex-Kinko's at the corner of Kennedy and Dale Mabry Hwy., in Tampa, Florida using windows software Microsoft Word. Fedex-Kinko's where "We make every Fedex experience outstanding." Derrick McNealy, Project Manager. Thanks to Milo Pirello, for all technical support and minor modifications, from Fedex-Kinko's in Tampa, FL. Raymond Claude Perdue *The Mans' Digest*

Cover:
    Coordinator
       . . . ."*The Great Hank*"
       . . . .*Photographer*
          Jeffrey Lapore
          "Pete" P. (212) 758-3420

        -*Photo Researchers,*
        Inc. . 60 East 56th St.
        New York, NY 10022

        National Archive Records Administration
        Joe@photoresponse.com
    . . . .*Asst. To Final Layout and print*
        Milo Pirello

PERSPECTIVELY

ACKNOWLEDGEMENTS

This is a work of fiction, conceived through the imagination of the writer. Any similarities pertaining to facts related to this story or its characters are coincidental.

Raymond Claude Perdue *The Mans' Digest*

PART I

Chapter 1

It was just before Spring on the fourteenth of March, and a brisk sun filled the sky at 8:45 outside of Mobile, en route to New Orleans, on Interstate 10. Frank and Soame had been riding all night. Frank had driven since they left Miami, and though he and Soame were making the trip as buddies, no one else had ever handled his ride. He was very reluctant to trust his childhood friend behind the wheel of his new Ford Probe GT.

After refueling in Mobile, Soame told him, "Say Frank, fatigue has gotten to you and you're burnt out. You should either let me drive or let's take a room here, so you can get some rest." Frank nodded and let Soame drive.

"You'll be handling it eventually, anyway," said Frank. "You know how I've always been leery 'bout my bike--now it's my ride."

"Yeah, we've been buddies a long time, dude. We go way, way back."

They were merging into interstate traffic a few miles later when Soame turned to his friend to remark on his pleasure at handling the smooth-driving new sports car. He saw Frank had crossed into "z-land" and was just about a note short of sawing logs. An old song, the Commodores' *"You Are,"* began to play on the radio. Soame settled back and let his mind drift back to the events that led to him and Frank getting together on the trip two days before.

He had just gotten home from "the joint." The eight year sentence he'd received was out of proportion to the non-serious crime. He still had five years to do on paper, plus over $5,000 to pay in restitution. Because of the overcrowded prisons, "gain" time resulted in "early release." This was common in the Florida penal system, which had become the state's largest industry, even larger than the lottery and tourism.

An affair with a woman sixteen years his senior had resulted in the prison term. He had been with her six years prior to the sentence. She had started experiencing menopause and neither of them knew how to handle it, even after they discovered what it was, which caused the ensuing problems. She experienced a really rough time with "the change" and refused to get help or use the professional help he found. Her unwillingness to accept that aspect of her life resulted in enormous pressures being put on the relationship. He tried to shrug the experience from his mind. It was over, at least that part of the ordeal. He drove on, listening to the music on the radio, optimistic as well as realistic about his uncertain future.

Soame was a college graduate, an honorably discharged U.S. Army veteran who trained with the Special Forces and had combat experience in Vietnam. He had previously earned a degree in Social Science and worked for the State of Florida, on two separate occasions, as a social worker. He had also worked in five major markets throughout America as a radio announcer and had, at one time, gained national recognition as the third best rhythm and blues D.J. in America. The native Floridian who simply had "caught a case." This happened in the Florida Panhandle after moving there from Miami with a woman who was half Cherokee and half Italian. She was originally from Alabama. After prison he had returned to the "Magic City" and, for sport, gone by "the corner" to the pool room and seen Frank. They had been raised in the Miami neighborhood called Liberty City. Soame, at thirty-eight, was a year older than Frank.

Frank's parents were from the Bahamas and they had a relatively large family with seven children. He was the fourth, with only one sister. After high school, Frank hustled jobs at restaurants, cutting lawns, waxing and polishing cars, and general labor. He then ventured to California for a while. Never marrying, after returning home nearly ten years later, he found his next oldest brother owned the neighborhood poolroom. Frank assisted his brother in operating the game room and billiard parlor. As manager of the place for five years, his duties were opening in the mornings, maintaining cues, stocking machines, and side hustling "grass" and "powder." The business went well and his older brother Curt was selling the place, when Soame came home and caught Frank about to leave for the coast once again.

The two left "home" without any planes. Soame had secured a room and told Frank it was "on the beach." Frank stopped by Soame's place on his way out of town to " do some toot," smoke a joint, and bid farewell.

Soame had applied to several employment agencies and found out that in the state of Florida a convicted felon could not get a government job on any level. This policy had recently gone into effect. There were no openings at any of the radio stations he had visited and called, but in broadcasting, you could never tell. Positions were mostly impromptu. The problem was, he could have a job the next day or two months later still be unemployed.

The fastest and easiest job for him to get was in sales, but he did not have the clothes.

Then Frank asked, "Want to come along and check out the coast? There are all sorts of jobs out dare, 'Blue.' I can even hook you up with the phone company."

Soame's nickname was "Blue," but only people who knew him as a kid made that reference to his dark complexion. He thought about the fact that he had a week to report to probation and had not done so. His intentions were to report after he had secured a job. Though he did not like the idea of the Oriental population that dominated L.A., he knew there were many more opportunities in California than in Florida.

"Ya know, I used to work at J. W. Robinson's, at the downtown location on Seventh and Grand," Soame announced. "I was out there after the war and got the job for the expected Christmas rush in 1973. I was the first black floor salesman they ever hired. Then there were only two stores and the other was in Beverly Hills. When I went back in 1977 they had opened a new store in Pasadena and guess what street it was on?"

"What street, man?"

"Hudson Avenue. How 'bout dat jive? Ain't it cool? Now tell me, ain't it? Having a street named after you?" Soame chuckled. "Heck, I ought to go with you, Frank. When I went back to L.A. in 1977 it was because Jose Wilson, Barry White's manager, invited me to emcee a show on Hollywood and Vine. The place was called 'Biscuits and Gravy.' Jose bought the place across the street form the infamous Brown Derby and wanted to add soul flavor to the taste of the name. Anyway, the three of us were in downtown L.A. at my insisting. D.J.s are a different sort of star than the people they present. Knowing she would be enthusiastic to meet Barry, I took him and Jose up to meet the chick who gave me the job in 1973, Mary Bumbgardner. She got so excited that she jokingly offered my old job back."

They both laughed and skinned.

"You know this stuff has got me really trippin'. It must be pretty good," Soame said.

"Heck, I know the Los Angeles area pretty well, Frank. When I left Robinson's that year I took a room at the Sheraton Huntington Hotel. The purpose was to be near Colorado Boulevard, so I could see the Rose Bowl Parade. USC was beaten by the Buckeyes that year."

Soame was experiencing his first coke high in nearly two years. His friend patiently listened with interest and curiosity as he babbled on.

"Later on I got a job at KGFJ and extended my stay. I lived off Krenshaw, in an area called 'The Jungle' just below Baldwin Hills. You know where that is?"

"Not really," replied Frank. "I've heard of Baldwin Hills and 'The Jungle.' I know that area's not as bad as it sounds. Nancy Wilson lived in Baldwin Hills, didn't she?"

"Yeah, she lived five blocks from where I lived on Santa Rosa Lia Drive."

"My brother and I originally went to Van Nuys, an area north of Hollywood, and from there we went to Napa Valley," Frank remembered. "There, both of us got jobs with the phone company and things really started happening for me. I had never made any real money before they trained me and all, even paid me to learn."

"So that's where and when you became a telephone repairman and technician, huh?" questioned Soame.

"Yep, certified and licensed," Frank said.

"Say, give me another hit," Soame said, "and, if you're serious about your invitation, I think I may take you up on it. I've got some 'ends' and we can 'cop' some more on the way out."

Frank spooned about a half a gram on the tabletop in the motel room and told him, "I've got plenty." He then passed Soame a joint and, as he lit one for himself, he said, "We've got a decent supply of this, too. So, if you really want to 'hat' up with me, you ought to get your rags together. I'm on my way out now."

Twenty minutes later they were cruising up towards Hollywood Beach on Collins Avenue. They would go from Hollywood inland and take the Florida Turnpike. North of Lake City the route junctures into Interstate 10, which runs directly to Los Angeles.

Soame, though somewhat out of practice, was an excellent driver. He had developed his skills driving across the country four times and in the many major cities he had been in and through. Driving had always been a relaxing outlet for the tall, broadly built, former athlete. After playing high school football, and having gone to college on an athletic scholarship, though it had been years since his track and field days with the shot put and discus, he had kept his body trimmed of excess weight. As a result, he still showed a decent wedge with broad shoulders, standing 6'1" and weighing 187 pounds. He had played only one year of college football. As an interior linesman, he played first string his freshman year, but during that period he weighed 217 pounds as an offensive center. Then he and the athletic director at the school had a dispute. After giving up his athletic scholarship, he finished through work-study, a state loan, an NDSL grant, and received a choir scholarship.

Following college, "Uncle Sugar" added his fine personal touch to Soame Hudson's life and drafted him. After two years of training to acquire a military occupational skill, he became a member of an elite force. With direct and absolute flawlessness with movements and physical skills , he became a Killmaster. After entering the U.S. Army in 1967, he completed his duties in June of 1973. During the time he spent in the military, the NCO rank E-7 was attained, sergeant first-class.

As they approached the city of New Orleans, the clock on the dash read 11:50. At that time, Soame had no idea that, within the next twenty-four hours, an extraordinary change would take place in his life--one that was immeasurable by any form of modern technology.

Chapter 2

"YO, Frank!!" Soame called out, awakening his traveling companion.

"Yeah, what's happening man? We made it to Louisiana yet?"

"We're outside of New Orleans, about to go down into the city. I come up on a sign that said Bourbon Street and The Civic Center Area. You still want to stop and spend the night?"

"Yeah, Blue, we may as well man, dis 'bout the best place between here and L.A. I want ta find me one a dem fine 'nellas' everybody's been telling me bout, running round here on Canal Street." Soame had noticed the signs, he passed Bourbon, took the exit onto Broad, and made the approach to Canal.

Soame then told him, "Um hungry, let's find a room and 'scarf' before we do any ho hunting."

"That's a bet," was the reply from Frank, who leaned over tying his shoes. "You're doin the driving." Neither knew anything at all about the town, and both agreed it would be best to ask for directions to what they were interested in. A sign read, "Free Car Wash with Fill Up" and Soame pulled into the station. They both got out at the self-service pump, stretched and looked around. After filling the tank, Soame went to pay the tab and get the token. Frank had checked under the hood and was at the vacuum, enjoying the sights of the unfamiliar city.

Soame was informed by the attendant how to get to the better part of the district they were in search of. He found out they were only five blocks from Bourbon Street. The attendant informed him about cheap third-rate rooms, but Soame asked directions to the better rooms and food. His choice was out of habit, developed through the years.

"What's the play?" Frank wanted to know.

"Suppose I told you we just left all the beautiful women and other exciting things we're looking for in Miami?" Soame jokingly said, after driving across to the vacuum and getting out of the car.

"I'd say you were lying. First, I've got a lot of exciting things right here in this car. Second, in the short while I've been standing here, I've seen three of the baddest bitches I've ever seen in my life, anywhere! No black ho in Miami can possibly look as tuff as either one a dese foxes and um bettin'." Frank then gave the sign asking for some skin. They dapped and grinned. "It's some bad bitches here, and we ant even started lookin' yet," said Frank again.

"You got that right," replied Soame, "Dude told me where to get a pretty good room and said the hoes gonna be on the stroll from two pm till four am."

The vacuum turned off and soon they had driven through the car wash, and were letting the afternoon sun and breeze dry the water beads off the sports coupe.

Within fifteen minutes, Soame was pulling into the parking lot of an independent motel, which showed the signs of being a quality establishment. It was a basic two-story structure with a lobby separated from the coffee shop by the driveway. Behind the lobby and along the driveway were the rooms, with an elevated pool directly across the way from the rooms. A side door from the office lead to the breezeway, where there were vending machines. The breezeway separated the office from the rooms of the motel and led to the parking lot. Frank had used the front entrance to the office. Soame drove past him, entering the drive and parking area, which separated the rooms from the pool. The drive emptied T-fashion, into a parking lot, which was partially behind the pool. From there the drive, in the opposite direction, continued behind the motel, carried through another parking lot, and emptied into the street they came in on.

Soame had backed into a parking slip and was leaning on a fender when Frank came from the breezeway; he showed his palms and shrugged his shoulders. Frank raised his hand and displayed a key, while indicating "up stairs" with his other hand. After giving a nod, Soame proceeded to the trunk, to get shaving kits and other small bags they needed to freshen themselves. Upon entering the room, the first thing Soame noticed was it was an adjoining room. He mentioned this to Frank, who replied, "Yea, the clerk said most of them are, if we don't mind." Soame then started toward the adjoining door, while Frank concluded, "said they lock from both sides, with a door lock and a slide bolt." He knocked to see if there would be a response from the next room. There was no answer. Frank then told him, "I've got to get something out of the car; anything you want brought up?"

The room was rather large and spacious, double beds, rather basic, with an office refrigerator; the air conditioning unit was located under a large picture window, which could be concealed by heavy plastic draw curtains; they were open. Soame checked outside, to see who was out by the pool. From the doorway, he also listened to determine if the air conditioner was in use in the room next door. It was not. He had already noticed the small group scattered around the pool, but this time gave a particular stare at two beauties casually relaxing in two fold out lounge chairs. He stepped back into the room, turned the air conditioner and T.V. on. When Frank returned, the lamp and ceiling lights were on and Soame was in the adjoining room.

Both rooms were identical, except for the location of the small table in each room. In the adjoining room, the table had been placed near a corner instead of in front of the air conditioner, as was theirs. The beds were on opposite walls in each room. "Hey, how'd you do that?" Frank asked, with excitement in his voice.

"What?"

"The door, how did ya open it from the other side?"

"I guess someone left the bolt off."

Frank then told him, "I'll be right back, I want to show you something." He hurried back outside.

The bathroom window overlooked the main parking lot and street with nearly a twenty-foot drop. Frank was nearly as tall as Soame, 5'11½" and though they both appeared to be about the same size, Frank did not have Soame's physique or the control of his body as Soame did, due to his athletic and military training. When Frank returned to the room, he took a telephone technician's kit from a shoulder bag. That was the beginning of his fun for the afternoon. It was a modern, direct dialing phone system display. After dialing eight on the room phone, the guest simply received a dial tone for a local call. Nine gave access to the operator, for billing long distance calls. Frank was in the other room two minutes, when he instructed Soame, "Dial dis room numba for me, will ya?" It was 12; they were in 13. By dialing 12, Soame activated a bleep that would record any incoming or outgoing calls into and from the adjoining room.

It was Frank's favorite thing to do; he had installed a "bug." He loved monitoring other peoples' phone conversations. "You sure you know what you're doing?" asked Soame.

"I do it all da time, when I get a chance; sometimes I run across some pretty hot stuff."

"I'm hungry," Soame told him. "You gonna come with me to get some grub, or play with that?"

"Bring enough back for two, I'm gonna finish settin dis up, then shower."

"Want anything in particular, hot ears?"

"None a dat greasy spoon stuff, otherwise…" he shrugged his shoulders.

"While I'm out I may do a little cruising on Canal, to see the outlay of the stroll."

"Fine with me. Hey man! Bring me a lot ta drink; I still drink a lot of liquids. Want a 'blow' before you go turfin?"

"Naw, I'd rather eat first. I'll see you in awhile," Soame told him, approaching the door. It was near one o'clock.

Upon his return, Soame was gladly welcomed with the Cajun dinners he brought. He had been gone less than an hour. A nearby restaurant specialized in "Cajun Carry Outs." After putting his order in, he had cruised Bourbon and Canal streets and returned twenty-five minutes later to pick up the shrimp fried rice and other Cajun fixins. While cruising, he stopped at a stand and bought fresh fruit. From a corner market he had gotten chips, candy bars, and two chilled quarts of orange juice. With two bags of unsalted peanuts, they had enough to last for snacks later on, if they stayed according to plan, which was to leave shortly past midnight.

Where the car was parked it could be seen from the bathroom window. Frank was informed of the sights his pal had "scoped out" while gathering food. Neither had ever had Cajun style cooking before. The hot rice was saturated with small shrimp. Their palates were delighted, their buds well pleased with the main course, side orders of biscuits, and a fruit salad. Orange juice washed the meal down with total satisfaction for both men.

"You say they're on every corner?"

"Yeah, and throughout every block. We've definitely got a fix on their location 'Unks', there some fine bitches out there man, and everyone I saw was beautiful." Soame went on to tell him, "I never saw so many collectively fine, black and beautiful women in my life, and look what time it is! Whatta ya think it'll be like six, or seven this evening?" Frank could tell Soame was truly excited, because he seldom used "splib" nowadays. "It seems to be too many of them to be true; you gotta see um to believe it," he concluded, looking at Frank, in bewilderment.

"Unks" was a name Frank's family called him. Outside of the kids in his immediate neighborhood, no one else ever used the nickname. Therefore, Soame captured his immediate and precise attention when he used the name. With a slight nasal accent he asked, "Whatta ya think bout us scoring couple a dese chicks with some blow?"

"Heck, cocaine is cash money, anyway you look at it, we're on man! We're on!!" He then began gathering clean underwear from his tote bag, and picked up his shaving kit. Moving toward the shower, he said to Frank, "I'm gonna get clean dude, so I can chill out and relax for awhile."

"Cool, ... yeah, dat's cool 'Blue'."

After the shower, Soame discovered Frank had ventured downstairs and was prowling around in the pool area; the motel also had a lounge. A small game room led from the coffee shop to the lounge and out to the pool area. More people had gathered on the deck of the pool. It was mid-afternoon, Thursday.

The line and device was rather simple, compared to other types Soame had seen and used. In fact, compared to some of the sophisticated equipment he'd read about, the bugging equipment he had was elementary. However, if properly installed, the surveillance equipment in the room could do the same job as any other: a white light meant a call was coming in, or someone was dialing out. There were two other lights; the red indicated there was a conversation on the line; the green light came on when the recorder was in operation. The red and green usually worked simultaneously. His check proved the machine properly installed. With that style and type monitor, sometimes the simplicity involved in its set up also allowed for error, which would result in no indication of a call and/or no recording. A conversation listening device had a recorder and these instruments were laced with fine filtered electrons, all were activated at the same time. A sensitive and very small device sending also to the signal indicators, when any break in the dial tone triggered the mechanisms. Frank had done his job well setting up the equipment.

Soame knew the possibilities of the results and wondered about Frank. They hadn't spent any serious time together since they were teenagers, then only at times in the poolroom and on the basketball court. As children they had played "Cowboys and Indians," shot marbles, roller-skated, hunted with B.B. guns, and did a hundred other things youngsters do as children, including going to school. The memory of them playing basketball together filled Soame's thoughts. On the court Frank was a shade or two better than Soame. His size allowed Frank to be more agile and faster to the hoop. Though they were equal off the board and rim, as teenagers Frank was slightly taller, leaner, and quicker. Twenty years was a considerably long time, but he knew that, even though Frank carried maybe 20 pounds in excess weight, he had a lot of heart. He could not shirk the thought of the possibility of them getting a "take," something of major importance on the recorder, or through Frank's listening device. They were both decent, clean-cut kids who had been raised in an upper-middle class neighborhood and surroundings. Both seldom went looking for trouble, which caused Soame to wonder why, at the age of maturity, Frank had developed a penchant for eavesdropping.

During the past 10 years, they had occasionally run across each other. The two socialized, when they had the chance, and being from Miami, the pair knew what the drug scene was all about, though Soame received the better part of his experiences through formal and military training and going overseas. Soame had only one brother, who was fifteen years his senior, and they were raised separately. They had the same father but were products of different marriages. He and Frank had known each other since elementary school. It was good to be free once again, enjoying the freedom of traveling and the changes of scenery life presented. It was especially good to be with someone who knew him as "Blue," as "Unks" did.

Watching the TV while listening to the radio was a thing Soame liked doing very much. Only soap operas and cartoons were on "the tube," so he reclined, fully dressed, across one of the beds. In a short while, he relaxed.

He was just getting into a full and solid sleep when he heard the key in the lock. "Check it out man, I got a bad chick down stairs at the pool," Frank told him, going straight to the bathroom.

"Oh yeah," Soame heard the toilet flush and the tap run, before Frank appeared in the doorway, drying his hands.

"Yeah, and she's got a friend. Want ta meet her?" Frank then stepped toward the bed with excitement and anxiety in his voice, "I've already bought two rounds of drinks. Man, I've got um primed and ready." He threw the towel on the empty bed.

Soame smiled at him, shaking his head. "Boy, I never thought you'd be that lame. You're from the city; you deal with hustlers all day long 'Unks'! You didn't pull her, the bitch is catching you. I saw them both when I came up the stairs, after you'd gotten the room. Did you notice the dude on the other end of the pool, under the shade lounge, with the deep roll high boy?" Frank motioned toward the curtains drawn across the window.

"Don't be stupid and peep out man! Then they'd really have us sized up," Soame said casually, after the harsh warning, then continued in a more casual tone, "It's been a lot of years since the sky piece he's sportin was in style. He's a northern dude, and that cats' no jitterbug."

Frank turned toward his friend now sitting on the side of the bed. "The girls are out of Philly, they're real estate agents for a development corporation that wants to buy into the rural perishes down here."

"And you've told them you've got some coke, and they invited us to their place, or are they supposed to come up here?"

Frank sat on the desk and table ensemble that housed the TV and shrugged his shoulders; "Shit, I feel like a kid, but I told um bout the dynamite weed we got, and they're waitin to see what you wanna do."

"I want to go to the hoe stroll, after six, get me one of dem beautiful fine bitches, have her give me some slow head, for $25.00 or less, and be done with it… Now if you want ta wine and dine some hoes, give um all the merchandise, beg um for some pussy, and pay um – $50 to show um you can be a cheap chump or a hundred dollar fool, I'll listen further to your idea, but don't tell um I'm your home boy." Frank opened his mouth to reply, when they heard the bumping of the furniture and the sound and vibration from the slam of the door next to their room. It was almost a quarter to five. It was Soame's suggestion, "Tell um we've got a call to meet someone across town, get their room number, and tell um we'll call um back later on."

Frank eased himself from his sitting position, indicated with his thumb toward the next room, and slid open the desk drawer as he asked, "Whatta ya think?"

Soame watched him take the goods from the drawer, and stated, "So that's where you stashed it."

Frank's reply was, "Since I was goin out, I thought this would be the first place you'd look, if you wanted some." He stepped over to the table and took a seat next to the only window in the front room.

While he scooped powder, Soame told him, "I felt contented relaxing for the short while. I was almost asleep when you came in. I hadn't eaten anything since noon yesterday, before you came by. I was really hungry and ready for the food we had. A couple of lines and a joint would be the thing right now though."

Frank looked at him, and with a big grin said, "A couple of lines… I told you yesterday, we've got plenty. Blue, chill out with dis till I get back." Frank hadn't moved, instead he looked through the parting curtains. He did a one and one, then told Soame, "You're right bout that guy, I saw him come into the lounge, when I was getting the second round of drinks, but I really didn't notice him, or think anything of it until you mentioned him." He then lit one of the pre-rolled joints.

Soame lifted a motel card from the tabletop, turned it on its side, and used the edge to fluff the powder. He then told Frank, "Seems like you've got company next door; I think I'd better help you with this before you start giving it to those bitches and their pimp downstairs." He then took a hit in each nostril, with the corner of the card. They both chuckled and grinned at the situation. It was the first time the both of them had relaxed together, during the trip. The drugs were of super quality. Frank's joint went out, while they both took a couple more hits. Soame lit a joint and had taken a toke, when Frank stood up saying, "I'll be right back man, um goin down, and take care dat." With that Frank was gone.

Their plan seemed to be shaping up fine, and all was going well. The idea they'd mapped out the previous night, was to get some rest in New Orleans. They'd rest a short while in Phoenix also, before crossing the desert. Both of them had been across the country before and had agreed to leave Phoenix about mid-afternoon. The schedules were set according to the travel experiences they had with the route. Good time could be made during the long ride, their calculated planning would also grant them the sight of the breathtaking scenery across the desert to Palm Springs.

Everything was really materializing for them. The car was new; had less than 5,000 miles. When Frank's older brother told him he was selling the poolroom two and a half months earlier, Frank had the car bought it in three payments. The last one was made the day Soame came home. In Miami, an individual cannot make an "on the spot" cash purchase of a new car. The person can only apply for the purchase, wait twenty-four hours while the dealer contacts the police for an investigation. The potential purchaser has to be not wanted in another state or the state of Florida. He or she must have income and credit. Following this procedure, if the applicant meets these requirements, he is then allowed to make the purchase. For that reason, Frank had stretched the payments into three, after the initial down payment and being financed. As easy and tranquil as the situation was, however, Soame had been a boy scout before he became a soldier. He knew what it meant to "be prepared." His experiences had shown him, time and again, how fast and serious the x-factor can show up and take meaning = the unknown. The tap Frank put on the line next door worried him for some reason. Some men have a built in alertness. Perhaps this was the reason he began to wonder about the situation once again. He attempted to down play his worry, figuring after being incarcerated for a year and a half, he was over-cautious. He had never gotten paranoid as a result of the drugs he did, which were limited to the two he and his friend were doing. His "clean" system was evaluated, with the vague possibility of paranoia. Nevertheless, his motivation and alertness for danger had been fully triggered. Knowing this he attempted to relax.

Downstairs at the pool, Frank really did not care about the pointed out panderer. In fact that's why he was there, "to play." He was a player, who now was fully in the game with total awareness. After working and hustling for five years, and had sent himself nearly nine thousand dollars, at his brother's address in Oakland, with a good set of wheels, a quarter pound of super good coke, a half-pound of superb reefer, and over three grand in cash and travelers checks with him, the game tilted in his direction. Certainly no one was going to take anything from him, he was positive of that, and with Soame as back up, playing the bitches and their pimp at the pool became an obsession. He ordered another round of drinks and rejoined the ladies. Frank had nothing else better to do for a while anyway. Besides, Soame had the room. Passing the time with the ladies, was much better than being cooped up with a "hard head," though it was his friend.

They returned his wave as he entered the lounge, and when he returned to the poolside table with the drinks, they poured on their charm, with delight and expectation. After joining them, he felt like taking the both of them to his room, but instead he chose to give the situation an even play, by waiting to see at least a few "nellas" out on the stroll. So, Frank explained the call as Soame had suggested, and told the two women about the expected call back. This also explained his partner remaining by the phone upstairs. He gave them each a joint, and extended the thought of one enjoying the "herb" in the privacy of their room, while he kept the other company.

Shortly after Frank left the room, Soame heard the connecting door rattle. The occupants of the adjoining room had checked to see if both sides were locked. Later, he saw the white light flash on and off, followed by the solid red, and then the green light came on. The red and green lights stayed on for nearly three minutes. Shortly after six-thirty Frank entered the room, smiling, while telling the story, how one of the girls was told by the other, as she had come from the room, they'd received a call from one of their prospective customers. An appointment had been tentatively set up, depending on the potential client's work schedule. The supposed call confirmed the meeting they had to prepare for an hour later. They were both amused and laughed at the probable frustration of the pimp, when Frank noticed the red light blinking on and off, on his machine.

"Hey did you notice this?" he asked, walking toward the device on the table near the TV.

"That's your baby," Soame told him. Frank took a small earphone with a plug-in jack from his bag, pulled the chair from under the desk portion of the furniture fixture, and sat down. He then inserted the earphone into the side of the machine, hit the rewind button on the recorder and, after the tape reversed itself, pressed the play button.

The fruit, which had been brought in with the lunch, had been washed and spread out on a towel. It was on the ensemble also. Soame casually walked over, grabbed a pear, and bit into it, as he continued to look at the pictures on the T.V. screen, and listen to the music from the radio. Michael Jackson was on, singing *Billy Jean.* He moved his hand, with the pear in it, with the rhythm, as he nonchalantly, but carefully observed Frank listening to the recorded phone message. Frank offered the listening device to Soame saying, "Do you want ta hear dis?"

"Is it something worthwhile?"

Holding the phone out to him, Frank answered, "I don't know, can't say for sure; you be da judge of that, Soame."

He knew Frank well enough to conclude it was worthwhile for him to take the time and hear what was there. He took a tissue from the nightstand, briskly wiped the earpiece, and watched Frank press play: it rang twice, then a male voice answered "Yeah."

The voice from the next room said, "We're here at the usual place, and we've got room 12; it's upstairs across from the pool."

The response was, "How's business Ed?"

"Ohhhh, not too bad, but a little short, is Joey around?"

"No, he and Willie are out getting ties together, we had a late shipment into port, there was some difficulty involved in docking and a couple of other unexpected impairments have back scheduled us three or four hours. They probably won't be able to get to you boys until about midnight, maybe as late as one. Besides that, there are no other problems I know of."

The voice from the next room replied, "We're not suppose to see our people here until ten or eleven in the morning anyways. The arrangement is anytime before noon, so the midnight meeting suits us just fine."

"Good." replied the other end, "Glad it doesn't throw your schedule off."

"We've had a meal, but later we'll have some sandwiches brought up, so we won't be going out."

"Great, you boys stay put now, I'll have Joey give you a call before they pull out."

The voice from 12 then said, "All right, we'll be right here."

"That's good, I'll talk with you later," was the last statement.

Soame took a bite of his pear, gave the earplug back to Frank, who was still seated, and said to him, "Well, well." He looked out of the window and saw twilight flowing across the skies and landscape.

Pulling the curtain back into place, he turned and looked squarely at Frank, who had gotten up. "It's getting dark outside, hoes probably crowdin' down on the avenue" Soame said, using a familiar Miami expression to get Frank's attention. Frank refused to give in to the ploy, and be trapped by nothing words, when he knew his roommate had stated meaningless tidbits, which was a long way from the issue. Soame brushed past him and turned the lamp on between the two beds, "Ya know Frank, the scene dictates early arrivals and late comers, but I'd gamble the absolute best time to catch the cream of the crop out there on the stroll, will be in accordance with New York curtain time."

Frank had to respond, though he did not like or appreciate the idea of his buddy toying with his mind. "Oh yea, and what time is that Soame?"

"8:30," he replied.

"Why, cause by den you figure the guy Joey will be done calling dis dude next doo?" Frank asked this rebelliously, as if hostile toward the situation.

"No," Soame told him, throwing the pear core into the waste receptacle, "simply cause that's what time it is, that's all, and it's correct procedure for people in the know."

Frank sneered at him, pivoted, walked to the door, opened it, and walked out on the porch to the railing.

The pool lights were on. It was a week before official spring and the evening air had a nip of chilliness to it. The pool crowd had totally disappeared. He noticed the atmosphere in the lounge had thinned out considerably. Though the door was open hardly anyone could be seen, but he heard Caron White's record, *"Super Woman,"* playing on the jukebox. He had cooled off when he turned back to the room. Soame had turned the bathroom light on. Frank went back inside. He took a cluster of grapes from the small bunch on the table and started to munch. He noticed the TV and saw the evening news going off.

Soame sat at the table by the window, fluffing another portion of the coke put there earlier. While doing so, he wondered very seriously about the entire overall situation, with his childhood companion. As children, they had enjoyed spinning tops, with a make shift "puey," in a game called "nubbing." They shot marbles and used the expressions "no dubs or tribs," "sound me loud as a church bell," and "scramble!" They shot sparrows and pigeons with BB guns and when the robins flew down for the winter, slaughtered them. A couple of times the two of them even sneaked off with the big boys and went swimming in the rock pit. It is said, "boys never grow up, only their toys change." He made six lines and, after doing two of them and lighting a joint, he said to Frank, who sat at the foot of the unused bed, "We're not too sure about anything. From what we've heard we are assuming these guys next door have access." He paused, did half a line in each nostril through a straw, took a long drag from the joint, and with Frank silently looking at him, he continued, "In my opinion, we are in violation."

Without saying anything, Frank looked at him with shrewdness. Soame continued, "I must tell you this because it is a matter which surrounds the entire situation. It is like fighting for the right, or defending justice. We have dared to listen in on someone's private conversation, and assuming they have, or later will have something we want, because we want it, we cannot overlook the fact, it is theirs." He took another toke from the reefer; Frank still waited silently. Soame concluded, "Whatever you want to do, and I think your immediate idea is to some how crash that room, I am with you, but I tell you for sure and this is certain and positive 'Unks,' I'm not going back to prison. They have a prison in this state called Angola; it makes even the 'East Unit' back home look like a boy scout training camp. Whatever is to be done, if it is to be in anyway successful, it has to have a developed plan, with a secondary." He did a full line in each nostril, took another puff, and crossed his legs, looking at Frank.

Frank removed himself from the bed, and sat in the chair opposite Soame. Reaching out his hand, with his thumb and index finger almost touching, he said to Soame, "Let me hit dat man."

Soame laughingly said, "Shit, you might have AIDS, mother fucker. You gave me this." He pushed the plastic bag containing nearly an ounce toward Frank and handed him the papers.

"I just wanted to see if you had changed 'Blue,' whatta yah think?"

Soame hesitated because he hadn't thought of what was on his mind during the entire trip, until Frank asked him that particular question. "This is probably the best move… Let's find out what's to be said when the other call comes through. In the mean time, we figure a way into the room." He then asked the question he had been hesitating with. "Do you have a 'piece' 'Unks'?"

"Yeah, but it's a small one. I shipped my Mack 10 and my .357 out ta da coast with my other clothes and stuff. Dis is all I got." Frank, while talking had walked over to the far corner and brought back an overnight suitcase. He opened it and was digging through his belongings, when he stopped talking. He turned back to his roommate, leaving the overnight case on the bed. In his open palm he handed Soame a .25 automatic. Soame took the pistol; turning the barrel to the window and ceiling, he took the clip out and unloaded the chamber. He then told Frank, "Ya know, people talk about weapons and how powerful guns produce devastating effect, but you know what 'Unks'?" He had broken the pistol down, removed the firing pin, and was examining it.

"What 'Blue'?"

"Sometimes it's not a matter of who has the larger 'piece', instead it's who's able to get to the gun the fastest."

In Florida, especially Miami, temperatures hardly ever drop below 45º. Frank had managed a pool hall, with fifteen tables in operation, from 8 AM until two the following morning. He had done this for a considerable while and knew practically every "jitterbug" from their side of town, if he was hip. At one time or another, nearly all the hip dudes from all over "The Magic City" came through the establishment he had managed. To be in control of his surroundings, Frank had to have the knowledge of what went on. He paid smaller dudes to run the "skin" and "coon kan" games in the back room. He also employed three housemen to rack balls, and there were constant poker games, which he did decently well at as a player. These activities included "crap" shooters who drifted to and from the back room and were thrown out two and three by the hour. "T's" (tailor made pants), designer jeans, and Levis were basic pants styles worn by these people, who were typically on the move. Soame knew why Frank had this particular style and caliber pistol. The .25 can be leg holstered above the ankle, worn in a pair of brief underwear, carried under a cap, or simply worn in a hip pocket, without detection. He knew also why the clip, which held seven shells, had long range, hollow points for ammunition.

After checking the weapon out thoroughly and reassembling it, Soame placed it on the table, and the clip with all seven rounds in it, next to it. He then said to Frank, "Yo, Frank," who looked up from his pistol. "Do you know that this is the home of the mafia?"

Frank leaned back in his chair and jokingly said, "What mafia man?"

Soame looked him directly in the eyes and said, "The real mafia."

Frank's face got serious, as he adjusted to the mood, and with wrinkles furrowing his forehead he asked, "You mean the one in Chicago?" Soame then did a one and one. He had re-fluffed the substance with the card, and used the 2½" straw to snort the coke. Still not saying anything, he lit the remaining portion of the joint. Frank then said, "Das why I asked which one, I only know bout the one in Chicago, das the one everybody knows bout, right Soame?"

Soame looked at him coldly, smiled, and replied, "You're kinda funny man." Soame knew the simplicity, as well as the depth seriousness of the entire and overall situation. He continued, "Now check this out" – but before he could finish his thought, they both noticed the flashing white light from the machine. They both heard the half ring of the phone next door, as the red then green lights came on the machine. The white light went blank.

Chapter 3

In receiving national recognition as an R & B DJ, Soame was once presented with a Dunhill cigarette lighter. The national promotions man, Larry Maxwell, did the presenting to Soame Hudson, who was then known as "The Mighty Burner." The gift was especially sent through Maxwell by the president and owner of the largest black independent record company in America. It had been almost twenty years since he had received it, but Soame still had the Dunhill. He had been many places and sometimes had experiences beyond belief, but somehow he had managed to hold on to the lighter. Twice he had it sent to England to be repaired. In recent years, the company had set up establishments in New York and San Francisco. Since then, the lighter had been sent to New York twice. Once an individual owns a Dunhill, the lighter is guaranteed for life. All maintenance and repairs are free, except for the cost of mailing.

Soame no longer smoked cigarettes. While the red and green lights were on and brightly displayed, he turned the lighter over and over, placing one end and then the other lightly on the table. Very seldom did anything worry this man. However, the actions and fate of his companion had became an issue that was fast taking priority. It was almost seven thirty when the lights went out. Frank and Soame looked at each other.

Instead of unseating the apparatus, and without taking a chance on unseating anything, they went to the machine. Sometimes it would lose the entire message, if the machine was moved. Frank pressed the rewind button. The counter reversed and the tape rolled back to the beginning. Before pressing play, Frank looked at Soame who nodded. They heard the full, then the half ring, and Ed answered, "Yeah, Joey."

The unfamiliar voice seemed to growl with hoarseness, "Edmond, I gotta your message and it was to give you a calla, says your expecting a company around before one." There was a slight pause, "Says you no do so good with collections, ah?"

Ed told him, "It's these people in Beaumont, we were there last night, they did nothing with the brown and only gave part of the bill for the company of the girl. I think you should send someone else by, get all that's due you, or the goods and be done with them. They are a constant hassle. I mean week after week after week."

"Edmond how much cash you got a, ha, to turn into me?"

"Ah, its pretty close to three hundred thou, Joey."

"Dats not so good"

"Yeah, but I told ya, Boss, we got all the brown back plus we've only been out since Tuesday, we had three stops this trip. We did the short route."

"Oh well, a then I see a, I see. Tella ya whatta you do Edmond, put all you gotta together, in one package. We gotta word about the people you mention in dat town. Day takin skim off the product." Again there was a slight pause, "We gotta bring it back for testing. We give you all fresh for the usual seven stops you make, except Beaumonta. That gives us thirteen between here and Albuquerque. You're the first, we gonna be done before noon Saturday."

Knowing Joey had delivered, Ed told him, "Ah tell you what now Joey we've got a little girl to come back with us, but she's not so much."

"She's a white, right Edmond?"

"Yeah, Joey."

"No problem. Just do lika I say, and we got no problem." Ed's boss concluded by telling him, "When a we knock and you say its almost three, dis a time I tella you its only da two of usa, you got dat Edmond?"

"Got it."

"Run it back to the knock, Unks." Frank did and they heard the play back. Soame then went to the bathroom, and turned the light out. When he came back by the table and desk, he turned the radio back up. The jack with the earphone had been taken out, so they could both listen to the recording aloud. He and Frank then went to the front table. "This is a really a big operation," Soame told Frank as he sat down. "Seems like it may be the chance of a lifetime, and if we make the attempt we are committed to go all the way."

Frank casually put his hand out with open palm showing up as a sign for Dap and asked, "Den we're down with dis job?"

"Down all the way."

It was just past 7:45. Both of them knew a plan had to be arrived at. It had to be positive, solid and a sure winner. "The first move is to figure a move into the room, and be there when Joey arrives. We don't want to cause any ruckus in doing so, which can be a main factor."

When Soame said this Frank asked, "How'd you do it earlier ta day?"

"By gaining leverage on the door, taking the pressure off the bolt, and very diligently sliding the bolt back. Should the noise be heard or the bolt noticed moving, then there's trouble. We don't know how they're situated in the room and chances are more than likely they're heavily armed. Their pieces are probably kept in their hands, or at least in comfortable reach." Frank noticed Soame was almost a step ahead of him toward the angles of a plan. Soame dismissed the room to room entry idea by concluding, "That way is much too risky."

Frank was fluffing the remainder of the coke on the table. He dropped the card, snapped his fingers, and excitingly said, "Got it."

His roommate picked up the card, stuck in a corner in the pile of powder, looked at Frank and said, "It's almost eight o'clock, Unks." The substance was sniffed before another portion was taken on the corner of the card. Soame looked toward his friend and inquired, "How long you planning to hold on to what you got?" He then sniffed into the other nostril.

Frank then told him, "The sandwiches! They're gonna eat. He said he'd have the coffee shop send up sandwiches, if not one has to go out." They both would probably not snort the gram and a half to two grams which laid ready to be consumed. Besides, they both knew enough about the drug to clean their noses with warm water every three hours. They had started shortly after six.

Soame made four nice lines. While doing so, he told Frank, "You're really on the one with that one." They both looked at the recording device.

Soame got up, went to the bathroom, and returned with his shaving kit. After unzipping the small bag, he removed the small mirror, telling Frank, "Here's an idea…have you ever heard of a spook?"

Frank laughed, put his hand over his mouth and pointed toward his friend saying, "The mafia, spooks, you know you still kinda weird. Ya know dat, Blue?"

"Kiss my ass mother fucker and get hip to this," he said moving towards the door. "Like you just said, one of um might go out." He stopped, turned and looked at Frank asking, "If he does, how are we gonna know Unks?"

"Let's set up a watch from across the other side of the pool."

Soame laughed. "Um from Florida, it's cold out there, I'm not gonna sit out there part of the night playing peepin tom to a couple of squares, Unks. Ft Jackson, Ft Bragg, and Ft Campbell were some of the worst experiences of my life, but they were also some of the best. They were some of the worst because of the winter training. Um gonna show you what a spook is!"

After turning the interior lights out in the room and partially opening the curtain, he took the mirror outside. Frank watched him place the object at the base of the rail between them and room 14. He then came back, sent Frank outside, and instructed him to adjust the mirror to his instructions, as he would a rear view mirror. The looking glass was propped against one of the railings, which lead up from the concrete floor. From a certain position, the entire porch could be seen, back to the stairs leading to the breezeway. Soame then cut a groove into a bar of soap, and placed the mirror in it, on the concrete.

The crude but effective surveillance device was set up and in place by 8:10. As they worked, Frank told Soame about the signs he had seen. While he was in the lounge, one informed the patrons and guests the coffee shop was open until eleven, and the other listed a menu with a variety of sandwiches, drinks, and fries. "One of us should watch, while the other packs," Soame suggested. It was agreed that Soame would enter the room alone, no matter what arrangements were made in getting the food in. By 8:40, all but the listening machine had been packed. As a contingency plan, they took out the bathroom screen and window. The pistol lay on the table and light filtered in through the particularly opened curtains. The porch light gave them more than ample light for their purpose. They waited and took turns watching the spook, smoking, and snorting.

Beyond getting into the room, they had no plan. Step by step toward the objective had to be taken. There was money and drugs in the room next door. The possibility of a stakeout on the other room was rejected. They knew exactly where the car keys were and all the luggage was positioned for a quick exit to the car. More money and much more drugs were coming in, so the initial move on the room next door would be a worthwhile score. The second phase could possibly make them rich. At this stage of their lives, neither had a wife and children. Frank had earlier mentioned an out of wedlock child as a reason for going back to California. Both of them had various reasons and wanted the "score," and wanted to go "all the way."

At nine o'clock Soame began his clean up procedure. He washed the coke from his nose to preserve the delicate membranes. Though he did not have any vitamin-E, he used simple petroleum jelly to lubricate each nostril. Frank told him he had discontinued the practice, after the long hours he had spent in the pool room and because of the regular and at times almost around the clock usage of the powder. However, he also "cleaned up" and they spent time on the conversation about the many people who paid for plastic surgery simply because they did not practice the technique in proper usage of the substance. Two towels were draped over the opening in the bathroom. The drop would be lessoned if either or both of them extended an arm's length and fell to the gravel below. Soame explained the "push off" to avoid the hedge. It was not a dangerous drop, if the precautionary exit had to be used. Once Soame entered the adjoining room and if he was successful, they would then have access to both rooms. The important thing was not to get "jammed" in either room, if anything went wrong. They snacked on peanuts, grapes, apples, and oranges while they waited. By 9:25, they were drying out their noses with the tissue, laying out more lines, and getting high again.

"Once we have access, Frank, we leave these adjoining doors open. You close the curtains, get the mirror, and fix the machine so we can hear what's said directly. Should a call come in, we should hold them at bay, and wait for Joey; I hope like hell he brings Willie upstairs with him. We don't let them know how much we know about their operation, all right?"

Frank answered, "We find out from dem and find out who dey are and what dey got right?"

Soame smiled. "Why do you use so much 'splib' man?"

"I like it, practiced it till it got to be a habit, who cares?" Something irregular happened. It was an unexpected stroke of luck. The white light came on with a blink and went off. In the darkened room it was highly noticeable. Frank had just bitten into a pear, he looked to Soame, saw the occurrence and looked back at Soame to see if he saw what he had seen. Soame did a line of toot. Frank started toward the machine.

"Be patient, Unks. I've checked the machine and the setup, it's right."

Frank continued toward his machine, but did not seem to be in his initial rush. Soame saw him visually examine it and said "Let's wait and see what happens."

Frank had already done two of the freshly made lines, and Soame did more with the designed straw. They both knew it was impossible for anyone to be on the corridor without being seen. Soame felt positive the machine was functioning properly, while Frank began to feel nervous about the equipment. Sensing Frank's nervousness his roommate told him, "I've seen a lot of flukes man. You have also. They probably started to call and thought of something they…" The light suddenly came on again. Soame walked over to the machine turned the radio down very low and adjusted the knob on the recorder so they could hear what was being said. It was a call to the coffee shop for a pastrami and pickles, a salami on rye, and two Alka-seltzers also. The gangster was told, "Your order will be up in 15 minutes. Thanks for your patronage."

In his suit zipper bag, Frank had a white, silk long sleeve shirt. Soame had noticed and commented on it earlier. In taking his shirt off, he explained the idea to Frank. He felt positive it would work, especially when it was enhanced with him carrying a serving platter. After dressing in Frank's shirt, he turned the collar under, displaying his idea. They had seen the boy from the coffee shop make several deliveries. Soame felt no uneasiness about being able to swing it. In fact, he was quite pleased to be approaching the physical aspect of the encounter. All his thinking during the wait had just brought him anguish. After doing the last of his lines, he cleaned and groomed himself. Seven minutes after the call, he was ready. He took the small weapon, put the clip in place, loaded the chamber, secured the safety in place, and told Frank, "I'll knock twice. Then you take the mirror in and see that everything else falls into place like we planned, alright?" Frank nodded and Soame was off, out the door, past room 14, to the end of the building, down the stairs through the corridor to the breezeway and the machines.

It was rather cool out. Soame called an international flight reservation at the airport in New Orleans, and got the usual recorded message to wait. It never sounded so good. From his vantage point, at the public phone in the breezeway, The waiter could be seen ten yards before he approached the front stairwell. Turning his collar back under, remained to be done. The cool breeze was brisk and felt good on his body. While he had been at the motel, many thoughts had passed through his mind. The first night in the motel on Miami Beach, he had scored from a hooker on Collins Avenue. Now he faced possible death. No matter what happened once he entered the room, he knew positively that he was not going back to prison. Soame knew he was going to enter that room. The brisk breeze made his body feel vibrantly alive.

The taped message to "hold please, someone will be with you shortly," and the soft background music made him feel at ease about his task. He knew once he entered the room, the job would be rather simple. The major concern was getting into the room without detection. This was the first time he had undertaken such a plan of action as a civilian. Finally, his military training would produce something he could enjoy the benefits of....the waiter with the covered serving platter came into sight.

Soame rested the phone at the base of the stand in the phone booth, approached the waiter and asked, "Salami and pastrami for 12?" The boy nodded yes. "I'll take them back with me. I'm in 12. I came down to get something from the machines." Soame withdrew cash from his pocket as he spoke.

"$7.49, sir," the waiter told him.

Soame gave the smiling face a ten-dollar bill. "Keep the change. Can you pick the tray up in the morning?" He took the tray and placed it on top of the coke machine during the exchange.

"Yes sir, no problem. If you need something else before we close, give us a call."

He had hoped the small tip would be meaningless to the waiter, but knew then he could be identified later if matters went bad upstairs. However, the waiter was already walking away. He placed the phone on the receiver, turned his collar under, and took the weapon from his pocket. He made the pistol ready to fire, and with it in the palm of his hand, he placed the tray on it. He took his handkerchief out from his left hip pocket and carried it in his left hand, holding the rim of the tray. He then proceeded to the stairs.

Though the men in the room sounded as if they were leisurely enjoying themselves, Soame knew factually they were hard at work, earning big money for the dangerous and hazardous job they did. Soame was the biggest danger they would ever encounter as a work hazard. He knocked on the door.

A really harsh voice called out, "Yeah, what do you want!"

Soame replied, "Your sandwiches, sir." He pretended not to see the darkening of the peep hole and knew only a partial black face could be seen behind a serving tray.

The door was opened against the chain and the voice inquired, "What do you have?"

"A salami and a pastrami, both with double chips, two Pepsi's, and a couple of seltzers."

The door closed while the chain was being removed. He saw the curtain move. The door reopened. A man stood partially behind it and invited him in. Half a step inside, he could see the person standing at the table near the corner of the room. He also noticed the person's hands were empty. That person directed him, "Over here on the table." He stood between the two men, after having made a step into the doorway. His left hand was at his side, a man and the door to his right and the person at the table to his left. The carpeting was not thick enough to slow the drag of the door which was to his advantage. He dropped the handkerchief, at the point of making the complete turn around toward the table. The stop and the fake move to retrieve the article forced the person standing partially behind the door to commit himself.

He was armed, but before he could bring the .45 into position to fire Soame had back kicked with a full squat thrust onto his kneecap. Because of the pain he was forced to endure, he could not concentrate enough to aim and fire the weapon, which fell to the floor. The kick twisted and broke his knee; his leg gave way as he struggled to keep from falling to the floor. He grabbed at the end of the bed, while he tried to stand, reaching with the other hand for his broken leg…The tray was thrown to the man at the table during the squat. That person caught part of the tray, and while he batted materials away, Soame had moved behind the man scrambling to hold the corner of the bed with one hand, hold his knee with the other, and situate his other knee to give him support. "Don't move!" Soame told the man in the corner as he leveled the .25 at his face. He then closed the door. "I mean it," he said with one foot on the .45. The guy left standing looked at him in terror and shock. His hand was on the handle of a pistol in his shoulder holster. "Turn your back to me," Soame casually ordered as a command. The armed man did. "Extend your right hand directly in front of you." As he did so, the one on the floor who had found comfort on his side cradling his knee with both hands almost in a prenatal position yelled "Oh God! Please don't let me die." The one standing hesitated.

Soame shouted: "Put your right hand up and bring your left hand behind your back, now!" The man in the corner did so and lived.

Soame then pulled the spread from the nearest bed over the man on the floor, stepped off the .45, eased it with his foot in front of him, kicked where he knew the broken knee was, and yelled "Don't nobody move!" The man under the cover cried out in agony. With his left hand, Soame disarmed the standing man, and forced him down to the spreadless bed. In doing so, Soame had him put both hands behind his back. "I told you not to move," he said to the man on the floor, when he saw movement beneath the spread. Soame tied the man's hands behind his back on the bed, with his own belt. He then picked up the .45 and proceeded to the connecting doors.

He had knocked twice after sliding the bolt back. While moving back to the occupied bed, Soame also surveyed the room. After checking the bathroom, he looked under each bed. He was undressing the man on the bed when Frank entered the room. The man being undressed had no shoes on. From behind, his trousers were being dragged down. A pistol was held at the base of his skull by the capturer. "There's your .357," he told Frank. The pistol had been tossed onto the other bed. The weapon used to hold the captive on the bed at bay was the .45. Frank picked up the magnum, balanced it on the palm of his hand for weight, looked down the side of the pistol and through the sights, and said: "Seems like we're in business, ha?"

"That things ready for action, John." He then motioned to the spread. "Under that cover is a fellow with a knee problem. Ease the spread off him carefully and I'll tell you what to do," Soame casually told him sliding the last trouser leg off.

It was 10:15. Both captured men were laid back to back, in a 69 position on the far bed in the room. They were tied hand and feet with a piece of sheet, cut and twisted for the added strength. Frank was at the breezeway collecting ice in buckets from both rooms. One of the men on the bed was in great pain. When he returned, Frank would come in as he had left, through the division, from 13. It had been relatively simple so far, but Soame knew better than to relax. That would be the easiest way to invite complications. So far, the men held captive did as they were told, but they had not been questioned, and though they displayed signs of resentment, they knew they could ill afford to show hostility toward the two who had invaded their room. When Frank returned he noticed an empty suitcase on the luggage rack behind the door he'd entered from. On the bed nearest the front door, he saw two Uzi machine pistols with silencers attached, an open 2 ½ foot circular tote bag with a lot of banded bills, and two bags of powdered substance. The powder in the smaller bag was white. There was a folded sheet of paper on the bed also; it contained names dates and figures. Frank could not see the paper, it was between the two bags. "Are we gonna doctor on dat guy?" he asked after viewing the situation with the added fixtures, and moving it to sit the ice buckets on the desk.

"I think we should find out what we have here first," Soame replied to him.

Soame placed the chair from the desk between the beds, nearest to the head of the injured man, who gazed at him still in bewilderment. "My name is Fred, my partner here is John, and we are interested in finding out certain facts about you." He paused, knowing what he had said would soak in with meaning. "Will you cooperate with us, and help our and your situation by answering some questions?"

"You've got all the goods, what do you want with us?"

"We want to know your names and other important information about you. Who are you?" Soame asked.

"Alston Watson."

"What's your partner's name?"

The victim looked away and responded, "Ask him."

"You seem to be in a great deal of pain. You can help yourself and him at this point, and things will be a lot easier for the both of you."

"I have nothing to say, get away from me, my leg hurts. Talk with him why don't cha."

There was nothing else to do. He'd done interrogations before and knew many approaches and techniques. An American hostage had never been the focal point of one of his interrogations, but the identical basic patterns began developing. He played the soft and easy approach, using the cat and mouse style, when the movement led to the uninjured man, who squirmed when Soame moved his chair. "John, bring me a piece of wire from the kit next door will ya?" Soame casually asked, placing the chair.

The brown powder was taken from one of the bags on the next bed. Frank stood on the opposite side of the bed holding a piece of wire, three feet long and so small it looked like a piece of string. Soame extracted the plastic bag from the leather carrying case, and unfolded it. He said, "Now I know you know what's going on, don't you? I know you know I want to know your name, and you probably think I'm going to ask you nicely, be sweet and gentle, promise you a lollipop and all those sort of good things, right?" The man said nothing. Soame talked a bit more, "I'm not very tired, but it's rapidly approaching my bed time. I'm usually in bed by 11:30. It may be needless to say your friend is in pain, and stands a chance of having the feelings reactivated in his knee, and he asked me to talk with you, do you mind?" The defenseless person still did not answer. Soame stood up reached over and hit his partner directly on the already aching spot.

The man cried out in agony, "Oh God please, please."

Soame then, with his thumb pressed into the calf behind the knee, pressed and pressed, eased up and pressed again. The yelling and screaming was so loud and intensified, Frank came around hurriedly and threw the folded spread over the man in extreme pain. They all heard him say, from beneath the cover, "His name is Ed, Ed. Oh God, please don't hurt me anymore, please." He sobbed, "Please don't hurt me anymore, man, please, I'll tell you."

After releasing the grip, Soame sat up and pulled the bed with the powder to him. He wet his little finger, dabbed it into the substance and tasted it. Alston's whimpering tapered off. It was decent stuff. Soame took a one and one and knew it was heroin. It was a pound and a half and it was raw. Soame knew it was heroin because he felt the urge coming on to throw up. "John, make sure they do not move, I'll be right back." He then went through the dividing doors, closed the division behind him and used the bathroom in 13. He knew he had made a mistake, and judging from what he had seen when others used smack, a nod would follow the regurgitation…fifteen minutes later Soame reentered the room. He went directly to Ed, sat down, and said: "Ed, you haven't been too cooperative. I've got something really good for you if you insist on remaining silent." Ed still remained silent. Soame reached out to Frank who had placed the bedspread on the desk.

"Dis guy kept complaining about his leg, so I put some ice in a towel and wrapped it around it while you was gone."

"Yeah, I noticed. Let me have the wire will ya, it seems to be time for me to doctor on hushed up Ed. I feel sure after awhile he's gonna have something to tell us. Got any idea what it is?"

Frank shrugged his shoulders, passing the wire, looking at Ed, and revealing a broad smile. Soame asked: "Ed, is this brown material raw?" The captured man still said nothing. He tied a loop in the wire, in front of Ed's face. The circumference was about three inches in diameter. Drawing the loop in, into a knot, he told Ed, "Now Ed, I'll be direct and tell you what it's gonna be like in about five minutes." He drew the fine wire in to a knot and caught Ed's attention with more words. "The next time I make a loop with this wire, I'm gonna put the head of your dick in it. Have you been circumcised Ed?"

"What do you really want from us?" Ed asked.

"Well, since I know you can talk we don't have to worry about forcing you to open your mouth, so we can fill and stuff it with smack, do we?"

Through a series of questions Ed revealed the plan. Everything was included except the knock when Joey arrived. Frank looked at Soame when Ed gave the wrong information about the knock. Soame pretended not to notice. After Ed repeated the involvements the second time, Soame instructed him, "Now repeat the part from the knock."

"Sure, they knock twice, we knock twice, then they say it's almost two o'clock, then we say its only three of us."

Soame then asked, "Alston, is that right?"

"Yeah, yeah, yeah, sure that's the way it goes, can he get some more ice in this towel for my leg, it's helping but I think most of it is about melted. It's like he said they knock twice from outside first."

Soame then patted the injured knee. The ice had really frozen it. "Now if we don't pack ice around that leg again, the pain would come back, would you like that, Alston?"

The man looked at him with bulging eyes and said, "We told ya, we say it's almost three, they tell us it's only the two of us, we let um in."

"How many will there be?" Soame asked.

"Two sometimes three, we never know, but he's never alone."

Soame was satisfied. It was ten past eleven. The leg was repacked in ice.

Alston was placed behind the far bed from the front door. Two pillows made a cradle for him to rest the ice pack between, under and on top of his knee. Frank had gone down and filled a pillowcase with ice. Soame cleaned his nose while Frank loaded the car. The only item left in the other room was the phone device. Ed was seated in a chair, between the beds, his hands tied behind his back, and looking miserable. For Soame, it was like old times, years back in the military. He had completed many missions and was thought to love what he did. He had survived only because he had gotten to be one of the best and, during those times, there was nothing he would not do for "Uncle Sugar." This night so far had been like a training exercise during the old days. Experience had taught him to remain alert throughout the operation to "arrive alive."

The coke Frank had was far better than that taken from the occupants of Room 12, although Frank had a straight up "one" on his and the bounty was raw. From his sandwich bag, he broke out a large portion, nearly an "eightball." They also rolled 10 joints of weed and decided to smoke only in room 13. They alternated watching the two men. The Uzis had shoulder straps and were ideal for the occasion of greeting the expected party, if any difficulty should arise. Frank had never handled one of the rapid firing automatic weapons. Starting from the thirty-two round clip, Soame explained the operation of the pistols. They arrived at what they calculated to be a sure plan in "jacking" Joey and his companions when they came for the pick up and drop off. As the major stratagem in developing the plan, Soame stressed the importance of surprise to Frank. The initial objective was to get Joey, his partner and the goods into the room. A gunfight outside the room would mean instant failure, but that possibility was also considered. At least the Uzis had silencers. Getting to the car and getting away with what they had would be the move at that point.

Since Ed had called and answered the phone it seemed logical he would be the one to answer the door. Soame wanted to ensure, as much as he could, the key element of surprise they needed when the time came. Alston was incapacitated because of his injury. They not only had the problem of not knowing how many men Joey would bring, but also how the incoming group would react, so every effort had to be made to control their captives to avoid giving away their intentions. To minimize any inside threat, Ed was gagged, placed under the bed, with one hand extended and tied to the middle leg on the opposite side of the bed. In this way, he would be camouflaged, with the aid of the spread. Ed's other hand was tied behind his back, and he was on his stomach, which caused the bed to tilt considerably. Soame would answer the door using the same procedure Alston had when Soame had brought the sandwiches up, except that Soame would not show his face or talk. For that reason, Alston was seated in the chair. Because of the knee it was not necessary to tie him. He had to be seen by the entering men, and he had to look natural.

Frank would be positioned like Ed, but slightly under the front bed. Both beds were made, but the covers were bunched up on one side to hide the men on the opposite sides. At eleven fifty, everyone was positioned for whatever was to come. The original two occupants of room 12 had been treated as decently as possible. Ed was a heroin addict and had begged for an injection to sustain him. Soame had obliged. A hole was made in a pillow case, Alston's foot was stuck through it, and it was brought up to his calf and taped at the bottom. Towels held a half pillow case of ice in place. The top was taped mid-way up his thigh. Though Alston's leg had been attended to, there was no doubt in his mind that Soame would kill him if he failed to do exactly as he had been instructed. Soame and Frank snorted coke from their positions, while they waited. Soame knew the men they waited for were professionals, but he wondered if Frank knew how professional their captives were. In the coming confrontation, everything could hinge on a single flaw occurring in a split second. Everyone in the room knew the two men with the guns were ready.

At 12:25, there was still no change. Soame thought this was a good sign. No call meant they would not have to worry about being detected. Joey would probably be coming directly up to the room. A final check showed everything in readiness. The car had been parked up near the office, close to an exit from the parking lot. This was in the event the bathroom window had to be used to jump and run for it. Frank had the car keys, a .357 magnum, and an Uzi. Soame had faith in himself, trust in the weapons, and hopes of bringing them both out of the room alive and with the goods they had already snagged, plus what Joey was bringing. Soame waited on the desk ensemble, where he could see the entire room. Frank sat between the beds on the floor.

Soame studied Frank, thinking how useless the one shot/one kill principle would be in this situation. Somehow he did not have the jittery feeling he had earlier felt about Frank. As kids, they had thrown and caught their share of punches. When his temper flared, Unks had always become furious and had to be subdued. This night he had been warned to "remain composed, and always think above the situation." At 12:50, Soame brushed past Alston, went to the ice bucket, and grabbed a handful of the small cubes. On his way back to his position he dropped nearly half on the bed for Frank, who immediately gathered them in his hand, shook them as though they were a set of craps, and tossed one in his mouth. At this instant, there were two knocks. Soame silently moved behind the door and observed Frank was responding well, easing onto his stomach partially under the front bed. Soame simply knocked back twice, moved to the corner of the bed, and covered Frank with the spread. He nudged Alston to respond. Soame's left hand made the adjustment with the spread. The hammer on the .45 was adjusted into position to fire. With the movement of Soame's thumb, Alston saw this action in front of his face just before the barrel rested on his temple. Alston gave the code: "It's almost three o'clock." Soame then moved to the door and looked through the peep hole.

There were only two of them. The one nearest the door responded, "It's only the two of us."

Soame turned the knob that unlocked the door, twisted his body, and leveled the .45 at Alston's face; he sat five feet away. Looking directly at Alston, knowing he would not be detected, he opened the door against the chain. Alston had been instructed what to say, what to do, and what not to do with the other parts of his body, in order to live.

"Twisted my knee, Joey. Open the door, Audie." Alston and Joey were looking at each other as Alston spoke. Soame could not be seen through the crack at the facing, created by the door's opening. He closed the door, took the chain off and opened it for entry.

Joey furiously marched in. "You twisted your ankle! Sitta around a broken up?" He was about to take his hat off and, in a direct path to Alston, he took his third step into the room. "Joe is a down da stairs, he's a waiting, we gotta hurry." He was then standing over Alston who was reared back in the chair, with his leg propped up on the lower part of the ensemble. The man in the rear was halfway into the room.

Soame rushed the door as the second man came through. By this time, Joey clearly saw the spread covering Frank on the floor. Joey had a briefcase in one hand and his other hand was extended to place his hat on the desk, near where Alston's foot rested. Soame heard footsteps passing the door. It was not known if anyone occupied room 11. At that hour, Soame knew slamming the door could attract attention. He closed the door without a sound.

"Freeze!" Soame demanded. Instead of doing so, the second man attempted to step away from him, turn, and pull a weapon from his belt. There was no alternative. Like a distant, tearing screen, the faint burst from the silenced machine pistol, threw three slugs into the side of the disobedient victim's head. The man did not feel the sting of more projectiles entering both his feet and ripping his ankles as Frank sprayed him also. Joey was in a turn, but had to either shift or drop the briefcase he carried, to increase his speed. He had successfully placed his hat on the desk. On his own, he probably would have lived. Soame had estimated his intelligence and knew he would have halted on command, but Alston, because of the ice packs and the totally frozen condition of his knee, had forgotten about his pain. Soame had not moved since he closed the door. Remaining in his tracks he saw the drama unfold, as if in slow motion, one that cost the other three men their lives.

The move Alston made was very unwise, foolish and costly, when he brought his leg from the furniture. His attempt was to stand up and charge head on into Soame: when his partner at the door attempted his step and turn procedure, Joey started his turn, Alston then made the move with his foot. Soame had strategically placed him in the chair, reared, to detect any move he made. Alston was the gunman with the initial two. He proved he had hart, though a foolish move, he displayed valor on his job, dedication as a professional, and devotion for his employer in the face of danger. Both of them were in clear sight of Soame, as Alston's leg gave way. He did not know his knee was broken. He fell into Joey, who dropped the case on the bed while turning, still pivoting and reaching for his shoulder holstered weapon. The blunder landed Alston on his face, in front of Frank, who was totally surprised with panic, and held his finger on the trigger of the Uzi. Frank had that instant, brought his face from under the bed. The commotion told him things were not right. Suddenly, Alston's face appeared within two feet of his. The Uzi sprayed Joey's ankles, before a sequence of slugs tore Alston's face apart. Totally shocked, dazed, and weakened from the injury, Joey attempted the carry through in bringing the pistol out, as he was falling. His body took more than twenty bullets, from midway his thigh to his head. Five slugs rattled his heart. After placing them there, Soame jumped on top of the table, and called out, "Hold up, Unks. Its over!"

The tearing screen sound finally stopped and Frank brought himself to a sitting position on the floor between the beds. Soame squatted. Holding the barrel of the weapon he possessed toward the ceiling he asked, "You all right, soldier?"

Frank, still mildly shock, said, "um cool man…um cool."

The most stupid event to occur in the room that night happened next. The bed next to Frank suddenly flipped on its side and leaned toward him. Before it fell on him, and would pen him to the next bed, he sprayed the Uzi once again. From experience, Soame had been firing in bursts of three's and five's because he knew the value of ammunition as well as the principle, "fire to the tracer, for placement." Frank knew nothing of this technique and emptied his clip. When Soame helped Frank to his feet they discovered Ed's riddled body.

They had been very lucky in one way, successful in another, and yet there was still another task. Somewhere outside there was someone called "Joe" who knew there were four men from his organization in that room. Soame knew they would have to find him. Frank had no thoughts on the matter; he was still adjusting to the situation. Less than two minutes had passed since Joey and his associate had entered the room. Soame gave Frank the briefcase and they went to the other room. The smell of gun powder and blood lingered behind them, saturating the air.

After scanning the parking lot from the bathroom window and noticing no one waiting, they came up with an impromptu plan. With Soame taking the over-sized briefcase out of the window to the car, and Frank carrying the monitoring device, the room would be completely empty. Frank was to go past room 14, to the end of the building and down the stairs. The lounge closed at one. Frank's job was to notice anyone in the parking lots directly in front of the rooms and in the "T" formation. The four men in the room wore suits. Frank was to nonchalantly look for anyone appearing to be waiting for someone to return from a room upstairs. The porch and entry to the stairs descending was to have given him the vantage point he needed to accomplish his assignment. He also carried the magnum in his belt, and his .25 automatic in his hip pocket. The car was the point of rendezvous.

Soame knew, that if Frank could locate "Joe," Soame could make the approach, with the advantage of surprise. He arrived at the car thinking, for once he was on a mission that would gain him something besides a laborious paycheck every two weeks. This is all it ever was to him, a job. The briefcase contained what appeared to be about six kilograms of coke. The thought of the "Jackpot" for the other twelve "drops" was the motivating factor. Besides, Frank had done something he really liked. They took two good hits from the remains of the eight ball they'd been doing. "I'll be at the car by the time you get there," Frank was told as he went out the door. The room keys were taken and it was a simple fall for him, from the bathroom window. He had rolled on the gravel and was on the front pavement, before Frank was at the bottom step.

"I saw him, it's gotta be him, Soame," Frank said approaching the car. "He's in a caddy almost where you parked when we came in. He's backed in and sittin under the wheel." His voice rang with excitement and anxiety--he had digested the kill.

"Ya know, Frank, we're not committed to anyone but ourselves. We have a lot and, unlike Miami, the one who drives isn't basically the scary one…that guy's sittin' on a lot of loot, and is probably very good at his job." Soame saw a trace of disappointment in Unks' face and added, "There's a lot of living in the trunk of this car, plus what's in this case, and most importantly we're safe now."

"Hey, Blue, you said all the way!" Frank smiled broadly to coax his buddy.

Frank had attracted Joe's attention leaving the room next door to the gangsters. Joe watched Frank walk down the stairs and through the first corridor. The breezeway was well lit, because of the machines and phones. In the breezeway Frank went back to the corner and peeped. Joe then became suspicious. That move caused Joe to come out of the car and lean on the fender. The driver was alert and every bit the composed professional Soame anticipated him to be. Though less than ten minutes had passed since the two men had gone upstairs, Joey said they'd be gone "a couple of minutes, both packages are prepared, we gonna drop and picka one up." Joe was becoming aggravated. He sat with one foot on the ground, smoking and chewing a cigar.

The plan was for Frank to give Soame time to go up the opposite side of the street. It was the same busy street they'd driven in on. It was also the same street the bathroom window overlooked. When Soame went far enough in the opposite direction, he had to have time to reverse his walk, and at a normal pace come in behind the Cadillac. Frank would then get Joe's attention, simply by parking next to him, and getting out of the car.

Soame had fastened the Uzi in the small of his back with the shoulder strap. It was undetectable, fitting tight as a corset. He used the opposite side of the street because there was still traffic, which he wanted to put between him and his objective. Frank's clip had been emptied, so they divided the remaining twenty-four rounds equally. Frank had his Uzi only as a precaution. The warning was, "under no circumstances are you supposed to approach or go closer than necessary to Joe." Soame sensed that Joe was the real killer in Joey's gang and probably the most dangerous of the men. There was a four foot wall separating the parking lot from a playing field. This was the practical reason that caused Soame's decision to go after Joe. Soame's approach was in going up the street far enough, not to be seen across the field as he crossed and reversed his direction, without being noticed. He had to also walk to the wall and "crab" along it until he came up behind the Cadillac. The car was seen as he passed the lot. Using his peripheral vision, he saw the man leaning against the car Frank had described. The driver appeared not to have noticed him. As it turned out, if Frank had waited one minute more, the situation would have been perfect. In fact, if he had parked the car and simply gone upstairs, all would have been fine. Instead, when he turned into the parking lot and saw Joe outside rather than in the car, this presented a challenge and excited him.

Joe was a large, big gross-looking guy. In stature, he resembled a Japanese sumo wrestler. When Frank saw him, he drove straight to him, pulled out toward the pool and backed in next to the Cadillac. There were four other cars on that portion of the lot, which had fifteen slips. Frank had on a windbreaker, concealing the Uzi on a strap hanging from his shoulder. Though it was concealed, it was not in a good position for him to immediately produce and fire; in keeping the weapon concealed getting out of the car. Joe recognized the windbreaker before he turned towards the pool. After parking Frank had the perfect chance to position, aim, and squeeze the trigger on the man pretending not to notice him. The shots would have been made from his passenger window. Instead, knowing he had rushed the situation, and to give Soame more time, he got out of the car with a cigarette between his lips, patting his pockets and stepping toward the man now standing by the Cadillac. Frank asked, "Hey buddy, got a light?" Joe placed both his hands into his pockets as Frank stopped before him. It was the last cigarette Frank would ever hold; nothing else was ever to be done by him, ever, nothing else, ever, following the last light he saw.

Many men know of giving and how to give their best. Some men think the best is all they can give. As the word "ultimate" implies so does the word "absolute" refer. It is often the degree one has to achieve in order to succeed. The type of movement done that night by Soame should have been termed as "dogging" instead of "crabbing" because he was on all fours. With all he had and with all the effort he could produce, Soame tried to get to the rendezvous before Frank. His partner sensed Frank would be impatient and not allow him the time necessary to move into position. The field could not be crossed; the risk was too great that Joe would see him. Immediately after ducking off the sidewalk, he heard Frank's motor turn in, off the street. Soame was behind the wall. At even a normal parking lot speed, he could have kept up with the moving auto on all fours, "crabbing" as he was. The engine was heard as it roared and raced seventy-five yards away. Soame very seldom panicked. Had he stood and ran he could not have made much better time with the effort and speed he used. When he was ten yards away, he heard gurgling sounds. He peeped over the wall and saw what he thought was Frank being choked. Appearing to weigh about 270 lbs, Joe towered over Frank, standing 6'4."

Soame then ducked and moved toward them, while un-strapping the weapon from his back. When he stood again he was directly behind Joe, who held Frank in front of him. Soame squeezed off four rounds in an even burst. He walked the rounds up, directly into the center of Joe's back, between his shoulder blades, smashing his spine with each projectile as it hit. Precision calculations and experience dictated that Joe should have been free of all movement in the upper part of his body after the first bullet hit him. That single round should have paralyzed him upon impact and freed Frank from his grip. Instead, only Joe's right hand stiffened after it fell to his side, violently shaking and trembling. The huge man's left hand still held Frank by the throat. He was weaving; the bullets had pushed him forward against Frank. Soame could not see Frank, and did not know what was actually going on. In horror, Frank had died; though still standing, he was a dead man.

Frank had walked right in on the big man, who flickered a lighter once and doused it. When Frank leaned in closer, Joe's left hand plunged a fillet knife into

Frank's throat behind his jawbone, directly under his ear. In dropping the lighter, which had caused Frank's temporary blindness, Joe reached for Frank's belt, and from the front of his trousers, Frank was pulled in even closer. The thin sharp knife was grounded in, cutting upward, until the point of the blade pierced and penetrated Frank's brain. They stood as if they were dancing. Soame did not see Joe's left hand fall to the side as the right did, because it was stuck inside his partner's throat and lower head, holding the knife that had cut and twirled into the dead man's cerebellum. Soame then immediately placed three slugs into Joe's head, walking them up from the base of his skull. The final shots sent the killer of his friend toppling forward to the ground. He watched for movement from beneath; there was none. Before he climbed over to the other side of the small wall, he knew both men were dead.

Standing over the men, Soame could see how his buddy had died. He had seen horrible sights before, but Soame knew then for sure, he had never lost a close friend. The impact of the fall, because of Joe's size drove the special type knife blade through Frank's skull. Four inches of the point stuck out of the back portion of his head. Sometime you want to stop, but you can't stop. How can you stop when there's no stopping to be done? We are all basically governed by habits, and Soame was trained and conditioned to good habits. Military training dictated his responding with sound judgment, and he knew his ability to survive depended on him making a secure move at that point.

The immediate danger was someone seeing and or noticing the scene. He walked to the driver's side of Frank's car and found no keys in the ignition. He saw the bullet-riddled windshield in his approach to the car. He then threw the pistol with the silencer into the back seat of the sport coupe. In Frank's right trouser pocket, he found the keys and quicken his pace. After pulling the car beside the bodies to shield them from view, he opened the passenger side of the vehicle. That particular model coupe was designed with reclining seats that lay out almost flat. The passenger seat was let all the way back to the extent of its measure. Sometimes it is not the strength, but the know-how that is the determining factor. Soame had to kick Joe's hand out of Frank's head. The big mans body was then rolled to the opened passenger door, it was doubled, and lifted onto the reclined seat. He laid Frank's limp body on top of Joe. There was an abundance of blood and grey matter left on the pavement. The car was then backed into the position from which it had been moved. The glove compartment was then emptied the compartment and Frank's wallet and pistol was taken from his pockets. Later he would send someone in his family the belongings and at least part of the money.

The personal items and the Uzi's were taken to the new Cadillac. Soame had seen the lights from the radio when he initially came over the wall past the automobile. The keys had to be in the ignition. It was general knowledge, that type car, the trunk could be opened by a button in the glove box. The trunk light revealed how much he had gotten soiled during the escapade. After transferring everything from the Ford to the Cadillac, he took a fresh shirt from his suitcase and closed the trunks. A towel was taken to the nearby pool. He dipped the towel and his new ankle boots and went directly back to the cars where he wiped his face, arms, and boots. After changing shirts, he wiped his Levis as best as he could. Exactly nine minutes after he had fired into the back portion of Joe's skull, Soame was exiting the parking lot in the Ford.

A half block from the motel, he drove off the side street into an alley. Soame used a 2 by 4 to knock out the shattered windshield of the car. After climbing up on the hood, and exerting effort in several attempts to kick the glass out, he found the board. He could only shatter the glass with his booted foot and the mass only sagged together. He assumed Frank tried to get the weapon into position to fire, but in his desperation, during the strain and pressure of the encounter, The only shots fired from his weapon hit his own windshield. Less attention would be paid to the car without the glass than driving it as it was.

It was parked a block and a half off Canal street, in a parking lot near a dumpster. Other than clothes, the two bodies had nothing on them. Soame removed Joe's wallet from his inner coat pocket. It was packed with cash, which Soame would use as a wad for immediate needs, rather than disturb the bundles. It created a slight buldge. In the small lot, Soame removed the license plate and wiped the car's surfaces. The interior was sprayed with lubricant. The WD-40 was noticed before arriving at the motel.

Chapter 4

It was 1:45 Friday morning, the 15th, as Soame Hudson approached a third rate hotel on Canal street. He had purchased the kidskin boots manufactured by Stacy Adams, less than four days prior. In 55 degree weather, with no coat, the dude from Florida was cold, and he was "stepping."

…Ever wanted to cry and couldn't, because you wouldn't allow yourself to? Ever thought about blame, knowing what responsibility is? Childhood goes back a long ways when you are past thirty-five, having been reared without brothers or sisters, and lose a friend you've played with practically all your life, because he asked to give you a ride… "Aw Unks, if we'd just…."

"Hey Blue, what it is…um cool, um cool, we goin all da way, um with you Soame, um with you."

"Maybe you should look where you're going, monsieur." The soft, low keyed, sexy voice said with a heavy and distinctive French accent. Soame, hurrying and lost in his thoughts, had this morning walked into a beautiful, fine, sleek, and voluptuous woman, who overwhelmed him because he could not figure out where she came from. On top of that he was mystified, fascinated, engulfed, and totally taken aback by her charm.

"Pardon me, ma'm," was all he could manage to say. Soame usually wore a hat, but since he did not have one, he could not tip it to her. They were in front of the Lady Baroness Hotel. There seemed to be very few people on the street. "I'm at fault, I'm sure, I honestly did not see you," he apologized.

"It is all right, but you should be more careful, you might just bump into a post, ha." The words rolled out, totally captivating him with her French accent and charm.

He smiled and asked, "Are you with someone, Miss?"

Sweeping her long lashes at him, she replied, "Maybe, what do you think?" Her reply delighted him, and made him feel light as a feather. He could have floated away, realizing she was a "hoe."

"I think anyone as beautiful as you, and with the charm you display, should have an escort." Smiling with a slight nod of consent, he added, "And if you are on your way home for the evening, it would be my delight and pleasure, to share my cab with you."

"Ah, oui oui, how gallant, monsieur." She said this while fluttering her long lashes at him, turning her shoulder parallel to his chest, and looking in the direction he had been going. She stood, slightly looking over her left shoulder, waiting for his response.

"My name is Soame, and I think you are very re-gal, Miss_____?"

"D.D." When she stated her name, it sounded as if it was being said fast in English, but the French accent was clear. She also added, "But Suarme, such pleasures for you, would delight me for a hundred dollars."

He looked at her with sternness, and, with gestures, assured her of his acceptance before he spoke. "Madam to spend some time with you this night, as inviting as you are, would be my pleasure. What you ask I consider a small token and ask that you reserve for me in the future, when for you, the possibilities of delight from me are unlimited."

She looped her arm into the extension he had made while talking. They strolled up the block exchanging glances at each other. She asked, "Perhaps you will show your faith in the idea we have in common, and extend half, oui?"

"Again that would be my delightful pleasure, but first don't you think we should take the cab?"

"I see no problem in that." After telling him that, she found out he was unfamiliar with the city, and basically only knew of the renown Bourbon Street, as an inviting lure "for raw social excitement and acquaintances." She took him up one block to a cab. In less than ten minutes, they were a block from the motel. He gave her $250.00, and she told him there was no motel on the corner, he had given the driver as their destination. He had previously told her where he lodged. His response was, "I like very much, the way you hold my arm, and I enjoy strolling with you, do you mind?" Her reply, in the back seat of the cab, was to place her hand on his member. Resting her hand between his legs, she snuggled her head in his chest. They listened to Michael Jackson's *I Want to Rock With You* on the radio.

They encountered no interruptions, and Soame noticed no irregularities escorting the beautiful woman directly to the car. After seating her in the plush vehicle, he gave her another hundred dollar bill, and from the open passenger door, said: "DD listen…I'm going up to my room. I'll be there for maybe ten minutes. Will you wait here for me?"

"Take your time, I'm yours for the night. I'll be here when you return." The room had already been wiped for prints. He replaced the bathroom window and screen, wiping and handling them with towels, as they were installed. The room had already been checked and double-checked, for any possible item that may have been left behind. The air conditioner had been purposely left on. He turned it off, and entered room 12 from the connecting door. Even with the air conditioner on, the room reeked with the smell of blood and defecation. Soame wiped the buckets, luggage rack, door chain, the middle leg on the far bed, and every item Frank had touched, or could have mistakenly touched. After doing the bathroom, he removed the serving tray and cover from the front bed. After wiping them, they were set atop the luggage rack. Soame then went to the front door; the "Do Not Disturb" sign was on the inside knob. He wiped it and placed it outside. DD waved from in the car. He had calculated the chance, with the potential risk, if she was looking. It would take much less time, to simply walk to the next room from the porch, than it would to set the bolt, from the room he and "Unks" occupied. There were two connecting doors. Both had a bolt on the inside. Soame re-entered 12, slid the bolt in place, pressed the button in the knob to lock the door, and exited the room again using the front door. With the towel he had used, he duplicated the procedure in 13. On his way out, he partially opened the picture window curtain.

At 2:25 am, he and DD pulled into her basement garage across town. She occupied a one bedroom apartment, on the second floor, in a very nice neighborhood. She had invited him to stay the remainder of the night, after he informed her he was en route out of town. Little did she know or expect that he wanted to take her with him. He had hinted though, "With all probability, I'll be leaving before daylight." From the trunk he gathered his shaving kit and other belongings for a complete change of clothes. He also carried up the quality coke, enough reefer for the time he would spend, and a bundle of the banded bills.

DD opened the door, and they were met by the barking of her little French poodle, and the very noticeable fact he or she had not been house trained. Little foot steps raced to her, over the sound of ruffling paper. As she turned the ceiling light on, from the front door switch through her laughter, DD called out "FiFi" and scooped the puppy up. DD was a real treasure, and Soame had noticed that fact about her all along. Now he had a chance to observe her motions and actions relatively close. The odor in the apartment covered the smell of blood, which had soaked into and dried on his jeans. He was filled with desire and anticipation. Along the way DD told him about the dog. He had only taken a step into the doorway when she turned, slightly looking over shoulder with the puppy in her arms. They both looked at him; DD said "Ma cherire," to the puppy. "This is

Suarme." The small dog swiftly licked its lips. DD then swerved her body to the couch, sat FiFI down, and said, "Come in, come in!" He did, leaving the door open behind him.

DD scurried about picking up paper, telling him chatterish things. Twice she stopped and rushed to the bedroom and kitchen, opening the windows. The ceiling fan was also turned on, as she scampered about. He became aroused every second, especially once the air began to clear. Her chit-chat and movement filled him with increasing desire, to see her getting about in her panties. The patch in her rear crotch showed vividly, each time she bent over, and soon he felt he could tolerate it no longer. When she had picked up all the paper, she stuffed it into a plastic bag, lit a stick of incense, got a leash, and asked, "Are you coming, Suarme?"

"Say, ah…I don't want to rush things but… can I rub your ass DD?" She knew he would do it anyway, and she would allow him to do anything reasonable he wanted to do. "Can I rub it just once, before we take her out?"

To his amazement, she did something that surprised, shocked, and fascinated him: She turned her back, hiked her partial mini-skirt up to her waist, and with one hand pulled her panties into her crack. Revealing her totally exposed cheeks with her other hand, she held her hair on the top of her head, in a gather from the back, and said to him, "Suarme, come here, my darling." After he'd made the approach, and before he touched her, she said very softly "Suarme, I am yours. How long do you want me ha?...tell me dat" He rubbed both buns with one hand, then put his palms on each, lightly squeezing them. She remained stationary as he moved, positioning her body to straddle his, with her shoulder forming a T in the center of his chest. With his right hand, he once again rubbed her ass. Her pussy was as fat as the filled plastic bag, waiting to be taken out. With his left forefinger he stroked it. Soame then gently bent over to her breasts. They filled a partly open silk blouse, held by a sheer, sky-blue colored bra, matched to her panties. He carefully bit the protruding top of her left nipple, once while he rubbed and stroked, twice after blowing into her ear, and the third time with calculated firmness, while taking her right hand from her head, placing it in his left, and moving it to his bone hard dick.

"If you are mine, you must choose to leave with me. I will be yours as long as you want me. How long do you want to be mine, lover?"

He was once again rubbing and stroking while he talked. Light kisses were delivered to her forehead, her eyelids, to the tip of her nose, and her cheeks, moving like a soft brush sweeping upon her lips. "Let me think a little, Su-arme. You could be dangerous, but you are gentle and I see the goodness in you. I tell you soon, oui?" With both her cheeks in his right palm, rubbing and squeezing, he slid his right forefinger in her pussy, back and forth through the moisture. He placed his left index finger in that moisture, squirming in the secretion to her clitoris, and there he toyed. "Oh Suarmmmeee, ooooh please, Suarmeee, Pleeeeeseee," she moaned. He then pecked her lips briskly with a kiss and quickly released her.

He returned to where she had invited him from. Still looking at the beautiful woman he had asked for. He did not want to simply go to bed with her, he wanted to make love to her. He knew that, she was vibrantly alive, inside, and could satisfy his needs. She further amazed him, by doing something he had never before seen any other woman do: She shook her hips in four even motions of grace. During the process, without using either of her hands, she brought her skirt down over one cheek then the other. He would later find out she was famous in the region. What he had witnessed was her trademark, as a professional. The celebrity before him was "Miss Dubanee."

She turned to him, licked her lips and said, "I like you."

He responded, "Yeah? ... If it pleases you to know it…I want you…lady." She then walked to him, grabbed his member and solidly rubbed it, and slowly with luring swirls, strolled toward the couch. Almost there DD stopped, looked over her shoulder and winked at him. Continuing to the puppy she bent over. When she straightened up he went to the kitchen and dining area, for the bag. He then joined her at the door.

It was a very nicely designed and furnished apartment. Though she was definitely French, the furniture was a combination of modern American and contemporary. Downstairs the building and lawn was nicely kept. There was scrubbiness, and he noticed the pool was relatively small, for the size of the complex. The building appeared to contain about forty apartments. Soame questioned the four-month-old puppy walking on a leash. He thought, "They had to be at least a year old!"

"No, No Suarme, dat is for the larger ones, and the basic age obedience classes require."

When they returned upstairs, he noticed the dog once again stayed where she was placed. DD went to the kitchen, put fresh water down, and poured a snack from a box. Soame locked and chained the door. DD displayed astuteness with her inviting hospitality, turning the lamp on. "Hit the switch, will you darlinggg," she purred. He turned off the ceiling light and she turned off the fan. DD then kicked off her shoes and walked nimbly across the deep shag carpet to her boudoir. Following her, he commented on the apartment, and asked how long she had been there. Hiking her leg to a crossed position, she responded; "2½ years," while sitting on the bed about to release her stocking from her garter. He sat at the dressing room make-up table, watching her undress as she revealed certain facts about herself. He pointed out he had traveled abroad on several occasions. Although he had not spent time in New Orleans before, he said: "I know an original accent from France, when I hear one." She was then sitting ten feet away, on her bed, with her legs crossed. Her hands were flat on the bed with the palms down, and she had undressed to her panties and brassiere.

"I'll not avoid the issue, which is seemingly obvious, but what do you really want, Suarme?"

He stood up, casually walked toward her, and stopped four feet away. He thought of the dried blood on his pants and wondered if she saw or smelled it. She was watching him closely, as he moved toward her. "Don't move, I'll be right back," he said. Turning, he raised his hand, pointing upward with his index finger. "When I get back, I want you to show me your pussy." Pointing at it, he continued out, toward the living room.

He returned with the items from the trunk. The bundle of bills he carried had a blue band around it, showing $10,000. Upon his entry into the room, she laid back on one elbow, hoisted a leg straight into the air, pulled her bikini panties to the side, and softly said, "Darlllinggg." Not taking his eyes off her, he walked over to the small cushioned piano-style chair he had been sitting on. It was placed about a foot from the bed, where he sat down. Except for the cash, the other materials were put at his feet. She was truly a beautiful woman by all physical standards. Not only was she "fine" and charming, the area at the vertex of her legs was displaying the absolute fattest pussy Soame had ever seen. Her's was laden with smooth and fluffy hair, like that on a baby's head or silk.

Soame had seen a lot of pussies before and knew they were not all the same. The hairy mound somewhat overwhelmed him; it was not like other pubic hairs he had seen, even his, which were kinky and burry, truly characteristic of blacks. She was exposing the area he'd requested by holding her panties to the side with three fingers. With her index finger, she tickled her clitoris. Looking at him stare, she called out, "Look Suarmmee," taking the tip of her finger, and twirling her tongue around it.

He smiled in appreciation and, with a casual voice, told her, "You're a very good bitch." Without hesitation DD eased gracefully over on her side. She gathered herself on her knees, then extended on all fours, with her rear directly in his face. Holding that pose only briefly, she reached back with one hand, and once again held her panties to the side, for the view he had requested in departing the room. "You're beautiful DD." She went back on all four and began rocking back and forth. Momentarily she stopped, eased her panties midway to her thighs with both hands, went back to all fours and rocked back and forth a little longer. She asked, looking back at him, "Do you really want me, Suarme?"

"I've asked you to leave with me." He said in standing up. "Sure, we can enjoy each other's pleasures for the next hour and a half, perhaps two. What I really want DD, is your lasting company, while I search for your true devotion. When I leave, will you be accompanying me?"

Breaking the visual trance, she fluttered her sweeping lashes. There was a momentary silence. She looked at him again over her shoulder: "I'm still thinking about it. Hold my ass, if you really want me, Suarm." He patted her right cheek and found he had to hold and squeeze it, because she ground herself into his hand. He placed his face against that same cheek, where his hand had been, and bit into her flesh. Soame held it hard, with his teeth. He bit harder until she yelled loudly and moaned to him, "Ohhhh, Surammmeee." He released her. Still on her knees, she pulled her panties up saying, "You naughty boy, naughty, naughty Suarme." She then turned, sat on the side of the bed, looking up at him, sadly.

"Yeah, that's what I want to talk with you about, but first I want to shave and get cleaned up. If you're really serious about coming with me, here's something I hope will encourage you. I don't have anyone, anywhere, and I'll be good to you DD. By the way, my name is Hudson, Soame Hudson." He extended the bills to her. As she took them, he reached down and showed her the drugs. "There's a lot of everything I'm giving you in this offer," he said. "I'll share it with you, but I want you to want me. I've had plenty of women, in a lot of different places. Like I said, I'm alone and I'll do you right." Once again the magnetism attracted both and held their eyes. Knowing she was totally aware of the issue and the security he promised, he did not pressure her for an immediate decision. "You don't have to tell me right now, just let me get cleaned up. You can join me in awhile, if you want to, I'll call you… You got any shampoo?" She rose and scooted past and under the hands offering assistance. After hurriedly taking four steps, she stopped, turned, and with a raised index finger, signaled him, saying, "Come on, bad boy." He was led to the bathroom, where she pointed out her toiletries.

He had finished shaving when she knocked. "You don't have to knock to see me, ever," he told her, opening the door. She wore a honey-colored, terry cloth robe. It was tied and hung midway to her thighs. DD had a handful of bills spread out in fan fashion. His shirt was off, he had just applied aftershave, and was about to take his pants off. "If I say yes, and do not choose just now, what would you say to that, Suarme." Fanning herself with the bills, she casually strolled in, and stood in front of him. He unzipped his pants, removed his belt, and while looking at her, in his stocking feet, he said, "Seems to me that leaves only you committed. I'd be very pleased to have your company, my dearest."

She had said, "If I say yes." This lingered in the back of his mind. Knowing she was a very experienced "Lady of Evening," he also knew that she was clever. Through experience, he knew she was either for him or against him. He could only hope, wait, and watch her responses. He kissed her forehead and the tip of her perfectly shaped nose. She had a pecan brown complexion. Her hair was black, worn in a beautician's style, with the back portion draped just past its shoulder length. "Give me those," she said, reaching for the pants. He had no idea what she wanted with them. Evaluating the circumstances, he decided to project the trust he knew they would mutually have to give and understand from each other, with reliance. He knew the .25 automatic was in the right hip pocket. The handkerchief separated it from the denim, to hide the pistol's appearance. She did not know he had it. In extending them to her, she stooped, picked up his shirt, and gathered other articles from the hamper. "I'll need those also Suarme, I'll put these in the machine in the laundry room up… Oh! It's so heavy." She had requested his socks, and after rolling the entire mass, she had taken the pants. Without saying anything, he retrieved the pants, removed all the articles from the pockets, placed them on the pink fur-like commode cover, and gave the pants back to her. She knew he saw her see the gun. Neither said anything about it.

"Did you say the laundry is in this building?" Soame asked. With a revealing sophisticated air, not realizing how deep her accent projected, she replied, "I shan't be gone long, the laundry room is up the hall, Ah?" With the money in her robe pocket and the ball of clothes under an arm, she moved close into him. Through his boxers she grabbed his rod, "I will need these and those if you want them done." He attempted to take his shorts off, but she did not release him. "Is it good?"

"I'll see you when you return," he said. After gathering the shed items, she placed a smacking kiss on his lips, winked at him, and walked out.

Entering the bedroom from the shower, Soame told her he was cold. After closing the windows, she asked if she should turn the heat on. He replied "No" and watched her walk naked back to the kitchen. Paw sounds on the bare kitchen floor, and whining from the puppy drifted to him. The floor had a solid oak finish. He decided they made a very nice couple, and gained pride in the thought of having her. Not only did she look gorgeous in her clothing, her body was captivatingly lovely. At twenty-six, she had no stretch marks, no scars, and only a couple of blemishes totally hidden by her clothes, and hardly noticeable when she was disrobed. DD was also very hairy, which he liked and appreciated. That included that she did not shave her legs. When she and the puppy entered the bedroom, she patted the stool, which had been placed back at the lighted make-up mirror. Fifi stood on her hind legs trying to get up. Soame found this amusing. He laughed and responded, "Oh, no." DD scooped up the puppy, said, "Ma cherire," and went kiss, kiss, kiss. Fifi then stood, prancing on the stool. Naturally, he watched with delight her fat, protruding pussy, when she stooped.

She stood with one knee on the bed. Both of them were still naked; he was laying on his back, visually locked into her stare. Soame's hand was extended to DD, who took it in a half turn, falling backward, with her back landing on his chest. The gaze was re-established; they kissed for the first time and it felt everlasting. When their tongues finally separated, he spoke: "We have to leave soon."

"Oh Su-armme," she sounded as if she was crying, and told him, "Have me good before we leave. I want to remember, and I feel I should never forget this time."

"I will, and we both shall never forget, but it won't be as good as either of us want it to be. There isn't enough time right now."

The beautiful woman, without make up told him, "I know, but after today, we will have a long time."

The apartment had been a furnished rental. She and her pimp had moved into it 2½ years prior, because of the location, away from the atmosphere and people she worked around and with. She had seen no clientele there, which is why they separated. He wanted her to start working from the apartment. When

Soame met her, she had been alone for three months: when they separated, she was very happy and pleased they were able to come to suitable arrangements. She was totally satisfied when the situation was finally finished. She had experienced many bad times, with a number of men who were professional panderers. She had began working at 15. Her mother was a prostitute, who came from France, because of a love affair with a white executive, from New York. DD was fourteen. Neither she nor her mother spoke English. Instead of marrying her as he had promised, the New Yorker wanted to put her to work, and turn her 14-year-old daughter – DD – on the streets, in New York City. Her mother was somehow able to get to New Orleans, on a discount tour to the Mardi-Gras.

"We came because the people here know and understand the French." She told Soame. "If not for you, I work for someone else. I like you because you say I can choose… Miami, ha?... Here I have been trapped so many times, I can no longer count them. I've been taken to towns, put into rooms for months, and did not know where I was." He listened without interrupting her. "I'll go with you because in being with you I am happy, Suarm. It is the first time ever I have left this town and could go because I want to go, and with someone who ask me." He heard the sincerity in her voice, and understood her interpretation of "choose." She said in conclusion, "I have been lucky, I go out twice, sometimes maybe three times a week. Eventually someone will take me, they 'lay down the law' I must obey… I am a whore, that is all I know to do. Until you, I have no choice." They both understood the situation. There remained a lot to be continued on the direct subject, but preparing to leave was the immediate factor having priority.

Downstairs, Soame had gone through Frank's things, and had gotten rid of other discards, rearranging the trunk. At 5:15 am, the trunk was full, but DD had a few other items, which she would carry. The car had an Alabama tag on it; it was titled to a company in Mobile. The title was in the glove compartment, with insurance papers. Though it was dangerous, he removed the tag from an older model "caddy," which had Louisiana plates, and used those plates on the one they would travel in. The .44 magnum found under the arm rest in the front seat, was with the other weapons, and all were accessible without difficulty. So were the drugs, except for an ounce, of which he and Frank had been using a quarter. This left about eleven ounces with what was brought from his home town. During the packing, DD had not been down to the garage. He made a number of trips back and forth, and was twice followed by Fifi; he found her company amusing. DD used the cocaine in the "main line." His response was, "I have no objections to it at all. Just be honest with me, and we'll never have a problem."

She smiled, hugged him, and said, "Oooh thank you Suarm, thanks very much." Being a snorter, he knew having only an ounce and a half of Manitol could possibly be a later problem, depending on where they were headed. A destination at that point had not been planned. The original tag was not discarded, but placed in fairly accessible reach inside the trunk, which was now secure. With an ounce of coke, an ounce and a half of "cut," papers, and an ounce of marijuana, Soame went upstairs to the woman he would, in thirty minutes, drive out of the city of New Orleans with.

Two full length zipper bags, an overnight case, two hat boxes, Fifi's dish, a bag with several cans of dog food, some dry dog food, and his shaving kit were all that remained to go. "That's it!!" she said joyfully, clapping her hands. He closed the door behind him. He had never before seen two creatures so lively. Fifi was more active than a kitten with a ball of twine, or pawing and chasing a rubber ball. The puppy played merrily on the rug, "arff, arffing" and scampering about, putting her nose in the air, looking out of the corner of her eyes, to see if she was being watched as she scurried about. Soame led DD to the glass top table in the dining room. She sat on his lap and he placed the drugs on the table. DD knew he had heroin, but when earlier he asked if she indulged, he was told it was not her preference, either. The mood was drawn to the serious conversation which he initiated: "Within thirty minutes, we're gonna be leaving. Stay as relaxed as possible, and try to think of anything you might be overlooking. Things like a note, telling the landlord you're out, and such of that nature."

"Oh you're a doll. I had not thought of doing it that way. The thought crossed my mind several times, and I've tried to dismiss it," she said, with both hands on her cheeks. He then eased his left hand further up the inside of her thigh. He knew the habits and routine of "snorting," and had through the years had been in contact with drugs on various levels. He asked, "Do you have your 'tools' and materials ready to travel in the front of the car with us?"

"Yes, Suarme." There was a pause, but he noticed she projected no uneasy feeling. She went on, "I have a pouch which contains everything, but the water, I will carry it separately."

"Great," he said. "This is more than ample to carry us through the weekend. Can you handle the responsibility of keeping up with it and being sure…"

She interrupted, "I've done it many times. No one will ever know we're 'holding,' if we're stopped, Su-armme." He kissed her, enjoying very much the feel of her body, and the wetness in her panties.

She rolled the reefer while he put a half cut on half of the ounce. The pure substance was much better for her means. After wrapping a portion of his, they put the remainder in a pill vials, from which it could be dipped with a straw as he drove. They both then got "high," in their individual ways. A "joint" was shared in doing so and after petting during and through the entire process, he stood her up, with DD's elbows on the glass top. He hiked her skirt as she spread her legs and held her bikini panties to the side, and they enjoyed a "quickie," before she left the building for the last time. When they finished, and after affectionately kissing her, he reached into his pocket. From the center of his wad, he removed two single dollar bills. Snatching the bills, he flung them on the table to her, and said, "Ha, bitch!!" She looked at them, angrily pouted her jaws, charged him, pounded him on his chest with both fists. Laughing, he caught both of her wrists and through the 'arff, arffing' of Fifi, asked, "What's wrong?" This was all after her cries of "Oh Suarmme, Oh Suarmme."

Through all this, in her frustration, she told him, "You give me so little after the first time, now you do the same thing. Then I said nothing, am I so cheap?!!"

Smiling, looking down at her, still holding her wrists, he asked, "Whatcha gonna do with all that money girl?"

In bare feet, she stood 5'10". Snatching away from him, she pivoted to the right toward the puppy. Swooping Fifi up she said, "Come, come, Fifi." Entering the living room, she stopped, turning herself and Fifi toward him. She said "Maybe we've found someone to share with." The dog yipped twice, then licked a flickering tongue, leaving it exposed in a pant. DD turned toward the front door.

Everything fit into the trunk, except the two hat boxes. He put them and the puppy's dish in the back seat. When all had been carried down, he returned to the apartment for her and her pet. In leaving the building, they separated on the first floor. Soame continued on to the basement for the car. DD had written a "notice of departure" and left it in the manager's mailbox. From there, happier than she'd been in years, she and Fifi walked to the front of the building, and waited for Soame. Had she been thirty seconds slower, they would have arrived at the front of the complex at the same time. He got out of the new car, went around, and opened the door for her. She held Fifi in both arms, with her purse draped over her shoulder. Soame and DD both were very proud and happy of and for each other. Both were in search of a new beginning; they shared this quest.

When he had taken his place under the steering wheel, in sitting Fifi on the seat, looking him directly in the eyes, she said, "Monsieur Hudson, … I am Miss Dubanee, I am very proud and glad to be with you, and thank you for assisting me."

Soame smiled and said, "The best is yet to come!" They were off.

Chapter 5

ACCORDING to the car's clock, it was 5:53. That morning they were on a ramp, entering Interstate Ten, leaving New Orleans en route to Baton Rouge. Soame turned the radio on, pressed the middle selector button, and whammo! There it was, one of his most favorite old tunes *You Are* by the Commodores. After merging on the highway, he looked over to Dominique, and said: "Say there, lady." With Fifi cradled in her right arm, she slid closer to him, saying softly, "Su-armm, oh Su-armm."

The gas tank was just shy of half full. According to the papers in the glove box, the automobile had been purchased within the past six weeks. It had less than ten-thousand miles on it. The Cadillac division of General Motors, is known as the producer of the finest built cars in America; its trademark is the standard for luxury. This style and make exemplified "the top of the line" in its class. The company produced only two other models rated above the Fleetwood Brougham D'Elegance. Soame and DD traveled comfortably with Fifi, in "the hog." People who own this car are known as the "money getters." Top flight executives usually set the trend with this style. Things happened for the person who operated a "hog." To understand the "happenings," one would have to experience handling this automobile, and be shown the awareness it dictates. This particular style and model automatically leaves the factory with everything imaginable as standard equipment, except for a cellular phone and radar detecting equipment to expose speed traps, Soame found everything else in place.

In his calculations, he felt nothing had gone on at the motel he had left the night before would be detected until 11:00 AM and 1:00 PM that day. The dried blood on the pavement was a projected thought. However, though DD's apartment was a considerable distance from the parking lot, while they were there, there had been a slight rain. He drove on, thinking that facts and the motel, in all probability, could not stand publicity that would damage its business. There was nothing specific to implicate him. He therefore had an unknown identity, traveling in any direction he chose, with $392,000 in cash. He also had almost seven kilograms of "raw" – pure – cocaine, and a kilogram of "raw" heroin. The "boy" or "scag" was in itself worth over a million dollars. Traveling with him was one of the most beautiful black women he had ever seen anywhere. He enjoyed very much that she seemed to love calling his name. Since the ride in the cab, his intentions centered around having her in that car, doing what they were doing. At her apartment, the attention and concentration necessary for the results he had gained with her, overruled thoughts about the escape. She had not been an easy gain. Mentally, it had been a mind-wrestling conquest. He had "played" at his best. The most fortunate aspect of all was her "unkept" situation. They enjoyed the ride, viewed the scenery, chatted about various matters, and relaxed in each other's company, while becoming more acquainted. The two people would become lovers for the remainder of their lives.

Almost certainly, they would not travel all day. Some time between 11AM and 2 PM, he would stop at a first-rate hotel and "lay over" until probably around midnight. His favorite lodgings were the Sheraton and Ramada Inns. He would need the rest, and it would be best to travel the region, this particular day under the protection of darkness. The black car, with a half black leather top, rolled along on Double E–agles. Knowing the car had to be specially ordered, because of the tires, Soame gave his attention to added features. Since there were none immediately displayed, he could not afford the time and attention above existing priorities. The executive wire-spoked rims cost nearly a thousand dollars each. One was almost twice the amount of DD's apartment. She had just "hit" for the third time. Storing away the "works," she said, "Suarm, you said to be honest and I feel like telling you something." They had been traveling for 45 minutes. He had just put a half joint into the ash tray, and he had done nearly half a gram from the vial.

"Let me share the goodness you feel, and hear what you have to say, dear." Fifi was asleep in the rear window. While slightly rubbing his chest, she raised up and peeked over their shoulders, to check on her puppy.

"I feel like a rich woman," she said. "I have never had this feeling before, though I have bought, for other men who had me, cars like this. I have made so many car payments they can't be counted. Funny, I think the bundle of money you gave me is not that much, when I actually look at it, but I have never had that much money before, for myself. Do you understand what I'm saying?"

"Sure." There was a slight pause before he went on. "Did you believe me when I told you the best, and it coming later?"

She liked the feel of his bone hard through the trousers. She toyed with it and said, "I believed it then, and I believe it now, Suarme." She had continuously attempted to squeeze the hard-on with one hand, and each time found she had to use two, to apply the pressure she wanted. This did not irritate him; it seemed to fascinate her.

She seemed entranced with what she was doing, when he asked, "Do you think the manager of the building will send the money to your friend Sadi?"

Tugging at his zipper, she replied, "The woman who manages is very nice. I think she will. The place wasn't damaged, do you think?"

He asked her to hold up with the exercise she was about to proceed with. They were nearly half way between the two cities. He would drive through Baton Rouge. To be sure of getting well beyond the city to a rest stop, he would have to refuel soon.

Sadi was a girl – a "working lady" – who helped DD catch "Johns" or "tricks" on Canal Street, when DD worked without a pimp. Sadi's husband did not mind her "working." DD would use one of their two rooms, paying them a fee. The woman's husband would keep away any pimps who tried "coming in" on DD. Without him, they would have taken her money, and forced her to work for whoever got to her. Sadi would send "Johns" she knew, who wanted DD, to the room, when she was there. DD would sometimes lean out of the window, and call a passerby whom she knew, or one she felt she could coax him up. This was the only way she could eat and pay her rent. Without the apartment, DD would have been forced to use housing on the "stroll," where she had lived off and on for eleven…

"The place looked really fine to me, I told ya," Soame replied. They were about to take an exit ramp. The station advertised an automatic car wash.

The puppy had never ridden in an automobile before. She had been purchased from someone in the neighborhood who bred gray miniature poodles. Two months had past since the breeder's son brought the prepaid puppy to the apartment. Though it had only been an hour, they thought it was a good idea for DD to exercise the still small, ball of fur. Soame sat in the car, and gloated at a woman he could hardly believe was not a movie star, or at least a person of similar stature. To himself, was "Wow, the kind of girl who always belongs to someone else." He noticed everyone else at the station also gazing at her.

"Check the hood, mister?" the attendant asked.

"It's all right."

The skirt she wore was not a mini, or even a half-mini, but its fit slightly above the knees complemented to her $37\frac{1}{2} - 23 - 38$ figure. No matter what she wore, her beauty was radiant. Soame held himself in check, and congratulated himself for his accomplishments. He opened the door when he saw Fifi squat. After getting out, he walked around, looking about and checking the car.

He particularly noticed when the puppy finished that DD did not bend over. With her knees together, away from any on prying eyes, she stooped. With Fifi in her arms, she turned and immediately saw him. She told the puppy something and pointed toward him. Many of the on-lookers turned their heads in his direction. The guy who had once been a radio announcer, a floor salesman, worked with a diamond group, and done public relations, as well as a few other jobs, was quite amazed. He smiled, waved the index and forefingers of his right hand. The quickly flashed inverted wave, signaled them: "Come on over here, you two," he called. With a voice heavy and deeply resonant penetrating the early morning air, the other onlookers, still dazzled by gazing at DD, could not help but turn their heads toward Soame, who walked toward DD. Fifi began squirming in DD's arms. He had never before seen anyone else reveal such pulchritude, not only in physical appearance; DD also displayed overall mannerisms. Knowing everyone was once again watching her, while almost to him she snuggled Fifi to her cheek; he grinned with delight. He had come from the rear of the car. Seeing her fine body in full stride sleek and swaying, in front of the Cadillac he held his grin, waiting for her. Taking a side position in front of the right headlamp, he placed his booted foot on the bumper and draped his elbow on his knee. The grin was a slight chuckle, when she arrived; only close could she see the slight movement of his head, and hear the low guttural sound. Ten feet away she had seen the grin fading back into the smile matching hers. "How about you, are you gonna go?" he asked.

The dog had been placed on the hood of the car. It was 7:10 in the morning. The attendant said, "That'll be $27.40, Sir. Would you like it charged?" While giving him $30, Soame asked him for keys to both bathrooms.

When the attendant was out of ear range, DD asked, "How did you know?" Fifi had walked to the driver's windshield with her shivering prance. The tiny leash was not fastened around her neck, it stretched in DD's hands, from one to the other.

He replied with a question, "You are mine, aren't you?"

"Come, come, Fifi," she called to the puppy. To Soame she said: "I told you yes this morning. That's why I am here, you silly boy." Rolling her accent at him, she clutched the puppy to her cheek. She stood really close into him, almost touching, between his legs.

"Well, sometime you gotta know bout whatcha got." He kissed her forehead.

They chit-chatted while Fifi playfully squirmed, throwing an occasional lick toward him. It was but a brief interval, before the attendant returned. The hot wash was $1.50. Accepting the keys, he told the attendant he would use the wash and "keep the change."

"Your car will be fine where it is, while you're gone and thank you, sir," the attendant replied. DD took Fifi with her.

When they returned from the restaurant, Soame got two coffees and a cup of ice. In the climate controlled car, Fifi would eventually take the melted water from her dish, on the floor in the back. DD had begun drinking her coffee when the machine started. Fifi was between her and the passenger door. *This Gun's For Hire* by Bruce Springsteen played on the radio. "That white boy is really getting down," Soame said.

"Oh look, Suarme!" The girl DD pointed at had caught her attention. Although the girl was nearly a hundred and fifty yards away, they could see she had schoolbooks in one arm, and was walking toward the Interstate. Since there was no building between her and the highway, combined with the fact that it would have been an irregular place for a school bus stop, sparked their interest. In her right hand, she had a long stick. Every four or five steps, she would strike the ground with the instrument, as if she was chasing rabbits from the brush. Because his hand was in use under her dress, DD fed him a couple of sips from her coffee, while they both watched. The song was finishing when the car wash machine stopped.

The girl had thrown her books over a fence and climbed over it. The fence separated the field from similar small growth, a cement ditch, and the Interstate, to which she was obviously headed. Soame directed the car onto the ramp, as the girl crossed the ditch toward the road's shoulder. Morning traffic had picked up, and was moving fast. The girl stopped about twenty-five feet from where Soame would merge into traffic. DD urged, "Pull over Suarm. Let's see if she wants a ride." At that instant, the girl stuck her thumb out. Stopping, he lowered the rear window on the passenger side.

The girl, seeing DD, said, "Hi, y'all goin ta Baton Rouge?"

Fifi whined and pawed at DD's lap. DD continued, "Do you want a ride?" Passing the puppy to Soame, DD said, "We are going there, if you want ah?" The girl nodded. DD turned, reached into the back seat and moved the hat boxes, for more room. Soame was disgusted, because the squirming Fifi prevented him from putting his hand up DD's skirt. He could only unlock the door from the panel and watch, without really noticing the girl. The door opened following the sound of the release. The boxes were stacked and DD invited her: "Come on in, there's enough room for you." After the door closed, the two females said "Hi," DD retrieved the puppy and settled into her seat. Soame said nothing and merged into traffic.

Initially, DD thought her name was Shirley. When Chairly clarified the name, she said: "Its like sayin chair, only with Chairly." She was on her way to see her brother, who had been in an accident, "a motor-cycle accident." The accident had occurred two weeks earlier, and according to what Chairly said, he was living with their aunt, "till he get betta and able ta come home." He was 19, and the town was Slidell, on the outskirts of Baton Rouge, on the way. When DD asked if she drank coffee she replied, "A lil bit, if y'all got some."

"Give her mine. I haven't opened it. My hands are full." Easing his hold, he indicated the steering wheel with one hand. Traffic had began getting heavy, with motorists traveling to and fro between the small towns and the major cities. When DD gave Chairly the cup of coffee she said, "No. No, das too much, I only wan a lil bit."

Soame looked at her from his rear view mirror for the first time. He briefly thought about what she had said. He immediately dismissed any thought of her, noticing DD kneeling in the front seat toward him, her skirt hiked up midway past her thighs, revealing a clear "shot" at her panties. He thought immediately of the towel he usually had in any car he operated, whiled he traveled. Being a "safe driver" he checked the traffic flanking him. This was not the first Cadillac he had operated. He knew only the El Dorado and Seville out-classed this particular model, with the Seville rating above anything manufactured by the company. DD had poured half the coffee into her almost empty cup. Noticing this, he said, "Let me help you." He patted DD's hairy mound, that the pastel-colored material covered. After passing the coffee back to Chairly, DD remained in the position; she liked admiring Soame's profile. Though she had tender feelings for him, she wondered without opposing thoughts, if this was the man she was to actually fall in love with. Several times she had felt the same way about other men and had the same thought. Each time she had been deceived. Her infatuations to this point had only been toward pimps. They were the only men she knew, except the "tricks" who paid her. Most of the tricks she had seen wanted her for themselves. Some were decent men. She knew deep within her, had she gone with one of the "Decent" ones, eventually he would only cast her out, to do the only thing she knew. Was Suarme really different? With all the style and class he presented and projected, was this simply another lure into the trap she had lived in as an adolescent, and throughout her adult life? Several times before the apartment, she had the chance to think there was a better life for her. Each time she'd ended up back on the "stroll" on Canal. This would be the greatest disappointment of them all, if he failed her. She compromised with the thought that, even if he was a pimp who had cleverly deceived her, she could still possibly love him. The sun was easing up behind them. The tinted windows enabled clear visibility of the scenery as they moved on.

At times Chairly would slurp. Other motorists darted and weaved in and out of various lanes, on the four lane road. DD noticed Soame held the car at an even speed, without cruise control, and seemed to carry the cars that flanked him through air, as if they were a flying squadron. He wore an undershirt, DD's coffee had been set to rest in the holder built into the open glove box. She had loosened the buttons on his shirt, allowing her hand to stroke his chest. With her head resting on his shoulder, she did not deprive herself thoughts of him. A deep feeling inside told her, if he was not a pimp, he would never allow her to work. That night he had told her he "wasn't, had never been, and would never rely on such means." He spoke so well, and seemed so much more educated than any black man she had known before. He had more true style and class, than any man she had ever known, period. Realizing this, DD knew, she could never give Soame anything but herself. Knowing she was like a hundred other women who worked that one street, and thousands in New Orleans and other cities and towns across America, she wanted this man for herself. He was special. The man she traveled with was rare and precious; though he knew her professional game so well, he was totally different. He was as rare as the true love she had never before felt for any other man.

"How's Fifi?" he asked.

"She's under you, asleep." When he said nothing, she continued, "She curled up directly in front of the brake pedal at the base of the seat. Are you happy with me Suarme?"

"More happy and pleased than I have ever been with any woman in my life."

DD raised up and checked back on Chairly, who was asleep. The cup was turned upside down on the stacked boxes. She said softly, "Oh Suramme."

DD knew about the healing, restorative factors of vitamin E. Her skin did not show a noticeable track sign, because of the care she gave it with the vitamin. Previously, Soame had used the capsule. DD had a four ounce bottle of the liquid E in her overnight kit. There was also a small bottle in her pouch, in the front seat. "I'm happy when you're high. If doing it is your thing, just be honest with me," he had told her earlier. He was a constant snorter, and had no reluctance toward sniffing the substance. Since finding Chairly in the backseat asleep, they had gone up twice. Approaching Slidell, DD attempted to awaken the girl by gently calling her. It became somewhat of a funny chore, even with Fifi pitching in with her yipes. Finally, with extended efforts in yawning and stretching, Charily asked, "Are we near New Orleans?" Once again she caught Soame's attention, from the rear view mirror.

They were ten miles past Baton Rouge when they heard what Chairly said was "all da story." Her mother beat her any time she did the slightest thing wrong. Her mother's boyfriend took advantage of her any time he wanted to. He and her mother drank all the time, and this morning he "did it" to her for the last time. She swore she would not go back, no matter what. The inside covers of her school books revealed her as Chairly Grivins. When DD asked if she had reported her mother's boyfriend's actions to her mother, she replied, "Twice he did it ta me in her bed. The first time I ran ta her for help, she told him, 'Go on Henry. Maybe you can make a woman outta her.' When he did it ta me the next time, she told me ta relax, and he would teach me how ta enjoy it."

It was a perplexing situation for the listeners. DD had the arm rest down, from efforts to awaken Chairly. Looking and listening through the space left by the upright rest, she would glance over and up at Soame, from time to time. Soame pretended to ignore DD's glances and nudging. However, he could not ignore the fact he knew that Chairly knew he heard her every word. DD knew also, and he knew that as well. The girl looked directly at the interior mirror during her talk. Each time he had nonchalantly glanced back, he caught her stare.

"The second time he pulled me in da room, and she jest watched an got undressed. Den he did it ta her; I had to stay on da bed, so he could feel on me."

He then spoke, "Chairly, listen. We're on our way out of state. I'm not like your mother's boyfriend; I won't take advantage of you, and DD will not beat on you. If you want to be dropped off, I'll take you to the bus depot in the next town, and give you fare to wherever you have in mind. Should you wish, I will simply give you some money now, stop and let you out. You must tell me now, where you want to go, or what is it you want to do." There was no reply from her, even when they looked into each other's eyes in the mirror. "Later on, around noon, we're going to stop for the day. How about if you think where it is you want to go, and let us know then?"

"How far ya goin?"

DD asked, "Do you mean before we stop at noon?"

"Afta ya stop fa da day."

He told her, "We might be riding for a few days, maybe a week. Right now we don't know." He then felt DD's hand in his crotch and continued, "We might decide to drive up to Oregon." Glancing back to see her response, he noticed she seemed not to be really interested in what he was saying. She was merely looking out of the window, not excited, not depressed, merely enjoying the ride and observing the scenery. He said anyway, "We've just gotten married, and we're on our honeymoon." There was still no reply. A short while later, Chairly was asleep again. The front seat lovers enjoyed each other as they drove on.

It was a beautiful day. So far they had encountered no problems. Fifi never returned to sleep. She was lively and playful. Because she continually pawed the back seat in an effort to climb over, DD tested her thirst. After Fifi had drank, she was placed once again in the rear window, where she seemed to be contented. It was near 10:30. Soame and DD concurred on taking advantage of an approaching rest stop. They all took the chance to walk and stretch. It seemed to be just in time for Fifi; who happily relieved herself. Using the men's room, Soame performed the necessary measures to preserve his nasal membranes. DD had used the vitamin each time she withdrew the syringe. Soame and DD agreed to have a good meal a short while later. They would wait until after they had gotten a room to continue the coke. This would allow for a healthy appetite. Though Chairly said she wasn't hungry, she had snacks from the vending machines. They drove away, without incident.

Toward eleven-thirty they were bypassing Lake Charles. Ten minutes beyond the outskirts of town, Soame saw the ideal place he thought for lodging. It was a Sheraton, with rooms on two floors. Though he did not necessarily like first floor accommodations, this time it would be most convenient, because of the car, and a parking place in front of their door, that the establishment afforded them. Soame was sure he could get a set of adjoining rooms, away from the main building, without difficulty.

Before booking a room he found a shopping center. They would order food in the hotel, but he knew it was best to get snacks, drinks, and other probable needs, before the room was taken. The girl had not been a problem. However, she was a major consideration. He did not know how she would act. She could go wandering off, or call someone. The story she told could have been true or not. She had lied about her destination being New Orleans. Soame knew through experience that women lie by nature. Chairly represented potential jeopardy, which could result in a catastrophe, but there was DD to aid the situation. He felt a slight urge for liquor, knowing after the meal he would become sleepy. The alcohol would further assure sound sleep, and since it would be only for a short while, he wanted the rest.

Soame's feelings about women could not be that wrong. He did not spend extensive time trying to understand them as individuals. The love game was won or lost, and the woman usually won. He simply accepted them for what they presented. Eventually he would have to trust DD, if they continued. Her first test had been the initial $250 he had given her and the wait downstairs in the car. A list of items at the grocery store DD and Chairly would shop for. He would also purchase items, but from a nearby package store, in the same complex. His choice in liquors was scotch, Red, or Black Label, preferably Black Label. He drank either of the two, when alone, during cold months. Accompanied by a female, he would drink vodka. Dark rum made Soame sick. During summer months, he liked Bacardi rum, only the light one. There had been a major difference since that brand of liquor was no longer imported from Puerto Rico. Americans do not make the liquor as well and now produce the product. Leaving Fifi in the car with the windows cracked, they separated to make the purchases.

Soame knew that he could fall in love with DD. He had loved many times before. Though he did not know it, this would be the first lasting love he would ever have. In a short while they had learned a considerable amount about each other. At times she drank Hennessey cognac, which was her favorite drink. With the Black Label he purchased for himself, he bought the regular Hennessy and a special 5 star Champaign mixture, which sold at $125 a bottle. From that day forth, when she drank, she would only drink that special blend. He preceded the other two to the car. He sat in the car and watched their approach. Noticing the front windows were down, Chairly pointed and left the sidewalk, in front of the grocery store, with an ornate grin on her face. He watched them step on to the pavement of the parking lot, and each motion his woman took he felt proud of.

One of the two large adjoining rooms they checked into was for Chairly. She was a factor involved in stopping east of the State Line. Immediately after entering their room, and securing Chairly and Fifi through the connecting doors, he and DD made wild and passionate love. It was so stimulating and wonderful, they both laid in dizziness for awhile after they were spent. Though she was multi-orgasmic, DD would only cum for a few men. She had never before had an orgasm such as she had when she came with him; the last time she came, and as she did, they came together. Afterwards, they laid there, in each other's arms. Meals were ordered and they showered.

Because of the abundance of attention Fifi received from Chairly, the puppy would spend the entire stay in the room with her. After the return to the car from the grocery store, Chairly began rubbing and petting Fifi. With the interest Chairly took in the puppy, they began liking each other. This allowed the "honeymooners" the privacy they wanted and needed, and eased Soame's mind somewhat, figuring the girl would be preoccupied with the day. One of the two large adjoining rooms they checked into was for Charily. She was a factor involved in stopping east of the State Line. Immediately after entering their room, and securing Chairly and Fifi through the connecting doors, he and DD made wild and passionate love. It was so stimulating and wonderful; they both laid in dizziness for awhile after they were spent. Though she was multi-orgasmic, DD would only cum for a few men. She had never before had an orgasm such as she had when she came with him; the last time she came, and as she did, they came together. Afterwards, they laid there, in each other's arms. Meals were ordered and they showered.

Soame slept a few hours, but the majority of the time was spent making love. They could not keep their hands, or any other part of their bodies, off of each other. The love they were searching for and establishing would never be doubted toward either of them. Nothing showed on the news about the incident in New Orleans. Slightly past one, Soame had gassed up, their belongings were assembled, and they were off again. In less than thirty minutes, they crossed into Texas.

"Dat sign said Orange County," Chairly informed them. At the hotel, she confessed. She had no place to go, no one to go to, and swore this was true.

She seemed to be a decent kid, so they agreed to let her travel with them. Fifi voiced her opinion and voted with an "arf, arff," and the matter was settled. The girl and the puppy made excellent company for each other. This definitely gave Soame a "free hand," if a matter needed his handful help with it. This volunteered help he saw cause to render directly after they re-entered the interstate… Prior to reaching Beaumont, they went north, changing direction. The new route carried them toward Tyler, Texas. They continued on toward the state line and just past dawn, and en route to Oklahoma, an amazing thing happened: Soame had gotten the map, when he refueled while registering at the hotel. In planning the impromptu route, that night before leaving the hotel, he had not paid strict attention, and not noticed the indication for the border patrol, at the state line.

They came up on the "stop for inspection" sign without warning. It was five-hundred yards away. The sign spaced twenty yards further indicated "K-9 assistance" and warned to reduce speed. He eased the small caliber pistol beneath his outside thigh, taking the safety off. Of all the incidents, circumstances, situations, and perils, he had encountered and been exposed to, Soame felt chances were this would likely be his last. Never before had his heart raced with such fury. The woman sitting next to him also saw the signs, noticed his movements, and with her right hand could feel the rage of his heart. Her hand had been resting slightly above his abdomen. DD moved slightly away from him, allowing space so there would not be criticism from the inspectors, about her being too close. She knew the coming danger, and as he had long before instructed her, "Always be prepared." She was as "ready" with the pouch, as she possibly could have been. It was situated in the center of the seat, slightly toward the passenger space.

She asked, humbly, "Do you think we'll make it, Suarm?"

Knowing there was nothing else she could have said better, he looked at her, feeling it was his last, if chances dictated, and said, "I may die. I want you to live; if there's shooting, get in the corner on the floor. Your personal money they cannot take from you, when this is over. It is enough for a start from where we met." They were three-hundred yards from the station. Turning his eyes back to the road, and admitting to himself he was falling in love with her, he said, "It would have been nice. I feel you would not have left me. That's all that's ever been important to me with any woman I've had; for her to have stayed with me. Be strong DD. Now do as I've told you. Stay exactly where you are unless there's shooting, or if you're asked out of the car." Nothing else was said. They were two-hundred yards from the station.

Soame knew with all probability, he would not live beyond the approaching lights. A hundred and fifty yards away, he buttoned his window completely down. The ash tray had long since been emptied and shut. The girl in the back seat was a mental disturbance, he had tolerated as company for DD and a keeper for the dog. To him she was of no other significance.

A hundred yards from the inspection station, the first warning grade in the asphalt, was encountered. Soame had been taught throughout his life, in application to the situation, to obtain and retain composure. He eased into a state of complete awareness, with total identity. After checking his nose in the rearview mirror, Soame Hudson was in structural readiness for whatever was to come. At that distance, having rolled over the short span of grade, he saw the only preceding car pull away from the station. There was no car behind him. From the northbound lane, the car he drove would be alone in the station. As he entered, there was no car coming into Texas from the opposite lane. There were two guards for each lane; each team had a detection dog with it. Soame proceeded to the "all traffic stop" sign. A guard approached the open window and asked, "Do you have any fruits, or live plants?" He looked into the car.

The other guard was then turning past the front head lamp, on DD's side, coming toward the passenger door. He was casually walking, but with spaced steps and had his hand on the butt of his weapon. Soame saw there was no safety strap on his holster. To the question, Soame replied "No." The guard was signaling "proceed," when the dog at his side barked – an indication that the car contained drugs. Fifi had been asleep between Chairly and the hat boxes, and neither guard saw her. The guard on the passenger side, was at the door. He saw DD and the girl in the back seat awakening with a yawn, taking a hand to her open mouth. Before the guard dog finished his initial bark, Fifi had nimbly jumped onto Chairly's lap "Arff, arff, arffing." Everyone in the car simultaneously said, "Fifi." Knowing the strength and magnitude of his voice, in application to the situation, Soame called twice. His last vocal projection was alone and ranged with authority, "FIFI!!" The German Shepherd then barked, which was Soame's intention, knowing the second dog would also react to the smells he was trained to identify, which had been calculated in reaching him from the car.

When the first bark was heard at the open window, the guard on the passenger side took a step back from the divider, and cleared his holster. The other team of guards was turning toward the car which was easing off. The guard in command of the situation was at the window. He had raised his hand to say "Halt." Instead, he used his raised hand, to signal the guard on the opposite side, with a pointed pistol. "It's alright, there's a small dog in the back seat that barked, that's all." He gave Soame consent to proceed.

Using excellent judgment, Soame did not accelerate, or put his foot on the brake pedal. From his rearview mirror, he saw the guard holstered the pistol; the car then picked up speed. There was less than a fraction of a second for three governing decisions to be made; if anything different had happened, they would have not gotten away. That was the absolute closest it could have been, for any situation, anywhere, to give three people in the car, the benefit of the doubt. Technically, they were supposed to have been stopped and searched. Soame had not had a chance. The rifleman in the tower, thirty yards away, had also taken position. The AR-15 he held, had been aimed.

Five-hundred yards beyond the inspection station, resuming normal speed, Soame looked in the interior mirror. The marked car beneath the tower did not pursue them. He turned the radio up, hearing a country and western station, and a duo, singing *You're the Reason God Made Oklahoma*. He and DD looked at each other and kissed, as she held his member in her palm. Fifi could be heard lapping water from the dish on the floor behind them. Chairly made a slurping sound as she bit into an apple.

Chapter 6

SHORTLY past eleven, they pulled into the parking space, in front of their rooms at the Ramada Inn Motor Lodge, on the outskirts of Oklahoma City. There they would stay until past midnight Sunday. The morning after having stopped to refuel thirty miles past the state line, they planned their activities. Soame needed the rest and very well knew it. The border patrol station should not have been over-looked in planning the route. An alternate would have been taken, had he been keen, as the planner.

Their activities centered around DD taking Chairly shopping. The girl needed clothes and, since they were traveling north, she also needed a coat and at least one sweater. DD also suggested that Chairly have her hair done. Unpacking and settling into the various rooms had become fun and exciting for Chairly. Caring for the puppy, finding security, and enjoying an atmosphere of luxury gave her comfort.

Soame called a cab and DD was asked to get instructions to a newsstand and a head shop. From the newsstand, she was to bring back a paper from New Orleans. Joker cigarette papers and pipe screens of all sizes were to be bought back from the head shop. The main reason for the trip to the head shop was to purchase Manitol. The driver would likely know where a head shop was. "Get a couple of boxes of papers and all but the extra large screens." Once they stopped wherever their final destination might be, Soame really wanted to lay low for a while.

Since the stay would be longer this time, Soame took several items he had not used before from the trunk including a small portable record player. Giving women money for sex was an idiosyncrasy he had developed over the years, with a host of woman. Since DD pounded on his chest, he had given her two more one hundred dollar bills. Though she had money of her own, he gave her five hundred dollars for shopping. Feeling that Chairly was not familiar with having money, he instructed DD to purchase her a bag and ladies wallet. DD was also told to give Chairly five hundred dollars and five singles. After the two females left, Soame showered and, returning to the room, found the puff of fur curled between the double stack of pillows on the bed where he had left her. She was asleep, preparing himself for sleep and "planning," he sat at the desk in the room, with the chair facing the bed he rested his feet on. He had Johnnie Walker "on the rocks" and listened to some music.

Soame reflected on the events leading them across the state line. He was very proud and pleased with himself, for having unbelievably fantastic luck of being in that room that Saturday morning. A short while after crossing the state line, they had stopped for fuel. Still wide awake Chairly asked DD, while they drove into the service plaza, "Did y'all see dat policeman back dare wid his pistol out, when we was at dat place?"

Soame and DD knew immediately who Chairly was talking about, but DD asked, "Who and which one honey?" DD was testing the girl, to see how she revealed the story.

"I don know who he was but…" And she went on with the story as to when she became aware of the situation.

What initially caught Soame's attention toward the officer's position, in his approach to the window, was the insignia he displayed on his collar. The spread wings of the eagle marked him as a colonel. It was the possible edge he had not expected, if the senior officer at all presented a ghost of a chance. Soame knew he had been given clearance to proceed. During the last word of the question, Soame shaped his mouth and used a slight indication of his head, to say "No." The fastest game ever handed down in the streets of Miami, is "Cop and Blow." As a kid, his street-wise learning taught him to "Do what's to be done and leave as soon as possible." In many ways, his formal training and experiences showed the same principle, revolving around that idea. A series of events took place, spontaneous and almost simultaneous, causing the flow of the scene. Even before he had finished the question in seeing the movement of Soame's head, the officer's hand had begun its upward move to indicate "move on."

Soame shook his head and said "No" with the signal to proceed. Then there was the "yawp" from the k-9 and the first arf from Fifi, just as Soame's answer had over-lapped the colonel's question. The three of them were harmonizing with "Fifi" while Soame's foot had released the brake pedal and traveled to the accelerator. Having worked as an announcer, he knew the projecting of one's voice. He had also been a professional soldier. In attaining his grade in the military, he knew how to give a command. When the overall situation broke, that is what Soame played for, after recognizing the colonel. Soame hoped to gain the colonel's professionalism and courtesy, if in outward appearance, everything else was in order. There were two other guards in the opposite lane, whom Soame knew also heard his voice preceding the bark of their dog. Attracting them and that bark was his calculated goal. After the initial bark, his hope was in the camouflage presented by the sounds from the interior of the car, and the people in it as a family with everything being in order, accepting the appearance of the driver as being a professional and a man of prestige. Soame had received the professional reciprocation and he "played" his total and absolute best for. Had the "full bird" (colonel) not been at that particular position with the car at that time, they would not have crossed the state line.

With his head tilted back and his nose filled with the vitamin, Soame allowed it to drop throughout his nasal and bronchial passages. "Coming down" he slowly consumed the alcohol and continued to relax. In a short while, he began to yearn for DD. Since he had been with her, the thoughts of losing a particular friend were suppressed. He knew he had done his best. Fate had presented a chance in no other direction.

He played an album by The Temptations, released in 67': *Whole Lot Of Soul.* Twenty minutes later, Soame got into bed. He positioned pillows under his neck, and with a q-tip like apparatus made sure his nose was totally swept. He slept, totally undisturbed for four and a half hours.

The partition door to Chairly's room was left open, as she had been instructed. The adjoining room's door was also open and slightly cracked. DD entered their room from Chairly's. Fifi was asleep on Soame's chest. Hearing the movement of the door, the puppy sprang to life and "arf arfed." Seeing DD, she pranced and whined. Before "Miss Dubanee" walked to the bed and scooped up her pet, Soame was reseating the .44 magnum. It was Chairly who was the first to speak. As DD ran across the room, the girl was two steps behind her saying, "Fifi, we're back."

At the bed, they enjoyed the excitement of being reunited. Fifi took center stage. She loved the attention and created ways to get a pet's, "smack smack smack" simulation kisses and a variety of hugs, from the woman.

"Well darling, she wanted it," DD stated, before Fifi stole the show. Soame was partly covered with a sheet and had a hand to his mouth, stretching as he yawned. His attention at that point had only been given to DD, who was enchantingly beautiful with her new hair-do. He had seen Chairly behind her, but noticed but a glimpse. His full attention was on the woman holding the dog. Discussing the possibilities of Chairly having her hair done earlier, Soame and

DD had agreed she was "too young." Now, it was stunning for Soame to see her. After DD's comment, he simply said, "You look very nice, Chairly."

The girl in the new dress asked "and hia, bout my Aunt Miss Dubanee?" She had pearly white even teeth, and seemed to practice the grin she showed. Chairly was almost as dark complexioned as Soame. He had already seen the new pumps when she was in stride behind DD, entering the room.

He then answered, "Your Aunt, you say?" She then followed DD in springing on the bed.

All the packages were brought from the next room, and the two females chattered about the trip. Chairly then took Fifi for a walk. She had been congratulated on her first hair do and praised for having been splendid company, and helpful during the shopping trip. The girl presented Soame with a gift from the "twenty" dollars she had received from DD. Alone with DD, Soame was at a loss for words, to express his appreciation of her new permanent. It seemed to be a hairdresser's masterpiece. The style was truly French including the roll, which was to the side and toward the top. The beauty of her face was totally exposed, with the remainder of her hair falling to the opposite side, parted from left to right and waved back where it fell. Its partly cut, curled like circular sideburns, and the rear portion taken over her ear, and included in the mash making up the roll. She was wearing a pair of neatly fitting slacks that looked as if they were tailored. Her long-sleeve cotton blouse, tied at the front and top in a bow. The DNYX earrings hung 1½ inches, and were encased in a triangular gold shell. The white blouse was peppered with circular, square, and triangular designs, which were 2 inch black objects. The slacks were charcoal grey. With her French designed stockings still on, DD sat on the side of the bed and heard him say, "My darling and most precious, there's something I want to tell you."

She leaned back with her hand supporting her from the other side of his thighs, and leaned her upper body toward his chest. Lowering her face to his, with a child-like meek voice she responded, "Yes, Suarme."

"There's something about you I've not overlooked, but I've failed to actually realize it before now," Soame declared.

DD purred her French accent in a babyish style asking, "What, what have you now realized Suarme."

"You have exquisitely beautiful, beautiful eyes. That with the other features about you, which are magnificently beautiful and wonderful, places you in my opinion as the very essence of feminine pulchritude."

"Oh Soarme, no man has ever used such words with me before. I'm sure I understand what it is you say, and I feel you would not tell me anything wrong, or something you did not mean, but I am not as learned as you, and sometimes you leave me so dazzled. Especially like now, when you compliment me. You make me so happy. I am so pleased and happy to be with you, oh Suarmmmm!"

There was a pause. During the interlude of silence they laid in a hug, with her face snuggled between his jaw and shoulder. Raising her mouth slowly to his ear she asked, "Did you really miss seeing me that much?" Scooting from under the covers and her arms, he kissed her cheek. Leaving the bed, he then walked to the window and partly opened the curtain with the cord. The lodge only had first level rooms in that section. He did not see Chairly and the puppy immediately, but he also realized there was grass at both ends of the building. He was not really alarmed, but as a precaution wanted to check on her. DD watched him put on his pants. When he reached for the shirt he previously laid out, she asked, "Do you want me to come with you?"

"I'm only going to the car," he said while tying the long-sleeve, tapered shirt in front. He stood in the open door, with one foot on the sidewalk, looking in both directions. By then he also saw that DD had gotten completely in the bed. Her chin rested in both of her hands, as she was propped on her elbows, at the foot of the bed. Her feet pedaled slightly in the air through the extension of her legs, bent at her knees. Though the afternoon was brisk, she knew the fresh air was inviting to him, and his body also enjoyed the sun. Finally, he saw Chairly approaching. She had rounded the corner in the front of the building. Fifi was in one hand held to her cheek. From the pocket of her new sweater, she pulled out a key and dangled it in the air. Soame and DD engaged in small talk until Chairly arrived, which he estimated in looking as she neared her room.

"DD sade fa me ta always keep ma key." The puppy licked her upper lip, seeing Soame look at her.

He then replied to Chairly, "That sounds like a pretty realistic idea."

After she had opened the door she told him, "I'll be ova ta git my thangs afta while."

"We may be going out, but look at your menu before you come over. We may have dinner first."

"Oh we don already ate," the girl told him. Soame looked at DD and felt a tingle all through his body. She had not moved and was smiling.

Looking back to the girl holding the open door in one hand and the puppy in the other, he said, "Yea well, I'll talk to ya later. You and Fifi enjoy yourselves."

Chairly went to her room and DD asked, "I thought you were going to the car?" Looking at her, he did not reply; he simply closed the curtain.

From the shopping trip, DD had also brought back two New Orleans papers. The cab driver had told her, the best newsstand was next to a shoeshine stand, in front of the major department store downtown. During their shopping in the department store, she and Chairly had their hair done. The store featured a tobacco counter, where she was able to purchase papers and screens. However, the tobacconist gave her directions to a flea market, where she could buy the items in bulk. She brought back two eight ounce plastic jars of Manitol. The flea market information attracted Soame's immediate attention. From time to time, he had browsed through more than a few. He had never gone to a flea market without finding something of interest.

Less than an hour after Chairly entered her room with the dog, they were all down town at the flea market. He bought four twelve ounce jars of Manitol. He also purchased four glass pipes, two large and two smaller ones. He then asked for and received a business card from the owner of the concession. With the materials he had in the trunk, his thoughts were toward the possibility of having a direct contact in the future. Obtaining the business card then could possibly save time and hassle later on. There was also an identification card booth at the flea market. Because of the circumstance DD thought "Chairly Dubanee" seemed to be a better and appropriate change for the purpose. The car was registered to " Stradford, Inc, Russel L. Furman, pres, 8723 Spires Ave the title and insurance papers showed the same person's name, but at 3917 Channy Dr. Both were Mobile, Alabama addresses. That afternoon Soame obtained a photo I.D. card as Russel L. Furman. On the back of the card in the "print identification" square, was his thumb print. The plastic lamination over the card, with the identifying information it contained made it look official. The card alone made the trip to the flea market worthwhile.

Before leaving, DD purchased a bag of Chews for small dogs. Fifi would delight in them. Soame's boots already showed a knick from an attempted bite into the kidskin, though she was too small to do serious damage. The puppy was teething and would enjoy the items designed for her.

Having obtained and accomplished these measures, they returned to the motor lodge. The department store and flea market would be closed the next day.

Fifi was with them during the time at the market, and showed a trace of disappointment, when she had to wait in the car with DD and Chairly, while Soame got his hair trimmed. In the barbershop, he did something he had witnessed as a boy. There was someone in the chair already, and three others waited. To be next he offered the three men five dollars each. The man in the chair then exclaimed, "Hell you can have my seat now for three dollars, if you're really in a hurry!" The car was filled with delighted laughter when he told them that story while riding through their ethnic group's community, en route to the lodge.

Though DD was in her mid-twenties, with both hands resting at her sides, a pencil could be placed under each of her breasts and it would not stray. They were the most erect "mounds" of that size he had ever seen. Sometimes she wore nothing, though it was only going to or coming from the shower, and this was done with him. Other times she wore his shirt, or a sheer, see-through top she had. Swimming was one of her greatest exercises and she did it as a form of pleasure. Except for the walks with the puppy, they basically stayed in until the following evening. Only a few clothes, overnight bags, and a zipper bag were accessible. "Miss Dubanee" only had three pairs of panties as a change. To Soame the amount seemed unlimited. Each time he would hide a pair she would come up with another. Some women look more sexy in their clothes than they do undressed. There was no way not to look at DD once you had seen her. She became the sexiest woman one could imagine. Though he had her in anyway he chose, Soame loved looking at her sleek well-proportioned legs, connected to the thighs that led to her swirling hips. She had a round mouth print of teeth on her right cheek, during their stay in Oklahoma city. The small gap he had between his two front upper teeth, was outstandingly vivid in the purplish blue imprint he left there.

Partly through a cat and mouse game of discovery, they played with each other and other natural items of interest they learned, they were able to gain more and more binding feelings toward their relationship. The course they took establishing their relationship, enabled them to develop respect for each other. These early days in the developmental stage of their lives together were leading to a mature bond. Both of them had searched for the bond they were then nurturing toward maturity. Once totally established within their unification, this cemented construction of feelings would be love. True love between two people can not be functionally disturbed by anyone, anything, or any outside force. The feelings

Soame and DD had already established up to this point were truly and totally functional toward true love.

DD's experiences were equal and almost comparable to those Soame had encountered. Until she was nineteen, she had not been kept by a black man. During that time and over a five year period, she deliberately caused the deaths of nine men. At twenty-three she was kept and made love to by another woman. After having fallen in love with that particular woman, for a year and a half, they became separated and never saw each other again. Their first night together Soame was told her last pimp had left town, and had received money from her to do so. The money was given not because he was her pimp; she gave it to him because she felt sorry for him, and did not want to see him hurt and humiliated further, or possibly killed. Soame would never talk with anyone who knew the woman he was sharing company with, when she lived and worked on Canal Street. He knew then they shared a motivation toward the attraction they had to each other. Truth was the catalyst; it was activated by faith in each other, based on the principle that he knew he would not lie to her, if she did not lie to him. She felt exactly the same way. In time, if either violated that simple truth, which was the commonness between them to themselves and toward each other, the absoluteness involved in the idea would cause destruction to one, or both of them.

"Miss Dubanee" was a notorious figure. Not only had she been trained to "get money" as a prostitute, she was a thief, a pickpocket, and a woman who knew more gambling ways to earn money than some black pimps she knew, who did not have the skills and courage to possess her. At seventeen she was taken by a pimp from her native country. He taught her to go into a room, "turn the trick," and be out in five minutes. While with him, any time she entered a room with a "john," her limit was five minutes to be back to him with the money. A quarter of the men she took behind closed doors, she could make ejaculate without them taking their organ out of their pants. It is simple to say "there is always the best in any working field or particular area." The woman in Soame's company whom he had removed from New Orleans was the best in her field, in the city, on either of its most renowned streets—Bourbon and Canal—which are major hoe strolls.

There were men who fought each other and lost their lives, whom she did not know about, trying to possess her. Other men who thought they possessed her, not in a physical way, fought with her, and were just as dead. It was definitely the change both of them were looking for, an attempt to adjust their lives, which now caused them to be together. Soame knew very well, long before meeting

DD, a person does not have to go to high school and college for a formal education, to be intelligent.

During their first stay in a hotel, before crossing the state line into Texas, all he told her about the financial security he could provide for their future was, "I have enough cash to allow us to live as comfortable people in society for the next twenty years, at least." He also explained, "I do not share my woman, in any way sexually, with any man. Any woman whom I consider to be mine, and accepts me as her man, and considers herself to be my woman, must understand that I will not tolerate a violation of this principle, which I strictly govern as a standard. Other than my mother's eldest son, and my father's first siring, who also bears my name, I call no other man in this world brother." He sat on the desk looking at her, sitting at the foot of the bed. Less than four feet separated them. Their stare was locked onto each other's eyes. "Do you understand completely what I have said to you, Dominique?"

"Yes, Suarm, I understand what you have said, completely. If it is your law, I am your woman."

The evening found them at a car wash, not far from the Motor Lodge. The car had been refueled, serviced, and checked. The mid-sized car wash serviced the local area with four stalls. Upon their arrival they found only one stall occupied, and five minutes later the "honeymooners," Chairly and Fifi, had the wash all to themselves. It was a fun thing to do, at the self service center, on the outskirts of town, convenient to traveling motorists also, because of it being next to the highway. Following the wash, Soame dried the car while DD and Chairly vacuumed. Though the vacuum was a lot larger than the one at home, and made considerable more noise, Fifi wasn't worried whenever the suction nozzle was held towards her. When she started barking and sneering at the noise and spout, Chairly thought it was wise and practical to place her on the hood. The car gleamed with the late afternoon sun casting reflecting sparkles from it. In preparation to leave, an odd occurrence took place. After the fun task had been completed, DD scooped her puppy from the hood, took Fifi to her chin, and went around the open door to the front seat saying "Ma Cherie." All four doors were open while Soame stood back with a towel in his hand, admiring the glistening wire-spoked, mag wheels. Seeing DD playfully enter the car with the puppy, and Soame's move to close her door, Chairly dove into the back seat, in her new Calvin Klein designer jeans; then it happened.

Knowing the back seat was completely empty, when Soame heard Chairly cry "ouch," he immediately hesitated in closing DD's door.

DD quickly sat Fifi in the driver's seat and turned to see what had happened, asking "What's wrong with you my dear?" DD was on her knees, looking at Chairly rub her tailbone, when she finished the question.

"The seat is kinda hard, but dare is a lump right hea."

Bending over her, Soame saw she was not hurt.

He said: "Scoot over for a second, and I'll have a look at it. When we get back I'll see what I can do about this."

Feeling the plush crushed velvet grey material, he discovered what he knew it had to be. Following their return to the Motor Lodge, when everyone was all settled, and while they all waited for dinner, the confirmation was completed. It was a specially designed rear seat. It was crafted to be held firmly into position by four one half inch circular bolts. When the bolts were removed a simple hard shove upward in the center, released the top portion from the snap fixtures, which centered and partly held the top in place. He had guessed there were special added features to the car, but had not been anxious to look for any. He knew he could do no more than he did then, if he had discovered it earlier.

Not trying to pry into his affairs, or in any way spy on him, DD came out of the room. She was in the bathroom when he came to the door saying, "I'm going out to the car for a few minutes." He had been gone for more than fifteen minutes.

She stood at the door ten paces away and asked, "Can I help you, Suarme?"

"Well if you close the door, and step over here a little closer, I think I might have something I wantcha ta do."

When she had done as he requested, and stood directly behind his half bent body, with his upper torso bent over the back seat, she asked, "How can I help you darling?"

"Show me your pussy."

Hiking her skirt up she told him, "Ah, but Suramme, you can see and have it also, if you come inside."

He was turning and in the completion of the turn, sat on the lower frame of the open door. "Those are nice panties, but the panties don't look like a pussy to me!"

"You must look closely, darlinggg," she told him, pulling the material to the side.

The bolts were fitted by a special wrench he had seen earlier, while closing the trunk. All the tools were stored for convenience and accessibility. This tool he remembered, because though he had seen one lug wrench for the special mags, not needed he subconsciously wondered, "Why two?" but the built-in, nut-shaped device, with a prong, was only similar.

He knew there were only three other cars in the parking spaces, on their side of the building. The curtains were drawn, on all the windows from where anyone could see the open door of the car. After looking "closely," Soame rested the top of the back seat on its face, against the back of the front seat. On the top was a furniture blanket. Beneath the blanket were burlap-covered stacks of carefully packed, heavy duty, green plastic bags, which were taped around the centers and ends. Twilight filled the horizon, casting a flamingo-colored brilliance across the setting sun's trajectory. He extracted one of the bags from the specially designed well. "Don't let Chairly come out, if she opens the door," he said to DD.

"She won't open the door, Suarme. I've told her for no one, or no reason, unless we know."

With his Case pocket knife, he cut a corner portion off the bag, telling her, "Here now, cup your hands." Popping particles glistened, from the chunk he removed, toward her hands. It would probably amount to a good "eight ball." He told her, "What you already have might be a shade better, if you want to try it. I'll be in when I put this back together. Take it inside." He then tasted a flake. The confirmation of the discovery was good, but for now, he could only replace the stash.

All the material was so well fitted together in place, he knew what plundering through it would result in. In the "cap" of the seat there was over two-hundred and fifty pounds of weapons. This was what caused the hard ride Chairly endured as a discomfort and never mentioned. The packed well of the seat should not have affected her ride, in the least. Replacing the "cap" caused Soame aggravation and frustration for the next twenty minutes. He was almost to the point of calling DD back to help him: it would take two men to properly fit the "cap" on. It had to be positioned directly over and into the specially made snaps; there were six, in total. Properly, two men could lift the top portion of the seat, and while one looked and directed, they both could place the cover in the position the designer had produced as an exact placement. One man could not see the snaps on both ends. Balancing the object from it's center and positioning and lowering it into it's properly designed receptacle, was a major feat for Soame. After finishing that task, he anchored the bolts into position, and went inside.

Chairly was there for dinner. Soame had seen a waiter deliver the food on trays and leave the wagon. Watching the waiter , Soame had pretended to be at some odd job, in the open door of the car. Upon entering the door, he saw the covered food on the table with a setting for three, and also noticed his still unopened present. It sat on one of the perfectly made beds. The gift was in the center of the bed, farthest from where he stood. Fifi was laying next to it, and sprang to her feet, with prancing bows and snorts as he walked through the door. Since the day of it's presentation the two females constantly urged him to open the gift. Alternately, he had said: "We've gotta go downtown, we're about to have dinner, let me shower first, let's wait till in the morning." Throughout the day there had been a few other excuses until, "Let's go wash the car, won't that be fun?" He did not need a Ph.D. to understand why DD rose from the desk chair, folding her arms over her breast, and Chairly rushed from the bathroom, pop-eyed, looking as if she was about to see the greatest spectacle of her life, which was becoming more enjoyable by the minute.

Soame's first step told them "No Dice!" Though he had glanced at the bed, the Stacies trampled three strides to DD, the door slammed, she cried out, "Oh Suarme!"

"I gotta wash my hands, what's wrong?" he called out.

Snickering, Chairly put her hand to her mouth to cover her exposed teeth, which her lips could not manage to do.

"You through in there?"

He noticed she looked toward DD, then back at him, then without speaking, she simply moved.

Finally, when the trays and covers were placed outside, DD refused to allow Chairly to walk the puppy, telling her, "No, no, not now dear. We have done something special for this man who provides for us. Suarme is our present not good enough for you?"

Knowing she had cornered him, he replied, "How can it not be, when I don't know what it is, DD?" He had moved to the bed, and taken the wrapped item with a bow, in his hand. "I've been a little busy, that's all, and I wanted to do it, opening it I mean, at a special time. Gifts mean a lot to me. It's been an awful long time since I've had one. When you two went shopping yesterday, I wondered if you'd think of me. I also thought of yesterday morning, just before sunrise." He looked at the only person in the entire world, other than himself, that meant anything to him, and continued, "Then, I had the thought of never again receiving anything. It's a very special present, that's all, I just wanted the feeling of someone giving me something to last just a little longer."

It was the only unsuitable quality she could think of about him, and knew it would be a while before he made the adjustment for himself. He had proven it the previous day, when he walked by the very same items, and a variety of similar ones, without notice. The gift she and Chairly shared in giving him, the day before, was a set of fragrances by Aramis. He had only a small bottle of aqua velva in his shaving kit. He used it both as an aftershave and for cologne. He very much appreciated the gift, and they both knew he was sincere with the expression of his thanks.

What Soame really wanted to do was geared to what he said and another motive. He had lost someone special, very special to him. That person would not receive any credit for the part he played. Soame was not worried or troubled, but had bad feelings toward the way he left his friend. Of course, he knew he had no other alternative in pursuit of the course he took, in adhering to the first law of nature. There is nothing he could have done for "Unks," that would have mattered. "But I had to leave him that way," is the thought he had to overcome. It had happened before with many others, in various places, and in different ways, but never with someone so close. He wanted to see if Unks had gotten the simple recognition of having been found; that would mean a decent burial, at least.

His motive had a dual purpose, outside the gift… in less than a week, Soame had broken a routine he had previously gotten accustomed to, over a period of a year and a half. He had eaten and gone to bed habitually, in gear, during the time he revolved in a systematic procedure. There was no doubt at all he needed the rest. The drugs he used also played a part in his considerations. His system had been totally free of other than prescribed drugs for a year and a half. Both factors – the rest and the drugs – he knew, if done properly, a gradual immunization would have set in. There he was, stuck. Knowing there was no time to rest, except that which had been taken. It would have been foolish and absurd for him not to take advantage of the stimulative awareness the drugs provided. He had ventured into a paradoxical situation, regarding his stability. Soame, knowing he was the only dependable factor he had, and would ever have absolute and complete confidence in, had played this enchanting game of solitary, in reviving his physical condition and totally re-establishing his mental composure.

There was a vital reason and structural purpose for the game he played with himself. It was in getting to read the newspapers. After securing them, he could not make a move until he knew for sure what had been reported. Rested, Soame was ready to travel. Knowing the size of the city in which the incident took place, he knew it could not possibly have been a headline, nor front page news. The car was the focal point. It seemed impossible for anyone to have been able to have given a description. Could he travel at least?

In the first paper he searched through, the story was revealed in the "C" section: It was a long way from being a feature story. The six inch article was found on that section's fourth page, lower left, last column to the center of the page. The caption read *Four found slain in guest room*. The story told how four men, who were victims of a drug related assault and robbery, were found in a local hotel, yesterday at 3:00 PM, by maids and hotel attendants. What surprised Soame was, along with there being no fingerprints, there was no jewelry, ID, or money on either victim. The story reported that the single room had been ransacked, with all drawers and tables torn apart. According to the article, the room had been rented to Oswort Hammock as a single party; he was one of the victims, identified by the clerk who had registered him. Hammock had been an occasional guest at the DaBloom Hotel, staying only one night at a time. No one knew anything about any of the other men. There were no leads, except blood was found in the parking lot, and believed to be that of the assailant who may have been injured during the gun battle, which apparently caused the death of the four men.

In searching through the second paper, he found basically the same story, though there was a better placement. The size of the letters in the caption were larger and the story was in the "A" section, page fifteen, and in the lower left center of the page. There was a syringe found in the desk drawer, with traces of heroin in it. There was also a gram of the substance in the center of the floor, imbedded in the rug. In this article, the T.V. was listed as missing, and stated: "The police suspect there was more than one attacker, because the assailant would have needed help to get away, according to the amount of blood found in the parking lot." Hammock was a traveling salesman from Phoenix City, Alabama, the article included.

Neither paper said anything about his lost friend, but in one, under "Deaths" he found Unks' name. The assumption was that it had been obtained as a check on the car and matched the description. "That's the only dog-tag that I could give you 'Unks', to get you back home; be cool!" Soame thought to himself, and felt he had accomplished his objective.

Except for the late lunch DD and Chairly had at a fine restaurant the day they arrived, all other meals were eaten in their room. Chairly had enjoyed the privacy of her room with the companionship of the puppy. It was the first time she had dined with the couple. Following the meal, she and DD finally enjoyed the much anticipated excitement and pleasure of seeing Soame open his gift. When all the thanks, smiles, kisses, and hugs, were done, Soame relaxed on one of the beds, while the females talked in the small sitting room, between the bathroom and the open closet. He had carefully stored the newspapers. When DD saw him getting the papers, she asked Chairly for assistance in setting the dinner trays outside. It was their last night together at the motor lodge. Soame appreciated the time in concentration and privacy to read through the papers; so far it rounded off his day.

Soame also enjoyed his privacy with DD. They both shared the thought of not being flamboyant and relished the times as an actual honeymoon. Neither was introverted, and both liked the exploration of themselves and each other. They were free to make love at a whim, the way they chose, when and as often as they desired; they did so compiling golden memories and receiving gratifying rewards.

DD only knew the car as being his. Besides the money he had given her their first night together, she knew there was twice that amount in the travel pouch on the passenger side of the front seat. She had seen it, and he instructed her to use the money as her own, if an emergency arose. Soame carried both a money clip and a slide; he had no wallet. In his clip, he carried seven $100 bills, five $50s and three $20s; inside his slide as small cash, he carried tens, fives, and singles. The clip was carried in his front right pocket and concealed his pocket knife. The slide he carried behind his handkerchief, in his left rear pocket, if he did not have the .25 automatic. He had not been without the pistol since he met DD. It and the handkerchief were carried in his right hip pocket. The handkerchief shielded the pistol from being seen. He had not gotten out of the habit of undressing in the bathroom, from when he showered alone. This was done purposefully this night, which was the second time they had not showered together. He would not allow the application of the fragrances until his body was clean. Through time, there have been many men who have had it all, and lost it because they trusted too soon.

When Soame came out of the shower, DD was sitting on the foot of the bed closest to the door, partly between the two beds. Her left leg was stretched straight out onto the carpet area. Her right foot was propped with a noticeable bend at the knee, on the bed next to the one she sat on. With her legs wide apart, she exhibited vividly the bikini panties she wore. She also had on a t-shirt top. Opening the door of the bathroom, he immediately saw her. He had on only a pair of boxer shorts, and across his shoulder was a partly draped towel. He was using the towel to dry his hair, when he walked out, and saw her leisurely holding a pistol. The gun was in her right hand. That arm rested between her and hand her elbow on her right knee. Street experience taught him "never buck a gun, unless you are ready and willing to kill or be killed." His military training taught him "how to buck."

A step and a half from where he stood rubbing his head with the towel, there was a drink in a glass. The glass sat not on a coaster, but on a face cloth. It was near the corner end of the desk, table, and drawer ensemble. They said nothing to each other, merely looking into each others eyes for no more than a second, then he looked away toward the glass. The only real oddity about the situation involved the fact she had the pistol. He flapped the section of the towel he was drying his hair with, to the back part of his shoulder. To remove the glass from the tabletop, he had to hold the face cloth down with one hand. Though he was then a bit closer to her, he was also sideways. With one hand clutching the glass, and the other holding the cloth, he asked "What's happening, you wanna give me some pussy?" Other than turning her head slightly, following him with her eyes, she had not moved. Their eyes were locked in direct contact with each other. Without sound, and shaping her lips only, in forming the words, Soame saw her reply "Oh, Suarmme."

He then raised the glass to drink. While raising the glass, she lowered her head, grinning, and while he drank she chuckled. Bringing the glass up, he saw the momentary smile she had, before it turned into the grin. The mirror on the ensemble reflected this to him. Lowering his glass their eyes held each other's brief stare once again, before she asked, "Is that all I can do for you, Suarme Hudson?"

"Whatcha got there?" Sliding the pistol to the side of the bed, holding the barrel to the floor on the far side of her, she told him, "It's my weapon." He knew then for sure, she knew what she held. "Present it to me for an inspection." Without turning, she brought the .38 snub nose to her direct front, pressed the cylinder release device, threw the cylinder out of the chamber with a flick of her wrist, and placed her left index finger where the ready cylinder had been. He was then standing over her, at her side. Turning toward him, carrying the pistol toward him in her move, he accepted it with his left index finger, in the vacancy, replacing her finger.

Carrying the "piece" to his right hand, Soame held the cylinder, pushed the ejection rod, while holding the barrel to the ceiling, and with his left hand, cupped the back of the pistol. Six bullets flowed and bounced in his left palm, with the rattling sound of brass. Soame then looked through the cleared cylinders of the chamber, and after snapping it back into place, held the beautiful thing in his widely stretched palm. The revolver was plated and made by Smith and Wesson. It was definitely a lady's gun; the pearl handle fit the description. A fool could see it, notice it's beauty, and mistake it as a toy. Certain men carry pistols with the described handle for that express reason. "This is a really nice weapon" he told her.

"If someone came unwanted, I could pretend to be shooting at them, and the noise would scare them away.... Then too, if that person persisted, I could stop him without worry. You Soame, are not afraid of guns."

"Any man who is not afraid of a gun pointed at him is either a fool, or a magician during the course of a trick, and I've even heard of some of them being killed in exhibitions." There was a pause and he said, "Deception and invitation has killed many men. This is rather large for a woman. How did you get such a weapon?"

She was up and walking, two steps past him, when he asked the question. She brought out from the top drawer of the dresser, a saucer she had kept from a tray after a previous meal. Soame tossed the pistol on the far bed, passing it on his way to the small sitting room. DD began with a story of how a guy had been her pimp, was also a policeman. This was the reason it had been a year and a half since she had worked on Bourbon Street. When Soame returned from the rear of the room, after combing his hair, he had put on a shirt to take the draft off his body. He left the bullets in his shaving kit. She was sitting in the chair at the desk. The substance from the back of the car had not been tried. It was as he had given it to her, in the saucer. She had just "fitted" the coke and was about to make her "tie." He sat on the tabletop, while listening to how she learned to use the pistol through the guy who gave it to her. She would qualify as a marksman on any range. When she finished the story Soame had taken out the record player. "How is it?"

"It's all right, but it's lacking something the other definitely has over it."

During the early 1960's until '68, David Ruffin had been the lead singer for The Temptations. Soame had made major contributions toward recognition of their music, during Ruffin's final two years with the group. Above all the records he had heard and played as a deejay, Soame's favorite was by The Temptations. However, David Ruffin was not the lead singer on that particular record. *Believe In Love* featured Paul Williams, a tenor with a high pitched voice, as clear as glass and as smooth as the most exquisite, flawless silk.

Soame had the only album by the Temptations, featuring that particular song; *Whole Lot of Soul* has it as side two, cut four. Looking at DD's records while putting her belongings in the trunk, he had recognized it, checked inside the jacket, to be positive the album was there, and considered it then to be an amazing night. He had not heard the record for nearly twenty years. He stored it, the portable record player, and several other records in easy reach for that reason alone. He suggested to DD, "Try what I gave you at your apartment." He waited; she had "spiked," and he knew she had the taste. When she began "jacking" the syringe, he knew the rush was coming on. He then played that record.

During the following hour and a half they talked, listened to music, did their drugs, petted, and made love. They listened intensely to the cut, four times before placing the needle at the beginning of the records. It was an enjoyable time, the feelings they had were fresh. The love they made was pure. That night they would leave Oklahoma City; they began to gear toward the preparations. A towel was placed over the liquor bottles, with her pouch and other materials at the base. The towel covered the mass like a teepee. In the bathroom, they shared a "quickie" over the bathroom sink, with him going in from behind. The two treasured the gratification from pleasures they gave each other.

A problem had developed with Chairly, though it did not appear to be major. When DD presented it as a "situation" to Soame, he lingered in voicing his opinion, telling her, "We three will talk about it before we leave." While he read the paper, DD found out, "I don kea whea we go I don wanna go ta school!"

It might have been a difficult task for the parents of a real family to coerce their child to remain in school. Neither of these adults had experience with children of their own. Beyond being a child, Chairly's adolescence presented a problem. Perhaps the adolescent factor was the problem itself; DD had been gentle with the girl, kind and caring, yet this tactic had not worked toward dissuading Chairly's stern view on the matter.

Soame said: "I think she's very intelligent. She seems to prove that fact, by knowing us better than we know her. I think that's quite an accomplishment in such a short time."

Evidently Fifi had been asleep when Chairly was called into their room. Even the dog could sense the talk as being serious; she sat at the girl's chair and gave a slight whimper in notifying her presence. Initially, Chairly was scared it would not go her way, knowing the confrontation with Soame would decide the pending factor she had won over DD, was what she had at stake. When the puppy came in, she felt she had gained the advantage, and gave the impression she had become bored with the entire matter. DD found this amusing and astonished Soame by saying, "Chairly, as I've told you before, if you stay with us, you may have to go back to school."

"She *may* have to go back to school? What is this? She has left home and found a burger king on wheels, which has rolled her from Baton Rouge to Oklahoma City, has beds and everything else for the convenience of her having it her way?" They thought maybe he had gotten a bit angry; he knew he had not. Fifi lowered her front legs, in a forward stretch to rest her lower jaw on. To have something to do, and hint at defiance toward his tone of voice, DD scooped the puppy up, saying, "Ma Cherre." DD held Fifi to her chin, as if the puppy had been hurt.

Chairly then made the boldest play of all.

"If I stay wid ya an DD, an um always honest whin I um old nough, can I have my very own ca?"

"Bit…" Soame stood up displaying full control of the matter, noticing their eyes, and Fifi's squirm. They knew perfectly well what he had started to call her. "I don't have to negotiate, compromise, or in any way reach a settlement to ride, house, feed, and clothe you Chairly. Do you understand that?"

"Yea sur."

"In extending my benevolent courtesy to you, over a period of years, at the end of that time I do, most certainly not believe it will be my obligation to purchase a car for you, if you've completed high school, which you will do, if you stay with us. Do you understand that, Chairly?"

"Yea sur."

"You may return to your room now. Start gathering your things. We'll be leaving in an hour or so."

Feeling defeated and looking depressed, Chairly rose. Soame told her, "The manner in which you've asked, very well proves you need to be educated formally. Learn the difference in using can and may. It's absurd for you to even think of not continuing with your schooling."

She was moving toward the partition when DD said, "But darling, she did not say she wanted a new car, she simply wants a car."

When Chairly walked through the adjoining door, she heard him say, "And I said she should learn to talk properly." Both of them had gotten their points across.

At the flea market they were only separated for a short while. In fact, it was DD's idea that she and Chairly check out an item of interest, which left him alone. The large box Soame appeared with was not wrapped; therefore, they did not pay strict attention to it, especially since he did not mention it. From the flea market, he carried it directly to the trunk. After DD gathered all the soiled items from both rooms, for the laundry, he went to the car and came back inside with the box. After tossing it on the bed, Soame said, "Let's see now." Knowing he had gained DD's full attention, he pulled the first coat out, "What've we got here?"

"Oh Suarme!!" He gave the coat to her, turned the box upside down, and dumped two more from it. "Suarme, how did you get these? They're so beautiful."

"This one's for you, Ha… give this to her." They each had car coats that were identical. The camel colored, half length, London Fog trench coats were what all of them needed. The evening air was brisk, and had a seasonal chill with it. From the room to the laundry, at the rear of the building, DD carried Fifi tucked close to her, under her coat. The dryer was started before the washer, and as it warmed the puppy was placed on top. The lovers enjoyed the short time out in the fresh air. Fifi kept them amused with her lively antics.

The puppy pranced around on the small area, and when DD drummed her freshly done fingernail tips on the surface, Fifi would charge to the sound, snarling and pretending to be furious, while biting, pawing, and yipping at the sound. When the drumming stopped, she would go to the edge of the top, look over to the drop below, and prance with high steps like a "Tennessee walker race horse" in the opposite direction to the far side. While prancing, she pretended she did not see them, glancing from the corner of her eye, also pretending no one watched her. Almost to the edge, DD would drum with her nails. Swirling back, scampering over the slippery surface, Fifi responded to the sound, as if she was a charging bull, going for the cape of a matador. Finally, she raced to the open hands of the only woman in Soame's life.

Soame's estimate of the coke from the back of the car, was that it was of the same grade he and Frank had gotten from the next room in New Orleans. Though it was pure, it ranged from 7-10% lower in grade, from that which they had brought from their hometown of Miami, "The Cocaine Capitol of the United States." In powder, as a form, there is no such thing as 100% pure cocaine; unless it's synthetic; 97 and 98 plus points are usually about the 'best' grades found, even in top quality markets. At best, that which DD tested would round out to be 85-87%. In Miami, that type grade would be basically good only for the "rock" or "crack" factor which had risen. "Base" cocaine could not produce a turnover sufficient to pay for the handling at such a low grade. Before going out to the laundry, Soame had three fingers of Black Label, in a regular drinking glass. While washing, he smoked a joint. He usually did this before snorting. He had gulped the liquor down. DD had just given herself an injection. When she reached for the bottle, he told her, "Wait until we come back before you have the drink. I'll tell you why, while we do the laundry."

The question was asked when he lit the reefer. "Suarme, why did you say I should wait for the drink, I really like the punch?"

"Liquor is a depressant, a 'downer.' Cocaine is a stimulant. That's why it's called an 'upper.' When the two are done together, you have a counter-reaction going on in your system. A 'downer' and an 'upper' trying to balance or counter-balance each other. It's a waste of money and time to get 'high' on coke, and no matter what type of alcohol it is, even beer, it's a 'downer'; I guess no one's ever told you this before?"

"No, and I listen to what you say, and it seems very true. I've done the coke with Hennessy for a long time."

In the room, the material left in the saucer was not to be wasted. With a "rule of thumb" measurement, he put a quarter "cut" on the three grams. DD had folded the clothes and began packing. He took from the stash he had put away and had not been using, three grams and combined the two into six. Though they were separate, he put the six grams with the stash, and put all of it away. He knew a lot about the substance he handled.

Usually "shooters" go "up" more than "snorters." It is because they enjoy the exuberance of the rush. When the packing was just about completed, DD said, "I think I'll have that drink now, we're just about ready."

"It's yours, you can have it anytime you wish, I simply thought I should let you know what happens, combining the two. How bout sitting on my lap while you enjoy your drink and whatever?" He was sitting at the desk, using the straw with the saucer in front of him. Chairly was asleep when they returned. Fifi was put on the bed, where shortly afterward, she curled between pillows as a "puff of fur" and was asleep also. With the new coat, his wardrobe consisted of a change of Levis, two pullover shirts, a couple of dress shirts (one long and a one short sleeve), a change of top and bottom underwear, and three pairs of socks. Some men are tailored because of style, or they like the prestige. It was a necessity for Soame to be tailored because of his large thighs and small waist. Another reason included the slight bow in his left leg, which made it a quarter inch shorter than his right leg. He did not like to purchase dress pants from the "rack." They never fit properly. He had measured out ¾ of a gram in lines, which he probably would do before they left. The saucer contained his original supply. The glasses, ice, and Hennessy 5 Star VSOP 125 was within reaching distance from his lap. DD was fully dressed in a rust brown flaring dress. She wore a three inch black belt with a large oval buckle in front, and black fish net stockings with heels. She used the same earrings from the previous day. Soame watched her put on the sheer, aqua panty and bra set, and gloated in seeing her fasten the garters, from the black belt she turned and twisted into place. They were comfortable and enjoyed their indulgences.

Chairly's newly purchased items suited her well. She joined them, in her new jeans and one of the new blouses, with her new coat. After displaying the new items she would wear, she departed their room. DD had done well in assisting her with the selections they made. The new gown, flannel PJs, socks, and both dresses were packed in a small case, ideal for the space allowed and fitted for her travel needs. The car was parked directly in front of the room. Everything sat packed and ready to go; it would take less than five minutes to load the items and be under way.

Forty minutes later, DD sat in his lap, and following three stiff drinks, she was about to go "up." It would be the sixth time they would listen to the record. Three times she had gotten up. During one of the times she displayed herself to him, as she had done the first night and time they were together. To him it was more exciting because she was fully attired, except for her shoes. DD knew exactly how to move her dress in more sensualistic ways, in time and movement with her body, than any woman he had ever seen. Soame had known burlesque queens, and had dated many dancers as well as frequented theaters in various places all over the world. DD tantalized him with entrancing delight. She was becoming his woman; it had been a very long time since he had thought of the possibility of having such a woman to himself. After her second drink, they made hurried, passionate love.

Knowing he had to drive, his last drink was taken before they did the laundry. The quick shower was invigorating; DD felt comfortable traveling in slacks. The disrobed garments were called "bag things," and while Soame loaded them and their other belongs, DD applied what little makeup she would use. By the time Chairly walked Fifi, the car was warm; they were ready to leave, continuing north.

Chapter 7

SHORTLY after leaving the motor lodge, their course took a northwest direction. Soame had known for a while that DD could drive. Though she said she was a good driver, she could not read a road map. The legend was the first item of interest he gathered her attention toward, in his initial attempt at explaining a map to her. In total, Soame had driven "cross country" four times. Prior to the last occasion, he had previously been through Oklahoma City. One of the routes he had taken before was from Alexandria, Virginia to Los Angeles. He then traveled through Pittsburgh to Oklahoma City, and from there took the renowned Route 66 through Flagstaff, and had driven on down to Phoenix. From the radio Juice Newton's *Break It To Me Gently* was strong and heavy on the country and western station they had homed in on since approaching the city they were then leaving.

DD sat close to him, rubbing his knee and stroking the back of his head. Though there was hardly any traffic, she was very careful as to when to be directly under him, when he manned the wheel. Driving is a very serious matter, at times requiring concentrated efforts. Chairly sat as comfortable as possible in the back seat, holding Fifi. She had been told simply, "We will make arrangements later, to make that seat more comfortable." He had traced a route away from all shown inspection stations. Being from the East Coast, the Interstate Commerce Commission stations were those familiar to him. There, cars were not stopped. The symbols were different on the map, indicated in the legend that he had not paid particular notice to. It was an almost total blunder. He had lived through his mistake.

There was no particular destination. Priorities at the time dictated his interest toward getting rid of the car and finding a place to "lay low" with the people and pet he was with, as a family. Soame knew his comfortable financial position, being able to provide for DD and Chairly, for a considerable while. Depending on what area was selected, and their style of living, he had a lifetime of security in cash alone. The drugs, to anyone knowing the distribution of drugs, were "automatic cash money." There were a few variations in his speculation on how to move at least twenty-five kilograms of cocaine, and the little more than one kilogram of heroin. The combined coke had slightly more value than the single "key" of "boy" or "smack." It depended on the market, which could make the single package out-rank the "girl" in value. He knew he could not tap any market, with such a vast quantity of drugs, without being detected. Law enforcement agencies were not his only concern regarding detection. The people who originally owned the drugs were definitely his biggest threat. Unless a spontaneous blunder or mishap occurred, Soame's new "family" was safe. There was enough cash money available, for him to take time in deciding how to convert the drugs into cash. This brought the car back into immediate prospective.

Soon the car would be reported stolen, if it were not already. The immediate threat, if the car had been reported would last only six months, eight at longest. Had it not been located in that period, the car would be taken off the police "hot sheet." Techniques and methods change over time. Before he received the prison sentence, he was aware of insurance companies waiting six months after the report of the stolen vehicle to list it. The automobile would then be listed in the computer bank of two agencies, of which the national computer check was the most thorough. Brand new, the car was valued at $37,000.00. Considering the low mileage, and it being five months old, his probable asking price would range from 30 to 34 thousand dollars. With the title and papers on a straight cash deal, he'd take between 26 and 30 thousand dollars. He would go as far as allowing the beautiful looking, driving, and riding car to be "stolen" from him by a fast dealer for twenty-three "grand." Gaining the cash from the sale would be a daring escapade. He had been considering the venture since crossing into Texas, but he had to put space between the car and what he had left behind. The problem was deciding whether to leave it abandoned or make a quick sale. Storing or trading it would be too dangerous.

DD had made it beyond the second stay at a motel or hotel, and had not been put out, or had someone brought in on her to turn a "trick." This had never happened before. For years she had become resentful, not only of men, but all individuals. She existed as a person, for a long while, though she had sought for a trace of kindness or warmth and decency from someone else, anyone. Each time she had reached out and taken hold of the hand she thought was there to help her, it turned out to be like all the other hands before: it delivered her into the continuous revolving cycle that had become her life. She was trapped in the web that led from pimp to pimp, tricks and other johns, madams, other whores, and males who were often gamblers who prostituted themselves. That night, when the confrontation occurred with her pistol, she thought her life had revolved back to the determination point. She had reached it so many times, and each time with all the mental and physical effort she had put forth to get there. The revolving door would always bring her back into the life she had been living.

That night in the city they had just left, she found herself farther than she had ever gone, without having to go back. She had everything except the keys to the car. She would either have to continue taking her chances with Soame, or get the keys and leave, having it all but him. She would have had to kill him for the keys, he could not be incapacitated to the point of giving them up. She searched through what she saw as evidence and what she knew of him. Comparing him with others, when they had reached that point, all the others before him had revealed evidence that they would turn on her. Rather than display gentleness as he did, in soothing and petting her, the other hands had slapped and beat, and caused discomfort, though it was not all physical. He continued to be as different from the others as she had originally thought him to be, the night she left with him. Within herself, she knew for sure she had to choose. She chose to take the best chance ever, to stay with Soame.

He had not and would not snoop, pry, or poke into her personal belongings. Had he, he would have seen the ox blood colored, leather gun case she kept the revolver in. The case was practically hidden in her overnight carrying case. The night they left Oklahoma City, he gave her back the bullets and watched her load them. She replaced the gun in the leather case, and stored it in its original place. The .25 automatic was the only weapon carried in the car; other than Soame's pocketknife.

The drugs caused a similar problem to the car. He knew enough about the "girl," to store it until the "heat" was off. With all probability, the "boy" could be kept in the same dry manner. Knowing values how to do basic research, he felt confident in being able to get to a general library, wherever he stopped, and do his research. He felt positive he could store the "scagg" for at least a year without complications or detection. The best fact about knowing what he had was, he knew enough about organizations to understand the changes that would take place in top positions and political environments with influence. No matter what, within two and a half to four years he could distribute in bulk, become wealthy overnight, relocate, and the entire matter would be done with. He and his lady could enjoy themselves during that time, and have the same ability to convert the drugs into cash when enough time had passed.

Shortly past six that morning, Soame crossed the state line into the fourth state he would drive through. He stopped at a rest stop, which was practically desolate, just after entering Colorado. While DD and Chairly used the restroom and walked Fifi, he changed plates, back to the original. Later he would discard the Louisiana plate along the way. Eight track tapes were being phased out. Cassette recordings were the "thing" with modern sound equipment. Compact discs and digital players were then unheard of by the general public. The Fleetwood featured a cassette player, but since DD had no cassettes and no one was interested in purchasing any, they enjoyed the radio stations and the car's quadraphonic speakers. Soame was traveling in an area he had never been in before. He greatly enjoyed listening to different announcers, from a variety of stations in other areas of the country, and each style and presentation of music. He could tell that DD enjoyed the easy listening music, which placed an assortment of orchestras in the elegant car with them. They were able to tune in to stations as far away as San Francisco, Mississippi, San Antonio, Cincinnati, Nashville, and Toronto, Canada. Other than the Jackson, Mississippi frequency modulating through to them, they heard little soul or rhythm and blues, unless broadcast from a top forty station. The "pop" and country and western music kept the car lively, and allowed Soame to maintain the perk in the hi's he obtained. He needed keen alertness to deliver them. Leaving the rest stop, he caught a country and western station from Colorado Springs, and turned the volume up to nearly a blast, when he recognized Bruce Hornsby and his band, the Range, doing *That's Just the Way It Is*.

Seven miles before entering Lamar they drove into a truck stop. They had stopped earlier and had breakfast, but to allow the others to stretch and have coffee, he invited them to take advantage of a 15-20 minute rest break. It was near eleven and they were more than two-hundred and fifty miles into the state. While pretending to use the phone, he saw exactly what he needed. Having done all types of jobs, including professional and manual labor, he had considerable experience with furniture moving, handling, and packing. He had approached several long distance drivers who had stopped for a break, meal, or "lay over," before he found one to assist him with what he was in search of. He purchased packing materials from the driver. The materials included three barrels, two regular cartons, one large carton, and four bookcases. He also bought tape and three furniture blankets. The air was cool with a true nip to it. They were at the base of the mountain area, which led up to Colorado Springs and on north through Denver. With a blanket over the materials tied down through the open windows, he drove into town. He did not know if their stay would be for the remainder of the day, or if they would stay over night. It was different and exciting. Neither of them had thought of going to or being in Colorado.

Chapter 8

THEY rented double rooms on the ground floor of a two-story building. Soame drove through Lamar and, on its outskirts, found a motel suited for his purpose. The rooms were nice, but not as plush as the ones they had occupied on the previous nights. After refreshing themselves, unpacking, and unloading some items from the car, they all rode back into town. Soame suggested they "temporarily" use another car. He purposely introduced the idea to get their feedback, while he looked for a used car lot. Forty-five minutes later they were enjoying the lunch they brought back to the motel

Having enjoyed the meal and a short period of relaxation with the two and Fifi, Soame began his chore. Chairly thought it was fun, fun, fun being with them, and had never had such an exciting time in her life. Fifi thought the chews were super fantastic, and carried one practically every place she went, from room to room, and even once to the "bathroom." Soame was unloading the trunk and hoped Chairly would get bored watching and retire to her room. No such luck. She was wide awake and gave no indication that she had the slightest intention of not seeing what was coming out next.

"May I help you?" she asked several times. Not wanting to hurt her feelings, and really beginning to enjoy the three of them and Fifi together, he said, "Naw… Why dontcha just be comfortable with your Auntee Dubanee over dare."

"Miss Dubanee, Monsieur Hudson, if you do not mind!" DD declared, watching his toil, from the only bed in the room. She was truly amused, seeing him walk back and forth through the open door, with her belongings each time he entered. The open trunk was directly in front of the room. Chairly was amused also, and attempted to be cunning with her tease. Fifi lay next to her mistress, with a chew clutched between her paws. She also watched Soame, shifting her gnaw from jaw to jaw.

DD came to Soame's rescue however; from one of the suitcases she chose a flowered dress and excused herself to the bathroom. After a quick change, she returned wearing the light, summerish, transparent piece. He had emptied more than two thirds of the contents of the trunk. Though it was difficult for her to escape the alert eyes of Chairly, who watched everything, DD moved about the room, doing various chores, at different angles, and would "hike," giving Soame "raw" shots when she gained the chance… The car's rear added music to the scene. When Soame was done, he sat in the open doorway and asked DD to bring him a drink. He lit a "joint" and listened to music from the open trunk. DD passed Soame his scotch on the rocks and said, "Come Chairly. Let's go over to your room, before that beast has a notion to have you reload the entire mess!" Having gained Soame's attention, DD grabbed the girl by the wrist, flaunted, swayed, and sashayed to the connecting doors, sending the girl first, and giving Soame a complete rear view look at her white bikini bottom. She had only been gone a short while. He was nearly finished with the drink and reefer. The only reason the drink lasted was because he used it to wet his mouth, while he smoked. Soame was basically a gulper, using the ice to chill the alcohol. DD stood over him, and his moist right hand found its way, tracing upward on her thigh. Just as it reached the goodies, stored in the front portion of the white material, Sammy Karshaw began singing *Border Town* on the radio.

Other than having to return to the truck stop for more boxes, there was no problem in their stay. The coffee shop and restaurant at the front of the building enabled them to have hot meals on the premises, which was a convenience. DD discovered that Fifi was becoming house trained. After leaving the apartment, not once had she "gone" when she should not have. Unlike the other places they had roomed, with the pavement of the parking lot basically at their doorsteps, this place was different.

The motel had a three and a half foot space between the building and the sidewalk. The sidewalk was four and a quarter feet wide. Beyond the sidewalk there was grass between the single parking spaces. Though the lawn surface had not yet recovered from winter, Fifi could be let out and watched from inside. She exercised herself, leaping and frolicking back to her chew. Registering, he had requested, "ground floor rooms, adjoining, toward the far end of the building, if you have them available." They occupied rooms 13 and 14, in the fifteen room, first floor unit.

By ten everything had been packed, marked, stacked, and ready to go. Chairly had finally gotten a chance to help, because Soame packed the illegal materials away first. It was an ideal fit for the bookcases. After dinner, he showered, laid back, and watched them pack DD's things. When she needed help, or simply as an irritating gesture, she would call out, "Darllllinnngggg. Soame, if you don't mind." The room was then filled with smiles, giggles, and Fifi prancing and barking.

When all was done, and after Fifi was walked to the cold brown grass before bed, Soame noticed something about Chairly and DD, which caused his heart to glow with warmth. With the puppy cuddled in her arms, saying goodnight, she and DD kissed each other's cheeks; holding the puppy then with one arm, she exchanged the woman's hug. DD pulled at the nap on the puppy's head saying, "Cherre."

Chairly looked at Soame and stated: "DD has taught me to say Daddy in French: Papa."

With a wide grin on his face he inquired, "What did you say?" She then threw him a kiss, waved, and turned to her room.

Lovemaking seemed especially good that night. With that and the other things they did, it was after four before they were off to sleep. Shortly after nine he was awake explaining an idea to her. At the truck stop, on his return trip, he purchased a cap, with a picture of a sailfish on it. Explaining his idea, she responded, "If you cut your side-burns, half way to your ears, it might help." He had also gotten a pair of reading glasses. With the cap and glasses, and carrying through on her suggestion, he hoped to change his appearance. He made the effort, despite being tall, very dark, with broad shoulders, and everyone who ever heard him knew his voice was unmistakable; it was almost impossible for Soame to disguise himself.

Before he finished shaving and taking the sideburns completely off, the clerk at the freight office was telling DD, "We can store it for as long as you like, and ship it any place in the free world." When the beautiful woman asked, the clerk also told her, "We can have one of our drivers pick it up in an hour, at that location. Shall I send someone over?" She relayed the information to Soame, who now felt positive about the matter. He nodded his head in assent..

Chairly was entering the room with Fifi, while Soame was on the phone making a fantastic discovery. What totally surprised him, was the casual assurance of the man regarding completion of the transaction.

"As long as the title is clear," he said. "That's why we're here as brokers." The broker added that it would take no longer than, "Ten, fifteen minutes at the most."

Seeing Chairly, his mind reflected back to the previous day, and how she had capped the day with her good night. She was beginning to make her presence known. Though she was a help with the puppy, she seemed to be deliberately placing herself in his path for attention. It was obvious Soame knew hardly anything about girls, especially adolescent girls. In fact, he seldom attempted to understand women. There was always a supply, and at times an abundance of them. He simply accepted them as mischievous, and those he had lasting relationships with, enjoyed the times together while they lasted. His preference was toward older women. However, fate had drawn DD into his life, directly after his serving time without women at all. That same fate was also molding them together, through circumstance, which basically cancelled his interest in any other woman. Now change presented him with Chairly, a female in her developmental stage. Peaking in his prime, chance was also allowing him to apply his simple tact, training, and practical experience toward a younger woman. The girl drew his attention to a different level, applying psychology, and knowledge borne of experience through the years. When Chairly said "Papa," she "knocked the ball out of the park." Soame had not yet sired. He was totally overwhelmed.

Soame honestly felt he did not have to give Chairly time, for her to feel he did not object to her being with the group. It was not the beginning point of his close observation of her. She displayed signs of potential and active promiscuity, but he had never known a woman not to be promiscuous, though it is not exclusively a feminine characteristic. The day before, after lunch, he had asked her, without prying, and with as much concern as he could project: "Chairly, your family at home, do you miss any one of them, who may have an interest in your whereabouts, or might be concerned as to how you are?"

She was not reluctant to talk about neither her brothers nor her sister, who had a baby a year and half in age. That was all; then her faraway disinterested look came into play. He did not know how much, or if she had been coached by DD. He decided to allow her in, with any game she had in mind to play, and find out how sharp and keen she really was, in getting what she wanted. He had established the fact that she had to be registered for school. Doing so, he had demonstrated his generosity, which was preceded by his word, the day they met. This concern had shown he was not the same low character as her mother's boyfriend. Chairly went out with the puppy. Soame took advantage of the time alone with DD, to explain his idea about shipping her belongings by freight, to their destination, after they had determined it and arrived. Meanwhile, the freight company could hold the materials in storage. This would allow them more room.

DD was not told exactly what was going on. After seeing the wrapped packages in the back of the car, and what he had told her at the border station's approach, she suspected he was attempting to camouflage some factor he would eventually tell her, or he did not want her to know. This was also when she was told that he would be selling the car. She said to him, "Then wait. I'll be right back." She went out to the car and returned with Chairly. DD had the money from the interior pouch, on the passenger's side. Soame nodded and began unloading the trunk.

Later that evening after dinner, DD asked Chairly to remain in her room, while she and Soame discussed something very important. While DD selected items she would use while traveling, he removed the special bolts from the backseat. Because of the location of the rooms, and the motel having few guests, there was almost complete privacy for them.

Although it is called furniture "barrel," it was cardboard and taller than a regular packing box. It stands nearly the height, and has slightly more room than a clothing trunk, stood on one end. Soame lined the barrel in a blanket, and loaded the contents of the well of the back seat into it. There was excess, which he loaded and stacked into a bookcase, rather than fill the barrel to the brim. A bookcase is smaller than a regular size packing box, also cardboard, basically used for the package, storage, and shipment of books. Tallying up what was packed, he had twenty seven "keys" of cocaine, three "keys" of heroin, plus a "key" and a half taken from the room before "Joey" arrived. With the quarter pound remaining from the "girl" they were using, and a half-pound of "reefer," it totaled a considerable amount of substance.

It was difficult getting the assortment of weapons out of the cap of the back seat. It took nearly twenty minutes, but finally Soame located the locks which held the springs into pace. Apparently, the seat had been turned upside down, and a blanket placed between the springs and the underside of the seat. The springs were then refitted into position, to hold pressure on the weapons, keeping them in place. A burlap sack separated the lower springs from the weapons. They were factory new. They included pistols, mini-machine guns, AK-47s, and M-16s. What created the lump, causing Chairly's discomfort at the car wash, was an old style, also factory new, Thompson automatic machine gun, also referred to as a "Tommie gun." Though it included the straight clip, Whoever loaded the Thompson could not, or did not locate the release for the clip. The cylinder clip was locked, into the weapon; it was not loaded with the .45 ammunition it holds. It was the weapon's protruding cylinder that had caused the lump in the back seat. It was hardly noticeable. After getting it all into the room, replacing the springs, and cap, there was no problem bolting the seat back into place. In his frustration of searching for the spring locks, Soame turned on the radio so the music might relax him. Though the station faded in and out, with occasional static, he tuned in on a top 40 station from San Francisco. During his endeavors in the back, he did not change the station. When the task was completed, he sat relaxed on the back seat, with his feet and legs crossed toward the other end. While the announcer did a brief news summary, Soame did a "one and one." After reporting the weather, the announcer gave a low swaging lead to a record Soame had never heard before. The deejay introduced the artist as Steve Winward. Soame, as the music crescendoed from a perfect signal, relaxed with *No One Can Make It Through*.

The room had materials of all sorts scattered everywhere, basically for DD's convenience. The drugs they would not immediately use were already packed. The assortment of weapons were stacked away from everything else, along the wall in the far corner. To allow packing space and room for her sorting, he pushed the bed to the wall entering the room. He began packing the weapons into two barrels, using three rugs in each. The rugs were used for cushioning and to create a tight fit. The stacks of newspaper he also obtained, on his second trip to the truck stop, enabled him to stuff tight all that he had packed. Except for packing DD's things, the job of packing was done. The records played on the portable machine, kept them entertained and relaxed the atmosphere. Through his suggestion, DD then asked Chairly over to select some albums and records (45s). The remainder would be packed and stored for later shipment. He was in the bathroom preparing to shower when she entered the room.

The best factor about Chairly, observed and analyzed by Soame, was she did what she was told to do, when she was told to do it. This impressed Soame, who noticed other good features about her, including that she was well mannered. He was aware of the Mann Act and the "white slavery" danger, which was the reason he did not go into Texas the day they met her. Compared to the other illegal acts he was involved with, a sexual charge would, hardly hold validity, to the others that could be stacked on him. Though they at times enjoyed themselves with the happiness they all shared, it was a very serious manipulation procedure with him. Clairty was a threat to their discovery. That he might not have found the weapons and other drugs, without her discovery, weighed heavily in her favor.

She and DD seemed to be entranced with either what they heard of the conversation, or his voice while he spoke into the receiver. Hanging up, he said: "Chairly, good morning and how are you, this morning?"

"Um fine, good monin."

Fifi then entered the room and was scooped up by DD, who briskly ran her fingers back and forth through the nap of her head. Soame said: "I'll clue you in on the activities we take part in today, which include our checking out at one." This seemed to perk her up. He had not before told her of any plans, but she had known at the other places that they would be there only for a short while, and she knew beforehand when they were leaving. Soame smiled in associating her attentiveness with that of a young Doberman pinscher, bright and alert. "In a little while, someone'll be here to pick up these boxes. In case you haven't guessed, we're having them stored, until later. Then DD and I are going out to buy another car. Remember us talking bout it yesterday?"

"Yea Sur."

"You don't have to, but if you're going to be that polite, it's 'yes,' and the other word is 'Sir'. It takes time and practice, but I think you'll make it fine. A simple yes or no will be enough for me, all right?"

Chairly nodded her head in assent.

"Yea, well anyway, while we're gone, you're to remain in your room. Do not use the phone, and if anyone comes to the door, tell them your aunt isn't here and she will be back shortly. Do you understand?"

"Yes, Soame."

"All right, now great! Listen now Chairly, if anyone knocks on that door, tell them exactly as I've told you, but if they insist on talking to you, don't play dumb or stu…"

She interrupted, "I know what ta do, DD told me ta…. I know what ta do Soame."

Realizing he had been slightly careless in letting her think that he might consider her stupid, he allowed her to finish.

He knew why she interrupted him, as well as why she paused and deviated from what she originally began to say. He said, more gently. "You were about to say DD told you something, which is all well and good, Chairly, but listen. It is a common courtesy to listen, in fact, when someone else is talking, especially when they are adults, to hear that person out, before you speak. Has anyone else ever explained this to you before?"

She searched his eyes, to see if he was as sincere as he sounded, or if he had really meant to hurt and belittle her. Long before now she knew Soame was not mean. She also knew he was not scornful and to her, he had been really nice. She caught a glimpse of his smile, and acknowledged within herself that she was in error before she answered, "Yes Soame, I been taught dat befo."

"Good. Well, sometimes it's just a matter of having the patience. Then you give yourself time, to remember what you've learned. Like I said, I think you will make it fine, you're doing well, all right?"

"All right, Soame."

"It's been breakfast time for quite awhile, but we've waited to see what you want, Chairly."

She saw that he knew he had her complete attention and only looked for her answer. With that response, she heard, "Right now we are communicating as normal human beings. Talking is the greatest form of communication there is. In a general conversation, one listens as the other person talks. This sets us apart, and makes us the highest form of intelligence on Earth. That fact, being able to communicate."

He watched her. This time she did not appear to be bored. She had learned something, and it pleased her. He said: "Now I want to tell you what to do if someone insists on talking to you through the door. Would you rather have breakfast first, have me explain it to you afterward, or hear me now?"

"I'll lisin, Soame."

He gave her the instructions.

At 11:20 that morning, DD and Soame returned to the motel with a six-year-old Ford LTD. There was a delay with the freight pickup. After being notified that the materials would be picked up between 11:45 and 12:15, he proceeded with his plan. They visited one of the used car lots they had passed the previous day and purchased the car. This was a complete turn of events for DD,. Witnessing and being a part of these types of happenings, was like being trapped in a fun house. Following her back to the motel, Soame discovered a dream: seeing this gorgeous woman driving the handsome "hog," he then knew exactly what he wanted to do, as soon as the first chance presented itself. The car was chosen for its trunk space. There was no excessive carbon blown from the tail pipes, when the salesman started the engine. This indicated the rings were good. The engine did not skip or sputter, but settled at a resonant idle, without choking. After checking the minor equipment, he hoped the transmission was good. In all, it appeared to be a sturdy, used car without excessive mileage, according to its age.

After fitting the small boxes on the floor of the trunk, everything else packed in perfectly, except one box. Chairly would have to share the space in the back seat with it. He then began a very serious conversation with DD. There was no doubt in his mind about her capability in comprehension. He knew DD's intelligence was far above normal, with a sharp wit. As he outlined the simple plan, the truck from the freight company arrived. They were in front of the room. The packed Ford had been taken to the parking space in front of Chairly's room. The trunk was raised on the Cadillac because he was wiping it. With all probability, if the car was sold, it would be detailed by its buyer. Fingerprints will last up to, and sometimes a bit more than twenty-four hours; this is according to the environment and conditions. The trunk presented a place his prints might be detected, if the interior was detailed, and circumstance led to dusting, within a short span. The driver used a dolly. In less than ten minutes, he had been paid for six months storage and had loaded the boxes and was gone. There would be a COD shipment later on when they found their destination.

Soame had already used the toll free reservations number to contact Sheaton. On the outskirts of Denver, near Golden, there was a hotel he liked. It was near the interstate. He had made the usual reservations for them, but in suites, and the reservations were booked in DD's name. He explained the plan to her while they wiped the interior of the car. She wrote the reservation confirmation number on a piece of paper.

DD understood that Soame would leave them at the motel, taking the Cadillac. She checked to be positive the keys to the Ford were in her pocket. DD was to wait forty-five minutes after he left, for his phone call. The highway led back through town. There was no problem in getting to it, because they purchased the car within view of the highway, two blocks away, and came directly to the motel. The road in front of the motel led past the used car lot to the highway. DD was to take the highway west, if he did not call, ride west on 50 for 150 miles, where she would meet Interstate 25. She would change her direction at Pueblo North, on the interstate, which would carry her through Colorado Springs and on to Denver. He explained how the hotel was situated, and why she would have no problem getting to it from the interstate. She had enough money to wait there until he called.

Soame reflected back to the last time he had given someone important instructions. That person died; not because he was not trained to do as he was directed, he gave his life because he chose not to follow simple instructions. He did not want to worry DD or make her paranoid. However, he did want to impress upon her the importance of getting to the hotel. He said: "These are specific instructions, you must follow. Above all, do not speed, or do anything irregular to draw attention to the car. When you check in, be sure to ask the registering clerk, if it will be necessary for you to pay in advance, for a collect call you will be receiving. Have him inform the switchboard operator of the expected call, while you are at the desk. Your first responsibility after entering the room is to call the hotel operator, telling her or him of the arrangements you've made for the collect call. Give them my name as the calling party, and check with each shift to see if the oncoming operator has received the accepting instructions. DD, I may only be able to call once. The call must be able to get through!" Ten minutes later Soame was driving the Fleetwood from the parking space in front of the room.

The plush carpeting in the Brougham, on the underside, had button fasteners to the floor and base of the seat. He had conceded to himself, he did not think it was possible. After knowing it was there and looking for it, the assembly could not be noticed.

Like in all zoned areas, more than several businesses of the same sort were located in the same block. He wasn't too sure of the one he had called, after the lure, not being on the alert. Because he had passed the first broker, Soame proceeded to the next establishment. His story was that he had been to Reno, and this was the only time during the year he could get a vacation. He could not vacation like regular folk, but they had taken him. He started to go home with his pockets dry, but will not let them get away with it. He was going back. It would take another day and a half, to get a draft of a sizeable amount to a local bank, his financial institution had an affiliation with. He would catch a plane out, be there, and have his forty "grand" back by then. There were two others like this one, and nine other smaller cars at home. He had a fleet of um. While he told the broker this, the broker had thoroughly checked the car out, looking into the interior, checking beneath the hood, and visually examining the exterior of the De Elegance. He never looked in the trunk.

In the broker's office, Soame faced the man sitting behind his desk. "Mr. Furman," he smiled slightly, pausing to examine the car title. "In about five minutes I can have you $30,0000 for your car, if you will accept my offer." Soame looked at him, twisted his lips to one side, then to the other. "I'd give it to ya right now, but my secretary has to go across the street and cash a check, it is a sizeable amount, sir."

"I've lost forty… because I bought three in the same purchase, I was able to get them at thirty-seven each. The car's only six weeks old –" The broker took out the company checkbook, called his secretary in, and during her approach told Soame, "I'll write this check for thirty-two, Mr. Furman, considering your impending circumstance, with travel arrangements, and if you are not 'comped' at your hotel, you'll have assistance in that way also."

"Do that and I'll close at that figure. Consider it a deal, and thank you for your consideration."

After the secretary left with the check, the title had to be signed over. In doing so, Soame started to reach into his back pocket for his ID. The broker immediately stopped him, saying, "Ah, that won't be necessary, sir." Soame asked him if he would call him a cab. Three minutes after the return of the secretary, the driver was at the door of the office asking, "Someone here call a cab?"

"I've got to get a pair of shoes as a present, let me out at that shoe store, will ya." The drug store he placed the call from was across the street, and three stores up from the shoe store. Over the phone he gave DD directions to the drug store. Leaving the empty rooms, with Chairly and the puppy, he drove them from that point. Though they no longer had the "hog," there was now considerably more cash, and a heck of a lot less pressure.

Chapter 9

It was past midnight when they arrived at the hotel. Because he had requested rooms with a city view, the reservations explained the panoramic windows. The suite Chairly would lodge in was not as spacious as that which the couple would share, but large sitting rooms adjoined both suites. Because of the late hour, the best they were able to order from room service included two turkey clubs, a BLT, and potato chips. This suited their appetites because they did not want to try sleeping on full stomachs. Beverages and ice cream rounded off the meal.

Exploring her accommodations, Chairly discovered the largest bathroom she had ever seen. Though she had not actually begun to use make-up, the separate ladies parlor filled her with a desire to borrow DD's lipstick and have one of her own. She was spellbound by the extra large mirror with the encased smaller lighted one. Soame informed DD of the paper being delivered that morning and during their stay. He bit into the fresh pear and with a full mouth muttered, "This is also one of the luxury features, DD. Over here is the wet bar and its fully stocked. Let's see if it has your Five Star." He carried the fresh basket of fruit with him to the bar.

"Oh Suarme, there's so much more to see, I've never imagined a hotel room being so large." Her bathroom had a spacious heart shaped Jacuzzi, which had steps up to it, as well as down into it. It was almost double the size of Chairly's. Though she had not seen the one next door, her dressing room and closet were larger than actual hotel rooms she had been in. Considering the extra large mirrors in each room were the same, the walk-in closet for DD made the difference in size. They would later find the room also had a regular size bath room.

Soame phoned the bell captain for assistance in bringing other belongings from the car. He leisurely enjoyed the drink on the rocks he had prepared and while on the phone noticed a box of cigars. Though the weapons were distributed between three boxes and now stored in Lamar, he wanted help with the light duty chore, for the satisfaction it brought. It was a top floor room in a two-story building. The two suites were across the hall from the elevator. Fifi bounced and sprang on the plush shag carpet while tagging behind Chairly.

"My room got a kitchen, too!" she exclaimed.

"Yea, well even though it's technically still a room, Chairly, these are actually called suites, and we have kitchenettes. That's either the bellboy or the food; if it's the bellboy, he's here to help me bring the rest of the luggage and things from the trunk. I'm going downstairs, you two."

"Oh Suarme, you make me so happy." As DD flung herself to him with open arms, he hurried to remove the cigar from his mouth where it had been between his teeth, while he talked. Chairly found this amusing and attempted to cover her grin. They were at the kitchenette counter, which had four high stools.

Because Chairly's belongings were packed with hers, DD unpacked the suitcase in the sitting room. They enjoyed the meal together and went to her room to shower and prepare for bed. Soame relaxed, half sprawled on the comfortable couch, with his feet propped on the leather cushion. He was totally mellowed out, steadily "coming down" after his first drink and the meal. Now he enjoyed a three fingered drink with a joint. The cloth materials cushioned the portable record player. The records were all DD's and each had its separate and special value. She had not yet told Soame which was her favorite tune. It could not be considered an "oldie goldie," because it had been relatively recent that the record was popular. "It really didn't do too much, considering the potential it had," Soame told her, listening to and remembering Eddie Murphy's *Party all the time*. DD said she liked the song not for its lyrics, but mostly because of "the thumping funk, with the locomotive beat." He found it odd that she would use such an expression and was amazed to see her rhythmic moves as she beckoned him to dance with her. He had never actually seen her dance before. She moved with soul and grace and intrigued him with her luring enticement. The same song was on both sides of the 45. Flipping the record, she turned the volume up and without saying a word used her hands and body and gestured him to dance with her, like no hula dancer would suggest.

Chewing on the doggie toy, Fifi had not accompanied Chairly through the adjoining door when she left. She was also busily watching DD with the remainder of the unpacking; for that reason the door was left open. After hearing the music, Chairly in her flannel pajamas came skipping over. She was dancing before she joined DD in the center of the floor. Chairly had come to Soame's rescue. He could no longer suppress the bulge in his pants that had become fully awakened. Chairly seemed to like the record more than DD. They turned the music up and tuned the atmosphere out. They partied down! As soon as one side played out, one of them would flip the record and the two of them would begin all over again.

Fifi ran around the beautiful woman and her dancing partner, jumping, yipping and panting. DD and Chairly competed with various acts and presentations, in an assortment of sexy positions. Every second was a visual delight for the man who refilled his glass twice, newly astounded by the girl. He smoked reefer with his drinks and well into the morning they were still dancing to the same song and entreating him: "Come dance with us Soame."

Though it was almost spring, it was cold outside. The spacious bedroom was lavishly furnished with one king-sized bed. It was near 2:30 in the afternoon when the couple awakened. DD was overwhelmed by the view presented in splendor from the terrace of their bedroom. Soame had drawn the curtains and opened the sliding doors, the cold air awakening DD. Soame invited her out for the view.

Later that afternoon, in a shopping plaza toward the city they shopped at a Neiman Marcus department store. The first items to be purchased at the expensive store were coats. Only because she was a "hand puppy," Fifi was allowed in the store. DD and Chairly also bought several pairs of warm slacks, practical for the cold weather. The simple visit for the coats turned out to be somewhat of a shopping spree, for all of them. DD insisted Soame be outfitted "from head to foot." He bought a pair of Rossies and a pair of Baleys, and worked from there up. There wasn't time to be tailored. Recognizing Soame's problem the courteous salesman catered to Soame's suggestion. He purchased the trousers two sizes too large in the waist. This would allow him ample legroom. He would return for the trousers, after alterations had been made to the waist. Soame accompanied the women from there to get shirts, socks, underwear, and handkerchiefs. Finally, he purchased a Stetson hat, which distinguished him in his usual style.

DD bought Chairly her first bottle of perfume. Chairly was also given $50.00 to spend as she wished. Soame also presented both with Lady Longine's watches, a gift to both of them "for being such wonderful traveling companions."

"Merci Beaucoup, Papa." The obviously attentive eaves dropping sales woman examined the private scene without reservation, while Chairly paused, then resumed after removing her hand from her mouth covering her grin.

"Aunt DD an me is very glad dat ya boght dese an the otha thangs for us, an we very happy ya enjoy our company. Thank you, Soame."

Soame simply smiled and nodded. He wondered while looking at them and Fifi, "Will they attempt to get the puppy into the restaurant?"

The fact was, they were all too burdened with packages, to consider dining. After making the trip to the car and depositing the items, once again he sent them to the grocery store, while he went to the liquor store. The hotel's wet bar did not have Hennessy 5 Star VSOP 125. Soame knew when they moved to another town, he wanted to have some Black Label scotch with him. It would be excellent scotch drinking weather; he would be traveling north. At the grocery store, an assortment of snacks was purchased, including peanuts, raisins, wheat thin crackers, and cheese. Those items and a few reserve cans of food for Fifi, completed the list. He stated to the person behind the counter, "Four quarts of Black Label and four bottles of Five Star Hennessey."

"I see you have exquisite taste in beverages." The woman told him in walking toward the scotch.

"Had I asked you for Dom Peringon and requested the year '56, I would feel that you were sincere in your compliment," Soame replied

"That we could not furnish you with without ordering, though it would only further confirm what I've said about your choices." Upon her return to the register, she noticed Fifi squirming, pawing, and licking toward the man beneath the Stetson. The attractive middle-aged woman complimented the miniature and permitted Soame to release the puppy to the floor. She then informed him of his being fortunate in buying the cognac there. That store was one in a chain of only three in the Denver vicinity that carried it in stock. "At other stores it is usually placed on order from our distributor, unless the customer is directed here, or to one of our other locations." Realizing the possibility of the later scarcity of fine product, which DD had stated she was more inclined to, he attempted to buy a case. The only case she had was open and was two bottles short of being full, which Soame accepted.

The interior of the car seemed more cheerful and lively than ever before. One subject lead to the next and Fifi was continually passed and petted from front to back seat and back and forth. Occasionally Soame would give a hardy laugh, or inject a story. Though she told him about her past, DD had not told him that she had not had a sexual relationship with one man for such an extended period of time. Other than with a childhood sweetheart, and before coming to America, that was a fact about her. She felt dazed when she realized with wonder that this event over-shadowed any doubts she had about being perfectly happy and totally content with Soame. Lovemaking had been especially good the night before. At times he could be a bit rough and she knew this. They were adjusting to each other. When he was sexually rough with her, she was able to react to control, and yet at the same time, allow his freedom with her. He enjoyed sex with her, because she responded to his sweetness in a caring way. Though he was sometimes rough, her confidence in him did not allowed her to think he would hurt her. With a full erection, Soame displayed a seven and one half inch tool. She was not selfish with herself toward his comfort. Though he was physically attracted to her radiant beauty, DD was very wise on this point, through her experiences in governing her actions, reactions, and responses toward a bachelor. This one she knew was not a homo sexual or bisexual person.

Soame had a vast amount of experience with woman, and DD knew other woman had attempted at corralling this worthy prize. In this way, she "peeped" him, and used keen insight to gain leverage at the one point all others had come to and failed. Eventually she would either succeed in knowing she had him, or allow him to drive her away. She knew Soame would never leave his woman. DD also knew she was his only woman. In succeeding, which she at that point was determined to do, she will have proven to herself the discipline within her. Her mind was made up, after leaving Oklahoma, to win him. To do so she knew she would have to "play" against herself and relinquish selfishness and any form of spite toward him. This would not be terribly difficult, because Soame was a truly giving person, toward his woman. She knew she had discovered a true man. He would not always be as pleasant to be with. No matter where he went or how long her stayed, he would come home. The realization of the victory she knew had to be inevitable, stirred in her completely suppressing jealousy, and this would be the total infringement she would have to make against her femininity.

In Soame's thoughts during the ride back to the hotel, he gave consideration to the valuable goods in the unguarded room. In fact, DD was more strict toward protecting the $20,000 cash in the travel bag she now stored it in than he was with the bulk. The large amount of money was distributed between three bookcases. The 45 rpm records were packed with them, to add weight to the boxes and disguise their contents. DD insisted on carrying the convenient traveling bag with them and securing it in the trunk, while they shopped. Soame could not see the practicality in lugging the three packed and sealed boxes downstairs, loading them into the trunk, and for the time they shopped, leaving the car unguarded. "Chairly most certainly cannot be expected to stay in attendance and Fifi would be completely disregarded if someone really wanted to break into the trunk or steal the car," he told the two females. "Besides, with the bag and the boxes together, if a break-in or theft happened we'd lose all but what we have on us, and I'll have to bring it back upstairs when we get back, cause then I'll be worried. And on top of all that, DD, all this lugging, locking, and worrin's gonna spoil my high. Now what's wrong?"

"Nothing Suarme, I simply want it and you safe, that's all."

He hugged her, patted, rubbed, and squeezed her in stimulating places and said, "Don't worry we are safe as we can possibly be right now. Don't become over worried by the fear of something that does not exist."

"I take the bag with us in the trunk, all right Suarme?"

That night, before Chairly came through the doors, DD danced for him, with her skirt lifted and held at her waist. The love they made and the sexual pleasure they experienced was truly exhilarating. DD revealed something in the movement of her body during her dance, she had not yet given during their intercourse. He now wanted the stored pleasure he knew she had and kept from him.

Only one other woman had ever shown and demonstrated such moves. She had not done it in a dance. He was then eighteen and she was two years his senior, and an upper-class man. Because of her reputation on campus, she was called "Dick Tracy" by the fellows in private. As a freshman, within a month after being enrolled, Soame scored the junior. During a three and a half hour period, at a rooming house, they had sex four separate occasions. During each intercourse session, only her heels and the top portion of her shoulders touched the sheet beneath her body. She threw pussy at him in waves; encircling his dick in surging thrusts. Soame was 6'1" and weighed 189 lbs. They had vigor, vim, and vitality in their youth. She was 5'9" and weighed about 107 lbs. During the engulfment, and as he petered, he was twitched and slung into a rotation which swirled his rod into a twirl. She then switched, swung, and swiveled the dick in the rolling wave, as it once again formed its delivering surge. When they left the room, the bed was soaked through the mattress. "Dick Tracy" never again went to bed with him. Occasionally he hounded her, though he was going through a series of woman. During his senior year she came back, to complete some additional courses, but she still said "no" and they never did it again.

"Dick Tracy" was the absolute best fuck he ever had. No one else had ever given him such an exciting conquest with her body. DD showed him she also knew how to do this. Had it not been for Fifi scampering toward the door neither of them would have noticed Chairly's entrance. She did the thing with her body and clothes he had never seen anybody else do but her. He was enthralled, and Chairly was overwhelmed with fascination, but neither of them said anything. Chairly began dancing toward the beautiful woman who never stopped dancing, after the precision calculated movements of her body, brought the tight fitting skirt, from her waist, over each separate buttock. The marvel in her doing this revolved around her not touching the material with either of her hands. The private spectacle bewildered Soame and for the second time left him completely mesmerized.

Chairly was permitted to take the record player and a few 45s with her when they were all ready to retire. It was past 3:00 am. Soame hurriedly took the dog outside for a brief walk in the bitter cold. He was freezing, and Fifi shivered when he placed her gingerly on the carpet in Chairly's room. After joining DD in the regular sized bathroom, for their showers she told him of her thoughts of Chairly being alone in such a large room.

"How can she be alone; she never been alone before," Soame asked. "This time she's got a record player with the puppy, a TV in her bedroom, an entire entertainment center if she wants to sleep in her sitting room. She can listen to the radio or record player, from the speakers in her bed room plus the doors are slightly closed and there's the phone too, DD. Now how can she be alone?" He was fidgety moving the tips of his fingers through the lather she had foamed on his back with the thick Turkish hand towel. "Is that a bump right there?"

Though it was not the hotel's bridal suite, the bedroom they occupied was elegant among the other lavishly styled and decorated furnishings. The king-sized bed had a canopy with fringes that dangled from it. The bed was Soame's focus at the time. This was not because he had been on the move for the past five days, did all the driving, and with the pressures he had, he had only slept intermittently. Instead, it was the gateway to the pleasure he had glimpsed in DD's presentation, during her dance. He had never rushed her to bed; this time was no different. Other than lipstick and eye liner, she hardly used any other makeup, during their traveling time on the soft fur cushioned seat in front of the extra large mirror. She did little meticulous things he had no interest in. The towel she wore wrapped around the permanent had to be undone. He had nakedly ventured into her room with her. In her terrycloth robe, with her hair wrapped, she showed the florid makeup light to him. He thought, "Yea the lights work great," excused himself, and got into bed. Because he played and toyed with every part of her body, she could not cover or wrap her hair in bed.

Sexual adjustment to and with a partner, if it's to be a lasting affair, is a very important aspect of the relationship. Man's greatest drives are food and sex; for some individuals, these are inverted. During the time they had been together and had sex in varieties of ways and positions, they were adjusting well. Each felt confident in the other's satisfaction, and the ability to deliver that satisfaction, without being asked.

DD entered the bed with conversation, which both of them shared as a preliminary to the foreplay they enjoyed. They knew the initial climaxes and ejaculation were a more in-depth form of foreplay, for what was to come. The atmosphere was totally conducive and anything and everything either of them wanted was within their immediate proximity. Their only interest at that time was each other, for the pleasure they stalked and knew would be delivered.

With her experience as a "working lady," DD knew she had received thrills with Soame that she had never encountered before, with a single individual. No pimp in the world can hold a woman, if he allows that woman to be satisfied by a man with an instrument, who knows how to use it, for the pleasure and satisfaction of that woman, and after doing so makes himself available to her. In her dance, as a show of gratitude for the pleasures he had given her she revealed that she had not given her all. In presenting the maximum for his visual inspection, she knew he was able to discern the quick flutter of various moves, because of the glint which appeared in his eyes, for only an iota of a second. She watched him as close as he was watching her; both for the mutual gain they knew was possible. A short while later she did it again. Realizing he had been caught off guard, she observed him closely, but he nonchalantly ignored the gesture, observing the outer movements and her hands and arms projecting the lustful craving he sincerely had all over his body, and especially deep in the pit of his groin. His vision moved, tracing her body upward to her eyes. DD smiled at him, and their eyes were locked into each other as her hands and fingers danced like the wings of a graceful bird. She did it again and again, as they both stared into each others eyes, both of them knowing each time it was done. Lowering her hands without making a sound, she shaped her lips "Suarme, Suarme." Then she puckered her lips sensuously, and the puppy moved toward the door.

It was her exact and express intention that he saw what had been seen. It was then his move to pursue what was there to be given. Their initial intercourse lasted about fifteen minutes. They had experienced sex three times. This was in Oklahoma early in the morning after their sleep, during the first night there. He was fairly well rested, and after that third time, which lasted almost an hour, she informed him "Suarme, I have never had so much sex so many times with one man. You make me cum so very much, I like it and I think I can love you." They had enjoyed sex the previous afternoon, and that night before sleeping also. The break this time before the second round lasted for nearly a half hour. Soame did not drink again that morning; he smoked a "joint" and snorted. They both enjoyed the easy listening music filtering in from the speakers in the bedroom. Separate strings on the violin, as well as plucks from the guitar and various sounds from other instruments could be distinguished. The music was soothing and relaxing to their minds. He became aroused through her administration of oral sex to him. She had technique and style, which was erotic and demanding. Looking at the sensuously beautiful woman, perform the act with grace, care, and agility and decreasing her up and down movements to revolving swirls, was an arousing treat in itself.

The second session did not involve anything they had not done before during their time together. As a Leo, DD was the most compatible astrological sign with Soame in practically every way. She had huge lips surrounding her vagina, which made it an awesome pleasure to look at and, unless positioned properly, that factor restrained his full penetration. However, this allowed her more grip; because of his length and thickness. Soame seldom used a full penetration to give satisfaction. He was a well experienced "dickster."

While in the "joint," Soame did not spend countless hours on the weight pile, like many inmates who wanted to display a muscle building torso, gained through the constructive use of barbells. Instead, keeping to a goal of fitness and tone, he developed a personal routine which he did privately in his cell. Push ups, sit ups, and knee bending squats, enabled his physique to maintain a sleek appearance. This practiced routine done in daily sets also enhanced his reflexes, which would have been sacrificed in developing a body structure through bar bells. Except for his sexual stamina when he initially met DD he was ready. During the single, double, and one triple session they had before Denver, he was able to build his endurance. In their repertoire, either the basic missionary or doggie fashion approach was the beginning point; one usually followed the other.

Their style entailed "The buck," not fully extended with only his arms looped at the back portion of her draping knees. On their sides, they then had intercourse with their arms on the bed extended his over hers, or vise-versa. This refreshing stimulation had a phase harmonizing their strokes with either in control. From that position, he spread her legs and got between them, both of them still on their sides rotating. In each position, DD climaxed; this was his reason for each change. He spilled into her while standing at the edge of the bed. She once again resumed the position on all fours, with her knees at the edge, spread to allow him in for the pleasure they found together. It was past five o'clock and the session had lasted nearly an hour. Both of them knew there was more to come.

After cleaning themselves and each other in the bathroom, they strolled nude in intimate conversation, to the bar. Soame prepared the final contents from the green liter bottle of Cognac. He munched on peanuts and fruit. Other than having complimented her on the dancing, and this was said to both her and Chairly, the enjoyable exhibition, danced earlier that night was not mentioned. They both were aware of the rest their bodies needed. Yet, they recognized the expectation neither of them mentioned, which they both gathered to be imminent.

On the loveseat in the bedroom, DD "fitted" her "works" while he smoked reefer. They always found tidbits in interesting matters to discuss. In Lamar, while waiting for the ride and pretending to be a diabetic, he purchased a bag of sixty disposable syringes. She had done a shot before he did a one and one. Soame prepared two of the syringes from the bag. She long before knew he did perfectly well, not only in fitting the "hit;" he also administered the shot with skill. All of their paraphernalia was then taken to the night stand. While he stood there, at the edge of the bed, DD sat and began performing fellatio on him on his tool. Later they extended this to that side of the bed, with both of them in the bed. The center of the bed was wet. DD talked also, during intermittent intervals, to the shaft sliding in and out, up and down, and sometimes rotating in her mouth. She sang, hummed, and whispered to the rod, and occasionally looked in his eyes while projecting other moaning sounds. The talking and singing she did in French. When his member began its incline from it's limp stage, he had her positioned to receive an injection above the calf, behind and just below her knee. He did one and ones, watched, listened, and enjoyed. The glow from the floor lamp, in the far corner of the room, reflected gleams of glistening wetness, each time she raised to the head and tip, where she swirled and twirled her tongue. DD would then lick, kiss, sing, whisper, and talk to him, while looking and smiling into his oh-so-pleased face. All at once, to the hilt, far into her throat, she plunged the rod, and hummed some more.

It throbbed with readiness, both of them knew what was available. He administered the second shot. Decades had past since Soame had realized that the best male cunnilingus expert in the world, could hardly surpass the average female performing the art. His philosophy entailed the logical assumption "If a woman wanted to be sexually pleased, by having her pussy eaten, she finds another woman. However, the best woman she can find, for the deliverance, cannot fuck her as well as the average male. With his fingers, he toyed with her clitoris. This aided her stimulation, to the point where both of them recognized the readiness in each other.

An hour and twenty minutes into their third intercourse session, they had repeated all the previous positions, in the preceding session, except for "the buck." After forming the position, Soame did exactly as he had done before; though it was not much room for her to work toward and from him, DD did well in delivering herself, aiding their coupling. He, after a short while in "the buck," moved closer and further into her with practiced skills and experience. By lowering his shoulders, carrying her legs further up in their hosted position, he encircled his hands under each of her arm pits and held her pinned, by the top of her shoulders. This brought his mouth to her ear, and her's to his. This also spread the vertex of her legs more, offering him a deeper penetration, and it basically took away the majority of her movement, what little she had. He did not rush in with a plunge, Soame eased himself further into DD, and after taking an appropriate number of measured and timed strokes to the hilt, he asked her, "do ya wanna gimme some pussy, DD?"

"Don't hurt me, Suarm, please."

They both spoke as lovers to each other, with the confidence each of them knew they had in the other, and expected from one another. He knew she would cum. He removed his hilt and stroked her, occasionally totally sinking his entire measure. Each time he did it, she chanted French in his ear, and it was an awakening feeling of inspiration for him.

With what he sought, there was another aspect of her sexual quality and desire that had not been released to him. It was not an inhibition, but through habit due to interior environments that she refrained from releasing herself verbally, as she desired to do with him. In various preceding hotels and motels, not excluding her apartment, she had realized she could be heard if she talked loudly. Chairly was always just above a whisper away, whom they gave respectful consideration toward in that bedroom so no one could hear DD, whatever she did in expressing herself verbally, but him. Soame indirectly presented the fact to her. His voice vibrated in her ear. "Talk to me, DD."

"Oh Suarme, I am talking, can't you hear me darling, please fuck me good, oh Suarm, my Darlinggg."

"Gimme some pussy DD."

She then talked in French and her tone became louder. He measured and timed his strokes with her expressions. Then she said in English, "Oh, but I am giving it to you darling, Suarm please have it, take it all." They both knew she said this in jest. Nonetheless, she talked to him in both languages, and they both knew when she was at the peak of her curve, delivering into her climax. In one swift withdrawing motion, he removed himself out to the edge of her vagina, and while doing so locked his elbows onto her sides, fastening her to the bed with the help of the weight of his torso. She could not move her body up to catch the instrument of pleasure she thought was slipping out of her. The entire action was momentary. She screamed at him, before she completed, "Oh Suarme, please don't let it go." He penetrated half way, released her shoulders, raised his body, had released the locking hold with his elbows. Slightly lowering her legs, he told her, "Now give me some pussy, DD." Still retaining the preliminary cap toward her peak, she gave him what he wanted, and he heard what she had to say in the uninhibited tone, and in two languages. She threw pussy at the dick, around it, under it, over and through it, and when they both knew she was totally satisfied, he knew there was still more. Through her pleasurable climaxing frenzy, she forgot that he had not ejaculated. She realized this when he began positioning her again.

In Oklahoma, he had given her the first g-spot thrill and orgasm she had ever received. He had to probe her left side, and switch to the right side of her vagina. There, in the lower side of her upper track, he found it. It was then DD discovered she had an erogenous zone. Though she did not faint like more than a few women he had established this awareness with, DD found the enveloped disclosure to be the most pulsating, invigorating, orgasmic release she had ever experienced. In releasing her from the partial "buck" position, only her right leg came to the wet sheet. His knee fastened to the bed slightly above her knee, holding her leg straight. His arm looped under her opposite knee, bending it carrying her thigh upward as if she were a high-stepping majorette. The hand, from the arm holding the knee up, was fastened to her bedded shoulder. Being placed into the position, she knew what it entailed.

"Suarme, you make me cum too much. I like it but it will be too much, Suarme."

"You gonna gimme some pussy, DD?" He stroked her.

"I give it to you Suarme, I swear I did just now; let me give it to you Suarme, I can do nothing like this, please let me give it to you Suarme, I promise, Oh Suarme, oh my god please fuck me please."

Nowhere in any place he had ever been was there a better "dickster" than Soame. Women with experience at lovemaking, who loved him, taught him, with his inclination, how to make love. Yet, he never pandered himself as a gigolo. Some woman detested this fact about him. DD was suspended in sexual animation, stretched out between substance and reality. She could not understand how, within two minutes after having such a monstrous orgasm, she was beginning to cum once more. Soame stroked her good and as hard as she yelled and screamed, telling him to fuck her. The surprise she encountered totally outdid her: calculating her peak once again, just before she topped her curve, he released her raised leg. This time there was no asking to be done. She was in the middle of a g-spot orgasm. She was releasing a poignant feminine odor which saturated the room. The sheet beneath them was already totally saturated with sweat and secretions she had released. Everything she had displayed in her dance, she now gave in its totality, screaming and calling, he saw when she arched her back. Her body was off the bed from the lower portion of her shoulders to her heels. She tossed, humped, slung, swirled, wound, rung, threw, and rolled pussy at him that way until she knew she would cum herself out of her wits. In one expedient motion, barely allowing her body to touch the sheet, she looped both her arms around his wedge, just above his waist. His elbows were locked, though he did not expect her to lift herself up to him. She could not stop cumming, did not want to, and switched, swung, and shot more, until she passed out.

This was not something he had not experienced before, but her fainting disrupted the ejaculation he was about to spill. The bone hard glistening instrument waved from side to side, before he grabbed it in a choke. He was scurrying to the nearest bathroom for a towel. Within five minutes she would revive on her own. He placed the cold wet towel on her forehead. As she laid comfortably on her back, he checked her pulse. She was as fine as he had predetermined her to be.

After his brief visit to the sitting room, where he changed the dial selector on the radio, to a soul music station, he returned in the midst of DD regaining consciousness. It was shortly past 7:00 AM. "Oh Suarme, I think I must have fainted. I have never fainted before, for any reason."

"Are you all right? How do you feel?"

"Oh you do it too much Suarme, you fuck me too good."

He was sitting on the edge of the bed, with ice water from the bar. Limply she threw her upper body into his lap, and while demonstratively sobbing, she softly pounded in his chest.

"Oh you beast, you hor-e-bal beast. Suarme you make me feel as if I were a little child."

Through her sobbing she laid the side of her face where her fists had rested and asked him, "How can this be, how can this be Suarme?"

Until then neither of them noticed the radio. The deep stringed resonating sound of a cello, caught their attention. It came from the introductory cords of Aretha Franklin's *Natural Woman*.

Not being able to get an answer, after dialing housekeeping, Soame talked with the bell captain. He could only commit himself with the promise, "Sir, I assure you, when the first maid arrives, I will have her up there, to accommodate you with a change of linen. Please be assured sir, I'll handle it." Soame then took advantage of time during the interim and ordered breakfast.

* * *

The conversation in the car, through the prating DD and Chairly did, had become a French lesson. Fifi rested in DD's lap, while her mistress petted and fingered her nap. They had taken an inward route for twelve miles, away from the expressway, back to the hotel. The proprietor at the liquor store had given him the directions, to view the scenery between Denver and Golden. During their talk, Soame found out it was the first time the owner had worked one of the registers in nearly three months. One of her regular employees was ill, and "my floating part time substitute has an engagement this afternoon in Boulder. When my husband was alive he handled these trivialities, but now since the entire operation is on me, it seems I'm left to shoulder the burden." Offering condolences, Soame was informed, "It's been nearly a year now, I've adjusted, and I'm fairly well comfortable, thank you." The route they had taken gave them a look at the suburbs. It was cold out; during the early days of spring, there was still snow on the ground. He had to re-approach the interstate for the last two and a half miles to the hotel. Everyone in the car was very well pleased about having taken the route. It was the most exciting and enjoyable afternoon they had spent together. Now they were all hungry.

To get to the hotel from the expressway, the exit had to be taken after passing the Sheraton. "Ant dat ourer hotel, Soame you pass in da hotel!" Chairly exclaimed, in her momentary tantrum of excitement.

After the curtains were opened, the extra large panoramic window presented the view he had been promised. The sights across the porch railing, over the parking lot, and beyond the expressway, toward Denver, were grand.

The following morning brought an especially pleasing surprise to DD. He was out of the bed near 9:30. When he had showered and gotten dressed, Soame disturbed her sleep by telling her he was leaving for a short while to "see about something kinda important."

"Will you be gone for a long while, Darlinggg?"

"Probably not too long, but I don't want you to worry, if I'm gone for more than an hour or two."

That would be the longest period of time for a separation between them, since they had met. She thought on that fact, but after his departing kiss went back to sleep.

Upon his return he went to the hotel's housekeeping office. The previous day, the woman in charge of that department arrived for work at 7:27AM. The bell captain had her immediately report to the night manager's office. At 7:35 she was rolling the utility cart from the second floor household service room on the wing Soame had rented the suites. Just as she finished making the bed, two other maids, sent by the bell captain, joined her. Because they were about to finish their breakfast, Soame suggested since they were there, they do the entire suite. It was a job for four maids, the supervisor called in the other two maids. She was tipped $20.00. Each subordinate received $10.00, and the bell captain was left $15.00 at the front desk. He was off duty at 8:00 AM.

Soame once again gave the housekeeping department head $20 and instructions to call the bedroom suite. He knew DD's response, and carefully instructed his aide to do accordingly.

"Ms Dubanee, pardon me for disturbing you, but yesterday morning my staff and I – "

"Who are you, what do you want, and why are you calling me, how do you know my name?"

"I'm the head housekeeper M'am – "

"Well my – " There was a pause when she started to call Soame her husband, "we don't want the room cleaned early today, come at your regular time, all right?"

"M'am, I'm calling to ask is that your car, out front directly beneath your suite? Ms Dubanee, could you please go to your sitting room, between the bar and the foyer to the window, it's very important for us to know who the car belongs to."

Because Soame was out, she began to worry.

"All right, would you hold on a moment." In her robe and bare feet, she found her way to the cord, pulled slightly, and stepped to the opening.

Looking up to her, directly opposite and across the parking lot was Soame under his Stetson. He had a big grin on his face, and in his new clothes and coat, he moved both hands, slightly bowing and ushering her attention. She then saw the cranberry and maroon colored car, with a half black leather top. It was five yards from where he stood. There was a ribbon around the body of the car, with a big white bow in the middle of the top. In a flash of a second, only the curtain moved, where DD had been. After seeing the door open, he became afraid. He thought maybe she would not stop for the railing.

* * *

To that point, it was the happiest experience they shared as a group. Fifi had no problem in discerning what was going on. It was near noon when he returned with the car. At three, DD was still in baffled amazement. Chairly, who rode in the front seat with her, still wanted to "less ride som moe chile."

Soame, who was being chauffeured, informed them, "Since you two seem to be in the spirit of riding, how about if we stop by the hotel and get our belongings." They had taken the expressway east toward the mile high city. At Commerce City, Interstate 25 begins a southeasterly loop, by passing Denver. DD drove on the loop to Aurora, where they had lunch. She re-entered the interstate, continuing it's southward route, until they traveled to the Lowry Air Force Base vicinity. At the southern most point of the loop, she reversed her direction.

Traveling northeast they went back to Commerce City, entered the expressway west, which took them to the hotel. Passing the hotel and seeing it from the expressway, Chairly encouraged DD to continue the enjoyable drive.

The car was a cash purchase. Soame simply phoned a cab from the lobby of the hotel. He had been informed of which of the Cadillac dealers would most likely give him the better deal, the previous day. The LTD was still a factor to deal with. At the hotel he began loading the boxes into the new automobile, while DD and Chairly assembled them for packing. There was no rush; the rooms were initially paid in advance for three days. When all the boxes were loaded, after telling them he would be back in an hour or so, Soame was off once more. Though she was thoroughly satisfied and truly happy from his previous outing, DD seemed a bit disappointed that he had to leave once more.

The previous day they drove through a section which was basically black. In the Ford, he went back to that area to find out who had "the baddest grass in town." Several opinions indicated the same person. A promise of "a dime bag," enabled him to be taken to that person, who had just gotten home from work. The job was his "front." The weed was a high grade, from Hawaii. It was super and of a better quality than that he had. He was candid in obtaining different prices in the market. The person taking him there assisted in the deal. Without a notary seal, the title of the LTD had to be witnessed by two individuals, other than the buyer and the seller. The buyer's girlfriend also witnessed the document, as a sale. With a promise of "a ride back to my hotel," the deal and exchange was made for the Ford and a pound of the Hawaiian marijuana.

It was nearing seven when he returned to the hotel. DD met him in the foyer. She was ravishing in her terrycloth robe and skimpy under things. "Hay DD I got some, Wow!! Hello dare mizz lady. Ah did y'all finish packin?" There was no one in the sitting room; music, soft, easy listening music, filtered through the speakers.

"DD, you won't believe the grass I go – "

"Come with me darlinggg, I've got something else I want to show you!" she told him softly, looping her arm through the arm of the hand holding the bag. Leaning her head on his shoulder, she also began steering him in another direction, from the bar high seat.

"DD this is the be – "

"Miss Dubanee" once again interrupted and directed him toward the bedroom, injecting, "Suarmeee don't you want to seeeeee what I have for you?"

Chapter 10

At 1:17 they entered Interstate 25, from the expressway at Commerce City. The radio announcer, over the musical introductory pad, had given the time and went on to say, "It's 31 degrees outside, in the Mile High City. Here are the Commodores with *You Are*.

"Hay, dats da first song I heard on da radio in da otha Cadillac when ya'll picked me up!"

* * *

After giving the cab driver a fairly generous tip from his slide, Soame had walked conservatively across the sidewalk onto the car lot. He had a rust brown tote bag slung over his shoulder. After looking at a Seville, and on his way to another one, a salesman approached him with his standard pitch and a lot of questions. When he had seen all three models on the lot, the salesman informed him, "Ah, sir, our showroom displays the Elegante. Would you care to see it?"

Since his approach the salesman had not rushed Soame. They both led each other at a moderate pace. Soame demonstrated something he had looked for in patrons when he was a salesman. The customer who "knows what he's looking for" is practically an effortless sale. Entering the glass doors, looking directly at the glossy, maroon Seville, with the half leather top, taking their first steps toward the beauty, the salesman made his sale with, "This is the very best General Motors and Fisher has to offer in style, comfort, and quality, through our Cadillac division. Sir, I'm absolutely positive you will be pleased."

Soame did not take the Ford with him as a trade knowing it would be a cash buy, and the LTD would be meaningless, if not a total loss through their standard sales devices. He did not want to bicker over an issue, already worked out to their advantage. Before entering the showroom he had been told about the "North Star Systems" still being on the designer's planning board. "Is a navigational comfort to give directional ease to the driver." There were two other models, one from each other series, constituting the display. Nearly a two-car space separated the three show room cars. Naturally, the Fleetwood was represented with the Brougham De Elegance. Between it and the epitome shown to Soame, was a 2 door coupe "El Dog." Noticing the El Dorado, Soame had an idea beyond the bargaining point. It was an almost obvious factor, with the cash weighing heavily in his favor.

The tires on the Seville were top quality steel belted radials. However, the El Dorado's tires also had polyester sidings. Goodyear is the standard tire issued on Cadillac assembly lines, unless the automobile is ordered, and Double Eagles are requested in the order. Knowing he could not get Double Eagles to complete the deal, Soame requested a gratuity.

The spoked rims brought his attention to the tires on the El Dorado. He compared the rims of the two cars, and though both had sixty spoke rims, the emblem in the center of the Seville's tires was noticeably larger in diameter. He preferred the smaller ones from the El Dorado. It took the mechanics twenty-five minutes to make the switch; the steel belted radials with the polyester sidings, the true sixty spoke rims, with the smaller emblem, were placed on the Seville. With that he rode away.

* * *

They were cruising forty miles north of Denver, when Chairly asked about the windshield wipers occasionally sweeping across the windshield and disappearing, until the following interval. Soame looked in the mirror, told her about the snow flurrying and the gusts of wind, and noticed Fifi. "I neva saw it snow befo. One monin I woke up and it was on the grown, but I show ant neva seen it fallin." She was excited and contented in her happiness even though she did not have the back seat to herself. One of the regular size boxes would not fit in the trunk; it allowed her two-thirds of the seat. Fifi's special place was close to the indication lights in the center of the rear window. When a flake momentarily stuck to the window, as it melted into nothing, she would paw at it, until she drifted off to sleep.

There was a dealer tag on the car. Soame remembered the address from the card he had received at the liquor store, and the title showed the owner lived four blocks away. It was titled to DD, and as the bow indicated when she received it, it was a gift from her bow. The automobile was uninsured. Though he did not mention that he would be leaving town, he agreed to send the license plates back to them within twenty days. He had left a lot behind that had become memories. Some were good and some bad; like other times, in other places, all that remained from the experiences were the memories. They were seldom good thoughts..

As love birds, DD and Soame always had fun in the front seat. The further they proceeded north the more it snowed. Speed had to be decreased because of the driving conditions. DD could not sit as close to him as she preferred, but at a comfortable half arm's length away, she was able to feel and clutch the meat, beneath the new wool flannel dress slacks he wore. DD looked picture perfect. Including the morning they left her apartment, she had never before looked so radiant to Soame. As a contingency, there were two blankets between her and the door, there since Oklahoma City, when the weather had gotten much cooler. Soame drove carefully, an alert driver with both hands holding the wheel. This hampered his fun with his lady, but increased their chances of arriving at their destination.

There was no particular place he traveled to, except the state line. It would be the fourth state they traveled through, his seventh since he departed from home. Loveland was the midway point on the route, between Denver and the Wyoming state line. The car had hydroplaned several times. Twice he pointed it out to them, in approaching the ice. It indicated the potential danger they traveled in, and why Soame decreased his speed to less than 50 MPH. Traffic was moving slowly in both directions. When snow reaches the surface of the highway, it melts. An accumulation of the water becomes ice in freezing temperatures. At times a solid sheet of ice lasted for twenty or thirty yards. In other stretches, it continued for more than a hundred yards. The driver can neither accelerate nor pad the brake pedal. While hydroplaning, it is best that the driver's feet be positioned flat on the floorboard. After having it pointed out to them, the passengers in the car could recognize the different feel of hydroplaning.

"Iz lak travelin cross da iron of a bridge, when ya ride ova a bridge in a ar."

"Yea, it's kind of eerie isn't it? Now listen Chairly, if and when you learn to drive, you too DD, if you ever encounter this type of situation: while hydroplaning, other than continue to hold the car in the exact direction it is proceeding in, upon approach onto the ice, the driver has no other control of the automobile. It is definitely the most dangerous condition under which a driver can operate a motor vehicle."

Climate control air circulating devices enabled the car to roll along at a comfortable 76 degrees. While at the shopping plaza, in the city they had left, noticing the weather was much colder and the fact they would be traveling north, Soame bought a coat for DD, to match the one he chose for himself. They each had Harbor Masters. The full length, light brown, overcoats, had removable black bear fur linings. The salesperson informed them, "They will be a warm and comfortable delight, in any freezing temperature above sub zero, even if you have nothing else on but your shoes."

"I neva knowed ducks stay so wom" was the comment Chairly made when she and DD joined him in putting their other packages in the trunk. She elected to wear her new parka. It was light blue, with down feather padding. She had never owned such a jacket before, and it seemed to brighten her world just a little more.

DD was curled up in her new coat. Soame's coat was stacked atop the blankets. When Chairly reversed her jacket and spread it over the top portion of her body, DD asked that Fifi be passed up front to her. They were twenty miles north of Loveland. The puppy was then attired in her smartly knitted pink body cover. In the window she was not cold, because of the temperature inside, and the defroster that heated the window glass. Fifi climbed from DD's lap onto Soame's coat. She extended her paws from the coat, while standing on her hind legs, and looked out the window.

During the winter months, many deaths are cause on the highway by motorists and passengers simply freezing to death, after becoming stranded. Encountering problems with their vehicles, in many cases motorists are forced to the shoulder. There are times when passing travelers will not stop to give assistance. Freezing temperatures are deadly. In most cases people who become victims are not prepared for the harsh and deadly weather, outside the warmth and safety of their cars. Troopers are at times scarce. Various reasons call them to different points on the highway. Unprepared for the harsh conditions outside, when no one stops, after a while the stranded motorist seeks the warmth and comfort of the interior of the car. At that point a dilemma exists: whether to remain in the freezing interior of the car – many times it seems safer because of conditions outside such as freezing winds, icy rains, and snow itself – or take the chance outside of the automobile, attempting to hail someone passing by. This situation has caused many deaths along the highways.

In Lamar, Chairly started bringing a pillow along. Though it was a factory brand new car, he wanted to minimize the extreme possibilities, if mishap did occur. They traveled along, in luxurious comfort, occasionally talking, listening to the radio, and hearing periodical, "Breaker, break, break," on the factory equipped C.B. radio. They thought Chairly was asleep, until he lit the joint. His smoking was not strange to her.

The Maui was a better than good brand of smoke. It is a top selling variety of weed recognized worldwide. DD had only once before attempted to smoke with him. During the last hours in the suite, and practically each time he lit up during the trip, she had rolled her French accent at him. "May I have a puff Darlingggg?" It was truly a high potency smoke. DD usually only had one drag. Soame hardly ever smoked more than a half joint at a time.

"Papa, I thank soon, I might wanna learn ta smoke," the voice came from the back seat.

DD slightly snickered, and because of the marijuana, began coughing.

"How is it you manage to keep your mind on things unbecoming to you, while you neglect the things you should have an interest in?" Soame asked Chairly. "I haven't seen you with a book in your hands since you've been with us. You're not an adult. If you were, you wouldn't have to ask to smoke. You'd have a job, and you could afford your own."

"Well, DD told me ta be totally honest with ya'll."

At that point, DD said "Shhhhh."

"No no, let's hear her out," Soame said. "Cause um tired a dis bullshit about every time she wants something she absolutely knows she can't have, she brings your name into it, and has gotten clever enough to associate it with honesty! Chairly. What the hell do you think I am?" Soame managed to control his temper, which had never flared before in front of them. DD raised to her knees and aimed a harsh stare at Chairly, who seemed to be only interested in what Soame had to say.

"You know darn well I'm not going to allow you to drink liquor or smoke cigarettes or grass, don't you?"

"Soame, you drank li-ka and smoke."

"What!! I'll tell you what, Chairly. When you want to drink liquor and smoke whatever, you simply get yourself a job, find yourself a place to stay, and drink and smoke as much as you want to. Is that cool with you?"

She did not reply. Fifi shook herself, yawning, after being awakened from a comfortable nap on Soame's coat. They all felt him take his foot off the gas pdeal.

"Did you understand what I just said, girl?!"

"Yea Sur."

"Are you sure you understood what I told you?!"

"Yea Sur, Soame."

They noticed he had not accelerated. In fact the car continued to decrease in speed, and he had changed from the far left, to the far right lane.

"Now as long as I continue to feed and cloth you, and keep a roof over your head, what are you gonna do, Chairly?"

"Um ga do like you say, Soame."

"And when it comes time for you to go to school just what are your plans?"

"You said I hafta go da school Soame. Um Goin!"

"You playin' me just a little too close Chairly. I don't wanna go through this with you no more. You betta watch yourself. Do ya hear me?"

By the time he finished he was talking really low. Everything else in the car was so quiet, as low as he spoke, every word was plainly heard. Still the car cruised at only 40 MPH.

"Yea Sur, I har ya mista Soame."

Fifi climbed down into her mistress's lap. They had hardly regained the 50MPH speed they were traveling at, when she felt the glide. With it she saw both of his feet move, and his elbows spread slightly, when only his palms held the steering wheel; his palms faced inward, projecting his thumbs up, as if he was giving the "high" sign, with both hands. The glide lasted for more than fifty yards.

After traveling twenty miles or so the subject came up once more, but this time with a different approach.

"How old was you, when you started smokin, Soame?"

"I don't really remember Chairly, twenty-one or two I guess. Why?"

"Cause I jes wanted to know, das all… but thangs change cause I been smokin off n on fa most two yeas. Me n dis girl and anotha boy we know use ta go out in da field and smoke all da times."

"Well it wasn't good for your health, and you can see it stunned your brain, because you can't keep your mind on the right things."

"My mama use ta leme smoke and she and ah boyfriend usta leme drink beer to!"

"Well it seems to me a short while ago DD and I gave a certain person a ride, because she was tired of being confronted with the things her mother and boyfriend did."

DD then came into the conversation, "Suarme, I think you and Chairly should come to some type of agr – "

"Hold on a minute! Why do I have to com – "

"How you ga cut somebody off when day talking? Do you remba das not comunekatin, Soame? Remba you said we must lurn ta comunekate?"

Soame sighed and said, "So what do you wish to say more, on the subject of your smoking, in communicating with me, Chairly?"

"I didn say I wanna smoke now, I said soon I might wanna smoke!"

"Well as soon as you get around to asking me if you may, or if you start smoking without my consent, soon, that'll be soon enough for you to start furnishing yourself with the things I've told you about on your own. Do you have any idea how soon that'll be?"

"Well if DD say I can smoke, how bout dat?"

"Let's just hear what Miss, Aunt, Dubanee has to say about the matter and coming to terms."

"I thought ya'll was married, you keep callin hur by har name. Don married peoples have the same name?"

Soame looked toward DD, as she reached for the sun visor, on her side. She flipped it down, took her lipstick from her purse, passed the puppy to Chairly, adjusted the blankets and coat, faced the mirror, and adjusted and freshened her makeup, ignoring them.

Soame had never seen DD present such a non-caring attitude. It surprised him that she would demonstrate such evasion. Chairly said, "Das what ya tole me Soame, yall was married."

"We're married by and through a common bond, which is at times strong and more binding than that observed and practiced in law."

"Das lack me not reely bein yo little girl ant it?"

"I never said you are a child of mi – "

"Suarme, Chairly," DD interrupted. "You two should stop this, you should stop it now! Chairly, before it gets you into trouble… and I do not mean with Suarme."

Though they were driving through patches of snow, during different stretches, they averaged 55 mph. Some distances they were able to travel the limit, which was 65 mph. The slowest pace was at 45 mph, which they did when they encountered ice. Soame became worried about Fifi and her possible need to be walked. In the rear window she was decorative and humorous. Twice since she had been placed back in the window, in her pink body cover, they had hydroplaned. The humor was pointed out by Soame, in coming in contact the first time, after she had been placed back in the window. He glanced in his rear view mirror, after making contact with the ice and glimpsed Fifi. Knowing the car was on a straight glide path, and there were no obstructions ahead, he called their attention to the puppy. By chance, that time, they did not get the full scale of her antics, but when they skimmed the ice on the next occasion DD and Chairly caught practically the full play of her capricious reaction. While awake she usually lay near the center light with her mouth open. Encountering the ice she closed her mouth, rolled her eyes slowly toward the front, and then to the opposite of their sockets. When her head and eyes centered, her head bobbed continuously until they reached the regular driving surface.

"She looks like a Jerry Mahoney doll," Soame commented through their hysterical responses, when he momentarily saw her again.

"Wyoming state line, 500 yards," Chairly read from the sign. "We almost in Wyoming. How fur we goin Soame?"

DD asked her, "Are you tired, honey?"

The question brought a giggle, from her mouth stuffed with gum. "Naw, Um jest like you, Soame's wundafo ridin companion. We got watches ta prove it, DD."

It was near 6:00 AM. Though there was no major increase, snow drifted down. Along the way it changed in degree. Some places there was none, but it was always cold outside. The new Cadillac he drove did not allow him to contemplate the probability of a mechanical or electrical malfunction. Soame was really tired. He was more tired after crossing the state line, than he had been during any of the previous stretches. He looked at DD's glossy nails when she pressed the station selector on the radio. He thought back to the erotic times in the bedroom suite, and how looking at her face and hands aroused him. The thought of leaving so soon, after being in such pleasant and plush accommodations, with her was almost haunting. It was all behind him, and he was still moving between Cheyenne and High Springs. Soon, he would stop for rest. Most likely, they would stay there for a while; longer than any other place they had been.

Raymond Claude Perdue The Man's Digest

Part 2 Chapter 1

Like many other welcome stations, this one was open all day and night. The service station provided clean rest rooms, maps, brochures, hot coffee or chocolate, and a warm enclosure also displayed large pictures of famous Indians, teepees – showing how they covered the land by the thousands, before the people who lived in them were forced onto reservations – and there were other factual relics and artifacts representing American Indian culture. There was a registry which "Samual A. Lightburn," signed as a visitor to the state of Wyoming, with four members in his party.

The atmosphere was similar to the traffic they encountered on the highway during the drive; seldom did they see anyone. They relaxed and enjoyed the coffee and chocolate from the dispensers. Soame had a road atlas, but he hoped the large state map and brochures he selected would give him some inside information, or identify that certain type of place he was in search of, to "lay low." His Stetson had a gambler's roll, and a couple of times during the drive, he wondered why he wore the new Rossies, instead of the ankle boots. In their overcoats, they were a handsome couple; accompanied by the girl and the dog, they looked like a family.

Cheyenne is situated a short drive east, where Interstate 25 junctures with Route 80. Soame's immediate destination was the major city. They were at the welcome station approximately twenty minutes. Nearly a mile after crossing the state line, they were greeted by a large green sign with white reflecting letters, displaying, "Welcome to Wyoming." Beneath the letters was a picture of a cowboy riding a bucking horse. The welcome station was a quarter mile beyond the welcome sign.

On the atlas, which is primarily a road map, the stretch between Cheyenne and High Springs appeared a vast openness. With the aid of the large state map, Soame found what he was looking for. The area he gave consideration to be south—because of its size. The map description showed it to be a small town or settlement, with possibly seven-thousand inhabitants. There were several similar areas, in the triangle formed by Cheyenne, Casper, and the small city of High Springs. His plan was to venture from one to the other, if neither of them suited him, he would eventually find the exact spot. Typical of his style, though he did things quick, he was in no hurry. He also liked this particular area because it was located near the largest city in the region. He would have to get supplies, and in doing so the size of Cheyenne would minimize attention.

Realizing a Cadillac dealership would not be open for two, possibly three hours, Soame drove to the junction, and exited I-25, then entered State Road 80 East. Cheyenne was then a short drive away. Predawn showed in the sky directly in front of him. Though it was not thick and clustered in rolls of drift, there was snow on the ground. He had mentioned the gum plopping to Chairly, who wanted to know if she could do anything right, but he was thankful it had not led to a long drawn out discussion. He drove a short distance on S.R. 80, saw a country dirt road, with snow on its shoulders and ditches, and turned into it.

DD had no interest in looking out the window, into the darkness dispelled by the head lamps, projecting a scene she had seen time and again. Though the soft velvet cushioned seat beneath her felt pleasant, she preferred the touch of the bear fur. Except from Oklahoma City to Lamar, since leaving the apartment, she did not wear slacks while riding. Like all the other times she wore dresses, she had on no panties. Her bare bottom sat on her coat. On open roads, when there was no danger, she laid partly under Soame's arm, with the side of her face just above his stomach. Almost immediately leaving the welcome station, she raised her skirt, wrapped the remaining coat around the top side of her lower body, and regained her usual position. She noticed the decrease in the speed of the car, and the change onto the exit ramp, and because he had told her their route, her estimation of the junction and the change in direction was precise. Again there was a decrease in speed, and she felt the change of the surface beneath the tires, and the crunching snow, as they slowed. She also knew they would be spending time waiting, to have the oil changed.

Beneath the hood of an automobile is a very delicate instrument. Though there are people employed at interstate and turnpike service plazas, these people are not necessarily mechanics. Though some are mechanics, their training and experience is not always up to date. Some station workers will change your oil just for the chance to look under the hood of a new car. Ignorance can be deadly in this situation. Trying to find what is to be done, at times other devices are tampered with, or in some way become noticeably disturbed. This can result in outcomes very costly in time and money, for the vehicle owner. There are many cases wherein the owner finally gets rid of the car, because he or she initially made the simple mistake, of entrusting the automobile into an unqualified person's hands. Not knowing what they were doing, these people often fidget with the wrong part or device. By the time the car gets to the dealer, two or three gadgets could be twisted or turned, out of place; this also comes about in attempting to find the original problem. In the process the two or three parts or devices, are the problem.

Motor oil is used to reduce friction, and lubricate the parts in the cylinder, in an automobile's motor. New motors lose shavings from pistons, and other fine particles, discarded in the cylinder housing. The discarded fragments and particles collect in the oil, and channel to the oil filter. Some drop directly to the crankcase, which is beneath the assembly. The crankcase is commonly referred to as the oil pan, because the oil from the pistons and cylinders drain down to it, for collection. In purchasing a new car, some dealers will instruct, "When you have driven seven hundred miles, have the oil changed." This is to discard all the shavings and particles, that have collected in the crankcase, which is the reservoir for the stored and used oil. Changing the oil drains the case, and the shavings and particles are discarded as waste. This eliminates the possibility of the harmful metals being recirculated back up into the cylinder where they can do long term damage. Frequent oil changes increase longevity of the vehicle.

Soame intended to change the oil in Cheyenne. It was a likely place for a Cadillac dealership, and he had no idea of what lay ahead of him, or the direction he would take, after leaving the large city. With the proper tools, he could remove the drain plug from the crankcase. With the replacement of the fresh oil, he would also need a new oil filter.

DD was thoroughly satisfied with her new prize. The car was a luxurious comfort, and it boosted her pride to be its owner, but Soame had become the meaning in her life. Even the love she imagined before meeting him could not compare with the feelings she had for the only man she would now accept in her life. To her the issue was settled beyond any conceivable doubt or competition. Twice she had risen up, to see where they were. The first time she lit a fresh joint and passed it to him. They talked in whispers, while seeing the new dawn filter through the tree limbs above them, extending out over the road they traveled. They also saw fences, trees, and open fields, beyond the ditches bordering the road. The second time she rose daybreak was making its appearance, illuminating the area around them. She could see better then how to use her "works," and hoped he would not discover the number of "misses" she had made. She had the feeling of a beautiful day. Her entire life had changed since she met him. At last she did more then just exist—she lived.

During the forty-five minutes he had taken the country road, making several turns from the main dirt road he turned onto, he passed only two cars, traveling in the opposite direction. He roamed and explored a bit more than an hour, before DD sat up, freshened herself in the rear view mirror, and initiated merriment that would carry through the day, ranging from a variety of conversational topics, to the fun, games, and teases they enjoyed in being together. Chairly was asleep; the loving couple in the front seat talked in low tones, occasionally tugging and bumping each other, playing, while riding at a slow speed on a deserted road. They passed through wooded stretches, and saw open fields covered with snow, reflecting the brilliance of the glow, from the rising sun. The scenic early morning drive took them across two wood bridges, and for a couple of miles traveled along side a babbling brook, which was in some places blanketed with thin ice. There were stumps, branches, and limbs in the water, and ice had collected around the protrusions. A light covering of snow from the night exemplified the serenity that existed in their lives at this time. This peacefulness not only was portrayed in the environment, it was felt within them, toward themselves and each other.

In the one lane road, he made a three point turn. He had been doing one and ones all along. A mile or so after the turn, Chairly spoke up, "Is dat cocaine you doin, Soame?"

"Why?"

"Cause I hea ya sniffin, and das what ma sista usta do when she did it."

"What?"

"She was doin cocaine, I jus ased das all."

"First of all, usually people observe common courtesy, especially toward those they know, greeting others with 'good morning.'" Soame slowly brought the car to a halt, placed the gear shift in park, and turned back toward Chairly.

Her eyes slightly widened, but Soame knew Chairly was not afraid. Long ago he had noticed the brazen nerve she had. Widening her eyes was a part of the charade she presented. He saw time and opportunity to confront her. With index and middle fingers, he eased the gamblers rolled hat further back on his forehead. "Good morning, Chairly." She merely stared at him. "Well, since you won't speak to me, here's DD up front here also. Do you mean to be discourteous toward the both of us?"

Chairly remained silent still, until DD began her turn toward the back seat. "Good monin ta both y'all," Chairly blurted.

"Well, it seems we've at least made that much progress," Soame observed. "Secondly, it seems you admire your sister's doings. It shows just how fast she really was. Didn't you also tell me she had a baby?"

Before Chairly could answer, Fifi sat up in the back window, and scratched her ear, as if she had a flea. Soame instructed Chairly, "Hold on... put your jacket on, take the cover off the puppy, and take her to the front of the car." Without saying anything, she made the preparations and the door was opened for her. At the welcome station Fifi only urinated. This was brought to his attention inside the building, where she was placed on the floor to exercise herself; she was carefully watched then by Chairly, but she did not defecate. Scratching her ear was the indication she gave. His door remained open as they all watched the dog shiver and practically dance a few yards in the tire track, away from Chairly. When Fifi was done, she rushed back to the girl's waiting hands.

"Izz cold out dare," Chairly said.

DD kneeled in the front seat, reaching for the squirming puppy, "Give me her cover, honey."

When the door closed Chairly began taking off her coat.

"Chairly," Soame said, "when I was a boy, knob toe shoes were in fashion, with three quarter length shirts. Girls wore crinoline, under wide flaring skirts, with either black or brown and white shoes, and bobbi socks."

Though she pretended to be fumbling with something in her lap, he looked at her and talked. "Jackie Wilson and Elvis Presley were popular names in music, and on the football field Jim Brown and Johnnie Unitas had become legends in their own life times. Allen Sheppard walked on the moon and Little Richard played in a Jane Mansfield movie."

Soame noticed Chairly's attention stray to her typical far away stare out of the window. He said: "I noticed a vast difference when you were buying those shoes at the shopping mall the other day. When I was a boy, the most popular brand tennis shoe was the All-Star. The other day I paid more than a hundred and twenty dollars for those air pump Nikes you have on your feet. The All-Stars cost $8.50. That's a pretty big change, in time and price. Do you know what crinoline is?"

Chairly suddenly erupted: "Soame, I ben gittin hi since I was twelve, I jus wanna get hi das all. I mean, I can sneak and steal yo stuff, and ya would neva know it, but I ased ya Soame, cause DD said it was da right thang to do. I know what powder is, um 14 and I know a lot, but I jes smoke das all, I da even like bea."

"Well um gonna tell ya Chairly… I'm a very private person. Very few people have ever known me well. I'm also an adult, and so is DD. Neither of us has lived with a teenager, or had close contact with one, outside our coming up as teenagers. I know that images are important, and I also realize what we project to you has an influence on your ideas of becoming an adult. Chairly, since you are so open and frank; I did not raise you, and I am not particular about having you in my private life. I especially do not care for the infringements you attempt to impose, in getting what you want. I've tolerated you, only because DD asked me to give you a ride. Soon, we're going to settle down somewhere, not far away. We will be there for a while. During that time, since you are here at DD's invitation, and because you've expressed yourself now, as having smoked marijuana before, I will accept her decision in regards to allowing you to smoke. In the meantime, I do not want you to confront me with the things I do, and these things you know I will not allow you to do. Are we communicating?"

"Das cool, Soame, thanks."

En route back to the highway they saw a raccoon crossing the road, toward a snow covered patch that had settled on the ice. The scattered debris surrounding the stump, limbs, and snow seemed to be its destination. "Das a coon," cried out Chairly, when DD called attention to the animal that was grayish brown with a black cheek patch and a black and white ringed bushy tail. The crunching ice, and sounds from the car, caused it to scurry along at a faster pace. This filled the interior of the car with excitement. Fifi was helped onto the dashboard and began yipping. An array of questions began pouring in to the driver. Various subjects revolved around his experiences as a radio broadcaster.

"You knowed the godfather a soul, pusonly Soame?" Chairly asked.

"That Godfather bit is just a self-proclaimed attachment. That Georgia boy has an official title by which he is honored as 'Soul Brother Number One', but that's not the title itself. It's the most distinguished and prestigious title and position a black music entertainer can obtain. It's the true goal of a black vocal artist. They all hope and strive for it, Michael Jackson, Prince, R. Kelly, Freddie Jackson, and all the others beneath James Brown as 'the king of soul' work toward that goal…sure I know 'Brown'. We're not buddy buddies, but I know him, and he recognizes my name well enough for me to go back stage and see him anytime we were both in the towns where he appeared."

"When was da last time you seen him, Soame?"

"Now Chairly, how much do you really want to know about Soame's personal contact with people who are stars?" DD asked her.

"No, it's quite all right, we've got the time, I don't mind telling her, and besides, there's a message I want to pass on to her about the real James Brown and his true feelings towards young people such as herself. The last time I saw 'Brown' was after he'd done a concert in Ft. Lauderdale, at the Sunrise Musical Theater. I was residing on Miami Beach at the time, went to Lauderdale and caught the last part of his act, to see if it had changed over the years. I sent word to see him, and for the first time I wasn't called to his dressing room. I thought it to be a bit strange, and I pondered as to whether it was an embarrassment. I was ushered to his Limo and instructed he would see me on his way out. The bodyguard waited with me. The car was in a secluded area in doors, behind the stage he'd just performed on. He is the absolute most dynamic performer you can possibly witness.

"Anyway, the mood changed as people began saturating the area preceding his appearance. Other guards escorted and followed him, and there he was. He had been recently married; his wife had moved through the crowd with him, and was seated by the driver. From the open door, he and I standing face to face exchanged greetings, and after a few other words he said, "You know um married now, man?" He then slowly swept his hand toward his seated beautiful bride, we both had to slightly bow, in looking while he made the introduction. There were other words exchanged in the friendly acquaintance, before he climbed into the rear of the stretch limo and invited me to Tampa. He offered the invitation with a stay at the Sheridan where he would lodge. I told him I might come, but the following day found I could not make the four hour drive, because of other priorities. That was the last time I saw him.

"It seems to me there's always been a James Brown," Soame continued. "As a teenager I learned to slow drag with *Lost Someone, Try Me, Bewildered,* and *Prisoner of Love.* I graduated from college and was on the air for the first time, on a small station on Miami Beach, WMBM. It was one of two black stations in Miami and the smallest of the seventeen stations servicing the AM market. I will not go into the stations, not only in Miami but practically across the country, that had almost stopped playing Motown and James Brown records. There was a syndicate in my home town, comprised of guys much my senior. Another guy you may have heard of, Les Brown, took me to one of the meetings. The big wheels: Fred Hanna, Nickie Le and Butter Ball, did not want me in the meeting. Les and I are the same age, he chose not to go to any other meetings until I was accepted. I never went to any of their meetings. In fact, instead I brought the attention of the black music industry to Miami.

"In '62, Stevie Wonder made his debut with Motown, on an album recorded live, from which wherein *Finger Tips* was produced as a 45. From that time no one else heard of Stevie Wonder, until I bucked the syndicate in Miami. I started playing Motown. I began with *I Was Made to Love Her*. Broke the record, and forced the other black station to play and chart it. Gladys Knight and the Pips had been off the scene for a considerable while; I did *Everybody Needs Love*. Both of these records became national sellers, from the air play I initiated. I also took the Temptations' *You're my Everything* and set it up as well. Now here's what's really interesting about these facts I'm giving you, because in a way it distorted one man's future, and gave a crown to another. Marvin Gaye was initially a solo artist, who was paired with a smooth and graceful alto by the name of Kim Weston. The duo did not succeed. She left Motown Records and went to MGM, where she released, *"That's Groovy."* This left Marvin Gaye as a solo artist again, still with Motown, which then matched him with Tammie Terrell. Their first record was *Ain't No Mountain High Enough*."

"This was all taking place in '67. Between March and that summer, the postman delivered a package to the station from King records. I had the 7-11 shift, and not only did I receive the package, I opened the package containing the first James Brown record I ever played. I broke a string of hits by Brown—*There Was A Time, Cold Sweat,* and a couple more, which enabled him to regain his popularity. It took nearly three months to break the Gaye and Terrell record, and in the meanwhile I did the Four Tops' *Bernadette*, but Marvin and Tammie began to spark. As it took off, I flipped it and carried both sides, *Ain't Nothing Like the Real Thing* also began to show. During that time Otis Redding, the reigning King of Soul, died in a plane crash. There was Wilson Pickett, Johnny Taylor, O.V Right, Bobby Bland, and Al Green had just made his debut with *Back Up Train*. The following year at the convention for the National Association for Radio and television announcers, because of his gain in popularity, which was aided with *Say It Loud*, and receiving a vote higher than Lou Rawls, James Brown became the King of Soul. That's why he's Soul Brother Number One, and will be as long as he draws breath into his body. No other person can share the title with him. Marvin Gaye was disqualified because he sang as a duo; before Tammie Terrell died they had a string of hits including *It Takes Two, You're All I Need*, and many others.

"I left MBM and went across Biscayne Bay to WAME, the larger black station in Miami. Les had gone up to Columbus, Ohio. He and I joined on a jumping sound he introduced me to, through the owner of the label, Bunkey Shepard. He and I got to be close friends; he produced a label bearing his name *Bunkey*. The record Les and I made a national hit was *Get On Up* by the Esquires. It was their only hit. I continued driving with Motown Stevie Wonder's *For Once In My Life*. This was preceded by another record I can't think of but the three were mine; I took time in breaking each of them and that's all it took for Stevie to have the name and fame he has today. I followed Gladys Knight and the Pips up with *Heard It Through The Grape Vine, Make Me the Woman You Come Home To*, and *House Of Gloom* by the Four Tops. A bit later 'Brown' had a concert in Miami. I would not see the show because it was a outside in a ballpark. In fact I did not go because the local DJs were to be introduced on stage. I always simply wanted to be the man who played music and talked from the box in the living or bedroom, perhaps too in the car. Around town people were claiming to be me, showing up on beaches and clubs using my name. Some who had gotten to know me wanted to even know what type and color toilet paper I used. Popularity has its disadvantages, especially in your private life. Anyway, I was then doing a midnight show and filled in for one of the guys in the syndicate who did not want to have 'Brown' on his show for an interview. While filling in I did the interview. It was the first personal contact I had with him.

"I found an interesting person within the entertainer. He explained how he came from a poor family background . In the winter when he was a boy, reared in his home state, Georgia, he and his family ate from the discards of whites who would slaughter animals, take the finer cuts of meat, and give Brown's family the leftovers. He told me of his people being so poor during winter months when they did not have heat, he would walk up and down the railroad tracks gathering coal to use as a heat supply. *Say It Loud I'm Black and Proud* was a top ten seller during the time of this interview. Naturally we did not talk about his impoverished childhood conditions on the air. When it was time for the interview, five minutes before I was to air it, I asked what he wanted to say about his record. He was sincere in telling me 'You're an educated man. I wish I could have gotten an education. My message is to the young people who will be listening, and it's not about the record. Will you help me relay to them the importance of staying in school, completing their education so they will be prepared for the rough world that's out here? The world has no feeling or regard towards anyone who's not prepared and the only preparation is a good education.' We did the interview, and as best as I could, I aided him with his message.

"That night during my regular show, he came to the station. I had been given specific directions not to allow anyone in by the station owner. Answering the back door there was Brown.

"Hey, man, why didn't you make the show? You were supposed to MC, I thought."

"I explained that I had to rest after substituting for Nickie Lee, plus I had to be there from twelve to five. I had a three and a half minute record on, and I explained that I could not allow him in. I was not rude but I had to catch my record, queue up, and present another one after commercial. When I got back he was gone.

"I saw him next after watching his show in the Coliseum in Los Angeles. It was the first time I saw him backstage. After the show I had no difficulty at all getting to his dressing room. I was waiting for a job I had been promised by a station there. Through his invitation, the following day I joined him at his mini-suite, in the Beverly Comstock Hotel, in Beverly Hills. We had quite a discussion which resulted in his sending me to Hollywood to see his manager, Ben Bart at the Holiday Inn there. Brown's instructions were for Bart to book me a room. I stayed in the room almost all month-long after they left town. Each year Holiday Inn selected and featured one of its many hotels as Inn of the Year. That year, the Hollywood Holiday Inn received the prestigious award. It was a new hotel, with a revolving circular top floor where one of its bars and lounges is located. Like the renowned Pontchetrain in Detroit, or Pier 66 in Ft. Lauderdale.

" James Brown represents something special me. I've known him to own a Lear jet and have access to a castle in England. Only the British government owns the castles there. He's also owned a chain of radio stations. One of his misfortunes was Ben Bart whom I mentioned. He was a Jew and robbed Brown of considerable wealth. The government also did considerable damage to him with back taxes. Plus, he did a bit of time here in his developed years. I've never met MC Hammer or had the occasion to play one of his records. I like that *Can't Touch This* and recognize his music. He was not around when I was working as a

D. J. I mentioned him because of the contributions he made to Brown's welfare. He's a sporting dude. Perhaps someday I can help him in some way. James Brown is a very special person to me. He represents accomplishment and that I can do when all turns against me and I have to establish my own independence.

"Chairly, I hope you've gotten the importance of this story. I took the time in telling it to you because of the message involved from Soul Brother Number One, did you get the message?"

"Soame, I got da message in Oklahoma. When we gon eat, hay Soame! Dare the Cadillac place you passin it, I thought you was gon get da oil change!"

"I thought you wanted to eat," Soame said. Fifi pranced, pawed and yipped in DD's lap, feeling the excitement Chairly generated while they rolled along the main thoroughfare of downtown Cheyenne.

Chairly's idea of breakfast was stopping at "Mickey Dees." This allowed the couple to dine at a hotel restaurant. Chairly had only seen the Cadillac emblem, but with it were the symbols for Chevrolet, Buick, Oldsmobile, and Pontiac. It was the General Motors dealership and service center. Soame was told it was the best automotive service center in town. There was an hour and a half wait to have the service done, but it was worth it for the assurance it gave him. There was also a maintenance check and fill up with a free car wash. Though they would spend the remainder of their lives together, the four of them would never again enjoy such times as those they were sharing, and would share during the first months they spent in learning each other's ways.

Chapter 2

THE sign indicated a population of 7,500 people. It was slightly passed noon when they entered a township 63 miles north of Cheyenne. Soame stopped at a convenience store to purchase a local newspaper. There he was told how to find the only motel in the area. He would have gone directly to the real estate office from the food store, but he was informed the office was open only on Tuesdays and Thursdays. The office was owned and operated by the town clerk. It was open while she prepared the latest issue of the newspaper which circulated once every two weeks. Sandra Fairfield opened the office from ten until noon and from two to three during those two days of operation .

Along the way to the motel they passed two houses on one side directly off the state road. The other was nearly fifty yards back. According to the directions Soame had received, the motel would be "The first building past the second house. All three buildings are on the left—you can't miss it. Past the second house take the first turn in road you come to. The motel sits sort of back and off the road. Old Indian Joe got drunk just before Christmas and tried to make the turn in. The guy who owns the place hasn't taken the time to put the sign back up. The ground is still frozen you know and of course we all here know where the place is. Mostly people just pass through coming from or going to Cheyenne. Dan'll be glad to have you. Had some crazy notion about putting up a secret hideaway for lovers. Fact about it is, Mister, that's the name of it-"Secret Hideaway"-come to think of it."

None of the rooms adjoined. It was a four-unit structure, and all the other rooms were vacant. The small rooms had only one full size bed. So that all could sleep comfortably, Soame rented two rooms next to each other. The accommodations were clean and they were that the propane gas heaters worked in each unit, and each had a mini office refrigerator. The nearest public phone was a mile away in front of the fire station. Its desolateness made it the ideal for what he wanted to do. While he scouted the area he could obtain the two or three days rest he vitally needed, while looking for better accommodations. Soame estimated they would remain in the town about a week.

They were at the foot of a mountainous region. Although the temperature was 39°, he knew with the mountains being west of them, by mid-afternoon the temperature would begin dropping. The sun would vanish and he would be asleep because fatigue had really caught up with him. The girl imposed stress. It was a different type of brain wrestling than any he had ever encountered. There was no reward or benefit. It seemed to be all at his expense until that "if" factor presented itself. In Oklahoma, if she had not led him to the discovery in the well of the back seat would he have found the treasure? The thought enabled him to endure and work toward getting the rest he needed.

All money and the interior of the car were unloaded. With that and the twenty dollars worth of snacks and canned goods he had purchased, they would be decently comfortable for two days, perhaps three. He had been given directions to the "widow woman's" home, but thought it best to catch her at her office. The owner of the motel lived twenty-five yards directly behind the building. He had a wife and three children.

Dan explained his availability and told him, "Mr. Anderson, I could have my wife prepare enough for you and your entire family. We are right friendly round here and we can do it for what ever you think it's worth."

Dan was thanked by "Charles Anderson" who said: "We do appreciate your hospitality, but we'll be fine." When the proprietor rounded the corner toward his house, Soame called to the others and they began unloading items they would need from the trunk.

Chairly had the choice between the record player and radio. After dark she spent time with her hosts, and when they were all tired, she and the puppy retired to the room next door. DD instructed Chairly to leave a night light burning in the bathroom. It was an item Soame felt foolish about not thinking of. They settled in for the night.

* * *

While DD and Chairly explored Neiman Marcus seeing what each section in the women's department had to offer. Soame went to the bookstore. There he requested a special book, of which there was only one copy left. He purchased that copy and had it gift wrapped … DD beat him to the punch with the presentation of gifts. In preparing for bed, she brought out her special surprise for him. She did not unpack it until after they were out of the shower. She hurriedly preceded him into the room. Soame came out of the bathroom with the towel partially around him. When he saw her his eyes widened with surprise. She was in her new, blue chiffon, full-length see-through robe. Underneath she wore the matching gown. The robe was gathered at the neck by a ribbon, and flared down the center, exposing the gown. Completing the ensemble was a set of white silk underthings. The outer garments did little to conceal DD. The only ribbon on the robe and gown matched the swank undergarments. Soame also noticed that she had purchased new bedroom slippers, with a 1½ inch heel and matching blue fur.

During that phase in their lives they enjoyed giving each other gifts and Soame did not fall short. What he gave her that night turned out to be the most socially constructive and beneficial contribution he could have possibly done for her, in the prevailing circumstance.

"A man is a product of his environment," Soame knew this, with a background in Social Science. Other than take her physically out of New Orleans the present he had for her would enhance the possibility of the goal being attainable; if she sincerely wanted to conform to a rehabilitative procedure. He scored really big in the only way the situation permitted him to totally capture the woman who was falling in love with him. He presented her with an updated edition of the renowned book by Emily Post on "Etiquette." With this book and her interest in its contents, the damaging effect of her past history could be adjusted. In time, this present would contribute to her mental stability, a development that begun with her physical withdrawal from New Orleans.

DD was now exploring a world she had never known as an adult. When she was nine her father died in an accident. Until then, DD's family had lived slightly below middle class. At the age of eleven she found out what a prostitute was, when her mother took up that trade. Before Soame, life had never been so good for her. When they crossed into Colorado, life seemed like the living heaven she had dreamed of and hoped for. She thought life with him had been splendid to that point. However, the book created an avenue for her to travel in directions and dimensions she could have never before envisioned herself as being capable of entering. The book raised the possibility of considering herself being sociably acceptable.

A "miss" occurs when a person injects a chemical into the arm, which was intended to be administered through the vein. Missing is a common practice for people who use drugs intravenously, especially those who administer themselves. Moving the position of the needle after the vein has been located and punctured, is the basic cause of the "miss." The result of a "miss" is a "burn." The "burn" is similar to a blister which arises where the chemical is injected, when the vein is "missed." In two, possibly three, days, the "burn" becomes a sore.

That first night at the motel after preparation for bed and the exchange of gifts, DD set up her materials to "hit." She was experienced enough with the procedure to know not to "go" in the same spot within a 24-hour period. This practice also aided the administration of vitamin E and its healing effect on that particular spot. With this careful preservation technique, tracks are eliminated or at least kept to an almost unnoticeable minimum. Being right-handed and incapable of "hitting" her right arm with her left hand, DD developed a problem through the continuous intravenous administration of the abundant substance they had. Only fresh air and sunlight provides immediate cure for a burn caused by a miss. Covering the spot slows the healing. The ones DD had were beginning to appear as blisters. As she began to tie up that night Soame saw the protrusions and questioned "what-cha got there?"

Embarrassed, DD replied: "a miss or two." Not knowing he knew exactly what the formations represented, she explained, "My tie loosened, and a couple of times the works moved."

"Undo your tie, DD. We're not gonna have this." He did not say it angrily or as a rebuke. She realized this and appreciated his concern.

The principle involved, was a mutual feeling towards and about each other, what they did privately. They accepted these openly shared facts which were of no one else's concern. The potential problem displayed with the burn would be someone else noticing it and from that point they would know she "used the needle." After DD un-did the tie he simply tied her right arm and "hit her." He had not before "hit" her in either arm. He immediately recognize why she missed. She had shallow veins and they rolled.

Soame was almost an expert at giving shots and identifying what he saw. At one time he had professional problems and "hang ups" involved in his career as an announcer. During this time he went on the "ruff" to "skid row." The initial station he had worked for would not accept him, and the last station he worked at, no longer existed. He refused to take an out of town position. This would not have been terribly bad, but he also refused to take a nine to five. Eventually, he lost his car. Next, he lost his apartment.

He lived on the streets, sleeping in parks, stair wells, deserted buildings, and one night in a phone booth. After starting, he never stopped smoking marijuana. In his adult life, as a result of being "down," this became his first hustle. His brother sold "grass" by the bales. He would get free reefer, in the form of "shake" from his brother. This supported his habit and enabled him to afford a motel room. Because he sold "nickel and dime bags" he moved about on the streets of Miami, from day to day, moving also from motel to motel, selling only in the streets as he moved. Everyone who saw him and knew that he was "holding," also knew he had good quality reefer.

When Soame's brother began handling "coke," the same principle applied. He only resided in hotels and motels, and moved through the streets, where people were, day and night. He knew every all night joint in Miami and on the beach where he later lived. Prostitutes on the boulevard "Biscayne" would run to him. Anyone who knew him, and wanted "the best," "scored." He also knew the toll that the white powder extracted from users. He did not use the substance, and wisely took his brother's advice, " Just the way you get it from me, that's the way you let it go." Soame never "stepped on" a piece of Coke he sold. He handled " Fire" coke. That was always on "the one". He established a route so regular, and he was so dependable, people along his way would refuse to "score" from others and "hold" for him. At all night strip joints, girls would spend their tips and offer him their pleasures. Pimps who got money from the whores would spend it with Soame. In learning to sell his quarter, half, and gram packages, he also had to learn how to "hit" some of his customers, for various reasons. However, his success was basically in making a quick sale.

Later, when "freebasing" became the thing, at times, he would sit in "smoke-houses" all night, instead of "shooting galleries." Soame had truly been around, and knew the game from practically all aspects. DD was discovering and about to grasp a point, she could nearly put her finger on, but it was a totally strange awareness to her. Soame was an honest hustler; she had never known, nor had she ever heard of one before. She would never know just how common "base houses" and prostitute were to him at home.

Soame and DD were up until nearly five the following morning. She always gave him splendid and beautiful sex. He never failed to delight her and bring her to pulsating orgasms, and satisfaction. At four she dressed in her coat, went next door, and allowed the puppy to "go" in the accumulated snow. She and Soame also discussed Chairly. Their agreement was to give the girl time to choose what she wanted, outside of school, that she would attend was an established fact. They would encourage her toward the "right things." Her previous circumstance at home might have created a mental block, but they would be stable for while and could afford more time and attention toward her. She appeared to be a decent kid and Soame strongly instructed DD, "She notices only what she sees as being beneficial to her. Though I'll care for the both of you, she'll basically be your responsibility. She's torn between acting like a child, and wanting to be an adult. It's a difficult stage of adjustments for her right now, and she rebels at the fact that I do as I please as an adult, and restrict her as a minor. I don't want close contact with her. She's your guest and you will have to begin molding her character towards maturity, if her ways displease you."

Chapter 3

DD enjoyed coffee. Her day started with at least one cup in the morning to get her going. Since no hot plates were allowed in the rooms at the motel, this meant either she or Soame would have to go to the fast food convenience store. By 9:20 she and the puppy were visitors, wanting to know what was on the morning's agenda. It would take an hour for DD to make the preparations to go such a short distance, for such a small item, though it was her need that necessitated the trip. Soame accepted the minor chore and it enabled him to pursue another goal at the same time—visiting the realty office. He was left alone to dress, while the girls went next door.

Sandra Fairfield was approaching 50, but looked nice. She told Soame how she and her two children lived in the house, back up the road, before the motel. Her son, who was the oldest of the two, was in his second year of college, in Cheyenne. Though he had an apartment with two other boys, he was at home at least three times a week. She thought that was due to her cooking. Her daughter was a senior in high school, in a larger town 40 miles away. She revealed that her husband had been killed in a logging accident, five years prior. He owned the company, but after his death, she sold it.

"This is basically a reservation. You're lucky you did not arrive during the weekend, or at the first of the month." She also explained that the sign indicating the population was incorrect and outdated. "Heavens, they're less than 5,000 people here. Nothing to attract and keep the young. They move out as fast as they grow up. The Indians constitute 70 percent of the population, and they're the economic means of the community. Young or old, they all get government checks at the beginning of each month. Then they each have more than a thousand dollars." She appeared to be a rather laid back person and liked to talk. Soame was in no hurry; he listened with patience, concern and interest.

"The Sheriff's 67-years-old," Mrs. Fairfield continued, "and has held the position for the past 24 years. The circuit judge comes through once every four months, for the quarter session, and the biggest crime in the past three years has been invasion of private property." Soame asked about the possibility of locating in the area, due to the declining health of his "daughter," who was " terminal." He said they had traveled around the country to see specialists. The best suggestion offered was fresh air, "Which I notice here in abundance."

The woman nodded and continued her story. "The most frequent charge is drunk, and drunk and disorderly. In fact, the judge really threw the book at two neighbors three years ago, they had been drinking and got into a squabble. One persisted in sitting on the other's car, parked in his drive way. The Sheriff walked a block, and booked them both on the same charge. Each week he has the same problem at the jail. He doesn't have enough space. He thinks the men simply want to drink and have dinner with their squaws and children. The motel stays full during weekends and at the first of the month; they get drunk and go straight to the jail; if the Sheriff isn't there, they lock themselves in. They're now beginning to fight for the cells, from what I hear, because it's so crowded during those times. You didn't see a sign in front of the motel, because Joe ran over it. He's one of the locals. Last session the judge fined him the $27.50. He was ordered to pay the fine, for the sign, to be fixed by Dan. He hasn't given Dan a cent. The next time he gets drunk and has to go in front of the judge, the judge isn't going to take it too lightly."

The woman talked with a slight western accent. Her carry certainly was not southern, and also was not as distinguishable as the true western accents he had heard the previous day, upon arrival. Hers was more sophisticated, with a smooth tone and even dialect. She was also quite graceful in her overall mannerisms. He had told her that he wanted to rent or buy a farm, but none she described suited him. He was discouraged, after judging the area to be so "ideal." During the short time he was going to be there, if he had a home built, by the time it was finished, he would be ready to leave. Mrs. Fairfield agreed with him; it would be a waste. "Most of the white folk around here are basically farmers. The smaller ones have either sold or died out. Nowadays the larger owners are cutting their crops under, and receiving government subsidies. I don't know of anything decent, in the way of a farm. They're either dilapidated, or there's no running water or heat."

Soame shook his head: "I had my heart sort of set on it, after the little bit I saw of the area yesterday. The air is so fresh, the feeling is so clean and invigorating. I simply can't get a place here I'll just have to move on."

He was about to leave, when she looked directly at him and called, " Mr. Anderson." She momentarily stared at him. All along, while she talked, he had paid attention to her small mouth. His gaze was taken from her green eyes, by the appearance of the tip of her tongue, which traced along the upper rim of her top lip, from corner to corner. The flang tracing seemed to take place in slow motion, the red projection, extending and tracing, partially around the small mouth. This was the second time she had acted in this manner. In each instance, the gesture was blatant, a luring invitation. He knew this time, this one would not afford to let him leave. This he counted on, and wondered if he would. It was but a brief second, before she continued.

"I'll tell you what, my husband and I lived in a hunting lodge. We expanded it into two bedrooms when our son was born. The place is in fairly decent condition; the propane heater stands in the old fireplace, and all my old dishes and silverware are still there. We moved where I live now, when my father died. He gave us the lodge as a wedding gift. During the years we've rented it out to hunters, who've all taken extremely good care of it. My son has used it quite often in the past several years, to get away from me and his sister. So you see… What I offer in my suggestion, is a place that is livable. I have the keys here, if you'd like to see it."

Twenty minutes later, Soame, DD, Chairly, and Fifi were in the car, on their way to what would be their temporary home, while they were there. It was a short drive from the motel. From town, the widow Fairfield's house was at the end of the short road, to the left, before the motel. That same road, 10 yards north, also turned right; its name was Derby Lane. It ran nearly 400 yards into the woods. Fifi had been placed on the dashboard. She sat on her haunches looking ahead. DD and Chairly sipped coffee, and 75 yards off the highway they passed a house on the right. They passed another potential neighbor, well spaced from the first house and finally, at the end of the lane, there is was, a place to call home.

"Dare it iz, dare it iz, I kin see it!" Chairly chimed. This started Fifi to arf arfing, in her turn to see what the excitement was all about. The place sat partly embedded in a cluster of trees twenty yards back from the lane. Had it been spring in full blossom or summer, they would not have seen it, in front of it as they were.

"It's supposed to have a running stream three feet deep in back, with lots of trout," Soame told them as they all got out.

Near noon, the temperature had soared to the 40s. DD wore beige designer jeans Soame had never seen before. She presented a tantalizing attainable treat to him, in her boots and white blouse. The blouse resembled a long sleeved shirt, with ruffles in the front along the button line and collar. They all wore their "foggers" and Fifi strutted around in her body cover, before she was scooped up and carried on the inspection tour. There were patches of snow around and about the dwelling. The wooded surrounding area was blanketed, but sporadic openings occurred here and there.

They walked around the outside of the house, circling it from the left. It had a log cabin appearance, but the front and back screened-in porches helped establish a more modern look. Soame walked across the porch first and unlocked the front door. With DD directly behind him, he swept her, puppy and all off her feet and carried her into the marvelously spacious living room. When she was placed on the floor, they stood looking into each other's eyes and kissed. Chairly had explored both bedrooms and the bath, before they finished the lingeringly sensual tongue twirling intimacy. Fifi squirmed and pawed between them.

Soame said, "The landlord won't be back in the office until two this afternoon. We have until three to decide."

Still looking into his eyes, she responded, "If the other portions are as nice as this, my answer is yes."

"Y'all oughta come see da bed rooms," Chairly called.

Soame replied, "I want to see the kitchen." He and DD then went in opposite directions, though his interest was not in food. A counter divided the living room from the combination kitchen and dining room. The dining area featured a medium-sized table with four chairs.

Soame saw the kitchen and by the time the girls joined him, he had taken a seat at the counter, atop one of the stools. He then fluffed and spread six healthy lines on the Formica top. While they explored the kitchen, he did a one and one. He then asked their opinions of the bedrooms. The furnished structure stabilized the sound of his voice. They were totally pleased when they returned to the counter.

Soame looked at Chairly. "We may as well get this over with, I'm not the one to evade issues or points. Chairly, in a little while DD is gonna give you a joint of weed. Before you go off half cocked, I want you to know, that I know exactly what you are doing. First of all, it's said that grass has a tendency to lead the individual toward hard drugs. It's like a person will drink hard liquor after they've tried beer. Some do, some don't. I guess the majority do move on to hard liquor, which doesn't necessarily prove the theory accurate, because the person had the inclination initially. Whether they wanted beer or hard liquor from the beginning, they were motivated to the alcohol, and I believe in most cases, unless it's a matter of affording liquor from the beginning, the person made the cowardly approach to something he wanted from the beginning. Instead of simply drinking liquor, they used beer as a stepping-stone. This brings your exact situation into perspective.

"Now we're gonna allow you to smoke this grass in this house and around this place. Chairly, you've got a big mouth, and you open it at times without thinking about what you're saying. Other times you've opened it to me after you're interpretation of all the angles being figured out, and you've presented me with your cock and bull story of what you want, because DD says you should be honest. Now um gonna be honest with you. I can make my own babies and take the time and raise them, if I was interested in raising a child. I don't need you as a headache, burden, or problem. You've to get along with the program, by watching and seeing the flow of our style and pattern as a student in school. Chairly, when and wherever it is you go to school, you keep your mouth closed about what goes on in our home! Did you understand what I just said?'

"Yea show."

"What did I just tell you, Chairly?"

"You sade ta leave what we do at home, an nobody is ta know what wez doin."

"All right now, that's good, very good. You've got the exact idea and don't you ever forget that. This stuff here is very good herb. You aint about ta get pregnant but um gonna tell you this anyway, Chairly. Later on in your life, if and when you decide to have a baby, and if you're a pot head, then stop smoking. The biggest harm marijuana does to the human body is its effect on pregnant women. It is speculated that pot may do chromosome damage to the unborn child. So you remember that and keep it stored for the years to come. Don't go jumping out into life being fast like your sister. You don't need a baby to get a welfare check, so you can sit on your ass getting fat, having more babies, adding more to your social assistance. You need to get your ass in school, learn something, so you can earn something and be a good woman for the man that gets you.

"Now, outside of the dangers involved with tar and nicotine, and their effect on your lips and lungs with all the billions of dollars American research has provided, those are the net results. However, you must take into consideration cancer is the number one killer in our race. Tar and nicotine causes lip, throat, and lung cancer. That's the way it's stacked up. However you feel about it, listen Chairly, hear me very well and good, I will only tell you this one time. You're intelligent enough to remember, and if you are dumb enough to forget this, I don't want you around me at all. At eighteen, you will be considered an adult.

Until you become an adult, and while you reside with me, you will do no hard drugs. There are no ifs, ands, or buts, no maybes, and DD cannot give you, and will not give you permission to override what I've just told you. Do you understand me?"

"Yea, Soame."

Chapter 4

THERE were dishes, towels, curtains, linens, and even a vacuum cleaner in the cabin. With their belongings, they only had to buy food. The stream behind the house was thirty yards from the back porch. Winter conditions rid the banks of brush. This left a clear stream of running water, which rushed past the ice along the banks. They smiled at the abundant trout just waiting to be scooped out of the shallow stream.

They all agreed on taking the place. Soame and DD had observed Chairly after the discussion. He explained paranoia to her and told her about it being a result of excessive use. He gave her a "three finger lid," saying: "Too many scientists say cancer is caused by the chemical composition of cigarette papers. These are made of wheat straw, which gives you a better chance of not contracting the disease." Accepting the ten packs of papers, she hugged his neck. It had never happened before; the gift or the hug. He was caught by surprise, also with "Thanks, Pa-pa."

That afternoon Soame paid the rent in advance for three months. Their belongings were gathered from the motel. Dan appreciated the tip. Soame did not ask for a refund at the motel. Dusk found them with all their goods stacked and spread about in the living room. The only items remaining in the car were the bookcases in the locked trunk. It was a major accomplishment for them all. A tranquil feeling existed within them and throughout the accommodating environment.

The gauge displayed sixty gallons of propane gas in the tank. Exploring the linen closet, DD found a small electric heater. After bathing and showering the first night in their first permanent establishment, they relaxed and enjoyed the comfortably warm and cozy residence. Because the majority of the 45s were packed in the bookcases in the trunk, their supply on hand was limited. Nonetheless, searching through the "singles" Chairly found a record she really liked. It had not become an oldie goldie, but was relatively out of play. They had snacks and heated can goods and "jammed." Whitney Houston's *How Will I Know* set the pace for the lively scene they shared. During the time, Soame had been looking forward to a good night's rest. By 10:00PM all the lights were out and Chairly was comforted by the warmth of the small heater.

While they were in Denver, at the mall, DD and Chairly had gone to the grocery store with a list. Included on the list, with other items, was a box of Arm and Hammer baking soda. The first night in the cabin was also a memorable experience, because of the production he was able to obtain, from the materials he had. In assembling his paraphernalia, he questioned DD, "Have you ever smoked base coke before?"

"I know it's a pulsating high, I've seen others do it, and I know it's expensive, but I've never had the interest. Why do you ask Suarme?"

"Sooner or later the girl will see you hitting. She adores you; with all probability you can do no wrong in her eyes. Eventually, she's apt to have the interest in 'skin popping.' I don't want her to go to 'the main line.' There's also another reason: your veins are very shallow. You've been exceptionally neat, and done extremely well in keeping your 'tracks' non-detectable. I'm surprised you have no collapsed veins. I'm well informed enough about the product through a vast amount of experience to suggest you allow it a rest for a while through that method. I'm cooking up an eight ball to see the 'comeback.' We can afford your smoking; it's a cleaner method, but um gonna tell ya, it's drastically addictive. I'll never see you without it, and though you can smoke it in front of her, you mustn't give it to her, or allow it to be available to the girl. Do you want to try it?"

"Base" cocaine and "crystal meth" – methedrine – were two of the most addictive substances found in American society toward the closing third of the 20th century. Other than its name and reputation, Soame hardly knew anything about methedrine, but Soame had a wealth of knowledge concerning cocaine. He knew very well how to make the conversion from the powder to the truly addictive rock form. Though he never smoked the substance, through a self-made vow, he was able to instruct DD in using the technique. With a new pipe, filled in its stem, with nearly four hundred screens, which he had burned to eliminate wax and manufacturing substances, he presented a rock and informed her:

"DD there's much more to this than meets the eye. I've never 'based' and I never will. I'll tell you why later. Now, I want to tell you about 'basing' and what to expect. You will only get truly high, once. It will be this first time, when the pipe is lit and you inhale and exhale; that will be the high and the reason you will smoke from that point on."

He explained carburetion and the importance of applying the technique. There had been times he sat and watched men and women pay thousands of dollars to teach themselves the method of getting high with "the pipe." The desired outcome is only produced by mastering the technique of carbureting. In addition, it is not a smoke held in the lungs, like marijuana. Expert "basers" take in one deep smooth hit. They relax and release. Some search for years and pay astonishing amounts of money to learn the method involved in smoking the pipe.

"In about a week and a half this pipe is going to start talking to you. It never likes to be left alone. Anytime you attempt to leave it, that's when you will actually hear it – 'take me with you', 'don't leave me behind', 'hay, you're forgetting your friend, I want to go too' – As you see, I already know what's going to happen. Believe me, I would not allow you to attempt this unless I was absolutely certain, number 1) I can afford you this pleasure, and 2) I know you are strong enough to see that I will never place an obstacle between you and I. Though you may become attached to this pipe, I feel your feelings toward me are stronger. Remember, it did not give itself. I gave it to you."

"Soame, will I like it?"

"You tell me. Enjoy the first one, best of all." He placed the rock and "torched" it.

During the weekend, they made meals of the fish they were able to snatch and trap. The deepest portion of the stream was four feet. It was fifteen feet wide at its farthest banks. The fish and the water ran down from nearby hills. Further on, beyond the property they were on, the stream expanded into a pond. In the storage shelter, there was excess screening wire, from the porches that were somewhat recent additions. Soame contrived a device similar to a carrying stretcher. The contraption could be held on each bank by two of them. When submerged into the stream and afterwards remaining absolutely motionless, looking into the clear stream, the fish could be seen and caught when they swam above the screen device. It was a matter of timing and sometimes not rushing for the catch. They caught two and three nice size trout at once. The longest period of time they fished was twenty minutes. After they were fixed, the fish became succulent, the trout lasted through snacks and the next meal.

That Monday morning found them in Cheyenne. Not only were they in the city for supplies, they also made a visit to "the good hands people." The car received total insurance coverage with Soame listed as an additional driver. A local hotel address was listed with the tag agency, from which the tag was purchased. The first item purchased while shopping was a small, electric heater for Soame and DD's bedroom. Early mornings were brisk, and since the one space heater was used by Chairly, on a couple of instances they had gone out into the living room for comfort. There was no freezer, but the refrigerator's freezer section would hold enough meats and vegetables to allow them up to six weeks without having to replenish their supply. At a slaughterhouse, Soame spent $75.00, buying beef and pork cuts. That and $200.00 worth of staples and groceries plus the fish would carry them from six weeks to two months. They each got leather jackets and he and Chairly were fitted for boots. He could not persuade DD to accept a pair of lady Dingo boots to match his. She insisted the ones she had were fine, and the ones she had were enough to be in the woods, the little bit she would be in need of boots for the woods. She finally chose a pair of ankle lizards from a nearby ladies apparel shop.

During the following two weeks they spent time adjusting to their surroundings. Soame was able to catch up on his rest and found ways to occupy himself without leaving the immediate area. The music on stations feeding in from Casper, Laramie, and Cheyenne was basically country and western, which he did not mind, but DD could not stand. The record player had significant value in their lives during this time. DD was a wonderful person to be with and share time. It was an actual honeymoon for them. They made each other's day brighter and carried the glow through to the dawn of the following day. The girl spent a large portion of her time outside with the active puppy, which was treated like a dog of a different breed. They played and scampered through the woods. She would call, "Here Fifi," "Yip Yip" or "arff arff" and the puppy, in it's knitted cover would hurry to her waiting hands.

Exactly two and a half weeks after they had been in the cabin, an event took place which cast them together for life. Because of the shortness in the remaining school year and the fact they would soon be moving on, Chairly was not enrolled in school. That particular day DD had run a tub of bubble bath. This was her daily practice, and at times she would enjoy tunes from the record player while relaxing with her pipe in the bath. The "torch" she used was of grain alcohol, a wad of cotton, and a five inch section of clothes hanger wire. Soame found this to be more practical than his Dunhill. This day he caught her about to get into the tub. She had all her useable items in easy hand reach from inside the tub. She was in her panties and in the process of loosening the sheer bra. While palming her cheek with one hand, he assisted her with the snap, using the other. Naturally she was familiar with the move because it was one of his standards for making intimate contact. Each time, with each method, through every contact they had in this way with each other, they became aroused and stimulated. From her ear to her mouth, his lips traveled on to her exposed breasts. His hand was inside her panties, exploring the mound he would never lose his fascination for. He used his other hand, also fully in her panties, to palm both cheeks and slide under them, where his index and middle fingers found the prize. He toyed and gripped her with both hands, using his mouth on hers and upon her breasts. He liked very much the feel of her silky hairs. Every day, throughout the day, he had her, she had him; they were seriously excitable lovers.

With her help he had gotten undressed. The bathroom door was closed and she adopted a position on her knees. The position was somewhat formidable for her, but she always enjoyed it after she had gotten her first eruption. Her knees were on the bath mat and her arm and hands stretched to the opposite side of the tub, the soap dish was between them. They enjoyed this "spread eagle" fashion from the rear approach, for nearly ten minutes. Simultaneously, they heard whimpering from Fifi. They both turned to the right, looking behind them. There stood Chairly. One of her hands held her dress up. Her eyes were closed and she appeared to be in a deep grin, gritting her teeth, in ecstasy. The other hand was in her panties; she was masturbating and began licking her lips, still with her eyes closed. The puppy sat between Chairly's spread legs, on her hunches, looking up at the girl, to them, licking her lips and back up at Chairly.

"What are you doing!!!" Soame immediately demanded to know, not moving his or DD's position.

Chairly's eyes bulged in amazement. Still holding her hands and body in the same position. Fifi then stood up on all fours. Chairly replied, "Uh… Ah… I thought I was gonna use da bathroom an… all…"

DD, with his instrument still plunged deep in her, then injected, "Stop it, Stop it both of you! It is high time we did something about this, and I mean right now!"

In making a motion to get up, she went on, "Every day this goes on with you two, come with me, Chairly. You too, Suarme." She stood up grabbing a towel.

Entering the adult bedroom, DD began giving directions. Soame was asked to the center of the bed, with his back almost against the head board. Miss Dubanee then laid with her upper body next to his stomach and upper legs. Chairly was instructed to take the same position, on his other side. She did so after taking her boots off. DD then took the half limp member totally into her mouth. It was fully erect, after fully enveloping it, to its full length, and rising on a single stroke. Raising up, looking at Chairly, she asked, "Would you like to learn how to give him this type of pleasure?"

"Can I DD, can I?"

DD then sniggled, and became acquainted with ménage a tois, and having Chairly with their man.

Twenty minutes passed after which, Soame interrupted the instructional procedure. "How about we take a short pause. I'd like to get a snack and some refreshments, and Chairly, you're wrinkling your dress."

Fifi had taken a resting position under a chair in the corner. She could not see the activities on the bed, because she was small, and her vision was hampered. When the three got out of the bed, she followed Soame to the kitchen. She enjoyed the small piece of fish he gave her. He then made himself a sandwich with plenty of hot sauce on the trout. The puppy continued on with him to the counter, where he rolled two joints, and poured a four finger drink. He also poured a stiff drink of Five-Star. He then fluffed a gram of powder in a saucer, and by the time these items were assembled, he had finished his orange juice and sandwich.

Returning to the bedroom, as he anticipated, he found DD had removed her smoking materials and the record player to be only a reach away. This was not at all unusual. There were accommodations she had already set up, which made the pipe and phonograph easily obtainable. It was a continuation of Chairly's first experience with ménage a tois. Though the sexual encounter prevailed as such, she did not partake in any form of cocaine. Everything else done in the bedroom, at that time, she had peeped and seen them do all along.

However, this was yet to be also another first sexual encounter for her. DD was somewhat profound as a captivating cunnilingus expert; that same afternoon, she delighted, thrilled, fascinated, and overwhelmed Chairly with the cunnilingus she administered. The girl became a woman joined in sisterhood, gaining a higher position in Soame's household. On that afternoon, a different type of knit began weaving their family structure. Through time, it would also sustain itself as a permanent soldered institution.

Four hours later, DD enjoyed the bubble bath she had originally intended. She was then joined by Chairly. Soame had previously showered and while they bathed, he entertained himself with the sounds from the radio, and lounged in the living room. Later that evening they enjoyed a steak dinner with a salad.

They knew from that point in their lives, sleeping arrangements would not be the same.

Chapter 5

SPRING came into full blossom during the next month and a half. The snow completely disappeared as the temperatures warmed, and sprouted green foliage throughout the lower foothills of the mountainous region. There were no problems encountered during their stay. They became accustomed to the landlady's visits twice a week.

Wednesday and Saturday afternoons, Sandra Fairfield had a routine of simply stopping by. She had carried the habit through the years, in maintaining her property. Naturally, Mrs. Fairfield had an interest toward his "daughter's sickle cell anemia." To her the victim appeared to be healthy and did not exemplify the yellowish appearance in her eyes. This was typical of patients suffering with the disease, with the deformed red blood cells. Though through their encounters during her visits, this was never mentioned, it was a noticeable illustration, which never arose in discussion. In some way, her visits were very helpful toward them. In fact, had it not been for Mrs. Fairfield's visit, Soame would not have been motivated to explore the location to which they would eventually move. Not only did she bring the most recent newspaper, but also gathered information and economic reports on particular areas within the region that he had an interest in. These areas included other sectors in Wyoming, North and South Dakota, and Montana. Knowing she was "well off," this was initiated when Soame paid her for the newspaper with a fifty-dollar bill. He had already explained his interest toward moving on, and the type of information he would need in finding the suitable area he was in search of, for perhaps a permanent settlement. It had already been established that he had been fortunate in achieving prosperity and an early retirement. Extending the bill, he told her, "If you would use the change to aid you with any expense you incur, I would be pleased to have your help and attention toward this 'personal' project, Mrs. Fairfield."

"Why thank you, Mr. Anderson. I'm sure it will be no problem at all in getting this information. As soon as I can, I'll have it to you."

They were sitting in porch chairs in the front of the house. Farewells were exchanged and she departed his company.

DD read and studied the book on etiquette, and Chairly also took an interest in the fine points of conventional requirements for correct social behavior. This brought about the most interesting change anyone with the best expectation of her could possibly have imagined. Day after day, the two girls would primp, tease, and question each other on "what the book says." They developed a lifestyle of imaginary pattern, from what Emily Post had written. This included and involved the "proper" thing to do, how and when. The two women took on an air of distinct sophistication, which at times left Soame in awe. He was so pleased with the accomplishments and future possibilities that he ordered volume two from the Cheyenne library. Chairly also did extremely well in perfecting her French, which improved her English considerably. At the table they flaunted themselves and the French with the care and grace of highly bred, polished, and sophisticated America. With this, and almost flawless sex, DD had created an entirely new and different creature. Chairly was not the girl they had met from Louisiana.

DD would dress and make Chairly up to look as if she were twenty years of age. Though she was sleek, she was still "budding," and in some ways, Chairly was undeveloped. DD spent time and developed routines, painstakingly assisting Chairly with the carry and movement of her body when she walked. She could sway her body in such a way, it would attract any man's attention within twenty yards. DD would not have been so persistent had Chairly not been so willing.

The appointment was made from the public phone at the fire station. On the first of June they drove back to Denver and visited, in keeping with the appointment. The creations they obtained at the hair salon of Neiman Marcus, left anyone who saw them dazzled. Viewers marveled at the two black women from France with the gray poodle. Though Chairly was pretty and developing, there was no actual comparison to the mature, developed, and well experienced DD. She lavished attention on Chairly, who never disappointed an onlooker. By then Fifi stood nearly eight inches. She adored attention and for the first time had a clip, with a ribbon, and her nails done.

Throughout the mall, the two females attracted attention every place they went. Because it was the beginning of the summer, DD was able to dress in a way revealing her well proportioned body. It was total pandemonium for some who saw her. Scores of men would actually crowd into shops, even ladies shops, simply to observe them. Others, who wanted to see more, waited outside the shops for them to reappear. They carried crowds with them in stores, moving to different sections. In shops they purchased jewelry, lingerie, and other expensive and fine goods. They made their own separate purchases through the money they saved. Soame had never teased Chairly with cheapness as he played with DD, during the beginning sexual encounters. Because of her sexual favors and rapid developmental interest, by the time they revisited Denver, Chairly had wads of money. During the entire trip Soame purchased a single item. It looked and draped like a safari hat. The Panama "brim" cost $200. They became so clustered with gifts and packages, Soame made a trip to the car and deposited them in the trunk. The two women sashayed through the mall with the unleashed miniature poodle. The small dog was then able, after constant playing with Chairly, to walk a considerable distance without tiring. When the leash was fastened, it was attached to her Zirconia collar; it glittered and she wore it proudly with her head and nose pointed upward and a natural gait. Returning from the car, Soame had no problem finding them; he simply looked for the herd of people. He was amused by the people who were fascinated by "his women." He was also aware of his falling in love with their fascination.

Through the information gathered by Mrs. Fairfield, Soame was able to select a specific area he had an interest in moving into. He chose the tri-state area, where the Dakotas joined Montana. There, within a sixty mile radius of the state lines was his destination, if it worked out for them. A week after he received the information, he told the members of his household that they would probably depart the following week. DD's relationship with Chairly drew the girl closer to him. Relief came through his understanding and acceptance of DD's bisexuality. She became warmer toward him, knowing he had no qualm regarding this fact about her. Though she had told him about a previous relationship, and mentioned other sexual encounters with other women, establishing the relationship with Chairly, and knowing he accepted it, DD did not have to masquerade. Instead, she proudly displayed her bravado with both of them.

Once, in a candid discussion of Chairly, while they both enjoyed their indulgences, he explained to DD, "I like her, I think she's young, vibrant, and fairly intelligent. To be frank, I do not like her sense of reasoning. To me she could never be more than the person we picked up along the way. She's common, and I've refused sex with women of her caliber, whom I could have had for a McDonald's spoon of coke. I don't see in her what you've have noticed. Because of her youth, her body is unused, but she is lacking the experience, and until you I've had a preference toward older women. She's a comfort to you. I like her only because she's your friend and companion. I would never allow her the trust and love in keeping my heart. She's simply not my type of woman; without you, she would not be allowed near me."

DD had never known Soame to lie to her. Though she saw his feelings being different toward her, and hers only grew for him, she did not and could not hold ill feelings toward his honest opinion.

Shortly after Sandra Fairfield's visits became recognized as a regular schedule, in private company DD told him, "that woman, Suarme, she wants you."

"Until and unless you refuse me, my love, no one else can have me."

"You have but to take her Suarme, I will not mind. No other woman will cause me to separate from you. For a time now, I've known that you are all I ever wanted; you will always be my man. I will always obey, what you have stated to me as your law."

During the week he told DD and Chairly of the possibility of them leaving on Mrs. Fairfield's next visit. The two women in the household were out back, strolling in shorts toward the pond. They had just yelled to him, "we won't be gone long." Through the open interior door, he saw the landlady's car drive up, and observed her knocking on the porch screen door. He was at the counter, and had began opening an eight ball, from which his plan was to section out a gram for the evening. He promptly downed a three finger drink of rum. He was also in the process of smoking a joint. He took a mint from a pack of certs, from the opposite end of the counter and said, "Come in Mrs. Fairfield." He then took a quick one and one, and met her almost in the center of the living room. Upon greeting her and in the beginning of the conversation, he felt an overwhelming impulse.

The widow woman was casually dressed and wearing sandals. It was very pleasant outside with a 75 degree temperature. Sandra wore a sleeveless white blouse and a string of colored beads around her neck. The beads matched her clip-on earrings. Though she had on sandals, she wore stockings. The dark brown color of the leather form her shoes matched the wraparound skirt she had on. Her purse had been left in her car, and her hair was always nicely done. It was the first time, since they met, Soame once again caught the smell of her perfume; which was Cotillion on the arm opposite her watch. She wore a pearly white bracelet. Relaying the information she had for him, he extended his hand, as if to shake hers. He caught her hand and brought it to his lips; kissing it, he stepped closer into her. In making the direct close, almost face-to-face contact with his left hand extended around her, he palmed squarely in the crotch of her cheeks.

While observing the open, flushed, surprise in her face, Soame explained,

"I've always, since the very first day I saw you, I've wanted to do things with you, Mrs. Fairfield."

"But Sir, Mr. Anderson, you have a wife and I…I," she paused.

"You would accept me and allow me to do what I wish with you Mrs. Fairfield, is that it?" he asked, while slowly massaging the center underneath spot in his hand. She opened her mouth and while looking directly into her green eyes, he lavishly kissed her; increasing the rotations of his feels on her backside. With his right hand, he cupped her entire left breast. Both her hands were then free. She did not resist him. She stood with her head slightly tilted, returning his kiss, accepting his embrace, nearly two inches shorter than his height. Her weight perhaps at one-hundred and thirty-five pounds. Soame separated from her lips asking, "May I call you Sandra?"

Before she could reply, he placed his mouth once again over hers, and lowered his right hand to her dress, lifting it, with the aid of his left. Through the lasting kiss, his right hand found the lower front portion of her panties. Only the sheer material separated his left hand from her bare ass; it once again massaged her ripe buttock, both of them with rubs and squeezes.

Easing his mouth from hers, he requested, "Sandra, let me make love to you. Will you?"

His right forefinger had slid beneath the thin material and was deep into lubricating her vagina. He withdrew it and took the juices to her clitoris. Circling it with swabs, his index finger joined in and further aided the stimulation of the sensitive button. He then "walked" both fingers into her vagina and fluttered them. The woman panted about to orgasm. Gasping for breath as he decreased and increased the speed of his fingers, in a deep voice she told him, "Oh please, please… I could not stand it if she caught us."

Knowing she had begun, he told her, "Grab my dick."

Frantically, without reservation, as if sexual in desperation, she struggled for the dick kept from her by the material under her grinding and squeezing hand. Once again, he cupped his mouth over hers, plunging deeply, then rolling with hers, turning and rolling, while he stroked and rubbed her sex organs. She held and squeezed his shaft, moaning with pulsating delight in giving his fingers her creamy juices. This filled the air with the musky scent of sexual fulfillment.

A couch sat at the immediate left, against the front wall, after the entry into the living room. Soame directed Sandra back to the empty door space. He sat on the sofa's arm and from that space, he lowered his pants to midway his thighs. Neither of them said a word until he instructed her, "take it out."

She extended her hand into the fly of his boxers and extracted his partly erect organ. He noticed the sensuous lick she gave her lips, with her inviting tongue, during her stare at it. At that moment the station broadcasting from Casper aired a record. He admired the piece as an oldie and remembered it being number one on "the Coast," when he came home from "'Nam." The Jazz Crusaders were on display with *So Far Away*.

He called her "Sandra." She then looked into his eyes and once again he kissed her. Initially it was a gentle kiss, and it grew with passion and became wild and through the kiss she displayed lust. The hardening dick in her hand added in stimulating her. With his legs on the inside, without releasing her mouth, she was brought astride him. Sitting on the arm of the furniture, his feet resting on his heels in the open doorway, the wrap around material flared from it's center front, when he hiked the skirt up to her waist. Holding the Khaki skirt with one hand, he held her panties to the side, and inserted his bone hard dick, with the other. Still holding the elastic from his meat, he released her skirt and cupped her left breast, telling her, "fuck yourself with my dick." She did and rotated her strokes with thrust and passion; a type of passion she had never known before. It was true passion being released.

The music played on, like an endless melody floating across the desert. Straddling him, she had an orgasm. He had her to reach inside her panties, and rub her clit. Still holding the rubber from the tool she rotated on, he told her, "wet your fingertips." When she applied the saliva to her sex stimulator, he felt the increase in the flow of her secretion and directly afterward her rotations increased, and turned into whirls. She bucked and humped, looking like a cowgirl on a jumping bronco.

"Call me, Henry," he said.

"Oh, Henry," she called out.

"What are you doing Sandra?"

"I'm fucking Henry. I'm fucking."

Feeling a steady increase in her revolutions, while she ranged the instrument into herself, he asked, "Who are you fucking, Sandra?"

"I'm … I'm fucking myself with your… your… your dick, oh Henry. It's so gooood, it's sooo good ta me, Henry."

He felt the heat inside as the shaft was then being gulped, thrown out, gripped, and swallowed, over and over again and again. He prevented the elastic from becoming entangled in the rapid gripping, twisting and twirling action. Her lips circled him, in and out, up and down.

"Sandra, cum for me."

She attempted to speak, opened her mouth, licked her lips, and he began squeezing her nipple with his thumb and index finger. Without releasing, he applied more pressure. She rotated faster, with plunging grinds, hilting to his fingers. She moaned and groaned until he covered her mouth with his, still squeezing her nipple. In her finish, she collapsed with him lowered to the hilt in her and her arms around his neck.

The land lady was escorted to the counter. She asked, en route, "Do you think I should stay much longer, I don't want to get on bad terms with your wife, Mr. … Henry."

"You haven't gotten into trouble by doing what I've asked you to do so far, have you?"

"No, in fact, it's been gratifying."

"Then relax and stay for awhile, let's enjoy ourselves a bit more, I like your company, Sandra."

Accepting the stool he offered, she could not help but notice the product he had previously laid out on the counter.

"Oh goodie, it's been so long since I've seen that, if it's what I think it is."

She was then offered one of several two and a half inch straws. Soame watched her eyes light up with gleams of delight. After taking a one and one, he excused himself for a quick change of pants. He was soaked.

There would be no longer than ten, fifteen minutes at the most before DD and Chairly returned. Soame and Sandra shared a three finger drink of Blue Label. Chairly had gotten to be quite "grown." No one told her when and when not to do anything. At times she enjoyed an occasional drink. She liked to drink the Vodka with him. This was her brand.

"I understood your name to be Charles; in fact, I made your rental receipt out to Charles Anderson."

"My initials are C.H."

They also enjoyed a joint of reefer. She exposed how she and her husband did the exact same things, at the same counter, which was the reason for its addition to the cabin. Following the drink and smoke, they snorted. Considering the time, with the probability of DD's return, he could not help but notice the efficiency in which she consumed the products. Other than the remainder already opened and displayed on the counter, there was another eight ball. He asked if she would meet him that night and explained he enjoyed talking with her.

"Do you really think we can, without causing any problems?"

He pulled the draped flap back, allowing her dress to expose her stockings, garters, legs, and where they came together at her brief, white, panties. Standing, looking at the exposure, he asked, "You know the area. What time, where, Sandra?"

Leaving, she received nearly an ounce of herb, two packs of jokers, the displayed and the unopened eight ball, and a pinch on her nipple. She favored the spot, as if she buckled at the knee on that side of her body, saying, "Shaaa. Are you sure you want me to wait until then?"

At the door she told him how periodically, in going through her son's pockets, when she washed, if she found a joint or two, she was lucky. "A year ago, I found nearly an ounce and for a short while, it was almost heaven."

During the brief span, she also revealed other interesting facts about her life. Her future showed her becoming more alone. Between 8 and 8:15 they were to meet 50 yards off the highway on the lane. Rubbing her rear, he kissed her forehead, she then turned and stepped off the porch. In her departing wave, from the car, their eyes met to say, "See you then."

Chapter 6

When DD and Chairly returned, Soame was finishing his shower. Fifi was sitting on the counter, with the two females standing around, when he entered the area, with a towel around his neck. He had on only a pair of dark blue silk boxers. "I can smell her pussy still," DD casually stated. She asked him, "Was it good?"

"To give my opinion, would be comparing another woman with you, and I would not do that, love of my life." Soame then extended his hand for a joint. Chairly and Fifi did not move, except following his motions with their eyes and heads.

"But I want to know, Suarmme," still inquiring while moving around to Chairly who was then separated from DD by him. An ice bucket on the counter held the small, personal packages of coke, straws, and papers. He lit the joint with his Dunhill and extracted some uncut coke and manitol from the covered bucket. She knew he would not ignore her question.

"What can I tell you for real," he said at last: "DD… we've never had an argument. Is this the beginning of one, or are you simply interested in having me certify the fact in words? You are my number one lady, and no other woman can possibly replace you"

DD did not fall for the pitch. He had been evasive and still did not answer her question. She stood her ground between him and Chairly, folding her arms across her breasts, staring at him directly, and summoned his further response.

"She's very lonely, has no one to provide her with these types of things." He indicated the ice bucket. "I'm supposed to meet her tonight… she's quite interesting to talk with."

Chairly motioned as if she was about to walk off. DD caught her blouse and tugged, and the girl returned to her seat on the stool, and sat, slowly stroking Fifi's head.

Soame began mixing "cut" with the coke he had measured out. DD still said nothing, and except for the tug, had not moved. "She's an all right woman, for her age. DD, you like her?"

"No Darlingggg. She's not exactly what I would call my style. I have what I want, and the both of us are totally satisfied and happy with you." She lowered her hand, slightly turned and rubbed Chairly's behind. This appeared to have moved both of them. DD then completed the turn in full, held Chairly's chin, and kissed her. He glanced at them, took a sniff of the material he was mixing and began straining it once more, with the small plastic sifter. When the two of them finished, Chairly asked, "Can I go start dinner now? Um hungry."

"I'll tell ya just whatcha can start," Soame replied. "You can start ya little ass in school, just as soon as we get to where we're going. You talk that bullshit French, you'd better learn how to speak English."

Strolling off, swirling, she flung a maturing hip; peeking back over her shoulder, she glimpsed his stare, with her rolling eye. Fifi sounded a "yipe, yipe." DD let her down to the floor. By the time she entered the kitchen, the puppy caught up with her.

While he dressed, DD instructed him, "Not in my car ha, Suarme… you have not yet even officially done it with me in the car and that is my honor only for the first time. Am I not deserving?" The moon will be out, it is partly full, the skies are open and scattered with stars. This is Indian country. She will want it deep in the forest with her back on the ground; take a blanket, do it to her Indian style."

Leaving the cabin, he had only his parking lights on. The slow drive revealed the sight of her car. He had traveled up the lane; the car could hardly be seen. It sat parked in the slight curve of the narrow country turn in. In it's almost concealed position, it also allowed any passing traffic access to the single lane. There was never a passerby, especially at that hour. He escorted her to the passenger side of the Seville. In enjoying the delight of being together, for a short while they simply conversed. During the thirty minute period, they indulged in a smoke and snorted coke. He shared the passenger seat with her, and after their first kiss, they knew it was time to go.

He was directed north, and from where they entered the highway it was about two miles, to where they turned right. The unused, narrow paved road took them across an old bridge, and once again they turned right. She then moved closer to him, and had him douse the lights. "This will take us two hundred yards above the larger pond, which flows into the stream behind the cabin. You can stop any place along here you choose." She was a very well preserved woman, and had not at all lost her beauty, which was evident despite her age. He allowed the car to roll along, with no acceleration. Being a constant snorter, it interested him that she snorted without reluctance; as if she had at one time had a continuous supply of the powder. While "tooting" they talked; basically, he listened. He was hearing how the trail they were on came into existence, when he brought the vehicle to a stop. The property opened up to fifteen hundred acres "this side of the highway," and had been owned by her and her now deceased husband. He heard how the small town with nearly 50,000 people flourished through the lumber industry owned by them. Her story was not a sad one, but there was remorse, not immediate concern, but as would be found in a story of life and times. Her lost husband seemed an accepted fact. Soame and Sandra petted and kissed. He appreciated the joy she expressed being in his company.

Her husband had been the richest man in the territory; he grew his own marijuana, and had private stashes of the powder, by the pound. Soame found out she knew exactly what "cut" was, and heard how the Indians would steal each marijuana crop she attempted to grow, until she ran out of seeds. During their embraces she shared her warmth, offered her considerations, and clearly enjoyed his company. They did not rush the evening. It was a beautiful cloudless night. Every star strung throughout the galaxy could be seen. Their final stop was where the old, completely unused logging trail ended, near the pond. Several times before he had ventured to the road. He knew it well and the surrounding area in which he lived.

Outside, leaning against the front grill, with her in his arms, Sandra came totally alive: the windows were down for the background enjoyment of the radio, tuned to a Canadian station, which carried very well on the car's system. Abba began *Dancing Queen*.

"Turn it up, Turn it up, Henry. Will you please?"

Of course, "Henry" did not mind, because it was one of his favorite oldies also. She had stepped back from him, after tearing out of his arms. Soame pivoted in the small space, and quickly increased the volume. She was directly behind him, when he removed his torso from the open window.

"It's my favorite of all." Sandra swayed, listened, and even sang with the music before it ended. She explained, "It was after my son's birth and just before my daughter."

Soame, while at the door, began gathering the blanket and other materials that would make them comfortable. He turned off the radio.

After finding a spot they both agreed on, the blanket was spread and the materials were laid out. In a short span of time, it seemed as if the ground had elevated them up to the heavens, and all the stars were at their fingertips. They further indulged, talked, kissed, and engaged in foreplay before their actual lovemaking. They repeated, there under the Milky Way, their repertoire of affection toward each other.

Much later the announcer said, "It's four minutes past four o'clock and 71 degrees outside." Soame sat in the car, looking into the rear-view mirror. Down the lane, Sandra's car entered the highway and she blinked her dimmer. She knew he would be looking. The voice on the radio belonged to Hank Williams, with *I'm So Lonely I Could Cry.*

Soame saw Sandra Fairfield twice more before he left—once for a short while to spend time as they did that night, and finally in parting. Both of them understood the probability of his never returning, but did not accept the possibility of it being "an overnight thing." He could always write, call, or send a package. Soame had given the area a great deal of consideration in regard to staying. He felt eventually there would only be Indians there, whom he did not at all resent, but his instincts dictated that he needed more space, and a bit more of a town to work with. Always, in a love triangle, if he was or became the second man, he gave in to the establishment of the duo. Sandra had a steady thing with the local Sheriff, whom she stated would, "give license to distribute the stuff, if you can get it in here."

Her news, the afternoon they "found" each other, was she would sell him the cabin, and the twenty-five forest acres it sat on for $5,000. He filed this option in his mind as a contingency. That night, in parting company, he gave her ¾ of a pound of New Orleans coke, and a half pound of manitol. He also gave her 5 oz. of "weed" from his hometown. A week later, in leaving, he told her, "This is my very, very personal assistance toward your being in heaven for awhile, without problem or interruption." He gave her three ounces of Maui-Wowee, and an ounce and a half of his best grade coke.

"If I had known this, believe me, you could have stayed and the place would have been yours, free."

"Don't underestimate or undersell yourself, Sandra Fairfield."

Soame then shook her hand, slightly nodded his head while tipping the Panama, turned about and walked out of her office. He climbed under the steering wheel of his lady's car, and as they waved in parting, he was gone.

Chapter 7

From the base of the Laramie Mountains, they moved northward, toward the region of the Black Hills. Had they continued on Route 25, the interstate would have taken them on to Casper, the heart of the oil region. Though Cheyenne is the state's capital and offers scenic outings, they had not been there to explore. They did not visit renowned places, such as the Hereford Ranch or the Jim Baker log cabin. However, though it was basically for the purpose of claiming books he had ordered, they all had a chance to visit the state library. He made it a point to allow the girls to tour the state museum. It was the first time Fifi had been left alone in a long while. For that reason, they did not stay as long as they would have liked. The library was only an interesting building for Chairly. She elected to stay with the dog, and was not motivated by the library's collection of interesting books. Soame noticed that the two books he and DD brought back to the car held her interest and she read both.

Shying away from Casper, Wyoming, they listened to a radio station from there. Soame noticed a considerable amount of promotions being done on "Hell's Half Acre." The city featured it as one of it's scenic locations. The car performed beautifully, as expected. It was always an eye-catcher. While it gleamed, it floated them through the scenic land they traveled; moving on upward to High Springs. It took careful itemized packing, but at least he had the privacy to load without being observed. This made the difference and enabled them to transport with them, everything they came with and the items they collected while they were there. Canned goods and frozen foods were left behind, but he was assured they would not go to waste. The car was lively, to an extent, but they all realized they had left the first home they had known together. They had no real assurance as to what it would be like where they were going. Nor did they know where that was. Soame simply told them it would be better. They were beginning to trust him. Though he had gained considerable confidence in DD, other than the all mighty, and himself, he trusted no one.

They crossed the North Platte River, and were traveling parallel to the Nebraska state line when Chairly became wise to the activities of the front seat lovers. DD and Soame never became tired of each other. This both amused and sometimes frustrated Chairly. By peeping, she discovered DD rubbing Soame's hand.

"How long dis been goin on?"

There she was, with her arms and face extended over the passenger seat, with a full view of DD's sun dress around her waist, no panties, and Soame's hand held at the wrist, by hers, in her twat. He was driving with his left hand and his right was extended to DD, turned at the elbow. She was close to him, grinding on it. Chairly had calculated, the precise time, when neither of them thought she would do such a thing.

"Now look kid, since the stork just brought you in, on, and into our lives, we don't see how and why other unnecessary arrangements should be made toward your satisfaction and our discom – " His reaction corresponded with what Chairly was really after, which was riding in the front seat. Since the first day she rode with them, she surmised this was one of the happenings in the front seat. After being taken into their sex life, she presented the matter, which was casually admitted as fact. Before leaving the cabin, she expressed her wish to ride in the front seat with them. Soame told her it was not a safe practice, with ample room in the back. This did not sit right with her, she let it be known, but it did not change his decision. DD had pinched Soame's arm, stopping his chastisement and ridiculed Chairly in French. Twenty minutes later, Chairly was asleep. They were cruising on State Road 85, nearing Lusk, the midpoint toward their coming rest stop.

They had relaxed together at the cabin for nearly three months. Each of them enjoyed the pleasantness in the congenial atmosphere they found. The environment had given them as individuals a chance to simply "air out," rid of their past conditions which they had been displeased with. This existed as the major bond among them as a group. The puppy, developing toward maturity, found her own position with the group. They were a family and they took refuge in that, as the strongest institution in the world.

Fate had finally placed prosperity in Soame's path. Opportunity had knocked for him before, but always time, circumstance, and position had prevented him from responding. It is said that "opportunity only knocks once." In fact, for Soame, there had been various times and circumstances wherein he had not been able to achieve success he desired, but he then sought another chance, each time from a different direction.

The stay in the cabin allowed him to put his life in perspective. His body was already in good physical shape. He also had to further enhance its condition and put it in tune with the drugs he was doing, which had been absent for nearly two years. The jogging he did, added to his daily workout schedule, and put his physical condition at a peak. His sexual activities only contributed to the conditioning. The money was very much an important aspect of the plan he arrived at. Also important to him at this phase of his life, was the woman with him, whom he hoped would not leave.

So far it had been an easy drive; he had no reason to rush. During previous drives, with the other cars and en route from Denver, he had not used the cruise control. On this trip he accepted the special feature, to the pleasure and comfort of his drive. They crossed the Cheyenne River, near Mule Creek junction and because of dusk and the tinted windows, they put away their sunglasses. They moved in a luxurious float, parallel to the South Dakota line. At New Castle, Soame would head east and enter the region of the Black Hills. By 9:30, he expected to be in the "gateway city to the Black Hills." They cruised toward that destination.

Even without a reservation they had their choice of three suites at an independently owned hotel. The luggage had been packed for easy accessibility and with the valet parking, Soame requested the keys to the automobile. There was a stipulation involved with the courtesy extended to them in view of the infraction against the hotel's policy. Though she had a pedigree as a miniature, Fifi was developing into a sizable dog. She was no longer carried around by hand, but at times lifted from place to place. Considerable time had been taken, on a regular daily basis, to training the intelligent puppy. Entering the hotel, she carried her leash. Her grayish coat began taking on the silver texture it would have when she totally matured. Seeing her, before they were allowed to register, the desk clerk called for the manager. The owner who happened to be there answered the clerk's call to the desk. The policy was explained, "since she is so well trained." In the man's examination of her, Fifi "sat" still, holding her leash. "However, even though she is very well trained, under no circumstances will she be permitted in either of our dining areas."

It was past 10 PM when they entered their selection, which was comparable to the previous rooms they had rented. This was in a single building hotel and the accommodations were basically the same. The sitting room and entry portions were recessed. In the foyer, they walked down two steps into the sitting room. Fresh flowers in a decorative bouquet were delivered, while the bellhop was in the bedroom with Chairly and Fifi, assorting the luggage. There were complementary cheeses of all sorts and the wet bar featured cans and bags of peanuts, pretzels, and crackers. Soame showered in one of two baths. Neither had a Jacuzzi, but one featured a combination sitting room, dressing room, and ladies bath. DD ordered their dinners.

DD was the early riser. The wake-up call was requested for nine. After DD made her appointments, she was then roused Chairly. At 10:45 they were leaving the hotel, in a cab, with Fifi. Soame did not get up until after one. He showered, and while on his way to the terrace for a sandwich, he discovered the hotel had a heated pool. He changed his mind about the snack and instead visited the gift shop and purchased a pair of trunks. It had been a while since he had been for a swim. Returning to the room, following his swim, he found the women and Fifi had returned. They had visited the beauty parlor and Fifi had received her second clipping. All of their nails were done and for the first time Chairly had a pedicure. Fifi's head nap had been bunched in the center and she sported a pink ribbon. Soame complimented the two women and received a gift in return. Once again he showered after giving his the dinner order to DD. It was 4:30.

DD had done a very good job in tutoring Chairly with French. DD aided the girl's education in other ways as well. A fact concerning Chairly's progress in that direction stemmed from her reading. She spent hours reading practically any informative material she came in contact with. The association in the conjugation process enabled her to subconsciously identify the proper placement and usage of words. The structure of verbs, vowels, and consonants, their usage in the English language, and how they were used differently speaking French, turned the tide toward Chairly's beginning to speak proper English. She did not exceed Soame's expectations; but the progress she made was considerable. In many ways, through DD's tutorial, Chairly became an adorable person. Every improved aspect about her was highly noticeable, including her manners. She knew enough French to get by in a general conversation, undetectable as a native except by someone who spoke the language fluently. Everything DD had, she wanted to show off. This included herself. She refused to sit helplessly by, having so much more than she had ever imagined, and have the occasion pass by wherein she could present herself and some of that which gained her pride.

When DD confronted him, between the bath and the bedroom, he did not display surprise.

"Suarme, I would like for all of us to go out to dinner."

He had on only a robe and walked toward the bedroom asking, "Where do you have in mind?"

"Downstairs, of course."

He noticed she had a complete attire laid out for him on the bed. The oddity was it consisted of more than his underwear, which was the standard they had developed.

"So you're going to leave your puppy?"

"No Suarme, but let me handle it, please, I want us to go and all they can say is no; if they do we can simply go someplace else."

He had started applying lotion on his body. When this was done he combed his hair. Chairly and Fifi then joined them as he applied cologne.

"Are we going out or not?" Chairly wanted to know.

Fifi had sprang up on the bed and sat near his pants. He disrobed and DD brought him his underwear. Lifting one leg, to climb into his shorts, he asked Chairly, "Is that what you're wearing?"

Not until he stood before the maitre'd at the main dinging room did he realize he was in the company of Madame Dubanee and Countess La Chair "share". He came to this realization after the dog was presented as a question of entry for them. The questionable issue was presented to him. DD interceded. She and the countess were inseparable and the countess was never without her companion Fifi, as it was explained to the manager. Soame was amused, but he was also hungry. Fifi, hearing her name, and guessing the scene concerned her, "sat." By then practically all eyes of the other diners were focused toward the entrance. The maitre'd then signaled for the headwaiter. DD lavishly flaunted French at Chairly, who seemed surprised, but made casual exchanges in private. DD monopolized the conversation while the headwaiter, who came within an inch of patting the dog's head, before a distinguished throat clearing from his superior caught his attention. Everyone noticed utter silence in the dining room. All the attention was toward them and the dog, stretched on her stomach, with fully extended paws. The Countess dared to unleash her. The zirconium stones were glistening. The entrance lights projected them as real diamonds.

Following an exchange of whispers with the chief steward, the head waiter said to them, "Sir, countess, madam… we would be more than pleased to accommodate you, if you will kindly accept my suggestion to dine on our terrace, where we assure you of a lovely view for your comfort." He summoned a passing waiter and went on. "The terrace is usually the gathering place of our bar patrons, but we have on occasion set up a table, which is our proposal to you at this time."

The countess then responded, "Splendid idea I'd say, would that meet your approval Pa-pa?"

At this, Soame was overwhelmed.

He merely wanted "to eat, relax, and screw both the imposters." Until that time, Soame had said nothing, other than having asked for "a table for three please." During the activity which followed, he fingered through his clip and guessed the bill he extracted and as being a fifty. In replying to Chairly's question, he simply eased the bill, noticeably by the head waiter, to the steward, "If you would extend your services and accommodations to meet our comfort, we would be appreciative." Ten minutes later, they were looking at the majesty of the Black Hills of South Dakota. The view was absolutely magnificent. Having driven in at night, Soame had not seen the most spectacular sight in the region, even though he had driven in through them. From their table they were presented with the thunderous sight of hills, spread in sequential proportion, growing bigger, one wave after the other, clapping toward the horizon, in waves of even larger formations. With the setting sun in the background, through an orange, purple, and grayish light mist, the exquisite sight rolled off into oblivion.

They found the duck to be succulent, with the special sauce DD requested. Fifi's display could not have been better. The leash had not been refastened. She sat and laid on her stomach with outstretched forepaws at attention, between her mistress and Chairly. At intervals they each gave her morsels. Each time she moved, the diamond-like glitter cast attention from the waving pink ribbon ends. Her silvery coat blended toward the flamingo purplish background. Their table was next to the rail. There were no other tables on the dance patio. No one danced. Everyone else saw them.

Because Rapid City is situated east of the Black Hills regional scenic attraction, which is renowned and the former home of the Sioux Indians, it is referred to as the Gateway City. Soame and his family sat near the railing, on the western side of the hotel, and viewed the Hills, beginning across a plain 15-20 miles away, and carrying on through hundreds of miles.

CHAPTER 8

THE morning following their terrace dinner, they were once again traveling. They left at 9:30 and moved toward the outer realm of the hills. This time Soame was in a very serious search and pursuit of a new place to call home. In their search, they ventured to, through, and around Sturgis. Leaving Interstate 90, they drove north on Route 79, crossed the Belle Fourche River, went to Newell, and continued through that vicinity to Castle Rock, a short distance from the geological center of the United States. In five days they had taken off roads, traveled back roads, and driven on country drives for miles and miles. Soame did not see a spot which he thought ideal. They took a route west to Buffalo and were again on 85, which they used as a passage through the Northern extension of the Dakotas. From Bowman they searched the Marmarth Area and drove along the Little Missouri River before using Route 12 to enter the state of Montana. From Baker they drifted south on 7 and spent a day of relaxation in Medicine Rocks State Park.

They had traveled through plain country. When not in one of the small towns for days, their view consisted of unobstructed spaces of land, until the sight placed the horizon into the sky. They had seen rolling plains, rocky plains, and plains that appeared to be totally barren. The expanses of emptiness they had seen were incomparable to the cities they had lived in, and traveled to and through, during their previous travels. They were totally amazed to see that the lands they passed through and saw beyond had absolutely no ornamentation - other than the plain lands presenting no elevation or depression - they were simply flat, level lands. In the park they enjoyed themselves and spent the night in its outskirts. It had been more than three weeks since they left Rapid City.

Soame was in search of a town – there were no cities of considerable size – the size of the area they had lived in when the town flourished. He considered finding a spot with a population of 40 to 50 thousand people, what he considered ideal. He found a significant population in each area. He also was informed there was a population decrease in effect at that time. Even these areas were limited to a few. Traveling through the outlaying areas of these places, they saw evidence of the dwindling. Buildings showed evidence of non-usage; they were unoccupied and dilapidated. They had driven across the plains from one town to another and found the same at each location.

Montana is called "Big Sky Country." At day break they were leaving the park area. Once again they drifted south into the plains toward Ekalaka. At times they had driven for miles and miles and not seen an approaching or passing car. During this stretch Chairly and Soame came very close to getting into their first argument. Already she and DD were alternating in front and rear seat; this began after their first week of exploration. It wasn't necessary since DD had gone soft and gave Chairly what she wanted. Besides, DD had an interest in the sound system in the rear of the car. To her, the amplification was better in the back, as Chairly pointed out. In Rapid City, she and Chairly bought a number of cassette tapes, which aided in the comfort of their ride.

For nearly two weeks Chairly badgered Soame about letting her drive. At times DD would relieve him for two or three hours at a time. Yet there were days he'd drive day in and day out, day after day. Motels were rare, and in some towns they passed through the motels were shabby in appearance. Near ten that morning, Chairly gave Soame a compromise, "Soame if you lemme learn how ta drive, just a li'l bit, only a cup la miles, I'll lick ya dick."

"What!! Are you raving mad? You share my bedroom. Four months ago you told us you never had oral sex before. Now that you've practically become an expert, after practicing polishing my knob, I have to sit and be propositioned to allow you to handle this car?"

"Soame, you got us way out heah in da desard where there ain't nobody but us. Takin' us back and forth ta places fa no reason. So why, Soame? Why can't I drive dis ole car sometime? Why!? Jes tell me why?"

"You're improper, you're belligerent, and as much a thug as some of my home boys in Overtown, Liberty City and the Grove. In fact, you are helplessly uncouth Chairly. That's what you are, totally uncouth!"

She thought perhaps DD would come to her aid, but she was in the back seat enjoying her pipe. They were all surrounded by music from the sound system; a cassette of Herb Albert playing *Rise*.

"I don't know what dim words mean, but Soame, stop the car. I'll show ya zackly how un whatsa neva it iz. I iz. Stop da car Soame!"

He drove on, ignoring her, without saying anything. Within five minutes she asked him several more times, in a demanding tone, "Stop da car Soame." Knowing she was being completely ignored, she appealed to DD. "DD pass me da toilet papa. Iz yo car tell him ta stop so I can use the toilet." She reached for the partical roll, saying "Will you two please."

That was all she said, and DD passed the paper. He drove on for nearly a mile before he allowed the automobile to coast to a very slow speed. He pulled to the shoulder of the road and applied the breaks, but the car did not completely stop. Chairly opened the door, saying, "Um ga Sho ya how un wha sa neva I iz Soama, um ga sho ya!" She slammed the door, marched to the front of the car, and onto the highway. In the center of the road, after taking five paces, she turned about; facing the car she lowered her pants and undies. They thought she would use the toilet paper to prevent the stain of urine onto her panties. They were wrong. There, in the center of the highway, between two road markers making a center line, she did it. In fact, she did both of the numbers. While she defecated, DD moved to the front seat. She did use the toilet paper. Everything, in a mass, was left there with the pile. Chairly returned to the car, but neither of them said a word to her. Falling into the backseat, she spoke in French and motioned to him. Soame did not see the motion she gave, but DD turned to the rear as she entered the Seville. She looked at Chairly, vexed. Soame shifted from park to drive and as the car eased off, he asked DD, "What did she say?"

"She said, drive on, drive on."

Changing their route, which continued south, but slightly southeasterly, they went through a series of small towns and farming communities before they re-entered South Dakota. They took 323, which carried them into 212, and at Belle Fourche, they were once again on 85. Along the way they saw towns and farming communities that were completely deserted. Even Soame had never before seen a ghost town. Tumble weeds actually rolled or gathered where people once had been. The experience brought on a totally different feeling. It was a sensation neither of them had ever experienced before. They had traveled north in South Dakota and gone over the North Dakota state line. From North Dakota, they went west into Montana. They headed south, southeasterly, and once again they were at the base of the Black Hills.

Soame had never completely failed at anything. He was determined to find what he was in search of. In so much land, there had to be the type of place he could call home. This time he went back into Montana and planned to go into the Hills. They traveled roads that emptied into trails that corkscrewed through towns and small villages. Though these places weren't to their liking, the view from the top was truly breathtaking. The amazing view filled them with glee for a considerable while. So far there had not been a major discord among them. Soame proposed an idea, "Tell ya what let's do."

"What Darlingggg?"

"What? What Soame? What?"

Fifi's ribbon had long since been tied and dangled from the rear view mirror. From DD's lap, she had learned to spring to the seat top, from there to Chairly's lap, and hop into the back window. A couple of bumps on the noggin, in the window, helped her perfect her hop, and lower her head in the move. "Arff, Arff, Arfff."

"The next town we come to that has R.V.s for rent, let's store the car and rent one."

He could tell by their reaction that they were not that enthused. He knew they knew that was the best offer available and the most he could present. With the offer they also knew there would be no let up. Chairly did not know, and naturally could not understand, their purpose in roaming. Once, when she became overbearing with her questioning on the subject, Soame told her, "We're still on our honeymoon. Remember, somehow you got to be a part and an extension of our honeymoon. That's all kid, you're a part of a honeymoon."

CHAPTER 9

THE trio was about to once again go back into South Dakota from the hills. Soame had a hunch. Even though they re-entered the state, his plan was to once again get back on 85. They went back to Belle Fourche; however, it was for the express purpose of going once again into Montana. He had the feeling Montana had more to offer for his needs.

Excitement carried through the interior of the car like a spark of electricity. Everyone was in a state of anticipation and no one but Soame really expected to find anything. He was driving fast, and though he was not exceeding the limit it was faster than he had been driving for a month. DD and Chairly were having a lively conversation in French. He never paid attention, in the least, when they talked, but could not help but notice Chairly's improvement in being able to speak the foreign language. In that way he felt good towards her achievements. As hard as they tried, to the point of purposely learning identifiable names, places, or other nouns, including his name, he simply tuned them out. He allowed their indulgences, and enjoyed the music they had taken control of.

They were still traveling at the legal limit, cruising with the floating sensation the Seville allowed. His Panama was well broken in by then, and under the "broke down sky piece," which was draped and to the side of his head, he wore dark sunglasses with a black frame. They were in Montana when a peculiar thing happened; of all the places they had traveled to, someone always noticed the population sign. They all missed it entering the city-township of Smath,.

Two minutes after they passed the sign, they entered the town. DD and Chairly had stopped talking. Fifi sprung from the rear window, off Chairly's lap, on to the seat, and from DD's lap she stood on her hind legs with her paws extended to the dash peeking. She had a clear view out the side passenger window. "Look," DD and Chairly both said simultaneously. Soame had seen the sign but the women were so much faster. The sign read "Unbelievable Deal on a New or Used R.V." The lot had only two. He pulled into the lot; and a smiling face came out to meet the car. The deal was so terrific that fifteen minutes after he pulled onto the lot he had rented an R.V. for a month.

Trying to be of as much assistance as possible DD suggested, "Darling, there is a real estate office across the street, why don't you check it out."

Storing the car on the lot provided them with daily security and the car dealership owner assured them it would be cleaned daily. The R.V. featured practically every modern mobile convenience available. The forty-five foot Tradesman included a color TV, a short wave multiplex band radio, which received radio signals from all over the world, and two separate living compartments, which comfortably slept six people. The features seemed to be unlimited. After parking the car at the side door of the R.V., the materials from the trunk were carried to the van.

The realty office appeared to be unattended when he entered. He noticed the entrance to the rear and thought, "Why would the front door be open, if no one was here?" After taking a few steps forward, he started to call out when he heard the toilet flush. A thirtyish looking woman of average height and build stepped out. She was casually dressed, and was wiping her hands with a paper towel.

She discarded the towel asking, "Have you been standing there long?"

"Maybe. Possibly a minute."

"I'm sorry no one else was here to greet you, there are only three of us now a days, and one of the others is only part time. I'm Camille Johnson. We're the only real estate agency in town. How may I help you?"

They exchanged smiles and handshakes. He used his actual name and explained his purpose in being there. "I'm the last one to leave for lunch. Five more minutes and you would have missed me." She went on to tell him what he already knew, and concluded, "For you not to be aware of the economic conditions, not only here but also throughout the entire west and Midwest, you would have to had drop directly down for space."

That statement summed up how unaware an individual would have to have been to not know about the economic crisis farmers throughout America were confronted with. The crisis was imposed by the federal government who was criticized and rated overall, "The absolute worst president to ever have been elected in America's history." Ronald Reagan had no problem whatsoever in defeating the incumbent democrat from Georgia. In fact, Carter had failed so miserably, even in the eyes of the public, that on the day of balloting, by 4:00pm—two hours before the polls closed—Reagan had already defeated the "peanut farmer" by a landslide. It was by far the largest overwhelming defeat in the history of the United States. It had been a fluke for Jimmy Carter to even become president. Republicans were so confident Gerald Ford would be re-elected that they relied on each other to do the voting, so both did not go to the polls. The largest black vote turn out in America's history put the Georgia governor in the white house. That was the closest presidential election in the history of the country.

True, it was in the best interest of the nation to allow the Reagan administration the "take over." Also true that it was the worst course the American public could have taken to allow Reagan a second term in office. Not only did this allow the Japanese the leverage, as creditors holding the mortgage on America, with virtually the ownership of California, but Americans suffered in many other ways economically. Major shoe companies were forced out of business because of the flooding import of cheap shoes. American people were deceived into spying on each other through the initiation of "crime watch," when in reality it was the government that created the crime through a corruptive system to broaden police agencies. The era also, through federal expansions and mainly through federally appropriated monies, enlarged prison systems throughout American states.

During the periods between 1980-88, the American farmer felt a devastation like never before. The small farmer was almost completely eradicated. Because of restrictions and sanctions imposed on and upon the small farmer, he was forced to sell his land to the large farmer. Even though the large farmer worked the lands, because of unfair prices—regulated by the government—the large farmer was forced to plow his crops under, to receive federal government subsidy. This caused a dilemma, for the farmer: to grow the crop, he could not get a fair price on the market to cover his expenses. He therefore plowed under for the subsidy, which did not cover his expenditure or expenses.

The government then had a convenient favorable solution for the farmer now trapped far over his head in debt. They created a loan program of foreclosure, which took the home, equipment and all the farmer had. What Soame had witnessed in his travels, north of the Black Hills and in the area he had lived, was the chaotic result the Reagan administration inflicted upon the American farmer.

The agent told Soame about the several "sights" outside the town. One consisted of sixty-five acres, a farm house with a barn, and running water. She described the dwelling as being, "a comfortable living facility." After receiving detailed directions to the described plot, they concluded their meeting and agreed to meet the following day before noon. She also explained and directed him to a house nearby. He had the keys to both entries.

"The other things were a bit too heavy for us darling." Greeting him with a hug and a peck, DD indicated the book cases, knowing he would want to move them and place them himself. "How successful were you," she inquired. The car was parked with the trunk open at the side door of the R.V. He removed the boxes, explaining about the keys he had and the other land he'd been informed of. She also expressed interest in seeing the farm.

Everybody was gung ho toward the idea of the farm; a shopping list was prepared for the adventure. There were no mountains in the immediate area. The extension of the Black Hills into Montana was south. Southwest, across the open prairie, were mountains. They sensed a scenic atmosphere as being near though they were more than a hundred miles away. En route to the plot they would be inspecting, the "family" group saw two other farms they knew could not be brought back to life. Those two were among the many amounting to hundreds that they had seen in other areas and states. The farmers simply gathered what they could and left. There was an abundance of wild life and thousands of acres of open land that had been cultivated at one time. They had seen barns that were falling apart and rotting. Dutch windmills hanging in shambles from lack of use and maintenance and unused dwellings decaying, many had fallen. They pulled next to a running stream, and enjoyed time they had shared on several other occasions. They picnicked and enjoyed the fresh air and being out doors. Afterwards DD and Chairly changed into shorts and went wading in the running stream, Fifi kept Soame company on the blanket. Watching from the bank, he enjoyed and relaxed with his favorite summer drink.

Upon driving the motor home under the large shade tree in the front yard and before bringing it to a stop, DD told them, "Something tells me, without looking any further we are going to buy this place." It was towards late afternoon. They were almost twenty miles from where they left the car. The weather was very pleasant at seventy-seven degrees. The house sat twenty-five yards from where they parked. Its light green color was highlighted by the knee high picket fence which separated them from the actual front yard. Two flower bushes were on each side of the walk to the porch, which was not screened, but appeared to be roomy. There was acreage of cleared land behind the house with fields of brown straw scattered all through it. A green forest of tall timber marked the property line, and the purple white capped mountains overlooked the entire scene, as the sun created a distant haze, in its sloping journey behind the extensions of land into the sky; that topped it all. "It do, somehow seem kind a different, don't it?"

Soame said to them both, "Well, anybody care to take a look with me?"

Fifi was the first with 'arf arf." He grabbed her from the front window, opened the door and climbed down. Chairly was directly behind him and saw the dog scamper to DD crossing midway the front of the coach. Thirty yards from the rear of the house, off to the right sat the barn. The rust brown color had faded in its appearance, but without being close one could easily tell, the faded color was not because of lack of inhabitation, it simply needed to be painted. They all liked the initial appearance because it looked as if someone still lived there. The flower bushes were quite overgrown, and though none of the windows had curtains, none of them were broken. The house was in the middle of two hundred yards of cleared land with fields of wheat straw behind it for nearly a mile where the fields were over shadowed by the forest.

They checked out and examined the entire house and barn area. With a spacious living room, the country-style house had a comfortable dining area with a totally separate and large kitchen, which still housed a fairly modern stove and refrigerator. There were three bedrooms, a bath and a half and they all especially liked the large fire place in the living room. There was also a hallway heater with connections where a heater had been taken out where the hallway ended, which was where the entrance was for the rear bedrooms. The large propane tank near the barn had a 650-gallon capacity to store fuel for the heaters and stove. A careful look revealed the house to be completely insulated with a roomy attic. After checking out the barn, they decided to spend the night. It was almost dark and they wanted to get the feel of the place.

The R.V. was parked near the entrance of the barn, facing the road. The night proved to be quiet and restful. They enjoyed the time and fun in being together in the motor home. They had previously spent fun-filled evenings and nights in the car, which had been well christened, but the camper was a large difference to the added pleasures and comfort. They, through habit, were on the move shortly after sunrise.

Arriving at the other available location, they found it had an immediate suburban existence. The main road ran directly through town. In the entire town, there was only one traffic light; it blinked at the intersection of the main road and the street the house was located on. A quarter of a mile north of the intersection, almost at the dead end, sat the house the group examined next. Though there were other houses in the neighborhood, no one else occupied a home within a hundred yard radius of the last house before the dead end. It was a fairly big house, but only had two bedrooms. They were very large and spacious. One of the other rooms seemed as if it had been converted into a study or library.

It contained all types of racks and shelves, which appeared to have contained books. The spacious dining room emptied into what seemed a parlor, or a huge sewing room of some sort. Though the porch was big and shaped the house like an "L," it was not screened in.

After walking through the place from front to back, DD told him while looking at the large bathroom for the master bedroom, "This is what I want if we're only going to be here for five years." She had not gone into the other bath or seen the storage areas, nor had she seen the large and spacious basement.

"Are you sure?" he replied.

"Look at how well kept it is Suarme, and besides, we've got the convenience of being right here in town, even though we are far away and secluded enough, not to be bothered by any of the locals or their affairs." Without replying to her, he stood in the doorway which separated both rooms. In the bedroom he looked at the paneled walls, as they were in each of the other rooms seen. They had walked through the house on a solid oak varnish floor. Fifi's paws slightly screeched as she stretched out on her stomach between his legs.

To his left was a lighted mirror, and directly behind him was a walk in closet. This created a short hallway because of the roominess of the closet, which had to have been for the lady of the house. It had racks for shoes, and shelves for hats or other items to be laced over head. Doors led to the closet from the bedroom and exited into the bath. He had not answered quickly. Knowing he was seriously pondering the matter, that he liked the farm so much, and knowing he would not deny her hardly anything, she reiterated with a different approach, "Suarme, it's been more than a month now. We've been on the road in three different states in less than twenty-four hours, we've found two places we've been searching for all along. You've said what you wanted; I like the farm also, but I like this place, this house so much better. You can tell the real estate woman we will use this as a home base, while you look some more. That's how sure I am."

She was standing in front of the mirror ten feet away. Had Chairly been present and the matter cast through a vote, the farm would have won. Because of its rural remoteness, she had already envisioned no school bus traveling that far for her. Neither of them would drive her each day; she would either not go to school, or have a car. The place had no furniture. He pointed this out to DD, "You won't be looking at night will you Suarme?" She was wearing jeans with a decorative blouse and flats. A strand of hair curled on her face. It had been purposely separated from the roll, partially to the side, but in the back portion of her head. The oval earrings complimented the beautiful face she had taken time to make up that morning. The ornaments jingled when she moved toward him, in response to his signal. Fifi sat up on her haunches to view what she knew to be imminent. He kissed her. It was so gentle but the simmering kiss lasted with the both of them. He felt and rubbed the sponginess between her legs.

"When you take the other keys back, Chairly and I will get the car."

Beyond two other houses in the next block, there was a huge shaded tree with limbs that extended out over the street. Its location was to the left just before the intersection and the caution light. She and Charily transferred some of the goods and materials back to the car while he revisited the realtor. The owner of the agency was present. Following the introductions by Ms. Johnson, Soame explained to them the issues, and how the matter stood towards a decision. "If the matter hinged on a marginal issue, it would be what to do with the land surrounding the place. It's in a totally picturesque and beautiful location, but I'm not a farmer."

"Oh, well, if that's the case and you're still interested in a place out from town, I have several more places that aren't farms, but the directions aren't as easy." With that she sort of caught him by surprise: two blocks west of the office, he had turned off the main road onto a dirt road. Twisting and turning the dirt road had many turn offs, and after bearing right past two forks he had gone over a wooden bridge, to a paved county road. This concluded a twelve-mile drive, during which they had seen ponds, streams, a doe jumping across the road, and the other various forms of wild life. Turning left on the paved road, they drove for two and a half miles and then took the first dirt road to the right. After a series of "S" curves and passing turn offs, they approached the first turn off to the right once more. This carried them up a slight hill, and around a curve. They had been through the woods, into a forest, and approached another wooded area, which led them into the forest around the curve. At the top of an incline, fifty yards off the road, they located the farm.

Noticing the surprise in his face, the owner of the office stated, "Camille, why don't you take some time this afternoon, and show him the places dear." In doing so the proprietor gathered her personal belongings and told them, "I have a lunch engagement."

The agreement was that Ms. Johnson would meet him at the house at one that afternoon. The three of them went out of the front door together. "Oh there's my date now." She indicated across the street, to the car lot. This time Soame was almost shocked but did not give any indication.

Near the car and the motor home he saw a sheriff's car and a uniformed man standing and talking with the owner of the lot. DD and Chairly stood watching them. The two bade Ms. Johnson farewell and walked toward the lot. In approaching the group, the broker stated, "Mr. Hudson I'd like for you to meet my luncheon date, who is also the sheriff of our county." In reaching to shake the hand extended to him, Soame also heard the uniformed man exclaim, "Beauford R. Allison, is the name and I'm pleased to make your acquaintance Mr. Hudson." With that they came to know each other on a first name basis. DD and Chairly had already been introduced to the sheriff. Fifi sat in the midst of the group, paying strict attention to the procedures.

"Oh what a beautiful car," the businesswoman said admiringly. DD was joined by Chairly in hosting the show of her car. This left the three men to continue their conversation. During the ten minute period in which they talked, Soame formed an idea in the conversation, which was the prelude to the actual physical construction of developing the idea into the project, which eventually lead to his legal fortune.

The sheriff appeared to be middle aged, perhaps an inch or so shorter than Soame. All three men stood with hats on. Only Soame and Beauford wore sunglasses. Though he was a bit shorter, Beauford was at least thirty pounds heavier than Soame. Anyone who ever heard him talk paid attention to what he had to say, especially when he was serious; not only because of his quality voice projection, but also because he knew how to apply reverence with the words he used and how to speak precisely about a subject, and deliver his message as directly and quickly as possible. Some considered Soame an eloquent speaker.

He had toyed with an idea for more than four years. In fact, he had done considerable research, purchased tools and equipment, then moved from one end of his home state to the other. With what he had he attempted to put the idea into effect, but personal domestic problems disallowed him from getting the project off the ground. Years passed before that day, since he had mentioned the idea to anyone. He captured their attention, when Beauford stated, "I've been told you're a retired radio announcer; this town's foldin', as much as I hate to say it, but in a couple of years ya might just be here alone. If ya stay, got any ideas in mind?"

Impromptu and in a matter-of-fact tone, he presented the produce jewelry box idea: he had an interest towards setting up a shop and produce jewelry boxes in mass. With the completion of the shop, and after mass producing, he hoped to expand. The idea revolved around the mini furniture concept, from the idea and principle used in designing and making early American style furniture. This included pieces like dressers, mirrored dressers, china cabinets, and actual size chests, all made from various woods.

The two men just looked at Soame when he'd finished. Beauford scratched the back of his head, tilting his hat over his eyes, straightening his hat, he removed his glasses and with his bare hand wiped his face as though he was using a wash cloth. With one stroke he came down from his forehead, hard and fast. Under his panama, and from behind his shades, Soame looked into the piercing blue eyes that peered at him. "Well, ah, if there's ever anything I can do for ya, just let me know."

"Sheriff I appreciate the offer. The idea calls for carpenters, and I'll need adequate building floor space to set up a shop."

"How many carpenters you figure you'll need?'"

"Perhaps five, maybe six."

The sheriff then looked at the lot owner, and back to Soame, with a smile, saying, "You do us a lot of service ya know that, not only do you come and extend our dwindling population, but you offer the possibility of jobs as well. Soame, this town is very glad to have you, and I am pleased to welcome you." When the Sheriff retracted his extended hand, a folded bill was in his palm.

"What's this?" he asked openly unfolding the hundred dollar bill.

"Have lunch on me, and if there's any expense involved in aiding me with the help of getting those men I asked you about".

"Mister this will practically buy the small café we'll be eating at."

The women were re-approaching the immediate area. Fifi preceded them and sat in their center. Beauford concluded "Soame, if you'll meet me here in the morning, between 10:45 and 11:00, I'll have those men here for ya, and I thank ya." With that they parted company.

He followed DD to the house. They went back and forth and out of room after room, while she told them of the different ways the house would be furnished. She'd heard how excellent it was for the three of them and Fifi. Though he did not at all object to the house in town, he really favored the farm. It was one of the few times Chairly totally agreed with him. However, they both knew they all would be living in the house they were unloading their belongings into.

Ms. Johnson was not late when she arrived. DD and Chairly had no interest in seeing any other places. "They will be like hundreds we've seen in the different places. They can hardly be better than this one, or the one we saw yesterday Suarme. I want to enjoy my pipe, and share the afternoon with Chairly and Fifi, since you will not be here." She had stepped close into him, and had her face on her hands in his chest. "Go on Suarme, have fun, we will be here when you come home."

The day before, she failed to give him the keys to the cellar, which had a separate outside entrance. They were off to the farm house. Camille Johnson enjoyed the ride in the recreational vehicle; she had never been in one before. En route she told him about the farming town and how two thirds of its population had abandoned the area within the past four years. Thousands upon thousands of farm acreage was for sale, and because of the abundance, farmland was being sold at twenty dollars an acre. Following her divorce, she and daughters and son moved into the area from Minneapolis. Her eldest daughter was seventeen, another fifteen, and her son was thirteen. She managed a real estate office during the later years of her marriage. Smath had been their home for the past five years. Other than being away from her ex, and being out of the city, she had no other reason for being there. She had already made arrangements at the end of the summer she too would leave. "There's no reason to stay, when everyone else is moving out. I hope this doesn't change your plans Mr. Hudson. I really do need the commissions since we all are dirt poor, but nevertheless, I must look out for my children."

"With the value of land at twenty dollars an acre, a house on a farm that size will hardly profit you any worthwhile commission will it?"

"Without my child support and alimony checks, I would have moved a year after I arrived. As I've told you Mr. Hudson, we are all dirt poor, to say the least for some."

He parked under the giant birch, and admired the white picket fence. Ms. Johnson prepared to leave the R.V. when Soame said, "No, wait a minute. You've just finished lunch. Would you care to have a drink with me?" From where he sat he could see that Chairly had nearly a half fifth in the back near the refrigerator.

"I'm really not cut out for drinking, my head spins rather fast, if I have more than a swallow, Mr. Hudson."

"I have a special soda pop chaser, which will keep you coherent and in control. Will you try some with me?"

"I don't mind, if you won't consider me a dead beat for company afterwards." Upon opening the door, Soame swirled the driver's seat and exited. He returned to the chair seat from the rear of the vehicle, with glasses, ice, orange soda pop, and blue label.

He poured a healthy four-finger drink over ice cubes in both glasses. "These houses on wheels have more room than I would have ever imagined." He then mixed the orange pop into the drinks. Near 2:30 they stepped out and he walked around to assist her. With both feet on solid ground, she proceeded in being escorted around the door and told him, "I know the water is not running inside, and I've got to use the little girl's room."

"I'm sure you realize there's no problem in going out here, if you allow me to watch." He stated this looking into her light blue eyes. To cover her slight grin, during her chuckling laughter, she placed her hands over her mouth,

"You would not Mr. Hudson, would you?"

"Does it seem strange? I'd like even to see it before the flow, and notice it afterward, to review the complete before and after effect, Ms. Johnson." She covered her face in a shameful giggle. "Besides it would give me the opportunity to find out what color panties you have on under such a striking outfit, which I'd like to compliment you on. I've wondered since seeing you this morning."

Suddenly she stepped five paces away from him. "Well, if it's not embarrassing for you, I'm game, and all for it." Stopping she turned about hiking up her red skirt, exposing her stocking tops, black lace trimmed garter belt, and matching panties. She lowered her panties with a thumb inserted on each side and squatted between her light pink patent leather shoes; they were high heel pumps. To get a really good look, he lowered himself in practically the same position and watched. They almost rose together. With a slight edge, Soame immediately stepped to her, as she was about to raise her panties. He had taken his handkerchief from his back pocket. "May I assist you in your process, Camille?" Both her hands still clutched her skirt. She was slightly bowed.

"Mr. Hud…" before she completed her say, she felt his bare hand rubbing and massaging the fresh urine all over her pubic hair and the lips of her vagina. Looking into each other's eyes, they kissed. It was a warm sweet and succulent kiss, which did not last long, but during its length, it unveiled a passion to be explored later, if they desired.

"Call me Soame," he said. He then wiped her vertex with the opened handkerchief. As she brought her panties up he wiped his hand.

Entering the front yard he inquired about the blooming bushes of flowers that resembled roses along the walk. "These are primroses, they are quite plentiful here. They are more or less in the herb family and as you see, have various colors; if you'll wait a moment I'll get the key to the cellar."

After opening the door, she produced a key on a string, which had been hung on a nail attached to the door frame. "Because of sudden winds that sometimes occur in this area, homeowners keep the keys to their cellars in this convenient place to know exactly where it is, and be able to get to the protection of the cellar as fast as possible."

In the cellar he discovered the family left more than a hundred jars of preserves and jellies. Beets, sweet black cherries, and other vegetables and naturally grown fruits from the area. He was told more about the family that lived there. They were not only unable to carry all the canned goods, but also they left two scythes and four sickles. Other farming implements and goods, that were too big or bulky to load, were also left behind. Soame also saw a cross cut—two man—saw. The basement was quite roomy. The house sat on a sixty—five acre plot, but the family had farmed more than two thousand acres. The house, with all of its contents, and the sixty-five acres surrounding it, could be bought for a mere $1,300.00.

It was there in the basement he kissed her for the second time. In doing so he made an arbitrary plunge by telling her he would close the deal if she allowed him to make love to her. She stepped back from him. Soame saw a look of frustration, humiliation, and anger, laced with malice. "Soame, did you say Mr. Hudson? I am not a part of the deal. I'm not to be bought or sold." She continued looking him up and down with contempt and resumed, "We may close this deal, if you chose to, if I have given you the impression that I am a woman to be had an—"

He stepped toward her saying, "Camille, Camille, it is me. I know who is at fault. I've said what I did not mean. Men are often fallible. I am no stronger now than an average man, attempting to use leverage in gaining what he desires. I'm not infallible. Will you accept my apology and pardon me?"

Though she had calmed considerably, she snapped, "Let's get some air, its gotten to be rather stuffy in this drab atmosphere."

After locking the outside door, they walked to the rear of the house. He was very glad and pleased he could display her attentions toward the beauty of nature in the daylight, with their surroundings. With the wealth of experience he had with women, he had played for the results he had obtained in the cellar. In using that specific tactic, he uncovered a part of her character she had not previously projected. He had reasons to search for her true persona. She had played well. In the back of the house he extended his probe. "That mountainous, far off area, is it Granite Peak?"

"Oh, no, Soame; though it's the highest elevation in this state, it's clear on the other side of billings, near Livingston. Those are the Rosebud Mountains. They're in Big Horn county, and an extension of the Wolf Mountains, which trail across the state line from Wyoming."

"This state offers a lot to the memory of George Custer. It's strange how in America's history book, a win for the cavalry was a noble victory, yet a defeat by the Indians, was seen as a massacre. He was driven by rage, and hatred, which are not components of a quality and superior soldier. I admire his gallantry, during the last phase of the civil war. Of course, he was not as renown and prominent as Phil Sheridan, but Custer's name ranged, somewhat before Little Bighorn."

They had walked out near the edge of the wheat field, she told him, "There are probably sweet black cherries in the hedge row at the timber line." There was a pause, the gentle breeze slightly ruffled the fields, causing waves in the dancing shoots, bowing and weaving, with gentle flows. She looked at him, seeing he had not taken his vision from the mountains. "I remember Sheridan, but I can't think of what he was noted for."

"He was a cavalry man. Lee had Stone Wall Jackson as a bulwark with the southern infantry. J.E.B. Stewart, was his rampart with their cavalry. Thinking he and his crew were northern soldiers, Jackson was ambushed one night, riding to a confederate camp, by southerners. He never recovered from his wounds. Phil Sheridan boxed, went in after, and personally killed J.E.B. Stewart. He did it in a suburban area of Richmond, the confederate capitol. Both Jackson and Stewart either won every encounter they had

Ulyseses S. Grant - Cold Harbor, 1864

with the enemy, or eluded them. For Lee, they were irreplaceable. No United States cavalry man, has ever earned a victorious reputation to equal that of general Phillip H. Sheridan."

They followed each other's eyes, and in turning back toward the house she stated, "We've had a few wars since the civil war, I'm glad we now live in a time of peace."

"There are only two types of peace. One comes about between wars. The other exists eternally after life."

Strolling he told her how the pink blouse she wore matched the light plush pinkness of her cheeks, and pointed out how the red sprinkled polka dots in the blouse not only matched her skirt, but made him think of an apple pie, with tiny holes in the crust. Approaching the front of the house he asked if she had locked the front door. When she replied no, he stepped up on the porch, from the ground on the side of the house, and replaced the stringed key on the nail.

"All of my friends back in Minneapolis have, at one time or another, and around here I've not even as heard or mentioned the subject. I've simply never had exposure to it Soame. It looks sort of like sugar." They were at the curve where the road entered the Ponderosa Pine Forest; the farm was a quarter of a mile up an incline, at their backs. After stopping and unwrapping the remainder of an eight ball, he did a one and one, and asked if she'd ever done or seen cocaine. "Want to try this Camille, it's really good and it'll mellow you out."

"If I do, will it make me want to show you my panties?" She inquired with a blushing smile, and immediately looked out of the passenger window, as if she was embarrassed.

"Hey, will they still match me in their color if you do?" Seeing her smile, she fumbled with the seat lever, swirled the chair towards him, and in slightly lifting off the high back, she brought her skirt to her waist. They enjoyed the indulgence. Soame appreciated, observed, and was charmed by the display, and learned that marijuana was quite plentiful in the area. As a common practice, she and her daughters were regular smokers at home. They began a slow drive back toward town, talking while they rode.

Midway through the joint, they were sharing, she told him she never thought grass could be so potent. They were entering the "S" curve, when he asked how the agency existed if no one bought property, which appeared to be evident one to the population decrease. He was then informed when she arrived there were seven agents working from the office. People paid to list property and a small fee each month enabled the "for sale" property to remain posted with the listings. The farm had been listed for two months; the house belonged to a doctor, and was a six and a half week listing. The only remaining male member on the staff, was also a local school teacher. No one expected the realty office to be open at the close of the summer.

Soame informed Camille that with all probability he would take both the farm and the house as well. He also asked if she could come up with a deal, which would profit her a thousand dollars in commission. With a broad grin on her face, looking directly into his face she told him, "Soame for a thousand dollars, you can have me and both my daughters as well."

He almost choked with surprise, and attempted to laugh. Holding the wheel steady with one hand, and attempting to cover his coughing mouth with the other, he asked, "For how long?"

"Pull over Mr. Hudson. Right here." She gave him all of her, in every way she knew how, and in every way he wanted. When they were both spent, and laid totally naked on the bed in the master quarters, she told him, "Soame, I am a good woman, I have no one, nor do I have a place to move to from here. If you can arrange your affairs with your family, where no trouble will be caused, I will be your outside woman. My girls are obedient and good children, I will not force them to decide, I will introduce them to you, and ask your respect towards their decisions."

"I want you Camille. We will have no problems."

The multiplex band radio was tuned in to a record mail order station, out of Gallatin, Tennessee. The announcer was introducing an album by Bobby Blue Bland, a blues artist and musician, taken from his album *Two Steps From The Blues*, and his tune *I'll Take Care of You*. Hearing that record, at that time, had an emotional effect on the internal atmosphere of the motor home; at that point the weekend was approaching. He already knew she did bookkeeping. He found out she'd gotten her house and the three acres she lived on, in a deal similar to that of the farm. Camille expressed her main interest in securing a future which she also wanted her children to be prepared for. Before driving from the spot he gave her $1,500.00, the remainder of the eight ball, and a small portion of the weed. They made arrangements to meet the following morning after he had met with the sheriff and the carpenters.

Chapter 10

WHEN he walked through the door, everyone greeted him with hugs and kisses. He had no idea until he arrived that the lights and water had been turned on. Hydroelectric power plants and steam plants that burn coal, supply the majority of "the Treasure State's" electric power. It was near dusk. DD told him with a big smile, "It was not difficult when I told them we were already moving into the place."

He immediately began preparing for a shower. Helping him out of his clothes, she told him, "I know Suarmme, what you have been up to, at least this time she is younger." She reached into his shorts as she talked. She palmed his organs and squeezed, saying "busy, busy, busy" each time she squeezed. "DD, I've got an idea toward redeveloping an interest I attempted, in trying to become an entrepreneur."

"Suarme, please, why do you use such words, knowing I do not know the meaning. I have never before heard of such a word, what is it you're saying?" she asked blushing and giggling.

In his boxers and socks he hugged her, and while holding the radiantly beautiful woman he had come home to, he explained, "It seems to be an almost perfect opportunity for a business venture. It will be a lot of hard work, of course, but if I can piece my ideas together, we can set up a business enterprise which will flourish in this area. It has to succeed because from what we've seen, and what I've heard, there's no other chance for this town being kept alive. We'll be here alone if the idea fails." He then outlined the jewelry box concept to her. She then called Chairly and the three of them showered.

The average temperature during the day ranged in the mid sixties. As they did the previous night the heater was used in the motor home to stay the chill. It made their nights cozy and comfortable.

When he drove the RV into the car lot the following morning, he saw the men standing outside the sales office. They began approaching the vehicle before it came to a stop. Beauford was not with them. Names were exchanged and he also introduced Worldwide Conservation and Energy, Inc. to them, which was the name of the company they would be working for; his company. He outlined his plans and idea. It was very interesting and worthwhile to find out two of the men worked for a furniture factory, in North Carolina, before moving to Smath.

They knew the operational and procedural involvement of the "assembly line" principal he mentioned. This was the method they would install, develop for, and work with, towards succeeding with the idea. He also found out that four of the six men were farmers, part-time. They each farmed less than two-thousand acres, but times caught them in both directions. The best any farmer could do was plow under, and collect the government subsidy. All of them seemed desperate for work. Though he had no immediate idea of opening the jewelry box shop, he took all six of them on for $75.00 a week. They signed on with 10W40 information, given to Ms. Johnson, in the reality office. They were to meet him Monday at noon at the farmhouse he was about to buy.

DD asked him to pick up a few items from market before he left home that morning. He made good use of his time, during the interval before seeing Camille for lunch, by making the trip to the market. It was there he met Pete Thompson, with his wife and daughter. Pete was also one of the men the sheriff had spoken with. Because of an immediate concern, with a higher-ranking priority, Pete could not meet at the designated place: he was far behind on his mortgage payment. Pete had been expecting the foreclosure for more than three weeks. Everything he had would be taken when it happened. The car was the only means he had to move his family; he was four payments behind and had been threaten with repossession twice. In telling Pete about Soame, the Sheriff also gave him a description of the vehicle he was traveling in. Through that description, he'd noticed Soame, when he pulled in the market parking lot. Pete had also just been denied credit for the groceries he desperately needed. Soame hired Pete on the spot. Not only because of his desperate circumstance, but also because Pete had experience in making jewelry boxes. He was from Alabama and stated he had spent five years in the prison system there. "During my bit, I made every style of jewelry box you can imagine. It was the only means I had to earn money." Due to Pete's state of desperation, Soame advanced him two weeks salary. This was to be deducted $15.00 per week, after his first two weeks, at full salary. He then took the carpenter to the phone station at the side of the building. They called Ms. Johnson.

Lunch with Camille brought a few surprises. She was vibrant, enthusiastic, cheerfully happy, and projected glee. She showed vigor from a stored resource of vitality. Soame was by far not lonely within his household, nor was he lacking in any way for attention or affection. Nevertheless, this new emotional addition to his life most certainly added spark to his day, which had already proved rewarding. She made herself a total joy to be with. He drove the RV a short distance to the outskirts of town and they lunched on foods he chose from the deli section while he was at the market. Though she knew his mind was practically set on the farm and the house, and part of the reason for being there was to close the deal, she had two other purposes in mind: one of the local farmers had stopped by the office that morning and listed his farm. His spread was considerably larger than the one Soame was interested in the house sat on one hundred and fifteen acres. The farm totaled more than four thousand acres. She had made a verbal commitment to the farmer, the third longest farmer in the area, that she would mention the new listing to Soame, since he was the first person to buy land in the area in a year. Though he would not be cheated, $20.00 an acre was absolute top price on land with running water and living facilities. $12.00 an acre would have been fair; $6.00 would not have been an unreasonable expectation. Regular farm land was available for less than a dollar an acre.

The second unscheduled reason had to do with the possible availability of an eight bedroom mansion. It had a direct "in town" location, but the listing fee had not been paid in four months. She had to contact the owner to find out if the place should still be sold. These matters were discussed over lunch. Afterwards, they shared a drink of vodka.

Her perkiness had not in the least decreased. With complete sincerity and apprehension, she nonchalantly with friskiness told him, "I will allow myself an hour and a half for lunch, so you can play in my panties if you want to. Don't ask me about colors. Let's see just how, and if you can be as aggressive today."

They were sitting at the "wall out" table in the kitchenette. While she undid her necklace, Soame kissed her. When they finished the joint, she had only her brassiere, panties, garter belt, and stockings on. He did one and ones. She only did ones. Each one she did, she exotically removed one of the remaining pieces of clothes. She began with her bra, and when all that remained were her panties, he assisted her with them.

They were sensually wild, and turned on to and for each other. Though DD had been a pro, Camille gave him something very few woman ever gave more than once. It was the second time she unleashed a passion with her lovemaking. Not only did she allow him to make love to her, she reciprocated by making love to him. She did this lovemaking freely, totally, and completely without inhibition or restraint. During the process of making love with him, she became totally void of any feeling of shame or embarrassment. She explored his body, searching for his desires and pleasures. Anything that pleased him, or she thought possibly desired, his most trivial whim was her demanding summons to satisfy with frantic, lustful, soothing pleasure. Her pleasures arose with his satisfactions. In that way they were totally and completely compatible. At times they were ruthless with each other; there was nothing wrong in their lovemaking, only the art of making love.

Soame once again took an arbitrary plunge, but this time, it was in a business-like fashion. It was she who played him, and his true character prevailed. She had noticed his admiration of the mountains, heard his words about men of gallantry and listened while he talked of a war that had been; he championed her with his concept of peace. Knowing the probable availability of the mansion, and his possibly buying it, when the probability became possible, he closed the deals on the properties he had already chosen. Camille found a good provider in the good lover. She found the superb tangibles would only enhance their relationship in both aspects toward the materialization of their goal. She could ill afford to lead him astray.

It wasn't until after 2:30 when she walked into the office. Both deals were closed and she felt very good about herself and her environment. The in-depth feeling of goodness she had, she could not remember having ever had before. Naturally the size of the house and its local boosted its value over the price of the farm. However, with the contingency in the background as a factor, Soame gave her a deal. At twenty-three hundred, for both estates they closed the deal with the presentation of the cash.

Entering her thirty-second year, she stood 5'8". Camille was a solidly built woman, with no trace of fat on her body. At 130 lbs. she measured 36-24½-36. Her brunette hair lay at her shoulders. It seemed as if Soame, in the short time he had known her, was filling an emptiness she held for a long while for the right person when he came along. She had encountered only one previous affair; it had been the first and only affair after her divorce. Soame's predecessor had been a local businessman who was also a town council member. Before the preceding winter, he closed shop and left. She uplifted Soame's life and stability with her bright and cheery character and warm disposition. He found her to be more than pleasant company and with her he felt he was worth something. He felt as though he accomplished something in merely being with her. They both felt the need they proved they shared for and with each other. He had never before seen in any other woman the passion Camille displayed. It took him to heights he had never dreamed of. It was very hard for any woman to gain that recognition and receive that credibility from Soame.

Her son was to spend the weekend on a farm with a playmate from school. The two boys had done this on several occasions through the years and enjoyed each other's friendship. She and her daughters were to join Soame and his household at the house the following morning at ten. It was the close of the week. It had been a terribly long time since she had closed a week, and for once could afford to pay off all her bills, give money to her children, and not be troubled by financial matters during the coming week, or month for that matter. September would be there soon. None of them had gotten new clothes in quite awhile. She knew of an ideal place, twenty-five miles out into the country. There they all could privately enjoy themselves with fun and laughter, without interruption. It was her ideal picnic spot.

The local furniture truck was in the yard when he arrived "home." The store offered almost give away prices, yet she did not go wild with spending. DD carefully selected bedroom furniture with a king size bed for the master bedroom, a matching sofa and chair, a recliner for him, a coffee table, and a complete dining room ensemble, with a rosewood table that extended to fit six. With the entertainment center and kitchenware included in the single purchase; she decided to wait until the following week to see how what she had fit in. Fifi stayed by her side while the owner of the store and his helper moved about bringing pieces in. Chairly was comfortably relaxed in the recliner. Because of the truck and the music Chairly had almost at a blast, they did not see or hear him until he entered the house. Fifi pranced across the varnished floor. DD greeted him with a kiss and a hug, and in his ear told him, "You should have a shower, I can always tell." Chairly simply set up in the chair, saying, "Look what we got." Fifteen minutes later with a generous tip, DD told the owner, "I will be back Monday or Tuesday for the other pieces I mentioned." Soame was very pleased with her choices. "Come Chairly, we are going to use the shower again with your pa-pa and spend the remainder of the day testing the new pieces in the bedroom."

Well after dark, the two women would not allow him out of the bed, except to use the bathroom, and make a final security check on the vehicles. Anything he thought he wanted, he had; he had it anyway he thought he wanted it, or they thought he might have a desire for it. The two women were instruments of endless pleasure. It was their first night in their very own home, their first weekend in

Smath, and they thoroughly enjoyed the night beginning the weekend. It wasn't until 9:00AM Saturday before he was allowed out of the bed.

After checking the cars that night, he told them about the picnic. They listened to the story with anticipation and enthusiasm. They discussed what appeared to be the matter in French for a solid thirty minutes,. Soame was somewhat surprised once again, in being able to notice with full attention, Chairly's improvement toward efficiently becoming fluent with the foreign language. What really captured his attention, and brought focus toward her improvement, was the gesturing she did; pantomiming in carrying through with the mimicking. He observed her closely and saw her doing this subconsciously in an attempt to really convey a true thought or feeling in the conversation. Gradually, she also improved with her English. This was most important to him. She was also becoming more reserved. He felt, in time, she would be all right.

Shortly after Camille and her daughters arrived, and the introductions were made, they were all ready to go. The Johnson's admired Fifi, who relished admiration. The eldest daughter Margaret, was about to enter her senior year in high school. She had no immediate plans as to what her life would be like a year from that point because she wasn't sure if they were going to move or remain as residents. At that point Camille injected, "We're going to stay here dear. Last night I told you I had come to a decision." They continued to chat, exchanging looks and glances at each other. Even though Chairly was the youngest in the group, she towered over Beverly, Camille's youngest daughter. The air was brisk for the Southerners. DD and Chairly wore short shorts with long sleeved sweat shirts. Camille had on Bermuda shorts, and both her daughters wore jeans. All three wore simple cotton blouses. Lunchmeat sandwiches, freshly baked biscuits, and pies, with a few jars of different preserves were the eats. The day before, Soame paid $20.00 for a watermelon, fruits, chips, nuts, and two gallons of lemonade. By ten, as scheduled, they were on their way to the outing.

The three adults occupied all but one of the seat-chairs in the front section of the coach. The remainder of the party was in the rear with "Yipes," sniggles, and occasional outbreaks of laughter. Fifi seemed to be their main attraction for a while. The two were allowed to smoke Marijuana openly, but Camille had not granted either of them permission to drink alcohol. After a date, Margaret had come home a couple of times with the distinct smell on her breath. She had not recently been out because of the scarcity of young men and boys in the area. Cocaine was heard of, but a totally unavailable commodity throughout the vicinity. Camille went on, filling them in on the "happenings," and the aroma of "Grass" made it's way to their section. Soame enjoyed the friendliness between the two ladies who did not project an iota of adversary thoughts or feelings toward each other.

In addition to his cut off knee high jeans, his Stetson, and the dark boys, he had on a sweat shirt with long sleeves, topped with a maroon jersey lettered with a white 51; he drove at a moderate pace following directions over roads and trails he knew had not been used in awhile. DD let it be known that she knew of the sexual encounters between the two of them. She also extended sisterly gestures, which he ignored, but saw Camille's positive response, and felt the two would get along fine. They had been riding for more than thirty minutes when he did a one and one. When he offered the tailored straw and vile to her, she asked DD, "Do you mind?" The French accent rolled, "No, no, no, for heavens sakes. I wish I could light my pipe without offence or embarrassment to your girls, as a matter of fact." Camille had never seen anyone smoke "base," even though she had heard about it. "Why not lace a joint, until we park and the girls are outside. Then we can party," Soame suggested. The three of them knew it was the practical solution.

The spot they drove to was truly beautiful. The small lake was approximately a half-mile in circumference. It's clear mirrored surface reflected patches of clouds and the dark blue firmament. DD strolled to the lake and found the water to be clear. She stuck her sandaled toes in it and found the water to be moderately chilled. The slightly wet foot was no comparison to the drenching splashes inflicted to her legs from Fifi's plopping plunge. It was not unusual at all for the dog to take a swim. Because of the season, her lion clip had been cut down to a modern style. It was the second opportunity she had had, and took full advantage of each minute to swim. Camille was surprised and in taking an available towel to DD, questioned the event. DD explained the word "caniche," meaning poodle, and in French it's derivative "canard" which means duck. The poodles breed is credited with originating in the marshlands of France. In learning this, while aiding DD, she found herself in need of a towel, when Fifi swam ashore, pranced between them and sprinkled them both, from her shivering.

The blankets were spread and somewhat distant. Noticing Margaret's trapped situation, her mother commented, "I thought she would be the one who would be ill at ease. I don't have a solution. I guess she'll find a way." Chairly and Beverly were full of giggles on one blanket, while her older daughter sat alone on the other; torn between the practical fun and laughter she had outgrown, which amused her sibling and their acquaintance, Margaret would not take the opportunity to join the adults, sitting under the canopy. She seemed pleasant and relaxed behind her shades, but they all knew she had to choose her company. Fifi found no problem in providing curly hairs, for the fingers that twisted and rubbed, while brushing through them. They had been there for more than an hour.

Responding to her mother's call, Margaret approached the shaded area next to the motor home. "It may very well be a special day for you my dear. DD and Soame have liquor here and have extended an invitation to you, with my permission, to join us in a taste of spirits. We saw you sitting alone, and with this offer you have my permission."

"You are heavenly mother, as are DD and Soame. I thank you both." She chose DD's five star and joined them. Their conversations varied from subject to subject, each bringing smiles that reflected good memories. They appreciated the warmth of the day. Soame removed his jersey and looked at the thermostat on the outside doorframe; it read 67 degrees. There were flowers scattered about, and rock formations, with patches of grass outlining the lake. Green, brown, and yellowish gold colors, from smaller trees and bushes, between the lake and the pines, added to the picturesque scenery, accompanied by the brilliance of the sun and projected on the encased beauty surrounding them.

DD smoked only in the confines of the coach. Knowing the objectivity of her intervals, Chairly used an excuse to once follow her. DD spoke to her in French that once, and she did not return. Later on again DD disappeared, and after five minutes Margaret excused herself from her mother's and Soame's company. Going directly inside the RV, she saw DD with a table lighter about to ignite the contents of the pipe. DD had heard Margaret excuse herself, and felt her rocking entry; she had not been caught off guard.

"I knew you were doing crack, I smelled it earlier."

"Then you know what this is?" She then lit and inhaled.

"Kids at school used to have it. Now no one can find it anyplace."

"Would you like to have a hit?"

"If you would, I will be your best friend, DD."

"But I already have a best friend. Chairly."

"Then I will be one of your friends forever."

"A friend is always very good to have. You do not necessarily have to pledge your friendship, but here try it, and let's see what happens in the future between us."

She took her first puff, and with the inhalation, they both heard Soame say in a loud voice. "It's about time we all take part in what makes this a picnic. Wouldn't you all say it's time we eat?"

DD squeezed her cheek lightly, before she exhaled. She blew the smoke out, and commented, "At a time like this."

They were all pleased with the preparations and lunch. There were leftovers, but no one had a doubt of them being put to practical use before the close of the outing. The perishable items were placed into a plastic bag and they all resumed their activities. Chairly and Beverly wanted to walk around the lake. Fifi indicated she'd accompany them, and with the warning to "be careful" the girls were permitted. They took two good size joints with them. DD privately said to Soame, "Margaret not only knows what the pipe is, she also smokes." He and Camille then went inside the travel home, and DD mentioned her and Margaret sharing a blanket.

The four of them could clearly see Chairly and Beverly rounding the corner. When Fifi streaked into a patch of scattered, knee high grass, he commented to Camille, "She's probably seen a rabbit. She chases everyone she sees; I've seen her catch several."

"I thought they were gentle show dogs," she replied, somewhat alarmed and surprised.

"The breeds smaller than the miniature are basically show dogs. However, the standard size poodle and this one are classified as utility dogs. In fact, some are still used to hunt and retrieve water foul."

While she still looked out the window, Soame told her, "My interest in being here with you 'miz lively nut' is not to observe Fifi. Would you still consider me aggressive if I asked for a panty inspection at this time?"

They were in the far rear part of the vehicle. Unfastening her Bermudas, she asked, "What will DD say if she catches us? Soame, are you sure you want to do this?"

"She'll probably not only want to see them, but also explore your body. I think she might already have given it consideration." While he spoke, the pink covered crotch was exposed to him. The loosely fitting shorts had fallen to her ankles. Almost directly in front of them, Chairly and Beverly were approaching the center bank on the other side of the lake.

"DD's a beautiful woman with a matching personality. She's open, very much alive, and I think she's warm. I'd be glad to share the sisterhood with her, if she likes me, and can get along with my girls." He then explained why Margaret laid on the blanket with her back toward them. It was a slight surprise, but Camille was not shocked. She and her daughters were very open and honest with each other, she told him this before. Making the observation, she stated, "Some time ago she talked about kids at school having it. She did not openly say she had done it, but she gave a clear indication to the effect that she liked it."

Camille then looked at the stiff glistening rod she was about to mount. His fingering between her legs motivated her to remove the briefs. The rear seat stretched across the compartment, much like the long rear seat of a bus. His cut off jeans and boxers easily went over his tennis shoe tops. He sat on the seat, while she took his penetration from the rear. Straddling it, she regulated the depth she desired.

Rotating and grinding, using the instrument as she pleased, she brought herself to two orgasms. Each time, she placed her hand squarely over her mouth and stifled the verbal release. The RV could clearly be seen rocking, and now and then a squeak would travel through the silence. Without halting their motions, they saw DD and Margaret stand and begin undressing. Beverly and Chairly were seated on top of a cluster of large rocks, two thirds of the way around, still on the other side of the water. "We're going for a swim," DD told them, while she and her companion climbed out of their panties. "We'll be watching" responded Soame. "Ohhhh. Ohhhh. Do it deeper, deeper, Soame, cause I love it so much. Fuck meee good, Soame. Oh please fuck me good and deep, cause I love it when itsss sooo good and hard. Ohhh please, Soame, please."

DD and Margaret initially paddled around and swam near the bank. When they began stroking toward the center of the lake, the two on the far bank resumed their progress. Fifi scampered to and from groves of bushes, patches of grass, and in and out of sections of small trees. Her gray coat was dominant and stood out against any of the colors around the lake.

Camille continued to squat and please herself with the best pleasing pole she ever had. Without removing himself from inside her, Soame rose upward, and standing he clasped her right shoulder and turned her around to the seat he had been sitting on. He instructed her to place her right knee on the cushion. In doing so, still holding her shoulder, he pushed her upper body down. Her right hand extended upward, to hold the top of the back seat. Her right knee, her breast – on her right side – and the left side of her face was all on the cushioned seat. Her left knee and hand supported her from the carpeted floor. Soame knew how to get pussy. He was totally capable of granting her request for the deep hard erection he maintained. His first big lunge caused Camille's supporting knee on the carpet to buckle. She cried "Oh my god, Soame." He knew she could not take the hilting pounds long. It would "bring her body down." He stroked and rotated in her several times with the full extent of his measure. He felt the smooth wall of her womb each time he hilted. She no longer cried out, she now grunted each time he touched the lower inside of her body. He allowed himself to relax and through his control, knowing she would climax also with the swell of his dick, he ejaculated. They both climbed to a light headed state of giddiness during ninety seconds of demonstrated masculine force. During her final orgasm, with the increasing swell of his knot, she could only whimper. Knowing he had spilled himself completely to their satisfaction, when the final bit from the tip of the head, was lifted out of her, Camille's last sound then, was a whimpering sigh. He released her shoulder.

DD and Margaret swam fifty yards toward the center, and were returning slowly, when the walking couple rounded the last turn in an approach to the motor home. Soame could only see the two in the lake. Stepping to the center of the coach, through the front windshield, he saw the other two walking. Camille was sitting up, stretching, to allow her circulation. She motioned him to her, and began her "clean up" procedure. It was gratifying for her. It gave her happiness and true pleasure in extending her fulfillment. He was truly deserving. She had never been so pleased, physically, nor had she ever encountered the sexual mental exuberance on such a fringe of erupting pulsations. The procedure she gratefully administered was but a mere small fraction of what she had to give, which was all his then: with her heart, her mind, her body and soul, and with all her strength, Camille, within herself, committed her entirety to Soame.

The swimmers were wading and about to step onto the bank when Fifi preceded the running, undressing Chairly and Beverly "Don't get out, we're coming in too." The two never broke their stride toward the blankets. Placing them together, DD replied, "You don't really need us to swim with you, do you? Go on, we'll watch." The other two did not slow down until the water was almost at their knees; there they hesitated until Fifi splashed them. The water had a vigorous chill to it. The splash was all they needed to plunge. Following a refreshing swallow of lemonade, Margaret laid unclothed on her back, with one knee extended up in a bend, and completely surrendered herself to DD. DD had laid beside her and covered her mouth with hers. It aroused Soame to see DD kiss, fondle, and stroke Margaret, who appeared to be enjoying every move. "I had no idea she would be so attracted to DD so soon," Camille said, watching with him. "Why, because they were not in a drab cellar, and needed some air?" They were dressing, and she eased into him, snuggling her head in his chest. "Well, since you put it that way Soame, I'm your woman, however you feel about it. I mean that with sincere and complete conviction. Whatever happens with this situation, you're in control." She looked into his eyes and continued, "She and I talked about you last night, and it was our agreement that if she liked you, you could be sh – "

He interrupted, by placing his index finger over her lips, and told her, "It seems as if DD has gained wind of the conversation you two had, and is not only willing to share, but also willing to be shared." The two in the water paddled a very short distance out and back to waist-high water. They began splashing each other, and thoroughly enjoyed the frantic delights. It was a true form of eroticism with fired excitement for them. Noticing the rise of the naked meat, after feeling it harden while fondling it, Camille took it again into her mouth. As she did in all her actions in lovemaking, she administered fellatio with robust vigor and aggressive sternness.

Chairly and Beverly paddled and stroked a short distance further up the bank, around and away from the blankets. Soame noticed them and watched them climb out of the water. He then brought Camille to a standing position, and with both their bottoms bare, they walked out to the couple on the blankets. His member was erect and pounced in front of him, with a slight hanging sway. Standing over the lovers on the ground, in only their tops, neither he nor Camille said a word. The people on the blankets said nothing either, but DD extended her hand upward to Camille. In her yielding to join DD, Soame took a position with and next to Margaret, holding her as she laid on her right side. The degree of her wetness told him she was completely ready. While DD assisted Camille from her blouse, he fondled Margaret some more, and with almost motionless effort on both their parts, she was on her back, with him on top of and inside her. He watched the inquisitive look turn to delightful expressions on her face, while they both carried him deeper into her vagina. The four of them gave themselves the pleasures of each other for more than twenty minutes.

Again, Camille used her hand to stifle sounds, from feelings of ecstasy. DD held her spellbound with cunnilingus, then sent her spiraling toward a paradisiacal pleasure. Such a reward of pleasure can only be attained through the expertise of an artist who knows how to skillfully use the tongue. Margaret was not a virgin, but she was quite lacking the experience and the true form of giving herself. Though her passions were simmered, they were potentially explosive. As gentle as he was, and as delicate as he could be, Soame erupted some of the explosiveness he found in her mother. She reached, hugged, clawed, and grabbed as she whined, cried, and begged for more. She craved for his jizm, in a feverish stupor, with wild anticipation toward the next orgasm she had to have, and pleaded not to be denied. She achieved several, before the final one with him. Then she exploded, and went wondrously, helplessly, and totally out of control into orgasmic oblivion. DD and Camille soon became spent. They positioned and locked into each other's arms without words or motion. Fifi lay several yards from the blankets looking toward the lake. Throughout the performance she looked, as she often did, and afterward pretended not to have seen.

They were practically dressed when Chairly and Beverly walked up, holding hands. Beverly looked directly at them, and told her mother, "We've also had fun." Everybody laughed and hugged. Fifi pranced around them and the few articles of clothing still on the blankets. Her happiness was expressed by "arff arffs." Soon they were all completely dressed, the belongings were gathered, and they were on their way back.

The house had not been completely furnished. Even so, through a unanimous decision, and with the convenience of the travel home, the Johnsons spent the weekend with Soame's household. They all fully enjoyed the experience.

Chapter 11

WORLDWIDE Conservation and Energy Corporation existed as a legal corporate structure six years prior to Soame entering the town. In establishing the concern, Soame's original idea had been to develop a business through the sales of shares in stock and expand the idea and company to the point of purchasing a radio station, with at least a down payment. The name of the structure exemplifies its purpose and the call letters, which were to be used for the station: WWCE.

He came up with the idea after leaving home as an experienced, nationally recognized announcer. Pursuing his quest, to become the well polished announcer he fantasized, as a "jock" he moved to various stations, in different cities, one after the other. Each station he worked with he pulled its highest rating. At each station, situations came about that produced problems. Management was always satisfied with his performance because the ratings increased commercial profit, the backbone of the industry. The other "jocks" he worked with always eventually turned out to be an aggravation. The number one position is always an enviable spot. It is a challengeable position, and often presents vulnerability from "out of towner," so he was subjectable. As a loner, he did not go for or socialize with the "brothers." He did not fraternize, and his social encounters, though few, except on business occasions were restricted to women. His reputation began preceding him in cities and he became a legendary outcast.

Through a fluke, because he really wanted to "make it" at home, he planned to re-enter the market there. The black station he had worked with had been sold, and the other one was doing religious formatted music. He had worked with a middle of the road station before taking advantage of his GI Bill and pursuing his master's degree. In Miami, he discovered that the top 40 stations had not integrated, so he did nothing, except create the Worldwide Conservation and Energy Corporation, and attempted selling his idea. The fluke was that how he discovered how his "homeboys," who were often junior high school dropouts, were making millions, living in fine homes, driving sports and luxurious automobiles, and had some of the finest women in town, on their knees at his "homies" door steps. Soame eased up in the drug game, and found out what life was all about from another aspect. He did not need a legal company to become a millionaire. However, he made money, and attempted to set up a legal business he thought would thrive and produce enough capital to get the station he dreamed of. He still had creative ideas toward becoming the "well polished" announcer he dreamed of, who articulated without depicting, race, region, or natural origin.

Soame was anxious to hire the men who were at the farm, waiting for work, as his employees. Starting them would once again put procedural development into effect to expand an idea he had. This would add to his personal achievement and self-accomplishment.

At noon on Monday, all seven carpenters were there. The house needed few repairs. They went over all that was to be done, including the paneling, which would bring a different look to the cellar. He wanted to keep them at hand. He could easily afford the several thousand dollars it took to find out which way the economic structure of the area would go in the following month, and keep them available.

They proceeded to the barn from the house. The building needed numerous amount of repairs. At one point, Soame thought and suggested the idea of tearing the building down and rebuilding. Even though they all laughed at the idea, they did not miss the sincerity in the presentation of his proposal. He knew that if his jewelry box idea was successful, which was the reason for their being there, they would need a place to store the product. The barn seemed ideal for that express purpose. He did not divulge his idea in detail, but kept it to himself.

They were to start the following day. His business structure had not gotten off the ground in a previous attempt. Nevertheless, as a organizational head, Soame knew the basic principals of employment, especially where his protection was concerned. He was totally aware of the risk and dangers involved with workers who used power tools and equipment. During the weekend he had discussed the matter with Camille, who was to sign each of them up with insurance and compensation. Each was to report to her before returning to the job site. In his own way, one by one, each found a way to have a private word with Soame, except Pete Thompson. Even though he knew it would have been bad policy, he looked at the favorable side of the issue, as a humane employer who was attempting a set up in a town he had been in less than a week. He advanced them all two weeks pay, with the exact conditions extended with Pete's loan. They were all happy and content with the relief in finding work. They displayed appreciation toward the generosity of their new employer, who was the first black man to have lived in the town, something Soame did not know.

While consulting with Camille, she mentioned once again the farmer who recently put the listing in. After stopping by home, and finding DD and Chairly perplexed by a problem, he visited the mentioned farm. It was toward the evening when he arrived. The sun was about to dip and glow behind the far away mountains. The Yates family had six members. The head of the family "Thad" Yates, had just come home with his two boys. Billy and Little Thad had been out to the barn with him, feeding the livestock. They had just slipped off work boots and shoes and had began to relax on the front porch. "Thad" also pointed out his wife and two daughters who were preparing supper. Soame was invited in and introductions were made, the issue at hand was discussed.

"I've got real good land here, not only to live on, but also to be farmed as well. This was my father's land, and I've expanded it a thousand acres or so, and brought up my family on the same site where my parents lived and are buried." Thad continued to tell Soame how hard times trapped them, like thousands of other farmers during the Reagan Administration all over America. "Fact is, even though Bush is in office, after being a puppet for Reagan, he doesn't show us any signs of relief, and we're starving to simply farm and sell our product at a reasonable price." He explained how terribly bad it hurt to grow thousands of acres of crops and plow it all under. Again, it was a lot easier to do that and be paid a supplemental subsidy by the acre, than watch the crops rot in the fields, or see the harvest go to waste in the barn and storage bends.

Soame did not know what the actual situation was with the farmer in America. Though he had seen the devastation, he had not put the evidence together with the picture and concluded. He had no idea of the firm control the government had with the regulation of farming. That evening he discovered what he saw in his long car drives was chaos. He had walked directly into a peril situation involving the American farmer. In listening, he understood the totality of Yate's plight. He had over four thousand acres of farmland, but Times and conditions dictated his move, to save his family, and do as two thirds of the previous farmers in the area had done. He wanted to sell because he knew his winter production would only take him deeper into debt. Soame could purchase the house, all the equipment, and the land at a "special" deal for $5,000 for the going prime rate. Yates only wanted to pack, and be able to move his family.

While he talked, Soame's attention was attracted by Thad's daughter, Cathy, several times. Her brother William was the oldest of the children, and approaching his senior year in school. She was a year younger. Her eyes sparkled each time he glanced at her. The girl would look at him, and shyfully look away and would smile. She was beautiful with her two long auburn plats in pig tails; she had green Christmas tree color eyes.

Not being a farmer, Soame told Yates of his interests and expressed his concern, but his inexperience as a farmer would only leave him holding land he could not develop or turn into a profit. "In a couple of days, I may be able to come up with a practical way to help in some way Yates, but at this time, I see no way I can. Let me think on it." They shook hands, bid farewell, and parted company.

That night Soame gave the overall situation serious consideration. He knew all along within a year he could be alone in the town. Also, he had "something to work with." In an attempt to barricade that possibility, at 10:30 the following morning he parked in front of the Yates house in DD's car. Cathy came to the door. "My Pa and Billy are working in the north 440 and my ma took Jennie and my baby brother to town with her. You can come in, if you care ta sit a spell, but I've got chores, and um gonna be goin' out ta the barn real soon."

"Can I come along and watch you at your chores?" He had just gotten to the front porch and placed a Stacy on the first step. She stood partially behind the screen door. "I've never lived on a farm, and it seems one this large would be a lot of work."

"Once you get used to it, it becomes sort of second nature, I guess." She then gave him a shy smile, and took a look back into the house. Looking back to him, she told him, "Sure, come on along. You can follow me out now, if you want."

"Thank you for the invitation." She slammed the door shut, and sprang from the step past him, barefooted.

"I wooda taken you through the house, but the floor's wet. I just got done moppin."

He was walking with and trailing her around the corner of the porch, toward the right side of the house. The night before, she wore a dress. Soame had noticed her beauty and estimated her fineness, judging from the full, not fat or bulging, figure the dress could not conceal.

"I've got ta check the garden, but I don't think any more tamatas are ready yet. Yesterday we got all the ready beans and some tamatas. So what city you from?"

The garden was in back of the house, a short distance off to the right. She had a totally tantalizing, voluptuous figure. The jeans she had on were merely another top layer skin covering. It was all natural, there was no put on with her walk and movement. Like a saucer, two thirds full with water, disturbed with tilting movement and touching the rim from side to side, but never spilling a drop, she moved smoothly and naturally.

"I'm from Florida, you all have real nice summers. This kind of weather is cooler than autumn or spring where I'm from. In Miami, these are like winter days."

They were ten yards from the garden. She stopped. Slowly taking three steps, and leaning towards an extended right foot she told standing Soame, as he watched, "I see one, and there's another one, but they ain't ready yet. They'll wait till this evening or tamorro morning." Turning back to him she told him, "I heard ah Miami, let's go to the barn. We got a nest nobody's found yet. Hen's spose ta be layin in the coop. One's been cackling out hea for the past three days."

In the barn he watched her bend, stoop, squat, and from a kneel with her face on the hay, look under a trough. He could not cover the protruding bulge, without bringing obvious attention to his crotch. He had an erection that throbbed to be enveloped and satisfied. She had taken glances at it for more than five minutes, casually smiled and continued the egg hunt. With her displays Soame saw she did not have a protruding mound. However, where the material tapered into her cleavage, she was fully stacked, with a fine gap, that left her thighs totally separated at all times.

He looked into that gap as she went up the ladder into the loft. Soame seldom lusted, but he ached to have the violently pulsating hard-on he had relieved.

The possibility of his intent wasn't too overbearingly blatant, but all along they conversed through a variety of topics that included a discussion on bitter-root, the state flower, and mangos, a luscious tropical fruit. She was bending over, looking between two bales of hay, for a nest on the floor, between the hay and the back wall. He stood six or seven feet, directly behind her. Still talking, she remained bent, and began backing up. He was not about to move, unless the floor collapsed. She backed into him, and contact was made against his jutting rod.

Without turning, she placed her hand on the extending spot and told him, "I think I found a nest mister, it feels like one anyway."

She was beginning to turn around and he took her opposite arm and assisted in the completion of the turn. When they were face to face, peering into each other's eyes, he asked, "Do you know what you're doing?" Her eyes were as green as pine needles. The hand on his crotch rubbed, grinned, and pawed. "I live on a farm mister, I know when times are right."

"Call me Soame, and what if your folks come home?"

Unbuckling his belt, she told him, "Ma won't be back till past noon, ta fix pa's lunch, and they won't be out of the fields till maybe one. They left, maybe thirty minutes befo' you drove up. People from the city talk aright and good, wanna look for some more eggs?"

His zipper had already been taken down, and she clung to him like a cat climbing a tree, lavishly sinking her tongue into his mouth. They both began tugging and pulling each other's clothing until they had each other's pants down.

She was a real wildcat in the hay. They started in the missionary position, and moved into doggie style. Soame could not help but notice her familiarity in getting into the positions. She moved her body with firing ease, accepting his measure with returning circles of thrusts and rolls, twitching as they tugged. With the experience she had, she was good. Her body was very pleasing, and she gave it to fulfill them both. She was not multi-orgasmic, and enjoyed the thrill involved with the toil. Soame waited for her, moving her into positions, for a comfortable release, which he was not going to deny. She worked effortlessly and feverishly.

The pants were then placed on two stacked bales of hay where she sat, allowing him into her with rotating pressing action that swiveled deeper with each swooshing stroke. He was standing into her sitting position. Cathy slung and humped to retain the placement of the measure she had lost during the transfer. She swung her hips at the instrument in her in a ringing, rolling hump, with bounces. With her fingers laced behind his neck, her arms stretched and her head thrown back, she appeared to be listless, but the lower part of her body had a continuous rhythmic move, that presented no doubt of her liveliness. When he cupped and squeezed her breast, she became verbally alive and locomotive with her lower body.

She told him how long she had waited and how desperate she had become. Last night when she saw him she knew he was the man of her dreams. When he squeezed both her nipples, she released her laced fingers and flopped back crying out, "Oh god! Please, Soame, fuck me forever. Please don't stop." Her propelled, synchronized, humped and swung rotations were slung, rolled and twitched so rapid, she appeared to be on her back in a shivering gyration, spinning with circular movement as her lower body revolved in a reel. She screamed with his swell and as they came they flooded. They moaned and groaned until they both knew the other had totally subsided. It was an incomparable sexual experience to the likes he had never before encountered.

Without separation, they kissed and had an intimate conversation. They kissed petted and toyed with each other through embraces, feels and rubs, until they felt his rise within her. Knowing it would be a lengthy encounter, he told her he would not take the chance on being discovered. Her pants were soaked, so she got up, removed them, kicked – with a push – the top bail off the stack. She sat again on the pants, orally satisfying them both. He then told her of a plan for his next visit; neither wanted to do without the other until then. It was rich, it was vibrant, and between them, it was totally alive.

When the remainder of the family came home, with Thad and Billy following Mrs. Yates and Jenny by ten minutes, they found Soame on the front porch enjoying a tall glass of lemonade. Cathy prepared the first one and because of the rattling ice, Mrs. Yates invited him to a refill. She had noticed her daughter marveling at Soame. Her last impulse, was in disturbing the exhibited continuity between them. He was older, true enough; however, she knew her daughter and respected her feelings. Soame had given Cathy twenty-five dollars. This was more money than she had ever received on any occasion. His address to Thad was direct and simple. Thad had talked freely in the presence of his family the night before. Soame had no reservations toward his expressions in the same atmosphere.

"I'm not a farmer, and will not experiment with the outlay of money, for the purpose of trying to learn how to use equipment I've never before come in contact with, and grow crops I know I can't raise beyond sprouts. You have explained your problems, and I understand what you have stated as management techniques you wish to implement for future stability, growth, and development, with a sound profit."

Each of them wondered at that point, where he was going with what he had to say, and hoped it would be beneficial to them. This excluded Cathy, who caught her mother's look in her direction, and emphatically motioned her head in an instant saying "Yes. Something good." In the same manner, her mother responded to her, with her eyes "Faint." Only the two of them saw and did this; Soame went on.

"I will not buy all your land, instead, if you will accept my proposal, I will accept half for $3000 and I ask for four-hundred of the seven-hundred prime acreage you've mentioned. I will pay you the sum in cash, and ask you to farm my half with yours as a co-op, which will make us as a cooperative partners, equally diving the profits from my half."

It was the answer to their prayers, and far better than any dream they could have conceived in light of their totally desperate situation. Not only would they not lose their home and farming equipment, the sale afforded them all their land and cash to operate with. Even Billy seemed pleased and smiled. The night before he'd seen Soame return looks to his sister, and attempted to be hostile with him until his father regressed his motivations. He was the first one in the spellbound and completely overwhelmingly surprised family to speak, "Paw, you said he'd be alright, and would come through." He then turned back to Soame, extending his hand.

Because he knew and felt their needs, Thad was given a thousand dollars there on the spot and the papers were signed. The remaining two thirds would be paid when the official papers were signed, which remained to be drawn up by a legal representative. He was a miracle worker to them. They all danced around in a circle and cheered.

As he was about to leave, Cathy said to him, loud enough so everyone else could here, "When you come back Mr. Hudson, would you mind giving me a ride in that beautiful new car?"

"Kathleen, you know better than th – "

"Pardon me Mrs. Yates, but I'd be happy to, if you and your husband don't object."

They both said at once, "Oh, no. No objections at all."

"Call me Soame. I'd be pleased to, and I'll stop by again next Wednesday evening, if it's a proper time for you."

Then as a surprise to them all, including Soame and Cathy, Jennie shouted out to him, "Can I go too Soame?" He nodded consent to Cathy's baby sister, and with a wave, got into the Seville, and was gone.

At home, the women were encountering what seemed to be problem after problem: DD and Camille got along beautifully, as did the younger set. Then the discussion of living under one roof became more than a probability. Camille had plans to move anyhow. Her son Richard would be spending two weeks of the summer with friends in the country, until mid-July. The issue remained and revolved around arrangements, which were presented for his decisions and approval. The matter concerning all of them living together was totally settled because DD had the larger house and it was the preferred housing for them all. The next issue was whether or not Camille's furniture should be brought over with their other belongings. The issue arose due to the fact DD had only purchased furniture to completely furnish one bedroom. The living room, dining room, and kitchen were all partly furnished. The question imposed toward the situation, was how to furnish the unfurnished rooms, and the remaining partly unfurnished sections of the house.

Certainly, the Johnsons going and transporting goods and materials everyday, throughout the day, was or scene to be avoided. Therefore, the simple choice had to be made from two solutions: rent a truck and move all of Camille's possessions, including furniture, over to DD's or 2) since new furniture was available at almost giveaway prices, buy and stock the house, leaving Camille's house and furniture as it was.

Soame physically displayed great concern toward the "turmoil and complexity" involved with the matter. He thought to himself how ridiculous it was, knowing he or DD would not hurt Camille's feelings, to not accept her furniture. He was positive DD felt the exact way, but was air like toward feelings. Margaret and Beverly watched her while she explained.

Chairly was laid back in the lazy boy, with her sunglasses on, listening to music from the stereo through headphones. Seeing her and Margaret in shorts and sheer sleeveless blouses with no bra, he began to become aroused. Knowing this, in a sporting way, because the girls were looking, DD teased. Gesturing and in an alluring fashion, she repeatedly exposed herself to him, while explaining the "problem." Had he not been soiled with the scent from earlier activities he would have reacted to her lure. Because he felt he reeked with his and Cathy's dried love juices, he instead chased Chairly from his chair. He then looked at the legs, crotches, and breasts standing around him. He could not help but notice the beautiful women tauntingly tantalizing the hardening tool they all saw with a bulging rise.

It was then he discovered the "real" problem: earlier, Camille had come by to have lunch with her, after which they walked several blocks to see the mansion. This was the first encounter DD had with either hearing of or seeing the most grand sight in the town. She had been totally captivated with fascination, simply viewing the exterior of the site. When Camille opened the huge double doors, she was thunderstruck and breathless. The large garden, shaded trees, and lawn, though it had not been recently done, all had her in a trance. Walking into the interior further pushed her into a complete state of total astonishment.

A sunken living room, almost as large as the house they were living in, marble floors, mahogany walls, and a fireplace she could almost walk into. She attempted to describe and explain the house, becoming breathless. As if they hadn't noticed and to get his attention, Chairly was standing between the two sisters. She nudged each of them, indicating their attention to the plain view of the erection he had. It was totally unconcealed, and even the trace of the circumcised head was vivid beneath the Levis. He laid sprawled back in the chair, pretending to be totally in tune to what was being said. They all knew what had to be on his mind. DD at that point pretended to ignore the unmistakable sign of his readiness.

She went on about the screened heated pool and how the place could be theirs for a fraction of what it cost to build it. Suddenly, the French rolled into, "except for the visit to the grand house, I've been with the girls all day, it could not have been either of us, and Camille was with me touring the place. Where have you been Suarme?"

The girls started giggling. She hurried him up, in a sitting position by his arm, saying, "Come with me, you need a bath. I will share my bubble bath with you now." Chairly flopped back into the chair, and reached for the head phones, while he was being lead away.

"But it was you DD, who said we would only be seeing places like we've seen before an – "

She interrupted with "But Darlinngggg, I am but a woman. It is a woman's right to change her mind."

"Then have you changed your mind about your love for me?"

She splashed sudsy water into his face, and leaped into his arms, saying, "Never Suarmeeee, never my Darlinnggggg, never."

He had always only taken showers. They had not before made love in the bathtub. DD delighted in the fact that it was the first time since meeting the Johnsons she had sex with him, and did not have to share with either Camille or Margaret.

Chapter 12

SAMUEL Stribbs, for a considerable while, had been an acquaintance of Soame. In fact, it was Congressman Stribbs who sent Soame the information concerning the SBA, when he wrote to him about setting up a small business. The distinguished statesman had been chairman of the Ways and Means Committee. Soame had only seen the senior congressman once, when he visited Tampa, Florida, the representative's district. They later discussed Soame's hail from the crowd, yelling "Sam!! Sam!!" while he rode along in the parade procession during the gala, annual festival known as Gasparilla. Stribbs rode in an open convertible, sitting on the back seat and trunk separation, waving and throwing various colored roses toward hordes of people cheering him as he passed.

Since then, with the retirement of Lawton Chiles, Stribbs had become the senior statesman from the "Sunshine State." Camille was rapidly becoming secretary and bookkeeper for Worldwide Conservation and Energy, Corp. During the evening, Soame had written a letter. Camille typed the letter the following day, and with his signature it was sent to the congressman in Washington, D.C. Since Stribbs was always prompt with his replies, Soame had confidence he would receive an expedient response.

The letter simply extended salutations and advised the representative he had relocated. Its purpose in stating then he was in Smath, Montana setting up business practices was for purposes of legal representation. Naturally, there were local inquiries; Soame asked for his political recommendation; someone he knew to be directly affiliated with the Democratic National Committee. Soame asked for his recommended choice as soon as possible because he had a business deal in operation, which was a simple merger. He needed legal representation to close it.

Passing by the office that day, he also found out that the Sheriff and Mrs. Tillman – the owner of the office – were lovers. "She's a widow and his wife very seldom comes out." In a very flauntingly gay way, Camille went on, "Oh Soame, everybody knows it." It was near 3 o'clock. He stood at the window, looking at them ride off in the patrol car. She was gone for the day, and had asked Camille to close up.

Unknowingly, Soame's function then was to aid Camille in her deepest and most long awaited fantasy. The door was locked, and after the blinds were adjusted, he sat on her desktop facing her chair. She took him in her mouth from a seated, working position behind her desk. He enjoyed enabling her unrestrained, exorbitant imagination. There was another function for endeavor toward her fulfillment. In the basic missionary style, she was extravagantly wild across the desk. When it was over, she confessed, "Every time I sat at that desk, I wanted to be fucked like that, thank God you came along."

Soame started circulating money in the town and area. Those who were left, were packing when he arrived, or at least they had immediate plans. Had he not come when he did, by the fall of the year the town would have been deserted. Mrs. Tillman had already told Beauford, "I can no longer afford to keep the office open. Paying her during the two week notice is the most I can do, with hope for the both of us." The day Soame came to town, at the close of that day, she was supposed to have received her notice. Her exact situation was dire at that time; even with the pittance of a salary without commissions, she hardly knew where her next meal would come from. Like so many others, she attempted to "give" her home and property away, at $1500. Within two months, she dropped the price to $650 and no one as much as proposed at making an offer. She was living month to month though her alimony and child support checks. Each month through and until the next, she prayed the checks would not be late.

The bit of money he'd put into circulation, encouraged the people in the area to give more effort toward the idea of surviving just a little longer. It kept the hope alive that "something would materialize." He did not know because the realization had not set in on him; everybody in the town and area knew he was there. The idea about the jewelry box "factory" caught on, and spread like wildfire. The people, hearing about it, gained a little more faith, and somehow, for that reason, had a possible inspiration to hold their homes a little longer. They still wanted to call Smath "their" community.

The helper on the furniture truck had been a regular employee at the combination hardware and furniture store for seven years. Three months prior to Soame's arrival, the salesman was laid off. It was the second time he had been called to work since then. DD purchased two sets of bedroom furniture. One was used in the converted library. The living room was completed and DD decided to leave the dining room as is because he told her he would buy the house for her – the mansion – if it became available, and if the town did not fold up. There were throw rugs scattered about every room, and bean bags all over the house. In the master bedroom, which Camille shared with them, there was an additional entertainment center. The room was basically the gathering spot for all of them.

Chairly and Beverly found a friendship which made them inseparable at times. Margaret displayed the same type of attitude toward DD, but it was generally known that Soame had won her heart. She would not outrightly compete with her mother and especially DD. Competition wasn't necessary because he never overlooked any of them. They all got along well. The family group had increased in size, and became more alive with pleasure and understanding. Each one sparking or igniting an ingredient to the other.

With there being no school in progress, there was quite a bit of leisure time at the house. The place was exceptionally clean when it was purchased, and with six females, each assigned to an area, the upkeep was relatively simple, especially with DD doing the inspecting. The day after the arrival and placement of the additional furniture, Soame stopped by the store and ordered a half-sized deep freezer.

Fifi became everyone's pet. Her price was relatively inexpensive at times: a rub, a pet, a simple name call, and she was ready for a frolic. Though she gave favor at all times to DD, when Soame was around, she shared her time in places near him without a rub or pet. They established a connection of sorts wherein when both were at home they were always in sight of each other. This brought them comfort in their companionship. A few times he had let her out, to do her "business," then watched her as she romped about.

During the week, he visited the farm twice. He advised the men of making a sound job out of what they were doing. He told them, "Break your necks in a rush to complete the job, and you'll have nothing else to do when it's finished." They all understood, and seemed to be satisfied earning a wage while doing something that showed promise. He had two prototype boxes coming in, but it was really Pete who kept their morale up and peaking. He related to them as one of their own and there was no difficulty at all in them seeing what Soame was attempting at setting up. The two who worked in North Carolina, added fuel to the fire. Soame did not know that talk, behind his back. It was Pete, who called to him the last day he was there that week, "Don't worry about work. There'll be plenty of that once those boxes get here and we get things arranged."

"You all just go on and close out the week, start your regular day Monday, and I'll be back out to see ya before Wednesday." It was mid-afternoon Thursday. He had posted a deposit at the hardware-furniture store while buying the freezer. Anything they needed for supplies and materials was available or could be ordered. He had not chosen a foreman. Climbing into the car he told them,

"Remember, safety is always first. You all have a good weekend. If you need me contact Camille Johnson." Each of them had earned and been paid their first week's pay. The agreement was that the taxes and withholdings would be deducted in six weeks, as he told them, "A liberal amount weekly, until you're caught up." They were establishing a bond. The mutual feeling was that all they had to do was stay with each other. He waved goodbye and drove off.

Camille and her daughters were basically "city girls." Some phases of city life they had practically forgotten about, after living in the small, country, farming town, for a while. DD was not reluctant in setting up an atmosphere for what turned out to be an all weekend pajama party. At one point, Soame hooked up four speakers to one turntable and they all almost blasted the building away with their favorite records.

Near noon Saturday, Soame and his household all went into a conference. It was the first assembly of the sort between them. The purpose was to bring them all into focus, and lay them abreast and totally aware of what was happening. The two groups were merging as one family living under one roof. Camille's thirteen-year-old son Richard was not present, but with his return from his vacation he was also a member of the family. Margrett was old enough to make her own decision about the matter. However, the law considered Beverly a minor. Though she was with her mother, Soame asked both daughters their choice in the matter. He made it perfectly clear as an option, he would finance their fare with pocket money to their father. Only they could give him their choice on the matter. Both easily elected to stay. Margrett stated, "He's remarried and will not have us, but I would not leave my mother or you anyhow Soame."

In accepting their decision, he then accentuated the fine points of honesty, trust and the value of understanding. Soame also brought their attention to alcohol and drugs and its usage in his house. He also covered the factor of discussions with outsiders – "Non family members" – concerning what went on in the house, within "our" family. He spoke directly to Beverly, who was not allowed to smoke the pipe. She had previously been cautioned. When school began, she could only use alcohol on the weekends. He was not abusive, nor was he lenient. He told them "Anything any of you wanted or gave the slightest hint of wanting, I have provided for you. I will not change toward you. Half of you will be going to school in two months. Enjoy yourselves, relax, spend the money I give you. I'll provide the clothes and other necessities. I simply ask you to respect me as the head of this family, yourselves in being a part of this live and functioning group, and the rules I've stated to you, which you've shown no objection for."

Shortly, they got back into the groove of their normal activities. Beverly imitated Chairly, strolling around in their sunglasses, as celebrities avoiding autograph seekers. They played many other private games with one another and Soame told jokes. Among the other varieties of fun they had, music was always playing in the background. The Johnsons brought many records from Minneapolis. Lara Branigan's, *Glori*a, nevertheless, the first record Margrett bought, after arriving in the small town they all went wild over the tune and played it repeatedly all weekend.

The construction of Worldwide Conservation and Energy, Corp., grew to be the largest responsibility Camille had at the real estate office. In accordance with procedures, she had filed for a local tax ID number. Other certified documents also had to be obtained from Helena, for the company to be legally recognized in Montana. This was an addition to the real beginning in paving the way.

Tuesday brought the delivery of the freight from southern Colorado. Margaret and Beverly had no idea, and never would know per se, of DD's profession. She and Camille had discussed her siren activities to a certain extent. No one knew as much about her past as Soame, who advised her, "Some of the things you've done, are best kept between you, me, and the bedpost." Camille told her once, "There were a few girls at business college, who earned their way through school on their backs. I almost tried it a couple of times, but could never muster up the nerve."

The story revealed to the girls was one of many incidents that had taken place in DD's life. She was a famed name in New Orleans. She once performed in a Burlesque show before the largest audience ever assembled in the city's history. When the clothes arrived, they were all surprised, almost shocked, to see the exotic array of clothes, costumes, and undergarments. It was more than they really expected, especially the dozens of minis, micro minis, and sensuously fabricated, form-fitted dresses. After searching through all the boxes, and not finding what she looked for, Beverly, with an inquisitive look on her face, approached the one she most admired, asking, "Where are the ostrich feathers DD?"

It was two years before, during Mardi Gras. During a concert in the Super Dorm, "Miss Dubanee," under powder blue and pink flood lights, was seated in a Roman styled love seat, when the curtain slowly lifted. She was dressed in a light aqua body stocking, that glittered with rhinestones. The stones were bunched around the nipples of her breast and at the vertex of her legs. She had huge ostrich feather fans, blended with white and beige feathers. DD, "Miss Dubanee," did an electrifyingly exotic, enchanting and alluring dance for nearly fifteen minutes. The fans brought men to the edge of the stage in groves and waves. Security had to stop the show. She had to be ushered from the stage surrounded by police. Her reply to the curious and approbative Beverly was, "My dear the fans are very valuable, and to me they were precious. My former landlady was also a friend of mine. I left them with her, as a token of my esteem. As you see, they would have been crushed and ruined had we tried to bring them."

That afternoon Soame was out at the farm house, with the two boxes. One was a dresser and mirrored back combination; the other one was designed as a china cabinet. They were exact duplications of colonial style furniture, except they were smaller in size. Presenting the cedar wood crafted boxes, Pete Thompson made sure everyone hear him state, "I was pretty sure that was what you were talking about, but I didn't want to give myself away. We made those at Holman, when I was in the 'joint' in Alabama, back home." The next day Pete started as foreman, with a $25 raise per week. He knew practically every conceivable design there was in relation to the type and style boxes Soame had. Soame stood listening to Pete rattle off for more than twenty minutes, about this type and how that type carries a secret compartment, and the oblong box having more shapes and sizes than any other type box, and how the rope jewelry holders are made, and so on. A couple of the carpenters walked off scratching their heads. Others spat tobacco juice so close to Pete's foot, the splotches caked on his shoes. No matter what, they knew he'd be their "straw boss."

All the men had a basic idea of what would be entailed in setting up an assembly line toward manufacturing the product. With the prototypes the experienced carpenters saw the idea as elementary; it was a revolutionary idea. The mention and hope of the idea would further carry throughout the area. They were in timber country. Nothing since the town was founded would have such great impact to keep its remaining people together. The idea had been brought forth, but they still had a ways to go.

The RV had gotten to be Soame's regular mode of transportation. When he drove into the yard at home, the car was absent. Seldom did he arrive home, and not find DD there. This time, the door was not locked and no one greeted him. He called out, "Is anybody here?" Walking through the living room, he received the response, "I'm in here Soame, come on in. I want you to meet someone." It was Margaret. Her room was the converted library. She invited him in from her room. He walked in and opened his eyes to a big surprise. "Soame meet Muff. We've looked everywhere for him. He usually only stays gone only for a couple of days. I guess it took him extra time to find us, since we've been over here." While Margaret talked, she pointed toward the bed. There, sprawled out on both pillows, was one of the largest Calicos he had ever seen.

The huge black, yellow, and white cat looked as if he weighed at least twenty pounds. It gave Soame a casual glance, before licking its paw. Soame was slightly startled. Muff's glance seemed to be saying, "Hello feller, as Margaret's told you, I'm Muff, and I live with the Johnsons. As a matter of fact you can call me Muff Johnson, got it?"

In a white cotton summer dress, Margaret then got into the center of her bed. She sat Indian style cross legged, in the lotus position. Sitting directly facing him, she clearly exposed a perfect view of her dark blue undies. Reaching over, pulling Muff from the head of the bed, further enhanced Soame's view; they were bikini's, with finely designed lace along the edges. Resuming the comfortable position, she rubbed and stroked the tortoise shell cat gently. "We've had him since he was a kitten. Everyone this side of town knows him cause he's the most popular pet in town. We've never had a dog, or any other type of pet, only Muff." A big hum suddenly came audible; it almost vibrated the room. Muff had a loud purr to match his large stature. "When mother came home early from the office, DD offered to take us all for a drive." She then looked Soame directly in the eyes, smiled, shied away, then with a slow sensuous motion, licked her lips shyly bringing her sight back to his. Capturing his eyes once again, she eased her vision to his crotch, saying, "I didn't want to go. I was sitting on the porch when, from no where he simply walked up. Oh Muff, where've you been?"

Because of his size, it took a little exertion to haul him back to the pillows. "I was about to go through some of DD's things in the basement. She said I could. Would you like to accompany and join me there Soame" she asked, leaving the open display at his sight.

He laughed to a roar, held her in his arms, and gently, with ease, lifted her from the bed. He brushed a swift kiss, streaking a pucker on her forehead. "From what I've seen of your proposal, wouldn't this be a more appropriate place? This is our house you know."

"But the others may soon come back my love, and I will not want to be disturbed." Not mentioning locking the door, he conceded to her desire in asking, "Shall we take some refreshments?"

"If you will, it will be a double treat and pleasure for the both of us."

They walked through the door, leaving Muff content on the bed.

The following day, coming out of the realty office, he met the Sheriff. Beauford stood perhaps an inch, no more than a inch and a half shorter than the man under the Stetson. The town and it's surrounding areas were his greatest, and always his immediate concern. Three years prior to that time he had twelve deputies. Some moved, a couple simply quit, and because of the continued depreciation of the county's budget, his force was reduced to three uniformed deputies and a radioman.

Reappropriation of federal funds had been applied for, through the local government, but because of the continued depreciation of the population, everyone felt the quarter of a million dollar grant would not be approved. By September or October at the very latest, the town like nearly a hundred others of it's size throughout the region, would fold up. By the holidays, tumbleweeds would be rolling in the streets. Beauford knew, this man and this man alone, who approached him, might have the key to the survival and success of his town.

"Soame Hudson I've heard about the arrival of your scale model boxes, and I'd like ta talk with ya about that floor space you mentioned the day you arrived."

They extended hands to each other. Both wore their glasses beneath their hats, and Soame wore a long sleeved white on white shirt, with a clearly visible sleeveless undershirt.

"Yea Sheriff, they came a few days earlier than I expected actually, but Pete Thompson say's he's done hobby craft before, and they all agree, setting up assembly line procedures may not be too difficult." It was quite serious and informative for the both of them, toward progress from each direction, with a matter of fact approach. "Of course now, that's only one of the involvements of the first step in production. There are other steps involved with marketing, which include sales and distribution. These make the finer and key points toward the success of the operation." Beauford began slowly easing his hand to the back of his head. His hat slightly tilted toward the front as he gently rubbed and scratched. Though hardly noticeable, there was a care-free swaying rock, as he continued to listen. "Nevertheless, we're in progress because somehow I've been really lucky in being able to get immediately, experienced man power, to go directly into operation.

We'll move step by step and hope to progress with each step and move, Sheriff. I do thank you kindly for your help."

"Soame, I have a personal friend. I shared my childhood with him. We both grew up together, right here in this little country town. I was best man at his weeding twenty years ago, and since then he's become the biggest farmer in the area." Even with their sunglasses on, it was eye-to-eye conversation. They both knew exactly what they wanted to say to each other. Each had something else to do, and wanted to be done with the conversation. Also, each was aware of their encounter probably being the most important event, for the both of them, during the course of the day. "Tom Blanchard is his name. I'd consider it a really big favor if you'd stop by to see him before Monday, and if in anyway you can help Tom, in his situation, you'd be helping the both of us. Soame neither of us is the kind of person, who ever forgets a favor." The newcomer was then given directions to the Blanchard Farm. In departing, Soame told him, "I'll see him Friday evening Sheriff."

Mrs. Tillman said, "Hi," as he passed her enclosed glass office. She motioned him to the back, where Camille was busy on the phone. In approaching her desk he heard her say, "But Mr. Merryweather, we're facing a situation here where there is a good possibility that in the next four or five months, there may not be a town called Smath." She then smacked her lips at Soame, and motioned for him to be seated. Her voice resumed over the phone, "More than two thirds of the few who were here this time last year, are gone. The only hope we have is the possibility of some type of new industry which would create an expansion. The request for reapportion has not yet been denied, but with our dwindling figures, no one has any real hope, Sir."

While listening to the voice on the other end, Camille took a sip of water. She responded, "Well, it may sound ridiculous. Even so, I would propose an unrejectable figure, such as $20,000, so he could not refute the undeniable bargain." Soame listened as the voice from the other end roared back. Shortly afterward she replied, "But there are damages now. I have not heard from you in four months. Last week I made a personal visit to inspect the premises and house. We've had a recent wind storm. A huge limb was broken from one of the overhanging trees out back. The limb plowed through the glass and screen, and is now partially submerged in the pool." There was an instant, pause, to see if he would roar back again; he did not, she went on, "That in itself is a large repair and replacement bill Mr. Merryweather, and you know the place has not been maintained for a year and a half, other than us having the lawn done. I called your attention to that outstanding liability along with your listing fee, and you've remained posted." Soame did not hear a sound, but noticed Camille's strict attention, during the interval. "I will be here then, and expect your call, sir. Good day."

When the receiver was placed in the cradle, she told her employer and Soame, "Let's keep our fingers crossed." Crawford Merryweather owned the eight bedroom, extravagantly luxurious mansion. Camille was finally able to trace him down, through his office in New York City. The beautifully huge place had been built less than five years before. Its purpose was to encourage Merryweather's wife to move there with him when he retired. He dealt in stocks and bonds, with a home base set up through the New York Stock Exchange. Following its completion, only his servants occupied the dwelling for two years. She joined him there for six weeks, and could not stand being in the wildernes and never returned. A year and a half prior to the call, he relocated his servants, had the place closed down, and listed it for sale. Camille informed Soame, "Twenty-thousand will not pay for the solid brass, and porcelain furnishings and fixtures in the house. The plumbing is a marvelous set up, but only a tiny featured weaved into the overall grandeur of the building and its presentation as a true mansion. He does now know, without the existence of the town, the structure is useless and totally worthless. For him to scrap twenty-thousand out of it, at this late date, is a very promising offer. I am sure he will sell."

That afternoon, he drove out to the Yates' farm. Cathy was ready to go, but objected because her kid sister Jenny had no right to be "tagging along, ta see what was going on." Soame did not object, and told her he'd already promised Jenny she could ride also. "There I told ya." Jenny said sticking her tongue out at her older sister. Soame promised Thad and his wife that he would have them back by ten. Jenny had been let into the backseat, and when they had driven out of the sight Cathy eased herself over next to him. In doing so, and while throwing a proud, right shoulder look back to her sister, she glimpsed the cassette cartridge, only partially into the player. Before she asked, he told them, "I'm not too familiar with the area, do you know of a pleasant place we can go park, and enjoy the sights?" Jenny then leaned forward and whispered in her sister's ear. Cathy suggested, "the Old Hodgesville Road," and gave him directions. Cathy asked Soame about the tape. It was a Fleetwood Mac tape, and when fully injected the car came alive with their favorite song, *Rhiannon*.

It was plain to see that the sisters were not as disagreeable as they pretended to be at home. When they arrived at the road they were to travel, which would take them deeper into the country, Cathy told him something special. She and Jenny were also best friends. Jenny knew everything she and he did in the loft. She also wanted to know if he objected to Jenny sharing the front seat with them. When he stopped, Cathy was playing with his hard, unexposed meat, and it was obvious she wanted Jenny to witness the activity she engaged in. They traveled the scenic country road for nearly thirty minutes, rocking the car with lively music, talking – sometimes at the top of their voices – laughing, and enjoying the pleasant drive. The road dead-ended at what appeared to be an old deserted farmhouse. "That's the old Hodges Mill. Our parents used to grind corn into meal here, before we were born. We thought you'd like ta see it." Soame had noticed, with strict attention, the attitude and real maturity of the two. He could not help but wonder, if they were really as mature as they projected in the car, or as childish as they seemed in the presence of their parents.

The sun had just began touching down behind the mountains. The sound of the rushing waters, tumbling over the Miller's grind wheel was loud with the fury of falling, uncontrolled, tons of water, roaring louder, with each step they took closer. Cathy yelled to him, "Billy got swept twenty yards downstream, a year or so ago. He fell through the floor one day, when he and little Thad were prowling round up here." Soame had never seen an old fashioned mill before, and looked into the interior. It seemed all the interlocking assemblies were there including the grind wheel. Although the parts were all disassembled, he saw how and why such a creative force was necessary to put the equipment to operation. They were massive pieces of steel and iron, except for the grinding wheel, which seemed to be a gigantic whetstone. He was totally fascinated. The floor was practically all rotted away. The equipment was shelved on the opposite of the building, in a higher structure at least five feet above the rotten floor. Obviously water and air had caused the decay over the years. The water streamed into a twenty foot shoot from a pond. Through the almost bottomless floor, he could see it stream rapidly under the building. At the back of the building it roared, falling twenty five feet, where it carried its force on down the stream.

"It's not safe to go inside, the floor's all rotted out, and it's a ten foot drop ta the rushin' water." Jenny yelled, standing on his right side.

Then Cathy told him, yelling while he leaned in her direction, "We bought it from the Hodges, when they moved away four years ago. It's good land around hea Soame. Pa said last night he might let you have it, as part of your share of the acreage." He hugged both of them in each arm. They simply stood and watched for a while, listening to the thundering sounds from the rushing and falling waters. "I've got a blanket in the trunk, would you two like to sit on it, and talk with me for a while?"

The skies were darkening. They scouted out a nice spot, ten feet from the pond, away from the immediate sound from the mill, and spread the blanket. Soame found fun and delight in talking with the two of them. He answered their questions, about his home state, and how much "schoolin'" he had. They both seemed bright, alert, and totally aware of what was going on around them. They knew about all the other farms that had closed down, and were deserted around theirs. With pride, they discussed theirs being the third largest in the county and the only one that did not have a mortgage or loan on it or their paw's equipment. "Pa never really lost at farmin', but 'cause all the others plowed unda, he was forced ta do it also. He would only break even. Each year we broke even, ma and pa had ta go into the savins, till this year, when it was all gone." Later on, through Thad and Billy, Soame would find out, Tom Blanchard was held responsible for a lot of misfortune in the area: they had carefully calculated a profit margin. Tom did not carry through with his promise on the idea of rotating. Not only the Yates, but also other local planters desperately needed that little bit of profit. Because Blanchard did not rotate, and planted the same crop in the previously planted area, he could not get the yield. Seeing this materializing in his early crop, he elected to plow under for the subsidy. That cut the necessary profit out of the destitute market. In one single year his actions wiped out half the farmers in the county. They were penniless, and even those who were fortunate in somehow breaking even, could not make a full payment on an already overdue mortgage. They could not sustain themselves or their family.

They sat and talked until it was a quarter past nine. Frogs were croaking and periodically they heard a splash, from one springing into the pond. "Have you ever kissed two sisters Soame?"

"Why do you ask?"

"Cause Jenny wants ta kiss you before we leave, and I promised her earlier today. I told her I wouldn't mind if you did."

"She's a bit young, does she know how to kiss?"

Jenny then injected into the conversation, "Sure, me and Cathy practice all the time."

"Jenny!!!" Cathy exclaimed in a disturbingly loud voice of protest. The sound penetrated the atmosphere with such a high shrill, it brought total stillness, except for the rumbling roar of the mill, seventy-five yards away.

There was warmth in the embraces, and he noticed both of their affections in each kiss. They were submissive in being passionate in their touch. To a point, it was he who was unyielding. Aside from being very young, Jenny had been invited along as a guest. Cathy tugged and even wrestled to take his penis out. He would not allow her; she carried her hand into his Levis, which became the height of their sexual activity at the Hodges Mill Pond.

It was shortly before ten. Along the way, Jenny swore she would never tell anything that would ever happened between the three of them. With her older sister sitting in the middle, she leaned over and kissed him good night and went inside. He felt she told the truth when she told him, "I had a real nice time with you and my first ride ever in a Cadillac, Soame. Good Night."

She had only seen it once before, when Billy had some. Some of the kids at school had often talked about it, but that night was the first time Cathy had ever done Cocaine. During the course of the evening, the three of them had smoked two joints. Billy grew it, and shared with all of them. "Soame we never had no 'pot' this good; it's like magic." Cathy was a naturally affectionate person. Being alone with Soame, in front of the house, she went almost compassionately wild with explosive passion. He in no way attempted to stop her this time. She displayed a craving for him he never knew could exist in a woman. "I've wanted all evening, all night, since last week, I wished and prayed for ya Soame. Oh please, you're so big. You're so good. You don't know what ya do ta me. Just let me have it once more. Once more. Oh please, Soame, give it ta me, and I sware I'll be your's forever," she said, among the other sexually influential stirring words and phrases while she stroked, licked, and sucked to her satisfaction.

They sexually enjoyed each other in the car in front of the house for nearly two hours. She totally refused to let him go. "What about your parents," he asked more than twice. "I have a one o'clock dating curfew," she told him the first time. "I told you honey, I'm yours till one. Please don't do this ta me, when I've waited so long," was the second response. "Don't worry, I wont evea get us inta any trouble, baby. Please, my precious Soame, just love me and make me yours." He did not disappoint her. During the last forty-five minutes of the date, he introduced the eight ball to her.

He allowed her to do a one and one, but was smart enough to notice her reaction to the stimulant. The potency of the grass, had already given her a temporary fixation of awareness; cocaine is commonly referred to as "the queen of all highs." Business people all throughout the world use the drug, as a the modern day "yuppie" trend, to "stay on top of things." Cathy found the composure to plead for more lovemaking. She handled the substance well, without falter in audaciousness and docility, exhibiting raw, rural, real, honest feeling toward the person she had truly become mesmerized with passion toward. "If you're gonna give me your love and this kind of loving forever, you'd better get used to spending money."

"What did Benjamin Franklin do ta have his picture on money Soame?"

"He did more than fly a kite, I'll tell you that. Now listen Cathy, this is for you, and I don't want you to go overboard with using this."

"But Soame, I neva had a hundred dollars before."

"I'm not talking bout the money, this coke I'm putting in this bill is yours also."

He knew it would be a fascinating turn on for her, and wished they could spend the night together. In a separate $5 bill, he gave her some for her brother as well. He had her promise to be quiet about it to everyone else, and she would also encourage her brother, through his instructions, not to tell their parents about it. "Soame I'm your woman for the rest of my life, with all the faith and conviction I have in love. I'll always only be yours, and you can depend on that throughout eternity. I got a sister and I ain't gone lie ta ya evva about nothing. I share all I got with Jenny 'cause she really is my best friend um gonna tell her about this and give her some do you mind?"

Soame gave her a bit of the Mauai Wowee and another small portion of the coke. He felt a possibility of disturbance from her parents who could have been annoyed, though they were in front of the house. He enjoyed and very much appreciated her company, but wanted to get her into the house, and promised to be back Friday. Then she surprised him. "I didn't tell you this before, but baby my favorite record is on that tape, I heard it three times already, but Soame please, let me hear it just once more while I have your dick." Soame thought it was the previously mentioned cut. It was not. That was her's and her sister's. Her's alone, by Fleetwood Mac was *Where the Rainbow Ends*.

On the porch, she rubbed his hand in her crotch, while she grinded her body into and on it, while kissing him good night. She did not know, but she must have wondered, if he did not have to return to DD, that night, would Cathy have stolen his heart?

Chapter 13

THE following day Camille closed on one of the best deals she would ever make for Soame. She brought the closing figure of twenty-seven thousand to him for the Merryweather Estate. The house sat on 5 ½ acres of manicured lawn in the heart of town two blocks north of the main road. It had shaded trees multiple gardens, and other attributes, which gave it a classic modern appearance, shared by no other structure within the neighboring three counties. That day, Soame gave Camille $27,000.00 to purchase the land and home, in the name of Ms. D. Dubanee; he was titled as co-owner and overseer.

It was a splendidly happy occasion that evening at the house for him, his ladies, Fifi, and Muff. During their short stay in Rapid City, DD purchased a table lighter costing almost $400. The gold plated, basket-weave pattern lighter, crafted by Dunhill, measured eight and one half inches in length. Sequential indentions carried all four edges, from top to bottom, including the flip top cap. DD was very proud of the present she bought herself. Soame had a pocket Dunhill which introduced her to the quality product. Hers was one inch longer than his erected instrument. She cherished the thoughts and lighter, and relished in and reflected on memories of Soame. He was her only man, her true lover and soul companion.

Chairly and Margrett constantly borrowed and shared the lighter. Privately, DD told Soame of her reason for the lighter and its sentimental meaning to her, so she asked him to purchase one for them. Soame came up with a better solution for them all. During a trip to the hardware section of the furniture store, the day of the house purchase, he bought four bottled canisters of propane gas. He also bought two small fire extinguishers, just in case. They no longer needed the lighter to smoke, if they did not burn the house down.

They celebrated and partied all evening. DD and Camille put on a private show and restricted themselves to his company for two magnificently electrifying hours. Soame then showered, and while having a light, nourishing snack was approached by Chairly. It was not unusual for her to be dressed in clothes that gave her a boyish appearance. She usually wore her sunglasses in the house past nine pm, energetically chewing and popping gum. She had Beverly with her who was in contrasting garb.

Directly after he showered, DD and Camille used the tub, for a relaxing bubble bath. In his robe he went to the kitchen, scooped a healthy portion of his favorite flavor of ice cream into a bowl, and on his return, noticed the remaining three, had left the living room area. Fifi trailed him after lapping some ice cream dispensed in her bowl. He had passed by Margrett's room, when someone leaned out the door and called for Fifi. A few minutes later, under his panama appeared Chairly at the bedroom door. He invited her in.

The chewing gum popping Chairly informed him, "Hay Soame, check dis out man. I mean really, I got som thin I wanna lay on ya man, an iz's real heavy."

"Alright cool, so what's it all about?"

"Yea well, dig it dude, um tired a bein you. I mean, I got dis ole lady a mine and evva day all day long, I gotta hea hur say, 'do it Soame,' 'I love you Soame, Soame dis and dat, can ya dig it?

"Yea I can dig it, you hi kid?"

"Yea um hi nuf ta talk with my ole man, you wanna lisen papa?"

To this point his relationship with Beverly was strictly platonic. This was established and revolved around him being the head of the household, wherein she resided as a member. He was aware of her having a relationship with Chairly, which was turning serious. She was totally aware of him having relationships with all the other members of their family.

Soame got the gist of Chairly's implication and allowed her to have her say. It amounted to her wanting him, to be with him, with her girlfriend. He was not personally inclined toward their desires, except for the involvement of Chairly. However, he would not overlook the exerted efforts toward the presentation of Beverly, who stood just outside the door. When Chairly called her in, Fifi followed her on the leash with the glittering collar. Beverly had ribbons holding her hair on both sides of her head, and behind her sunglasses she wore lipstick and full make up. She had on one of DD's teddies; it was purple and fit her loosely. The hand opposite the leash, held a cigarette holder, containing a lighted cigarette. The garter belt, stockings, and heels seemed almost a perfect fit. They were Margrett's. Chairly locked arms, and escorted her in, with Fifi, gay and lively as ever, leading the way. She stood with one leg slightly extended before the other, and standing back in the anchored leg. Chairly took a step from her, toward him. With a bounce, extending her outstretched arm and hand toward Beverly, Chairly told him, "Dis ma bitch man, we got something ta tell ya." Beverly looked like a hooker on any street corner in America trying to pull a trick. She put the holder to her lips, took a deep drag from the cigarette and exhaled. She flung her head back, looked directly at him, and made a statement in French. Soame looked at Chairly puzzled and asked, "What'd she say?"

"For your service, you may have our autographs."

The master bedroom was not the only lively spot in the house. The party was all over the house all night. Soame was basically stationed in the bedroom, where he was constantly and continually entertained. Shortly after midnight, he once again made his way to the kitchen. This time he asked Margrett to make him a sandwich. She had to cook what he wanted. Her reply to his request was, "Only if you'll have it in my room, when it's ready." After entering the room with the bacon, cheese, and lettuce sandwich, she locked the door.

Camille arrived at the office after ten that morning. The money had already been turned over to Mrs. Tillman who would collect realtor's fees, pay commissions to Camille, and forward the balance to Crowford Merryweather. Camille's other responsibility in the office that day was the preparation of the checks for the seven carpenters. They were scheduled to stop by anytime after three.

Before leaving the house that morning, hers as well as everyone else's attention was attracted by an encounter between Fifi and Muff. Even though Fifi was not a year old, and bred as a miniature, she was then almost as tall as Muff. Fifi evidently thought Muff got just a little too close to Chairly while she and Beverly arranged themselves for the oncoming day. Fifi had pranced into the room from the master bedroom. As was her daily routine, she simply wanted to check things out. Muff heard the prancing paws on the hardwood floor, then muffled by the rug, and again on the floor to the doorway. It initially was a simple acknowledgement of presence from all in the room. Entering the room, she took a few paces and relaxed back on her haunches. Beverly wanted to remain in bed. Chairly had a reason for them to be up, and stood at the foot of the bed explaining. Muff, from the corner, swayed to Chairly, and caressingly eased about her legs. Fifi immediately pounced toward the streetwise and skillful Muff, who had intentionally lured her.

One swipe stopped the "arff arffing." But Muff did not expect such fury from such a pretty thing. Realizing she'd been struck, and rather than whimper, she proceeded to attack. The black nose, which had already been precisely struck, and the eyes were the only places Muff had already realized he could hurt Fifi. The nose attack did not phase the charging dog, who bared her teeth, twice Muff's size, in a very serious growl.

Muff was on open ground and swiftly retreated to a better position. There was space under a chair in the corner. He made it under the chair, over the brace and positioned himself boldly, deep in the crevasse. Fifi was less than a foot away when Muff shrieked, bowing into a defensive stand. Chairly swooped the puppy up.

DD scrambled, Camille rushed, and Soame knowing what had taken place, according to the sounds. "Ma Charee" cried the lady of the house, who grabbed the pooch. "Muff, Muff! For Christ's sake, what's gotten into you." Cried the upset Camille who entered the room and saw her daughter standing in the bed pointing toward the corner. Then came the explanations. Beverly simply said, "Well, you know how he is." Chairly explained to DD, "Fifi was standin hea and starded barkin," etc. Soame finally found his way to the doorway, blocked by Margrett in her short nightgown. She was in a comfortable place for his hand to rub and squeeze her cheeks.

When DD padded Fifi's nose with a Kleenex, and found a trace of blood, Soame asked, "Has Muff had his shots?" All the Johnsons looked at him at once, as if to say, "What shots? That's Muff. Muff is our cat and doesn't need shots." No one said anything, Soame pointed to the cat laying on Beverly and Chairly's bed licking his paw and asked again, "Has that cat had shots yet?" All eyes then shifted to the bed to Muff, who seemingly realized he'd become the focal point and looked at Soame as if to say "Now look here a minute feller, I think you are sadly mistaken. First of all, everybody's told you, I'm Muff. Secondly, what the hell are shots?" By that time Fifi was squirming to get to the floor. Camille politely told him, "We never thought of shots, Soame." Then she turned to DD, "I'm so sorry DD, if only–" Soame asked, "Who's the vet?"

They all knew the house they lived in belonged to the town doctor. The doctor who'd taken his place, was a Vietnamese refugee. He did not have a state license. Soame got dressed, drove to the realty office, and after using Camille's keys to enter, called the hospital to locate the nearest veterinarian. The one in the nearest town, had moved several months prior. There was one in Miles City, which was north of them. When he carried the news home, DD elected to travel to the one in Rapid City; she was familiar with the route and wanted to check into the hotel, have lunch, and have Fifi clipped while she was there. She had a house of volunteers to accompany her. This left Soame and Camille at the house alone, until she arrived at work. She was the only one who could not spend some of the money she had.

All the carpenters had been paid by 3:15. While closing the office, she called across the way to Soame, in the car lot, "I'm going home, and get some rest." He was standing at the RV talking with Pete. Two other workers were in on the conversation. "When everybody gets back, tell um I had to go out to Tom Blanchard's place, if I can find my way, will ya?"

"I know Tom, I'll tell DD. See you when you get home." She was waving, then entered her car and drove off.

Thad and Billy were just bringing the tractors in when he drove up. He wanted to see Cathy and wanted to be tantalized by her some more. He knew that she knew he'd be there. "It's Friday, we came in sorta early ta get feedin done, and relax toward the weekend with other chores." Thad climbed down from the big International and they approached each other, and shook hands. "Thanks to you Soame, we can see a future in our own place." He began beating the dust out of his hat with his bandana. "We'll just have to see how things work out, Thad. I hope we all can make it from this point." Soame then began telling him about being en route to the Blanchard Farm.

Cathy and Jenny could only tell him a small portion of what the Blanchard issue was about. Thad gave him his opinion on how stubborn and stupid Tom Blanchard had been. He had been totally reckless with an idea they all had carefully put their heads together to come up with. Yet Blanchard was forced to get another mortgage; Thad got stuck in the predicament Soame met him in, and many farmers simply lost out. "If you see him, it won't do any good, if you're thinking bout helping him. He's the biggest farmer around here. He'll have to work with us to get fair prices. He pretty near ruined us all. Lot a good men lost their places and had to move their families, because he's stupidly stubborn. You bail him out and he don't go according to plan this time, it'll wipe out every farmer in the county, and some others in nearby areas. Soame, you be very careful in what you do now."

"Thad, the first thing I learned about business is the meaning of the word itself. Experience taught me how to apply the word 'business' and its true meaning to terms such as outlay, income, and profit. I don't have any experience at farming, like I told you, but I've paid a hell of a price in learning to manage what I have. I can't afford to lose right now in anything I invest. I'm gonna be watching this guy closer than you've advised me to, partner. I want to see what he has to say about what's happened, and what he plans to do in the future. I'll evaluate what he says, and use the information and advice you've given me in the evaluation. Respect is the most I can give either of you. All I really expect and want from either of you is respect. I will not disrespect my money. I will not purposely allow anyone to make that infringement. I will do any and everything possible to stop the trespass. Thanks for the information and advice. Let's see what happens from here, Thad." They shook hands robustly.

He had spent the day at home until 2:45. Camille was with him from 11:30 – 1:00. He had a short while to be to himself and do small things like shine his shoes and brush his hat, while listening to particular tunes. He liked the Stacys he had on they were beginning to break in to a totally comfortable fit and wear. The denims were showing signs of wear and tear. In Montana, during the summer, temperatures dropped to the mid and low 50s. Over the light sweater next to his undershirt, Soame had on his car coat. The Stetson topped it all.

"Cathy probably knows you're out here, I'll send her out, if ya want a see her Soame." Brushing the dust from his overalls, Thad smiled and started walking toward the house. "Thanks, I'd appreciate that, Thad."

"Give me five man," the youngster said walking up, with a chuckle. Soame slapped the extended open palm.

"Where'd you get the snow?"

"Here and there. It shows up in some of the strangest places sometimes. I hear you've got a green thumb with reefer."

"Yea, but what I've been growin ain't nothing like the pot you gave Cathy. Man you've got the best drugs ever past through these parts. I heard you and the ole man talking bout Tom Blanchard. Hell, that's how he got rich and why he don't know nothing bout farmin'."

They both saw Cathy coming out of the backdoor, and before it closed Jenny was behind her. "Billy you gonna help me feed up?" Little Thad was going out to the hog pen.

"I've got something for you, but it's in the RV, if you can come out to it with me."

"Thad junior you go and start feedin, I'll be right back to help and finish up." He shouted to his younger brother, while he and Soame walked toward his sisters.

The motor home was adjacent and to the right of their approach. The boy then grumbled and kicked dirt up while continuing on to the pen. He glanced over his shoulder at his older brother. Though he got more attention than anyone else, as the youngest member of the Yates Family, Thad junior felt always left out in real matters of concern.

After greeting Cathy and Jenny, they strolled to the coach; Soame was holding Cathy's hand. He told Billy the importance of not allowing anyone else to know about the "merchandise." He also told him it was not for sale, it was his personal stash. He would share some with him but under no circumstance was he to let his parents find out. "If any questions come up about me walkin' out here ta the RV with ya, I'll just tell um I've never seen the inside of one before, and I asked you to show me. Thanks buddy, you don't have ta worry. You can depend on me, and I'll keep these two busy mouths quiet for ya too."

"William Yates you just shut that blabber mouth of yourin, it's the biggest and busiest mouth around these parts," Cathy retaliated.

Soame gave him an ounce of the "girl," from New Orleans, and a small portion of the dwindling "weed." He was about to climb down from his "inspection" of the RV, when Soame told him, "Tell your folks we're just riding off a short ways, and won't be gone for long."

After finding out Billy grew herb, Soame sensed he was "hip" and knew of the local drug scene in the area. He always presented himself as someone who stayed in tune with his surroundings. He would be far better as a source for the activity Cathy was restricted to have knowledge of, because of her being a female, without liberty to circulate as her older brother. Soame had taken a bit of a chance in sending him the drugs, but the hunch paid off; the effort was well worthwhile. Soame knew men and always took notice of the character and personality of any man he met. Billy was a rare kind of white boy. He did not need to be under his father's roof with his dad nearby or in the company of other family members to display disapproval and resentment. On a one-on-one basis, with odds against him, he'd speak up and his courage would prevail. That was Soame's opinion in "sizing" him up, the reason for giving him the ounce. The information Billy gave him aided him immensely. Soame was able to find out there had been a drug flow in the area. Through that flow, a person had gotten rich enough to elevate as top seed in the local industry. On top of that, not only was it the person he was en route to see, but also he had a direct approach.

They had driven to and parked along one of the hedge rows of the Yates' nearby fields. Other than saying "Hello Soame," when he and Billy met toward the RV, Jenny did not say a word. Along the way Cathy maintained a lively conversation on how her day was spent. She excitingly made gestures and used gestures she knew were pleasingly arousing to him, though they had not been in physical contact. As soon as the vehicle was brought to a halt, and the hand brake was applied, she was all over him with kisses that smothered him with delight.

He was polite toward Jenny; showing his consideration openly, he asked casually about her younger sister, who sat in one of the seat-chairs behind them. "Why's your sister so quiet? Jenny, is there a problem of some sort? What's the matter?"

Cathy told him, "Oh she's suppose ta be in love, and I told her I would only share so much of my man at a time." She had unzipped his fly and was about to openly expose his tool.

"Hold on, I'm interested in finding out more about the situation here." He'd barely finished when Jenny leaned to the opposite side of his seat sobbingly calling him

"Oh Soame" and smothering him with a lavish kiss. "Here, take a hold of a handful of this, since you're up here." Cathy directed her hand to his exposed and erect dick.

Other than an occasional glance at her baby brother's, when he was an infant, Jenny had never before seen a male's sex organ. She had a shy, snatch back, hesitant touch and feel approach to holding the rod her hand had been planted on. He surmised in fact, before that moment that she had never before come in contact with one. He could feel the her breath rapidly increase. Then the limpness of her watery kiss. What he did not know, but had a general idea of, was that neither of them had never gone out with a black man before. At fifteen, she was three inches shorter than her sister. Her bra size had developed beyond the pre-stage of maturity and progressed to the size above the training bra. She was a bit more softer than Cathy, but she wasn't as filled out. They shared the same soft, reddish brown, textured hair. Jenny's came to her shoulders.

"Hold on. I think since we have the room we should go to the back and discuss this." Soame suggested, taking hold of the situation.

"Talk as much as you care to Soame Hudson, but um first, you're havin me first, and that's the way it's gonna always be with the three of us. You're my man, and she's just joinin' us." Cathy was very serious, and there was no doubt between them. She had pulled her dress over head by the time she finished talking. She threw it to the side, and had her finger pointed to the tip of Jenny's nose, and asked, "Do ya understand what um sayin?" Jenny was casual and appeared to be familiar with her sister's personality and displayed no fear. In addition, she did not show aggressiveness, she simply looked back, returning her sister's stare. Cathy did not have on a bra, and looked very pleasing standing in her white flats and pink panties. Soame rubbed his hand over the material, squeezing her cheeks, and licking the nipple of her left tit.

"How about that idea of us going to the back?" Cathy took his jaws, squarely in both her hands, looked him briefly in the eyes, and stuck her tongue into his mouth, as hard and as far into his mouth as the twirling tongue wrestle would allow. The multiplex radio was in tune to the pioneer radio station in the state. Throughout the state there are only ninety-five radio stations. The signals carry with relative ease because the bands and frequencies are not crowded. KFBB fed in with a totally clear signal; Johnny Rivers was on, singing *Memphis*.

After holding them almost breathless, gulping inhalations only through their noses, for the duration of the record, she retracted. Looking him directly in his eyes, while they both almost gasped for breath, she told him, "Soame, I know you got a family of women in town, but I love you and take you as my man. I'll go anywhere you tell me ta go, and I'll do anything you say, when you say do it, if ya just don't eva leave me or walk out on me. I'll always be nobody else's, only yours Soame. I swear I love you." Jenny then told him, "Me too Soame, I love you the same way."

They had been in the back of the motor home for thirty minutes. On occasion Jenny had drunk some of the berry wine her father made. Cathy had gone out on dates and brought back some beer, or at times Billy would leave some in the truck, knowing she liked it. That day she received her first drink of hard liquor; Soame gave it to her. Jenny also smoked nearly a third of a joint, and watched her sister ride Soame's rod, from the sitting position, in his lap. Twice before, she had sneaked a look, watching her sister with "Boys, who hardly knew what to do." Looking at them in the coach was not spying. Cathy loved sex with a driving, impulsive passion. When her climax began, she called her sister to her, and kissed her lovingly, until the totally explosively eruptive orgasm was finished. Soame did not ejaculate. Jenny kept on her bra and green panties. While she was being kissed, she grinded her wet crotch on his forearm. She was captured spellbound in a kiss. Feverishly, they receded the pulsations of their successfully accomplished lovemaking.

Cathy had already shown Jenny how to snort the powder. They both sincerely felt that doing the powder with Soame, was what life was meant to be. That evening, the two of them taught Jenny how to give fellatio. Cathy gave instructions along with demonstrations. Jenny had natural abilities and interests, which would in time, develop her lacking experience. The date nights were agreed on as Wednesdays and Saturdays. No matter what happened, unless it was totally and completely unavoidable, Soame would be by to see them. Cathy's vigor was not surprising, nor was her vim rejected. Being with her was his purpose in coming. This time they showed Jenny the missionary style on the bed in the driver's quarters. In fulfillment, she locked her legs around the lower wedge of his back, and when they were done they were both wet with sweat.

Jenny was satisfied in the promise with the suggestion to wait until the coming Wednesday to surrender her virginity. Her hope was to have it last and be a memorable experience. This also gave Cathy more assurance in her status. The younger sister had never before had $15 to spend as she pleased. With the weekend at hand, there was more than $150 between them. Cathy elected not to give the money with the content he had given her. With what they had, Billy could be encouraged to take them to any place of their choice. "Somehow I know, wherever I go, I know I will only want ta be with you Soame. Wednesday seems like a awfully long time away, and we haven't even said goodnight yet." They all smacked lips. Going through the front door of the house, they waved and blew kisses, saying good night. Billy had left in the truck . The two Thads and Mrs. Yates were seated on the front porch. "You all have a good and safe weekend," Soame said.

"You too Soame," they replied.

Chapter 14

THE blazing red Irish Setter barked with the approach of the motor home. When Soame pulled into the horseshoe style driveway, the front porch light came on. It was past eight o'clock. The ranch style, modern, CBS, split leveled designed home was attractive, even at night, with path lights at each end and at the center of the driveway.

"Who's there?"

The barking quit. Soame had stepped out of the vehicle.

In a loud voice he responded, "I'm Soame Hudson. I'm new in these parts. The Sheriff asked me to stop by to see a Tom Blanchard."

A man wearing dress slacks, a long sleeved shirt, and house shoes, stood in front of him on the front porch. Soame approached the porch explaining his purpose for being there. The farmer appeared to be in his mid-40s, slightly balding on the front top of his head, about 5' 10" tall, with a rather straight and erect posture.

"I'm Tom Blanchard, Mr. Hudson. Beauford said you'd be by some time today." He moved toward Soame extending a welcoming hand.

"I know it's a might late, but the dela –"

Blanchard had opened the screen door, "We're mighty glad you could take time when you did Mr. Hudson, please come right on in."

Soame entered the house and removed his hat. "Call me Soame, Mr. Blanchard, and thank you for the invitation into your fine home. I commend you on it."

The house was not in any disrepair. Not only was the exterior and interior structurally nice, but also the inside décor was eloquent.

The furnishings were modern contemporary, with a slight blend of French provincial style. Two female figures entered from the patio area. As they drew nearer, Soame noticed that they looked like sisters.

"Please allow me to present my family, and call me Tom, Saome, if you don't mind." Soame looked at him, nodded and was ushered toward the advancing ladies.

After meeting Janet and their daughter, Cindy, Soame sat in the Blanchard living room. They were magnificently beautiful women. Further conversation revealed that Cindy had graduated from high school the previous semester.

Shortly after the talks began, she and her mother excused themselves to prepare drinks. Only Janet returned with the serving tray. Soame had asked for rum.

The two men had talked about all the introductory subjects, when Soame directed the conversation to the reason of his being there.

"Before coming to Smath, I requested information, maps, and brochures concerning this tri-state area. I've driven through town after town; more than two-hundred of them. They've varied in size. From what I've seen, Rapid City may very well be the nearest town or city still standing in the next ten years. I'm practically retired. I've done better than expected in broadcasting and sales, but I have business interests I have not yet completed. I am not wealthy, but I am independently stable."

Cindy was with Janet when she returned with the second round of drinks. "Even though I saw the devastation to farming towns in immediate areas North and East of here, I've only recently been informed and brought up-to-date on the plight of the American farmer, his diminish during the Reagan administration, and the continued struggle to survive now under Bush. I am not a financier. However, since the Sheriff personally sent me by and in doing so made mention of your personal friendship, dating back to childhood, how may I help you Tom?"

While Janet was out, Soame carefully eased a piece of foil onto the coffee table. There it rested and remained while he spoke. The foil contained two grams of cocaine from the original New Orleans product. He did not expect Janet to come directly back. Cindy's return with her was, naturally, also unexpected. Before he answered, Tom removed the foil from the table, asking, "Is this for my examination?" Due to the presence of the women, Soame was almost flushed with embarrassment. He had been brief and chose the direct method. He could not cower from his advance. There was no hesitation with his reply, which was not coy, "Why yes, if you care to. It may be to your interest and liking."

The foil was folded in the traditional style, known worldwide to people who use the substance of the sort. Keeping the piece on the table, Tom unfolded it, hoping for its contents to be what the wrapping implied. The glittering crystals fulfilled his hope. Not only did his eyes gleam, but also Janet involuntarily clasped her hands together and bowed her head. Raising the rum to his lips, Soame saw a wild grin on Tom's face after he wet the tip of his little finger, placed it in the glittering powdered rocks, and took it to his tongue.

There was nearly a twelve second interval before anyone spoke. Cindy was seated on the arm of the sofa, above her mother. Soame caught her attention. She looked bashfully away, and then back at him. She stared into his eyes for a few seconds. She then softly rested her vision on the top of her mother's head.

"This may very well be a happy day for us all Soame. Thank God you're here." Tom looked at his wife, motioning her in a way Soame did not understand. He then said, "This is the quickest way around here for a man to get rich. It's also the fastest way I know of for a good man to lose a fortune. I've done both, and thank God I still have my family together." With Tom's motioning Janet left the room.

Soame told him, "I know other men in other areas to also discover profits from the product Tom, but may I make a suggestion."

"Whatever your proposal is, I'm sure from the numbness of my tongue, if you have access to some quantity of this quality, you have a definite set up, development and expansion area right here, as poor as you may think it is. I hope you will take advantage of it. I also hope you can and will bail me out of the unfortunate situation I am in."

Soame, knowing he had struck the heart toward the true depth, wanted to evaluate. It was not as simple as Tom described in, "Because of the lateness of the hour, and my being expected at home, I would like to continue this meeting and discussion at another time. That way we can discuss all the points involved in the matter, and give it our full attention."

"When do you propose, Soame?"

"How about tomorrow afternoon? Around 2:30?"

"That sounds reasonable. If you'll be coming back out this way. I'm presently hampered for transportation." Tom stood as he spoke.

Rising as well, Soame told him, "That's no problem. Now that I know the way, I can be here at that time."

"2:30 it is then."

They shook hands.

Janet and Cindy were called out to say goodnight. Tom escorted Soame to the door and into the RV. The conversation had been casual, until they stepped off the porch.

"I main line it. I know how to distribute around here, but it will take time to build up clientele. The note is due on this place Monday, and I cannot get another extension. That's where the situation stands with me. If I can get your support, and if you are able to, it will most definitely be a lifesaver, Soame."

After starting the motor, Soame asked him, "How much is the note, Tom?"

"The entire note, principal and interest is thirty two thou; but forty-two hundred for the interest, will cancel my foreclosure note."

"Then you really don't have a problem in either case. We shouldn't have difficulty in arranging something. A man surrounded by the beauty you've engulfed yourself with shouldn't have to worry."

They shook hands again.

"2:30 tomorrow."

Fifi's nose was no longer a major concern at home. She had lost the minor scuffle, but benefited from the engagement because on the bed were three new body covers. She sported a new decorative blue ribbon, freshly done enameled paws, and a clip with circular trimming. She was high-spirited and lively as ever and as glad as everyone else to see him, when he arrived. There were all sorts of new items for everyone else, including Camille. She received gifts from everyone else. Beverly purchased her first teddy and there were even a few items for Soame, as tokens of appreciation.

Muff, however, was terribly disappointed with a lot of firsts. DD told Soame about Muff's adjustment to his first car ride. DD was gay and whimsically imploring with her descriptive antics. She entertained him in full view of the undrawn curtain, while he showered. The ride hadn't been so bad, if it hadn't resulted in Muff being at a strange place for the first time. It was his first time encountering the guy in the white coat. That wasn't too bad until the encounter lead to the first "shot" everyone raved about, since the "mutt" got the paw in the "puss." Upon their return, Muff scampered away, and had not been seen since.

Proceeding him from the bathroom, she went directly to the entertainment center. After their return, late that afternoon, she had noticed him leave an album on the stereo turntable. Other times he'd played that record, but with interest in a favorite tune. When he stepped into the bedroom, DD played the selection *Wonderful One* from the Marvin Gaye *Greatest Hits* album. Camille and Margrett were preparing his dinner, and a snack for the remainder of them. He noticed Chairly and Beverly leisurely lying across their bed, watching TV, with the polished, clipped, and freshly ribboned Fifi between them.

In the living room, after they had dined, Camille took an album, O.C. Smith's *Hickory Holler Revisited*, from the rack. She liked it because of a particular tune, *Little Green Apples*, which mentioned her hometown, and the birthplace of her children, in the lyrics. They all sat, drank, smoked, and enjoyed themselves.

The tunes on the recording were well-arranged. Soame was very familiar with not only the recording and artist, but also some interesting facts about the company. As an example, the company had released Aretha Franklin to Atlantic; a move which started her renowned career. Soame enlightened them about Columbia Records.

Following the release of Aretha Franklin, they were compelled to notice the mistake they had been making, in not properly promoting the storehouse of black talent they had. Aretha's *Sweet Bitter Love* on Columbia, would have, with all probability, surpassed *Natural Woman* on the Atlantic label, on which *Respect* is found and was drafted.

Not only did Columbia not promote blacks, but also they were housed separately on a subsidiary label called Date. Soame knew Granny White, who promoted the subsidiary, carrying Peaches and Herb, and Hines, Hines and Dad. The Columbia Broadcasting System had always been a huge company; they could well afford their ploy. Personal times and conversations with "Granny" disclosed him simply not being funded to handle his job properly, with Date records.

Soame's purpose in striking the conversation, was the information he gave them which revealed his personal contribution toward the extension of sales of that particular album. The fourth cut, on the second side features a tune that had earlier been done by Bobby Goldsburrow. As a working announcer, Soame took notice of it after moving to a second place of employment, in Miami. Smith had debuted with *Little Green Apples*, which resulted in the album through the singles sales and popularity. During his transition from MBM to WAME, the record and album had risen, peaked, and fading with sales. Upon his arrival at black broadcasting powerhouse "Champion Radio! WAME, Miami." At the ebb of it's fade, Soame, "The Mighty Burner," caught the selection *Honey* and presented it with so much impact the album soared on the charts. The favorably unexpected rise, because of the cut, forced Columbia to release O.C. Smith's second hit on a 45, which had become a hit before it was released. However, Smith was never heard of again in the record world.

Chairly and Beverly masqueraded for more than hour wearing their new sets of sunglasses. Beverly sported her new pumps, garter belt, stockings and teddy. Over and over they played the relaxing tune. Soame's memories reflected back while he lounged in the recliner. At the time of the "Bring back" success of the album he was seeing a girl in college who was also seeing Muhammad Ali. Ali and Soame had confrontational words about the lass, but only in a gentlemanly manner. Following his induction into the armed services, she became the first black Miss Florida. No on in the house knew about that part of his life. Nonetheless, each of them knew it had been a rewarding day, except the absent Muff. With all probability, he would have raised possible hell, implying, "Ah, now look here… that damn shot, throws questions into that 'rewarding' issue."

DD's idea of a quiet weekend was visiting her house and planning how to redecorate it. Her attitude had in no way changed. She, in fact, was happier and they were all pleased to be with her. The day before, Margrett and Beverly had been in a hotel room suite for the first time in their lives. Camille agreed with Soame, she should wait and get professional help, from an interior decorator. He also told her, he would send a carpenter over, to hear any ideas she had. The finalized papers for the deed weren't expected until the close of the following week. It was a total steal, if the town did not fold up and leave them and the mansion – the only occupied dwelling in Smath. They all went over to see the tree limb, and the damage it created. It was the first time Soame had seen and visited the estate. He was pleased.

Five minutes early, he drove up in front of the Blanchard home. Janet greeted him at the door. It seemed the beginning of a casual afternoon. He was led to the rear portion of the house, beyond the dining room area. It served as a spaciously enclosed patio and porch. There, Cindy was sitting comfortably at a glass topped table, talking with another woman whom Soame had not met. He was ushered to the woman, after greetings were extended to and from Cindy. The woman was then introduced as Teressa. A short while later, Soame noticed that Teressa had not spoken during the friendly general conversation between the three participants. Tom had not made his appearance, and neither of the other two mentioned him. He asked Janet, "Has Tom been called away by something unexpected?"

"No silly, I'm right here," came Tom's voice, from Teressa.

It was a complete surprise to Soame, who was absolutely startled. The two women laughed hysterically until Tom sent them for drinks.

"It's logical that you would sooner or later ask, how the biggest farmer throughout this area got big and rich from cocaine, and ended up broke."

Because of his natural poise and erect stature, his head automatically tilted slightly up and back. This was enhanced through the "queen's high," which aided his composition in maintaining a calmness. While he spoke, Soame observed closely. Had it not been for the wig, liner, rouge, lashes, and lipstick, and contoured brows, Tom may not have been exposed. The voice was the most obvious of all.

"This, next to cocaine, is my biggest vice. In fact the two are paired with me, and whenever we three are together, Teressa comes alive. We all have the little things, we as individuals do."

Janet returned with the drinks, and placed them on the table where Tom was seated at the head. Soame was seated to his right, with an empty place setting between them. They had ample space for the placement of the drinks to be within comfortable reach for them both. Tom wasted no time and spoke openly and directly.

"My wife here is a nymphomaniac, and she is totally wild about you."

She was between them. Janet patted the side of his jaw lightly. Looking him directly in the eyes, she smiled gracefully pivoted, and again left them alone.

Tom removed his drink from the serving tray. When Soame joined him, they made a toast "to understanding and success." When Soame had removed the glass from his lips, he said, "Continue Teressa, if you will."

"Rather than try and explain it in any other way, I thought you would have more respect for my directness. It is said that a single picture is worth a thousand words. My wife and I knew each other's interests before we were married. They've never interfered with our love, attitude, or patience toward each other." Without interference he went on, explaining how, in the past ten years, he had bought a twenty-five hundred acre farm and expanded it to almost ten thousand acres. He built an empire and stacked money for eight years. Half of the land he'd acquired in the past five years was as a result of the governmental siege on the farm industry. It all came into play as a result of him taking a Christmas trip to New Jersey and purchasing a half-kilogram of cocaine. He began a turnover with the money that started flowing in. Small farmers could not afford to farm at a loss, so they sold immediately. Those who had less than a hundred acres could not be subsidized. The lucky ones practically gave their farms away, and were able to leave with what little savings they had. Those who had prime land were able to save only the acreage and hold on to their equipment. They later sold it and in most cases that profit amounted to more than they had accumulated in their savings. Prime land was the factor and small farmers owning prime acreage constituted the farming population.

Strings of them began to fall at once. Equipment began losing its value, and then it had to be offered with the give away price of the land. Within a two-year period any small farmer still around was trapped with a mortgage he knew he could not pay off.

The conversation was not restricted to farming, though it was the central topic. Soame discovered that Tom knew his business with the other influential involvements. He was surprised to find out that agriculture accounted for only one percent of Montana's gross product. Though there was somewhat of an interest, the media took a lackadaisical interest toward the choking situation. The state, being the fourth largest in America and having less than a million people with Great Falls as its most populated city, had less than fifty-five thousand people in it. Its "Tribune" and "Gazette" out of Billings constituted the two most circulated papers in the state. The state governmental body ranked second in service industry with 17% of the state's gross income.

Soame compared the local situation to that of his home state. Small farming for a while had been being pushed out as vice president George Bush with the aid of a Miami newspaper "The Herald," set up and put into effect the first drug task force. This was during Reagan's introductory "crime watch" divisionary tactical maneuvers. This in effect forced people to watch each other while the government created the crime and threw public attention in its direction. Like an experienced, skillful, magician, the Reagan administration did this with drugs. Blind Floridians voted Robert Graham to the U.S. Congress in spit of the fact that he had done less as a governor than any other governor in the history of the state. He was elected governor based on his platform against crime. He expanded the prison system in the state through federal appropriations. The single industry, through such schemes and appropriations, became the largest industry in the state; the lottery. Voters were taken in with the promise of the lottery offering tremendous help toward aiding the educational system in the state. Teachers did not receive pay increases. Materials, schools, and implementations did not rise in quality, except for security measures. No means were made available for kids to have summer jobs. On the other hand, police agencies on the city, county and state levels increased. The skillful magician holds the voting public spellbound as he maneuvers.

Though Soame's reflected on his native state, he maintained strict attention to Tom's delivery. It was the purpose of his being there. "Do you understand, or know the term *oro y plata*, Soame?"

"No. I don't recall ever hearing it before."

"It is our state motto. It means 'gold and silver'." He talked about several things for more than an hour and a half. Some related to the farm industry, others helped Soame validate his establishment in the state. It was revealed to him that Montana was the forty-first state to enter the union. In 1803 its eastern area became a state through the Louisiana Purchase. It is the largest of the five Rocky Mountain States, and gold was discovered there in 1862, a year after the beginning of the civil war. Montana received its statehood in 1889.

The large farmers who bought small farmers praised themselves in affording prime land to grow sugar beats, potatoes, and hay. Soame was informed that two thirds of the state of Montana is grassland. They range from buffalo grass to western wheat, with blue grama as a standard grass. Wheat is the state's most valuable crop and barley its second. According to Tom 79% of the gross state product was in sale and retail trade.

He had gone over maps, charts, and other economic information with Sandra Fairfield. That specific detail had not been mentioned. However, he did know that the state had a 19% service industry, and that one fourth of the state is covered with forest. The contributing factor was that specific area had not been noticed during their search of the general tri-state area. Soame's enterprise dealt with the production of jewelry boxes, which are made from wood. He had stumbled into the perfect location to develop his dream.

After the first round Soame only requested ginger ale; they were into their third round. Though he did not have alcohol, he constantly did one and ones, while Tom consumed the gin and tonic mixtures. When she placed the tray for the third time, Tom told Janet, "This'll be the last for me unless Soame wants another ginger ale when you return. Why not join us and share our company in about ten minutes. my dear? We're about to wrap up our discussion."

The talks drew to a conclusion with a discussion of the irrigation process involved in growing a large percentage of crops in the area. The water was abundant, but the cost of irrigating systems and maintenance fees were considerably expensive. Tom briefly touched on the ranching issue, which had not been terribly damaged. However, people who raised beef and dairy cattle also felt the crunch and had motivations to cringe. In the immediate area there were sheep ranchers who naturally marketed their wool. "You're from Florida, so I've heard. Got any idea how it is around here during the winter Soame?"

"The information I've been able to gather indicated an average 20 degree temperatures in January."

"You're 40 degrees off. Try 20 below, and believe me, there's a hell of a difference. We've got a short farming season around here because of the early and long winters. I've already given you the basic method the government used to choke the small farmer out. The large farmers started falling the same way, except the majority of their loans didn't come through the local banks. Reagan skillfully set up loans and mortgages through the federal government. Immediate foreclosures, without as much as first extensions, wiped them out like a falling domino sequence. I'm at the top. I bought some of them out as they fell. Prices were almost better than the meager amount they paid the small farmer. The sale of the coke in this area enabled my expenditures and sustenance; and now the very hope of my continued existence, and the only possibility I know of, for an idea of survival, comes down to this meeting with you and your decision to help me. I extend to you my hospitality and everything I have with graciousness, toward your favorable consideration. Sir, I'm at your mercy."

"Teressa, how'd you lose it all? Why did you have to mortgage?" Tom only had nearly a third of the packet remaining when their talks began. He had consumed most of it during the course of their discussion and was about to make his last injection. Soame saw this and removed the eight ball from the pocket of his wind breaker and passed it to him.

"You're most kind," Tom responded. He began answering the question, as he further indulged, "It was a young fellow in his early twenties. I met him in New York, during a trip for a 'key.' We had a fling and enjoyed each other. I stayed a week, and two weeks later moved him out here."

"I got taken Soame. Really big time. Because of the thought I had of our mutual feelings toward each other, I stupidly closed my eyes and would not accept the obvious fact that he was robbing me. I sent him back to New York twice, to make purchases. Each time his story was that he got robbed. I was paying $60,000 a key; each time I sent him, it was to purchase a full key. A couple of times the stuff he brought back wasn't worth putting out. The major clients I had, to whom I sold directly, were all prominent and reputable people. I had workers, three of them, who distributed on a small scale. I was concerned of my reputation. I was this area's only major source. At the time I actually didn't know how much cash I had on hand; it certainly was a lot. When it came in I put some here, had a hiding place there. Between the house and the barn there were several places I'd tuck away five and ten thousand at a time. I couldn't deposit it in the bank because it would show, and its source would have been questioned if I was audited. Janet stayed busy with household responsibilities and until stacks and piles began not only diminishing but also disappearing, I didn't realize what a bind I had gotten myself into. It's impossible for one man to handle a farm this size. There were eleven workers on my payroll as farm help. I was constantly busy; between taking care of matters here with my household, farming, the coke, and an outside lover. There wasn't any time to count money. I foolishly let it slip away."

"I tried to take control of the situation, and could have been on the way to recovery. But I refused to leave him alone, which was the first problem. When it was all over, I saw it, and still see it, as the total best; as I said I refused to see the problem at the time. Had I simply carried through with the choice I took I may have been able to initiate a comeback. But I failed to carry through, when I scraped together everything I had left, and this time accompanied him to purchase the goods. I stupidly stayed in a hotel in New Jersey and allowed him to go across the river into New York for the buy. When I had not heard from him, realizing there was no doubt about what had happened, I called here. Janet scraped up bits and with the rest of our savings, I was able to cover hotel expenses and catch a flight to Rapid City. The car was brand new. I had it less than six months, and hadn't taken the time to have it insured."

Janet came to the table. But Soame had asked another question so Tom told her, "Give us a few more minutes, will you hon'? When you return, I'll have another tonic." When Tom answered Soame found the same story, other than love, that has foiled men throughout the annals of time. It is the story of lust and greed. It happened the previous season. Tom's financial standing had began to slightly diminish. Contrary to rumor and Thad's theory, Tom did not have a mortgage at the time because it was later impossible to get a second mortgage on the house, farm and remaining equipment; never carried more than the note which was then about to be foreclosed on him. Nonetheless, with devious intent it was Tom who started the circulation of the idea that there was a mortgage on his farm prior to the previous season. His purpose in doing so proved fruitful, but later proved to be to his disadvantage.

His scheme allowed the few remaining large farmers to take him in with good faith. With their confidence he approved their plan and consented toward the feasible profit margin. Tom had never been the biggest farmer in the state. His entire method of operation was geared toward the takeover he envisioned. His plan was to gain fifteen thousand additional acres. No one in the state had a farm or ranch so vast. He purposely plowed under to destroy his counterparts.

Had not it been for his failures through his lover, he would have overwhelmingly succeeded. His downfall took place over a nine month period. In January Tom went to the local bank and applied for a loan, but it was only for a six month period. He could not harvest until August. The subsidy would not be available until after harvesting. The first extension on the note was for thirty days; the next gave him half that amount of time. There would be no more.

When Janet returned to the table, he was in the midst of telling Soame how he'd purchased a $175,000 tractor, with attachments, for $5,000. He had to later put the equipment up for sale. "No one in this area could buy it, and wouldn't buy it, if they could have." He described a farmer coming north, across the state line, from Spotted Horse to examine the huge John Deer. Assuming the farmer would make a reasonable offer, and hoping he was not aware of his destitute circumstances, Tom asked him to propose a figure. $3,500 was the offer he refused, but used as a base. The man from Wyoming immediately said, "Good day, sir," turned and walked toward his truck and trailer. The tractor was sold for $2,000. That sent him to the bank for the loan. He had not gotten to be the biggest farmer in the state. However, his reputation carried not only state wide, but also throughout the region. "Soame you're the only one, other than Janet, who's ever heard and knows the true and whole story."

He noticed Janet had brought him another ginger ale on the rocks. While Tom finished the story, Soame could not help but notice she continued to look at him with admiration. "She's dying for you to reach out and touch her. Go on I won't mind. We've discussed it, and decided to be totally open with you," Tom said.

She had a smile on her beautiful face. Janet took his hand, and finding no resistance, placed it under her skirt. He felt her garter as his hand was being taken up. She was fully dressed, and her skirt was cream colored. "You don't mind doing this with me; while my sister prepares something for me, do you Soame?" His body tingled throughout when it made contact with the wetness and silky material between her legs. She clasped his wrist with her other hand, and grinded on his hand, with hunching revolutions. Soame noticed Tom was preparing a syringe, brought in on the tray. He was almost speechless, but managed to say, "I feel I am at a terrible disadvantage here, with such beauty, and in such lovely company."

Tom appeared not to have taken his eyes from the preparation. Soame shifted two of his fingers around the elastic rim, onto her mound, and inserted the middle between the walls of her vulva. It sloshed into her vagina. In less than thirty seconds, he had been lodged with plunging surprise into the seductive enchantments of the indulgingly apprehensive woman. His index finger was also added. The increasing rotations and hunches brought more juices, and with them a slight moan— the only sound heard at the table. He looked at Tom, who was about to place the needle onto the soaked cotton bud. He squirmed his thumb around the elastic, through the hairs, over the mound, and withdrew his fingers. It sloshed in the slush, but the rotations and hunches became humps when the middle finger found its way up her anal canal. She threw her arms around his neck and with her face next to his, she whispered, "Oh Soame, thank you for not refusing me." She whimpered tiny feminine grunts of satisfaction. Tom filled the syringe.

"I'd like to see you upstairs when you're done," she balanced the tray on one hand, and patted his jaw with the other. Janet had taken a step, when Soame asked, "May I make a suggestion?"

It was Tom who responded. "Why sure Soame I've told you, anything you desire."

"This will probably be more to your and Janet's interest. I have another eight ball I'd planed to leave with you. How about letting her take part of that package and I'll replenish you with the other one?"

"You're an absolute dream, Soame," responded Janet.

"Teressa, I'll talk plain and simple. Like I told you last night, you no longer have an immediate problem, with the potential disaster." He saw a smile on the feminine face for the first time,. "We also seem to be getting involved with a phase of our personal lives, which I cannot stand to be publicized. I do not and will not participate in homosexuality. The act in front of you with Janet a while ago is the first time I've ever allowed to be witnessed by another man." Tom attempted to speak, but Soame interrupted, "I will listen to you, if you allow me to finish." Tom gave him the courtesy.

"You have two charming and beautiful women in your family. I will not decline the opportunity to be with either or both of them, but I am discrete. I will not allow the people in town, or those throughout the area, to know my private affairs. I will not be observed by you for entertainment. There's other business to discuss, but since the situation has given lee way to thrash this issue about, I want you to know my full feelings toward the matter, in gaining the understanding we drank to." There were four joints on the table, he lit one, and did a one and one.

"Soame, Beauford saw Joey around here a couple of times because he lived on one of the properties I bought. Other than that, no one else knows of my personal activities." Soame thought of his meeting with the Blanchards being mentioned to Camille and Margrett. Neither mentioned anything about the Blanchard's personal lives. However, Margrett brought to light the fact, Cindy had been the high school queen, and never dated any of the local boys; a boy from Rapid City had escorted her to her junior and senior proms.

Tom continued, "Janet is practically a city girl. She's from St. Clair Shores, an area just north of Detroit. I got turned on to coke when I met her. I've never regretted either experience, and hope you understand me loving them both. When we want to party with another couple or individual, we simply travel to another area to avoid being detected; it's usually an over night thing. It's been a while since we've partied regularly; we're no longer a young couple. Cindy is a combination and extension of the both of us. We don't allow her to date boys from around here, and since she's been of dating age, there have been hardly any around here. Both of us want her to be in college, when she becomes 'aware of herself.' I want her to be with other youngsters from fine and decent homes."

Soame was finishing the second Maui-Wowee joint he'd ever completely finished after lighting it. He'd been "toothing" continually, and said, "Alright, here's what I propose to aid your immediate situation. I'll buy a third of your farm at $4,500. With that I request at least half of the third in prime acreage. I'm involved in a co-op with the Yates. I'll rent another third, at $4,000, over a five year period. This will leave you immediate access to a third, with $8.500 and a personal loan from me, with no interest. This should enable your transportation, and your daughter's matriculation into school in September. What do you think?"

Tom's eyebrows rose inquisitively, "Soame, I think you're a pretty smart fellow. Now what was that word again, you used in reference to Cindy and school?" It was Tom's natural voice, not the falsetto he'd been using.

"The word is matriculate. It simply means enrollment or registration. Cindy's enrollment or registration; her matriculation into school. Of course that's what it's all about isn't it? You want her in school. There are also agricultural schools; would you by chance be considering matriculating?" The serious look took on an expression and almost brought Tom to a laugh.

He simply replied, "Well I've never," and was feeling quite effective with the projection of his feminine composition.

When the jesting subsided, Tom positively focused back on the question, "Ah, you've mentioned a loan sir, to cover my daughter's tuition, and provide me with needed transportation. But you didn't state the amount."

"$3,500. We're talking about a total of $12,000 in your hands, two days from now, at your appointed time."

With a stern but sincere look Tom asked, "But what about the coke?"

"Teressa, how many grams are there in an ounce?"

"There have always been twenty-eight, why?"

"How many grams are there in an eight ball?"

"That's the size of the package you just gave me right?" Soame nodded his head. "Well, I'd assume it's four, maybe as much as five; it's certainly more than the two you left last night."

"That's the point. Though you've made money with the product, you really don't know the business. A skillful person will take advantage of your ignorance, detected through your lack of knowledge in simple terminology. An eight ball is the standard measure, in the business, sold above a gram. It's a three and a half gram measure."

Through the discussion on cocaine Soame found out that Tom had seen a triple beam scale used in New York and New Jersey, but didn't associate it with anything in particular in the sale of drugs. His "method of distribution," was measuring by a potato and vegetable scale, which resembled a large clock, with a plate on its top. However, he was right with his measurement spoon idea, for small pieces, but had not heard of the term "bag weight."

He made a point home by telling Tom, "They don't grow coke in Jersey or New York. I'd never pay sixty grand for a key."

"You know a lot about coke then, ha Soame?"

"Teressa, I know more about cocaine than Tom will ever know about farming."

Tom had a serious look of contention that also revealed awareness and inquisitiveness. "You've told me you built from twenty five hundred aces. Restructured and reinforced your existence, doing what you know. I've mentioned a five year period to you. The community needs you for its survival. The people in the community need you as a productive member of their population, rather than an adversarial force. You know farming. Put into action what you know, and we all will be fine. From my personal stash, I will give you coke from time to time, Let's work together that way with agreement."

"Mr. Hudson, if you will extend the favors, and grant the courtesy you've mentioned, it will save my life. I would be extremely grateful, and forever in your debt. I sincerely thank you for the benevolence in your consideration and favors."

They stood and shook hands in agreement. "What time do you have to be at the bank, before foreclosure, Teressa?"

"It closes at three; the money has to be posted before closing time. Can you meet me here between ten and let's say noon?"

"I'll see you before eleven Monday morning."

"I'll be here at the table for a while. Someone's waiting for you inside, if you're interested." Soame excused himself.

Passing through the open glass sliding doors, with a six inch step up, Soame walked through the modern styled dining room. The room contained a contemporary table with Louis XV style chairs. The furnishings were highlighted by a chandelier. To the left of the dining area, he noticed the tall stools at the breakfast counter, separating the well equipped and brightly designed, spacious modern kitchen. Cindy was pacing in the deep carpeted living room, which was not separated from the entrance by a foyer. It was the first time he had seen her since drinks had been passed out. She looked almost identical to her mother, except she carried seven to ten pounds less in weight, and though her hair color was the same, Cindy's fell slightly beyond her shoulders. She had it styled in two braided pigtails. She wore jeans, a t-shirt with no bra, and bobby socks. She turned and saw Soame.

He glanced at his watch, it was 4:27. At eighteen, and a half inch shorter than her mother, Cindy Blanchard exemplified beauty. At thirty-eight Soame hardly felt as being a prospect as her beau. He was enjoying the favors of the young, pretty, and delightful lasses in his stable, who charged and rocked his sparkling world. Other than speaking, he had no expectation of a deeper confrontation with her. She approached the center of the room. He was about to turn to the three steps leading to the second level of the home.

"My mother said you should be coming out to join us pretty soon; she went up to the guest room, and said if I didn't want to keep you all to myself, I should bring you up." In that brief, spell, they relaxed in each other's presence. With a pleasing smile and a slight blush, she asked, "How'd you get such an unusual name, Soame?"

Walking toward her he replied, "When I became of age I asked, and was told they didn't think my name ought to be Henry." Noticing each other's smile, he continued, "So I am Soame."

Following the short laugh, he asked, "What college do you plan attending?" The question removed all signs of happiness from her face.

"Seems like I probably won't be going." They were approaching the couch.

"When you enroll, if you will major in marketing, I promise you a job with a guarantee in your future." They were in the process of sitting. Her bottom barely touched the cushion; she jumped straight up running and yelling to her farther.

"What's all the noise about?" He turned toward the steps and saw a set of beautiful legs, in stockings, with a garter belt, and white brief panties. A hand went up, taking hold of a brassiered breast and squeezed it at him. He saw a sensuously protruding tongue, tracing the brim of the top lip, in the welcoming face of Janet. She did a slow turn, patted her outer hip at him, took two slinging strides, and almost slung it against the door facing, as she entered one of the bedrooms. He was about to place his foot on the lower step when he saw Cindy rounding the walled corner from the dining area. She appeared to be attempting to control her composure. Janet aroused him to an immediate erection. "I'd like to use the bathroom, if you don't mind." She directed him up the hall, next to the room the vivacious Janet had gone into. "I'm drinking ginger ale, would you mind bringing one up, with one of those home made cigarettes, at the table near your father?"

He used the bathroom and while there "cleaned up." Opening the door, stepping out into the hall, he saw Janet. She had not changed her clothes. Her arms were folded, and one foot supported her as she leaned against the door frame. She gave the appearance of a fifty dollar beautiful San Franciscan whore.

"That was a neat trick with the hundred dollar bill. Placing it on the tray like you did with your handkerchief. I dropped it in the hamper. That's how sure I am you'll be back. For the record because I want to know Soame. Was it your intent to try and have me feel as I'm some cheap floozy?"

He walked up to her. They stood almost touching gazing into each other's eyes. "No Janet, it's merely something I do, even at home, after every sex act with any woman in my household. The handkerchief was soiled, after I wiped my hand. No more, no less; Shell I leave?"

"Come on in here, I may get filthy rich with you."

Cindy trailed in behind them as they entered the room. "He doesn't smoke, so I brought them all." She had four joints in one hand and a dark colored drink in the other. "I remembered from last night you like rum and coke. We're out of ginger ale."

He had turned around, almost bumping into her. He had never seen her face with a grin on it. It was so pleasing that he became momentarily startled. Janet witnessed their encounter. She walked around him with a step and a half and removed the drink from her daughter's hand. "Well, are you gonna just stand there, or would you rather me lay on the bed and masturbate for ya?"

"Pardon me, both of you. Cindy you're so astonishingly beautiful, and it's impossible to compliment one of you, without extending one to you both." He looked at Janet who stood with them in a triangle. When she smiled, he thought of the tease she engineered at the door, and returning the smile asked, "Is this some form of deception or prank? Are you two putting on a mother and daughter act?"

Cindy took a hand to her mouth in an effort to stifle a laugh. "No, smart ass he's my husband, and her father. Close the door baby, I'm gonna make sure you get done right this time. This one's a real stud." When Cindy turned back to close the door, he wanted to grab her fine ass. He did not know exactly quite what to expect from her.

Instead, he reached around and palmed Janet's rear and squeezed as he rubbed. "He's going to give dad my tuition mother."

"What?!"

That changed the complexity of the entire scene. She almost tossed the drink to Cindy, took Soame in her arms, and gave him a kiss like he never had before.

"Oh Soame. You are positively a dear. I've never been so worried about anything in my entire life. I will never forget you for helping us this way."

When the first kiss was over, she led him to the bed. When they both sat, he said to her, "Janet kiss me again." The last one was shorter, but it was of the same fascinating quality.

"We've got something special for you to. All of us will remember this day. Soame, I'll satisfy you in any way you want, but let's watch my baby for a while." In high school Janet had been a cheerleader. Cindy had always wanted to be one, after seeing pictures of her mom. When she was in the eight grade the school discontinued football because there weren't enough boys to play. The year she was to try out, the basketball schedule was stopped, for the same reason. She and Janet were restricted to times at home, having fun together with the pom poms.

After removing the homemade creation from the closet, Cindy sat the balls of various colored ribbon to the side, and began removing her t-shirt. Lifting the shirt over her head Janet yelled, "That's it baby! Show him you're not afraid of guys and you're really hot stuff." Soame took the drink from the night stand, and gulped it down. Seeing the erect nipples, on the lusciously bouncing 34 "boobs," filled him with electrifying explosiveness. The hint was so blatant; he had no problem comprehending the obvious play toward Cindy. He sat and watched her cheerleading with intensity.

Janet began fondling him. "You're terribly huge Soame. You're any woman's dream. I've got to see this." She signaled Cindy to remove her jeans, and began unbuckling his belt.

When his pants had become unzipped, he took his windbreaker off and she began unbuttoning his shirt. Cindy was doing turn around bendovers and forward squats. When his shirt was taken off, he stood up and walked to her. His dress trousers dangled, but like hip huggers clung around his buttocks. Taking her into his arms, she submitted to his kiss. Neither of them had said a word. Janet continued to undress him. When his pants were at his ankles, he lowered the front of Cindy's panties to the extreme round of her hips, and inserted his penis in the crotch. He had never stopped kissing her, and brought the elastic up only enough to hold his protrusion where it had been placed. In a four month period his skills had been rejuvenated, and his body was primed. Janet saw the gentle easiness in which he handled her pride and joy, and her embracive responses, then sat slantingly against the dresser top and observed with estrous glee.

He released her tongue, looking into each other's eyes following the kiss their breathing was deep and rapid. Each swallowed simultaneously. Soame palmed both her cheeks, and guided her face with his into his shoulder. There again, she surrendered to his kiss. Her arms extended upward, behind his back, with her hands curving, and latching on to this shoulder tops. With his finer tips in the round of her cheeks, he swerved her hips into a rotational grind against the erection between her legs.

Cindy became suspended during the entrancing kiss. The elevating height of intensity swelled with warmth between her legs. Other than administering her own stimulations, she had not before been lifted toward a climax. It was not his intention to penetrate her. Maintaining the rotational grinds, with one hand he reached under her cheek into the crotch of her panties and resituated his member. The head, knot, and top of the shaft were placed within the folds of her vulva. Each of them knew the instant the contact was made between her lips because of the hunching rhythms she responded with. Janet thought he had penetrated her, but knew it to be almost impossible because of his size and Cindy's delightful and casual reaction. The intensive curiosity whirled her into a masturbating fenzy.

It was an almost smothering kiss. Neither of them could hardly breathe. Cindy would not discontinue because it was the catalyst motivating the raging heat between her legs. The head and knot lodged between her folds rubbing and massaging her clitoris; triggering her body with a sensational, wild, vibrating fire. Each time she slid on the head to the knot shivering delights spurred her onto the shaft. The back stroke movement brought the most thrilling, electrifying bump she had ever experienced. In a very short while she had become extremely proficient in sliding up the head, onto the knot, and on the shaft, back over the knot. She did this with pulsations of delightful thrills. She began a whimpering grunt. Janet recognized the same sound she had made a short while earlier, when he removed the insertion of his thumb from her vagina. He had used the lubricating juices to caress her clitoris with his thumb. This sent her back against his inserted finger, with back and forth action climbing into a cozy covert of dynamic pleasure. She was transfixed; captured by curiosity as to what the couple was doing, and entranced by the whimpers, sighing, moans and grunts Cindy made.

The erotic scene had gone on for nearly three minutes when Cindy attempted to pull her mouth from his. Soame did not give way, but this did not prohibit her. Once again she began returning his kiss, but suddenly, in a gasp, she tore away. Gulping for air, her hunching was a smooth wave of vibrating rhythmic measures, "I'm comm—, I'm going to com—." Janet was also finding release, "Me too baby!" Soame saw her lick her lips. They stared into each other's eyes. Cindy began jerking on the instrument between her legs, "Oh Soame, you're making me and my baby girl cum. I'm cumming Soame. Help her, let her cum please like me." Cindy gave a shrilly "eek" and went limp.

He gathered her in his arms and called Janet to the trousers around his feet. He stepped as she tugged, and in two strides Cindy was delivered to the bed. Janet checked her pulse, and Soame told her, "Just get a cold compress, it's happened before."

"Not here, put this under her feet. It'll lessen the possibility of delirium, if she comes out of it on her own; she's fainted." Placing the pillows, he looked at her with question. "I'm a nurse silly, did you penetrate her?"

"No, but I'm gonna fuck both a you bitches, before I leave."

"What?! You've got a beautiful piece of meat, that I'll admit, but the both of us, come on, you're not an android of some sort are ya?" She said it with a smile, glanced at her watch, and laid Cindy's arm at her side.

He gestured with a shrug and told her, "You are a beautiful pair of women. I wouldn't pass up this chance for anything material that I know of. We don't have to rush do we? What about Tom?"

"For you, anything in the world and as you already know we do—"

He interrupted, "You haven't lost anything. It'll be all taken care of Monday. It's been arranged between us."

"Oh Soame you're an absolute doll." She threw her arms around his body. They held each other. "There's something I want to get straight with you. He called me a nymph. He says that because he also likes men."

Soame took a seat on the bed, and began gazing into her crotch. "Janet, let me look at your pussy will ya?"

She leaned over, placed the back of her hand on her daughter's forehead. Satisfied, she gently smoothed the palm over it. Resuming her position directly in front of him she said, "Here, it's the same as hers, only she came out of this one." She lowered the white briefs just above the mid of her thighs. "Now if you want to see some more, you'll have to look long distance. I want a shot." Leaving her panties about her thighs, she strolled to the dresser. "This is some really good stuff you got here, Soame."

"I was telling you about the times we've had, and him calling me a nymp. You're the third person, and I haven't as much as gone to bed with you yet. There have been two others. Ten years ago we went to Jersey. Tom begged me to go to bed with one of his associates. Two years later, at a wheat farmer's convention in Kansas we met a couple. I couldn't stand the woman; she and I talked while Tom and her husband were next door in our room for an hour and a half.

"Four years ago in Rapid City, we picked up a complete stranger, took him to our hotel room, and both of us had sex with him for $50. Ten months ago he met a female impersonator and fell in love with him. That's where the wig he's wearing came from. Big exchange for a new Marque. Tom moved him from New York and put him in a farm house we have seven miles on the other side of the stream you saw on your way here. He ruined us, but Tom is my husband, and I'll always be with him. He's allowed me an affair with you. Both of us can tell that you're not into men."

She made the injection and once again walked over and checked on Cindy. "She'll be fine. She'll sleep for a while and be all right when she wakes up. Standing back in front of him, she reached for his hand. This time there was no skirt to block the view of what he touched. "She's a very good kid Soame. I'm her best friend. We have a lot of fun keeping each other's company; there's no one else out here for miles. I want to tell you something before she wakes up, and want you to understand why we came on to you like this. Do you think it's strange?"

"I've enjoyed women in a variety of ways. For me it's different because you're mother and daughter, but it's not strange."

"I'm glad you see it that way. Beauford said that the Johnson's moved in with you. That oldest girl has quite a reputation, according to Cindy, but that's not the point here. I've never as much as dated a black man. I'm not prejudiced. I've simply never before had an interest in one. They're none around here, and Detroit's heavily populated with them. My interest now is my baby." This time he wiped his hand on her panties, but it was less stained. Soame rose, and on their way to the dresser, he removed a vial from the pocket of his windbreaker.

He had done a one and one, and about to light a joint. Janet was about to "splike" and asked, "What did you do to her by the way?"

"She had a clitoral eruption. I put the head of my dick in her panties, and straddled her pussy lips over it. She rubbed until she got off, that's all. I figured she had not been penetrated, so I wanted to see what kind of natural moves she has."

"Yea, but I saw the kiss. You two were buried into each other. But you're sort of wrong about the penetration, and that's the problem. I've been so worried she'd become frigid, or develop some other type of mental impairment that would have lasting damage. A year and a half ago, her boyfriend penetrated her, but pre-ejaculated. In less than a minute she says he was through. Janet was once again resting against the dresser at the foot of the bed. When Soame took a seat in the only chair in the nook, turning toward him, maintaining eye contact, she slightly propped one leg on the dresser. Wiping his hand, he had pulled her panties up squeezing her ass. In shifting her position, to one foot on the floor, it gave him clear and open view at the pleasing sight. He glanced and she continued.

"This past school term, after dating a boy from Rapid City for over a year, he escorted her to the prom. They took a room at the only motel in town. This boy was drunk and practically did the same thing. He didn't even as much penetrate. He simply lay on top of her, and before he got it in, came all over her. She managed to get him dressed and out of the room, and drove him here about 2:30 that morning. He slept in the car until Tom went out and woke him up. So you see, it's been one bad experience after another. They both got her keyed up. Now that you've put the idea of college as a prospective, I've thought about it since she's mentioned it. She'll need to keep her mind on her studies, Soame. Attempting to have sex could be an off setting interference I'd like to eliminate."

"It appears you two are pretty close."

"I'm her friend, her sister, her buddy, and most of all, I'm her mother, Soame. I love her. She's the only child I have and there probably won't be another one for me. However, I'm not her lover. Neither of us is bi, or is a lesbian. I'd rather throw her into a scene of voyeurism as an effort to circumvent and alleviate that possibility with her."

He looked directly into the vertex of her legs, beginning his question with, "Well," his eyes slowly crept up to her brassiered breast, then on to Janet's beautiful face. "Then how about you. Are you interested in me?"

She glanced at her watch and replied, "She'll be awakening soon. Soame I know a good dick when I see one. You don't have to be naked, or sitting around in your boxers, for any woman to see you're very well hung. I'm in love with Tom because he's my husband, but I'm starved. Even before that he—she came into the picture, Tom had been neglecting me. It simply made the situation worse. It came over more than several times flaunting and pretending to be more feminine than Cindy and I. We tolerated it with hospitality only because of 'Teressa.' You see Teressa is our sister too, and has been for as long as Cindy can remember. We're that honest and open with her. It shouldn't be hard for you to understand. You're a prize I will enjoy having. I feel sure you share and agree. Since he—she, it hasn't been particularly worse, but it most certainly hasn't been any better, especially with the disrupting devastation it has left us in."

Janet looked to Cindy. She was resting comfortably. She had on only her purple panties. "She's the real prize, and mister, you're the guest of honor."

"Does she smoke week or do coke?"

"No, and she's never mentioned wanting to try that, alcohol or cigarettes."

"Would you mind if I offer her a toot?"

"Well, I won't object, but I don't want her to take and make a habit of it. All the kids around here and practically everywhere, from what I see and hear on the news, are on crack. I don't want her into that bag, that's for sure." She walked over and removed the pillow. Though she was gentle, it slightly disturbed Cindy. "If you do, wait five or ten minutes. I want to be positive she's totally coherent." He did a one and one.

Janet excused herself to use the bathroom. She had been gone no more than a minute, when he noticed Cindy's hand raised to her brow. "Oh, Soame, I must've fainted. Where's my mother?"

"You have been asleep for nearly ten minutes. She checked you and decided to let you awaken on your own. Had you opened your eyes a minute ago, she would have been here. She just stepped out to the bathroom. How do you feel?"

She sat up on the side of the bed. Wiping the side of her face then stretching into a yawn, with the hand remaining over her mouth, she told him, "I feel fine. Sorry I went out on you, but we really didn't do anything, did we?" She had a smile on her face, and looked at him with anxiety and curiosity.

"We did enough, and I believe we both enj-"

She fell back on the bed, giggling with embarrassment covering her face with her palms, "Oh no, this time it was me, I can't believe this."

At that instant Janet walked through the door, with a damp face cloth and a glass of water. "Hello Stranger."

The atmosphere of the room became settled through congenial conversation. Cindy had gotten catalogs and applications from more than a dozen schools. She requested the information because she liked each one. After receiving the information, her selection was narrowed down to three schools. Her interest was in nursing or surgical nursing. She idolized her mother and wanted to pursue the field her mother practiced, as an R.N. her college choices were Villanova, the University of Oregon, and the University of Portland. They lounged during the twenty minute discussion. Cindy sat in the chair, Janet moved from the bed back to the dresser top, and Soame lay across the bed. Janet graduated from Wayne University, in Detroit. Neither of them had heard of Soame's alma mater, Edward Waters College, in Jacksonville, Florida. When he told them that the city is the largest in the United States land wise, they were astounded.

He did a one and one when he got to the catalog from the University of Portland and offered some to Cindy. She shrugged her shoulders, looked over to her mother, and back to him, saying "I've never done it before." She then looked back to her mother, and asked with a cheesy smile, "What do you think?"

"It's your party dear, however you feel about it."

Looking back at him, she rose, and approached the bed with a big smile. She told him "Alright, I'll try it with you Soame, cause you're special to me already."

Janet talked to Soame about the differences between Portland State and the University of Portland. However, Janet merely mentioned the size factor, with Portland State housing over twenty-thousand students. Both schools are in Portland, Oregon. Soame brought to light certain standing factors they had not noticed. Besides having less than five-thousand students; it is the sister school to Notre Dame. The school was rated as second in America, only to MIT, in engineering. They had only noticed its outstanding rating in nursing, but its school of broadcasting rated number one, on the western coast.

By this time the three of them were sitting on the bed side, with Soame in the middle, their eyes glued to the UP catalog. He laid the booklet in his lap, and did a one and one. When he extended the invitation to Cindy, Janet went for her paraphernalia. Cindy told him she did not feel anything and delivered a smacking kiss on his lips. He turned back to the cover photograph; it was a low aerial view of the campus. The Willamette River was in the photo with the University of Portland sitting on a bluff overlooking the river. He then turned to the information on the inside flap. This was the reason, he told them, as to why he examined the catalog, with scrutiny. The information revealed the campus being rated within the top ten most beautiful campuses in the United States. When Cindy read the fact to them aloud, she looked at him, letting him know, "Its mother's preference also."

He replied, "It's the most plush, highly rated school, I have ever heard of. How do you feel about it?"

With a quick, quaint smile, she briskly looked back to the catalog and began fanning the pages. "It says, 'all applicants and admission fees must be submitted before the close of July.' Today's the 27th."

"Cindy I asked you how do you feel about the school?"

She was taken aback. As if only the two of them were drifting through the heavens on a cloud, she gazed, as in a trance while placing the book aside, and snuggled into him, as if they had been lovers for years, telling him, "It is my choice if you will send me, and I will be very pleased to go Soame." She kissed him. The kiss was short, but burned both of them with fire.

"Would you pass me my pants?" Janet had already noticed his erection. He glanced to his left, and she smiled at him. He extracted five, one-hundred dollar bills from his side, and gave them to Cindy. "You should have your application filled Monday morning; I'm sure your father will mail it for you. I'll be here to take him to town."

Janet then slapped him with her elbow, unfastening her bra strap. "I was waiting to see if you had lied to me. Put that away baby, we've got some unfinished things to take care of here."

Sitting at the foot of the bed, he relit the "roach." Janet was leaning against the contemporary dresser, she was doing a shot and he was snorting. Cindy had gone from her room to the bathroom. They both heard the door close behind her. "Let me look at your pussy Janet."

Taking her panties to midway her thighs and softly protesting, she asked, "Are we back at this again?"

When Cindy came through and closed the door, Soame extended his hand and asked, "Are you going to join me?" Instinctively, she clasped both hands between her legs, slightly bent over, shuffling toward him, with a shy grin, she told him "Would you believe I've never done this before?"

She rested one knee on the bed, and while placing an arm midway across his shoulder, Janet called out, "Don't worry, sweetheart, I've got his attentions trained in this direction."

She responded, "Oh yeah," while taking his chin, and placing her lips on his.

Knowing he was trapped, the kiss served its purpose. Soame had a lit "roach" in one hand and a straw in the other. The open vile was between his socked feet.

Cindy held the straw for him; he reached for his pants, went into the pocket containing mints, and offered one to them. He told Cindy, "Try one of these, and it'll keep your mouth moist."

"I want to try the coke once more, I still don't think it's doing any good though."

Ten minutes later the three of them were nude and in the bed. Their bodies mangled and tangled with rhythms. Janet swirled her slithering tongue all over his body, giving him pulsating sensations, even when she twirled her mouth into his hairs, and carried it on down the shaft. His succulent kiss brought moaning sighs from Cindy. He did not kiss her nearly as hard before. She adjusted to a gentle persuasion, and responded with vivaciousness. He used one hand to toy with her breast and upper body. He carried it between her legs, and into her secretion. Janet's head rose from his shaft, she tugged with her hands, and when he looked, she motioned "no" with her lips.

It was a simple, easy, gentle, and basic position they formed for intercourse. Nevertheless, Soame did not place any weight on the inexperienced woman, who had been primed to deliver herself onto his instrument. He felt Janet leaving the bed, as he inserted himself. With distributed weight between one elbow and his knees, he straddled her spread legs. Only his head was inserted. She had begun moving into him before he rested the elbow. She had taken a quarter of him into her, when she gasped. The freedom of movement found its way to her senses. She only had to move for the pleasure she was in search of, had wished and longed for; it was the pleasure of her desire.

She moved only slightly. Her juices supplied the comfort she needed to move more. Her body and mind enabled her to know it would be alright. When she had taken half of him, he began a slight rock. This excited her. Though he did not rotate, the rocking action with her movement began to create a harmonious rhythm. There was still no weight. She moved freely with him, looking into his face and wanting to smile with him, but she was feeling sensations she had never before experienced. They were jubilant feelings of delight.

Cindy called to him, "Oh Soame."

Through the smile he responded, "Are you all right?"

"We're doing it Soame. Where's my mom?"

"I'm here baby girl, I'm here." Janet was seated in the chair, and dared not to move, for fear of foiling the synchronized movement she had witnessed them create.

"Mother I'm doing it, we'r-"

He gave a slight, half rotation into her, and knew by then, she was not multi orgasmic. She hurriedly grabbed the tops of his shoulders as she had done earlier in the kiss. With natural instincts and abilities, she twitched from the deeper penetration, and threw herself onto the rod, taking it further into her.

"That's it, um gonna teach you how to fuck. Um gonna fuck you Cindy. Wanna fuck?"

"Oh Soame do it to me, please." He did a full rotation of his hips. When Janet saw it, it appeared to be a loop in an instant, like magic. It excited her to the point of masturbation.

Cindy cried out, "Oh God Soame, please."

He had made a three quarter penetration, in almost ten minutes. "Please what?"

"Do it to me Soame, please."

He then began rotating. "I told you I'm fuckin you. What am I doing Cindy?"

"You're fuckin me Soame." Once again she naturally synchronized her movements with his and began rotating.

"Um gonna make you my bitch."

"Oh please, Soame, please."

"Please what?"

"Please fuck me, just fuck me."

"I fuck my bitches really good. You wanna be my bitch Cindy?" She moved her hands from his shoulder, and hugged his lower back. Her rotational strokes increased. "I don't fuck no other man's bitch. Are you my bitch?"

"I'm your woman. Just let me be your woman."

"Um gonna stop fuckin you." He did, but he knew, Janet knew, and the delivering Cindy knew what she had developed. Without weight she looped and whirled rotational strokes onto the instrument.

Her eyes were droopy, Cindy's lips were folded under, and she waved her head from side to side. She was at the base of the bell. "If you can't be my bitch, you don't need this dick, um gonna take it ou-"

"I'm your bitch, Soame please fuck me." He stroked her slowly; she was reciprocating two strokes to his one and climbing. Placing one knee in at a time, without disturbing their movement, he climbed in between her legs. "What are we doin Cindy?"

"Oh Soame please fuck me."

"Where?"

"In my pussy."

"Is this my pussy?"

"It's your pussy. Please fuck me Soame, please." She was moving toward her peak and lashed whirling strokes at him, three to his one. He would not give her the swell of his head; knowing a deeper penetration would satisfy her just as well. He rotated deeper into the spread legs.

"You say you're my woman?"

"I'm your woman. I'm your bitch. I feel sooo good Soammmmmme. Please fuck meee." He rotated the penetration in, until their stomachs were slapping.

She did not scream. With grunts and moans she tossed her head feverishly from side to side, and in arriving at her zenith, she bellowed "Oh Soame please, my God yes, yes, yes, yes, yes, yes!!"

Janet then reached her third orgasm. This time she was standing over them. Her hand on his shoulder asking "Are you a mother fucker?" stroking herself into ecstasy.

So far it had already been a magnificently beautiful experience. Cindy had been stroked until the total completeness of her grunts, moans, and satisfying whimpering cries, perfected the final stage of the subsiding ebb. When she was finished and satisfied, Cindy rounded her arms around his neck, and wrestled them on their sides. "I did it, I know I did it this time. He's pleased me and made me happy mother. I never could've imagined the feelings I've just experienced." Janet then kneeled on the bed, next to them. Cindy looked him in the eyes, and then lavishly plunged her tongue into his mouth. The instrument still held them jointed.

Triumph reigned and the room was filled with the delight of fulfillment. Janet had timed the event, and was pleased with its efficient results, "It was more than twenty-three and less then twenty-five. I don't know for sure, so lets just round it off at twenty-four minutes. You were great, more than spectacular in fact, I commend you."

"Don't be too fast with your commendation. I've told you, um fuckin both you bitches. In fact, to show and prove to you um a real motherfucker, and I really know how to break in a brand new bitch, um fuckin you twice."

Cindy had excused herself to use the bathroom. Janet knew he had not ejaculated, and used the face cloth she earlier brought in to clean the still totally erect dick. They were still nude, sitting on the side of the bed. She casually looked at him with a rolling glance, from the corner of her eye, and replied, "Oh yeah, now you just do that mister."

"Fact is, as soon as she walks through that door, you're gonna start showing her how to give me head."

"Soame I'm not an eighteen year old girl. I've never been a whore. Before my husband I became effective with my body, and knew how to perform dutifully with efficient results. The years have only bettered my experiences. You may have hope, but I'd say what you're thinking is impossible."

"I don't talk sex, I do it. I've never had another man's wife as my bitch. We're going to be alright, Janet."

"I never said I was your bitch, and I do not cater to the term."

"We'll see. We will see."

She had not told him wrong. He was not disappointed in Janet's dutiful response, and the efficient manner in which she displayed her experience. When Cindy entered the room, he stood, moved to the head of the bed, adjusted the pillows, and rested himself in a reclined position against the head board. When Janet saw him motion Cindy to him, she leaned back and began fondling the pleasure instrument at her convenience. Cindy kneeled next to him at the head of the bed. She attempted to kiss him, and he instructed her, "Watch now, this may be important for you."

Janet was beautiful, not only in her appearance, but also in the smooth, relaxed, submissive, and orderly way in which she demonstrated the artful act of fellatio. At times she obediently cast her sweeping eyes to him. She had various ways of holding, shifting, and positioning her shoulder length, dark hair to display the beauty of her face. The two did coke while watching. The older woman was most effective in demonstrating not only oral sex, but various ways she was able to stimulate herself. She moved completely into the bed, and it was there he found her to be completely uninhibited. Janet straddled his torso in a kneeling sixty-nine type position, and with two fingers spread her vulva; the three of them knew she was definitely ready. The two had been watching for more then fifteen minutes. Soame asked Cindy to the chair.

He took an upright kneeling position behind her from that same position, on all fours,. She was brought upright. There in upright kneeling positions, he entered her from behind. She was tight. There was no doubt about the experience she had mentioned, and each knew beforehand, they were sexually compatible. Her lubricants eased the copulation. He easily had access to cup and toy with her breast from the position. She took him into her with his revolving rotating thrusts. She humped up and down taking him in as he back stroked out. Soame kissed, blew and sucked on Janet's ear, and when he pinched and squeezed her right nipple, the mini orgasm caused her body to quiver. She also responded "Oh yes Soame," and went forward for the deeper penetration. At this point, both realized there was no room for deception by either. A pussy slinger and a real dickster were engaged. There would be serous toil for the gratification. This was the position Janet had opened herself to him in, on all fours, "doggie style."

Her intent was obvious to him. Therefore, Soame gave her the measure she expected. She had kissed, licked, and taken it deep into her throat, and knew every inch of it. She was not disappointed with what she received. This gave her and Cindy a closer look at each other. All along she had been calling him lover, and referring to herself as his girl. It was not easy, but she had taken him, and if he hilted, it would be no more than a half inch more at most. She baited him, in close view of her daughter. In a whispering voice, she over and over used the terms "lover" and "your girl." Up to this point he had not uttered a word. The two women knew he was performing. Janet was positive, "I'm a married woman Soame please, just fuck me and have me as your lover." He said nothing.

He did nonetheless send her forward. She was sprawled out on her breast, and the upper section of her stomach was flat on the bed. Her arms and hands extended out, as if she was in worship. Her buttocks could only lift up. After several rotations, delivering his extent, he parted her cheeks with his palms. To Janet, this was exhilarating. Her second orgasm erupted, shattering her body through and through. In extending his all, they both knew he had expanded her as much as he could. Janet had never before seen a penis the size of Soame's. Not only was it long, it was thick in diameter. Before that day, she had no experience enveloping a dick his size. She was thrilled by that accomplishment alone. Not only did he want to see all she had, he also wanted Cindy to witness the experienced use of it. They shifted into the basic missionary position.

She made sweeping rounds of whirling thrusts onto the rigorously punching strokes he made with rhythmical impulses. Janet threw her arms around his neck, and looped her legs around his back. She slung riveting thrashes of circular rotations, to meet the measured pumps he threw into her. She never discontinued praying in his ear. To him the whispering was relaxing, and he enjoyed hearing what she had to say, though he did not verbally respond. Their bodies began to perspire, and slap with noise when they came in contact. He looked at Cindy whose excitement induced her to begin rubbing between her legs. "Don't do that um gonna fuck you good again, as soon as this is over. Tell me you're my bitch."

"I'll always be yo-"

"Yes I'm your bi-" Janet interrupted Cindy.

With another interruption, Soame reminded her "Naw naw; I was talking to my bitch. You're the married woman remember? Now come on and gimmie some pussy, and your lover is gonna make his girl, his bitch later on taday."

Janet had long before realized she could not out match his stroke. He seemed to accelerate with ease, and each time she slowed her momentum, he adjusted to her flow. This infuriated her with passion. A sensation took control of her body.

She raved with her heaves to, around, under, back and forth on him. He shortened, lengthened, and doubled his strokes in response. Far away, her sensations relayed the beginning tremble of a pulse. She knew that when in full bloom, its eruption would overwhelmingly consume her. She knew then exactly how her daughter felt earlier when she attempted to break from his kiss.

The want to stop moving her body was suppressed by the anticipation of the furthermost thrill of the day, within a year, perhaps ten years, maybe in her entire life. He broke his motion reaching back for a pillow. The penetration slid out, to the knotted head. Janet scooted and hunched into him crying "No, no God no, please don't stop fucking me Soame." He placed the pillow under her jack hammering ass, and removed one of her legs from his back. Using the grounded foot as leverage, she frantically gave herself to him, whispering into his ear. When she told him "I'll be yours, whenever, wherever, however you want. Just don't stop Soame, please fuck me, please don't stop."

"I haven't stopped yet, have I?" I'm your lover remember? I just want you to be my girl for right now. Come on gimme the pussy." Her feelings became more intense, like electrical impulses sending sensitive, increasing micro-shockwaves throughout her body, and she began to feel herself tremble. Sweat dripped and rolled from them both. He looked into her face, double stroked her with a hunch, and following the fully penetrated rotation he removed three quarters of the shaft. As she moved to gather it back, he plunged. This amplified her shock waves. "I'm about to cum, where's my baby?"

Only he could see Cindy, who had been snorting coke, twice within seven minutes, after he had stopped her from masturbating. He plunged his tongue into Janet's open mouth, in search of the exuberant kiss she had earlier invited him with.

Cindy saw both of them shaking, as if a massive tremble had taken effect on them. A closer look showed her mothers hips completely off the pillow. Her back was bridged, and she braced herself upward from her shoulders. She came, moaning through fulfillment, with their mouths embraced, fanning sweeps of propelled, rounded, hammering throws. He had no intentions of matching if he could.

It was not yet over. When she moved groggily into the position they began in, he inquired "Are you alright?"

"I'm fine Soame. How did you get the stamina?"

"I guess a lover has to have staying power, when he wants to make his girl his bitch, ha?"

She did not reply but allowed him to cast her into the "doggie style" position. She had a stockpile of juices trapped within her folds, but more secretions had to be activated.

Less than two minutes after his penetration, his torso leaned down against her back; this forced her to the bed, almost flat on her stomach. Soame extended her left arm toward the foot on the bed. Slightly easing her toward the foot of the bed and to the left side, he moved her right knee up. He had previously explored and tickled her erogenous zone. This resulted in the second mini orgasm she had. He stroked and eased directly into it. Janet instantly felt the beginning eruption and whispered, "Oh Soame, already? I don't know if I can stand another so soon."

"You asked your lover not ta stop fuckin his girl didn't ya?"

She had never before experienced a G-spot orgasmic thrill. Instinct alerted her of the most sensational sexual event in her life. The abrupt suddenness tossed her almost into fright. "Soame I'll be your bitch," she whispered, looking back and up at him. Only then did she realize she was being sexually captured by the most sexually productive force she had ever encountered. Though his strokes were gently slow, erotic waves of passionate intensity were vibrating through out her body. Again she whispered back to him, "I said I'm your bitch Soame, I'm married, but I'll still be your woman and your bitch. Oh God Soame, please talk to me." Janet turned her face toward her daughter, "Baby we'll share him like we said we would, I told him we talked about-"

"You sure you wanna be my bitch?"

"Soame, I'm yours honey."

"Your what?"

The first orgasmic wave hit her, drowning out any and all other feeling and thoughts, of anything and anyone, except the one who filled her furthest pleasure with delight.

He did not break his slow, even rhythmic strokes. Other than looking at him, panting, with a slight tremble, she did not move, in her surrender to the man, and the engulfing feelings of passions he had brought into her. "You said you wanted me to talk to you, I am, are you all right?"

"I'm flowing. I've cum so much, I don't know what to do. I want to tell you to stop, but it's so good. Soame you're fucking me too good. I don't know what to do. It's never happened to me before."

"Are you still my girl?"

She continued whispering to him, "I'm your girl. I'm your bitch. I'm your woman, Soame."

"For how long, Janet?"

"For as long as you want me, oh God please don't ever leave me, please"

"Well you come to me when I call?"

"Every time, any time, wherever, I'll come. I swear."

The final wave surged, erupting violent trembles throughout her body. Janet began pounding clenched fists on the bed. She attempted to drown her heaves of sighing moans into the bed covers. He gave the pillow to her. The soft material yielded to her, and accepted the screams of consuming pleasure found in the apex she attained. She threw her body into the instrument in whipping waves of frantic circles of gratification. He had stopped his movement when she began screaming. The pillow absorbed the screams, moans, cries, and hollering. The trembling subsided, her pace slowed, and only when she was completely done, was she still.

Cindy stood at the foot of the bed in front of her. Knowing she was finished, she inquired "Are you alright mother?"

With her face still smothered in the pillow, she was unaware of Cindy. Looking up, seeing her, she extended her hand. "He triggered my erogenous zone. It was an encounter with sexual pleasure I've never before had. I'll be fine, just get me a towel will you?" Neither of them had ever before smelled the existing odor in the room. Its origin was obvious. No one questioned it. She gave a bashful look at her Beau and her mother's boyfriend and exited the room.

Upon her return, Janet was seated in the chair. She was finishing the water brought to the room earlier. Soame was on the far side of the bed, placing the wet pillow on the head board. The saturated spot near the bed's corner was then seen by Cindy. Soame's body glistened with perspiration; his erect member shined, and a look into his eyes told her he wanted to be pleased. She was then more desirous of him than she had ever thought of being, for any man.

Walking toward her mother, she noticed Janet's hair and body was soaked with perspiration. They had been talking when she entered the room. She stood up, accepted the towel and gave her a hug, "I'm wet with sweat. I've got to use the bathroom. Thanks, dear."

As her mother left, Soame approached her. His lips gently brushed hers, and went to the nipple of her left breast. They both knew the spot activated the passions in her. He found that his finger sloshed in the secretions in her flaps. He directed her to the center of the foot of the bed. "Let's make this complete and cum together." He instructed her to a position, with her knees on the bed and her legs extending over its edge. This doggie fashion allowed him to stand.

He eased on into her With the penetration,. She had no difficulty rocking back and forth onto him. Cindy learned to revolve herself in this style. She gave moans, sighs, and whimpering sounds of delight. This time he did not talk to her, but she found his caressing her sides, cupping and fondling her breasts to be just as invigorating. After seven minutes of stimulating intercourse, he showed her how to go from her outstretched arms to her elbows. She took the deeper penetration with ease and loved it. Janet entered the room, with her hair wrapped in a towel, and a glass of water in one hand, she seated herself in the chair. Their moves became rapid and from the sounds Cindy made, she could tell she was about to experience her second copulating orgasm. What she did not know was the driving force had begun to swell. Moans, grunts, and sighs filled the room. Then she heard a sound she had not heard from him.

Cindy extended her hand for the remaining pillow. Throwing it into her face, she lowered the pillow and her face to the bed, suffocating the screams. With her elbows spread eagle on the bed, gripping the pillow, while she tossed her head back and forth, screaming into it, she whirled herself around at the exploding force within her. "Um cumin," was the deep guttural sound Janet had been intensely waiting to hear. Almost simultaneously, there was another sound. It was so loud. Its almost deafening penetration overruled anything else to be heard in the entire area. The window panes rattled, and in the quiet stillness, created as the aftermath of the roar, Cindy scooted off the protrusive instrument within her. She rested her face on the pillow, and took deeper exercising breaths of air into her lungs. No one expected the thunder that shook the house. Soame and Janet saw the rain outside. Janet also saw the glistening extension from his body. She swiftly moved to the bed and seated herself before it. She displayed pleasure toward the "clean up" sequence. She comforted the pleasure stick as it subsided; it had taken her to heights and thrills beyond her belief.

It was pouring outside; he and Cindy were at the bottom step when she dashed toward the basement for an umbrella. Janet then came up and walked him to the door. Departing wishes and waves were extended between Soame and Tom, the confirmation of the deal was again mentioned and nothing else was said between them. At the door the two stood a usually spaced distance apart. Before they left the room he and Cindy had gotten dressed together. After giving her three-hundred dollars, they proceeded to her parent's room. They allowed ample time because Janet had told them of her "quick shower." When they arrived they found she had also done her face, and added lipstick. She was fully dressed except for her shoes and one of her stockings. She was seated on her bed running the stocking up. He brought his clip from his pocket, and while she fastened the top of the stocking to the garter, he flung three hundred dollars to the bed, next to her.

"Don't you ever throw anything to me again."

He took a fifty, and threw it near the spread paper, saying "Here bitch."

Putting on one shoe she told him, "I told you you're going to make me filthy rich." When she put on the other shoe, she stood, straightened her skirt, and raised it to him. Her pink panties were exposed to him while she asked, "Think you've had enough today?"

"Its getting late Janet, I've got to be getting home." He handed her a twenty.

"I've never before had a Saturday as nice, pleasant, and as exciting as this one. I don't think I'll ever have one in the future to top this one, but if I do I'll never forget this day, for more than one reason, Soame."

"Are you sure you're my bitch?"

"Just tell me when and where you want me, and see how fast I come."

"Can you drive?" Cindy was there with the umbrella.

"I was going to teach my baby here this summer."

"Well, I'll let you know Monday. I've got to say good night now, see you then."

They smacked air kisses to each other, "Thanks Soame, goodnight." He and Cindy went out the door.

She had complimented him on the plush interior of the Seville. "Soame I was looking at this car when you came through the dining room earlier, after you had left my dad. I was wondering if I should ask you to take me for a ride."

He leaned over and opened the glove box. "It's kind of mystifying, how things turned out. Cindy you're eighteen and I'm thirty-eight. Soon you'll be off to school and dozens of young boys will be trampling over one another to knock on your door."

"Then the things I said to you, don't mean anything to you?"

"What you said to me means more to me probably than it does to you. Remember, I gave you the words to say."

"Soame I'll always be your only woman, you mustn't ever be worried about that."

"When you think you love me, let me know."

"I think I love you now, but you may think it's too soon for me to know. When I am positive Soame, I will tell you. I do know I have never had feelings toward anyone else, that are as strong as my feelings for you, and I don't think I could develop stronger feelings for anyone else." He took her in his arms and kissed her.

He had taken an ounce of coke from the compartment. In a bill, he poured a portion over the face of "Sam" Grant. The largest portion was left in the container. "You keep this money, but give the powder to your father. Give this in the plastic to Janet." He instructed her on the use, and importance of Vitamin E. He also explored the difference between "cut" and "raw" cocaine. Soame then took a hardy one and one with her, and gave her the vile.

During the course of the kiss that followed, he placed his hand between her legs. It interrupted the kiss. "No, no, I'm way too sore. Do you know what you did to me? No one's ever done it before; at least all the way."

"What did I do?"

"You fucked me my love, you really fucked me." This resumed their kiss. When she waved from the door, he completed the drive in the shoe, was on the dirt road, and gone.

Chapter 15

DUSK had taken the skies by the time he arrived home. In the short distance between the car and the house he was drenched. Inside, Soame went directly to the bedroom, disrobed and went into the shower. The others were watching TV except DD. When he came out of the bathroom she had a Stevie Wonder record on the turntable. "That's my record; the second one I did for him. The preceding one brought his name back to the public. *Signed Sealed and Delivered* was the booster, in launching his career. How'd you know to play that particular record?"

"I'm a Stevie Wonder fan also; you did not mention it before. Chairly!! Bring your papa his dinner. He will be in the boudoir for the remainder of the evening!"

Fifi's latest habit was in sleeping on his chest, when no one else was in the room. They had been sleeping for nearly two hours, when DD awakened the pooch. The dog in return stretched on his chest, waking him up. Following the use of the bathroom, he complimented her in her new, blue, short night gown. He also noticed and mentioned her hair style. It was the first time she wore it. In their bedroom attire, they settled in with small talk, relaxing in the atmosphere of home.

The two were lying across the bed, with Fifi relaxed between them. The volume was off while the television played, with soft, well blended, mood music, played in the background. "Darlinggg who have you been with?"

"You've never been so direct before. You don't appear to be angry. Are you?"

"I don't know but I have a reason for asking." He explained Beauford asked him to visit the Blanchard Farm from start to scratch. The situation there with "Teressa," the loveliness and beauty of Janet and Cindy, the sex they had, and the business agreement they had arranged to be carried through on Monday. They indulged in their highs, while he explained. When he completed the story, she treated him with her oral delights.

Soame stipulated confidentiality between the two of them in regards to "Teressa," in the event she wanted to disclosed any part of the information to Camille or Margaret, who had also become a growing factor with DD. "Now my dearest, I want to know why you asked."

"It's the situation here. Camille is satisfied with either of us, but we both know I only pacify her in your absence; I think she was miserably unhappy until we came along. Beverly doesn't know what she's doing, and doesn't really care. Like me, Margaret shares a feeling for you that's deep with silence."

"Oh, so what is this silent feeling you have that's so deep?" He was practical in his jest toward her because she remained shy in telling him of her love for him.

"How it would be for each of us to have you for herself, my love. We have all at one time or another thought or wished it. That is the point of this, and the answer to your question is Chairly. She amuses herself with Beverly, to suppress her interests and feelings for you. She's my girl, but there are times when I can neither satisfy nor pacify her. Soame, she is helplessly in love with you."

"That's my last concern. It's infatuation and I seriously doubt if she at least feels that. I'll tell ya what she's 'helpless' about; it's coming up with a new scheme to get something else she wants. Tell that hussy to use her smooth tactics in getting out, and getting a job, we'll see then how much love she has." He pushed up on his extended arms. "In fact, I'll tell her myself. I want some ice cream."

"No, no, no Suarme." Then Fifi began barking. "I will get the ice cream, and I will bring Camille back, and we will give you other treats." Darting out of the door and around the corner, she lifted the tail of her nightgown up, exposing the matching beautifully laced undies.

Camille's nightgown matched DD's. It was white with the pink trimmings DD had on her bottoms and vice versa. He was laid back on pillows leaned against the bed board. One knee was propped up with an arm extended over it. Camille went directly to him, sat at his side and delivered a long sensual kiss. The affection relaxed him. He appreciated it in more than one way. Some thing really puzzled him, and he needed to be relaxed for the concentration he wanted to give. Camille did not take to smoking the pipe. When he began eating the ice cream she delivered the same type of sensuality to the only member she would ever accept as a satisfying tool. After DD smoked, she joined her. They alternated, and at times both shared the administration. During one interval, DD sent sensations throughout his body with the stimulating pulsations of her tongue. Camille smoked a joint of reefer and snorted with him. He asked "Do you know of Tom Blanchard selling coke in the area?"

"Through Mrs. Tillman. I know he did pretty well, but that was before we moved here. She's often commented 'if he was as good at farming as he was at selling drugs, he wouldn't have the problems he's faced with.'"

DD took a measured piece of "base," placed it in the pipe at the night stand. She asked, "Is there something worrying you about that guy, you said you weren't going to deal with him in that way."

"Not from that aspect, but something's been said, that's a possible key to this entire situation, if we aren't to be stuck here with a car, farm, house and a mansion. I noticed it when it was said, but too many other issues had precedence —"

"Suarme, what, I don't understand how the pres-" Camille explained the term.

He concluded "It had to be instrumentally important. I would not have remembered it as a key factor, if it weren't. I've been trying to sort it out, I'll get to it. I feel that I must."

When he completed his say, she said to them, "I hope the input added can be of some help. I'm going to be busy for a while, if you'll excuse me." She then lowered herself to his midsection.

DD lit her pipe, and after exhaling, said to him, "I wish I could help."

Camille gurgled "M… t…"

He replied to them, "You are helping."

DD knew exactly how much money there was and kept tabs on how the money was spent between the two of them. She did not know how he had gotten it or the drugs. In Denver, after the sale of the "hog," she asked him, "What was the purpose of the reservations and instructions?"

"Forget about it. It's no longer important; let's just enjoy what we have. There's a lot behind us; let's leave it there." That was the only time she had questioned the origin of the material items they enjoyed. Soame discovered DD to be a very budget-oriented person.

He calculated his holdings very carefully. Detection seemed to be no problem, from where he was located. In a week he could travel east to Chicago, Philadelphia, Baltimore, Detroit, or New York, and for a quick sale, get rid of one of the four and a half kilograms of heroin. This would immediately increase his cash holding to between three quarters and million dollars.

This gave him little consideration toward the lack of money. He had developed a natural interest in his surroundings, through his knowledge of the social structure. Plus the environment was ideal for his adjustment in being financially secured, and offering almost perfect camouflage as he maneuvered. Because of him being black, if he could have aided fellow members of his race, besides DD and Chairly, in his immediate vicinity, he would have cheerfully done so. His circumstance and situation did not involve a racial issue.

Just past midnight, there was a knock at the bedroom door. When the boyishly dressed Chairly was asked in, she trampled directly over to the entertainment center, and without saying anything set the turntable in motion. They saw she had a forty-five record in her hand, as she traipsed across the floor. She wore a baseball cap turned backwards on her head. On the previous trip she had purchased a pair of penny loafers which were on her feet. She also had on jeans, one of his soiled white shirts from the hamper, and Camille's top of her green suit. She popped gum and announced "Um out walkin my bitch, and we thought we might as well stop by and look in on you common folk." She then placed the needle on the Rick James record *You and I*.

Through the door, with a canister of bits of paper, came a person they thought was Beverly. This time she did not have on shades. The long sweeping eye lashes could be seen, as well as the mascara eyebrows. She had false nails that flashed and glittered when she placed the fashionable cigarette holder in her mouth with flamboyant swankness. Camille totally disregarded the "put on" because it was the norm practically everyday, especially when Soame wasn't around. That afternoon they had almost been excessive with it.

No one had to guess, it must have taken them an hour, to cut the bits of paper Beverly began to toss as confetti. It could be seen through the clear glass jar; it was large. DD and Soame had overcome the shock in seeing her, when she threw the first batch. DD also noticed Camille ignoring the treat, and this time it was special. Camille never stopped exercising the performance she was administering. Her back was to them, DD tapped her on the shoulder. When she lifted her eyes toward DD, she pointed. The music in the background was thumping. Chairly had a knack for blasting the speakers. Camille looked at Soame, who indicated to the duo with the movement of his head. Dislodging from the tool, she turned and was initially trapped in wonder. She glanced over at Chairly, to be sure it was the right couple. Confetti drifted down in front of her face as she looked back at the person standing over the bed. She cried "My baby, oh God what have you done to yourself." Beverly sprinkled another douse of synthetic confetti over head.

She was wearing a teddy none of them had seen before, new pumps, a pair of fishnet gray stockings, and from DD's boxes, an almost white feathered stole across her shoulders. None of this topped the platinum wig she had on, but nothing was comparable to the person behind the lavishly expert makeup job.

Final bits of paper streamed over her shoulder, from her flaring them with an over the shoulder glance, as she ran away to Chairly. She and the pumping music held them in a slight trance. Beverly exchanged the jar for Chairly's shades. What they saw next, none of them, except DD, had seen before. Camille could not imagine her daughter, at that inexperienced age knowing how to present herself in a dance with such lasciviousness. It was a step from being vulgar. She humped, hunched, and rolled with the beat of the music. The stole was used between her legs back and forth lewdly, with her harmoniously moving body. After straddling it, she twirled one end, as if it was a watch on a key chain, and characterized herself as a hot shot gigolo. At the fade of the record, her back was to them; she held her ankles in a squat. Then slowly she raised her rear, still holding her ankles until her legs were straight. She moved her hips from side to side as she rose. Her hands were brought up tracing the inside of her thighs. At the end of the record, with one hand she took her shades; the other was used to raise the outside corner of the teddy. Looking over her shoulder, she winked as the record ended and the top of the teddy fell. The people in the bed would have easily expected her as a woman between 22 and 3 years of age, had they not known otherwise.

From the coat pocket, Chairly walked to her with a pad she had extracted, and a pen. "Mizz fine Johnson, my bitch, will now give you peoples hur autograph."

"Ah, say sport, while your Ms. Fin-" Camille slapped his thigh. "Yea, well pardon me, while your people here does us the grace, will you pass me my pants." Chairly jumped with exuberance, dashing to the love seat, where he usually placed his pants. By this time Beverly handed him a piece of paper with "Mizz Fine" scribbled on it.

"Whas da pants Soame. Ain't no pants ova hea."

"Oh yeah, ah-" DD pinched his arm, rose and stepped to the night stand. "Say ah, check this out big time; if you're done, how about giving us back the service of our equipment, that is if you and..."

He looked at the paper, turned it upside down, sideways, finally Beverly stated "Mizz Fine, if you don't mind!"

"Oh yeah Mizz Fine, thank you for this precious remembrance." DD handed him his slide and clip. Beverly snatched the holder from her mouth, and threw her head up exhaling smoke.

After turning the TV and radio back on, with her record, Chairly walked to the bed. He gave her twenty dollars. "Ah, shell I give this to you or your agent here."

"Gimmie da money Soame, you know how it go."

He gave Charily another twenty dollar bill. "Das all, iz dat all, Soame, fa all dis work?!" Beverly's cigarette was burning low; she walked to the dresser, removed the cigarette, and while snuffing it, glanced at her mother.

She had a feeling her mother could have been peeved. However, neither of them said, or indicated anything to the contrary. "What do you mean? You march in here with Ms. Sling nasty, play a three and a half minute record, I dish out forty bucks, for something you think is the pot of gold at the end of the rainbow, is that it?"

Everyone knew Chairly would not accept his response, including him. It had been a really good show. "Soame, um ga tell ya." She stood bowed back in her legs pointing an index finger at him. "I ain't ever seen a man as diconsirate as you, but we love ya, and wez good wemin. We gota be ta stay wid somebody like you."

"Here you are dear." DD removed a hundred dollar bill from his slide, and passed it to her.

"I'll tell you what, since you're so liberal to their cause Mrs. Super Fine Bitch of Mine! Monday morning, you put these two in that car out there, and I don't care where you take them, between here and the state library in Wyoming, but when you get back here." He was talking to DD in a tone of voice which she knew was serious. He had never raised his voice to that level to her before. Soame was pointing at the other two standing at the foot of the bed.

"I want them each to have a book, do you hear and understand me Dominique?"

"Suarme I hear and understand you very well. It's also Saturday night. The girls simply wanted to have a little fun. Plus they wanted to entertain you, most of all."

"I'm not criticizing am I? In fact, I've paid for the performance. What I am telling you and them is, I will not see Chairly and my second lady's daughter afforded with a one-sided view of life. You two have bodies, that you seem to know. I want to make sure you realize that you have brains as well. It takes the combination of the two. Do you understand me Beverly?"

"Sure I understand you hot shot."

"How bout you, kid?"

"Ma name ain't kid, Mr. James Brown."

"If you're done, I think you'd better get your asses out of here."

Chairly waved the fanned bills at him, and sensually licked her lips on her approach to the door. Beverly was a step in front of her, and at the door she stopped abruptly. Chairly almost bumped into her. Looking over her shoulder, as sexy as any hundred dollar hooker, she said something in French, tossed her head up, and took a step before giggling Chairly pushed her into the hall, saying, "Gurl, you crazy."

Except for monsieur Hudson, he pretended not to understand what she said. Turning to DD he asked, "What'd she say?"

"She simply said, 'My dear Mr. Hudson, you are such a cad.'"

He scooted out of the bed, marched to the open door, and roared through the hall and house, "And you two panhandlers tell that make up artist and beautician of yours to fix me a sandwich, and this time I'm having it in here!"

It had happened. He was pleased with himself. Once again, an encounter with Chairly had netted fruitful results. Over and over he had gone through each word held in the conversations between him and Tom. It was not who stated, "Shit you got will open the town up again." It was Billy, but Tom did say, "If you have access to quantity of this quality, you have a definite set up, developmental and expansion area right here." Chairly had been instrumental in disassociating his thought pattern toward Tom. Instantly, when he recognized the portrayal of the resemblance, she and Billy shared as characters, it came to him what Billy had said.

With what had been said by the two of them, combined with the fact, Tom had never had more than a "key" at once, and at best it had been "stepped on" at least once. He saw the possibility of "developmental growth and expansion." The dwindling population of the county was less than 1,500 people; when Beauford Allison was elected sheriff, there were more than 17,000. That was the heart of the situation, and it was rapidly losing its vital fluid. It was not quite a new discovery, but in finding a solution, one must know the exact problem.

Closing the door he went into the bathroom. When he re-entered the bedroom, the women saw the cheerfulness on his face. Since he had been home he seemed dull and depressed; past midnight Soame had come alive. Seeing the brightly expressed grin, DD and Camille looked at each other. It was DD who inquired, "Darlinggg, is it you have solved the problem?"

"No, I haven't solved it, but I know at least what it is, and what I want to do. I can't do anything faster than the pace I'm at, but now I know what the goal is, and I have method to get to it." He had walked over to the entertainment center. The record DD played earlier had been one of the two he scanned through Camille's box and found. They had been in the record holder for three days, but the mood was not in cadence with the flow of the music. The Rick James record set them off. He put the James Brown record on, and his two ladies saw what they had never seen before.

It was very conservative, and would have been acceptable with almost any style music; his dancing was very moderately casual. He called them to the floor with him, and replayed the music. Then with them, he got absolutely, atrociously vulgar. They all knew none of them could not out dance DD. With naturally applied rhythm, she had moves Fred Astaire had never dreamed of. Their vulgarities matched exquisitely when the arm tripped to play the second time, she said "Wait, wait, wait, I will hit my pipe, and I will show you." He increased the volume and he and Camille got it on. She danced more like a Hawaiian hula dancer, attempting to do the shimmy; with impressive style, she maintained his encounter.

On the third round of the record, Margaret came through the door. On a platter, she had a sandwich, potato chips, a glass of ice tea, and a side dish of ice cream. Between the next playing she said to them, "You all seem to be having fun."

"This my dear, is a record I used and made this guy the King of Soul. This record alone, is why James Brown is soul brother number one."

"What's the name of it Soame?"

"*There Was a Time*." The food had been placed on the dresser. He went toward the food, leaving the two on the floor who seemed not to miss his company. Margaret saw DD's pipe on the nightstand, and signaled her for its use. DD "shooed" her toward it, granting her consent. She had gotten turned on to the fantail strumming beat of the music. The lyrics voiced out: There was a time I danced, pranced, and made romance, but any kind of weather, we all get together, and we all do…

They had no routine set for Sundays. Camille and her daughters had gone to the local Baptist Church occasionally, but the minister had also been a small farmer in the area. When he moved no one resumed his position. DD had not been since she was a child in her native homeland. Chairly mentioned having gone to a Methodist church frequently. Soame was held to, and had a firm, unyielding, religious concept and belief in the Almighty Amon.

* * *

He and Camille once discussed the matter thoroughly beyond reproach. He explained to her, "Christianity is a farce. People in America basically accept its exploitations and close eyes and ears to religious practices and customs that were in effect thousands of years before and idea such as Christianized came about. I am an African American. I have a religious creed with my culture, which is the establishment of civilization, on the planet we live on. White America has done any and everything possible in stealing, distorting, and to the possible extent of destroying that which leads and traces back to us, Blacks, establishing these ways and patterns of life. In doing so, Americans take the greatest and most precious freedom of all for granted; it is our freedom of choice.

"Terms such as 'heathen,' 'pagan,' 'barbarian,' and any other specific term of the sort, refer to only one particular race and ethnic group of people, the Caucasian division. The smartest of you, even with modern day science, cannot trace your civilized origin further back than Athens; your civilization begins with Ancient Greece. Remember now, we're talking about religion. You must first trace to where the concept began. Since you do not have a civilized culture before that period, surely the civilized existing cultures had a religious concept, before the name Zeus was arrived at. Our history and civilization dates back further than the pyramids, which is symbolic only of black culture. Thebes was the first trade center in the entire world. The city later became Memphis, and today is known as Ethiopia. You might wonder what these established historical facts have to do with religion. With such a vast background in civilization, what is the accepted religious practice of the black man?"

Camille hesitated in answering "Christianity."

"How can that be so Camille? When the practiced empire of Christendom is the youngest practiced religious faith in the world, with less then a tenth of the world's population, members of the Christian faith. Asians practice Buddhism. The people of India worship Brahma, through the practice of Hinduism. The third largest practiced religion in the world is done through the descendants of slaves, who were outcasts as mulattos. The black side of their ethnic heritage is not that of a slave bond. Blacks were first in the world to use slave labor. Long before the design and construction of the pyramids, we had slave labor in force.

Anyway, the members of the Islamic faith worship Allah. They are only part black; the real population of the black man, throughout the world is staggering, but our original faith is not Christianity. Do you have any other ideas?"

She shook her head indicating "no," then asked, "Where does the word Amon come from?"

"It is the name of the first idea and religious concept ever uttered in praise or worship toward a higher form by civilized man. Whites have stolen bits and pieces from a variety of heritages and cultures, and through time, in becoming civilized, distorted, arranged, and adjusted the form of culture now used, to the convenience of the race. The land we live on is like the religion he uses as Christianity for only his benefit. Because he is more sinful then any other race of people, he has constructed and put together a principle revolving around sin and forgiveness, with the reward of heaven through confession.

"What I say to you here today will not phase or have any impact, or bearing on the religious world whatsoever. I do not talk religion; I practice my faith in Amon. It is not a forgiving worship. One who believes must do as best as possible to abstain from sin. I'll conclude in showing you the farce I mentioned. The basic guide book in the Christian belief is the Bible. Within the first fifteen chapters is the book of Genesis, wherein the imaginary tale of the creation is given. The story's setting is characterized by birds, bees, valleys, mountains, rivers, seas, and all the gatherings beneath the firmament, and the place is called Eden. Then there was Adam who slept, and Eve was put on the scene. Lets stop right there because I know you are educated to the point of knowing beyond doubt, you and any or everyone else, who knows how to read and write, has to be taught to do so. The question you can't overlook, unless you close your eyes to reality, is who taught Adam or Eve to read and write? Since they were the only two there, in the garden, who wrote the story?

"I'll take it a step further and tell you of the most renowned 'con' man, throughout the pages of history and time. He was born a slave and raised in a Black king's household. With the first rate education and skills he was granted and acquired, he sought freedom, for slaves who were not as fortunate as he. These slaves were not blacks, by the way, they were imports of another ethnic group and they were not mongoloid. Anyway, Moses parted the Sea of Reed, or the 'Red' Sea, so the story is told. A while later he was to have gone up on Mount Sinai, and there received the ten commandments. A learned person at this point would surely have to put aside the teachings of Hammurabi, which became the law, and accepted as code, but he was Black. However, in the first commandment according to the recognized 'con' artist Moses, it mentions 'the land of Egypt' and him being led 'out of the house of bondage.' Equate that with what has been stated about imported slaves, and see for yourself what Moses was really all about. Also, Paul whose name was a conversion from Saul, had heard of the coming of 'the Messiah' joined in with eleven others, as his follower. How could men like John, Luke, Mark, James, and so forth, who were common or less men, write so eloquently? According to their scriptures, words such as thoust, thou, and thee and others of the sort, weren't used as accepted English language until the days of Shakespeare.

"These people who were said to be followers of Christ, say he walked this earth for thirty-three years. During that time a woman at a well was said to have offered him her body, and he refused. That's too far beyond my imagination. A person of the sort, disguised as a man would truly be a freak and a pervert with devious intentions. I can and will never find a way to recognize the sort as a hero, and it is beneath the knowledge I have, with respect to my race and culture, to be led in such religious folly.

"At the end of each Christian prayer, the last word stated is 'Amen.' The Caucasian, as uncouth, treacherous, wicked, and mischievously cunning with his intelligence, in his vain attempts seeks to pay homage to such a cleverly contrivable scheme. Even in such a trivial way, his meaning in Amen is stated as 'So be it.' It is so, he shall not be forgiven. That be so, as an inspiration from Amon.

"I have taken this time in telling you this Camille, because of you, your daughters, and your stated faith in religion. You will have to relay this to them, should they question my faith, with you. It is your choice, in how you worship."

"Soame, and if they ask you, how will you answer?"

"As I answer anyone who asks, I believe in the Almighty Amon."

* * *

By 9:30 that Sunday morning everyone was up and about in the house. An hour later they were dressed in jeans and casual wear, had eaten and were ready for the surprising day he roused them in promise of. None of them had ever been west of the county line. Piling into the car, Chairly called out "Wait, wait, DD lemmie use yo key, I fogot somthin." She returned from the house with a Prince *Purple Rain* cassette. After adjusting herself directly behind him, in the back seat, she made a statement at Soame, in French. Except for him and Camille, giggles, sniggles, and stifled laughter broke out, as he eased the car into motion. Margaret, who had slept in the master bedroom for the first time, was sitting at the other end in the back seat. Understanding only the word "James" in Chairly's remark, he ignored her, having a good guess toward the implication.

"Aren't you going to ask for an interpretation of what she said Soame?" inquired Margaret.

"Naw, but I find it really strange how you all can understand her French so well, and I can barely interpret her English."

"Ha Soame, I bet you know what I say when I ax ya da play dis tape fa me." Seeing him ignore her, DD, sitting between him and Camille, extended her hand back for the cassette. It was the first time all of them had been in the car together. At the main road caution light he turned right.

"Whas we goin anyhow?"

"You'd better be careful kid, before you find yourself on the hood up here, being used as an additional ornament." This brought giggles and snuffed, grunted laughter, from those who heard and witnessed the two, everyday, practically every time they came in contact with each other. It had rained until 2:30 or so that morning. It was a partly cloudy, but beautiful day. Traffic was scarce. Soon after entering the thorough fare, leading west and out of town, the odor of herb drifted to the front.

"You girls be careful back there," instructed Camille.

"I have you know, you are addressing Mizz Fine Johnson and her attendants."

"Da gratast sho lady in da state of Montana, also known as Chairly's pride. Gurl wha yo glasses?" *When Doves Cry* was thumping through the speakers. At the fade of the record Chairly asked Beverly, "Wha yo money Bebly, I kno ya got chh money don't cha?"

"I don't need money, I've got Soame."

"Dat cheep skate, how can ya say dat. Ya saw what he did lass night. Das what I say bout train ta innatain cheep skate lo class peoples." That set the mood and was the atmosphere in the car.

With the "star" and her attendants in the back seat, they enjoyed the scenic drive. He entered Highway 212, drove through Ashland and on to Lame Deer. Before entering Interstate 90, they spent nearly a half hour at the Custer Battlefield National Monument. Interstate 90 took them directly into Billings. In their approach to the city, the highest point in the state of Montana could be seen. All along the way it had been cloudy, at various intervals. When the clouds lifted, they saw Granite Peak briefly. They encountered patches of rain, and the low clouds made the scenery more beautiful.

He had become accustomed to drifting down ramps from passageways, onto utility roads that outlined suburban areas of the many cities and towns they had traveled through. This occasion was no different, except it was a leisurely Sunday drive with his family. Fifi jumped from lap to lap and sprang from back to front, onto and over the seats at her will. She was really considered the "star's" mascot, but favored anyone who called her name, or whom she felt would be obliging with a pet, rub, or scratch. They were less than five miles outside the city when about fifty small light bulbs blinked sequentially on a mobile rectangular sign that read "Book Store." He glanced over at DD who had seen the display also; she lowered her eyes to the knee of the egg shell colored jeans she wore. When she originally purchased the pants, they appeared to have been glued on her. Since then she had lost between seven and ten pounds. The day he introduced the pipe to her, she never again used the needle. She was a regular smoker; in fact she had become a constant habitual smoker, and smoked almost around the clock. He had cautioned her about it. Not the cocaine, he was satisfied with the amount she, Chairly, and Margaret were consuming. Because he knew how much he had, and was the only one who knew how to produce the "rock" conversion, he knew the amount she smoked would do no serious harm to the supply he had. Chairly smoked less than any of them, and seemed to do it only to demonstrate at times to DD that she could. Camille questioned him about Margaret's regular participation with DD, and on her own; she had her own pipe. One DD had given her. His concern was of the effect it would have on her when she began her senior year in school. Soame informed her then, through DD's information directly from Margaret, she had been smoking two years prior to them merging into one household.

It was the regular eating habits he had cautioned her about. When the weight factor was brought to her attention, she claimed not working and not wanting to get fat was the reason. "Streamlining" her figure was the reiterated convenience she used, to take her further up the avenue. His feelings and trust were too strong toward her, to trespass into that area. On the other hand, she loved Soame. DD would have chose death over living without him. She unmistakably knew, he knew, he had gotten his point over to her. Her feelings disallowed her to not yield to his cautioning.

The soul match had been waited and hoped for by the both of them throughout their lives; the bond only grew stronger. She found comfort, grace, relaxation, company, and fun being with the girls, during times he was not there. They occupied her time and gave her pride, in showing herself to younger people as the true person she was, and the persona she illustrated, as the rich lady she was. The preceding night they had rubbed each other closely without irritation, when she took money from his slide, superceding his decision with the amount of money they were given. She was honestly doing her part in bettering their lives. He had bettered all their conditions. She could not teach them what she did not know. Beverly idolized her. They all shared common feelings toward each other that were almost invincible. He was the stratagem. It was he who had brought them all together, and again in seeing her demonstrated point he was able to relay his message. Both points captured everyone, without infringement against any of their feelings. Their family bond was also increasing in strength.

"Perhaps you didn't notice it Soame, but there was a book store a couple of buildings back." As she started to inform him, he had begun merging to the left lane, on the two lane street, the store they all saw was on the right.

"Aw mom."

"Well I'm sure Chairly's pride, Ms. Fine Ass, as bright as she is, doesn't object to a visit to bookstore."

"He wod na miss dat sine fa nothin in da wold, as smart as he is."

Soame was approaching an intersection A U-turn was not possible legally, but he did have an entry into the lane going the opposite direction, after a turn around, "Yeah Camille, I saw it, just had to get right to make this turn. As for you young lady with ill reputed thoughts toward pandering intentions, I'd like to point your interest in another direction."

"Na Soame, you kno done no body in dis caa know wha ya jes sade. Sides, I like da way ya aidin me already." As she nudged Beverly, and they began sniggling, DD spoke to her in French.

At the store Camille and Margaret joined his invitation to go in and browse. DD exercised her pooch. "Don't nobody wanna go in dat ole store Soame," was the answer he received from the "star's" manager, who spoke for her also.

DD had returned to the automobile when the three of them rushed out of the store to the car. A woman came out of the store and locked the door. They had been inside less than fifteen minutes. When DD asked what happened, he explained "I asked for four books, she doesn't have them. Two are out of print.

She suggested the library, and I asked her to call and check." He started the engine and as the windows ran up, the woman from the store backed out of a parking space. Their car tailed her. "We've got ten minutes before the library closes. She's gonna check the books out on her card. I gave her $300."

It had been years since Camille had read a book. In the store she saw *Valley of the Horses*. It was not the title, but Jean M. Auel's name that caught her attention. *The Earth Children Series* began with *Clan of the Cave Bear*. Camille suggested the first book of the series for Margaret, took the second one for herself, and the agreement was, whoever finished first would have first chance at *The Mammoth Hunters*. Soame had already told them he had selected books for "the star" and her agent. Margaret was not totally surprised when she was informed that one of the books was for her. It delighted her because it would be not only a gift from him, but also she was inquisitive to find out what reading he had in mind for her interests. At 3:21 they parked in front of the library. On Sundays it was only opened until 3:30. The store owner signaled him to "wait."

Handing the books through the window, upon her return, he tipped her another twenty dollars. The first dispense was to the person sitting next to him, "Do you think I will like it darlinggg, it is so big." That brought giggles from the back seat. After giving her the Frank Yerby book, *Darkness at Ingraham's Crest*.

The sounds in the back seat quieted when he passed *Forever Amber* to Chairly. "Na wait a minit Soame, I neva thot day made books dis big. How ya think um gonna read a book dis big?"

He turned sideways in his seat. "You seem to do a pretty good job at handling other big things you come in contact with."

The Johnsons saw Soame get really serious with Chairly for the first time. "You'd better start growing up, and watching your mouth. It's a part of that growing up I'm talking about. All this being cute, and these little antics and acts of make believe you are coming up with and putting on, Chairly don't go too far and loose contact with yourself. Now I want all you to know, I'm not raising a house of loose women. I've shared my bed with each of you. I know what all of you have and how well you use it. I want to see some ladylike characteristics in you sometime. I'm not asking or telling you to stop what you are doing at home. I'm telling you to put something else with it, practice the new ingredient at home because when I take you out or you leave home without me, I want to be proud of you outside, as well as I am pleased inside."

He started the motor. Compared to cities the southerners had been in, it was almost tiny. They enjoyed the view. Before he gave *Reluctant Goddess* to Beverly, he told Margaret how he had planned to give her the Kathleen Winsor book because she and her mother had three books; he felt Chairly could handle it. Beverly seemed to appreciate the paperback, when it was handed to her. Margaret knew she would never be disappointed by him. When he passed *Western* to her, both hands flashed to her jaws, in a momentary violent tremble. It was also a Yerby book. "Both of them are exciting stories of interest. I think you will especially like *Western*, Yerby writes superior to any other author I've ever read. That book you have is different from any other he's written. It's a story of love, with factual information, in a western setting. You'll find out a lot about the beginning of women's liberation, and how Kansas held laws protecting negros and women before and after the civil war."

"Oh thanks Soame, I'll let you know what I think when I'm done."

It had been an interesting and pleasant drive. All of them appreciated the chance to be away from home. The majority wanted to take the scenic route they all saw, advertising the Custer National Forest. It was past four o'clock when their exploration of the city of Billings was done. They decided then to return home. The southerners did not know the forest was so near Smath. Retracting their route, the interstate took them on an easterly course. They were approaching Hardin, when a question came from the back seat. "I jes think you tryin ta be meen Soame. You ain't red dis big book ya got me, an ya kno it. Whas it bout den, if ya red it?"

"It's about a peasant girl in a village, who is noticed by a nobleman who takes her to a larger city. Her adventures lead her to Buckingham Palace, and finally she journeys to America. You'll really like the story."

This marked another beginning for Chairly. He had noticed and DD brought it to his attention, how well she learned French, but was lacking in her native tongue. She had actually improved after reading the books, but after meeting and being with the Johnsons, she retrogressed in her English speech, while still steadily improving with French. It was the personal identity she was trying to maintain in her establishing her black roots. Reading the book enabled her to keep that identity, and channel the projection in another way. She made the attempt at growing up. This was not a difficult thing to do, with the adjustment of her speech. Her normal course in her environment would automatically do the rest. She would do anything to impress Soame.

Chapter 16

THE following morning at 10:10 he drove up to the Blanchard Farm. There was a huge barn, fifty yards to the right in back of the moderately designed home. Because of the rain during the weekend, he did not see dust which should have been created from the far off humming sound that got his attention when he arrived. Someone was operating a very large tractor, and it could be seen nearly a half-mile, in an open field, behind the house, between the space within the house and the barn.

"He's been at it since dawn. Says he should be able to get a late crop in on at least twenty-five hundred acres, if he can break and plant in time. Until January we had three remaining helpers. When he sold one of the three tractors we had left, he knew we could not afford them this season. The ground's just right; the weekend rain put us to thinking to start from scratch, with what we have."

He and Janet were in the living room, after she answered the door letting him in. "Tom said for you to make yourself comfortable, and if you're in a hurry I'm to wave him in. I've waited for you all morning; you are going to stay a while aren't you?" He attempted not staring at her. She wore a pair of short shorts which revealed that she wore no underwear, evidence by her pubic hairs. When he finally drifted his eyes up to her's, she again greeted him with a smile, this time with a wink. He started to say something, but she interrupted, "Cindy ran upstairs to her room, leaving me to answer the door. We ordered these by mail two years ago. We were just trying them on for fun, when you ranged the doorbell."

As she spoke they moved toward each other. "Well you're in the privacy of your home, and I think they fully expose a dazzling pair of legs."

"Well thank you Mr. Hudson, and this is in appreciation of your complement." It was the kiss he expected, after seeing her eyes melt with dreaminess. With both hands he palmed, squeezed, and massaged, her front and rear. "Go upstairs, I'll be up soon, shall I bring you something to drink?"

"No I'm alright. Do you have anything left from the weekend?"

"I've got a little, Tom's dry, we've been sharing mine. It was so good to be back on."

"Well you're still on; I brought you this." He gave her one of the two ounces he brought them from his jacket pocket. It brought happiness to her face and a smack on the lips.

There were three bedrooms at the top of the stairs. One of them he had not been used before. Soame found her easily. Standing in the doorway looking at her, he spoke, "Hey kitten, what are you doing?"

Her hair was not braided, the top was combed to the left, and hung slightly over her eye. The back portion was tied in a pony tail. Cindy was buttoning the top on a long sleeved tapered shirt. She shyly looked at him, brushed the hair back from her eye, and replied, "Waiting for you Soame; it's been a very long time since Saturday." Opening her arms, she met him. She was lifted up, turned around, and kissed during the embrace. To him the one-hundred and nine pounds seemed lighter than fifty. The action was so swift, Cindy found herself to be dizzy, but did not know if it resulted from the embrace, the spin, or the kiss. With him her spirits were so uplifted, it did not matter. His mere presence was an inspiration.

Locked in each others arms, she expressed her happiness, "Oh Soame, you've made my head spin since you've been in the room. You're real and you are finally here."

Holding both her hands in his, he stepped back casting his vision down on her body, then back to her eyes. He then said, "Aren't you now? Yes, I am in your presence." Under the shirt, she had nothing on. Cindy lifted the tail end, showing him.

"If you want to, I'm not sore anymore. I've waited only for your return my love." There was no spin in the stimulating kiss that led them to her bed. She helped him with his belt, and proceeded to pull the covers back, while he undid his boots and climbed out of his jacket and pants. Cindy told him, "I'll tell you now, and you must believe me. I will never ever have anyone else but you. You are all I have ever wanted."

They had been upstairs together for thirty-five minutes, when Cindy's foot touched off the bottom step. She had on the same shirt, tucked, loosely, in a pair of jeans, and white flats. Janet had changed into a flared pink skirt, with a blouse that had a laced front, covering its fastened portion. The short sleeved piece had no collar, with it and the skirt, she remained in the same sandals. "Do you care for a drink of something now, lover boy?"

His response was, "Do you know that you and I are the same age?"

When she greeted him, there was a cheerful grin on her face. The complexion of her mood changed, and when he added, with his smile, "Sure, I'll have a glass of orange juice, if you don't mind." It brightened, as it had been. Opening the refrigerator door, she responded, "That shouldn't have been too difficult to figure out, since I gave you my nursing school graduation date."

"Yeah, but it wasn't the date, it was what you said about Cindy being born, during your second year at Wayne. How about yourself lover girl?" The three of them found the chit chatting amusing.

"How long do you think it'll be before Tom comes in?"

"Probably in about an hour or so. The bank closes at noon. Then reopens until three. My guess is you two will catch the afternoon session, unless you want to leave earlier, do you?"

"This is all I have to do all day. Again, I'm enjoying the company of you two lovely ladies."

"Yeah mother fucker, I'll be a good bitch, and go out and check to be sure."

Three smiling faces were silent, as she took prepared foil and assemblies with her, "See you two in a while," Janet told them leaving out the back door.

Even though it was a turn on, when they were together, Cindy was not into coke. She was really actually falling in love with him. They were laying across the bed, necking, "tooting" and he was telling her certain aspects of his life when Janet returned. "Am I interrupting?"

"Come on in mother, Soame was telling me some of the things Beauford didn't know." Janet stood with her arms folded, her back against the facing of the door.

"He is just getting to the part about Camille Johnson, her daughters, and the two other women living with him. One is his common law wife. She's the one with the French accent, according to Beauford, is that right dear?"

"I see the sheriff has given you all the background information concerning my family structure and situation. Do you still think our relationship will fare, blossom and remain active and prosperous for the duration?"

"It's conceived in faith, truth and understanding. With me it's an eternal arrangement Soame. Here in the presence of my mother, and in the sight of God, I tell you again, you are the only man I will ever have." They smacked puckers, Cindy then continued, "No matter what happens, we will have to deal with it from this point, with the understanding we have. Can you accept this understanding with me?"

"Yes, and we will deal with it from this point. I appreciate and honor your understanding and faith."

"Congratulations you two. Now just where do or can I fit in?"

Soame took a snort and looked at Cindy, who responded "My bed and the one in the guest room are duplicates. Do you feel as if you don't belong? Two days ago you proposed sharing him. We've talked about it before and since then. What's the problem mother?"

"He says he'll be in around noon, so there won't be any problem in getting in, during the afternoon session. Now, if you two will excuse me for a minute or two, I'll be right back and join you."

He lit a joint of reefer, and asked her about her opinion on oral sex. "I can hardly wait to try it, but I don't want to rush. I also look forward to it, when it's only the two of us."

"I've done coke for a bit more than five years. My tolerance level is a great deal higher than yours. You naturally can't do as much as I do. You should not feel as if you should 'toot' as often as I do. On the other hand I've had sex with several young women, not quite your age, who were also inexperienced. Your response is better than any beginning sex partner I've ever had."

"Maybe it's because I've waited so long for you to come along."

"Oh, you knew it would be me?"

"My mother and I have always been open with each other about sex, and practically everything else. She's always said 'having the right person to explore the dimensions of sex with, is perhaps the greatest gift a woman can receive besides childbirth. They are the reasons behind purposes that satisfy our basic drives.' In an alien way, you thoroughly satisfied the both of us, in a way neither of us has ever been pleased before. She says the sensation you gave her is equal to, if it doesn't surpass the thrill involved in childbirth, except with you there was no pain. To me, each time we do it, it gets better." He threw a mint in his mouth.

"There's no one else Soame, it had to be you. For me it'll always be you, only you." They were still kissing when Janet reappeared, in her brown bikinis and sandals. "It's 11:15 you two, I want to be dressed when Tom gets in."

"With the combined beauty between the both of you, and all the sexual experiences we have, put together, will one or both of you show or explain how I am to fuck the pair simultaneously." By the time he had completed the statement, Janet was in the center of the bed with her knees arched. Her fingertips crept into the elastic, while he watched her casually flex them through her pubic hairs. With his rise, Cindy also stood on the opposite side of the bed near the head board. "My daughter understands quite well what we are doing Soame. She also knows you have one of the best dicks anywhere for any woman." She lowered to her knees saying, "We discussed this thoroughly yesterday and this morning before you arrived. She knows I want some of your dick right now will you please come on and fuck me?"

When Tom came in, Janet had arranged his clothes, and prepared everything for his shower and departure. Only he and Soame would be going into town. She and Cindy had also refreshed themselves. When Tom came downstairs, the three of them were sitting comfortably relaxed in the living room. Cindy anxiously awaited her father. He was to take her application and envelope. His responsibility also was to convert the cash into a money order, and mail it with the application. It was a tremendously big day for the Blanchard household. A minute after he came down the stairs, he and Soame were rolling out of his driveway.

"Of all the things to forget, I forgot to bring a glass or get a cup of water." They had been driving along on the dirt road for ten minutes. The countryside was beautiful; it was Tom's land. Roving fields of unplanted acrage. Redeveloped germination in patches, looking ready to harvest, which Soame had also seen on the farm property he purchased. There was a running stream, less than twenty feet, and parallel to the road they traveled. Soame had no problem in deciphering Tom's implication. There were disposable cups in the glove box. He had given Tom an ounce, and again left his personal stash with Cindy. Stopping the car, while lighting a joint, he instructed Tom to the cups. Soame also opened a three and a half gram portion for himself to "toot" from while Tom went to the stream. The two relaxed in pleasant conversation, and enjoyed the rise of the afternoon portion of the day for fifteen minutes. In conclusion of their talks Tom expressed his verbal thanks and appreciation for the courtesy being extended to him. Soame replied, "I've been helped by strangers also, who extended favors that meant almost as much at the time. I remember twice, after accepting the favor, I was told, 'When you are in position and able to, pass it on. All of the men who aided me, when I was in need, were not black."

They were two and a half blocks from the main road intersection, on the east side of town. They saw Beauford in his patrol car, fifty yards away, in their approach. The cruiser was parked on the shoulder of the road, facing them, on the right side of the road. He flashed his lights and signaled Soame to pull over. Doing so, driving to within ten feet of the patrol car, Tom humorously told Soame "I figure by now he would have gotten the word, and seeing us two together gives him no better chance to crack." Soame, naturally had no idea of what was going on. Beauford stepped back from of his car, and with a big grin on his face, walked toward the driver's side of the Cadillac. When he lightly touched the hood, in his stride, Tom said to Soame, "Yep, he's a lookin." The sheriff then began chuckling, and Soame was totally expecting anything, and considered everything a possibility.

Beauford casually draped his left hand into Soame's open window. Without bending down, he looked in all directions, while exposing his palm, asking "What can you do for that, if you really want to help a fella out, who's in need and bent inta bad shape?"

Tom yelled "Get out of here with that crap!" Plainly seen in the palm was a twenty dollar bill. It was folded in the exact manner as the hundred dollar bill, Soame had given him two weeks prior.

The sheriff then bent over, with a casual smile, with his left hand still in the window. "Mornin Soame. How ya doin there old buddy?" He had also hailed Tom across the seat.

Soame then responded "Sheriff, I just got back from a fantasy. In my wildest dreams, or farthest imagination, I never thought I'd be called on to respond in a matter such as this."

Tom then yelled, "Don't give him a damn thing!"

He then casually leaned over, and with a low tone voice, having a sarcastic look on his face, told his childhood friend "Suffer, no better for ya." Sitting up the look became a smirk, when he looked toward Beauford's car and said, "You left your lights on. I'm a county tax payer; why don't you go turn um off, before us tax payers have another battery to buy."

"So I did. Damn sure did, didn't I?" Beauford said, turning and walking back to the patrol car. He had dropped the twenty in Soame's lap.

In lowering the passenger window, Soame also grabbed his personal stash, from under the arm rest, and was about to throw it out of the lowering window. "No, no, what the Hell are you doin?" Give me that, and the twenty." Making a hasty decision to do as instructed, Soame fumbled between his legs, for the money. Tom snatched the foil from his hand, and began opening it. Expecting the bill from Soame, he poured half the contents of the foil on Jackson's face. Beauford was approaching them, midway between the two automobiles. The sheriff wiped his face with his open palm. He was not grinning or smiling.

"Over this way ole pal," Tom waved while calling Beauford who had committed toward the driver's side, he changed his direction with a slight skip, and proceeded to where he had been called. Soame was totally dumbfounded, when he saw another patrol car turn off the main road, headed in their direction. The car was approaching at a rapid rate of speed. Tom saw it also and asked, "Who's coming?" Bending over to Tom and the open window, he glanced, and replied, "Awe, that's just Rudy."

Comprehending what he had seen, he straightened up questioning, "I wonder where he's goin?"

Maintaining his stance, watching the speeding deputy, he told Tom, "I have you two to know, I've been waitin for you two since eleven this morning; Jack told me you got word to him you'd be in by noon, or when the bank opens at one."

The county cruiser screeched, with it's halt. "Ah Rudy, where in tarnation do you think you're goin? You know I haven't had my lunch yet."

There was hardly any traffic. Only one car passed, since they had been parked on the side of the road. Rudy stopped in the road, with the patrol car's hood almost parallel to Soame's hood. "Yeah, well Beauford, that's why I'm here to tell ya, Widder Tillman says, if you ain't there in ten minutes, the governor had better declare a national emergency, cause there's definitely gonna be one here in Smath."

"Well then just tell me why you came trailblazin down here ta tell me. What's wrong with your radio? Or Fred's at the station?"

The sheriff's hands were flat on the hood of the Seville. He gazed at the cranberry coloring, shaking his head in disgusted frustration, while talking to his deputy. "Ah sheriff, my radio's fine and Fred's never had a problem with the dispatching equipment. It's just that you've got yours turned off again."

Soame watched the both of them during the verbal exchange. It was typical of a small town. Beauford again surprised him with his impulsive, reflective jump, looking toward his car. "Oh yeah, so I have. So I have haven't I? Call dispatch and have Fred tell her I'm on my way, and thanks Rudy, thanks." Instead of Rudy proceeding past Soame, he reversed, while talking on the car radio. Beyond Beauford's car, he did a three point turn off the asphalt. He then peeled out, as if he was a fourteen year old kid on a dirt bike. Rocks, dirt, and dust flew and drifted all the way back to Beauford. He turned his back, fanning his face with his open hand.

"That boy, I believe he would do the job for free, just ta drive that cruiser."

At that moment, Soame felt considerably less worried, but had hopes of the sheriff not keeping Mrs. Tillman waiting. "Here ole buddy, have lunch on us tax payers, and I'd advise you not to keep the lady waiting any longer."

"How long you gonna be in town?"

"Depends on how soon Jack can see me, and how long it takes me to handle a couple of matters at the bank. I'm paying my note, thanks to you and Soame here. I really do appreciate you getting to him and sending him over."

"Soame I've asked you ta call me Beauford, and like I told ya before, it's an awfully big favor for the both of us."

He began backing away from the passenger side of the car, toward the county vehicle. With his wave, he told them, "I'm mighty obliging ta ya, I'll have ta see ya all later."

Starting his motor, he snatched the gear shift, and did almost a do-nut off the shoulder, onto the pavement, in making his turn. He kicked grass, rocks, dirt, and scattered dust, fishtailing toward the main road. While Soame raised the tinted windows Tom commented, "And you think he's got the nerve to talk about Rudy."

Taking the extended foil from Tom, Soame did a one and one. The interior of the car was silent until he responded, "Awe, yeah."

Chapter 17

PULLING back onto the pavement, the car approached an ally-type lane "Turn here, turn here," Tom instructed him. Forty yards up the drive, from the turning point, there was a huge tree. It had not been cut or trimmed in years. Because of its size and the hanging limbs, it almost concealed the front of what appeared to be an old warehouse. "I use to come this way when I came into town sometimes. I've sat right there, under that old shade tree, and made as much as twenty-five hundred dollars, on Thursday and Friday nights."

"What was there Tom?"

"A foundry. The old Smath Foundry. The town's named after the guy who established it."

Soame drove slowly listening to the story of the history of the town. "The original settlement was Berrydale, it's still in existence, twelve miles west of town. During the civil war, the secretary of war, Edwin Stanton, encouraged Lincoln to set up a safe operation for the production of bayonets and other rifle parts that the Union Army used, during the time. Olston G. Smath was a steel producer, and this was the place designated for the appropriated money to be spent. For two and a half years, not only did this place produce rifle assembly parts, but also parts for cannons and stirrups for saddles. When the war ended the place was used for the production of farm equipment.

"The settlement around the foundry began to grow and prosper in fifty years, when the old man's son started producing sewer covers. When I was a boy, men traveled as far as eighty to a hundred miles, worked here during the week, and returned home for the weekends. The town developed and expanded with industrious growth. Other men working in the foundry had small farms. That lasted for a while, and then large steel mills began pulling the contracts for the manhole covers. This place supplied every city in the Rocky Mountain Region, and some in a few other states. Mills in Pennsylvania, Ohio, and Indiana, because of their size, offered prices our foundry could not compete with. It went under." When Tom finished with the information, they were at the real estate office. He ended the story by saying, "The modern times, with upgrades in transportation methods, was the key factor in shipment, which was a large part of less expense for the big industries."

"Hello Darlinggg." It was 1:10, he glanced at the clock in the dashboard, while lowering the window. Tom began opening the passenger door. DD descended the steps, and walked toward the car. Upon her arrival at the car, Camille was on the top step. "Mrs. Hudson" Tom said, in nodding his head. "Well you can say that," "Tom." DD and Camille said almost the same words at the same time. It had been Camille, who added his name. Soame then made a move to get out of the car.

"Camille Johnson, you still around these parts?" Tom asked.

"Tom Blanchard, allow me to present the instrumental woman in my life, we simply call her DD." Before anyone else could say anything Camille added, "She answers to Miss Dubanee, if you want to be formal Tom."

They all laughed, and with her arm linked in Tom's, he escorted her around the car, where DD stood with Soame. While Tom extended his hand to DD, Camille told him, "I'm very proud she's my sister also Tom." It was then he noticed a very distinguished French accent. "Mr. Blan-chard."

"Oh, please call me Tom, DD, I'm so pleased to meet you."

They talked privately inside the office. The women basically described the events of their day to that point. Soame was very pleased in showing them off. It was the first social function of the sort him and DD had been involved with since they had been together. Even though Camille and Tom knew each other, it wasn't an in-depth acquaintance. The town was small and everybody knew what everybody else did. Word of mouth was the accepted as well as the expected norm. The exciting news was the answer from Washington. Both of them wanted to be present when he read the reply from Congressman Stribbs. They knew Soame would eventually stop by the office that afternoon.

The appointment was made with Jack Stillman. Tom's lawyer set the time for two that afternoon. The temperature inside was almost the same outside, without the sunshine. With three windows open, allowing a comfortable draft, it was 61 degrees inside. Whereas outside the rays from the sun allowed a 4 degree increase. Camille's outfit was conducive to her office environment. Her long sleeved dress was light brown. White pumps matched not only the string of pearls around her neck but the earrings as well. She had a watch on one arm, and an assortment of dangling bracelets on the other.

DD had on a light, sky blue, short sleeved dress, with a cream colored cashmere sweater. Her ear rings dangled ¾ of an inch from her lobe. They were of the same topaz, which matched her necklace and bracelets. The cream color of the low, two inch heels was identical to that of her sweater. Both ladies had taken time to assist each other with the other's hair. They were French styled. One had a ball and was tied to the back. The other wore a roll, which was waved to the right. Soame had excused himself to use the restroom. Upon his return he said to Tom, "Um gonna make a stop at the car lot across the way, if you'd like to join me." The ladies excused them, after hearing they would be back, following the arrangement of the affairs.

Crossing the side street Tom told him, "I was glad to get out of there before Mildred got back from lunch. She seems not to be able to stand me at times."

"Got any idea why?"

"Well, the latest thing was the loss of the car. When the town started folding up, she got to be the only insurance representative. I kept promising her I would but never did stop by to get the car insured. Then it was too late."

"Soame is that Tom Blanchard you've got there with you?" Tom did not wear a hat. On his feet, he had on a pair of John Connely shoes. He wore gabardine slacks that gave the look of sharkskin. The fifty dollar tapered shirt was topped with a khaki brown colored light player's jacket. Tom's watch and diamond centered ring glittered in the sunlight. It was Carl Willis, hailing them coming toward his office. They were stepping spryly.

"Well fan my brow, if we just didn't accidentally wander onto the lot of the tradingest used car lot dealer in the state of Montana," Tom said to Soame, loud enough for Willis to hear it. It was seldom during the week Soame did not have on Levis. He usually wore white shirts. The Stacys he had on had become a very comfortable wear.

In a pair of brown press slacks he replied to Tom, "You can surely say that again." Willis met them a few feet from the corner of his office.

Exchanging handshakes Soame went on telling Tom, "I came here to rent a RV for a day, perhaps a week. Somehow I ended up with one for a month." They all three laughed, and Carl found another reason to shake his hand. It was in congratulating him in becoming a local resident.

"I thought I'd come over to put a deposit on something I could use as a run-about buggy. My friend and associate here is also in need of immediate transportation and work equipment. What can you do for us?"

Willis was a tall slim man who wore a hat. It was the basic Empire design that had been blocked in a triangular fashion, with the front point favoring the alignment of Willis' nose. He was an inch and a half taller then Soame. These outstanding features about him fitted him the remainder of his casual appearance, as a used car lot owner and salesman. Hearing the question, he looked down, pushed his hat to the front, shading his eyes, and gave the appearance of being in deep concentration.

The truth in the matter rested in the fact that Willis had not sold a car or done any other business at all for a month before Soame came to town and stopped on his lot. Soame had also been his last customer. When he looked up Soame's Stetson tilted up for him to look into Willis' eyes. Carl Willis wore glasses, and had just passed his fifty first birthday. He gave Soame sort of a long stare before he said anything. "I'll make the same kind of deal, with you all, as I did with you before Mr. Hudson. One you can't afford to turn down."

"Sounds good to me. Let's see what you have."

The bank was a block and a half into town from where they were. After looking at a few of about fifteen cars and trucks on the lot, Tom test drove an El Camino to the bank. He then went to the two o'clock appointment next door. Soame worked out a deal with Willis for the El Camino and an International four-wheel AC-J5 series Jeep. They had given the jeep a test drive on a country road, and had just gotten back when Tom pulled onto the lot. The two vehicles were set in a package deal, for less than $2,000. The price was less than the cost of the jeep alone. It was three years old, and had fourteen thousand miles on it. The green El Camino had a white, wide, strip, in the center of the hood. Tom stepped out smiling. Soame felt at that point that everything was alright with him.

"Before you say anything, Cindy asked me to remind you of the application."

Willis had gone into the office to prepare the papers. "I'm glad you did remind me Soame, I really am. I've got to go back up town to get some stamps. I'm sending it certified delivery. That's the only thing I forgot to do."

Tom reseated himself in the car—a pickup type vehicle. Before he turned the ignition, Soame leaned to the open window, telling him, "If you like this El Camino, Willis is making the papers out on it right now; I'll buy it for ya, but you've got to get your own insurance. He gave us a real good deal with this and a jeep I've got." He waited a few seconds before he continued. "Mrs. Tillman will probably let you have the stamps in the package with the insurance Tom, if you want to handle it that way."

Tom got out of the cab of the vehicle, shook his hand, and assured him he would never regret helping him as much he had. It had been a long time since he had needed help, but he was more than appreciative Soame showed up when he did. The lawyer would not have the papers ready until Thursday because of Soame's choice. The interest payment on the note had been met.

"Isn't that the jeep Ben Edwards use to hook a snow plow to?" Tom asked Carl Willis.

"Yep, I've told Soame ole Ben, on a couple of occasions, had to use this to go in and pull the county sow plow out, after it bogged up."

When Soame told Willis he was from Columbus, Ohio, he replied, "Mister you haven't seen snow or felt cold weather no where in the good old USA, until you've spent a winter in Montana." Soame looked at the two other men, smiled, and didn't say a word.

To insure with the same company, he gave Willis DD's name for titling the jeep. By 3:20 everything had been completed. Mrs. Tillman advised Tom of the early mail pick up, which went directly through to Billings.

"It is processed and goes out the same night. There will be another pick up at 9:45, when the Greyhound passes through, en route to Rapid City. That mail usually doesn't go out until the following morning." Later that afternoon the three of them were together again. Tom told Soame that he and Beauford swam in the same pond. The both of them described adventurous escapades of thrill seeking youngsters, throwing the meeting into a laughing session. As it turned out to be fact, it was Tom, who was best man at Beauford's wedding. The sheriff had reason to part their company. An hour later Soame, said good day to Tom, and sent him to the Sheriff with five ounces of the grade from New Orleans. Soame's social inclinations were quite limited. It had always been his practice with other men. He also had certain principles involving direct contact with a law enforcement agent, in such a manner. In sending the material, the matter would rest between Tom and Beauford on settling of the score.

It was 5:15 that afternoon; he was enjoying the comforts of home. DD and Camille had recently arrived, and were changing clothes and freshening themselves. The tempo at the office had picked up for Camille. Her days had become complete with a sound work schedule. Margaret was in the kitchen preparing the evening's dinner. He was comfortable in the recliner, with Chairly and Beverly sitting on each arm rest. The two were in competition, telling him of the exciting experiences they had found in the books they were reading.

"Pa-pa, there's someone out front." Chairly had seen the car pull up, from the position she was sitting in.

They stood, allowing him to rise from the recliner. Both of them would have been totally disappointed if he had not palmed their rears when he stood. "You two stay here, while I see what this is all about." In his slippers, Soame walked out and off the front porch to greet Tom and Beauford, who were in Tom's El Camino. The two came right to the point and asked Soame if he wanted a maid. The town doctor, who had previously occupied the house, had an Indian house servant. She had been unemployed since the doctor moved. According to the both of them, she was fine, trustworthy and totally dependable except at times she drank a bit. Neomia also had a daughter in school, who was training to become a doctor. Beauford told him, "We've got over 37,000 Indians in this state. The majority of them live on reservations. She's Cheyenne, and by rights I should have her on the reservation over near Lame Dear. Her monthly check goes toward her daughter's tuition, books and board. I tend to overlook certain things at times, and everybody wants to help her, but we're all barely hanging on ta what we have, by tooth and nail Soame."

"I've got enough feminine hands to do everything necessary. An addition in any capacity may be dangerous in upsetting the chemistry. I simply won't take a chance on that possibility." When they mentioned the rumor he had purchased the mansion, he could not have been more honest in telling Tom and Beauford, "I don't know how long it'll be before we move into the larger dwelling. The idea you are presenting, is totally impossible for me at this time." The two men looked at each other, knowing he was right, and had called the imposition to their direct attention.

Beauford started to make a statement, but Soame preceded him with the question, "Why not take her into your home?" He and the sheriff were looking directly at each other. "She's the best cook and cleaning woman around these parts. I'd just do that, except we already have a maid. My wife don't let no body in her kitchen, not even the maid we have."

Knowing the die was next to be cast in his direction, Tom hastily injected, "I'd probably give the matter consideration, but I don't have a place for her to sleep. I surely wouldn't have her sleep in the barn."

"Gentleman, then the problem is solved." Hearing Soame say this, Tom and Beauford looked at each other in bewilderment. Beauford took his hand to his hat, to move it forward, allowing him access to scratch the back of his head. When he looked at Soame, the man standing in bedroom slippers explained to Tom, "I've got seven carpenters finishing up on the farm I bought. By 10:00 in the morning, I'll have three of them at your place Tom. You can have them prepare a basement apartment for her." They exchanged serious looks. Soame continued, "To boot, I'll let her stay at the farm house until the place is ready. How bout it?"

"Soame, you just seem to keep giving. I'm so far in debt with you al-"

Soame cut him off saying, "You are actually doing me a favor with this one. I couldn't stand to see her put on the reservation Beauford's mentioned."

Beauford stated, "I feel the same way." With that they settled the issue, and Tom hired the first maid ever to work at the Blanchard Farm.

The following day, Soame had Camille give Roland Burtrume a call. Burtrume was the local attorney Stribbs recommended; his office was in Billings. The letter DD spoke of when he and Tom arrived at the reality office was opened there in Tom's presences. However, the name of the recommended attorney was not mentioned until that night, at home. She had no problem in getting through, but Burtrume could not see him until the following week. In consideration toward the overall matter, Soame saw no problem with the appointment, which had been scheduled.

The matter was then placed as responsibility resting on DD's and Camille's shoulders, to make arrangements for school clothes, and coats. The Billings Gazette was one of the state's largest circulating newspapers. It was used as the local newspaper in town, distributed at the local supermarket. Each evening the Greyhound dropped of bundles, including Smath as one of the papers circulation points. Summer sales on coats usually resulted in great buys and fantastic savings. It would be something like they had never before imagined for the three southerners who had never spent a winter in such climate. With the paper, DD was able to seek out the sales, and found an "end of July, first of August close out" at a department store in downtown Billings. The sale included furs.

It was not until Wednesday when he turned in the R.V., in exchange for the CJ-5 series Jeep. The Custer National Forest was nearby, and he wanted to give DD the out-of-door feel in the Jeep, which had no rollup windows. They were headed to the forest, and on an impulse, he turned off into the parking lot of the local motel. "Darlingg, waa, what are we doing? I thought we were on our way to the forest."

Looking at her, and hearing her, on that same type "spur of the moment" impulse, he became aroused. "This is the next place I am going to fuck you."

"Oh, Suarmeee." She responded and he kissed her.

"Give me your pussy DD."

"Sure, but not here in the parking lot, when a motel is so close."

Camille had already told him of the place being for sale, at an almost give away price. Not only had the place been available for more than a year, there hadn't been twenty guests since Christmas. The two-floor unit consisted of eighty rooms. A breezeway and staircase separated the front from the rear forty rooms. The up and downstairs factor allowed the building twenty room quarters. Only the owners remained on the premises. They were without maids or any other caretakers.

The place had been purchased from an independent chain of motels, six years prior to that time. The owner went on further to tell Soame, "We did really well, until the foundry completely closed. Then seems like the farming around here, as everywhere else in these parts, a couple of years later, started going downhill also. We retired a year and a half before we bought this place. Everything we had is wrapped up into it."

It was 10:30 that morning, Soame had chosen a room. The price was $23.18. "Sure you can have any one of um you choose, or all of um for that matter," the motel manager said with a smile and passed the key to number forty.

Later that afternoon when they were leaving, DD asked "Can we stop back by tomorrow Darlinggg?? It's been so nice, because it's been so long since we've had time to ourselves."

He rubbed and squeezed her cheeks while palming them, and asked "Do you want to put Charily up for adoption?"

They were in stride strolling to the Jeep. She slapped his shoulder; he threw his arm around her. They walked snuggling with DD crying out "Oh Suarmmmme."

He was sure he had found what he was looking for. He and DD showered. She and the girls would start preparing dinner, while he visited the Yates place. One reason for going was to inform Thad, the papers would not be ready until he visited the lawyer, the following week. The new merger, with nearly seven-thousand acres of Tom's farmland being added to the co-op was also big news to be relayed to Thad and Billy. Going out the door he told them "Don't hold up dinner for me, I will probably be late."

"Suarmmme. We will wait for you to have dinner."

"But sweetheart, there's a lot of plan-"

It was Margaret who interrupted, by telling him, "I know Kathleen Yates, Soame. Are you sure you don't want me to come along?" She had stepped out, onto the porch, with her hands on her hips. She was standing next to DD, who had her arms folded across her breast.

"Kathleen. Who are you talking about Margaret?" Inquired DD.

"Wait a minute, no-"

Once again Margaret interrupted, "Youuuu know perfectly well who I'm talking about." She broke into tears stepping from the porch, in an approach to him. Directly in front of Soame, she began pounding in his chest with clenched fists. "You're wrong Soame. You're such a horrible person; I never thought or expected you to be this way."

She was sobbing, in frustration. He could do no more than hold her wrists. Chairly and Beverly were then standing in the front door, watching the scene unfold. "Now do you see what you've done? You've hurt poor, young, dear, sweet, and innocent Margaret, who's done no more than given you her heart," commented DD, rolling her accent at him in a slightly more than casual tone.

"Um hurt to" murmured Chairly, above Margaret's sobs, as she turned and went back inside the house.

Beverly remained staring at him, and could plainly be heard saying, "Oh but Soame, I love you sooo dearly." Even she had tears in her eyes.

Knowing he had to say something, and he would never lie to them he began searching for their reasoning. "I never thought I'd be accused of being untrustworthy. I'm ashamed of what I've asked you to believe in, if you can't believe in me, as your man."

Margaret then raised her face from his chest, and asked, "Can you tell me you don't know Kathleen Soame?"

"Not only do I know Kathleen, I know her mother, Mrs. Yates, her father, Thad, her baby brother little Thad, and her other brother and sister Billy and Jenny. I also know that I have a heck of a lot of responsibility toward the Yates family, and they all depend on me. I've never owned as much as I do now. Not only is the Yates family dependant on me, but seven other men I've hired as carpenters, earn a small salary from me, who say they could not have lasted another two weeks if I had not shown up when I did." Soame would not be audacious enough to play too far from Margaret's sentiment; he realigned his pitch back to the issue.

"Sure the issue is not if I know the Yates, but if I go to bed with Kathleen. You fail to see my responsibilities beyond this household because they are outside interests, and meaningless to you. I have never, before you became a member of my household and will never as long as you are a part of this family Margaret, put anything or anyone as priority to my family and household."

She began looking at him with somewhat perplexed admiration. "What you might not want to see and admit is my responsibility toward you. I may not always be here when the sun sets, but you've never known a sunrise, since you've lived under this roof, that I wasn't in calling distance, or next to you. Chairly says she's hurt also; is she hurt because of Kathleen or you, Margaret? If you want you can have me in your room, or DD's who told me already, to be back home for dinner." Margaret was then looking into his eyes. She made an attempt to speak. He overrode her with his conclusion.

"I prefer you to wait until I return because there are very important matters I must attend to. I'm asking not only in your waiting now, but also in all the times to come, don't ever wait for me with malice on your mind, jealousy in your heart or vanity in your greeting spirit. In that type of waiting you will never have me. Wiat as my women, in our home, who knows I will always return, and whenever I'm here or away, also know and be assured, my first and best effort will always be toward your security and well being."

DD then walked up, put her arm around them both, kissed him on the lips, and said softly, "I told you we would wait Suarme." Taking Margaret's hand, turning toward the porch, she asked, "Coming inside with me dear?" They both then saw Beverly, turn in the doorway, and return into the house.

Walking toward the Jeep, he told them, "I'll see you all after a while."

Thad and Billy had not completed their work day when he arrived at the Yates farm. Mrs. Yates gave her consent for little Thad, Jenny, and Cathy to ride with him in the Jeep, out to the field where her husband and eldest son were working. Cathy was learning how to drive, and enjoyed the experience in handling the Jeep. After Thad had been filled in on the development of the situation, he appeared to be pleased with the fact, the co-op then controlled a large percentage of the farming land in the county, where the average farmer tended twenty-five hundred acres. No individual farmer was in control of more land operated or held by the co-op at that time. Thad's idea was to put the land into productivity as fast as possible. Blanchard had an extra tractor, but no manpower. This meant the possibility of more men and at least two more tractors. Seed and fertilizer were also factors as calculative investments, which could be deducted from the late summer crop profits. Thad also felt positive he could round up the three or four men necessary to put the idea in motion by the weekend. Soame agreed to rent two other tractors. It was near "quittin time" when their talks were done. Little Thad wanted to ride home on the back of his brother's tractor. They tailed their dad in. Cathy further extended her driving practice, in pulling off in another direction.

"Jenny's on the rag. I didn't want ta tell ya back at the house, or while little Thad was with us," Cathy told him, as they bumped across a head row, toward a field road.

"I can talk ya know. Besides, Soame never asked you to tell him about me and his personal business." Jenny informed her, in sitting straightness on the matter.

"Ha, well excuse me. Miss Bloody Two Shoes, but can you just tell me please ma'am, how did you ever get to have any personal business, with my man?"

The road lead to another freshly cultivated field. In the middle of the field was a clump of trees, giving the appearance of an oasis. The Jeep had a covered top, but a cloth and plastic window fixture, snapped, and zipped into place, for the enclosure. The gear shift separated the individual front seats. With Cathy having her hands full, operating the vehicle between rows of freshly plowed filed, toward the clump of trees, Jenny took advantage of the situation.

There was no door or window assembly in place. Except for the seats, floor, and top, there was also a running board. "Sugar babe, do you want your sweet thing called Jenny ta keep your company, in that big ole front seat, while this 'dangus' gal tries to handle the lil o bitty automobile."

By the time he knew for sure it was Jenny, her arm was round his neck, and she had walked around on the running board, while talking to him, and was in his lap when she finished. Her back was to Cathy who yelled, "What the hell do ya think you're doin?"

"You wanna kiss your darlin sweet baby Jenny?" He then felt a mouth full of sweet, succulent, tongue.

A sudden bump told them all Cathy was no longer straddling the rows. "We'll be there in just a little while Miss Red Ass, and I've got somthin for lil ole, sweet Miss Jenny, just you wait n see."

While she wrestled the wheel, she gritted her teeth, in talking to her sister. Cathy then drove into the shelter of the trees. The sun was just dipping behind the peaks of the distant RoseBudd Mountains. "Get the Hell off of his lap! You brazen hussy!" She shouted, pushing Jenny off his lap, into the pine straw. Cathy began kissing him, and unbuttoning her dress at the same time, obsessed with having him right there, right after she got out of her clothes.

"It won't be fair if you don't let me do the first part Cathy. You yourself said it's the only right way ta do it. At least let me do the first part." Jenny, sadly looking at Cathy, sitting on his lap, in her panties, told her while she attempted to undo Soame's belt buckle.

"What do you think is fair honey bunch?" Cathy asked him, after pulling the snap away carrying this zipper down.

"I think since the three of us are here, we should all have fun and enjoy ourselves. Let's step out, so I can get out of these pants, and have a look at your beautiful body." Her nipples were shiny with hardness. He pinched one of them shuddering sensations throughout her body. Cathy shivered and sprung to the ground, where she stood next to her sister.

"We can do some 'toot' and see just what Jenny has in mind." Cathy gave a rational glance toward her, and then tiredly looked at him replying, "I'm pretty sure I already know what she has in mind."

When he had climbed down, and out of his pants, the three of them snorted, and were enjoying themselves in the secluded atmosphere. He sat on the running board, with Jenny in the praying position in front of him. Cathy directed her involvements, while Saome played in the crotch of her soggy panties. The wetness added gloss to the texture. Glossiness and the exposed red protruding pubic hairs added height to his aroused condition. When she kissed him, he lowered the white briefs midway down her thighs. "We're going to the front, Jenny. Want to come with us?" he asked.

Jenny could only stand and watch them place Cathy's elbows flat on the fender. She was bent over in a wide legged position, where he made a rear entry. Jenny observed the thrill and exciting way in which her sister gave herself to their lover.

It had been a dusty evening in the fields with Thad and Billy. His boots were mucky. "Darlinggg, I can tell by your boots you've been in the fields. There's also grime, and no doubt there's grit on you from the dust. Why don't you have your shower. When you're done Chairly will have your dinner ready. We can all eat then."

In a very high pitched mocking tone, Chairly responded, "Ha!"

Camille told him, "I will lay your pajamas and robe out for you dear."

The meal was rather normal and quiet until Margaret commented, "Soame, I have no problem whatsoever in accepting what you said earlier. I've totally freed my mind of any vanity or jealousies in my personality, those words simply no longer exist."

"Margaret, you're still seated, and remain at this table. Such expressive thoughts displayed earlier could lead to a vacancy where you now sit. You have been blatant with your criticism without even knowing what the overall situation is all about. Here now you mention your personality in its outward appearance. Being free of vanity and jealousy. My advice to you sincerely, is to search your mind and heart for your true feelings. Equate those feelings with the fact that each day I incur a six hundred dollar expense toward your upkeep. With your profound astuteness, I'm sure you will have no problem in venturing to Billings next week. Your mother and DD have a shopping trip arranged for school clothes and coats for the winter. Sure your 'personality' is a vital contribution to this group. However, I am also carefully concerned with you getting your mind in gear."

It was Camille who spoke, "I'd like to say something for Margaret."

"No, no. We allow her to say and do any and everything else around here she's capable of. Don't restrict or restrain her expressing herself now. I don't think she needs an mediator, or do you Margaret?"

"Soame, I apologize, my words and actions were totally out of place."

"Your apology is accepted with this warning: I've never denied you, or anyone else at this table, a chance at speaking to me in private conference. Before you step out on the wrong foot again at any time, remember I will not allow you or anyone, to attempt to belittle or degrade me."

Chapter 18

EARLIER that week Soame met the carpenters at the farm house; he had not been expected. Pete Thompson had them all reporting to work on time, and Soame was very pleased with that fact. Thompson was there. By a quarter of and sure enough, at 8:00 all six of the other carpenters were at the job site, ready to start their day, which lasted until 4:00. On Fridays they were scheduled to report to the realty office, where Camille issued their checks, between 3:00 and 3:15.

Everything at the farm was practically done. In fact, they were merely passing time with the job, as had been instructed. Soame had Pete take two other men with him that morning to the Blanchard's when the farm was completed. They each were promised a fifty dollar bonus if the Blanchard job was completed by the weekend.

It was early Friday afternoon when he drove out to the Blanchard Farm. Neomia had already begun working as their maid. In the mornings Tom would pick her up from the farmhouse. In the evenings Janet dropped her off. Until she answered the door, Soame had not met the colored woman. His introductory statement was, "I've heard quite a bit about you. I'm Soame Hudson here to see the Blanchards, and Pete Thompson, the carpenter foreman."

"Why Soame, please come in."

Janet approached the door from the center of the living room. "It's fine Neomia. Have you met your landlord?"

"No I haven't until now, and thank you Mr. Hudson. I've heard quite a bit about you also. It is my sincere pleasure to meet you. I am extremely grateful, from the bottom of my heart, for allowing me to stay at the Kent place."

"Your credits speak to your worthiness Mrs. Mesa. It is my pleasure to help my own."

Janet then looped her arm in his Soame's explaining, "What a pleasant surprise, come on in and see what your men have done." Neomia took his hat. The basement entrance was located in the kitchen; they strolled in that direction. "Will you have a drink before going downstairs?" Janet asked.

"How about if I take a rain check on that until I've seen what progress they've made."

"You'll be surprised. They are nearly finished," she told him, opening the closet door to the basement stairs.

"Boss man!" exclaimed Pete when he saw Soame. Tuesday morning, Pete had also addressed him in the same manner. It was the first thing Pete had ever done it unknowingly, to displease his employer. He was told then, not to use the "handle." "Oh excuse me sir, but it sort of slipped out." There was no doubt about Pete was glad to see him. The pleasing grin on his face assured Soame of that fact. Everything was going well. Janet remained at the top of the stairs. Soame did not change his stride in looking and inspecting. He had not been in the basement before. Nonetheless, he was quite pleased with what he saw.

"How are you all coming along?" Five of the men were in immediate hearing range. They made gestures of satisfaction. He then asked Pete, "How about it?"

"Yes sir, we're almost finished, Soame. Matter of fact, if the bank didn't close at 4:00, we could stay and be done by six."

Soame contemplated the matter. "So if you pick up your checks now, by noon tomorrow, you can be finished here?"

"Unless you or they have something else to be done, I'd say so, yeah."

"All right, knock um off, go get paid, you all have nice evenings, and let's see what tomorrow brings."

Before Soame could finish, Pete, displaying a big grin once again, replied, "Thanks boss, I mean Soame. All right! Let's clean up for today, and go get paid."

Upstairs on the patio, Neomia brought the drinks in as Soame complimented Janet on her refreshing looks. She had on a gray dress with an eye catching bracelet of bright green emeralds, and a necklace which matched. There were no earrings, but the soft pattern leather shoes consisted of various colored patches of green, gray, yellow, and brown. Her hair looked casual, without ribbons, bows, or pins. "I can hardly believe what I'm looking at," he said as Neomia sat the drinks down. "If the right album is in that cover, this is my lucky day."

Some of the stored goods had been brought up from the basement and placed on the patio. What he saw, which sparked excitement, was a picture of a multi-colored face of a mandrill.

In 1967 Aretha Franklin's sensational new album on the Atlantic Label, broke record sales. It was the first commercial album to sell in the south for $4.50. Later that year, during the summer, Fleetwood Mac made their debut with an album that also smashed record sales. The cover of the album featured the face of the multi-colored, ferocious mandrill. That album sold in the south for $6.50. Without touching the drink, Soame walked to the stored articles, along the side of the wall in the patio. With a broad smile on her face Janet asked, "Soame, what is it?" She remained seated sipping her drink.

"You know, that's what Cindy is doing right now. I never told her you are here. She's in her room listening to old records." Not looking back to her, he examined the contents of the album cover.

It was one of his rare, seldom seen, best features; Janet gazed at him, while he was in complete happiness. She was captured in awe, and taken aback, while looking. Neomia had been sent for Cindy, who walked in. "She said she would put that there just for you Soame."

Hearing Cindy's voice, he turned toward her, "Hello there young lady. How have you been?"

With glossy eyes she replied, "I'm fine Soame Hudson. My mother told me, if you're really whom she knew you would be, you could not resist that record."

He said to them, "Let's hear it." They played *Hypnotized*.

Twenty minutes later they were still listening to Fleetwood Mac's first number one hit. "Have you thought about what you're going to do with those articles along the wall when the basement is completed?"

"Tom will probably move it all to the barn. You can have the album, if you want."

"Nonsense. The guys will be back tomorrow. They'll build storage racks for the records, and compartments for the other goods." He had started with his second drink of light rum. "What type of furniture are you going to use? Are you going to continue with the modern contemporary décor?"

It was Cindy who answered, "There's no furniture around here like ours. The patio furniture is wrought iron, and made at the old Smath Foundry, but my mom ordered the interior designs from the east coast."

Janet then told him, "We've talked about moving the suite down from the guest room, but we haven't come to a decision yet. She's going to take the weekend, for traveling to Cheyenne. Her daughter is taking summer courses there. By the time she gets back Monday, we'll have it all worked out and ready."

He told Janet, "With the bargains they're having, at almost give away prices, you can hardly not afford to go on and do it all the way. Two hundred dollars will furnish the entire apartment, and you will get the style of work from the quality of her surroundings." The two women were standing near each other.

Soame moved from the speaker toward them saying, "With the El Camino, and two or three of the workers lending a hand with their trucks, it'll only mean one trip. Why don't you and her select it now, and tomorrow they can pick it up." He then gave her three hundred dollar bills. Ten minutes later Janet was on her way out the front door, with the maid. After selecting the furniture, Janet told him she would drop her off at the farm house. Tom was to have her at the bus station the following morning at 5:30 for the trip to Cheyenne. Soame and Cindy were left to enjoy the music and keep themselves occupied until he got back.

Dinner was being prepared when he arrived home. After a quiet and relaxed evening at home, he found himself "grounded" by the lady of the house until one the following afternoon. His plans were not altered. At 2:30 he was en route to the Yates place, to let Thad and Billy know about the co-op meeting Soame and Tom had agreed on for the next day at the motel. That visit also resulted in Soame taking Cathy and Jenny back to the mill pond. There, downstream from the falling waters, after the three of them had gone for a nude swim, Jenny, on a spread blanket, beneath a tall spruce, with lilies, lupine, and daisies all about, surrendered herself to Soame, and found no displeasing quarrels from her sister.

"I knew you would truly love the feelin, and you'll remember it and the three of us always bein here this day, together. Oh Jenny, I'm so proud that you're my sister, and um so glad I could share this time, and my man with you."

Because Soame owned the largest percentage of the land in the co-op, he was nominated as its president. In order to give Billy recognition, and insure his stability toward the future growth and prosperity of the organization, Soame declined in his favor. Tom was elected secretary, and Thad was the elected business manager. The post of Sergeant at Arms was charged to Soame. He had left word for Tom to stop by Saturday morning, when he brought Neomia into town. It proved to be a worthwhile visit for all of them.

Chiarly instigated the idea of a installing a phone line. Margaret relished the idea, and cheerfully presented it to DD and her mother under the pretense of helping ease the burden of Soame's responsibilities. In New Orleans DD did not have a phone in her apartment because she did not want her work following her home. When the idea was initially presented by Soame two weeks prior, the decision then was to wait until the move was made into the mansion.

Chairly's and Margaret's obvious course was in detouring Soame's frequent visits to the country; their main interest, the Yates place. Soame had not used a phone, as a piece of residential equipment, for some time. Camille had given hers up, almost a year prior to Soame and DD's arrival. The matter was resolved and Camille was responsible for contacting the phone company for installation. She was also to set up a charter that week, making *The Farming Cooperative of the Surrounding Areas of Smath,* a subsidiary to *Worldwide Conservation and Energy.* They all knew Tom and Thad would have to be included in the link up. The expense incurred was deducted from holdings of the mother company to be reimbursed from profits at the close of the farming season. This aided Camille's skills as the bookkeeper for both structures. Her biggest job and responsibility for that week was getting the paperwork prepared for all the involvements. The constituents as a whole body were to be presented to Bertrume, in Billings.

Usually when Soame stopped by the office, either Mrs. Tillman was out or leaving for lunch. Because of his regular visits, Camille was not too anxious about the phone idea at home. However, she did not mind giving in to the idea knowing Soame would do as he chose without restriction. Sharing his bed afforded her the leniency toward the younger women of the household. The office was the one place she was able to have him to herself. That Monday, after stopping by, he was off to the Yates place, to let them know of the phone being reconnected.

Turning into the Yates place, forty yards in front of the house, off the right, there was a patch of sweet black cherries. Soame saw little Thad picking cherries and yelled to him. "How's Ricky?" yelled the youngster.

He stopped the Jeep and inquired, "Who?" when the boy explained it was Camille's son, Soame noticed a slight giggle. He then told Thad of Ricky being on vacation with friends in the country, and after accepting a handful of cherries proceeded back to the Jeep and drove on to the house.

"Hello Soame," cried out Mrs. Yates, as he drove up. She was standing on the porch, in a summer dress with an apron.

"Mom we're getting the phone turned on," yelled Thad, as Soame stepped out of the Jeep. Mrs. Yates had a broom in her hands, and was about to sweep the porch when he turned off the dirt road.

"How are you this morning Mrs. Yates?"

"Oh, I'm fine. What's that he says about the phone? Cathy and Jenny are out back,on their way to the-" She never finished. Like two playful puppies, the sisters galloped up, pushing, holding each other back, and tugging, tussling as they ran. When they matched each other to the corner of the house, where

Soame and their mother could see them, they suddenly stopped, and were at total peace with their existence with each other.

"Oh there you two are. I was about to tell Soame you were on your way to the barn to collect eggs."

The sisters then greeted him, "Hay Soame." "Mornin Soame." They both waved with a smile, in speaking.

Cathy swept her red lashes over the dreamy green eyes, while her sister sparked, looking down, up, and down again, before Mrs. Yates asked, "What's that about the phone bein reconnected?" The statement was directed to him. He replied with the information he had come to deliver. He added his opinion of the co-op being able to function better with direct, immediate communication between its members.

"One of the men Thad hired to help him and Billy, just this morning said how much of a convenience it would be if we could all get our phones back to working again." Soame appeared to be pleased with the fact she was content with the idea.

"Do ya want ta see the inside of our barn and help us hunt eggs Soame?" Cathy asked, nodding "yes" out of her mother's sight. She pulled on one of her pig tails, and rocked from side to side when Mrs. Yates looked in her direction.

She was dressed in jeans and a tapered shirt, and almost bumped into Jenny, who was still trying to woo him. Jenny had a pony tail with bangs. Her wide tailed, laced embroidered dress had once been used for church or school. She added glow to the approaching noon. Her sister stood next to her barefooted. "Soame's got more important things ta do, than go egg huntin with two farm critters such as you," Mrs. Yates answered.

He looked up at her, smiled, set his hat back on his head, by raising the front brim with his index finger. Soame then looked at them, and back toward her, and was about to speak when they all heard, "Ma I got both these buckets full. Do ya really think we need another one?"

"Your pa said three little Thad, now you come on in, empty one, and that'll leave ya only one ta go."

"Awe ma, nobody ever uses the stuff anyhow."

"Those cherries are awfully good. I'd give you three dollars for a bucket, if you didn't mind letting me have one little Thad."

"Mind! Three dollars, sure Soame, take one of these."

When he passed the money to her son, Mrs. Yates extended for the pale, telling Soame, "I'll put these in something for ya." She then asked Thad, "Now how do ya feel about doin what your pa told ya?"

"Sure ma, thanks Soame."

They both started inside, Soame said to her, "It just might be an interesting thing to do, and if you don't mind Mrs. Yates, I'll accept that invitation to the barn. I'll get the cherries on the way out."

"Well you go right along, if ya don't figure you'll be wastin your time. Those two can show you around out back if you all like."

By Wednesday there would be seven carpenters idol for two days drawing a full salary. The basement at Tom's place was completed Saturday. They had even helped with the moving and placement of the furniture. The co-op hired four men and rented two tractors. Two of the men leased their tractors and equipment to the organization while they were on wages. The carpenters remained on the Blanchard Farm, building shelters for the added equipment, and doing minor repairs to Tom's barn. They were progressing on schedule. At the close of their work day Wednesday, the job at the Blanchard place would be completed.

Following a visit to the job site, he went directly to the motel. The idea Soame presented to the motel owner was accepted with a grin and a shake. After carefully considering the matter it was not the purchase of the motel that interested him. The structure had an east and west side. Each side was equally divided with the owner occupying the "Manager's Quarters." Soame wanted space at the establishment, and a free hand to do renovations to make the space he needed accessible to him. The idea he formulated made the motel very important and essential as a part of his operation.

Through Camille's brokerage he leased ten rooms for a period of five years. He stipulated in the agreement that be allowed to refurbish and make the rooms adjoining as he desired. All the arrangements were specified and noted. His offer was $4,000, in cash, to bind the agreement. This was accepted with the heartiest of thanks, the most sincerity, grateful appreciation, and the very best of luck in being successful with whatever plan he had in mind. The motel owner was a camel's straw from losing the place with a double mortgage.

After the meeting at the motel, Soame took Camille home for lunch. They had already discussed the proposal. She was then briefed on the meeting and given the notes of the agreement. That afternoon it was to be made a part of the presentation to Roland Burtrume, the following day in Billings. That morning,

Jack Stillman had dropped off Tom's paper work at the realty office. Following lunch, he was on his way back to the Blanchard Farm.

The carpenters then had a new job site. Thursday morning they would meet at the motel. Soame explained to Pete what the renovations would be. The directions to Pete were to get the men to the job site Thursday morning. They were to survey the site and spend Thursday getting their materials together. The immediate plans involved the last two rooms, up and downstairs, on the west side. These two rooms would be joined by a circular stairwell. The last room upstairs on the west side, was opposite to the east side upstairs room. These two rooms were to be adjoined by double doors.

Soame would only be gone for the weekend. The carpenters could only do so much, Thursday and Friday. They both were aware of that fact, including gathering the materials Thursday. With that in mind Pete was instructed to see Mrs. Tillman Friday, who would issue their checks. Pete then called the men together. Soame informed them of the arrangements of the checks, mentioned the new job site, and directed them to Pete's supervision. He gave anyone who wished a chance to speak with him private "until Monday." They appeared to be in agreement and when no one asked to speak with him, he wished them a safe and pleasant weekend.

"Oh Soame, you'll never know how much of a dear you really have been, and how kindly we will always think of you for the many favors you've extended." Her true happiness and expression of gratitude brought tears from her eyes. It was a total surprise to Janet to find the line operational. Cindy stood looking at the both of them wanting to express the same gladness. Neomia was tending to her responsibilities, and out of ear shot.

He noticed the care and concern displayed on Cindy's face, while her mother spoke, he addressed them both. "I'll be out of town for the weekend. Finding out about the concerns of the men and their progress, is only one reason for my return. I have a personal interest in being here."

"Is it the binding of the agreements you've mentioned, through your attorney in Billings, Soame?" Cindy asked.

As she inquired Janet approached him directly "Alright 'mother fucker,' be with us before you leave; I can think of nothing better, and I'm sure you feel responsive to two bitches."

Cindy said, "Oh mother please, Soame are your plans to spend some time with us before you leave?"

"Those are my plans, wishes, hopes, and desires for the remainder of the afternoon." The addition of Neomia allowed her to resume Cindy's driving lessons. This was the excuse she would use to the maid. She told him where to meet them in twenty minutes.

He had noticed the side road each time he drove to and from the farm he left. The rendezvous point was a mile off the turn. Cindy had been taking driver's education at school. She had not gotten her license before the class was discontinued. The El Camino pulled up with her behind the wheel. Janet seated him in the middle, and they proceeded in the direction they were headed. Janet made the trip a delight, which was transmitted to Cindy, who really handled it well considering it was her third time driving in nearly three years. Until she turned onto the road leading to the lake and picnic grounds, he had no idea of their destination. They only told him it was a secluded spot and a surprise. Their play led to fun, joy, excitement, and thrills capped with total satisfaction that afternoon at the lake.

It was nearly dusk when he arrived home. Preparations for dinner were under way. DD and Camille were making last minute checks for four day supplies of everything. They had an abundance of all they needed. They simply had to dispense enough to themselves to last for four days while they were away from home. Camille merely wanted the vacation away from the environment, and to be in DD's company with Soame. Her job was all done. The papers were ready, and in his brief case, a gift from Mrs. Tillman.

Muff was back on the scene and since his first exciting car ride, he and his friend Fifi were almost inseparable. The two of them were sprawled out in the center of the living room floor. Everyone scrambled over and around them through each other in the kitchen. Soame made his presence known by kissing cheeks, feeling behinds, and rubbing crotches. Margaret seemed more reserved toward him. She was not unresponsive, and he did not force himself upon her. Since their quibble, they had been somewhat distant. She had not invited him to her room, and he did not shun her. They both knew who was dependent and that factor alone distinguished her from his independence. Even DD could not advise her, for she had never been caught in such a predicament with him.

"Remember my dear, when you sat alone on the blanket, and you were invited to a drink? Since I've known him, I've seen no difference in the same man, who told your mother to call you over." It was Margaret's right buttock he squeezed. She casually looked up at him, after being void of his physical contact for a week.

When he massaged both cheeks with the same hand, without removing it, she moistened her lips with her tongue, and looked sleepy eyed at him, inviting his kiss. "Are you gonna be alright, taking care of this house while we're gone?"

"Sure Soame, we'll be fine." Chairly had on shorts, slippers, and one of his soiled shirts. He stepped to her, placed his hand under the shirt and held her vertex with hand, "Are you really my pa-pa?"

"Next time we're in bed, call me big daddy."

"I ain't callin you nothin Soame!"

Beverly's main function in the kitchen seemed to be making the iced tea. During the days they basically spent their times reading and practicing French. After dessert they all enjoyed their favorite drinks at the table. It was then Chairly asked the question, "Soame, are you gonna see da sho?"

"What show do you mean?"

"Well, Mizz Fine is makin a special appearance in the neighborhood. Da finest sho lady in da state can be seen fa yo advance admission."

"Oh yeah, well I'll tell ya. For the fact alone, Mizz Fine's manager's grammar shows a noticeable improvement, I just may consider it. By the way, what's the advance admission?'

"A hundred dollars."

"What?" That's outrageous."

"No it ain't Soame. See in dat way, we liminate all cheap skate and hecklas."

"Alright, alright. I'll take three of your advanced tickets. No wait. Margaret, would you like to view the appearance of the greatest show lady in the state of Montana?"

"Sure, I'd like to very much."

"Make that four tickets, but this had better be worthwhile."

That night at eleven sharp, "Mizz Fine" was presented by her manager. With the exception of DD and Margaret, the audience did not expect a burlesque act, with no confetti, and a costume, altered to fit, including gloves. The wig, stockings, and shoes all matched or were in direct contrast with the pink chiffon, and white stole. To the sound of the Archies, singing, *Honey* it all came off, and down to a teddy. Then "Mizz Fine" Johnson sensationalized her appearance, while capturing applause, with graceful movements in enchanting harmony, with Marie Mouldurne's *Midnight at Oasis*. While signing her autograph, she collected bills totaling of a hundred, two fifties, and a twenty.

The short trip to Billings was along the same route they had taken for the

Sunday outing. Soame, DD, and Camille drove out Thursday morning around six, and at 9:15 they were registered at an independent hotel. Suites had become a standard for DD, who admitted she also had begun looking forward to "being away." Reservations were not made because Soame wanted to select a place near the attorney's office.

Directly after settling into the hotel atmosphere, he contacted the local Cadillac dealership. Arrangements were made to have an oil change and service check on the still smart and flashy Seville. He was promised if he had it in by noon he could have it serviced and back by four. The appointment was within that frame, but neither posed an inconvenience to the other. DD had no immediate needs, except being with him. Camille had not had a beautician do her hair in three years. Within thirty minutes after their registration, she was able to find out that the most creditable hair dresser in the city was located two blocks from the hotel. Permanents were the specialty of the shop. DD only wanted a rinse and set, and could have gotten a chair that afternoon. Because she and Camille wanted to be together they took appointments at 10:30 Friday morning. At 11:20 Soame delivered the car, and taxied back to the hotel.

He chose to walk to his appointment and arrived ten minutes early. Burtrume saw him five minutes after his arrival, and from that point on the meeting was a total success. Soame intrigued the barrister with the story of DD's uncle in France, who had passed within the last eighteen months, and left her a small fortune. He was impressed with the establishment and relocation of WorldWide Conservation and Energy. "Oh, call me Roland Soame, and you say she's purchasing five shares of the stock in your company, at twenty thou a share? That'll send the par value of your remaining holdings up at an incredible rate. It's a worthwhile venture for the both of you. Time will tell, through your production."

The co-op charter, land agreements with the papers from Stillman, leasing contracts and receipts pertaining to all the involvements in the relocation and expenditure, were presented. Camille's bookkeeping records were also reviewed and copied with the other forms and documents. Burtrume made and observation, which drew light on his keen abilities as an expert in his field: "Now see Soame, these little notations." He was directing Soame's attention to markings shown in the ledger. "Most keepers of records commonly omit or neglect to insert these marks. They are essential audit abduction findings, and will save countless hours and hundreds of thousands of dollars. You are uncommonly lucky to have such a skillful and crafty person who has this type of expertise in the field."

The corporate seal was the only item not presented. When the attorney inquired, Soame explained his circumstance when, and how the seal was either lost or misplaced, and was not seen again. The incident took place three years prior to the meeting. "Well, naturally the date will change on the seal but that's not a relevant factor. Here's an address on the other side of town." Burtrume began writing on a pad from his desk. "This office supply has an office development section. See Carmen, and she will not only help you replace the seal, if you will describe your logo, or choose from a book she has available, she'll make arrangements, to have your office stationary made and shipped to you."

Shortly afterwards, and during the discussion, the $20,000 fee was announced, for corporate and personal representation. Soame wanted Camille's and DD's coverage included, explaining "Ms. Johnson" as the bookkeeper, and the broker to whom the motel contract was leased. The attorney then was given the complete address of the Tillman Realty office and casually responded, "Yes, yes, I saw the C. Johnson, but had no idea…alright then Mr. Hudson, the fee will cover your company, it's single investor and I will also represent the three of you, in any personal encounter. Mind you, this is a retainer's fee."

Roland Burtume stood 5'9" with a very stocky build and a barrel belly. The texture of his skin projected rich, easy living. The quality of his clothing and fine décor about his office, exemplified his success and position within his field. In presenting $10,000 in cash to the distinguished attorney Soame invited him to dinner at any spot he considered to be the finest in the city. The offer was accepted. With a tone almost equal to Soame's in resonance, he roared with laughter, extending appreciative thanks toward the invitation.

Following their meeting that evening, Soame found the initial cash payment to be substantial, in covering the retainer fee. The hearty laugh he had given earlier was trivial toward accepting other gratuities, which were brought to his attention. Before they parted company, Burtrume offered to contact the office supply, arrange for the seal, stationary, and his papers to be delivered in a single package. While Soame drew the logo on a piece of note paper, he explained how he would thoroughly finish setting up the contracts and detailed works for signatures. The evening dinner and meeting completed his business stay in Billings.

Chapter 19

DD and Camille were awaiting his return. They had gone shopping earlier during the day to be out among the people of the city. It was thrilling for Camille although Billings was not a quarter the size of her hometown, its size compared to Smath was staggering. DD was relaxed and comfortable and found men had not changed with their lustful looks and gestures. She turned heads every place they went. They honked horns, whistled, and emitted other recognizable sounds that would compel any woman's attention to the fact that she was very much a desired creation. They did tid-bits of shopping, buying small items, pricing here and there, until they stumbled up on a lingerie boutique having a half price sale. They were almost impatient to display their new goods to the man in their lives.

It was the first night in Camille's life she had ever been up all night to see the sun rise. During the night, she admitted that even on her wedding night she was in bed by 3:30. On both her prom nights, she was in by 2 am. That day, after his initial meeting with Burtrume, he did not tell her how her work had been complimented. A bunch of flowers had already been sent to the suite, complements of the manager, directly after their check in. They were an assortment of colors. Knowing he had a dinner engagement, and looking forward to the favorable results, that afternoon he also purchased a gift for them. The presentation was not made until after the evening meeting. This led to Camille's first all night escapade with Soame and DD.

He was surprised. Everyone had eaten. Silk robes and pajamas were dressings he'd never seen either of them in. They wore new slippers to match each other's robe and pajama set. The diamond stud earrings he gave them both as a matching set made their ensemble complete. The gems sparkled each time the crystals pivoted with the turn of their heads. Champagne and caviar were gratuities of the hotel. DD had brought along two bottles of her five star. Soame and Camille shared the wine, while during the course of the night DD enjoyed a record player playing records she brought along that were favorites to each of them. They partied and made love, without reservation, hesitation, and because of the size of the enclosure, the sounds were totally uninhibited.

During their appointment, Soame notified the front desk of the check out, and packed all their belongings. They were to call him when they were done at the beauty salon. When he arrived there they encountered something unexpected. "Ladies, since the business here has been complete, and this beautifully fine vehicle is all serviced and gassed, I have something else in mind for your pleasure." He was double-parked; it was toward the close of the noon rush hour, and he had opened the door for them from the inside. Getting into the car, DD could not help but notice all the flowers from the room decorating the back seat.

As Camille closed the door, DD asked, "Suarme, are we to leave without shopping?"

Easing in line with the downtown traffic he replied, "We can shop anywhere, anytime before September; even by catalog if we choose. Do you hold a mere shopping spree in comparison to the fun and exciting adventure I'm promising you?"

He had a big grin on his face. "No but I thought—"

"Good! Your hair does look good. Now let me see your panties, both of you."

He was not disappointed in the display of their new underwear. With DD's pants lowered, and Camille's skirt raised above her waist, they moved with the traffic. They drove from downtown Billings, entering interstate ninety. They proceeded west to Laurel, where their direction changed southward. The two had begun relaxing with the remains of the five star and the champagne before they changed direction on the outskirts of the city.

Ten miles south of the interstate, he found a convenient place to park and retrieve DD's pipe and his traveling container of powder. The two women walked about, enjoying the breeze and afternoon sunshine. They were traveling parallel to the Yellowstone River, which was in the background scenery. The flowers, the car, the beautiful pantsuit and dress were all parts of the pictures taken with the beautiful women. Each kept three various colored roses. Expressions were being made in happiness; having taken a scenic route, the long way home.

Route 310 took them across the state line into Wyoming. Their destination for the day was Casper. At Lowell, they had a mid-afternoon lunch, and enjoyed the sights of Lake Big Horn. The northwestern extension of the Big Horn mountains could clearly be seen southeast of them, plowing into the skies stretching southward. They traveled with and crossed the Big Horn River, and again re-crossed it, and ran parallel with the river to Worland, and on down to Shoshoni, never losing sight of the Big Horn Mountains. The waterway detracted from the bleakness of the expansion of the planes, on both sides of them. After breakfast that morning, Camille napped "for a couple of hours." She had never thought a ride could be so joyfully refreshing. The front seat had never been so lively.

At Shoshoni, Route 20 throws into eastbound 26. The merging of the two composes route 97. Directly across the plains, they took the almost straight drive, across the Powder River, on into Casper. There was an abundance of daylight remaining for them to picture the mountainous region, which then sat north of them, crossing the Powder River. That was their last sighting of the Big Horn Mountains.

It had simply been fun for Soame being with his two most favorite women, on an adventurous ride filled with pleasant sights. To DD it was an expansion of a live dream, in an episode of real fantasies with the man she loved and one of her girlfriends. To Camille it was the most absolute extravagant presentation, ever unfolded to her, outside of childbirth. The satisfactions she encountered following their registration into the hotel were stages of life she had long ago abandoned. There were exciting and thrilling firsts also, which carried serious impact on her stability.

That night, Soame informed her of Bertrume's praise of her work. Soame gave her $1,000 and instructed her to spend that on only herself. He told her, "I feel you will never intentionally disappoint me. Not only will I be disappointed, I would become angry, and I fear my feelings would change for you because of your willful disobedience. Spend this money only on yourself Camille, and let's remain happy and in harmony within our family."

"Thank you Soame," she was barely audible through her sobbing.

"Don't attempt to save it. I'm telling you to spend this money only on you."

"I will. I promise you I will. Oh please Soame, I'm so happy and proud you care."

Near four that morning, when she thought their sexual repertoire had come to its closing stage, Soame introduced her to anal sex. It was a jubilant discovery with her first female lover ever. Administering the most exotic cunnilingus, she had ever given her, DD stimulated herself with excitement and inflamed him while he watched her masturbate. He climaxed at the peak of their curve. Camille shook and shivered with his releasing eruption. She shattered into trembles, and went limp in her jerks. Neither Soame nor DD could distinguish if it was the money, the ear rings, the hair do, or the new sexual experience that activated her already vibrant personality. They both noticed the thrusting change. In addition, it had been a refreshing ride for all of them. Until that day, neither of them had ever entertained the idea of ever spending a night in Casper, Wyoming.

They found the city comparable to the size of the one they had left. Casper was more western, while Billings had a more northern, compact feel and appearance. The first move Soame made was in refueling and driving through an automatic car wash. The women stretched and relaxed while he vacuumed, and within ten minutes, they were on their way to explore the sights. The main street indicated the presence of tourism. The area was industrialized with refineries. At the close of a business week, between six and seven in the evening, only certain sections of major cities are bustling. There, in those cities, it is the hustle that creates the excitement.

The lodging they selected had a pleasurable atmosphere, after a comfortable and relaxing drive, following a sleepless night, filled with romantic activity. The view from the terrace of their upstairs suite overlooked the North Platte River. Before registering, they decided to have a quiet meal, sharing the time with only themselves. The women enjoyed private talks during a long bubble bath, in a plat formed, step down, spacious tub. Soame had showered and was enjoying his second rum and coke while smoking herb, when they went into the bedroom. He had ordered the meals, which were delivered by four waiters, before the women appeared. He was dressed in his pajamas and robe. They were stunning in their sheer negligee ensembles, purchased the day before. The meal and the alcohol they had to follow it, was all it took to entice yawns from Camille. Twenty minutes after her drink, she was sound asleep beneath the covers of the king size bed.

Soame and DD were up until nearly 4:30 in the morning. To them it was basic and routine, except for the drive and changing atmosphere. Five and a half weeks prior to the time, even those factors would have coincided with their methods of procedure. Without using the bed, the lovemaking through the night was raunchy. The petting they engaged in between the three sessions was compelling. From the couch in the sitting room they began with the conversation on the love seat in the bedroom. The lovers also made love at the bar, after they had gone out on the terrace.

Saturday morning Camille called home. After a conversation with Margaret, and finding all was well, she found Chairly wanting to talk to DD. She and Soame were asleep; it was only 9:30. Through Chairly's persistence and insisting manner, Camille went to the bedroom and told DD about the awaiting call. Soame lay half-asleep, dozing through the conversation. That got their day under way. They had brunch and ate a restaurant that had attracted their attention coming into town. That afternoon they took a tour bus and saw the refineries. Casper is the center of the oil region. After dinner that evening the trio did something, neither had done in years. They enjoyed a walk.

Sunday, they visited the Pioneer Museum, and on an afternoon drive, stopped at a roadside rodeo concession. There they took pictures and bought souvenirs and browsed. The trip had been rewarding with total relaxation. Soame was motivated by his feelings to simply drive and get away for a while. Through his inspiration they found peaceful relaxation in a tranquil atmosphere. They were removed from perplexities, stress, strain, frustrations, and other mental infringements that each had to cope with in their individual lives.

Though this relief did not void the existence of the matters to be dealt with at home, it did positively reform their dispositions. This perspective directly affected Soame. However, the two women with him were the major physical components in his life. To succeed without either or both, from that point, would have been more than difficult, if not impossible.

Because he wanted to see the western side of the Black Hills of South Dakota, they planned for a late arrival at home. They also considered that it would be an impressive sight for Camille to see, and he knew DD would enjoy and appreciate the scenic ride. It was she who called and spoke with Chairly and Margaret, telling them they would be home by noon the following day.

At midnight they left Casper traveling east. From interstate 25 he took route 20 to Lusk. He and DD had traveled 85 before. This time the northerly route would be continued through the Black Hills, directly west of Rapid City, on up to Belle Fourche, and from there, home. The excursion had been an endless honeymoon.

Chapter 20

AT 11:45 Monday morning Pete called "Lunch break!" From the end top floor room at the motel, where he stood discussing matters with his employer. The two other members of the crew, working in the room, went out to tell carpenters in other parts of the building. The work had well gotten under way. Pete had been taking Soame to various sections of the project for thirty minutes explaining the procedural involvement in spacing the men, and the central idea for the location of the materials.

Pete was then instructed to pass word on to the men to keep their specific duties to themselves. The "cover" information to be passed for anyone who inquired was the expansion of some of the rooms, making them into apartments. Unaware of his doings, this started the circulation of a rumor that got the immediate attention of everyone within an eighty mile radius of the town.

Since the week of his arrival into town, only two families had moved. Everyone in that section of the state was waiting to see if developments made would keep the small town in existence. The thought of someone reopening the foundry was the most any of the struggling families could hope for. The rumor restored and added strength to their faith and hope.

The news was of special interest to the town counsel. An emergency meeting was called. A federal survival loan of a quarter of a million dollars was submitted for reconsideration. The minimal amount to be applied for by a township was its only hope of providing salaries for education, maintenance, and security. Without the loan, the town would fold.

The counsel appointed Beauford to check with Soame concerning the possibility of the reopening of the foundry. The sheriff received a unanimous vote when he nominated Tom Blanchard to fill one of the three vacant positions on the counsel. It was also Beauford's proposal for the enlistment of Tom to make the approach to Soame concerning his business affairs, "Since Tom is a member of the co-op, which is apparently already breathing life back into our community, I think he is in better position ta question the business undertakings of one of his associates."

When Tom was informed of his delegation, Beauford gave him the information to relay. The town counsel needed an industrial plan to be submitted to Washington for a federal grant. The plan would ensure the town received a half million dollars. To receive the recognition, and the money, the plan must employ at least fifty workers. The industrial grant was a guaranteed issue. There was something special offered to Soame, by the town, if he could make the presentation. The community leaders would lease the Smath Foundry to him for fifty years, at $5 a year. As a personal tribute from Beauford the directions also included, "Tell him, with the plan submitted, he can do practically anything here he wants ta do, outside of burning the town down and committing murder, intentionally."

This was far better than even the loan because the amount was not only double, but also non-refundable. The primary factor involved was the guarantee. Tom followed instructions, and immediately tried contacting Soame. An invitation was extended to Soame to visit the Blanchard House Thursday evening. Soame had presents stored at the farmhouse for Janet and Cindy; he had not had a chance to deliver. DD and Camille were fully aware of his "outside" interests in the Blanchard women, and the gifts he had for them. Wednesday he spent the later part of the afternoon at the Yates place. After they had driven away from the house, to a nearby secluded area, it took that long to thank him for the presents and nice things he'd brought them from Billings. He had only been home long enough to shower, which relaxed him for dinner, when Tom called. Tom described the situation, and expressed his feelings. Along with the dinner invitation, he informed Soame how he felt like dressing for the occasion, but felt Neomia wasn't ready for the person whose descriptive voice he was then using on the phone.

Soame looked deep into the situation, and saw his friend's frustration. He had spoken with Cindy and Janet since being back, but being busy with the carpenters, and keeping up with the home scene, held him at the house directly after the trip. While he talked on the phone, DD and Camille were in the bedroom, Beverly and Chairly were preparing the dinner they were about to have, and Margaret's lap was resting his head as he talked. He was lying on the living room couch. "Yea, well like I told ya Tom, until today I've been in. Today I went out to see Thad-"

"Soame will you please excuse me, I think I'll go help Bev and Cherry in the kitchen." Margaret slid out from under his head, stood up directly in front of him, raised her skirt, and looking him directly in the eyes, patted the crotch of her panties. After she lowered the skirt, she sashayed to the kitchen. He was totally dazed.

"Soame, are you still there? Are you still with me?"

"I'm here Tom; I had to get myself together, ah Tom, how about I call you after dinner. I'm sure we can come up with something."

It was obvious that Margaret was teasing him. In his position, with his physical capability and resources, he would not allow himself to "freak" with anyone, especially one of the members of his household. He would permit the tease, but to find out her true intent Soame went to the kitchen. She had positioned herself between Chairly and Beverly, about to handle the preparations. "Aren't you going to wash your hands before you touch what they've carefully put together as our meal?"

"Thanks Soame," remarked Chairly.

"What do you mean? How do you know I didn't wash my hands?" He asked her back out into the living room.

"You got something you want to show me?"

"Not really. Why?"

"Let me look under your clothes."

"Since when did you find time to have an interest related to what's under my clothes? I was under the impression that you found Kathleen more to your liking."

Since the return from the business trip and mini vacation, he had been casual, as with everyone else. He and Margaret had not made love. She smoked with DD, and did all the other things she normally did, except enter their room late at night or invite him to hers. Once or twice he had patted her rear, and at meals they caught each other's eye. Whenever they made love, it was with passionate explosiveness. They were lovers, and Soame was very much a force Margaret did not know how to deal with. She was inexperienced in too many areas, and insufficient to gain either the independence or control over him she wanted. Both of those she knew she would never have over him. She could do no more then yield her femininity to the masculine force that was driving stimulation to the love she angrily suppressed.

"Do you want to show me your panties again?"

"Maybe." He turned and took two steps toward the bedroom, "No Soame, wait."

He stopped without turning around. "Aren't you going to look and see what you asked for?"

"Bring it here in front of me."

Walking to him, she asked, "Why are you so cold to me Soame?"

His voice had carried through the hall into the bedroom. Chairly walked out into the hall and stood with her arms folded. Camille looked from around the corner. DD said something to the dog in French; she sat between DD and Camille. Everyone in the house waited for two weeks to find out what was to unfold between these two.

She stood before him, displaying her elegantly long, beautiful legs, and panties to him. "What are you doing?" She gave an impish indication, gesturing with a slight shrug of her shoulders, a quaint flash of a smile, and in a fraction of a split second she turned up her nose. "Isn't this what you asked of me?"

"I want to see your pussy."

"Are you coming to my room tonight?" She could see her sister and Chairly peeking around the corner.

"I might. If I do, let me see what I'll be coming for."

Taking the skirt down, turning her back to him, taking a step toward her room door, she told him "You'll be coming to be with me!"

"Dinner's ready!" yelled Chairly.

Immediately following dinner he returned Tom's call. They agreed to meet at the farm house the following evening. They played spades in the living room, listening to records the remainder of the evening. DD and Soame played Camille and Margaret the first game. The games were worth two hundred dollars to the winners; the first pair to three hundred and fifty won. DD and Soame beat everybody twice, until Chairly added the jokers to the deck. They had been playing "Ace high." After losing with the added two cards, he left Camille as DD's partner.

Walking down the hall, he called Margaret. She unleashed her passions in his bed. He thought about the possibility of being away from her too long. Margaret besought him not to be cold towards her in any way again. Before that night, she had come to reconcile within herself that it was her jealousy that placed a barrier between them. However, he did not confuse her accusation.

That evening, Tom totally exposed all the information to him. Soame was surprised, and somewhat shocked, to learn of the overall involvement in the availability of the grant. He carefully sketched out a legal plan of operation, explaining to Tom as he proceeded. Janet sat at the kitchen table with them, after adjusting the presentation from the living room. Cindy stood behind his chair, with her hands on his shoulders, looking and listening.

The co-op was already in operation employing four men; with the addition of carpenters already with the company, it totaled eleven. He included himself and his secretary. With the thirteen people already employed through his corporate structure, Soame demonstrated in a diagram how he could manufacture nine different style boxes using seven men to assemble sections for each design he produced. Tom gave him the dimensions of the building space. On paper, he fitted the idea into the dimensions, and set aside office space. A notation was fixed with sketch citing, "These figures and diagram do not include office workers, salesmen, a maintenance crew, or warehouse stockmen – fifteen manpower increase. This plan can become operational within six weeks."

The plan was to be turned over to Beauford the following morning. Beauford was to relay it to Jack Stillman, but Soame was not to have been told of the procedure from the point of Beauford receiving the material. With the information Tom added, with a big grin on his face, "Ah hell, it beats pony express, no matter how you look at it."

Soame chuckled and responded, "I'll bet you can hardly wait for Halloween." The wide grin turned to a look of confusion. It was not until Cindy snickered and Janet nudged him, before Tom jumped up jigging. The house had a mini bar with three stools. Janet had examined the wall to wall carpeting in each room except where they were and the kitchen. He jigged off the edge of the large center rug, onto the varnished and waxed floor. "You know I've been trying my darndest to come up with a way." All along the women had been bringing drinks to the table.

Janet asked, "Shall I get another round of drinks?"

She was drinking with them. Cindy was having cranberry juice. "Let's all go to the bar, unless you all are ready to leave." It was 12:30 AM.

Though they had mentioned Neomia's drinking, during the week she was there, she drank less than a fifth of liquor when invited to "help herself" from a fully stocked arrangement. Cindy sat in his lap while he explained his idea to operate in the town, on a twenty-four hour scale. Tom had never heard of a town or city in the region with a "round the clock" pattern. With the motel, he could offer a house of leisure. His successful point was in finding the right person with the exact expertise to run it. That person had to be well versed in management in that particular field, to make the plan a workable idea. None of them seemed to reject the idea, but neither displayed an inclination toward it.

Tom was noted for having more farm land than anyone else in the area. Nonetheless, he had never before been a member of the town counsel. That night, with mid fifty degree temperature readings, Soame drank Scotch. He toasted Tom in his occupation of a seat in the counsel. Tom then proposed a toast, to the success of Soame's plans. At the close of the meeting Soame presented the ladies with gifts he had in store for them. Except for the presentations, and the bit of congenial petting he and Cindy did, outside at the car, the evening had been all business.

He knew DD would be awake when he came home. She thought he would go to the shower. It was the first time either of them had gone out during the night without the other since they had been together. Soame had been gone for more than nine hours. They both knew hardly anything would awaken Camille. The lovers did not think about sleep until daybreak.

Jack Stillman was not only the city attorney; he was the most prominent lawyer in town and a member of the town counsel. Beauford had seen Tom, had the plans explained to him, and had the papers at Stillman's office at 8:30 Friday morning. Like everyone else, Stillman was enthused with the idea of a jewelry box factory being in the town. With all probability, he had a better insight than anyone else, toward the potentiality of the idea. It was he who called the emergency meeting for Tuesday night. Stillman scrutinized the plan with the keenness he had used in obtaining it.

While in Casper, DD noticed the Cheyenne and Denver papers at a newsstand. She purchased a copy of each, and because Soame carried them for her, and commented on her packing them, she thought they would result in more interest for leisure time at home for him. He was at home with them, but there was very little leisure in the schedule he arranged. He waxed the car, polished his shoes and boots, and performed other maintenance with household fixtures. He had helpers and assistants, he also "checked" and "repaired" or "polished," along with the normal functions he engaged in. They were all pleased in having him around the house. DD enjoyed seeing the girls with him, and seeing him happy in such a way brought her pleasure.

Friday morning she was up, while Camille prepared for the office. Rather than disturb him, when her girlfriend left for the office, she had another cup of coffee in the quiet of the living room. Unless Chairly got up early, the house usually did not come alive until ten or ten-thirty. Relaxing on the couch, scanning through the Denver paper, DD saw something that excited her. Then she was glad they had not shopped in Billings. DD presumptuously called and made a three day reservation at the hotel where they had stayed in Denver. She originally asked for suites they had occupied before; only one of them was available. There were available accommodations to her preference, on the opposite side of the hotel, at the opposite end. The adjoining suites she reserved were on the third floor.

A short while later she went to her boudoir and found him in the shower. Margaret entered the room almost directly behind her. Like he always did, Soame came out of the bathroom drying himself. The two women had made the bed, and DD had underwear on the covers for him. Margaret was sitting on the bed with Fifi, reading the advertisement in the Denver paper. Morning greetings were extended and received within the trio and Soame began applying lotion to his body. DD, still in her robe and gown, was sitting in the love seat. When he began applying lotion, Fifi hopped from the bed, and sprang to the seat, in keeping company with the person she had been with all morning. It was then DD told him about the fur sale, and mentioned the fact Margaret had the ad. He was not in a hurry, but Soame wanted to get to the motel, to see what progress was being made. Dressing in his underwear in front of Margaret, he inquired as to when the sale was over, and what type of furs were on sale. It was the only fur sale of the summer for Nieman Marcus; it would last until Monday. Margaret added, "All the furs they have are at a 40-60 percent reduction." Putting on his pants he asked DD to disrobe. It was a common practice, if not quite routine.

Getting into his shoes, he asked DD to continue her poses from the bed. Margaret knew because she was there, she would be next. She had gotten excited watching DD, and seeing him become aroused. She was somewhat disappointed when he asked her to bring him a glass of orange juice. DD wanted just one 'toke' from the pipe. She knew what he wanted to see and the various ways he wanted it displayed. She wanted to artfully please him. She knew also, if he wasn't going to take her to Denver, she would have known at that point. He had never denied her anything. The white shirt he chose would require cuff links. It was being buttoned when Margaret returned. Accepting the glass he asked, "Can you do that."

DD was then propped on an elbow, with a leg extended upward, when Margaret also noticed the arched foot. "I can try."

"Let's see."

After removing her night shirt, and getting onto the bed with her female lover, DD changed positions and did something simple for her to duplicate. Fastening the links, he watched them on all fours, with their rears to him, expose their vaginas. While he dressed in the jacket he wore, and consumed the juice, they posed in four other positions. Soame walked to the bed reaching to his hip pocket. Long before his approach they knew he was fully erect. DD knew he would not take the time to please them or himself. Also, she knew no other woman would have the jisms they had aroused. He flung four, one hundred dollar bills on the bed. "Teach her how to show herself to me. How about making up some sandwiches? Pick Camille up for lunch, stop by the motel at 12:15, and bring a blanket. We'll have a picnic lunch and see how she feels about Denver."

Soame found no problems at the motel, which was what he expected. It was a delightful afternoon for a picnic, even if it would only be for an hour or so. It was the close of a work week and pay day. Earlier during the week he hired a plumber, and the hardware store had to order a jack hammer from an equipment rental supply in Rapid City. The separations butting the east and west top floor rooms had to be fitted with a ten foot adjoining space, according to Soame's plans. Between the walls of the two rooms, the carpenters found pipes that took a skilled plumber to redirect. The poured slab of concrete separating the top from the ground floor could only be cut so deep with a concrete saw. Pete sold him on the idea of the efficiency of the jack hammer. He was satisfied with the progress he had seen, and climbing under the steering wheel, he asked, "Which way to the picnic?"

East on the main road they immediately approached the caution light. Through it, at the end of the block on the left was the realty office. At the next corner he turned left, and proceeded two and a half blocks to the huge house they would soon move into. He was not surprised when he had seen all of them in the car. After Camille told him, "Let's go to DD's new place." Everyone laughed and they were all surprised when they heard, "Good, um telling you all right now, I don't see no sense in going on this shopping trip-"

"Ha!" came the sarcastic sound from the young black woman in the back seat, who still was the age of a girl.

"I thought I mentioned this to you before. It's not only impolite; it is outright rude on your part to interrupt in such a manner."

"Why Soame?"

"Why what?"

"Why an we go ta Denva?"

During the course of the short drive, the exchange between the two went back and forth. The others sat and listened with deep exhalations, sighs, faint fakes, and moaning motions. When the car stopped in the parking area in front of the garage, "You don't hafta gimmie no money Soame!"

"Well, if you don't have any money, you don't need to go to Denver to shop. Let's have the picnic, shall we?"

"I got my own money, das all um sain."

It was not the picnic or the exchange between the two of them holding Camille's immediate concern and interests. Helping Camille out of the car, she informed him, "Jack Stillman called the office this morning."

The three in the back seat climbed out, on his side, behind him. The trunk had been opened from the glove box. The others passed by with the goods, while she waited for him to assist DD. He walked between them toward the screened enclosure. The girls were preceding them to the lawn beyond the pool which they had to walk around. On the back lawn Chairly, Beverly, and Margaret spread two blankets and set the containers in place. "He asked me if you would be available this afternoon. It sounds pretty important. He said to ask if you can that he will give you a call at home between two and three."

As it turned out they would be taking the trip, but the items they purchased would be requested to be shipped in six weeks. This was to avoid moving the goods into one place, and out and again into another. They all had a wonderful time during the hour and a half outing. Leaving the jeep at the motel, after dropping Camille at the office, he went home with them.

"I've looked forward to meeting you since making the Blanchard papers out. There's a matter of utmost urgency involving the plan you submitted to Tom last evening. I'd like to get the material off in the mail as soon as possible. I've been reviewing and working on them all day. I think it's important that we have the plans in Washington by Monday morning, it's to all our advantage. Would you come by my office and give a final approval on the idea we're proposing. I'll need your signature before mailing it."

"Sure, glad you called. I can be there in ten minutes."

"Good, thanks Mr. Hudson, I look forward to meeting you personally. I'll see you then." The call came at 2:05.

Stillman was an impressive figure, for a small town lawyer. In his mid fifties, he stood five foot eleven with a slender build. He had a mustache, and there was no gray in his black wavy hair. He seemed to have composure but one could tell he had been toiling, and stress was seen in his face. Even though he greeted Soame with a smile, Soame could see he was a firm, hard, and direct person.

Soame had been in the office twenty minutes reviewing the drafted plan and proposal. After signing it and taking the seat across the desk from Stillman he commented "You make it look and sound so technical, Jack."

"It really is, Soame. No one in this district in the past six years could come up with a plan of the sort. In the past year our resources have extended appeals throughout the state, and your idea to this point is the best we've come up with. It probably seems simple to you, because you have the business aptitude, and a sharp sense of industrialization to develop an idea like this for expansion. Future times will more than likely prove you to be the salvation of this town and area. I'm very proud, in this minute way, not only to work with you, but also pleased to welcome you here, and I wish you well with us. I am pleased and proud indeed." Soame shook the extended hand.

Chapter 21

FROM Stillman's office he went directly to the realty office. Carl Willis moved about on the lot, and waved with a broad smile as he got out of the car. He knew Mrs. Tillman listened with a keen ear, as he explained the details of his meeting. The bank had not received his company checks from the printer. It was the Tillman realty checks being issued to the carpenters each week. It was Mrs. Tillman's smile that alerted him of his first arrivals for pay. The checks each had a fifty dollar bonus added. Mrs. Tillman had also heard about the trip. She gave Camille Monday off, wished them a safe trip, and when the last check was issued, she closed the office. Beauford was waiting outside with a big grin on his face. "I got your message."

"Well now, you just do things right, and we'll be all right Soame. I told ya, we never forget favors."

Having a fine house, with a spacious bedroom, containing a king sized bed, which was relaxing for hours of sleep comfort, Soame Hudson was in no way egotistically inclined to load his entire family in an automobile, and attempt to take and eight to ten hour drive, on a Friday afternoon, when he had not slept or eaten in the past twenty-four hours. The trip would also include Muff, who was due for a second rabies shot. DD had spent more than a half hour on the phone after the picnic, locating a veterinarian in Denver who would administer the shot.

After returning home with the car, he drove to the motel and retrieved the jeep. He went to the hardware store, where he was able to get a harness that was able to fit the large cat. He also purchased two nice sized pieces of sturdy luggage. Margaret and Beverly were in need of the traveling gear, especially to transport school clothing they would buy. When he returned home and showered, they all had dinner. His excitement in anticipation of the relaxation, thrills and pleasures, interrupted the comfortable hours of sleep he knew his body required. The two and a half hours of electrifying entertainment and stimulating satisfactions were heightened and climaxed by the exclusive one-time only appearance for the first time ever, anywhere, of the dynamic duo "Mizz Fine" Johnson and "Cherry Blast." "Mizz fine" alternated the stage with "Cherry Blast." After performing to the music of Cool and the Gang's *Fresh*, and Roles Royce's *I Want to Get Next to You*, there was an encore and she unexpectedly did very well dancing with/to music of Olivia Newton John's *Lets Get Physical*.

"Cherry" immediately noticed something after "Mizz Fine" had finished her act. Her final record was done one before "Cherry." The patrons were live and all responsive to the show. However, only one extended the three hundred dollars for the show, and that same one gave seventy-five dollars for the autograph. The same person signaled the announcer over, and dressed in her teddy, fishnets, heels, and wig, she was given two hundred dollars. "Cherry" had already danced to Elton John's *Philadelphia Freedom*. Her presentation was to have ended with Stephanie Mills' *Sweet Sensation*. She was to received an encore, which was expected. She had done extremely well and shocked Camille, who had seen them all having fun, dancing at relaxing times. "Cherry" was a fully primed, natural exotic artist thanks to the careful concern, influence, and tutorial of "Miss Dubanee."

Chairly did a spellbinding rendition to the music of William Bell and Judy Clay's *Private Number* for the encore. There was a stillness in the room, following the mind capturing delivery of her slender, budding body, in such a grandiose exhibition. Two of the people in the bed greeted her with smiles, and the pride she held was uplifted when one of them nodded her head in consent of the performance. Next to him, it was DD the pseudo-celebrity wanted most to impress. "Mizz Fine" was seated on the love seat, and, with everyone else, waited to see what else the presentation would bring.

In one hand he held both his clip and his slide. She stood at the foot of the bed, clad only in the thug bikini panties, given to her by her tutor. The swank piece was dark blue and seemed to be tailored. He snatched a bill from which holder no one else saw, nor did they see the denomination, before he balled it and tossed it to the foot of the bed. They all knew what it meant. Even Chairly knew, the best move was in leaving it laying, and walk out of the room. He knew she would not resist the confrontation. How it would result, no one knew.

She passed up the chance of the draw, and reached for the bill. Uncrumpling it, she looked into his eyes and clicked her roving tongue. "Dis ain't right Soame."

"What do you mean? You said we don't have to give you any money; on top of that, there, look at it. I've even given you some, now what's the problem?"

"I meen dat was before we knowed fo sho we was goin shopin."

"I knew all along you had good sense Chairly. Now tell me just how does knowing whether or not you're going to Denver effect your talking to me in such a manner. Um getting pretty tired of having to tell you to keep your mouth shut when I'm talking. Now what do I have to do? Slap you in your mouth to get you to understand that?"

She had been profusely chewing the gum in her mouth. Sulkily, and without answering the question, her jaws slowly stopped moving. It was absolutely quiet in the room. Everyone knew Soame was very serious. They knew Chairly also, and wondered if she would cross over the line. It was so casual, so smooth, so even, and so clear, even Margaret, who stood as far away as the entertainment center heard it. The amazing thing was that it was said so low, and yet the magical tones traveled so well.

"Did you hear what I asked you Chairly?"

In a flash, her eyes stretched. The indication was she would have trespassed, but his approach was totally different from that which she expected. Yet as a warning, it was also inviting. Quickly the young woman regained composure and said obstinately, "Soame, I gave up ma position an neva sade a word. Sides DD, um da bes bitch you got Soame, and da way ya treatin me, it ain't right, it jes ain't right, das all um sain."

"Alright, I'll consider what you say about Camille, but no one can replace your standing in my heart. You're younger, and when we moved into this house, it was you who said you wanted to share the other bedroom with Beverly. Camille works, and as an older woman shares this bed which has never been off limits to you, nor has that door ever been closed. You could come in when you want to, at anytime. No one can replace your position in my heart, but you can remove yourself.

"Now I don't give a dam about your evasiveness, and I'll give you every possible chance you want, or need, to win at these little games you play. Believe me Chairly, I know what I'm doing. However long it takes you to play whatever game you choose with me, you can have the time; it'll always revolve back to the point. The point here now is, what does Camille have to do with your talking to me crossly?"

"I jes wonted ta let ya know how I feel bout it, an you, das all; an um glad ya put thangs strate."

"Charily, the point is, did you hea-"

"Soame, I don't kea bout you hittin me in my mouf or anywhea, cause ya my man, an das yo right, but ya ain't gon call no otha woman yo second lady front a me no mo, an das da point to!"

She folded the bill in half, held it up toward him, and in having her say, marched over to the love seat, and began gathering garments saying, "Ya go takin sum otha woman outta town an evva whea else. She callin back ta dis house, layin up with ma man. Come back hea wearin dimons, an cause I ax ya bout Denva, ya wanna slap me in da mouf."

She slung everything over one of her arms, except her shoes. She stood wide legged, with her back purposely in direct alignment with the straight head look he was giving her. The sleekly developing long legs did not bend, when she bent over for her shoes. At the cottage she had learned to please him very well, in a variety of ways. With her free hand, instead of picking up her shoes, she reached to the elastic between her legs. Chairly looked him directly in the eyes from between her legs, and called "Soame." Stretching the elastic, she placed one side with the other, fastening it to the crevice between her vulva and her thigh. Exposing her genitals to him. When she stood with her shoes, the lip still held the panty part in place, where she had put it.

At the foot of the bed, she stopped, "Ah, Soame can I see ya cross da hall fa a while."

"I've told you about that also. It's 'May I,' and um serious about what I told you. Keep your mouth shut when I'm talking."

"Well ya don tole me bout school too, an it don't start till next month. Ya commin papa?"

"I'll be there in a minute." Then she surprised them. All of them looked with total fascination. None but one, thought anyone could emulate DD's walk. She casually strolled to door in that fashion, with the slender slightly bowed thighs exposing a flashing peak with each stride.

With Soame, Chairly was not afraid of anything, or anyone, anywhere. That house had become her natural environment; she had adapted well, and was at home. When he left the room Margaret put an album on. Twenty minutes later, the sounds began creeping through. Chairly had no restraints in unleashing herself to him. All of them knew how wild it would get, and before the real noises began, Camille told Margaret, "Turn the music up a little, will you?"

She and Beverly were smoking grass, watching muted TV. DD and Margaret were sharing DD's pipe. They were all listening to the Bee Gee's *Saturday Night Live*. "No, lets hear them for a while," said DD.

Midway through the second side of Al Green's *Al Green is Love* album, Chairly cried out "Big daddy, please." Three of the women in the room snickered.

DD touched Beverly on the shoulder; she was on a beanbag. "Now, if you want to, turn it up." The volume stayed at the same level. He had been in the other room for an hour and a half before he went to sleep in her bed. She joined them simply saying "He is sleepin." She had gotten the five hundred he took with him. At 12:30 am Soame was up and about. All the packing had been done. Money had been deposited into the Tillman account, for various uses. On this occasion, she used one of her credit cards. Soame did not see the practicality in purchasing expensive coats or jackets for Chairly and Beverly, who would wear them for a season or two and then outgrow them. "It'll give them something to look forward to. They're pretty 'fast' right now, as it is."

Richard, Camille's youngest, and only son, had requested to stay in the country, for the remainder of the summer. Three weeks prior to the Denver trip, Soame had given her five hundred dollars to be sent to the parents of the boy's friend, for boarding, during hard times. Each week she sent him twenty-five dollars for his personal money. The decision was made to allow him to continue to stay because of the move to be made into the larger house.

Margaret, Chairly, and Beverly had "chipped in" together on video equipment for nearly a month. The camera was fun for a while, but the books came along, and exciting adventures in reading set less interesting occupations aside. They were taking the camera for the trip, "Mizz Fine" wanted to be filmed on a live set, the lavish hotel suite. None of them had experience in walking a cat. They figured the harness would restrain the cat in the event he jumped from the arms of the person carrying him. At 1:15 they left the house for the three-day trip.

The route was almost a straight shot. A short drive took them to the junction of 212 and 59. 59 went south and met with Interstate 25 in Douglas, Wyoming. The car was livelier than expected. Jokes were constantly being told. Outside Cheyenne, when everyone unloaded to stretch and the car was being refueled at the service plaza, Muff scampered through the open door. They were on a merry chase for twenty minutes. It took them through the open door of the building complex. Calling "Muff, Muff," almost running, five women saw him duck in the hall, as he sidestepped, dodged and maneuvered from people who with agility, in avoiding the oversized frightened, feline, moved into each other, and after bumping, jumped into the path of the yipping poodle, and hopped once again, in almost humored amazement.

In the restaurant, heads turned, feet shuffled, and one man spilled his tray because the gray curly hairs briskly brushed his leg. Sliding on his side, after skidding around a turn, Muff regained with leaps and bounds to and out the glass door.

Soame, who had removed the Seville from the service island to a parking spaced across and adjacent from the door, simply got out of the car, and was about to sit on the hood. He had seen them dash through the door when it cracked. Fifi looked when he called, but because Muff leaped down the sidewalk, she yipped and strided behind him. Then came the women. "Suarme, aren't you going to help catch the puppy?" She asked almost frantically, trying to decide whether to look and go to him, or in the direction the two had gone. Beverly and Chairly whisked past her. Camille hopped and skipped behind them after noticing him indicating the direction. "Yea, sure. Fifi, Muff, here."

She could barely hear him, and femininely waved him away and was on her way. That was all the men needed, to be on their way, gloating behind the two women who appeared to have nothing on under the jacket and windbreaker. Margaret tossed her nose and head up at him, as she turned and was a step behind DD.

Young boys, teenagers and at least six men including two service station attendants, all looked in his direction. They pushed and shoved at each other to see and catch up with the sensuously walking beautiful black woman and the elegantly smooth, long, fine legs behind her. Ten minutes later, from the opposite corner of the building, around the open bay of the service garage came at least twenty people.

Boys were skipping and jumping almost playing leapfrog in front of Chairly and Beverly. In Billings DD had talked Camille into buying three mini skirts; because it had been years since she wore one. She also got her to wear a knitted V-neck pullover sweater that revealed the lusciously bouncing breasts. Each time she folded her arms across her bare midsection the "boobs" would rise and swell, and eyes popped in lust. The miniskirt DD wore was at least four inches shorter than the light jacket she had on. She had no problem walking from the house to the car, and on to the registration desk, in the "heels" that lifted her heels a full three and a quarter inches, broadening her calves, and causing her to throw her hips with calculated precision. Her beauty was stunning to those who could not decide, if the view she presented was pictured best, from the front or rear of her.

"Suarme will you please whis-sell for the dog?" Ten yards away, in her approach to him flanked by Camille and Margaret, encircled by at least twelve men and teenagers. "Yea, sure."

The men looked at each other, as he took his circled middle finger and thumb to his mouth. Not since the puppy scampered about, in the woods with Chairly at the hunting lodge, had he called her in such a way. The sound he made was piercing with shrillness. Heads snapped. He looked at Chairly, who displayed her palms and spread fingers, and with a limp movement, leaned her head briefly to the side.

Except for a passing freighter behind the building in one of the lanes going in the opposite direction, all was completely still. Trailing the sound was a far off distinct "arff arff". The bark repeated and two of the boys broke out running toward the initial corner they turned. Fifi turned the corner with a serious gait. There was mud up to her knees, but that was not the cause of the abrupt stop by the two boys, who were fifteen feet from Fifi when Muff rounded the corner. One of the men asked, "What is that, that just came around the corner?" Even a hundred feet away, the yellow, white, and black striped cat looked exceptionally large.

He had galloped around the corner, and in turning saw the youngster, who looked at him simultaneously, and froze, with bulging eyes. Their bodies appeared to have trembled into rigidity. One of the other men replied, "Well, will you look at that, it's a cat isn't it?"

"What do you think we been looking for?"

"Beats me."

Soame then told Chairly to get the towel out of the car. Fifi tilted her nose, and moved past the boys, without turning her head. As muddy as she was DD had never been more proud of her pooch. The building had completely emptied to see what was happening. In the restaurant, blinds were lifted, and people stood on chairs to see over the people along the sidewalk.

Muff's gallop had changed to a haphazard trot, until he was within ten feet of the boys. When the pace changed, the boys slightly moved in toward each other. His steps were cautious and prepared, as he swayed and looked until they were behind him. He heard the French, and knew his buddy was being scolded, and bounded into a leaping trot.

"Oh Muff, where have you been?" It was the woman in the short shorts and windbreaker.

Twenty feet away, he heard Margaret. He broke his trot into a walk, took three choppy fast cat steps, stopped, and as if to say, "Hay Fifi, look pal let me she ya how it's done" laid down, rolled onto his back, and began to roll on the pavement.

"Oh Muff," cried Margaret stepping to him. Chairly giggled and Beverly said, "Muff aren't you something?"

"Who was the last person to feed the cat?" asked Soame.

After seeing both animals, many of the spectators along the sidewalk, and on the pavement, started back inside of the building. People inside the restaurant stepped off chairs until Muff began rolling and turning. The mass once again turned back to the scene. People inside, seeing the attention outside, sprung back into chairs. Then an amazing series of events took place. Margaret and Beverly were almost fifteen feet away, near the clowning calico. Camille had taken two steps toward her daughters and their pet. The cat's belly was bulging; he saw it, and disgustingly, with his voice to carry through the harmonious crowd tone, to Margaret and Beverly, asked. The base bellowed, and for a long moment, everything became motionless. Chairly had delivered the towel to DD, who had on no panties.

She turned about, Fifi circled, and stooping, she aligned her crotch to him, thinking no one would step between the rising miniskirt and him. The dog was not only muddy, she was soaking wet. She told her to "stay." Taking three steps toward the trunk she said to Chairly, "I need another towel."

Fifi was sitting alone when Muff trotted up, because Chairly had responded, "I'll get it," went toward the passenger side of the car to pop the trunk. She was the only one of them to see the approaching trooper. Patrolling the southbound lanes, he had seen the crowd outside at the plaza. He had entered the one-way exit from the plaza, in the opposite direction. Still sitting on the hood, Chairly knocked on the inside windshield, to get his attention. "Da police," she mimed and indicated the direction. He did not turn, but had noticed the cat's potbelly as it approached. The state trooper's cruiser was the only soundless movement in a lot of at least 150 people, until Fifi shook and sprinkled the onlookers near her.

They backed up and stumbled into each other. Because people were bumping and stumbling into the patrol car he hit the cherry. Soame hopped from the hood, took four strides past the dog, and during the midst of the Johnson's discussion on who had not fed Muff, took Muff by the nape. "Can somebody tell me what's going on here?"

"These people lost their dog and cat, but they came back. Biggest cat you ever want to see."

"Is that so? Well I'm glad they got the animals back, but you people have to clear the drive and entrance here."

Soame put the cat in the car, and extended his hand for the towel from DD. "Close the trunk."

As the crowd thinned the trooper eased the car up to position where he could see Soame energetically rubbing the gray poodle with the towel. "Is everything alright?"

Only Chairly was inside with Muff. The remainder of his household stood around him. "It's fine now officer. Good morning." The two nodded at each other, and he continued. "Must have a pond nearby, she went for a swim, trailing behind our house cat, when he jumped out at the crack of the door and went hunting, I think that's what they were doing."

"Well ya don't say? That just about beats it all doesn't it? Well, if you are all right, drive safe and have a pleasant trip."

"Thanks for the concern, officer."

There were a few people looking from the hall through the glass. Cars were pulling out. The flamingo pink and purple skies, with a hint of gray, indicated dawn. The trooper did a turn about, waved and exited. "Anybody got to use the bathroom?" Ten minutes later, fully refreshed, they were on their way.

Chapter 22

It was a short fun-filled drive to Denver from the service plaza. The cat had not been fed. According to Margaret, "He wasn't in the kitchen when I cooked." Chairly fed Fifi before Margaret went in to cook, and he simply did not indicate to anyone he was hungry. Each one thought the other had done it. He and Fifi traveled in the rear window from there to Denver.

He had no intentions of leaving the hotel Saturday. It was DD's reservation. Entering the city, he once again refueled, and drove through a car wash. They all vacuumed and cleaned the interior. Soame then took the passenger seat, and when the registration was completed, before the luggage was brought up, he was in the shower. In the sitting room, lounging on the sofa, in his pajamas and robe, Soame had a "private" panty show. "Fifty dollars for each modeling, in a different panty, no teddies, no bras, and no briefs." He knew it was unlikely for each of them to have more than three pairs on the trip. It was such a surprise to Chairly because she intended to purchase new undergarments; she had only the ones she had on. Then came the nude idea. Because she could only do that fashion once, a less expensive "pose shots" idea was presented.

When he made the final offer, he got tricked. The offer was toward the lowest bid, to accompany him to the bedroom. The bidding opened at four hundred dollars. The women gathered at the bar, and after a brief discussion, all of them went to the bedroom, calling him from his relaxed position on the settee. By 10:30 they were all ready to visit the vet, see the pet groomer, and do their shopping. He warned them, "See what you think you want, put a deposit on it, or shop and compare, before you buy. You can go back this evening or tomorrow after you've thought about the item or compared prices." They each had leisure money in addition to the money they brought with them.

He spoke with Cindy and Kathleen on the phone, who had no other choice but to understand that he was out of town. Cindy said, "I'd rather be with you, if I had my preference, even though it's the weekend. It would probably be unlikely if you were at home. We haven't seriously been together for more than a week Soame. Would you please see me when you return?" Cindy spoke in a matter of fact way about the circumstance. He could not decide if the gift won priority over his presence with Cathy, but he understood her, and was concerned about her needs.

He called the liquor store and was fortunate because the clerk was able to contact the distributor and have his order delivered to the store. After one, the distributor would have been closed. He ordered two cases of the Hennessy 5 Star 125. Margaret had also taken preference to the cognac. She was quite feminine, but her biggest fantasy was in having the roles reversed in "her" household. DD would be a woman of sophomoric standing in her court. Soame would be one of many lovers attending her. Camille would be totally outcast. Margaret's Americanism and ethnic identity enabled her to imagine and hope for the scenario. Also, it was identification in a capitalistic system, which revolved around her "reality."

The real fact was that she had nothing except what was given to her by the people she wanted to dominate. Her mind was drab, but it was not deranged. She smoked "rez," after being told how by Soame. Her real problem was patience; she could not content herself with the hospitality of the people she wanted to immediately rise above and dominate. She would have Chairly's back flogged to ribbons of them all, if her fantasy were to be made complete. Her jealousy was a vindictive approach to the younger woman's courage and intelligence. She detested her ways with Soame, despised her being DD's favorite, and had a contemptible attitude toward her for being her sister's lover.

It was comfortably relaxing in the bedroom of the suite. Soame had a few gulping rounds of rum, played easy listening music through the sound system, and in tidying himself, found he needed a hair cut. It was no major concern, but it would not hurt to spruce himself up. DD did a fine job in keeping the ends clipped, but a barber could do the fashionable job. Peacefully under the covers he drifted into sleep.

The rest was undisturbed. Had Fifi not pounced on the bed, he probably would have slept another four to six hours. Also, had it not been for Fifi and Muff, "the girls" would have eaten dinner before returning to the hotel. Chairly and Beverly window shopped while the other three shopped and browsed in the department store. The two actually enjoyed it. Though there were not any autograph seekers hounding their heels, they were rather flamboyant in their casually mod dressed appearance. They caught eyes with the company they were in. Muff had never been bathed and groomed by human hands before. Muff was tuff and he knew it. He was carried until he felt the curious onlookers should watch him tug against the harness. After walking for a while, , the two seemed to have an innate sense of communication. Somehow, he seemingly transferred the message, and each time she spontaneously responded, "Say pal, now remember, we don't have to go to them. In fact, we get more of um when we stop. Beause they stop, and the others stop ta see what they stopped for. Let's stop again so I can do my thing."

Sure enough, the two would stop together. The two holding the leashes would skip in a stop toward them. Then in a chain reaction, people stopped all around them. Other people began tiptoeing to peep over shoulders in front of them. Kids wiggled through different pairs of legs to get a close look. Muff's initial presentation was sprawled on his stretched side licking his paw. He saw it was not necessary to lick his paw, so he simply lay sprawled. "Mizz Fine" was not allowed to smoke in public, but what celebrity, behind flashy sunglasses, and a classy cigarette holder with an eye catchy feline, wouldn't follow through and flaunt her flirtatious puffs?

Muff moved Fifi started out, and Chairly said to Beverly, "Chile, I kant wait ta get ma hair done." In a couple of months the lion-style clipping Fifi received grew out naturally. The time span would allow the rings to grow out, for her winter coat. The fur, the blue polish on her paws, and the fancy blue ribbons on her ears, was what Soame saw, when he turned on his side and saw her sitting up on the bed.

"Darlinggg, you are awake?" There was a dive onto the bed with a big hug, followed by a juicy kiss. She told him that she had driven over to Commerce City, to the fashionably pretentious little dining place, with the terrace, where they had lunch before. As it turned out, they could not be admitted even on the terrace because Fifi was no longer a puppy. When the manger came out and was considering the matter, Muff unexpectedly sprung from Margaret's arms. The manager had not seen the other pet, as Margaret stood behind Camille. "Where did that come from? That was a cat wasn't it?" yelled the manger.

Chairly, with her permanent wave, brought the dark brown, full length leather coat in, "Som body sade dis should be yo's pa-pa."

The once again hungry Muff, dragging his leash, went through the foyer and into the dining room. Then came Margaret and Beverly with boxes. He had never before seen them with their hair styled. Margaret looked ravishingly beautiful. Beverly looked grown up without excessive makeup.

One man saw Muff, stood up, and called for the waiter to remove the cat from his presence. Muff walked to him hopped up into his chair, saw the red snapper, and began eating. The waiter was afraid of the large cat.

Camille then came in with many small boxes of various lengths, and sizes. DD then explained, she tipped the manager and hair stylist expert, paid her in advance, and because Camille only needed a wash and set, with DD's restyling, the woman would open up for them "tomorrow at one." By the time Margaret got to the table, where two other people remained seated in astound amazement Muff had eaten his fill and was about to hop down. She courteously paid the check for the table of three. She had also shopped for him, like no other woman had ever done for him. Detesting the fact, Camille told him, "She wouldn't allow either of us to throw in, or buy you gifts on our own." Then came another hug, and a kiss that told him she knew the money spent was only a pittance between the two of them.

Before Camille brought the assortment of small boxes, he smelled the barbeque. He had already seen various colors of long sleeved shirts, was told the altered pants could be gotten the following day, and examined the thermal and flannel underwear and wool socks. As he opened one small box, DD would whisk another at him. The smallest contained a set of diamond cuff links, with a matching stickpin, and tie clip. He had opened it first. Then there were the leather gloves with virgin wool linings. There were ascots and scarfs of various colors. One box contained two sets of earmuffs, and the largest box contained a two and half gallon gambler's Stetson. "Darlinggg, we're all starved, and I remembered you saying when last you had Bar-B-Q. We stopped at a pit. Have you eaten since we've been gone?"

Camille had placed the foiled wrapped slabs in the oven. She and Margaret had already returned to the kitchenette. While he washed his face and prepared for the meal, Beverly and Chairly told him of the crowd of people that followed DD, Camille and Margaret out of the department store. He assumed that the ten to twelve people were men, even when Beverly described the wild whistles outside in the mall. "We were approaching them with Muff and Fifi, nearing the spot we were supposed to have met them. Muff had stopped along the way, and refused to be carried, so we waited a few minutes until he was ready."

"He don dat bout five times all ova da mall makin fokes look at him."

"Yeah, but outside the store four or five more people either turned around and joined the crowd or moved in from the sides and behind. I heard the whistle, like everyone else, but Cherry gave my sister Fifi's leash, stepped between her and DD to the woman, and after removing her sunglasses with her right hand, asked the woman, 'Yeah, so whaz up?' She was a beautiful longhaired redhead, taller than Margaret, in pants. Cherry was chewing, and almost patting her foot to a rock, when she talked to the woman who was about twenty-five. DD had turned around, and mom, who was on the other side of her, stood sideways. The woman looked at DD, back to Cherry, and looking at DD once again moistened her lips, when she looked at Cherry the next time she said 'Well, excuse me!' She turned and walked through the crowd. They followed us all over the mall, all afternoon. Mom and DD took the packages to the car, while we had our hair done; it was an hour and forty-five minutes because we also got manicures and pedicures. When we came out, we didn't have to look for them, we saw the crowd."

He had washed his face, brushed his teeth, and groomed. DD stood with him, in her stocking feet, passing the towel and assisting him. The two stood in the door, and when he finished, he stood and listened. "So where's Muff now?"

"I don't know. When we all came in, I removed his harness and leash, the door is open to our suite, and he walked toward it. Mom said not to open the doors to go out, until we know for sure where he is."

On the way to the kitchenette, DD told him she remembered seeing a fish market, on the utility road they had driven on. While driving to the hotel, she stopped by and Camille bought three nice sized perches.

Bar stools aided arranging them all at the counter without difficulty. The three slabs of ribs were piping hot. Soame gave praise to the Almighty Amon for the food they were about to receive. During the meal DD had them all laughing with her description of Muff at the table in the sophisticated dining room. "His hind legs extended him upward from the chair to the table, where he stood slightly over the table, on his forepaws. When he started eating the guy's food, he held his hands as if he was about to choke Muff, and made a move toward the table. Muff casually looked over to the fellow as if to say,'Now listen fella, I'm having a meal, if you don't mind.' The guy hopped back, and by that time the waiter was there. Like all the people in the restaurant, we were all so fascinated. We stood with the manager, where the foyer empties into the eating area, and watched. The waiter looked at us, and told the manager, 'I'm not going to touch this cat.' By then Muff had eaten over half of the fillet. The manger, very casually looked at us, and in a stern, low, voice, said, 'Will one of you ladies, please remove your cat from this establishment?' Camille moved, but Margaret said she would do it. When she had taken two steps, she called him. Muff looked, took two more heaping mouthfuls, and by the time she was two feet from the table, he was pushing his paws away. I called the customer, telling him the meals were paid for, and gave the manger a hundred dollar bill. I told him to keep the change because of the inconvenience."

They shared a large tossed salad with the meat and chips. There were two gallons of ice cream for dessert. To see some of the school clothes, he had to visit the sitting room next door. Some were to be sent later by the store, with Richard's clothes, and the two full-length coats. Margaret did not wait to have her fur jacket shipped. "It's too precious, and I know I could not stand to torment myself waiting for it." The leather coat he received was with lambskin lining with a mink collar. It was one of the few items left for men included in the sale.

That evening was filled with fun galore. Chairly would never again be caught without "undies." Not only for the "panty parade," but also he allowed them the chance to replenish their partly depleted stashes. All the new items were modeled at twenty dollars a showing. Naturally there was a presentation. "For da first time in Denva, an neva befo seen anywea, Mizz Fine Johnson, and Muff da wonda cat, fa excitement and yo fassenation." When she set Muff down, he simply climbed onto the hassock, licked his paw, and flopped down, draping part of his tail, legs and paws, over the cushion edges. They were in the setting room.

"Mizz Fine" had a lorgnette added to her act. She and her manager could hardly wait for the two-record show to be over. Returning from Commerce City they passed a "blue movie" video shop. Their favorite stars were Gaynor, Constance Money, and Ginger Lynn. DD was persuaded to stop and purchase the movies for them. It was not a difficult task because all of them enjoyed the movies from DD's collection. Venessa del Reo substituted for the unavailable Ginger Lynn video. The two wanted to see the recording they had made during the day as well as the new tapes.

Soame had a better idea for them all, and it captured their spirits with the mood he put them into. He did it with records. Ones he selected and brought along specifically for the satisfaction of not only listening, but also for effect. The first record they listened to was Gladys Knight's *With Every Beat of My Heart*. Before starting any music, he told them of the story and his experience in seeing a particular artist perform, and how he caught his attention like no other. He was the third act in a concert; Sam Cook was the star attraction, of the show held at the Jacksonville Coliseum. Following the second act, all the lights went out, in the building, except three spotlights that formed a circle, in the front portion, center of the stage.

Evidently the singer came from behind stage, through the unfastened seam, in the center, where the curtains met. In his dark suit, no one saw him, until he entered the lighted circle, and approached the floor mike. There was a crutch in each of his hands. "I never fond out what his affliction was. At the time he had a record on the charts. I was a senior in college. I'll play that record, but I'm going to precede it with another, to give you an idea of his music. I've never before heard anyone sing from mid baritone up to mid second tenor with such smoothness and accuracy. Even though I had heard his record, while he sung, I noticed the entire audience was motionless and transfixed by his singing.

The records were all played. The second one, *Speak Her Name*, was recorded by Walter Jackson. The third 45 on the spindle was *I Honestly Love You* by Olivia Newton John. He then played a cut from a Jackson album *Moonlight Over Vermont*, and did Millie Jackon's *Hurt So Good*. It was a short soulful mood, kept light with clear and smooth penetration. He began easing out of it with Nat King Cole's *Rambling Rose*. Brightness filled the atmosphere when he played *It Takes Two* by Marvin Gaye and Kim Weston that's groovy. With that record Chairly and Beverly began dancing. When Margaret asked him, he did not refuse.

He had never known a barber shop anywhere to be open on Sunday. When DD suggested the hair stylist trim his hair, he thought the idea to be practical, but somehow remained reluctant to have his hair cut in a woman's beauty salon. The liquor was his first purchase. After that they split up.

Three of them went off treading to shops for fun, relaxation and spending. In two hours they were to all meet in the vicinity of the department store's front. Three of them went into the department store. Inside, Soame ventured about, doing bits of shopping, while DD and Camille went to the fourth floor to keep their appointment. He was to also get his trousers. In an hour and fifteen minutes his shopping was complete; he had even gotten the pants, and found DD had carried a pair with her the day before, to be sure of the measurements for the alterations. He went upstairs to check on their progress, and found a black woman as their beautician. With a degree in cosmetology, specializing in hairstyles, he allowed her to trim his hair. DD had not mentioned her being black.

Denver was a good idea to him, for a number of reasons. He was really thankful that the mishap the morning before had not been a catastrophe. Twice before in his life, he had been at the threshold of success, and an irregular incident destroyed his build up. Had he been in Florida, the minor incident the day before, when the police came on the scene, it would have resulted in further inquiry. With all probability it would have began with the fact the animals were not leashed. Being "dirty" in Florida and other places, one has to be nearly impeccable to get through. When he bellowed the question, he had glimpsed the possible "fall."

Soame's grass supply was running very low. The women in the house were smoking a considerable amount, as was he. Tom and Beauford agreed that it was the best he had ever had. There were the three Yates of course, but no one but him knew, there was less than a half pound left to be shared and distributed.

Soame brought money and items of trade, to negotiate a deal for a hefty amount, if it was to be had. Muff had a litter box, and was the only one to occupy the two suites during that afternoon. They thoroughly enjoyed themselves, and were at the hotel at 6:30. At 6:50 he was walking out the door. He simply told them, "I've got some business to take care of. I won't be gone too long." His destination was to find the fellow whom he had traded the LTD for marijuana, several months before. In the back, on the floor of the car, under a large bath towel, was a black forty-gallon trash can liner. It contained a quarter pound of raw heroin, one pound of cocaine, and in a brown paper bag there was four thousand dollars in cash.

Some schedules never change. There are people who buy drugs daily. Others make their purchases during the weekends. Thursday evenings through to Sunday evenings are always busy times for drug dealers. They usually "re-up" Wednesday or Thursday, and Sunday or Monday. Considering the amount he exchanged for the previous time, Soame calculated his contract to be a Sunday "re-up" probability.

He did not know the direct address, but had no problem in locating the area, going directly to the house. He spotted it, parked at the end of the block, and walked back with the wrapped black bag. It was very good he arrived when he did. He expected to be fortunate enough to catch his contact with a "fresh" package. Luck for him was better that day. The contact was about to "re-up," he had not received the package, and had very little.

Twenty minutes after he arrived at the connection, they were en route to the supplier. It could have been a very dangerous thing to attempt to do, but there was no better way to get exactly what he wanted. In his hip pocket there was an automatic .25. Slanted through the front belt of the Levi's, he had a .44 magnum. The supplier did not want to initially meet with Soame, but when it was discovered he had "boy" and "girl" toward a trade, or cash, he had no problem getting up front to see "the big man." The pound of girl was traded for six pounds of grass. The coke was the New Orleans grade. The trade was three pounds of Acapulco Gold and three pounds of Panama Red, in the exchange.

In Miami, at that time, prime cocaine was being sold at twelve to fifteen thousand dollars a kilogram. A bulk buy – five or more "keys" – would place a buyer in a position to purchase at ten thousand dollars per "key." The New Orleans coke rated 84 to 87 percent, and was a pure substance, but would be considered "garbage" in the Magic City.

As pure, the coke was acceptable as "good" in the Denver market. In fact, the deal went so much in favor of "the house," that Soame was given the choice of selecting an additional pound of either brand of "weed" to compensate. He chose the Gold, and adding yeast to his favor, he asked that "the house" throw in the scale being used. It was a triple beam weight measurement utensil. When the supplier appeared to be trapped, pondering over the two hundred and fifty dollar item, Soame said to him, "Check this out man, um not going to walk away from the deal that's already offered and made. Um through here every three or four months. I've always got good drugs. You can make yourself a couple of thousand, like now, each time I stop by. Do you want to throw in the scale and call it square?" With that agreement the deal was closed with a shake of hands.

In Miami, at that time, Columbian High grade grass was being sold at nine hundred to one-thousand two-hundred a pound. The marijuana traded in that room, was far superior to any herb being sold in Miami, and the Gold or Red could not be obtained unless through special connections.

Soame was almost a connoisseur of herb. In Miami the grass he had would have easily sold at eighteen to twenty three hundred a pound. Back at his original connection's house, he made an offer. The supplier would not release any more of his product, because he had regular clientele, and he would not put "strain on his house." The approach was to the connection, who then had six pounds of grass, three of each. "The 'boy' I have will take a thirty, and nothing in the streets in the city will touch it." The guy knew it was a fact; he had seen and gum tested both products before they left.

"I'll trade you a gram, for a pound of each."

"You give me two grams and I'll let you have three pounds."

He set his newly purchased scale up, set the gram measure, balanced it with a hundred dollar bill, and weighed up two and a half grams. "Say dude, thanks for the connection, and I appreciate this deal."

Each time, to a degree, the house had won. His purpose that evening was in getting grass. He knew the weed he had was top quality. But brick mason cannot lay bricks without a trowel. A carpenter cannot build a house without a saw. A plumber cannot tighten or adjust a pipe without a wrench. Someone who deals drugs, cannot deal accurately without a scale. Soame had no intentions of selling grass. This was a tool of a trade he had learned, and gotten away from, because of other interests.

He had been gone two and a half hours. At the hotel he discovered he was the happiest shopper of them all. Though he had viewed and smelled the buds, he had not smoked any of the weed. The Maui-Wowie compared second or third to the Panama Red. The Gold is superior in its class, to any other type. The Gold from Acapulco out rates the Maui-Wowie by far. He had a coke high and knew it would be many hours before he ate, after he smoked. He had DD order club sandwiches and chips. He did not roll the hairy red buds from Panama. The Gold almost glittered like sparkling powder. He rolled five joints from one bag, and told them they all could not smoke the five before daybreak. He had ten pounds of marijuana; six of them were gold. No one in the suite knew how much he had. They only saw the pound he rolled from. Soame took a shower.

Jackie Dushannon's *Put a Little Love in Your Heart* was blasting in the sitting room, when he came out of the shower. "I was in junior high when it came out. It's the first record I ever bought."

Camille and DD were bopping in the bedroom. They had toked on the joint in the ashtray. Explaining the purchase of her fist record, she also told him she had only had one hit from the joint. "DD did two. It's really good."

He groomed, dabbed on the Paco Raban cologne she had purchased for him, and dressed into underwear and his robe. The two of them accompanied him to the bar. Everyone else was in the adjoining suite watching movies. Muff had the large couch to himself. Fifi padded alongside DD, who instead of bringing her pipe, had the remainder of the joint. Soame had one of the sandwiches with orange juice. No one else had eaten one. There were three other joints where he had left the five. He knew they would be up practically all night. Camille played *Good Morning America* by an only hit artist while he had ice cream.

It had been a considerable while since he had seen DD in a marijuana high. She became cuddlesome, with the aid of his shoulder, and nestled under him while he ate, and after preparing the ice cream, leaning from the close stool next to him. They had just begun relaxing on the couch. Soame had a drink, but the joint still had not been relit. Without protest, Muff had given up the couch and wandered off. Chairly came through the doors, with Beverly trailing behind. They looked about the bar, shook their heads at each other, and shrugged their shoulders. Chairly grabbed one of the remaining joints, and they began retracing their direction. "Hold on, wait a minute, what's happnin?"

"Dat gurl don lost da join." They were clad in new long sleeved tapered shirts, with contrasting colors; new panties, and no footwear. The two would have been comfortable anywhere on a beach, at noon, behind the flashy sunglasses. The reflections from the sun would have captured anyone's attention, bouncing from the costume jewelry they wore on each finger. Chairly was madly chewing and plopping gum.

"So ah, just tell me now, ah, cool stuff. What do you plan to do with the one in your hand?"

"We ga smoke it Soame, we redy fa a notha hit, ya sade itta last till monin."

"Yeah, but check this out. Before you start on that one, you've got to finish the other one."

"Soame, Margaret's lost it. We've looked all over for it."

"She ain't been no whea but da bafroom. I believe she flushe-"

Then came dainty, smiling Margaret through the doors, in a flashy laced teddy, and a sheer, half length robe type cover, which fastened with a matching belt, leaving the lower part of the teddy exposed. The three looked like fairy tale characters; especially with the hair do's. Holding the "roach" so they could see it, she giggled while telling them, "I found it, I don't know how it got in the medicine cabinet, but I checked, and here it is."

It did not take Camille long to logically ask, "When did you last brush your teeth?"

While she threw her hand to her jaw, as if shocked, Chairly marched to her. "Gurl gmmie dat, ya always playin."

"Ahhh hold on there, ah, sporty black, one at a time."

"Soame dis da bes reffa in da worl."

"Yeah, alright, finish the one, before you start the other."

DD knew what was in store for her and Camille the rest of the night. She did not know if Margaret would join them, or sleep on the couch next door, as she had done the night before. Margaret cherished watching videos with homosexual men. DD had several, which Margaret brought. Two had been purchased the day before. The combination of liquor, marijuana and cocaine was an aphrodisiac for him. She had not openly discussed the matter with Camille or Margaret, but it had been hinted at with the both of them separately. Neither of them could get around his control factor. Even when he had done the three, the two, or only one of the combinations, his release was generally at his discretion. Then there were times in the mornings, before Camille went to work, when she would arouse him by dressing and posing, and he would alternate between them both causing her to be late to work. She would have to re-shower and dress. Those times he had simply been awoken from sleep because she fellated him, or he woke on his own, through some slight noise Camille made. Those times he had nothing. Once again they relaxed on the couch. He was drinking the rum slowly. They had not yet relit the joint. DD was held in the thought, wondering what it would be like, after he began smoking, until daybreak.

Another reason he was in compliance with the trip to Devner was because it was a less than four hour drive from Aspen. There was a package he wanted to mail, and he wanted to mail it someplace no one was likely to see the sender ever again. Margaret had a lovely script. Her writing was unlikely to be associated with anything shady. Before the trip to Billings, he had asked her to write a short letter for him:

"Dear Kirk,…Frank and I were friends. We spent some really good times together, and I sincerely wish he was alive today, but unfortunately, as you probably well know by now, he did not make it to California as we planned. You do not know me, and we will never meet. Your brother and I planned something, which did not work out for him. We both knew the risks involved. We promised each other to do this, if one did not make it. He mentioned his kid in California, and you knowing how to get part of this money to him. The other part is for you all not to forget that he lived…From a true friend."

The letter was packed with standard crate paper, Frank's wallet, his other personal belongings, and thirty thousand dollars in hundred dollar bills. The items were fitted compactly in a box selected, to contain the contents through delivery.

It had been an interesting evening and night. All of them enjoyed themselves. No one in any way disappointed. At 4:30 he gave the news to the three he was in company with in the bedroom. Margaret came over while they were still in the sitting room. It was just before midnight. She and DD were first to leave for the bedroom. Neither of them smoked the pipe, after the grass was lit. After informing them, he went next door. He saw Muff laid out on the sitting room sofa, appearing to be more bored than anything, including sleep. At a pet store,

Camille had purchased catnip for him. He had never had any before. No one had seen him go near it, after it was rolled to him and he got the first wiff. Fifi saw him also and hopped up. He lazily flicked the very end portion of his tail, slightly turned his head, looked over his shoulder in her direction, and plopped his head where it had been. Soame was impressed with the fact, "At least the cat's content. I think." Fifi sniffed Muff and looked up to Soame.

Walking through the hall to the bedroom, he notified them, "Company coming back."

"Dis room iz off limits ta all men!"

The other voice answered, "Except one, and your name must be Soame to enter."

"Ha!"

There they were. The covers were neatly pulled back. Double pillows were leaned against the headboard. They lay in the king sized bed with a space the width of a single bed between them. They were reclined against the pillows in almost identical positions. The two looked like the chocolate and an off pink colored M and M, in candy colored shells. Just like at home, in the master bedroom, low background music filtered in, softy through the sound system, and they were watching "Blue" movies. In the center between them, was one of the larger ashtrays, from their sitting room. "You two know you're not supposed to be smoking in bed."

"Das when ya go ta bed ta sleep. We ain't sleepy."

"No, that's when you're in bed, in the event you fall asleep while you're in bed."

"Das what I sade, look Soame." Chairly extended her fingers into the ash tray, and her freshly done, multicolored nails held a "roach." It was a third of a joint.

"Those glasses are going to ruin your eyes."

"They're sun censored. We can wear them any place without worry about eye damage. They adjust to the light."

"Well, well, let me look at those." Chairly, whom he stood nearest, handed hers.

"Ya know, I noticed, but I disregarded the thought. I'm very proud you two paid some attention to yourselves."

"Mom took us into the optical center, since you said to shop and compare and we could go back today, but it only took two hours for them to put the lenses in the frames we selected. Pretty sharp ha?"

"Yeah, how much?"

"Mine were eighty-five. Cherry's cost one hundred and twenty."

"Yeah, we kin evon wea um in school."

"Hay listen, you two get up, pack your things. We're checking out. Now you don't have to rush. You've even got time to take showers, but I want you to get all your belongings together, we're leaving soon."

When he saw the two looking at each other, knowing he was serious, he added, "When you dress, wear something comfortable for leisure outside the car. We're stopping along the way, for a picnic." That brought smiles to their faces.

"Have you had fun?"

"Sure, thanks for bringing us shopping."

"Why we levin so soon Soame?"

"I've got a drive to make, and we can't have a picnic here in the hotel. Now have you had fun?"

"I have fun all da time when um with you."

"Good you wanna call me big daddy?"

"Ya betta get outa dis room, fo I call ma ole man. Sides, me and ma peoples hea don wanna be bothered."

"That's cool, now be sure and check twice when you're packed. Bring your cases to the sitting room next door, and let us know. I'm very proud of you both, and both of you look really ladylike with your hair do's. Let's get ready to leave."

During their travels, the original three had seen quite a few sights they considered splendid. All those in the car were impressed with what they saw and appreciated the traveling comfort of the car. Near 6:00 AM they left the hotel, with dawn scarcely breaking in back of them. None of them were, or expected to be, sleepy. Outside of Golden, a real scenic drive began for them, with an early morning look at Mt. Evans. It was fascinating to travel through the Eisenhower memorial tunnel, and beyond Dillon Interstate to Route 91. In clear daylight they traveled south to Climax, and at Leadville the scenic view was grand. Their travels took them to an approach to Mt. Elbert. Just on the south side of the mountain, Soame turned onto Route 82. In a valley area, in the midst of ski country, he drove in scenic surroundings to Aspen.

"DD give her the package." They were at the post office. He did not park directly in front. With other parked and moving cars, and people moving about, perhaps they would not have been noticed. There was a faint possibility of someone remembering Beverly getting into a new Cadillac. Eliminating the chance, he said to her, "Beverly, I want you to do something for me. Are you with me?"

"Sure. What do you want me to do with this?"

"I'm going inside to place a phone call. When I go through the doors, I want you to come behind me, go to the counter, mail the package, first class, and ask for a hundred dollars of insurance."

"You mean have it insured for a hundred bucks?"

"So you got that?"

"How ca Mizz Fine Johnson, da gratest sho lady in da state of Montana, forget a line like dat, mista hot stuff?"

"Here's a ten."

The route was retraced back through Independence Pass, to 91 and on Interstate 70, instead of going on to Golden, he put Mt. Evans at their backs, and went north on 40 through Idaho Springs. At Grandby, still trapped in scenic wonder, he asked, "We'll be traveling through here or drive on to Rocky Mountain National Park. It's your choice, what do you all want to do?"

Chapter 23

THE week after the Denver trip went by rather fast. He took three carpenters from the motel to their future residence. Two men were hired to re-do the lawn and flower beds, and Camille spent Thursday afternoon with "Ricky." It was their second visit with each other. However, another interesting event took place, which led to Camille placing ads in two out of town, largely circulating papers, the *New York Daily News* and the *Chicago Tribune*, two of the most circulated newspapers in America. Three members of the household, plus Richard when he arrived, would hopefully be going back to school in three weeks. The matter was contingent upon the federally approved loan, or the federal grant, of the submitted proposal. With Camille working at the realty office, and Soame being away from the house at various times during the day, the task of the housekeeping rest on the lady of the house. During the picnic at the Rocky Mountain National Park, at the close of the Denver shopping trip, the matter was hashed out. It was resolved, thanks to Camille, that they submit ads for a butler and an upstairs maid.

Work at the motel neared completion. "In about ten days boss—I mean Soame. We'd be done in less than a week, if the crew hadn't been sent to the big house," Pete told him during one of his daily visits to the construction site. He was totally satisfied with the efficiency of the carpenters at the motel. Their work was thorough and beautiful; there was never a complaint from Soame.

He and Pete divided their time between the motel and the mansion. Pete had to be on hand at the house to receive instructions, or notes from DD or the decorators, who had come in from Rapid City. It was an exciting experience for DD, to shape and form an already grand work, into her idea and liking. During trips she gathered *House and Garden* magazines, and other reading material, to give her ideas for the style she wanted. A couple of the ideas she had in mind had to be revamped because of the original design of the house. The floor plan and blueprint were available through the local courthouse. Pete and the three carpenters reviewed the schematics, and were helpful to DD in arranging alternate plans that were just as efficient as her original idea.

That Wednesday, through a call to the Yates, he found out Thad, Billy, and a couple of the hired farmers were working in the fields out on Hodgesville road. They were in the middle of harvesting the wheat crop Thad would have left in the fields, had Soame not come along and aided him in stabilizing his existence as a farmer. Cathy wanted him to stop by on a visit, and take her and her sister with him, but in declining the suggestion, he promised he would see them after he talked with Thad and Billy. Even little Thad had temporarily joined the work force of men, in gathering the crops.

Wheat is the world's most important food crop. It covers more of the earth's surface than any other crop. Sandra Fairfield provided him with the information, when he looked to the tri-state area to move in to. The farmers he was in contact with informed him that wheat is Montana's most valuable crop. Even so, part of the plight they had encountered dealt with the importance of farming in the state. After evaluating the facts, Soame did not find it odd in picturing why farmers could not get state and civilian support within the state. His unanswered question was: why wouldn't farmers on a national level, band together in protest, of the federal government's strangling them out of existence?

America is third behind China in world production of wheat. The Soviet Union produces more wheat than any other country in the world. Montana trails more than several states, in the production of wheat. Kansas, North Dakota, Texas, Oklahoma, Minnesota, Colorado, Washington, South Dakota, and Missouri, outproduce Montana's wheat input into the world market supply. A full quarter of the state is covered with forests. Grasslands cover another two thirds of the state. Though barley is second as being the state's most valuable crop, the U.S. ranks second in the world in its production, and Montana is the third ranking state in America, with the production of barley. Other crops grown and produced in the state are hay, potatoes, and sugar beats.

The fields were golden brown with ripe wheat. Thad could only wave and yell "I'll have to talk ta ya later; too busy with this thing right now."

He was operating the giant combine, skillfully handling the tractor and equipment. Billy and Thad were seeing to the rented trucks being loaded. Soame gave him a joint of the gold. He openly lit it, coughed, and took another drag. "Mannn, where in the world did ya get this, I'm high already!" They chuckled; Soame relaxed and watched the gathering process, while Billy climbed further into his high taking another "toke."

Little Thad brought over a main stem, and explained the additional stalks being tillers. He also explained the roots, stem, leaves, and head process involved in the development of the spike. "The spike is actually the wheat head. It carries clusters of flowers called spikelets." Soame turned to see Billy send a loaded truck off. Thad went on, "Spikelets branch off the joint, containing wheat kernels wrapped in a husk. An average spike bears 30-50 kernels."

The boy then told Soame "After this harvest, this will be your land. It's a clay loam, some of the best land we got. Pa said this is yours cause you asked for some prime acreage. The fallow will hold the moisture, but it won't be long before you can set in winter wheat. Pa says it'll be a late winter, so if you set your furrows deep, you'll have hardy plants to survive the cold in October and November." Little Thad shaved kernels into his hand from the stalk in his hand. Extending his open palm to Soame exposing the wheat, he said, "This is hard red spring wheat. We planted it in April; it won't grow in the winter cause it gets too cold for it to survive."

38 ft. V type dump trailers were being used. There were three of them alternating loads to the depot. Farming had been a success in the area for a considerable while. "Old man Hodges settled this area, even before my grampaw moved out this way. During the early 1900s this was a thriving community. Even before Berrydale came into existence the grand mill attracted people from as far away as a hundred miles, according to Paw." It was Billy explaining the settlement of the land, from the Indians, and how it was developed into a farming community. "It wasn't the farming alone to set up the railway station just east of town. The foundry you're reopening, and the prosperity of farming around here did it. Like I told ya before, North Dakota is second in America, in the production of wheat. One of its major producing belts extends into this state, and end in this county. You're standin' in the middle of it right now, on your land."

"On your acreage you bought from paw, you've got both clay and silt loams. In this state, you can't ask for better soil to grow wheat, barley and sugar beats."

"So where does the wheat go when it reaches the train station?"

"Wheat's probably different from any other base crop grown down your way in the South. We don't just take it to the market and get paid. The grain is stored in storage bins. You can see them from the highway, during the winter months when all the leaves are off the trees. Soame, I thought the other grass was better than good, but this is unbelievable. I never thought smoke could be so potent. Where'd you get this?'

"There's a saying 'Now and then, a stranger comes along.' Yea, I admit, it is pretty good. I've got an ounce for you in the Jeep. I'll give it to you before I leave, and I don't want to keep you from your work, but what happens from the storage bins?"

"Well, the purpose of the bins being near the railroad is for the wheat to be belted into box cars and transported to terminal elevators, located in the large grain market shipping center. There the government inspects and grades it. You can see how the department has control of the prices, because it's bought and sold on the basis of the grade. Prices are determined at the grain exchange."

Because of the uncertainty in staying, Thad did not tend the planted crops he had in the fields, as of a month before Soame's arrival into the area. He then saw the operational costs and possible repairs as necessary money he could not afford to ignore without further endangering the possibility of being able to move his family out of the area. A loam, is much decayed organic matter, plant or animal; it provides nutrition for the wheat plant. They had been farming that particular tract of land for three years. It was a mystery to the Yates, as Billy explained it, how the bearing spikes had 40-60 kernels. The previous year they had been forced to plow the fields under. They did not know if the bearing increase was due to the fallow retaining more moisture, or simply the production of the rich clay loam, enhancing the growing plants during the time it was unattended. Winter wheat has a yield of the sort, but spring wheat producing spikes with so many kernels made the harvest a possible and very profitable experience. Supply and demand was the governing factors at the grain exchange. Only time would tell if it would be a profitable harvest, which was to have been done in July, for sure, this year they would not plow under. The farmers were proud for that fact alone.

After leaving the fields, he drove over to the Yates' home. It was midafternoon, and Cathy and Jenny were done with their chores. He sat and talked on the porch with the girls and Mrs. Yates for a while. The chatting led to the presentation of gifts. Mrs. Yates overjoyed when she opened the box and saw her watch. He'd noticed that she did not wear one. There were boxes for both Thads which contained a pocket watch for her husband and a pellet rifle for little Thad. In total there were three watches; all from the same manufacturer, but each with a different design. The present had not been given to little Thad in the field because surely it would have taken him from his work or other fun. Openly there on the porch, he told them of the gifts to soon arrive by mail or parcel service.

Mrs. Yates had no objections to Cathy practicing her driving, and Jenny riding with them. Seeing them walk to the jeep, she brought to Cathy's attention that Kathleen had no shoes on. "Kathleen, you'd better come back, and put some shoes on your feet, since you're gonna be in respectable company with a gentleman."

She kept walking, looking back over her shoulder, she replied to her mother, "Awe ma, this ain't no hi falutin' gentleman, it's just Soame that's all, sides....he don't mind if I don't wear no shoes." Leaving the yard she turned to her sister in the back seat and said, "What'll she say thirty minutes from now, if she knew I won't have a stitch on?" Jenny leaned up, putting her arms around his neck and replied, "She won't have time to say a word about you cause she'll be too busy runnin her mouth bout me in my birthday suit with my darling lover." She then squeezed tightly, and after kissing his jaw told him, "I'm comin' out of these pants just as soon as we round the corner, so you can have a look at what's hot and ready for ya."

With that the two began arguing. Cathy drove and fussed for twenty minutes. She took them to a spot behind a field even Jenny had never been before. By the time they arrived, neither of the sisters had on a stitch.

Tuesday morning he walked through the mansion with DD, after dropping Camille off at work. The decorators weren't expected until after nine. Fifi padded about, but basically remained at their sides. Muff had not been seen since shortly after midnight, upon their return home. Turning off the main road, onto their street, the harness was taken off of him. When the door was opened, in their front yard, he was gone. The decorators were early by fifteen minutes. He walked through the house, and listened and watched, while she explained her notes and ideas to them. Twice she asked, "Darlinggg, what do you think about the idea?"

"It's your house my dearest."

He had already given her his idea about a sound room and library. At 10:30 Pete and the three other carpenters arrived. The tour began again, this time with the decorators expressing DD's ideas to the carpenters, with their own style notes. They presented their suggestions to DD, moving from living room to hall, in and out of rooms, the kitchen and pool area, back to the foyer, up the curved staircase, in and out of the bedrooms, and once again through the same old process. On the last round Fifi sat with him at the top of the stairs, and listened to the chattering, on the business subject of redecoration.

At noon, after picking up Camille, he treated them all to lunch, at the local café. The eating-place was across the way, directly in front and eastof the motel. A few of the carpenters who ate there were invited as well. With Mrs. Tillman and Beauford, the place was crowded.

His thoughts were to Cindy and Janet at the farm house on Thursday. After lunch, he saw DD back to the house, dropped Camille off at the office, and then went to the motel. Except for the stocking of the bar, carpeting, and exchanging the bed, the upstairs east and west, adjoining rooms were completed. This was to be his office. The kitchenette downstairs was done. He had not decided whether to use a carpeted floor or not. Following a brief conversation with Janet, she yelled upstairs to Cindy. When the receiver was lifted, throbbing sounds filtered through into Soame's earpiece. The rhythmic sounds were thumping and explosive with the lyrical message *Urgent*, by Foreigner.

"Hello"

"Say there kitten, what's happening?"

"Hi Soame, and you don't know what's happening ha? Even with the music, didn't mother just tell you?"

"I have no idea, is there a problem of sort?"

"Well that surely depends on how you look at it, listen to the music, for clarification of the message." Their voices were still, when the saxophone began soaring through the bridge in the song. Of course, he'd heard the former number one record over a hundred times before.

"I finished mine two days ago. Hers started the next day. Do you mean I asked you all the way from Denver, and you still don't get the message?"

"Hold on a second now. Are you telling me you were on your period when I spoke with you last? And now Janet's on hers?"

"That's right, women do have these occurrences, and they're called menstruation cycles, Mr. Hudson, and that's the message. Mother has cramps sometimes with hers. She's not feeling well, and I want to be with you."

"Well, well, I guess we learn something new everyday. I do appreciate being enlightened. She only said she wasn't feeling too well, but tell me why did you lay such a guilt trip on me for being in Denver. I at least called to let you know I was thinking about you and was concerned. "

"I think of only you, all the time Soame, and we don't necessarily have to be sexually involved together, which is the point at hand. Are we getting together or what? You promised."

"Thursday at the Kent place was my idea. That's what I just told Janet, but since the record has aided you in relaying the message so well, I'm trying to think of a place, where we can meet this afternoon."

"What's wrong with the Kent place today?"

"It'll take you too long to get there, and coming and going will tie up almost three hours for you. I think the lake will be more practical and it's just as secluded.

I've got to stop by the house for about ten minutes, why don't you get yourself together and meet met there, if it's alright with Janet."

"I'm already together my dear. I've been waiting for you to call since nine this morning. She'll be happy to see me go; she can't stand for anyone to be around when she has the cramps. I'm glad we have Neomia. I'll meet you there. I'm leaving now."

He stopped by home for a full twelve minutes and was still at the lake ten minutes before Cindy. Through the stillness he heard the sound of the approaching vehicle, and when it came into sight he rose from the spread blanket. After assisting her out of the El Camino, he sat on its hood and fender. She had on sandals with her jeans, and a short-sleeved cotton blouse. Her hair was loose, and the gentle breeze occasionally tossed strands into her face. Standing between his legs and in his arms, she spoke softly to him before he said, "I'm very pleased to be alone with you. This is a far different impression than what I received over the phone, both Saturday and earlier today."

"Does the new impression you have allow you see me any less than your bitch? Come on; let's talk about it over here. I'm not out to impress anyone else, and I most certainly don't want you to get the wrong impression." She pulled him off the fender, and led him to the blanket.

There were very serious stages of petting, and the removal of items of clothing during intermittent pauses. Sex was added to their passionate love making, and they enjoyed a nude swim. The cool water invigorated them and made them feel refreshed. The temperature was between 65-70 degrees. Neither of them thought to bring towels. While Cindy, laying on the blanket, sun baked the droplets on her beautiful body, Soame put on his sweater. He also went to the jeep, and returned with two small gift wrapped boxes. The suave ermine jacket for her, and the full length sable for Janet, were being mailed by the department store. Because she would be off to school in a few weeks, he'd asked for immediate delivery. The delivery would be the only way of them finding out about the fine gifts. They were still waiting for an acceptance letter.

In the early morning hours, when Beverly described the sun-protected lens to him, it was a double surprise. After shopping in the department store, he had done a brief spell of shopping before joining his ladies upstairs. He had gone to the same optical shop Beverly mentioned, and chose a pair of regal sunglasses for Cindy. However, they were much more conservative than the other two pairs.

The first box she opened only contained the case. It was obvious there were glasses inside. She was delighted, and had not before owned those kind.

The real excitement came when she saw the platinum charm bracelet, even though she mistook it for silver. It already had two charms attached with it. Fastening her fingers to the dangling cherry, she hugged his neck saying, "Oh you're the only love of my life, and we share this in a sacred way." There was a kiss and during the course of their foreplay, he said to her, "I've got something I want you to try."

They had not done drugs together that afternoon. Soame had a fresh joint and his vile with him. "I've got some smoke here. It's about the third best rated smoke in the world"

"I thought you said the Maui-Wowie is a top grade smoke?"

"I did, and it is. This is a gold brand, and other than golden rod, no other gold is better than the gold marijuana from Acapulco. Surpassing it is the Black Ganjah from Africa, and I've never smoked any better, or ever heard anyone else say they've smoked or heard of grass anywhere, outdoing that in Vietnam."

"It's that good ha?"

"This or the Vietnam smoke?"

"Soame, I'm into you. I feel in some way giddy to a certain extent, when I do the coke and grass. I know I get stimulated. None of it surpasses the natural emotional high I have when I'm with you. I hope you don't mind me talking about it. I've drifted off into a world of you Soame, and not even she can direct me. I try not to let it be frightening, but I must share this with you."

He lit the joint, she went on, "We both knew the details and boundaries, and since the beginning we said we would nourish our relationship within all those circumstance. In accepting them, we would not allow them to interfere with us. I'm so into you, I feel stretched out, and now I often wonder if you feel like I do, and what do you really think of me. I can't understand now how I existed before meeting you, and I don't what to exist without you. I masturbated before we made love; since then I haven't. No other man has ever seen me naked before, but I've gone to bed with two guys, in attempts to have sex, before meeting you."

Soame was sitting over her body. His left arm was extended across her mid section. The joint he lit and took two puffs off of had gone out. "So here we are, relaxed and comfortable, together. That's what's frightening to me at times. When we're apart I wonder if it is a fantasy being with you and feeling this way? Will I ever have to be without you completely?" He relit the grass; she was wearing the sunglasses, and in sitting up, asked for a drag.

"Only we can handle our relationship. I've always been and will always be open and honest with you. The foundation of our establishment, which you've mentioned is trust—"

"Soame, I'm so high already."

"I know, but understand that it's no fantasy." They kissed.

"So, the Asian and African grass is better than this?"

"You'd be looking at me in 3-D if this was Vietnam weed."

"I'm sorry I interrupted you." He did a one and one, and she said, "No thanks, not right now, this is super."

He did another one and one and continued. "The book charm on the bracelet represents the night I gave the plan to your father. There is quite a bit of uncertainty about this area. Our future here might very well depend on the results of what happened that night. Soon you will be off to school. You are far beyond cute; you are totally beautiful with an exquisite body. Cindy you can always depend on me, in accepting my home life as it is, whether I'm with you, or five thousand miles away. I can see you when I can and when you want to, without imposing on my home life."

Soame once again relit the joint. Offering the "roach" to her, she replied, "No, no. I'm afraid to. It seems I'm still climbing form the first pull."

"Take it easy, you'll be fine. I told you its good weed. Better than that, it's good to know when you're high, and realize when you are stable without doing more. I've had this for two days, and I haven't been able to smoke more than half a joint, within two hours." After he'd done another one and one, she rested her head on his shoulder, with her arms around his neck. With his left hand extended across her thighs, onto the blanket on the other side of her, they were sitting facing each other. With his free hand, Soame played with her hair, and stroked her backside gently while talking softly to her. The glasses had been laid to the side.

"It means a lot to me what you said earlier about waiting since nine. I know it means a lot to you for us to be together now. It is a mutual feeling. I could not call before I did without imposing. I'm sure, long before now, many people have told you of your beauty. I'm suspended in wonder—"

"Darling please, I want to do it. Light the joint and give me a hit of your coke. I've wanted to do it since I told you I would. I thought it would be the first thing we did this afternoon, and I've been waiting since we came out of the water for you to ask." He passed the reefer to her. Because she took a big "toke," she coughed; he chuckled and reached for the joint. "No let me try it again."

"Soame, I can't stop you from wondering, and it means a lot to the both of us to hear each other's honesty, but look into my eyes…Soame Hudson, I, Cindy Edwina Blanchard, am your woman. I'm your bitch. I'm your girl. No other man can or will ever have me mentally, physically, emotionally, or in any way. Not only do I promise, I vow these words to you with God in our presence. Now say what you want to about it, but I'll prove the vow I've made to you, through time, and if you ever hear of anything different, ask me first."

Before then he had not heard the seriously expressive verbal side of Cindy. She extended her hand for the vial and did a one and one. "Call me bitch Soame, and tell me to suck your dick."

He took another toke, did a one and one, and said, "Get on your job, bitch."

She had seen the actions put into motion, the day of their initial copulation. He was sitting back, two-thirds of the way up the blanket. She was lying before him on her stomach with her elbows resting on his thighs. He saw and felt her honest endeavor at attempting to please him. To find out what natural ability she had he let her continue for ten minutes. They then relaxed while enjoying the marijuana and coke. Soame from that point directed Cindy. With full engulfment of the partially limp member, she progressed to the "lollypop" licking technique and learned to use her teeth gently to the sensitive head. She was taught to use her tongue along the side, up and down the shaft, and twirl at the top. They both experienced sensual feelings.

Once again they relit the "roach," and at that stage, before taking hits of coke, he flavored the moistened head with the substance, dabbed her tongue under it, and her upper gum. This time when she did the one and one, and attached her mouth to the penis, she felt the magnetism of the cocaine. Applying what she had learned she became very efficient, and could whisper sweet and impressive words, and talk romantically, during the procedure.

Following their change in positions, with Soame resting back on his elbows, and Cindy gathering her knees under her, he resumed talking. "I'm gonna tell you something. You don't have to promise me you'll do it, but at least you can take it as advice, and if you can practice it, in the long run, it'll save you a considerable amount of inconvenience time, and possibly your being expelled." She cast her eyes up to him, and gave him her attention. When he began talking again, he cold not distinguish if her eyes were closed, or closely watching with squinting dreaminess.

"You are supreme in your class my dear, and with your local experiences, you are truly sophisticated. This is a rural area. In school you will be in the company of urbanities who are polished and prominent. There are games people play of which you have no idea. I'm interested in your establishing your independence, and circulating within your group, without exposing the fact you have knowledge of, or do drugs after you leave home. During the course of your studies, while you are in school, there should be no one for you to become friendly enough with, to the point of admitting you know about or do drugs. Remember, an ounce of prevention is far better than a pound of cure. To eliminate any possibility of any of your colleagues ever finding out, never get into a conversation with anyone on the subject, and if someone for some reason asks without the question being provoked answer them directly and say sternly, 'No I do not know about drugs, nor do I do them,' then leave their presence.

"Cindy, I am positive you are wise enough to understand and know exactly what I've just said. One of the games I've mentioned your not being familiar with is the drug game. You will have top quality merchandise. You do not need to exchange, experiment, or search for another source. You will have won the game through your possession. You can only lose by exposing yourself to anyone. Do you understand thoroughly what I've said?"

"I promise dear, I won't tell anyone no matter what. I really like this, my jaws were getting tired, but licking is almost as gratifying. I'd like to do it all night, or at least for hours. Is it good for you? Can I make you cum?"

"Before you leave, we'll spend a day together at the farm house. In time you will develop proficiency in the art. Perhaps when you've become that good, on the first erection you can. Beyond that one, you have to be profound. Do you want to get that good at it?"

"I'll show you."

"Well alright, neophyte, turn around here, so I can look at that beautiful pussy of yours, while you practice."

"It's yours Soame, I told you. I'm all yours."

She turned to him and they both relaxed, sitting up, facing each other once again. Another round was shared with the substances. The joint had almost been consumed. After doing hits of the powder, he began placing the cap on the vial.

She extended her hand for it saying, "Let me have a little. I'm going to put some more on this dick." After lightly coating it, they lay in a sixty-nine fashion on their sides, facing each other. Cindy took his directions, and brought her knee upward, bringing her foot near the ground. Soame began gently stroking her body.

"Even though you may not see it as such while you're in school, these are the better years of your life coming up. You'll be on your own, with the responsibility of making it to your classes. Years later you might reflect back, and consider them the best years. Take the time and get the schooling; there is no rush. You will be anxious and excited to complete your courses of study I know, but during the first semester of this freshman year, minimize the number of hours you carry from twelve to fifteen. In the process, take two of your elective courses and carry them with a minimal number of your major subjects. This will be a period of adjustment for you. I feel certain you will have no problem adjusting to the educational atmosphere. Tom and Janet say you will spend the first year on campus. Hopefully you'll get a compatible roommate."

"Yea, the idea stinks, but I've made up my mind to suffer with it. The informational guide says there're no single room dormitories, but I'll be all right. I can handle it."

"That's the spirit. The minimal schedule will allow you the latitude you may need in handling any difficult situations you might encounter. Most importantly, you can concentrate on the courses you began with and work toward establishing a high grade point average. You'll have three and a half years to either maintain or improve that average, and make up the one or two major courses you sacrificed in getting adjusted to college life. Does that make sense to you?"

"Sure, Mom says practically the same thing, but she's skeptical about having the time. We're afraid Soame we don't know how well Dad'll do from this point, and your plan might not be accepted you know? "That's putting the real issues up front."

"You do what um telling ya, and if you tell this to Janet, she may be obliged to tell Tom. I don't want him to become dependent on me. It'll destroy his initiative, and I see a lot of drive in him as a good man. Whether the plan is accepted, or I stay here or not, I'm financially secure with collateral involvements to secure us for the rest of our lives, but I want you to be formally educated. So you see it's no problem. Can you keep that between us?"

"Ouch!" She slapped the topside of his fanny, and applied pressure with her teeth to the protrusion in her mouth without removing it. She soothed the spot, then licked and kissed it, and resumed her normal administrations.

"Not as a beginner. You've got a really good 'head,' you could make me cum, but I want to fuck you."

"No, not now, let me do it some more, I really like this because I'm crazy about you. Then you can do it."

"Which?" She did not reply. He had been stroking her body and fondling her breast and nipples. His hand moved to the area holding him in trance, between looks at her spellbindingly beautiful face, with him in her mouth. His fingers began toying with her clitoris.

"As a measure of contingency I want to tell you this. The state of Oregon is one of the most liberal states in America. Let's hope this does not happen, but if you became the attention of the police anywhere in America with drugs, and were arrested, you would not go to prison as a first time offender with the small amount you would have. There's quite a bit I could tell you which you do not need to know now. We've taken care of circumventing the possibility of exposure by eliminating the knowledge of anyone else knowing you smoke or snort. In the event the mishap takes place and any drug is found in your possession, the absolute first thing to remember is not to panic.

"Cindy, if it's taken out of your hand, not to mention your pocket, your hand bag, your belongings, or anything else your only reply to any question asked concerning the substance is 'I do not know how it got there.' To be arrested, you must be read your miranda rights. Within your rights you will be informed that you have the right to remain silent, and you have the right to an attorney of your choice. Whatever you do from that point do not say anything except, 'I wish to place a phone call.' They'll try and scare you with threats. They may attempt to butter you up with promises. You may even spend a night in a city or county jail, but you will be out within twenty-four hours. That my dear is how you could be expelled. Now do you understand why I have taken the time to tell you to keep your drugs to yourself, under lock and key? If no one else knows, you shouldn't have anything to worry about." She nodded her head while looking into his eyes. Along with fondling her genital parts, he caressingly stroked her thighs and legs. He moved his tongue from her knee to her ankle, and asked, "Do you have any questions about what I've told you?"

"If it happened I would call my mother and ask her to call you, but it won't happen. I'll be extremely careful, I promise you that Soame Don't worry I'll be alright."

They knew the other was ready. He eased his kissing tongue up her body, pausing at her breasts, taking them into position for the intercourse neither could no longer resist. When he began nibbling her nipples, he moved up to her neck with kisses, and blowing on, around, and into her ear, she inserted him into her. When he kissed her cheeks, nose and closed eyes, she was moaning. He'd never rested more than a quarter of his weight on her. They rotated together marvelously. He was more than she had ever wished for. She was his sexual creation.

Lovemaking that afternoon totally satisfied them. Unrestrained and enthralled with thrills, Cindy slung her body to him and onto the shaft within her. Without hamper she called to him in exclaiming delights, saying what he had taught her, and expressing her personalized feelings about the intercourse they were having. It was not wild, neither was it frantic. As lovers they'd developed passionate rhythms. Some of the routes they took to ecstasy were through various positions. Her rapidly experience increased and each time they copulated, she found a new position for exploration, and triumphed. As in the initial session that afternoon, the last was also exuberant.

When the blanket activity was over, they walked to the water's edge and cleaned their nostrils. It had been a wonderful day, for the lovers. They were dressed, the blanket folded, and because he asked her to, Cindy walked Soame to the jeep. He had a package she was to give to her father, for Beauford. Leaving the blanket, and with one of the joints from the pack, an ounce of gold for her and Janet until Thursday, and the package for Beauford, they strolled to the nearby El Camino, with her arms around his waist. He explained exactly, the quarter pound of gold and the half-pound of red reefer, to be delivered to Tom. After seating her, he went around to the passenger side and sat in the vehicle. She had not seen the ounce. The ounce was what he'd been smoking from since Monday morning. The package for Beauford had been made up that morning, before leaving home. Soame then exposed the single joint before lighting it. He offered her his vial to take with her.

"No, no, I've got most of what you left me with. It's good, but I'm sooo into you, it's something I look forward to doing with you because you make doing it so much better." Janet had told him she and Tom were comfortable with their supply, until Thursday when the three would be together. Soame then asked

Cindy to turn on the radio. While she tuned in the Rapid City station, he asked, "Do you want to hit this before we leave?"

"You say the Asian grass is like 3-D ha?" He simply waited to see what she had to say. She leaned over and kissed his lips. He knew there was no downer. They'd been going up all afternoon. "With you I've done so many things I hadn't done before. I've had hidden emotional feelings; some I kept suppressed. Others I never knew existed. Some of what I've done with you, like the oral sex today, I've waited to do as a woman. After obtaining the sexual heights I've already achieved with you, I think what a blur my life would've been, if it were not for you. It is beyond my imagination to envision someone else satisfying me." She had been avoiding his eye contact, bashfully shying away to look at other elements in their immediate surrounding. Sternly, she returned his stare, telling him, "Before I'd ever submit to another man's romantic touch, I would rather turn frigid, and go totally insane."

She extended her hand to his, and he felt her squeeze. She continued, still looking at him with a slight smile that reminded him of Tom, "I guess I've gone a long way around to answer your question, but Soame these are small fractions of my thoughts of you each night when I lay in my bed. During long days when we are apart I spend time thinking of things I could have said, or should have said, the last time we were together. I cherish these days above any others I've spent.

"You can take me with you on a space ship, in flight to the moon. I'd go bobsledding with you from the top of Mount Everest. Each time you leave me, I'm accompanied by anxiety, until we're together again." She released his hand and looking at the bracelet, with a broad smile, told him, "Maybe you should have gotten two cherries." They both laughed. Soame took the vial from his pocket and removed the short straw from his sock. After doing a one and one, he fitted a portion on the designed straw and held it to her nose. After the first, she inhaled into the other nostril.

"In essence, that's what I've been is that before meeting you, I had no thoughts of ever doing drugs. I tried beer, but can't tolerate the taste. I like the grass and coke, but nothing surpasses the feelings I have for you. I'll do anything with you. I'll go with you anyplace you take me, and be there when you say. My feelings toward you Soame are unyielding and will never change. So now you know a bit of how I feel." With that he noticed Janet's casualness in her, but was too aware of the depth of her seriousness. He lit the joint.

The days were long. The August sun was sinking in their faces, nearly thirty minutes above the tall pines on the western side of the small lake. Cindy had turned the radio down while she talked. He reached over and turned up the volume. They caught the first note of the musical pad to the record by Nicolet Larson, *Hot Child in the City*. Cindy jumped and moved her mid section in a "hootchie cootchie" fashion. "That's my record Want to see me dance?"

"You mean without the pom poms?" Turning the volume up, she jumped out, ran around to his side, and displayed her stuff to him. He found it pleasing, looking at her from the open door.

When the record finished she came between his spread legs and looped her arms around his neck. With his arms around her waist, they heard the beginning of a Dee Clark record, from the 50s, *A Lover's Question*. "Come on, let me show ya how kids danced before you became a dream."

He demonstrated the "hunch," and after a bit of the "funky four corners," he asked her to "swing" with him. At the end of the record he brought her body into him, ballroom style. They grinded their bodies into each other, and became entangled in a kiss. They could not because they would not suppress their motivations. They removed their pants, and once again she practiced fellatio, with him sitting in the passenger seat of the car.

Soame retrieved the blanket from the jeep, and again they allowed themselves another lovemaking session. This time, except for his administering cunnilingus, and giving her a g-spot thrill, he had sex with her in every way,and in every position the surroundings afforded them. When they were spent, their bodies went limp. Again they plunged into the water to refresh themselves.

That time after seating her under the steering wheel, he did not take the seat on the other side. He thought of the lovely company they could have keep in each other's presence. His home life was at peace. He simply could not afford to disrupt the serenity. Dusk made its infiltration into their surroundings. Placing her hand on his, in the open window seal, the charms brushed with a sound, against the paneling. Looking at the bracelet, and back to him she held on to of the charms asking, "After the third one is added, then what?"

"That one should signify completeness. How do you feel?"

"A little sore, but otherwise fine."

"This is the second time you told me you were sore. Bitch, you getting good to me, and you get better each time. Let's see what the future has in store for us. At 9:30 the day after tomorrow, I'll be at the farm house. I'll see you then."

Leaning in to her, he kissed her forehead, the tip of her nose, each eyelid, and her lips. "I'll see you then."

Raymond Claude Perdue The Man's Digest

Part III

Chapter 1

EARLY Saturday morning, Soame called the Yates. After talking farming activities with Billy, and being further thanked for the weed, he then spoke with Cathy. She understood when he stated, "It'll be best to wait until tomorrow," and said to him "We will be expecting you then."

That morning by ten o'clock, the entire household, except Muff was at their new home. With the employment of the two yard men, the women had gotten into gardening. Each had a special section that had been turned and tilled by the yard employees. Her duties at the office kept Camille from progressing as far in advance as the others, who were spending considerable time at the place, which would soon be their new residence. They had carried along lunches, snacks, and with the foresight of DD, they also had a watermelon, it was like an outing, because the caretakers had the day off.

When procedure got under way, Soame visited each of them in their separate plots. The ladies were wearing short pants, cutoff jeans, short shorts, and Camille had on boaring culottes. He deemed himself the "official pussy, ass, and grounds investigator." Announcing his position, he informed them, "My duty and function is to inspect and investigate all crotches and cracks, to see if the holes can stand tampering, and will allow planting." Toward noon he had examined them all except Camille, who ignored him. Soame wrested her to the ground, and removed the combination pants-skirt. This revealed the sky blue bikini panties worn, which she was forced to display for the remainder of the afternoon.

Toward one o'clock, they all gathered on the pool patio area for the lunch break. The wrought iron furniture was in very good shape. He assured them it would be sanded and repainted. There was a glass top table, which had been barely missed by the falling limb. The piece was unmarred and though the limb had long since been removed, the glass and screen, in sections, had been taken out, but had not been replaced. The decorators were to bring their designs and creative ideas back, the following week. The family members sat around the drained pool, having fun and at the table, in conversation. It was mentioned, one of the decorators interest in Fifi, who had already gone through her first estrus cycle. Free stud service had been offered to DD, in exchange for the pick of the litter. However, decorators miniature male was white. They enjoyed the sandwiches and for dessert there was the melon.

In the waterless pool, Soame had each of them dance to one record, and they all enjoyed it, including him. The portable record player had been brought along. Chairly's Marcle was wrapped in a scarf. The jeans she wore were cut to expose the lower sections of her brown buns, and the pink, sheer fabric covering them. She also had on a rainbow colored shirt. It was she who initiated the idea, when she walked into the pool, while the James Brown record was being played at the table. "Turn it up," she called out. Soame stopped the music, took the portable to pool side, and in starting the record from the beginning told her, "now let me see ya get down." He replayed the part, "any kind of weather, we all get together, and we do, the James Brown." When she finished that time, Margaret was asked to take the center stage action, in the pool. Like DD, she had on short shorts, and at the close of the record, did her version of the "slide" and "bird leg." Three weeks prior to that time, he had demonstrated the dance to them all. Beverly's pants were not cut as short as Chairly's and she made a grand showing. They all applauded her backward, forward, "moon walk," combining the "slide" with the actions, and when the record closed, she stood on one leg, doing the "bird leg." In Denver, Camille had used tact, for the special appointment for them both. Once she got in the chair, the hairdresser found she wanted a permanent, and another style; it was worth the beautician's while. The blue panties could only be seen, when she bent over, because of the tapered shirt. All week she had been sporting the hairdo. When her turn came, she left the sun hat at the pool's rail, and rather than try and outdo the younger women, she did what she knew would excite the man in their lives.

"Camille you knew this would happened!" DD was braless; her nipples were vivid, through the silk blouse. He had asked her to be next. All of them knew, no other figure there was comparable to hers. She replied to his request for her to dance in her panties asking, "with these shorts Suarme, what else is there to see?" Then her compromising point was, "I will, only if you dance with me." She had on thongs. He followed the swaying swivels of her hips to the four foot section, where the others had made their entrance. He took one step down, she abruptly stopped and turned. Giving him a serious look, she asked, "Why do you still have on your pants and shorts Suarme?" They were a lovely couple together, no matter what they did. None of them knew if he would be conservative, or become outlandishly outrageous. He was extreme with the presentation of style in both ways, and in the song, one verse sanged "sometimes I dance, sometimes

I talk, but any type of weather, they all get together, ta watch me do, my camel walk." Until then, none of them had ever seen the "camel walk" demonstrated.

"Alright, up until now it's been all fun, games, shopping trips, and a lot of lollygagging. I'm glad you all invited me along with you today; the fun will continue, but I thought I'd take this time to tell you, this family is about to go into action, and our combined effort will be directed at producing money." The others sat along the wall of the pool, with their legs draped over the edge. When the record was over, he'd asked the player to be turned off, and held DD's hand, telling her to sit on the floor, assisting her.

"I'm not going to make this a long drawn out ordeal. So not to bore you, I'm going to make this plain, simple, and direct to the point. I want your direct attention, without interruption. Some of the matters I'm involved with here in town, other than Camille as being book keeper, do not concern you. Because of your direct involvement, pertaining to the matter I'm about to present and generally outline, I am taking this time in telling you before hand, what I say is not to be repeated or discussed with anyone. You are hearing it now first hand. All of you are intelligent enough to comprehend what I'm about to say, and when I'm done, if there are questions, ask me.

"I have acquired ten rooms in the motel, on a five year lease. The idea I have in mind, when put into force with it's operation, will be a place where all of us will work and earn money. It's a creative idea, which will further establish this town. DD and Camille's work will basically be, keeping up with the rest of us. My plan is to make this town a twenty-four a day operational spot. It will take as much as a year and a half to fully develop my idea, but when the plan is fully developed, Smath will have become a place like you have never imagined. To envision the concept I'm presenting, you will have to have lived in Chicago, New York, Atlantic City, or Vegas. As small as this spot is, in comparison to the cities I've mentioned, with all probability, the first question to enter your minds is how?"

"The motel is being refurbished, to allow us access to the ten rooms we will have in operation. Next week I will take you over, and show you our planned procedure of operation. This will not interfere with your schooling, and I am sure all of you know, if there is to be a public educational system, it will no doubt be delayed beyond next month, due to a loan and a proposal submitted to the federal government, for financial support of not only the school system, but for the continued operation of the town itself. I'll be simple, honest and blunt in telling you, the space I've leased is for the sale of cocaine. I have a vast knowledge of the product. I've talked with people in this area, and places nearby; I know the market value, and the impact of availability, and how this will effect people as far away as a hundred and fifty miles."

"Coke is not the only marketable idea I have in mind, but it is the only aspect of my business operations you will assist me with, except for Camille keeping books. You all will see, handle, and make, more money then you could have, in your wildest fantasies imagined or dreamed possible. Um telling ya this up front: when the money starts pouring in, guys are going to start making and presenting all types of propositions, and want to do all sorts of favors, and make any, and every type of offer to get up under your clothes, and in between your legs. No man in his right mind will tell any woman, she can't give her pussy to another man. I know better, because I know, if a woman wants to be with another man, there's nothing the man she's with can do to stop her. Knowing that, I'll openly tell you this, if I ever catch either of you, in the bed, the arms, or even the car of another man, you can pack all you have, and move, and in doing so, not only find another place to live, but you will also have to find another means of supporting yourself. There is no possible explanation I will accept, as a reason toward any excuse for the misbehavior, I've told you never to get involved in."

"Though it will technically be an illegal operation, we have the backing of the local town officials, and its' law enforcement agency. The other involvement, which will be a new phase of operations for me, and you will have no dealings with, will be prostitution. I mention this, because later you may hear rumors, as they circulate, concerning the matter." He took two steps toward DD, and was standing directly over her. His genitals hang in position for her oral consumption. Soame gently touched the side of her face, with a soft pat. "Suarme here, now, are you sure?" "You wanted to get at what's under my pants and under shorts didn't you? I'm sure you didn't ask me down here just to dance; now what's the problem?"

He looked up, and saw Beverly's open mouth, as she threw her hand to her jaw, as if she was in astonishment, and DD saw his rising member, in accepting the invitation. "In concluding, I'll tell you now, there will be no prostitution at the motel. You will in no way come in contatct with that phase of my operation. This is a five year plan; during that time, when you like, with the money you will have earned, you can take a vacation anywhere you choose. Are there any questions?"

"You sade we ant soppose ta be in no otha man's ca. It gits cold up hea Soame. I ant bout ta stan in no sno fa you an nobodie else, ya betta kno dat now!"

"There are three cars and a jeep at the house, as well as a phone. There's also a phone at the realty office and the motel. I don't care if cold and snow is stacked up as high as this house, and it gets to be forty below. I just took you shopping for winter clothes. You can think um jiving if you want to. You'll find yourself living in the cold, and that same snow you say you can't stand in. That's what you'd better know! Are there any other question?" This time Chairly stood up, and with her fist on her hips, lashed out at him. "Yea, I ant don yet! Why kant ya jes buy us a car, so we kin go back and foth, den we wont have no problem!"

"I don't see where there is a problem with what you say, no problem at all. Especially with you earning your own money, to spend it the way you see fit, and if you want a car, when the time comes, surely you'll want it included as an affordable item, for your personal upkeep."

"Soame, Mista Linkin free da slaves ova a hudud yars a-go, ya ant got kno bisniss puton us working in da cold an sno!"

"Yea alright, I'll tell you what. You get your little narrow ass out or those clothes you have on, and come down here. Bring that Miss Fine bitch of yours along with you, and when we leave here today, you go tell Mr. Lincon what I've got business doing. That goes for you other two as well, out of your clothes and into this pool." He began chuckling. DD held his instrument with one hand, and while looking over her shoulder, said to Margaret, "Bring the pipe dear." They all rose while Chairly began untying and unbuttoning her shirt. While she climbed out of the cut off jeans, she asked him, "what cha gonna do when we git down dea?" Projecting the continued defiance, indicative of her character, though she was not bold enough to contest his will." I'll tell you what um gonna do, ... as the investigator, um gonna do a preliminary inspection. I want you to get down here, and put your palms against this wall, I think you're holding valuable evidence, and to be sure you bitches got what I want, um gonna frisk ya, and confiscate my goods, before it turns cold and start snowing, and your Mr. Lincon sends the Union Army to seize my properties and goods." He was laughing so hard his shoulders bounced up and down. Seeing the other nude bodies file past her, Chairly stepped out of her panties, and after balling them with both hands, whirled them at him.

His eyes stretched, looking through the tears, seeing the pink material coming; he did not duck. They flattened on his face. Soame held them with one hand, to his nose and sniffed. The brazenness of Chairly was further exemplified, as she continued to stand on the ledge, in the nude, with her hands on her hips. He sniffed twice more, shook the garment, and placed it over DD's moving face. The other three were approaching them. He said to Chairly through his continued hysteria, "I'll bet you call me Big Daddy before you leave this pool; now get down here."

"I bet ya kant make me do nothing I don't wanna do."

"Bring my powder, those two joints on the table, and stop by and get my lighter out of my pants, and just keep on rappin." DD clawed the material from her face, rolled it again in a ball, and hook shot a dab, smack into his face, again. As he had done the first time, he held the material to his face and sniffed. Stepping back, he extended his hand. "Alright, up against the wall." DD took his help in getting up, turned and took two steps toward the pool wall, and veered to Margaret. Soame strided one giant step, intersecting her approach. "My pipe Soame, what aobut my pipe?"

"Haven't you heard, all the protesters are getting ready to see Mr. Lincon, before it turns cold and snows. I've got to hurry you all off; up against the wall I've got a pipe for ya, and it's not for you mouth this time."

"Suarmeme!" He motioned to the other three, "All right, up to the all, and you! Leave that gizmo right there!"

It was well past dark when they returned home, DD and Chairly were shivering. In route, he ducked slaps, avoided and dodged rocks, and limb portions thrown at him. Muff was laying, with his fore and hind legs, tucked under his body, on the porch railing. Long before their arrival he heard their playful laughter; had listened to the gleeful screams, and caught the plea frolicking cry, "No Suarme please no, I will never do It again, just don't throw me in that ditch, please, please, I promise." There were the continuous "arrfs" form his buddy, and after the "grrr," he heard, "You'd better not tear my pants! Tell her to stop or I'll toss you in right now!" Two, very closely related, voiced their encouragement, "sick him Fifi, sick him," "Atta girl, eat 'im up, get him girl, get him." Muff had once grown though a stage with the Johnson's, between kitten and adulthood. Those had been adventurously plundering times. Times with the Johnson's were bright, full of joy and almost as happy as he'd seen, in them living with his buddy, and her group. He heard something that made him think back to the time he climbed up on the pantry shelf, and the flower can, without it's lid on, overturned on him, making him white all over. The lady of the house was cooking it was her laughing that caught his attention, and caused the reacquired thought. He had not heard her laugh so hard, since the "white Muff" adventure.

"Ya bet not hit me wid dat switch, um gonna bus yo hade opin width dis ro—ow! Bebly whea ya at gurl, com help me ow! Ouch! Ya betta stp." Awe, here come my people, at least to of um. Why are you two running? There's nothing or no one behind you. I guess I'd better jump down, and when the big one opens the doo—opps, here we go just like that. Hay! I know after all that excitement, and it's past dark, you've got to be hungry too. "Slam," "Slam." Ah Margaret, remember, "Muff, where have you been?" That's your favorite line. Hay Bev come on out; nobody's out here but me, and I'm hungry. Oh yea, here's one of the black ones with the hairy legs, ah say--." "Bebly opon dis do chile, Beb"—"Slam." Hay listen, remember me "Muff the wonder cat," and all that. I'm hungry! Great, now I can eat here's the lady of the house, and the lady of our hous—say you two are passing the kitchen. You know, food, eat, kitchen, me Muff I'm hung—"Slam."

Yea, hay Buddy, ok, ok, I like you too, but watch the dribbles with ya licks will ya. You hungry too? Now, I know this guy's got to have an appetite; where ya goin Buddy? Come from behind the couch, this guy won't hurt ya. Why's his pant leg torn? Hay um goin with him come on Buddy. "Hay old boy, what's happening" Nothing's happening if you're not hungry, and the name's mu—ahh, yes, I know anytime you wash your hands it's yum, yum, Tim—"Want some ice cream Muff?" Do I want some ice cream? And he called Muff well can ya beat that? There ya go fella, just take Muff's bowl on up and load her with ice cream. "here you are Muff hope you don't mind the pecans." Now here's a guy who really knows how to enjoy, yum, yum. I guess you're gonna stretch out on that lay z boy and enjoy your cream to ha! That's what life's all about, pussy and yum, yum. Yea, pussy and cream, that 's all there is ta life, pussy and cream.

Chapter 2

SITTING in her recliner, listening through the headphones, while enjoying a heaping bowl of ice cream, Soame enjoyed two records. Though it was early, no one else in the house made a sound. While in the kitchen, he had heard Fifi's paws on the hardwood floor in the hall, prancing toward his bedroom. The barely audible sound of the metallic clic, when the door was opened, following her whines and scratching. When he finished the ice cream, it was the first time he used the hall bathroom for a shower. It had been an interesting day, filled with fun and excitement. However, it left him ostracized with the cat, in the house.

"*Rhinestone Cowboy,*" by Glynn Campbell and "*The In Crowd* ,"with Dobie Gray, were the only two records he listened to all evening, and before eleven o'clock he drifted off to sleep, in the nude, on the couch. Comfort was found in sheets and a blanket, taken from the hallway linen closet.

Around 3:00 AM DD touched him asking, "Suarme, are you coming to bed?"

Looking at his watch, he responded "Come on, put your robe on, I've got something I want you to help me with in the basement." They were off to the bedroom, where he dressed in fresh underwear, his robe, and slippers. "If you are going to do a hit or two on your pipe, do it now because for the next thirty minutes or so, you won't be able to. We're going to wrap a package, and before we do that we will wash our hands. After that, we will only be touching the items we will be using." On the way to the basement, he took foil from the kitchen cupboard.

"Do you have any idea where this is going?"

"Since there are also ladies sunglasses, and I still have the phone bill from the hotel, I have a pretty good idea. You talked for twenty-three minutes, from 4:45 until past five in the morning. It was the day we left."

"Yeah, I used the executives room in the other suite, while Chairly and Beverly were getting ready and packing."

"So, how is she?"

"She's fine, and even at that hour in the morning, said the call was long overdue. She was concerned to hear how we are faring it."

"We, or you Suarme?" They were discussing Sandra Fairfield earlier that preceding week, Soame clued DD in on everything he said in the pool, the previous day. She knew the plans almost in detail. Camille also had considerable forehand knowledge of what was said at the other house, but did not know as much as DD. Except him, none of them knew the probable course of action to be taken, with the encroachment of winter, if none of the plans worked out.

It was obvious, the cash was rapidly going out, and to that point there was no income. It was harvesting time for the farmers in the area, who had planted spring crops of wheat. In fact, the majority of the small farmers had already gathered their harvests, stored them, and shipped the grain to the shipping center. It was a fortunate year for the American wheat farmer: the previous season had been a catastrophe for European and Asian wheat growers. A worst than harsh and extensively long winter effected the world's two top leading producers of the grain product in a retroactive prospect. Their productions had been of poor quality and grade, far below their expectancy, in the world market. Because of the U.S. surplus storage, of the grain, which had been nearly depleted, the market remained basically stable. After a less than normal productive season for the two top growers in the world, the impact did not hit the American wheat farmer until the close of the harvesting in July. Except Thad's, the majority of the local farmer's productions, had been graded at the grain market, bought, and shipped. At the beginning of August, the news of inadequate supply began breaking as prices rose. The government had held the news for almost eighteen months. The thought was, the Soviet Union and China would have a productive year, to compensate for the previous farm productive downfall. With them breaking less than even, when Thad began his harvest, prices were rising.

Little Thad had told Soame, in the field, it was the land his father was contemplating him having. All afternoon he pondered the thought, and that evening, in explaining it to Camille, took her to the office for the duplicate papers on the Yates transaction, which were still being finalized by Burtrume. "Yes dear you own the land and the crop they've harvested. It's a conclusive fact. The property has been assigned to you. There's the date, his signature, and witnesses. Soame, because they live so far out, no one knows them extremely well, except for that oldest girl having the reputation of being the biggest floozy in this entire area. Otherwise Thad Yates is a reputable person, and no other farmer would dispute his standing. I'd advise you to see what he has to say rather than listen to implications by his youngest son. I might be a bit worried if the thought was projected by William." They were in the living room examining the papers.

The matter had been practically straightened out that previous morning when he spoke with Billy over the phone. "Soame, man this grass is so mellow, I can't believe nobody would have any smoke this good. I've already taken out every seed that was in there. Oh! By the way, ya know ya made a lot of money this week with that crop out at the Hodges place don't ya?"

It was then Billy explained the upward fluctuation in the market. He also talked about the target price and PIK, which is an subsidy alternative to plowing under: in lieu of plowing under, the federal government simply paid the farmers to leave their fields unplanted. That year there were no paid in kind distributions. "Ma told my paw to call you and break the news, but he looked at Cat with a grin, and said he had a feelin you'd be round pretty soon."

They both laughed, and through Billy's chuckling, he asked Soame, "What'd you do to her man; I mean truck loads of guys use to come round here, now they're more scarce than flying cows, and when one does come, she sends Jenny to run um off-"

"William Yates you shut your blabbing mouth, give me that phone!"

Later that day he would get the full scope of the matter from Thad, but what was of immediate interest was the package they had prepared, and how Sandra Fairfield related to their progress in their surrounding area. He had purchased half of Thad's land' the two-thousand acres being harvested for Soame, were to be shared equally in profits, by Thad. This was the means of the cooperative agreement they made, with the buy and selling contract. When expenses would be deducted from the profits, for farm labor and equipment, Soame would show a gain, but it would not be enough income to support the new comers lifestyle or involvements. The Wyoming area became a "safety valve," if all failed, and the dead of winter caught them in a none existing town.

No matter how successful the farmers were, not overlooking the fact Tom did not plant at all, and the majority of the small farmers sold their crops before the increasing surge, without the loan and, or the grant, the town would surely fold. He explained it as "seed money" to DD, and it being an affordable outlay. "The land, the three houses, and all we have here that can not be put into a van, taken to Wyoming and stored, we may simply have to leave behind."

"So what did she say about us coming back? Did you tell her about Camille and the girls?"

"Sure, but I told her there are four others. I explained the entire setup; she called me a lover boy, and said before we left she offered the place, and the only change now is that it can be had by me at half price. I told her I'd send her a package in the mail, and if questioned, she does'nt know any one in in South Dakota. So that's the move we might have to look forward to. It'll give Camille a chance to explore Cheyenne, if she wants to work. The girls and her son will have the convenience of schooling, and when you all are safely put, I'll have to make a trip. In Philadelphia, Detroit, Chicago, or New York, I can get rid of a pound and a half of the 'boy,' and we'll have a million dollars, to make it through the winter, and plan. What do you think?"

"I think I have never had a million dollars; it will be fun."

"Good, the odds are in our favor the grant will be approved, but there is a possibility it will not. Don't sit your mind on anything permanent, until we see if the town's going to stand, if not, that will be our retreat." He kissed her. "Do you want to ride with me tonight, into Rapid City?"

"Let's go in the jeep. Cool nights here remind me of France, when I was a girl."

Gimmie some pussy."

"Suarme, here in the basement, let's go – ah Suarmmeeee."

Before they went up stairs she was informed that he would let Camille in on the developmental move, as the situation progressed, and if it became necessary. It was understood by DD, the matter until then, if it materialized, was to be kept strictly between the two of them.

Nobody had awakened before 10:00. After she and Chairly had their breakfast, they began reading in the quiet of the house. Because her older sister would not let her read *Valley of the Horses*, she was midway through one of the two Ken Follett books Camille bought while in Denver. No one else bought a book during the trip. Beverly had already finished *Reluctant Goodness* and *Clan of the Cave Bear*. The other book Camille brought home was *Night Over Water*. Chairly was climaxing the final chapters of *Forever Amber*. By 12:00 everyone else was up, except Soame.

Near 1:00 he brunched with the three who chose to wait for him, and dine. They all knew he was not really sound asleep, because around ten, it was the sounds from Camille, that caused Beverly and Chairly to began stirring about. The mid portion of the day was spent lazily around the house. When Chilry finished her book, she found her way to the video equipment. She had not taken time to check it, after Soame brought it back late Thursday afternoon. It had taken a really hard "tooth and nail" sale to convince her of the pretense, the equipment was to be used that day to tape the harvesting of the first crop he had produced, as a co-op farmer. "Bie yo own stuff, dis our's Soame. Ya jes kan tak our stuff whin ya feel lak it, an do what ya wanna."

In all actuality, it was Janet and Cindy he used the hundred dollar rental fee toward. There the tactic wasn't as demanding, after he taped them from the porch of the farm house, arriving and getting out of the El Camino. A considerable amount of persuasion had to be used from that point, and with the nude and action sex sequences they all participated in: "Now listen, twenty years from now when features have changed, you will be proud of these captured memor-"

"How about you and your features, won't they change as well?" Cindy interrupted asking.

"Yea, but I've got ta take the pictures."

"Bullshit Soame, no fair. What's good for the geese has got to good for the gander."

"You complimented this elaborately compact bar last week, let's have a round of drinks."

"Drinks my ass." Janet wasn't buying his pitch, exactly the way he wanted to make his sale, especially after Cindy initiated the questionability of his non-participation.

"Come on baby, get his camera. He'll be first in fact; I'll get him out of these nonessential featureless clothes. Catch him being disrobed ." that sat the trend for the mode of their day. They videoed inside, outside, under the shade tree, and in the barn. There were various stashing compartments built into the house, basement, and barn. He showed them one of them, with the assurance it was the only place the cartridge would be kept. Only one of the carpenters knew of the hiding places. Soame had paid him extra, and felt confident the secrets would not be revealed. The storage place was shown to them for other reasons, as well. They discussed, in depth, the situation again, with Cindy being away from home, with coke and reefer. Though the cash had not been stored in the compartment, it would be a storage place for $10,000, for Janet to have immediate access, if an arrest situation occurred.

In the event she and Tom went "dry," it was also a spot where she could claim two ounces of "girl," without having to contact or wait for him. Cindy had never drank before. By noon they were all "lit up" with Blue Label Vodka. Around that time, Soame presented Janet with a breacelt identical to the one Cindy received two days prior, except for the charms. With it he gave them the catalog for ordering the charms. Janet also received two charms. Her's were a pillow and a dog. After he explained the pillow as being a token of the first day she laid with him, she added "Well these two are of the same meaning."

She said it with initial wonder, changing to a huge smile, then humorously stated, "You're a real mother fucker, ya know that mister?" She then melted her nudeness into his, with electrifyingly lavish kissing. It was the same type of kissing experience he had been thrilled by earlier, when the second round of drinks were taken to the bedroom. Cindy gave him oral stimulation for twenty minutes before Janet began kissing him. When Soame ejaculated, he was not sure which was the cause.

Chiarly found the recorder to be in good working condition. This motivated Beverly toward selecting various scenes. Knowing the indirect object of their ploy, Soame moved from the Layz Boy, and went outside. While he cleaned the jeep, they started washing the car. Suds were splashed, water was sprayed, and it became a wet, fun activity for Chairly's camera.

Toward four o'clock, he drove the Seville into the Yate's yard. Cathy and Jenny moseyed out to meet him. Thad greeted him on the porch, and there was a "Well hello Soame" from Mrs. Yates, standing in the open screen door. She explained being busy with supper, and knowing why all her helpers had run off. Before he finished rendering his reason for declining the invitation, little Thad squirmed past her with "Hay Soame, and thanks a lot for the rifle. Paw won't let me use it on the Sabbath, or I'd show ya how good I am with it."

"Yea, you're a real prankster, do you know that?"

"Grinning with impishness he replied, "Awe, I was just jokin with ya Soame, everybody knows you're about the smartest guy around these parts."

"What's this, what'd ya do this time."

"It's really nothing," Soame answered Thad in the boy's defense.

"I slipped a little, and wasn't paying particular notice to what was being said at the time. Later I had to catch my thoughts, but the experience brought me back to the realization, I should keep my concentration on my immediate involvements. There's no problem, really."

Thad gave me a casual warning to his son, and directed the focus on the previous weeks productivity. Cathy and Jenny listened from a swinging double chair, on the opposite end of the porch. Little Thad took seat on the demented siding of the steps. The conversation began with the Hodges acreage, which was Soame's. Of the thousand acres, which had all been planted in wheat, there were four-hundred acres of clay loam, which in southern farming terminology, is comparable to "bottom land or soil." "Soame, I'll tell you, those spikes in that clay loam had up to 60 some as many as 65 and 67 kernels. I've been farming all my life, and I've never before seen tillers carrying spikes so loaded."

Three hundred acres remained to be harvested. Thad told him by noon—dinner—Tuesday that field would be cleared. The silt loam was surpassing it's expectancy in production as well. Spikes had another thousand acres in two other fields to be harvested. Of that, three-hundred acres were clay loam. Production was almost as good, but the Hodges land was the best farm land in the county. Tom owned an adjoining twenty-five hundred acres. The crop he planted after Soame's arrival, had secondary roots, and leaves that were bright green. In that type of loose richly organic soil, when matured the roots would grow as deep as seven feet, to support a five foot stalk.

The county storage bins were holding Soame's wheat. Because of demand for the grain, other farmers had shipped and sold. Thad's crop had not been taken from the fields. This was all in accordance to the planting procedure he had used. Thad then thoroughly explained target price to him: government price, when the production of wheat was not low in America, which is the world's third largest producer. Because the Soviet Union and China, were below par with their productivity, and those two leaders in wheat production had not gained from the previous season, United States wheat was being bought as fast as it could be hauled to the shipping centers. The market did not have a stable target price, because of the continuous boost in price the grain exchange was placing on the commodity.

Thad did not see any way for the prices to plunge. Soame's accounting was being measured by the number of truck loads coming out of his fields. The question presented by his equal sharing partner was, "Do you want to send the Hodges harvest to the grain market shipping center, Tuesday?" Now too, you can wait, and store the other thousand acres we'll be takin out the fields, till the middle of next week, and ship it all together." Soame noticed the keen smile on Thad's face in presenting the choices. Before he spoke and with the hesitant movement of his lips, Thad interposed, "Ya got another option, if you want to hear it."

Soame was not baffled in the least. Having experienced games of romance with Cathy and Jenny, and knowing the sharp witt Billy displayed, and after the encounter with little Thad, he was well aware of the tree, from whence those offspring came. He knew also, Thad was observing his facial expressions, and they projected him thinking. He could not estimate if the wide grin on Thad's face was from the projection of thim obviously concluding the remained two-thousand acres of wheat, to be harvested, which had not been mentioned, with the daily rising prices, but he gave it a casual shot. "Well Thad, I guess since we're here, and this is what it's all about, I'd appreciate it if you'd enlighten me."

I've got my fields to take in also. The prices are higher now, than they have been in the past ten years. We are a small percentage of farmers, with crops still in the fields and storage bins. There are farmers that could not have waited, even if they knew prices were going to be this high, toward the close of harvest. They had mortgages to pay, other debts, and their families to feed. Compared to exchange prices at the beginning of this season and prices in the past five years, in July, when harvesting began, prices were remarkably high. They've almost doubled since then. Sure farmers are glad they got a better than fair price six weeks ago, to pull them out of debt, to a certain extent. They are also sick, because they could not store until now. The way I see it, by the time Im around to getting my crop out of the fields, with the steady climbing the prices are makin, it seems the price of wheat will double what it is now. We can call for enough box cars, at one time, to take all we have to the shipping center, if you want to do it that way."

The decision was practical, and based on Thad's explanation, and experience in the involved matter. Happiness was shown through out the farmer, after hearing the choice. He extended his hand to the man who had saved his experienced livelihood saying, "Partner." Thad then called to his wife, telling her to bring out the surprise. It was a gallon jug of sweet black cherry wine, with glasses for all of them. There was only one chair on the porch. When it was offered to Soame, he honored it's reservation for Mrs. Yates. Jenny and little Thad, by that time, were coming through the screen door with two chairs each. Cathy was holding the tray. Thad had poured all the portions to the people seated, when little Thad appeared once again, with another chair. The wine had been chilling since Thursday for three consecutive years, he had won blue ribbons at the regional state fair, with the wine they drank. Thad explained that year's batch undergoing fermentation, and what was being consumed coming from the previous year's award winning producct. Soame would leave with a gallon, for each year the wine won first prize. It was the third time he had noticed the unconceivable brightness in Mrs. Yates smile. She was very proud of her family. Soame was very comfortable, being with them. It was the first time Thad presented himself humorously to Soame. He saw the admiration of the Yates for twenty minutes, exercised toward the head of their household. He told true stories of his children, that encouraged them to blush, become squirmy, fidget, and call out "Aw paw."

Once Cathy cried, "No pa, please."

Mrs. Yates called his attention to the ready meal. "Well why didn't you say so; I've been sitting here runnin my mouth."

He had stood up. She rose wrapping an arm affectionately around his waist. Thad coninuted, "Since you say you're not going to join us, my guess is there'll be one eatin late."

He was looking at Soame changing his direction of vision to Jenny he asked, "Jennifer will that be you?"

"Paw I want ta go for a ride with Cathy and Soame."

"I never heard a ride mentioned, but if he wants to take you two for a ride it's fine with me."

Soame then stood up, "Mrs. Yates, Thad it's been a fine afternoon, and a pleasure being in your company. Once again Thad extended his hand, "Soame you're welcome to this house anytime. Each time I've been with you, I've been pleased being in your presence. You can get the wine when you come back. Thadeous, you commin?"

They chose a Michael McDonald tape to listen to while they waited. Soame told he also wanted to see Billy, after receiving the message from Cathy, Billy wanted to talk with him before he left. It was near 5:30 when they drove away from the house. Soame parked three quarters of a mile from the turn off Billy would have to make, to get home. It was a spot Cathy chose, because Billy's approach could be detected, and it would give them ample time to arrange themselves, before he arrived. Her menses showed that morning. She asked Jenny to the back seat, for her comfort in leaning across the front seat, to affectionately have him, the way appropriate to the overall circumstance. Jenny was relatively quiet, but he could tell. The wine was a fantastic prelude to the grass, they also all had smoked. They were M-E-L-L-O-W.

Long before he turned in, the rooster tail of dust could be seen, exploding above the hedge rows. Soame was looking through scattered trees along the turn in the road he was parked on. Across an open field he saw the hedge rows, the rising dust, and intermittent flashes of gray, as the five year old Chevy truck streaked along the dirt road, revealing itself now and then through breaks in the bush. After nudging Cathy, and saying, "He's on the way," she sat up, swiped the new lipstick from the dashboard, flipped the visor down, and began applying freshness to her face. Jenny had been giving him a clear, direct, shot at viewing her panites from Denver. While she adjusted herself, and with her sister calmly using the lighted mirror, Soame wiped the shining wet hard with his pocket hankerchief. During his attempts to place the "stand up" stiff, and adjust his pants, Cathy turned to him, after flipping the visor up, and asked, "How am I lookin, Daddy?"

It was a surprise; she had never before used the reference with him. He was almost standing on the floor, with his back high on the back seat. The gray truck fish tailed, enteering their direction. He looked over, "Ya lookin fine chick.'

"How bout ya darling sweet Jenny. You bout as sweet as our paw's sweet black cherry wine, you know that sugar?"

"Shut your mouth! How do you dare talk to my man that way, in my presence." He had glanced back at her with a smile, and was buckling his belt. "You look good sweet thing."

Billy had to be sitting close to the wheel, leaning against the door, and the controlling the steering wheel with either an attached knob, or the heel of his palm. When he straightened our, he was still "Haulin buggy." He had to see them. Soame began raising the windows, knowing the dust would drift. "Soame what's happening man?"

"Shit, you tell me dude, who's chasing you, the sheriff?

"Hell, the sheriff don't work on Sundays man, didn't you know that? The only way to get Beauford Allison on a Sunday, or any week end past noon, Saturday, is to call the jail, and have whoever the jailer is that weekend, to call him at home. Then, he'll probably call one of his men, and send him out. He's only got so many men, and each week end they alternate jailers, he'll be the only one working till Monday morning. That's cause nothing ever happens round here."

"Yea, well I got your message, thought I'd wait around for you. Your dad makes some really good wine. He could stop farming and market that stuff. Wow! Its really plush."

"It's the best in the state. I'll talk to you about it later but right now, how about comin over, and let me put something in your ear."

"What you got that's such a big secret from anybody William Yates. Ya ain't doin nothing but running over ta Berrydale selling grass, and ya better gimmie and this baby girl the hundred dollars for the coke ya took, right now! Soame he took our cocaine."

Billy spong from the truck seat, digging into his pocket. By the time Cathy finished, he was leaving into the window, looking Soame in the face, with his hand extended over the steering wheel. His hand held considerable amount of loose, crumbled, and some folded, bills. "Pass this to her for m-"

"Hold on a second, she doesn't need the money and I want to get something straight right here. Did you take their stuff dude?"

Then the rattling argument began with the two Yates. The third one pitched in from the back seat, and intensified the heated verbal leashing confrontation. Soame gave a long blast with the horn, and all was quiet. "I want to tell the three of you something, and I really don't want to be involved with this, and I hope you all don't put me in this type of situation, because I know, just as sure as before I came along and became a part of your lives, the fact prevailed you are sisters and not only a brother, but older brother. I am positive, when this is all over, and I'm gone, it's still going to be a family matter. The question um asking you Billy is, did you take the coke I gave them, like she said?"

"Why Soame?"

"That's my ole lady dude, and you see Jenny in our company it must mean something."

"You didn't have to tell me that man." Billy stepped back from the car.

"They way these two switch and clown around the house, talking about their 'man Soame.' This is the first Sunday you been by. Did they tell you they spend their Sundays in Berrydale? Soame this, Soame that."

Billy turned around twice, with his hands extended up, his fingers trembling, in giant wavey shakes of hallelujah fashion, saying, "My man Soame blah, blah, blah. Man, everybody in this territory know these two red head country girls belong to you. Since you mentioned company what you proably don't know is-"

"Shut your mou-"

"Let him finish, now you be quiet for a minute. Say what dude?"

"Man them two is the biggest drug dealers in south eastern Montana, South Western North Dakota, and North Western South Dakota. Your ladies, my sisters."

He sensed it was true, and he was completely shocked. Soame had been half leaning out of the car window. He casually looked over his shoulder to the passenger seat, then glanced a view to the rear to hear seat passenger. He then looked back at Billy. "Did you take their drugs?"

"I had to Saome, people were waitin. We had to take the phone off the hook, they were callin askin when we were commin. We expecteed you by one or two, I didn't leave till four. I'm sold out, totally dry. I had to man, you don't know how mnay people are waitin right now, for me to bring them."

"Alright now, that is the exact point. I'm not going to overlook the fact, I clear and specifically told the three of you, these products were not to be sold, they were for your personal use only. The real point I am interested in is your taking what I gave them. It's not right Billy. You say you had to, and you mention the phone. Why didn't you simply call me?"

Billy looked off and around, then directly back into his eyes, "Cause that's the way I did it man, that's what the situation called for at the time."

"Yea, well I can handle that. Now check this out if you will. You're growing into your adulthood. You don't have to promise me anything, and I think you've got a good feeling toward the sense of responsibility. I attempt at taking care of the responsibility toward these two, with the claim I make on them. I want you to do me a favor young man; if your father or Mrs. Yates don't take what I give them, don't take anything else I give to these two. Is that cool with you Billy?"

"Hay yea man, that's cool. I apologize, you want the money?"

"I've told you before, the money is not the issue here. Um the one that's givin you money, remember? Anytime, and if I'm in the company of someone else, you can always ask me to the side, and what ever you want, if I can do it, I'll help you. Hold on, let me take care of this and I'll see what it is you want to tell me."

He leaned over, went into the glove box, and extracted a small brown envelope. He had put a "one" on a gram. The envelope held two fifty dollar bills. In them were two grams of coke; each held one, wrapped and secured with a small piece of tape. He gave one to Cathy and one to Jenny. "You two know you're not selling anymore drugs, don't you?"

Cathy slightly shrugged her shoulders, while looking at him, and replied, "If you say so."

Soame looked into the back seat "I did it because-"

"It doesn't matter. I said you're not selling anymore drugs, right?"

"Well I would na done it for the first place, if she didn't tell me ta."

"It was mister know it all, William T. Yates, who started the whole thang."

"What or however, I'm interested in the understanding you two should have from this point you are not to sell anymore drugs, do you understand that?"

"Yea."

"Alright Soame."

He removed four fifty dollar bills from his slide and clip, and gave the two in the car a hundred dollars each. "Now there's your hundred bucks. There ain't nothing else about this ever again, right?"

"Thanks Soame."

"Thank you darling."

He looked up at Billy and asked, "This entire issue is over and completely dead, and we're square, right?"

"Yea man thanks."

"You two sit tight um gonna talk with your brother for a minute or two."

After getting out of the car, closing the door, and after taking one step, he heard the giggles. In taking the second step toward the truck a voice screamed from the car's interior, "You ain't shit William Yates!"

Billy had been cutting the powder with Vitamin B-1. They were selling nickel, dime, and quarter pieces on occasion, was a big sale. He explained the lucrative spot and it being his established spot for more than three years, earning extra money with the marijuana he grew. Soame sent him home for foil and succors. They were less than two miles from the Yates house. In Denver he had spent almost $1,500 on the two sisters. Wool dress slacks, gloves, dresses, skirts, blouses, fine slips-full and half-and of the matching sets of under garments, he brought back two pairs of panties each. They had been gift wrapped at the store, and not presented with the Elgin watches, in the presence of their mother. In route to them also were sets of long underwear, and boots and shoes. Because there was a variety of footwear for each of them, Jenny's was purchased a half size larger. The sale person's suggestion was, she would grow into them, without discomfort while wearing the top quality and fashionable items. He had gathered all their sizes, through various times he had gotten the information from them. Sweaters, coats, and parkers on the way, would fix them for the winter.

Three weeks prior to that particular Sunday afternoon, Beauford relayed word through Tom, concerning an incident resulting in an arrest: because of the weaving car, a state trooper "pulled" a driver to the side, on Route 20, west of Buffalo. The driver was tested and proven to be intoxicated, beyond legal limit. There was also a passenger in the automobile, who had been asked out of the car. Following the arrest of the driver, and during a "Terry search" of the vehicle, marijuana was found. The passenger was then also taken in, for questioning. The two Caucasian males were 19 and 20 years of age, and were in route to Reva. They could have told authorities they were coming from Frankfort, and were in route to London. They definitely would not have gotten the electric chair, for a less than half joint of marijuana,. Information was revealed, they had been to Berrydale. The alcohol content in their bodies was beer, and the marijuana found in the car came from "Billy" Yates. The North Dakota agency, through procedure, contacted the Montana local agency. This threw Beauford into the picture, who discharged the involvement through relay. It was nothing serious, but the event had taken place.

He directed Billy in using the implement and material brought back. Food had been dished for his sisters, who ate and danced in front of the car, with the unwrapped food on the hood. Billy used it as a practical reason for the foil. He and Soame were sitting in the truck parked behind the blasting sounds of David Bowie's *Fame*. Crafting the 1 ½ inch squares, Soame informed him of the Route 20 affair. There was really nothing either of them could do about the past occurrence, "But if you sell another piece or joint of grass I give to you, and I find out, I simply will not give, nor will I sell you anymore. It's that simple."

When twenty-five squares had been made, Soame took one, placed a dime portion of coke in its center, and demonstrated the sandwich lock fold, with double tucked ends. When Billy was informed it was a $10.00 piece, and three could be had for $25.00, Billy became excited and told him, "Hay man! That's almost a quarter piece right there!"

"Alright mister, let me get this point over to you. Before I talked with you, in the listening presence of your sisters, and none of us really wanted any true agitations to erupt, with this being the first time we all being away from your house, and all that. My respect is no less than it was then." Both of them were entirely in tune to the over all situation. Billy was partially aware of what was about to transpire between them, and taking advantage of the opportunity to fill him in, Soame disregarded his anxieties for an immediate return to Berrydale, and attempted to talk business sense to him, calmly. From the vile he did a one and one and offered it to Billy.

"You're pretty bright; tell me this, how much coke do you have to sell."

"That , if you're going to let me have it."

"So, you don't have any, and the answer is none, right?"

"So what's the point Soame?"

"That is the exact point. You don't have any coke to operate with, and from this point on, if you haven't come to the realization of the fact, I want to assure you, I know exactly what I am doing. When you talk about farming, I listen, and don't try and tell you how to do what you have been doing all your life. Billy, I know more about cocaine, and on top of that, I know more about people who use cocaine, than you know about anything, in this world we live in."

Billy, after their initial meeting, had not been arrogant. He had never displayed belligerence again, and Soame found in him an energetic character, with considerable drive and stamina. Nevertheless, he did not have future plans beyond farming. "It is my intent to put you to work. You should work with me, for yourself. Are you interested in working with me?"

Hearing his positive response, Soame noticed both car doors open, Cathy sitting under the wheel, and she and Jenny were slouched in the seat with their heels propped between the door frame and the body. "Now check this out. Just as sure as I know what I'm doing, I know you have thoughts of taking the packages I'm to leave you with, and redo them with the vitamin B-1 you have there. It's this simple, what I leave you with, and anything I give to you from now on, don't open the packages. The only way any one else can see what's in your packages is to make the purchase. You can get smart, and try all your little tricks, and cause both of us to loose time and money. I'm telling you, do not open the packages, after they have been made up."

With that Soame passed him the dime piece and instructed him to open it. He could not properly. Soame exhibited the proper method of carrying the flaps, to expose the full compressed contents of the foil. Before unlocking the final fold, it was held to Billy's nose. He inhaled the burp, when the coke was displayed. "I actually smelled it man."

"Yea listen, if you go to Istanbul, Peru, Paris, New York City, or London, you will find coke in either this or a capsule form, if you purchase it in a small quanity. Just like your dad's wine, it ferments in the package, and when it's opened it's ready for consumption. It's not to be open before then; in that way your package will remain fresh. Now give me ten dollars."

"You mean I've got to buy this?"

"That's my way; any package I make I sell. There are no samples. Once it's opened it's sold. You should practice that, and if you are not satisfied with the contents of that package, you can have all your money back." He then gave the younger man a stern look. "Billy, once a person tells you he is dissatisfied with any package of coke I give you to sell, you give him his money back, without question; never, under any circumstance sell to that person again. Gimmie my money dude."

That marked the beginning, for Soame's distribution of the product from New Orleans, as a saleable commodity. The half ounce had been ment for Billy's personal gift. The sixty-forty percentage was agreed on, with Soame receiving the 60%. He directed Billy in making up his remaining twenty-four package knowing he had money, Soame optioned him for the up front payment, then all the packages would be his. The payment was made, Soame gave him another hit from the vile, and instructed him. "Those are $10.00 packages. Do not sale them for more. You can sell three for $25.00. You do like I say, people will start flocking to you. You do the things I've told you not to do, you will have demonstrated you can not handle my product. In that way you will remove yourself from the business. I'll be by Wednesday evening, you can call me before then if you need to see me. You be cool, and make money for yourself."

Soame did not allow him the remainder of the half ounce. He felt that Billy was capeable of rising to support himself. He had given him a source.

The car was put into a slow roll, back toward the Yates' house. Having declared the Berrydale matter closed with the two riding with him, Soame was compelled to stress the situation being deceased, after Cathy insisted on clearing the insinuative remarks presented against her and Jenny. In front of the house they sat and talked for a half hour, on other time passing matters, before the sisters went inside, for the three gallons of wine. It was not a favorable parting, when they were left with a joint of grass each. He explained, "If you don't have it, you can't give it to Billy to sell. I don't believe you think I'm really serious. Why don't you give him the coke I give you, and prove to me you don't need any more of it either. I'll see you Wednesday, if you want to practice your driving Cathy. You two stay out of mischief, and leave trouble alone."

Before leaving home, the statement to DD was, he would be back before 8:00. Because of smudges, ashes, stains, and dirt in the carpet, he stopped by the motel, and cleaned the car. Chairly was found ready, and insisted on going with them. Soame was persistent, through out their final preparations, in renouncing exceptence of excuses for Fifi being taken along. The package being mailed contained a quarter pound of Gold reffer, a half pound of Red, and a pair of sunglasses in a case. It had been weighed on the triple beam scale, and a small amount of excess postage had also been affixed. The glasses had originally been intended for Janet. The decision to send the package was impromptu, after the shopping in Denver had been done. To him Chairly had always been an imposition he had excepted. They all knew, once the dog was in the jeep, DD nor Chairly would attempt at controlling her, as they promised.

DD had helped him prepare the package and knew it's contents. The chance was well far and remote of dogs being used in inspecting articles being sent from Rapid City, or arriving in Cheyenne. That distribution point, sent mail to Sandra Fairfield's area. Soame wanted to nil any possibility of a dog not only sniffing the odor of the contents of the package, but also catching the whiff of another dog. He had direct presentation to anyone he came in contact with. No one knew anything he was doing in complete detail, except him. His origin was not that with a confessional back ground. Soame had no conscience toward the aftermath of an activity he became involved in, when through it's course, he'd used his precise judgement, to make whatever decision there was incased. He trusted only one person he knew. The fact he'd instilled toward his existence, was concentrated within the idea, he knew no one other than himself, worthy of his trust. Until that evening DD had progressed further than anyone else, in gaining as much trust from him as he would allow. Her failure to relinquish concede in the idea of a possible detection, caused by her puppy, disappointed him. He left the three of them with the Johnsons. Cindy was called from the motel, and later met him on the outskirts of town. After depositing the package at the main post office. The Seville was driven to a motel, that had been noticed en route. The lovers enjoyed three hours of romantic pleasure.

Business wise, Soame was on the move. Some situations in his personal and homelife inclined toward tenseness, and in avoiding stress he found outlets. It was his ingenuity used in setting his structure up. Had he not been able to function well, within the realm of his creation, he would have automatically failed. Soame Hudson was the only vital part, in his involvement.

That morning, he was awake when Camille began moving about, in preparation for work. She developed perceptiveness in entertaining him, when he was up at that hour, as she dressed for the office. His final request to her, after their smacking kiss, and as she approached the bedroom door, was in checking on the allocated properties for Tom. He was spicificly interested in the Hodges tract. Soame was sure the twenty-five hundred acres had been mentioned by Tom, as being assigned to him. The question was, if the assignment was through lease or purchase. Before she cleared the front porch, he was in the shower. News and information the previous day, created more drive in him. The farming report gave him an uplift. The movement of his product was a gratifying feeling, though the packages were small in value and amount, it was a beginning, and if Billy carried it through, the area would expand. That previous night he had celebrating in mind, which he did, but his intentions were in being with DD. Through out the day he'd looked forward to them being away, alone together. She had never before questioned a decision he made. Never had she been disallowed her, liberty in choice with him. DD was the center of his home life. It was his opinion she had faltered. She would never know how deep the penetration of hurt carried. Her man had allowed her to become too close, to acknowledge disappointment to himself. The incident, in ways, was trivial true enough. How be ever, to his calculations, another time in an event with more significance, when the cost would be more than feelings. The fatal blow, would then be inevitable. Soame would not position himself to await such a disaster. Soame had never before deserted any woman he'd been with. Nor before had he cared for anyone, as much as he had feelings for DD. She allowed him to think of her as a "write off." The car, the houses, and the money she had accumulated. That's how fast his thoughts and moves were. She had learned about more than a bit about him, of it all she had not explored the opportunity of finding out, Soame was almost without compassion. His moves were geared toward business and pleasure. The main woman in his life had treaded too far into his character, with demands of sacrifice in his best interests, for attribute he was almost lacking. Her feminity was her greatest asset. He pondered her reasoning. Activities in the past twenty-four hours, had given him a glimpse at a flicker, of a spark, that might have been at the other end of the tunnel, if the darkness he'd been working into was'nt complete oblivion. She'd chosen a really bad time to present an opposing confrontation. He would not lag with her, or allow the drag, with his move. An adjustment would immediately have to be made, and was imminent. Soame was totally motivated.

Chapter 3

He had been at the motel a half hour, when Beauford stopped by. In exchanging greetings he told Soame, "You truly amaze me.. I've never seen someone, come into a drastic situation, take control, and plan toward success, while I've taken part of its development, as you are demonstrating, your capabilities. You are an encouraging figure to be around. I'm very proud to know ya, and I consider you a true friend, Soame."

It was completely unexpected, but he felt he knew Beauford, well enough to see in him, the true sincerity in the expressed words, with the communicative gesturing he used. Following thanks and exceptance of the kind words, Soame escorted him on a tour of the building, displaying the renovations, and explaining the use of each room. Private lines with modern phones had been installed in three rooms, in the rear of the building, which was Soame's combination office suite. Thick, rich, honey colored, carpeting, covered the upstairs west room, which was a combination bar, office and lounge area. There was a wall sofa, a recliner, and a round, glass top coffee tabe, with a regular office desk as basic furniture in the room. Florescent tubular lighting had been added to the ceiling. There were two floor lamps in opposite corners. The northern wall, behind the desk also holding a lamp, was painted egg shell. The southern wall was hidden by ceiling to floor pleated draping the pruple material had a glittery appearance in its texture, and could not be distinguished between velvet and silk. From the outside the door appeared to be standard, as others in the building; the entrance had been sealed from the inside.

Unbreakable ¾" plexiglass replaced the picture window; it was tinted, and fitted with Levelour, 1 ½" blinds. The surrounding west wall was cedar pannaled. Between the bar, which was centered by the plexiglass, and the south wall, there sat an entertainment center. Duel speakers projected stereo sounds in the west room, as well as in the east bed room, which was the only portion of the three room arrangement housing a bathroom. With a king size bed, plush carpeting, a love seat, a cushioned sitting chair and hassock, the room was quite plain. The same type window and blinds as in the opposite room, had been installed, and a burglar proof door and lock had been added. A sliding glass petition and pull drapes, was the separation for the two rooms. Other than a floor lamp, the lighting fixtures remained the same. Since "the girls" had the house and the move to their larger home would basically provide them more room for family folly, Soame did considerable in giving the place a bachelors appearance.

He knew there would be times when they spent time there with him. There was the kitchen and dining room for those occasions. The spiral stair way descended from the northern wall, in the eastern corner of the west room. The normally expected fixtures were in the kitchen, which was separated by a carpeted dining room. The linoleum floor in the kitchen, carried to the matching carpet in the bedroom. The table, with the added leaf, was designed to seat six people. Richard had not yet moved in with them. Soame was confronted with the perplexed situation involving DD. With her gone, it would surely be also, good riddance to her riding companion Chairly. As in the up stairs rooms, different colored bean bags were here and there.

Beauford saw that portion of his renovation, and liked it. The onlooker had been basically quiet, observing what Soame presented and explained. The stairway took him by surprise when they entered through the modernized door, in the dining room. It and its upstairs match, were the initial changes explained the hoist. All three picture window replacements were identical. At the bar, which curved on one end to seat one, the two men sat on two of the six stools. There they had the chance to talk, and listen to each other.

Without Soame telling him, Beauford knew it would take years to generate noticeable capitol, and worthwhile reconstruction, according to the submitted proposed plan. The idea behind the hope of the grant and, or loan was in gaining immediate relief, to allow the continued function of the local government. This would automatically provide and support the local school, and medical facilities. They had been talking ten minutes when Soame told him, "Even with mass production, if we had twenty-thousand boxes for sale today, I would first of all have to be able to market them. At that point I would need a convenience for the distribution. It would take years, after going from city to city, meeting with department store purchasing agents, jewelry shop owners, and other businesses of the sort as an outlet, to set up orders and shipments."

Beauford noticed Soame did not look discouraged at all, as he stepped behind the bar, and from the office size refrigerator, took out a carton of orange juice. He removed two drinking glasses from a mirrored shelf. There was cheerfulness exemplified in pouring the juice and continuing. "If I could afford to sink $300,000.00 in salries for a year, and purchase and pay another $200,000.00 for equipment and maintenance, sure the idea will employ fifty or more people.

With that, after setting up, and over let's say a 9-12 month span, I figure the production would range between 7-10 thousand boxes. Where do I store? Sure, I'll have the boxes, but that's all I'd have, with the headache of storing, marketing, and distributing my product." They each took a swallow of the chilled juice.

"This new idea I'm showing you will put immediate cash into flow, in this area. This will also provide toward the stricken welfare of this community. It'll bring loafers and drifters into town, who are still good people with worthwhile contributions, but suffered the same plight the remaining people of the area, are hoping to evade. Some will be drawn merely to be near the excitement; the glamour of what I'm about to produce through the operation of this motel, and another lively adult spot, will cast a trancing magnetism, that'll give some the warmth, just in being close to the liveliness, even during your coldest day, during a long winter." With that the sheriff gave a big grin and began chuckling. Neither had removed their sunglasses. Both were hated, and except for the adjustable, table top, fluorescent lamp, all the other lights in the room, including the rotating light which changed prismatically, while turning and shining through a spectrum. Beauford nudged his hat up off his forehead, and onto his hair line. After wiping his mouth, he said to his sitting company "Man! You're some kind of a salesman."

"Yea, I have been and with all probability, I'll have to develop a sales pitch, and go into action once again, peddling the boxes that are going to be made right here in this town, in that foundry I've leased; all over America. The point is Beauford, this is a live idea and it's about to start happening really soon. This is the now idea I'm about to put into effect, and it will give the remaning people left here a reach into an actual cash flow. It'll put bread on their tables, food into their hungry stomachs, shops will open, businesses will develop and flourish, and once again people of this community will be earning wages and back in the main stream. You probably already know the farmers are on the rise, if it continues. Those who farm will not again feel the dread of deserting their homes, and the fear of their schools being closed." He struck fire at home base.

"Alright, I understand what you're saying Soame. I don't know which is stronger, my hope or my belief, in ya doing it. I'll tell ya this for sure. I do not believe you've invested the time and money in what I've seen, and other projects I know ya been working with, and did it not being able to carry through with your developments."

"I feel sure this idea will work, with sugar." In Beauford's immediate presence, he referred to cocaine as sugar, Soame went on. "I'm very glad I've got your support, and I'll tell you this: with this idea in force we will survive until the federal government decides on the loan or grant. It's obvious without either, this town nor any of my ideas will exist. Except for the properties I've secured, all of this will have been in vain, that's the chance I took, with my forwardness."

"On the other hand, if either is granted, through this operation, which will be in effect within ten days, I will generate enough capitol to pay the salaries, produce the equipment and provide the maintenance in the open shop I have shown you the plans for. Once we move off in that direction Beaufrod, which will be with continued forwardness, let's not look back."

"Well now that's what I've been waiting to hear. In fact, it's nice to see what ya doing with the building and all, but we've got senators and representatives from this district, and that's what I came ta tell ya. Jack is in contact with all of them. We applied twice for the loan, and each time Jack hammered at them day after day, and that went on for months. His phone bill could've paid my salary for six months." They both gave a slight indication toward the rejection humor.

"It seems then we couldn't get any support. Now Jack is the one receiving the calls. The plans and proposals not only got to Washington, but through a congressman from another state, who was once chairman of the Ways and Means Committee, and is now the Senior Statesman from your home state; by the way, do you know who I'm talking about?"

"Sure, you mean Sam's gotten wind of the actual plan?"

"If that's Sam Stribbs, I want ta tell ya, indeed he has. Soame, I've never seen Jack Stillman so excited. I knew of him when I was a kid, and no one around these parts is more respected, and that's with all due respect to you coming a very close second. Jack thinks you're the miracle itself Soame. Your congressman was instrumental in getting us the backing, so when the insignificant measure hits the floor, with our town and livelihoods depending on it, Jack feels sure we will get the grant. Now how do you feel?"

"That's really good news Beauford, that means maybe the school's will be open on time. It means also you'll be here in your town with me, seeing this whole thing through, how do 'you' feel?"

The issue was kicked back and forth with humor. They descended the stairs and outside, the host at the building, explained the mecca of the operation. Approaching the breezeway, they stepped from the corridor. Looking to the end room, on the second floor, Soame explained it as being used only for security purposes. Convexed mirrors would be used to observe the activities of the breezeway. The breezeway was to be the focal point for the activity, at the motel.

They walked to the front of the building, Soame showed him the four rooms to be used there. He named the "women" of his household, who'd be working evenings and weekends. In using the term "women," he saw through the tint in the sheriff's glasses, as he unconscienecly returned a sleepy eyed look. When he finished talking Beauford asked, "Ah, ya mentioned school, upstairs. These women ya just spoke of, will they be going ta school?"

"They're not grown enough to miss school, I promice you that."

He had not spoke to Thad or Mrs. Yates about their daughters, but he told Beauford he felt there would be no problem, in them working the same schedule.

In and out of the building, everything was shown and displayed to the guest, who found it to be fascinating. He saw all ten rooms, went up and down another stairway, had gone through a secret passageway, and talked with Pete, and the other carpenters at the work site. He had even talked with Soame, through 2" of plexiglass, over the intercom system. An hour and fifteen minutes after viewing the exterior of the security room, from the parking lot, they stood in the breezeway, concluding their talks.

"It's a pretty interesting looking set up. I've told ya before, I have no doubts about ya being able to make it work. Tell me this Soame, will ya be depending on me ta assist and provide ya with security, or do ya have private ideas in mind?"

"Two years from now this town will be crawling with so many people, you won't have time to keep up with the stedy pace of my operation... besides, I won't take advantage of putting you up front, in this type of activity. Some people won't see it as a true value to the community, and acknowledge the service it will bring." Bueaford then placed his hand behind his head, eased the back of his hat up, forcing the front brim to contact and rest on the frame of the glasses. He tilted his head back, continuing to look and listen to the man before him, in the new 2 ½ gallon Stetson.

"Today, in five major cities throughout the country, I started running ads for personal I'll use as security. I think that'll handle the situation. You can help me though, and I'm in somewhat a bind, in this spot. It'll bail me out, and at the same time, you will give someone in town, the chance to earn some good money. Um in search of a barbeque cook, do you by chance know one?"

It was then, Soame saw in depth, how cool, calculative and possibly dangerous, Beauford Allison the County Sheriff, really was: all along Soame had been hinting bits of information, as luring measures, attempting to intice Beauford in with inquisitions. With his craftness, Soame provided the answers, or fill in statements to the questions and blanked information, he had intentionally left out. It is a commonly practiced technique, but the method and applicational level on which it was being used, surely should have received more fruitful results, from a "country boy," like Beauford; in Soames estimation. The sheriff did not budge, with the implication of curiosity, from the initial outside showing and explanation of the security room, until the final stage of their conclusion.

It was Beauford who fished him out, in his use of the word "private." He'd told the southerner, he'd never forget a favor. Word had been sent, he would have liberty to function. That day, at the close of the meeting, Beauford asked a question , and indicated he would go to the extreme, by not saying "security for your private ideas." The manner in which Beauford asked the question, left Soame thunder struck. Soame was a military veteran. Through one of the MOS's, he received training in applying the technique and through past experiences, used the method efficiently. Logical thinking would dictate the sheriff's position, and continued re-election automatically placing him, as at least a reasonably intelligent person. Soame sought beyond that established exceptence, and dove into the statistical involvement of his position. This exemplified only his persona, in is position. Soame needed to know who he had working with him, and how far they would go. A man can only go as far as his true character will allow him. Being from a city housing well over a million people, and the largest county in the state, it was almost a staggering thought, for Soame to actually be in the fifth largest state in America, and it housing less than a million people. That was the breakdown, leading to the character analyzation of Beauford, who used his natural rural finesse, with the assertion of his professional experience, in displaying what his associate in presence, was searching for.

It hit Soame like an anvil. He had to re-enter; for positiveness, there was such little time. The evasive stall was through the answer he responded with. Thinking as he spoke, he had the man power and the capitol, to back the serious ploy he endeavored, in using tact toward the on the spot reaction. It was also an exalted retaliative counter surge, toward a lost reversed effort, offending his personal esteem.

When Soame fed his question, Beauford could not shun his optical involuntary movement, though he quickly adjusted. In a flicking instant, his eyes flashed through enlargement. Bam! Soame had scored, and he well knew it. To keep his jaw from further dropping, he moved it from side to side, within two – slow motion – seconds, Beauford became internally raged with anxiety. When Soame faked a brisk smile, he pivoted right, took two steps east, quick turned, and marching back to observing Soame, he snatched off his glasses. Face to face, he slightly jabbed once with his index finger, toward the man he was getting to know. "You! Are totally amazing; that's a fact Soame! I just saw Neil Jefferies before I came to see you. He let his younger brother operate that little restaurant there." It was the only public eating facility in the town. They were standing less than forty-five yards from the establishment the sheriff was pointing at. Soame had informed him, he was going to have a wooden fence built west of the drive way, between the motel and the café's parking lot. This would disallow eating patrons the opportunity to complain of the motel's activities. A clear view of the breezeway could be had, from the across the way parking lot and building. It was also the direction Beauford had taken two steps toward, he went on. "He's the best barbeque man in this territory. Neil's live here for almost twenty-five years. Opened a bar in the middle of the next block, after he gave this small business ta his kid brother."

Though he was calm and in every way collective, Beauford took identical steps in the direction he had pointed and gone earlier, telling Soame before he stopped, "A year and a half ago, he closed the bar. He's got five kids and about ta leave town." He had been talking with his back to his host, without turning back, he signaled "quiet," with a sweeping fanning motion. He then moved with stealthiness, through the remaining breezeway, and stood in the center of the eastern corridor. While he scratched the side of his head, tilting his hat to the side, and rubbed his neck, it came to Soame; through a passageway of potential echoes, he had moved without a sound. Nothing rattled or jangled; moving with quick steps which were soundless, he had not tipped. Turning toward Soame, still looking in a fixed northern direction, his head slightly bobbed, before he leaned into a noticeable rock. Evidently one of the carpenters appeared from the end room. There was meaningless confabulation, other than the purpose it served, and the sheriff proceeded back. "He's got a wife and five kids. I knew it would be important ta him, hearing the news from Jack, but he's got the same ideas about time, and the materialization of development, as we talked about."

"Would you find out if he hasn't gone, and if he's still here, tell him this town's going to need him real bad, and soon. I'll let him have whatever he needs to hold on, and build a pit, if he'll stay and work with us."

Beauford had stopped, to hear him finish. The official hat and the Stetson then slightly dipped. Soame was taking particular notice of his movements, in carrying his body. He appeared to be a kid, who had grown into a job; probably an ambition he always had. It was easy to summarize, he was not a bully. However, with the same summarization, he had always had a sizeable body, and knew how to handle himself. The pistol he carried did not add, or take away from these summations; his true character had been very closely scrutinized, by someone who had training and vast experience, in the observation of men. "We'll meet you back here after lunch," said the sheriff, stepping off the corridor walk, onto the parking pavement, toward the patrol car.

It was 10:45, he felt good, not only inside but under the sweater, striped shirt, jeans, and in the underwear, socks and Stacy's, he felt vigorously alive, and primed for the remainder of the day. A portion of the vim stirred from the 62° temperature, whipping the gentle winds through the breezeway. A contribution had to be given to the carpenters, who were finalizing the remaining detail portions at the site. Walls were being torn down in the mansion. In two days they were all to be there, to meet the decorators, and examine their formal plans. Soame went to Pete, gave him $25.00 and instructed him to take all the men to lunch, at noon. "Gee, thanks Soame, you make a man feel glad to work fur ya."

In his office he poured his first drink of the day. On top of it, fifteen minutes later, he had eased back into his reffer and coke high. Several of the Blanchard albums had been brought and kept on loan for the office. The smooth and comforting sounds of Nancy Wilson were used to round out his morning. The "*How Glad I Am* ,"Album featured it's title selection when the chimes sounded, and he noticed the motel line blink on the phone set. "Helloo."

"Whuch you doin?"

"Why?"

"Causee I jes wonna no, das why, anch ya glad ta be taukin ta me on da phone?"

He thought of two things: it was the first time he and Chairly had conversed via phone, and that day he would buy a small recorder. "Long time ago, I was suppose to have gotton a point over to you. It remains, the first thing you say to a person in greeting them, especially in the morning is, good morning."

"Good morning darlingggg, how are you?"

"Oh, Hello."

"Suarme, I asked how are you?"

"That all depends."

"I tried to contact you a half hour ago, but before that fellow at the front desk ranged, he said he was sure you were on the premises, but he was almost certain you were in conference. I had tried before then to get through to you on the company line. Don't you feel well, or do you? On what does your feeling depend on darling?"

"Dominique don't badger me, I was in a good mood before this call."

"That's what I mean, I want to talk with you Suarme."

"You have the right to do as you please, I've never restricted your rights, have I?"

"That's exactly what I want to talk with you about; I want to see and talk with you."

"Now, you get this straight, as long as your given rights, do not interfear with my course of action."

"I said I want to be with you darling, I'm coming over."

"I don't see where you would be in violation, so what's your problem?"

She hung up. The voice on the extension said, "Um, commin to."

"For what?"

That phone was placed in it's cradle also, without reply.

Chapter 4

TEN minutes later he was standing on the upstairs porch, when the cherry maroon colored Seville, drove into the main parking lot of the motel. Across the parking lot, from where he stood, there was an abandoned house of considerable size. It was the last building on the left, on the western outskirts of the town. The parking spaces near it were not marked. When at the motel, Soame parked the jeep center broadside of the house.

His habit was always in backing in. DD drove up, and reversed in on the south side of the jeep. He'd already seen the silver gray dog standing with her fore paws extended to the dashboard. She was first on the pavement. She scampered and pranced around, and when DD and Chairly were midway the lot, to the breezeway, she did a number. The breezeway was the only stairway entrance to the upstairs rooms on both sides. It wasn't until Fifi finished, and began a gait toward the two, when he whistled. She jumped into a prance, in his direction. DD and Chairly stopped, looking up at him in surprise. They were less than three steps from stepping onto the downstairs porch walk. "Use the door downstairs." Though she knew what rooms were to be used, she did not know of the renovations. To kill time until their arrival, he had opened the dining room door, gone back upstairs, and through the bedroom door, he walked the eastern corridor, through the breezeway, to the office door, and stood, as a deception. He had intended to harass them by having them walk to him, and back around. Them finding their way upstairs, and the short while he gave them alone, in the suite to explore their way, served the purpose as well.

Entering the bedroom, the first thing he noticed was Chairly behind the bar, in the opposite room. His attention had been call to her by the light, which poured in from the fully opened blinds behind her. He left all the lights on in each room, before leaving. After switching the bedroom lights off, the Stacy's padded across the plush carpet, through the divider. DD was sitting behind the glass top desk, in the hi-back, swiveling, recliner executives chair. "Darlinggg, what you have done here is beautiful, I congratulate you, and I think you should have a picture on this wall."

Her indication was to the north wall. It was a bright suggestion. He was pleased with the observation he found no fault in. "I noticed it about the walls in the eating room as well, when we came in. We've seen the entire place Suarme. I really like it."

The chair had a designed piece of plexiglass beneath it, to allow freedom of movement, so the rollers would not become entangled in the carpet. She pushed the chair back from the desk and crossed her legs, after making the statement. She was very well dressed for occasion, without at all giving an over dressed appearance. She wore the diamonds he had given her, and some she had purchased, with a string of pearls. DD looked elegantly rich, beyond her beautifulness. She had never slouched with her appearance to him; he was not dismayed, or in any way the least stunned. To her praise and suggestion, Soame commented "Oh yeaaaa."

It was obvious to him, Fifi had been commanded to the hassock, where she sat, on her haunches. Otherwise she would have been at DD's side or on the new long couch, which would have been a very pleasing alternative for her. Where she sat, the growing pup looked like a circus pooch. "I ain't neva seen no glassas dis lil."

The four 16" shelves held leaded glasses, decreasing in size from ten ounce fillings, to three two ounce shot glasses. The matching decanter was in the center of the fully stocked bar. It's twin set was at the farm house bar. Chairly was filling one of the shot glasses with blue label; she had just broken the seal on a quart. "That's called a shot glass. In many bars, its basically used for measuring and pouring."

Through experiences at different hotels, she'd become aquainted with lited mirrors, and their aid and effect in applying make up. She and Beverly purchased an entire makeup kit, during the shopping splurge in Denver. It was one of the items brought back with them. Though she intentionally did not speak with total excceptence, Chairly was very debonair with the presentation of herself, in all aspects, especially her dress and make up. The makeup, without over bearing, was used effectively to inhance her age. Easily, she was excptable as being between 19-21. She shopped for only expensive items. Anything reasonably, or moderately priced, even on sale, was beneath her taste. The three quarter length cashmere sweater had been laid across a stool. Her rings and other adorned jewelries glittered, shined and sparkled. She had on a long sleeved, silk, shirt, which was light brown, with brown ladies slacks, and a pair of lizard shoes. Without seeing them, Soame knew she had on the best under garments the mall and department store they all had shopped in, displayed to her. They would be some he had not seen.

The shot glass was taken to her mouth, and it's contents gulped down, as if she was a dance hall floozy, in a western movie. "Get out the way."

He had walked up behind her. She expected him to pat, or feel the cheeks she presented to him, in his approach. "Whut, ya dunt wont me hind is ole bor ya got, in dis fine place ya don bilt?"

Soame sat the bottle she'd poured from, on the counter. "Drink from the the other side."

"Haa!" she expelled in a mocking way, throwing her head back. She then squeezed past him, grinding the hips he refused to touch, onto his crotch.

They each knew what the situation was about. There was no doubt in either of their minds; it was a show down, and it was completely foreign to their encirclement. He knew the person sitting behind the desk, in the slacks and soft leather jacket could not see him, and was taunted with displeasure, because of that fact. DD could only hear the ice cubes being removed from the tray, and deposited into the glass. Chairly had taken a seat at the bar, gazing at him. He had poured a stiff, four finger drink, and was adding the orange soda, when DD walked to the stool next to Chairly. The two women knew of the probably expectancy, for him to be pouring Vodka,. His hand shaked rattling the cubes, chilling the alcoholic mixture. No one said anything. DD and Chairly, during the short interval of chilling the drink, became transfixed in watching him, and the rattling, produced by his trembling hand. The charm spell was over, only when he removed the glass from his mouth, engulfing it's entire contents in the single drink.

The display was not intended to be macho. Nor was it a bravados act of meaning, with any particular significance. It was simply a carry through, with the actions arrived at the lure DD from behind the desk. None the less, in serving it's purpose with the inducement, the consumption appeared to have melted Chairly. She had been whisked to the land of spangled lightheadedness. DD remained totally composed in her outward appearance. "Suarme, what are you doing?"

"I just had a drink."

Under the jacket, she had on a purplish chiffon blouse, with a 2" band that may have been used in drawing the material closely around her neck. She wore it in a very loose tie, over her exposed cleft, caused by the unfasten button at the top of her blouse. She took a step toward, posted both hands on the bar counter, and leaned between the empty stool and Chairly, peeping over the back portion of the counter, in search of some apparent mystifying magician's apparatus, he was attempting to conceal. "He ain't got nothing," explained Chairly.

He then indicated with his out stretched hand, a slight turn and bow, to two bottles of five star. "Would you like to have a drink?"

She looked around, and over her shoulder, to Chailry, and ordered "Fix me a drink." When DD moved to have a seat on the stool, Fifi jumped from the round leather cushion, Chairly moved, and Soame sat his ice cube containing glass, directly in front of DD. She would have seen the placement, but the scratch and the padded percussion sound, from the movement of the dog, demanded her attention. It was the first raised voice, to be heard in the newly decorated atmosphere. She raved in French. The dog scurried back, resuming it's position.

"Dim's sho's sum pretty curtens," complimented Chairly, on the dichromatic drapes. Soame had exited, before she turned, to enter the bar serving section. There were three large fluff pillows, on the brown soft leather couch. The coffee table was low, and the 42", round, glass top, was held by a three spreaded T-pee top formed device, which gave it an insubstantial appearance. It could not be distinguished as being placed with the use the couch, an aid with the recliner, or a separate furniture item, serving its individual purpose. On the table was an open pack of cigarettes. Soame pulled the table to the couch, removed the vile from his pocket, sat, and unzipped his boots. When he gulped the drink they knew sex would not be a part of the routine. Looking at his adjustment on the couch they knew he was situated for whatever there was to come.

"Chairly why don't you go over to the next room; I'd like to talk with your pa-pa, alone for awhile. Suarme, can the curtains be drawn?"

"Not only that, there's a sliding glass patrician behind the drapes. Hay kid, slide both ends together, and pull the draw cord, it's that simple."

A remaining two thirds of a joint had been in the pack. He lit the roach as Chairly left the room. DD was tehn forced to turn to him, unless she spoke over her shoulder, or removed herself from the stool. Hearing the divider slide in its track, she stood up calling to Chairly, with brief words in French. There was a reply, "Here Fifi, come, come." The dog spanged toward the opening.

"Suarme I want to talk with you." She had taken two paces to the recliner, and placed her knee on the end of the seat.

"Yea, well how bout passing me an ash tray from up there, will ya?"

DD daintily moved about, granting his request. The distinctive characterstic of the furniture arrangement, rested in the fact, it allowed no seating facial alignment, without the adjustment of a turn, unless the second party was seated on the hassock, or one of the stools. After she'd placed the ash tray, he said to her, "Why don't you go and see if she's closed the partition securely. There's a latch; when its fastened-"

They both heard the click, securing the patition. The room then became almost sound proof. "Take off your jacket and go check to be sure. I want to see you walk." He did a hit of coke.

"I locked it as well."

"Good, she's grown and developed quite rapidly these five months. Seems strange, I started to tell you how, and to lock it, but I did not know if it would have been offensive to either of you. Relax, take of your shoes off, is this going to be a long talk?" She had to sit on either the hassock or the recliner, to unbuckle the straps, if she didn't walk around and join him on the sofa.

Sitting on the recliner she replied "I don't know, it depends."

"Where is your pipe?"

"I do not need the pipe to speak with you, Soame you are my man."

He had been continuous in doing one and ones. "Well listen,… before we get into the merits of this disquiet confronting us, I want you to know whatever you have to say, keep in mind the proficient manner in which you just carried out the two duties I asked of you. You did both without hesitation, or rebut. You did them with efficient thoroughness. The absolute bottom line, from my stand point of view is, when these talks are over, as well as this instant, if you feel you can not do what I tell you to do, when I tell you to do it, the cash money you have, the houses in your name, the car, even the jeep if you want it, with all your other possessions. You can have them in our eternal separation. Do you understand what I have said to you DD?"

"Some of the words you have used, like always, I do not have a perfect understanding, but put together with the other words, I have a clear understanding. So yes, Soame, I have a clear understanding of what you have said… that is the point." She stood before him in her stocking feet, hearing what he had to say, and presenting her opening remark. Knowing he would not interrupt her say, she began pacing, as if she was a top flight executive addressing the board, or an attorney, making a presentation to a jury. Soame kicked his shoes off, propped with his back against the vertex of the back of the sofa and its arm. His feet comfortably rested on the sofa.

"I am a twenty-seven year old woman." The statement caught him by surprise and dazzled him. It wasn't until then he remembered her birthday, a bit more than three weeks past. He attempted not to be overwhelmed, but knew she presented the fact knowing he'd forgotten. "All of my adult life, until I met you, I was a prostitute, a thief, a gambler, a woman who was taught to scheme, rob, and do more things than the majority of women can imagine, in ways to get money. I was filled with dreams of America, the land of the rich, big buildings in place of the province. Here people were supposed to be free to live as they wish, and seeing Americans when I came here, I thought one day perhaps I somehow might become wealthy also, and drive a fine car, and live in one of the big houses, or tall buildings. I had lost, and totally forgotten about those long lost dreams, until I met you. I have much more to tell you, but I am haunted by what you said about our possible separation, and I tell you, you will never leave me, that is an impossibility, clear your mind of the thought. I will cook your food, wash and iron your clothes, tend to all of your needs and cares at home, and in time, I will bare your children. Now I only know one kind of work, but I would learn to do any, and everything it takes beyond what I know, to keep you Suarme. Nothing, no one, no where can take you away from me, and keep you, because I will always be in your house, and you will always come home to me. I will nev-ver leave you, and you will nev-ver leave me. Nev-ver Suarme nev-ver."

Standing directly in front of him, she paused to hear what he had to say. Knowing she was not finished, he casually returned her look, and took another hit of powder. On her way to the bar, she told him "I need a drink."

When she returned to his immediate presence with her drink, sitting the glass on the table, and after stating she had prepared a double, Soame sent her to the bedroom with a message for Chairly. Having delivered the instruction for her and the dog not to leave the room, DD returned finding the Lay Z Boy, moved and repositioned to seat her across the table from him. "She said she was about to come over for her sweater; that's what she had in mind. With only the TV, she's bored. Thanks for the seat."

After seating herself, conveniently for the reach, slipping her drink, and informing him she'd later want a "puff" of his marijuana and a hit of the coke, Soame responded, after looking at his watch, "One of us will have to call Camille, she might have plans with one of us for lunch. I've got an afternoon appointement, that might get underway around 1:30."

Both of them knew the real estates office well enough to calculate Beauford's having Mrs. Tillman back at work by then. "That's what I mean Suarme, you, are totally different from any other man I've ever known. I've known other rich men, and a few of them have been wealthy. They knew me only as a woman to be used for, and to excite their pleasures with all the promices and offers they made. There was no attraction of warmth, and I knew I could not feel I belonged, except in being used as a tool. You are completely different, because I feel a part of you. I know your feelings and reactions; I know what responses you will take. Your mood is one of assurance, and I can depend on you. My darling you have not failed in giving me already, all that I have ever dreamed of. On my birthday, you did not mention it, but Camille took me over to the house. Only twice in my life before then, have I been in a house so grand. I had to be carried in through the back entrances, and escorted to the only room I saw in either. So you see, I've only seen other houses like the one you have bought and used my name,… from the outside."

There was a pause while she sipped her drink. DD was not being evasive, even though her approach was not in direct presentation to the issue. She was very bright, high spirited, and with her keen wit, fascinated them all at home when ever she exploded with laughter. Her natural, exquisite, beauty, was her best charm, and the most eloquent fact about her poise, figure, and personality rounded DD off to be a marvel. She was well aware of herself, and an amazing fact in her composition and personal array, there was no phoniness about her. As such, with her genuine sincerity, she had a developing trend, toward a flaw, which could become paramount with maturity. She would then be useless to him, and a deviating means to devastation. Though it had been a trifling encounter, it's meaning and purpose was explicit. He saw it, and it's meaning vividly. Soame had heard some of the things she was saying before. Other than in the respect given to hearing her out; nothing she was saying had significance over the point, which he patently a waited her arrival.

"You did not mention my birthday, but you brought more happiness into my life on that day, than I have ever experienced. It exceeded the car, and diamonds are always a positive thrill for any woman. I've never before known a rich man to be a superb lover. You exceed even my expectations in fulfillment. You have shown me another way to live. Sure there have been times in the past, before I met you, I experienced times of happiness, but with you, it is continuous, with joy and pleasure. You've had a birthday also. We were moving then, across the country, and I did not know. I have with me, a present for you."

She gulped the remaining portion of the drink. DD then reached down and lifted one of the legs of the pants she wore. A scabbard containing a knife was revealed. A tug on the adhesive strap, unfastened it. The ash tray on the table held the remainder of the reffer he'd been smoking. In passing him the knife assembly, he was asked for the ash tray. Soame removed a fresh joint and passed it to her, from the cigarette pack, removed himself from the couch, stepped around, and extended a light from his Dunhill. Soame then placed the roach on the cigarette pack, went to the bar, emptied and cleaned the ash tray. He brought the hassock with him, and placed it and the ash tray aside the recliner, affording her the ease in sitting back in the chair. He removed the vile from the table, took two hits of powder, and placed it also on the foot stool. His hankerchief was unfolded once, placed on the cushion with the other items, to hold the 4" straw. DD watched as he examined her gift. "I wil call Camille now," she said, leaving the area.

Soame became more attracted to the brand name on the object, than the weapon itself, after seeing the eagle. Upon her return he thanked her, and added "I did not know American made stilettos." I've had pockt knives manufactured by them; they put out good products, thanks again."

"The one you carry in your pocket is causing a fade in your jeans."

She noticed him balancing it as he said, "Yea but my pocket is always-"

"Suarme, that is very good, I have never seen you throw a knife."

"Well, you see, we're suppose to learn something each day. I've learned something about you today also. The knife really desgined to be used close in; it's actually not a throwing knife, except for people who know how. The blade probably would have broken if I had missed."

"You took such a chance, to throw it in the left of the stool?"

"I appreciate the gift, but it would be dangerous to get to, if I needed it in a hurry."

"Will you ever use it?"

"There are practical purposes for it here, opening letters and I'll keep it stored, to be handy. On occasion I may carry it, but I hope not to have to use it for the purpose, for which it is designed." The dagger had a six inch blade. DD took two large hits of coke.

"Suarme, yesterday when you left home you said you would be back around eight, and I should be ready to leave. About 6:30 I had my bubble bath and while I was getting dressed Chairly came in. When she asked, I told her only that you and I were going for a drive. She said she was going also, and walked out of the room. You know that we are lovers, and at times I do not want to break her spirit. I thought it would be best for you to decide. She is strong willed. I am not the first female friend she has had. She's told me of a girl in her school who is Cajun. They took deth vows toward each other. I know you think that if I should leave, she will come with me, but she is smart as a woman, in a girls body. She's growing into her smartness. I know both of you. She's totally wild with her love for you. Me nor anyone else can draw her away from you, as with us all. You also know that Margaret does not like Fifi. You said you were leaving and would wait in the car for me, one minute. You did as you said and left alone, because I was not there."

"You do not give me credit for handling the situation, yet you did not refuse her from going. I know you well enough to know you had been with that farm girl, and if we did not go, you would not go back to her, you would call the Blanchard women, or one of them, if you did not go alone. You say when you tell me to do something, do it. When I have not, Suarme, when? I would have ran to the car, if you had called me, but you did not. In the basement you asked if I wanted to go, you did not tell me to come with you. This morning we watched Camille pose, I offered you my head, ad you pushed me away. You were cold to me, and you have never been before. I am your woman, and I know deep inside you there is hard, cruel, meaness. Beat me Suarme, take away the pipe, do as others have done and lock me away in the closet. I never felt for any of them, and I will never feel as strong for anyone as I do you. Anything to please you, I will do gladly, but as yours, don't take away what you have freely given, and allow me to expect and appreciate, as the right to think for myself, when you have given me a choice. You punished me this morning, and it hurts worse than you can imagine. I have done nothing for you to be cold to me, and if this is the way you now choose to live with me, I will except it and go on living with you, because I will never leave you, and I have told you, I will nev-ver allow you to leave me. That is what I came to tell you my darling; however you may feel." DD then did another large one and one.

She was very positive in stating herself. There was no apology, nor did he expect one. Her presentation was stern, without an implication of watery eyes. It was her, in complete alignment with her character. It was not unlike talks they'd had since they met, but on a totally different matter, towards her close.

Soame stood, walked to the hassock, did a toot of coke, and found the exact position he'd been resting in, after he took his shoes off. "Hay girl, um gonna tell you somthin. First of all you are a black woman, and like my history and origin does not start here on Indian soil, your culture does not begin in France. I'm not saying I would have been a Ramses, II, or not denying your possibilities as having been Hatshepsut, if we were born on African soil. You are the most beautiful woman I have ever seen, Dominique Dubanee. I will be as short and accurate with words I know you can understand, in addressing the issue: You are smarter, in general ways, than most women I know, who are college graduates. I have put forth effort to place you in an atmosphere, according to your intelligence, wherein you should function extremely well, with the experience you have. In fact when this initial occurrence took place, I over looked it, because of your position in the house. It is defiance on your part, we are now confronted with."

"A short while ago, I offered Chairly a small amount of money, after she had danced. You defied me, by removing money from my clip, and giving it to her, opposing what I had done, over ruling my decision. Let me give you an example, or a very good illustration. Have you ever seen a surgical operation in effect?"

"Only on TV, maybe once in a movie."

"Good, then you've seen the doctor, and round him you saw nurses and technicians. At times there are other doctors assisting with the operation, but when the single doctor is operating, of the other nurses, there is but one, head surgical nurse. When the doctor requests an instrument, that nurse has the freedom to think of flowers, movies, sex, reminisce on any topic she wants to, before and after that operation. When he calls for that particular instrument, her duty and function is to have it in his hand, without obstruction of time.

"You are my head surgical nurse DD. You do not have the training or the experience, to rightfully oppose me. When you do, you expose much more than you realize to jeopardy. There was a reason I offered the small amount of money to Chairly. She's a very bright kid, and I know she and Beverly idolizes you, and what you have told them of your past, but I want them educated, so when they are of age, their minds can place them in positions to earn a living and gain independence, without using their bodies in such a manner. They love you for encouraging them in that way now, but later, they will want someone else to blame, besides themselves."

"Suarme pardon me, but you are wrong. I mean about their minds, and educating them with the help of books. Especially Chairly; with her I am firm with that. She likes to read but I make certain, each day for at least two hours, she reads. I read also Suarme, we all want to be smart like you. Camille helps me with words at times, and I always use her dictionary to find words you use; I learn them that way. I read the book you gave me about slave living in this country, and I wonder over and over, why you have me read such a book. Wes was also smart, but until I got to the part where he falls in love with Fobbie, I still do not understand. Then uh la la, I like it. Now I am done with it. Chairly felt the same way about her book; then she could not stop turning the pages fast enough. Now I am reading the book. Already I am to the part where Amber has the baby."

"You must have been reading a good two or three hours?"

"Some when you left yesterday in the afternoon, some last night. The books are interesting, and I do not smoke as much when I read."

"Tell me how did the book idea come about?"

She was stunned, there was a pause, "Alright Suarme, I got the picture when you used the doctor example."

He sat up directly in front of her. "Then why didn't you stop? Why have you just been so persistent in trying to show and explain how well you are trying to culture their minds? It's because you really don't have the picture DD. You have a way, and you have ideas of your own about inforcing your way. When we met, I gave you $10,000.00, and told you, you can pull up, and leave any time you want to. Since then, its compled considerably. You've mentioned never, several times during this talk. I'm going to ask you this one-more-time. It will be the last time, ever, I ask this question. Be sure, be absolutely and totally positive about the answer you give. Do you want to take all you have, with that I've mentioned to you before, and separate from me?"

"Nev-ver Suarme, and you will nev-ver leave, without coming back."

"Alright, now um gonna give you the real picture, in 3-D. Yesterday I asked you if you wanted to ride with me to Rapid City. You did not say yes, but you presented the impression you would. All this switching out, and too, each time Chairly has been in the background, and whatever you two do, as long as it doesn't interfere with my plans. I've got to move, not only to protect and provide for myself, I've got you and others to support. When you attempt at having your way, you hinder my planned operations. That causes me to have to just readjust with more planning. In that way I loose time and essential rest. You've done it twice, and this second time, it's led to this talk were having, which I'm about to show you how, and why it will never happen a fourth time."

"You have been well schooled at being a ho." It was a shock to DD, he'd never used the term; she praised that fact about him, and knew he was about to hurt her more. "You are crafty with your intelligence and that what you have learned before me, you now attempt to use it against me, perhaps to take what I've given you to another man."

"No, no Suarme, no, no, please stop it."

"You lie God dammit, and I know enough ta know a ho ant nothing but a ho, and that's all she'll ever be. As good as I've been to you bitch, you've lied by pretending. Now you want me to except some ho story, bout you weren't told. You lying bitch, and I know enough about bitches to know, if the whore lies, the bitch can never be trusted."

"Please!! Please Suarme no!! Please no!"

He had risen, walked around the table, and stood over her as he talked. Soame had not raised his voice, and in suppressing the carry of his voice, in containing his anger, he talked through his teeth. Tears came to her eyes as he brutalized and tormented her with words, words she thought far beneath him to use. The terrible hurt came from his use of the words as description of her. DD stood up, pleading to him, and attempted to throw her arms around him. He back peddled away.

"I told you I have the picture Suarme. I was wrong, I admit it, I was wrong."

"What wrong do you admit?"

"I wanted to find out what you would do, that's all, I just wanted to find out what you would do."

"Twice you did this, you did this purposeful disruption twice."

Being out of the sun her complexion and his had lightened. Her skin tone raised to the shade between light brown and a dark beige. Soame had a non fixable hue between black and charcoal gray. She had fallen to her knees, weeping. "It is a woman's way Suarme, you know so much, you must understand."

"I do, I really do, and I tell you what; I know you will try it again. I do not know what type of games you play down in the bayou, but between here and Wyoming, there is a lot of land, and from there through Colorado, there's more land. When you try that stunt again, I will warn you by saying remember. You be brazen with your woman ways, and disregard the warning, and I'll take you for a ride. You want to be a whore, playing ho games with me, I'll treat you like a whore, and a hole will be the last thing you'll find. I promise you, it will be painless."

"Is that what you did to Aunks Suarme, is it."

"How do you know that name?"

"At times you talk in your sleep. You're my man Suarme, I watch over you I protect you. I am a good woman you will never find a woman better for you than me. I give my all to you, but I have nothing to give, but me. Trust me darling I will obey, no other man. I do what you say, I will not mislead you. Don't worry Suarme, never will you have to say remember. I am yours, I can only give myself, please do not be cold to me, or call me that name. I promised myself in Oklahoma, I would be totally faithful and true to you; I have failed myself, I will not fail you. You are the only man I have ever wanted, I will not fail my man, I will die first. Promise me Suarme, you will not be cold to me, and you will not call me that name."

"I have done nothing wrong, why should I have to promise? I tell you this."

He began unbuckling his belt. "You are forgiven until you violate; you know my law. Get out of your clothes." He went to the couch, and undressed from his waist down. "A thousand times, you will tell me you were wrong, and count each one. Your riding buddy in the next room, get her over here, and when you crack that door, tell her what she was to do five-hundred times. Say it loud enough for me to hear it, and tell her she's gotta say, I'm going to, why. Repeat to her exactly what I've said."

The loosely fitting tie on her blouse had been undone, with two buttons. The blouse had been pulled out of her pants. She took two strides, a skip, and hurriedly paced to the door. "Chairly Suarme calls for you. You must lick, kiss, and suck his dick five-hundred times, count each one aloud, and tell him I am going to, why." He had stepped out in the center of the floor, midway between the partition and the bar. She stepped through the glass door, sweeping the curtain from her path, telling DD, "I ain't doin nothing! What he thanks dis iz-" "Plap" her heels went into the air, as her upper body fell back, and down.

"Ooo lawdy plese mista Soame, I ant done nothing." She'd began scrambling, dragging herself cowardly, back toward the devider. She had been slapped side the face and head, directly over the ear that still ranged.

Soame took one step asking "Why!!?"

"I on no mista Somae I on no."

"I hear, every time that car our there starts up, you feel you have the right to be in it." Chairly found the glass door, and attempted to pull herself from the floor. "You better not go back in that room. Sit still! Um talking to the house I paid for, on the phone I had installed and you! got the nerve to hang up on me, why? Um gettin bout fed up with you. You been puttin on airs since ya been in that house. I try and give you every thing you want, let you do as you please. You want to be grown, I give you the freedom to do that to. You want to act fancy, and be better than the white people living with us; well, you don't have sense enough to know and appreciate what you have. I am sick and tired of your foolishness and air clowning. You can continue to make a total fool of yourself, but you are going to stop disrespecting me, with your sly remarks and your arrogant ways. I'm not going to embarrass you in front of the Johnsons, but you are a black woman, and blacks are not as stupid as you pretend."

"The very next time DD tells you to do something, whatever it is, if I see it, or word gets back to me you didn't do it, you're going to take whatever you have on, and get away from me, and anything I own. The clothes on your back is what you leave with, when you can't do what this woman tells you. You understand that?"

"Yas sur."

"I thought she just told you something I said for you to do, now what'd you tell her? You'd better not lie to me girl?"

"Um go-"

"You got one minute to be out of that shirt and those pants, or you can wear it out of here, and keep on going." He looked at his watch, and over at DD, who stood gasped, "What's your problem?" She continued with her buttons.

Rather than unbutton her shirt Chairly pulled it over her head. When she reached behind to undo her bra, he said "Leave that alone, where are your shoes?"

"In dare."

"Get them shoes girl. Anytime a woman pays $273.00 for a pair of shoes, she should wear um, don't you think so?"

"Yas sur." While she scrambled to her feet, trying to take the pants off, and simultaneously attempting to go through the devider.

DD asked, "My brassiere Suarme, do you want it off or on?"

"Well I don't know; is it one of these $37.00 brassieres, like the one the sensational Cherry has on? Are those $17.00 panties you have on under there – what's taking you so long to get those lizards on your-"

Chairly appeared through the curtain. She appeared to be doing the "funcky chicken" dance, wipping her eyes, climbing through the curtin, avoiding his direct path. With the gray and black shoes, she had on black stockings, a beige garder belt, matching the bra, which featured a little bow in the front.

DD was somewhat relaxed with the idea the hectic scene was over, but fretted the remote possibility of the ignition of an uprising, through an unseen mishap. She knew them both, and sympathized with Chairly still being partially shocked and simi-petrified. He had not demonstrated before, in such a manner. There was no question of and, or about it's meaning. It had gotton to a point of amusement for himself, in further quailing his fully displayed aggravated temperament. When she unzipped her side zipper he asked, "Ha, just out of curiosities sake, mind you I don't care how you spend your money, it's yours, but how much did you pay for the pink undies?"

"For the set Suarme, which was on sale, it was $23.00."

"Oh yea, well now tell me, do you have any idea, where the sensationalistic Cherry here," with an indication toward her, Chairly slightly jumped with fright. "Where she gets these expensive ideas, with her refined taste?"

She knew she had guessed wrong, it was truly Soame, and this was one of the times he was unpredictable. "As you told and showed me, I told her to shop for brand name quality merchandise."

"Yesss, well then, did you tell and, or show her, quality does not necessarily mean expensive, or the most expensive is not necessarily the best."

She stood looking at him for a moment, then asked, "What do you want me to say to you Suarme?"

Soame turned to Chairly, "You learned anything today?"

Both her hand went to her face, she slobbered and whined, with snotty sniffs, "Yas sur."

"What'd you learn?"

"O -- --" she whined distortions.

"Get your hands from your face," saliva ran from her mouth, snot drained from her nose, and her face was marshed with tears and the two liquid elements. "I don't have any children and I don't have time, and I really don't care for the idea of taking another man's thrill, and shaping it, into a suitable form of life for society. I try and treat you like a woman, and ya don't have sense enough to present the pride I give you, back to me with respect. God dammitt don't you ever disrespect my woman again bitch, you hear me!?" She put her hands to her face, and her sounds were again unaudible. "Get your hands out form your face, I told you that! When she said she and I were going for a ride, what'd you tell her?" The slap.

The slap wasn't nearly as hard. She fell to the floor out of fear, and avoiding him. "I want you to fuck up, so you can get your ass out of my house! While you are there, don't you touch that phone again, until you think you know for sure, you treat whomever it is you're talking to with decent courtesy. Now get your linky frail ass over to that couch. Your aunt Dubanee is going to show you what it's like to be respectful, after being disrespectful. This better not happen with either of you again."

DD had stepped out of only one of her pants legs. When he looked back at her, she dropped the leg she was holding mid her thigh, and rushed to Chairly, dragging the pants, saying "Come on Chairly, before he has us picking up paper, outside, around the building, in our underwear."

"You first with fifty, then she'll do fifty, and in that way you will rotate, until each of you have done them all."

Chapter 5

WHEN the phone chimed, DD had done 187. Chairly got stuck in her first set, convincing herself she could talk properly, in applying the effort. I am, substituted "um;" going was found to be the applied, right word, for "goin." It took a while to get over her stubbornness, but with the idea injected, "You will do it, until you say it right and from that point you will complete the number assigned to you. No matter how many times you do it over." She complained of being tired, after repeating 7, 26 times. He was not dogmatic, to the point of driving her in such a way. After DD's substitution, and progressing to the 100 mark. Chairly began thinking straight, using the right words. She made it to 150, before he answered the phone.

It was Billy, who had been out of product since the night before. A few people had been to the field inquiring. "I tried it the way you said. There was no way for it not to work, but to me it seems a waste."

"Don' let that thought phase in and take effect on your direction. A month from now, you'll see exactly how ridiculous it is; I'll be sure and remind you. Now listen, we're on the phone and want to be as direct and expedient as possible. From the drift I get you want me to see you later, right?"

"Now if you can, you know you left me with only what I had."

"Yea, and I'm tied up right now, and this afternoon I've got an appointment. Let's do it this way; you'll be home by dark, so how about I give you a call then, and you be ready to meet me at the turn in, from the hard road. That's about midway for both of us, and I'll be ready to leave home, when I call."

"I'll be here."

"I'll call you then."

That was the snag, resulting form the previous nights alteration. After leaving the Yates, his plan was to take ample product with them to Rapid City, there he would show DD how to "scale and bag" the dime bags he knew Billy would need, if he carried out the instructions. It was 12:20, the adjustment had been made. When he returned to the couch, DD told him, "Oh Suarme, I forgot to tell you Camille will not be taking lunch. She is taking the afternoon off, at least part of it, and coming here, when Mrs. Tillman returns from lunch."

"I heard you tell her that."

"With your 1:30 appointment, we won't be able to finish this."

"Are you tired already?"

"No, no, I mentioned it, that's all."

"Well, there's tonight and tomorrow; tonight you will dance, tomorrow I have nothing planned. Later this afternoon, we three are going back to the house. I have something I want you to help me do."

"Since ya an—don't got but one woman ya don't need me; since I lak ta ride an all."

"Yea, you stay here."

"Soame I wanna go too."

"I said that from the beginning, what's the problem?"

"Gimme some coke."

"You don't need any, because you don't know how to ask for it."

"I was wrong! Two hundred. Your turn Chairly."

"Can I have som a da coke Soame?"

"If you figure you're tuff enough to get that vile, let's see you try it." In snatching the vile, Chairly spilled a small portion of the powder on the table, because the container overturned, when she misjudged her reach. "See whacha made me do? I know what ta do wid it."

At 1:30 the two left out the bedroom door. There was no food in the refrigerator, DD was to have had lunch ready ,Camille and the arrangements had been made to spend the night. After shopping with Camille, they were to stop by the house and pick up Margrett and Beverly. Before they left, aside from the money he gave them, and while Chairly was using the bathroom, Soame gave DD a hundred dollars, and instructed her to buy a small recorder, so Chairly "can hear what she's missing."

He was in the front of the building, downstairs in the "accounting room, when Beauford drove onto the parking lot. There was a front seat passenger in the cruiser. He parked in front of the breezeway, before seeing Soame come out of the room. The sheriff had a wide grin on his face, as the three men approached each other. "If we'd waited another hour he'd a been on his way ta Boise." He then made the introduction.To stay, Neil would have to have his lights reestablished, and all his goods had to be unpacked, but he was in agreement with the sheriff and Soame, to at least hear the idea, before unpacking in Boise. There, his sister had extended an invitation, for him and his family to reside with her family, while he found something to do. He did no have immediate employment waiting for him anywhere. In giving him verbal assurance toward the idea,

Soame discussed the potentially successful idea with the construction of the bar-b-q stand. Neil already owned the property, but the idea of selling coke from the motel had not been thoroughly presented to him, even from a general outlining view. Beauford then explained, "he's got a U-Haul truck loaded ta the hilt, with his car hitched behind it on a tow bar. I figured the best thing was ta stall him, get him here, and let you tell him about it. Neil in this way, after you've heard what we've got in mind, I believe you'll stay at least until this operation opens up, then you can better see how the bar-b-q idea will come in the picture."

"Well, then let's hear it, here I am." They all chuckled.

During the course of explaining the idea, Soame was put somewhat on the spot, through the use of the word "sugar," as substitute. When Neil gathered the conclusion, he became excited, asking "wait a minute, you keep saying sugar, do you actually mean coke? You've got that much coke to put into operation, from Smath!!!?" Soame would not go all the way still, in the presence of Beauford, and there was also then, a witness. "Let's just say for now, I have access toward the availability."

"Well, why didn't you say coke? You're darn right the idea'll work, people will be coming here by the droves. I'll stay, don't worry about that. You got some coke now? There hasn't been any around here since Tom stopped. Let me try a piece of it." Soame's reluctance was obvious, and had been to Beauford, who prevailed. "I've got some I'll let you try, wait'll we leave."

"Do you need cash to carry you through, until this materializes? Soame asked Jefferies. "I sold my truck, and have enough to carry me for a couple of months, will take longer than that?" By then you'll be roasting ribs and chicken. I'll tell Smitty to square you away with three rooms, until you get your lights turned on and unpacked."

"Great, then Beauford and I'll just see you later." Soame went into his pocket, with his right hand saying, "that's a good idea also, because there's another part to this operation, and I'd like to discuss it with the both of you, since we're going to be in close association."

He was extending a hundred dollar bill to Neil, "Have dinner on me." Beauford had frozen. After Neil accepted the money, with thanks, Beauford asked, "ya mean ta tell me, there's more ta this plan?" Putting the money away, with a big smile, Jefferies commented, "I'm making money already, let's hear it."

"Here's a better idea than now; I haven't had lunch, and I've got a couple more things to do this afternoon. How about if we arrange our schedules to meet back here, tomorrow morning at 10:00, if it's convenient for the both of you also?" The agreement was made, for the appointed time. Soame then edged toward the commitment, in the presence of the sheriff, "Beauford, if you'll set him straight, to tide him over, until I see him back here later tonight, I can see to him being situated, from that point." That brought hardy handshakes, big smiles and, "I'll go home, undo my car, and bring my family over. It's been a pleasure meeting you Hudson, and I look forward to a continued growth in friendship, through success."

"Same pleasure and hopes here Jefferies, see you later tonight, and Beauford, we'll see you in the morning." That was the first meeting with the three of them.

Possibilities and hopes were beginning to brighten; actions were gaining pace. Without going upstairs he drove directly home. Margrett and Beverly were leisurely awaiting their ride to the motel. Articles had been gathered for the overnight stay. They seemed excited, even though it was not an out of town trip. He had them prepare sandwiches, and asked to be called from the basement, when the snack was ready. The purpose was in preparing the package for Billy, and a portion for Neil. He for this, "broke up and spooned out," two ounces, which he would put a one on, for the 100 dime packages he had in mind, and an eighth, which would be cut the same way. This would give Neil a quarter of an ounce, and four ounces of marketing product. With the sandwiches Margrett prepared, Beverly also dished a bowl of ice cream for him. When they began talking and asking questions, about the books they'd read and were reading, he conversed with them at the dining room table, during the meal. Following the conversation, he returned to the basement, and began compounding manitol to the substance he'd already separated.

To do it properly, both the cocaine and the manitol should be strained and sifted, at least twice, before they are sifted into each other, then the compound is once more sifted. Tiny particle are lost in the air, during the process, even when the atmosphere is without a gentle breeze, to float the powdered particles away. Although he worked in the basement, Soame estimated he'd lose a full dime bag, in that way. The process was well underway, when he heard the others come in. The stereo had been playing at a moderate tone. Less than thirty seconds after their entry, it was blasting. A short while later, DD called form the top of the steps. She was invited down, and in having seen him apply cut, time and again, she was very well acquainted with what he was doing. However, during the entire time together, she had not before that point seen the quantity of exposed cocaine. They had been at the same table two nights prior, putting the reefer package together. DD was sent for foil, scissors, and waxed paper.

The lady of the house went up, delivering the option to Chairly, to join them, or leave with the Johnsons. What was being done was explained to all of them. They had already been informed in their participation in distributing the product from the motel, and Soame felt because it was used so commonly and freely in the household, there was no reason to be coy.

Chairly returned with her. The process was relatively simple for the both of them to carry out. Soame had long before thought of the latex gloves, which he'd used handling the previous package, and when DD left and returned, with a pair of Camille's scissors, they practically whisked through the task. 1 1/2" squares of foil were cut by Chairly, while DD cut the 1 1/16" squares of wax paper. Soame set the triple beam on 1/10 of a gram, when the cutting was done. DD was then shown how to take the powder form the scale plate, and place it in the center of the wax paper, which was being set in the center of each pice of foil. The paper subdues and enables the compound to contain, the oil from the coke, while it ferments in the locked foil. It also keeps a more fresh "package." These are valuable considerations toward the buyer, with the fact, the paper saves particles from going into cracks, caused by crumples, when the package is sometimes roughly handled, or in someway caused to wrinkle. Though it was not good, money making, base cocaine, the packages Soame was folding was "fire" coke for snorters, anywhere in America. In a full twenty-four hour span, in the locked package, the cut-manitol will have been eaten by the oil and other chemicals, with the natural elements of the cocaine itself. That package is then fermented, and though there is still a manitol element in the compound, it is a more potent grade of coke, than when the package was initially locked.

The majority of street buyers do not experience the excel of the fully fermented coke. The most outstanding reason is, the dealer makes and "offs" his package, as soon as possible, for the "turn" of the money. Small amounts, such as dime packages are sold usually, within four hours after they're made. Another reason, which is also outstanding for not gaining the experience, has to do with the buyer immediately opening the package, and either tasting or smelling the substance: the package is then burped. With the belching, should come the snort, for the true test and taste of the worthwhile of the package. The day before, Soame told Billy, with experience, how to sell the package. In time, customers would rely on the product from him, and in that practically only way, will they take it, leave without a peek, taste, or smell, and be assured of having what their money was spent for. Soame knew how to do a few things extremely well; handling cocaine was one of them. To his estimation, it would have been impossible to for Billy to sell 25 of the 100 packages that night. Then it would be "green." The packages he sold would be "ready," from Tuesday night on. Either case, they were "fire."

An important element involved in their procedure, was the cleaning of the scale. After all the packets had been counted and placed in a brown paper bag, and Neil's portion separated. Soame took careful time, and prepared three quarters. Chairly resumed completing her previously assigned assignment, while he explained in detail, the step by step involvement of use and adjustment of the scale to DD. They scaled out a gram of coke and a gram of cut, and arrived at two grams of product. This was the applied one. They measured out ¾ of one of the grams, and applied ¼ manitol to it. When it was mixed and sifted for the final time, the mixture was placed on the scale, and came up, just shy of a full gram. He explained why, and the distinctive difference between the "quarter cut, on a one" and the "one and a quarter cut." The packeted three separated quarters, from the quarter on a one. A remaining almost full quarter was mixed with the other full gram, and given to Chairly. "Here, leave my shit alone." Because she'd regressed her pace considerably, she stopped that time at 262. DD was naturally keen with aptitude, projected with a budgeting mind. "Everything we do, form here on out, with product for marketing, is your responsibility through this scale. Everything that's to be sold you will weigh it. You will also keep tabs on every package, weighted by this scale. Do you understand your job?"

"Sure."

"How many packages have we weighed to be sold, and for how much each?"

"What is to be done with the three quarters?"

"They are samples; that's very good."

"How about the large packages."

"Excellent, now, let's go up to the front, and I'll show and tell you how this little gizmo is to be cleaned and stored, after each and every time you finish using it. Soon, this too will also become yours, and only your responsibility.

"How bout me Soame, what um goa be doing."

"238 more apologies for one thing, and with and after that, you'll be working on, and improving your speech." They were walking toward the front of the basement, he looked over to DD, "Did you get the recorder?"

"It's in the car." Camille had visited them, to let them know diner had been rearranged to be served upstairs. It was consented by them all, their first meal, in a new kitchen, shouldn't be prepared with haste. Following the dismantling of the disassemble parts of the scale, the cleaning procedure was shown, and while assembling it, he explained why the evidence should always be removed after use, and why the measuring instrument should be kept in a separate area from the drugs. The triple beam scale, is the most commonly used device by drug dealers. Basically, they are the only ones with need for such a sensitive apparatus, for its practical purpose. When one is discovered, the location of drugs is almost a certainty.

Directly after the meal he left, with plans to join them at the motel later. The bedroom door had been left unlocked for their convenience of entry. It was past 6:30; even with the carpenters long since gone, he felt the chances were far beyond remote, of anyone plundering the rooms. Except for the liquor, there wasn't anything else to be taken, without revealing the thief as a burglar. It was not that sort of atmosphere. Rather than wait for Billy's call, Soame decided to be at the Yates' home when he arrived. There were several reasons.

That afternoon, the parcel service delivery had been made. There were smiles, hugs, and kisses galore. Mrs. Yates did not appear to be upset with the idea of Jenny receiving gifts as well as her eldest daughter. Some of their types were totally implicative in the removal of any doubt about the open, triangular courtship. He did not have at least a small present delivered for the lady of the house. This fact he regretted, but noticed she did not seem displeased or disappointed. With her daughters, she was very jubilant. Little Thad arrived once again with Billy. The two men had been talking more than ten minutes, when the smaller tractor was heard turning off the main dirt road, onto the road leading only to the Yates' home.

Thad had informed Soame of the less than three hours work remaining, with the conclusion of the crop on the Hodges place. The wheat had been gathered and transferred to the transports properly, Thad expressed no disappointments. What caught Soame's strict interest was the subject on potatoes. The field was planted through Soame's help, with the loan. Though a bit late, for himself Thad planted 400 acres of whole tubers; he put 27 bushels in each acre of the all loam soil plot. What attracted Soame's interest toward potatoes was the introductory measure Thad used. "Yea, if my potatoes do well, I might be able ta bring in a pretty good year. Did ya know potatoes is one of the worlds most important foods?" Of course Soame knew of no such thing, and answered, "I thought the peanut was."

"It ranks with the peanut, but the potato is the world's most widely grown vegetable." He then went on talking about the more than several hundred varieties grown in America, and how the leafs would have to be killed on the Nor Chips he planted, before frost hit the plant. Thad told him about the 110 days it would take for the crop to mature, and he had gotten 5-7 tubers per plant in that field, in an average season, but during good seasons, he had gotten as much as 11-14. He explained decreasing the chances of rot and disease, as being the reason for planting whole tubers, rather than pieces. The Soviet Union produces 25% of the potatoes in the world. China and Poland preceed America in production of the vegetable. Idaho, Washington, Maine, Oregon, and Wisconsin, preceed Montana, with the USA's production. Thad rounded off the topic by telling Soame, "If my potato crop does half as well as your wheat, I'll call it a pretty good season. Looking at the wheat in the fields, it'll definitely be the best I've had in the past four years."

It wasn't hard for Thad to summarize, Soame was there to see Billy, who'd been delayed because there was a rented tractor and harvester in the field, to load two trucks, which was Billy's responsibility. During "rounds" he'd seen various vehicles and people drive out to the end of the field to see Billy. Soame was on the porch with the women, when he wheeled the big international in. Soame met him coming in from the tractor shelter, which was a lean-to attachment to the very large barn. There was a tall Larch nearest the barn, and a smaller Alder closer to the house. The two men met near the midway point between the two trees, which were some thirty yards apart. The women had gone into the house, after a wave from Mrs. Yates, which Soame could not see, in his approach to Thad. He found Soame always to be an interesting person to talk to. Other than the fact, he was the first black man he'd ever spoken to, they were partners, and the real oddity was in the fact, Soame was a "city boy," who really displayed a sharp interest in farming. Thad had been a farmer all of his life. Had Soame impressed him as a "city slicker," he would not have been tolerated around the house.

Thad amused himself, little Thad and the women in his house, with conversational stories, jokes, and antics about Soame, whom he could not find the least fault in, or about. This was done especially when Cathy and Jenny became too sassy with their raves. Time and time, without employing detection, he attempted to "stump" Soame, but had not been successful. "He would look at me and look off, and I could declare he was gonna," etc. This was his course of disruption, in amusing them with his opinion of how bright he thought Soame was. "The darnest thing he ever did, when I knew I had um, was ta look off and back at me when he said 'Thad, I just don't know.' I coulda went through the ground. Even I woulda said something stupid, I think, but he just," etc.

Little Thad had been more successful than his father, with a verbal prank. Practically each time he held the stock of the rifle to his shoulder, he thought of the day he received the gift he'd been asking his parents for, more than three years. Times were hard for them, when the boy came of age for the present he wanted most. There was a hush, when the men heard the sound of the smaller Massley Furgerson, the brothers were coming in on. A far off sound then also penetrated the air; it was a Western Meadowlark. Thad had over seventy-five head of sheep. There was time for feeding and a bath, before supper. Hogs and cows also made their presence known, and being fed was on their minds. With barley, the rotational crops Thad talked to Soame about, when they initially met, were clover, corn, oats, timothy, and soybeans.

The conversation was about sugar beats, when they heard the other tractor. Soame had not been aware, until Thad informed him of his home state, being the largest producer of sugar, in America. The sugar beat is second to sugar cane in the production of sugar. America follows the Soviet Union and France, with its sugar beat crops, which is grown through an irrigation process. The day before, Soame and Thad's daughters sat and awaited Billy. When he was spotted, it was a sugar beat field, Soame looked across, and saw the dust. Thad was telling him how two employed helpers were "topping" the clustered dark green leaves—the crowns—to ensure a good crop in late September, or by mid October. "Sugar beats are grown for the sugar contained in the large and flashy roots. There's about 225 acres in the field ta the left, before ya turn inta the big road." Oregon is the leading sugar beat producing state "stateside." When they saw the tractor turn in toward the house, Thad said to him, "I've seen cars and trucks drive out ta the field all day; I've got an idea you and Billy are doing something. Now I'm not pryin or anything. He's already out of school and grown, I haven't said anything ta him and probably won't. I know my son, and I don't believe you'd lead him wrong, but you all be careful with whatever it is you're doing."

"Thad, being a stranger in these parts, before I make a move, with anything, in any direction, I try and do it with as much information and certainly as I can. I've got a lot of respect for you and your household. I would not expose any member of your family to the threat of danger. Any danger involved, I would set up obstacles, barriers, and blockades, to stop even the threat of the possibility of that danger. That threat, if it availed itself, I would immediately shout down any activity I am involved with, to eliminate any harm arising form the threat. Any, all, and every means I know of, I would not meet the danger, and if it finds me, it will find nothing incriminating. Your family members, whom I'm in close contact and association with, are also within that scope of protection. I appreciate and understand your advice, which is adhered, and I will Thad,, we will be careful, thanks."

"Paw, we should be done before 9:00 in the morning. Everything loaded out just fine. Hay Soame!" Little Thad jumped form the tractor, and ran over to join them. Clutching the machine to a slow roll, allowing the dismount, Billy waved and yelled, "Be right back." And the Furgerson kicked into motion. "Well ya got feedin' to do. I'm going ta the house. Billy's got the figures for ya Soame. Ya got more company here now ta really talke farmin ta ya. Again, it's been a pleasure partner, I'll see ya later." Thad had taken four steps, with his last words, he looked back with a smile and a wave. The Duck overalls and long sleeve khaki shirt were cluttered with dust. Nearing the small Alder, he hit twice with his hat, puffs of dust flew, and drifted with the breeze, until they were no longer seen. Little Thad was telling Soame he wished he didn't have to, "feed up, then I could show ya! I can hit anything Soame, even a dragonfly on the clothes line." Thad was at the top step when the screen door opened. "Lor-dee me," little Thad turned to his father's exclaimed voice, "Cat in Jenny's got new clothes! Hay Billy come quick, and look at Cat and Jenny!"

"I see um, I see um. You better go get started, I'll be there soon, alright?"

"No, it ant alright. Ya never come when ya say that, least till all the work's all done. Soame I'll see ya later, ha? Then I can show ya."

"Come on, I'll help you. I want to talk with you, and this'll give me the chance, without keeping you from your chores. You can show me Wednesday little Thad; how bout if I give you all a hand, and make it a little easier for ya right now?"

"That'll be swell." Little Thad was about ten paces ahead of them, going to the barn.

He figured the girls would be showing their new clothes to their father, and suggested the offer of help with sincerity. Billy assigned Thad to the sheep. They were diary cows; eight of them. They were fed in an area next to the far side fo the barn, under a shed, similar to the lane-to for the tractors. Two of the cows had calves. Billy explained the two usually being milked in the morning and evening at feeding time. Because he was there, they didn't have to separate and hold the calves back, while Cathy and Jenny milked. The chickens were fed a mixture of corn and meal, broadcasted over the same area the cows were fed. Soame had always heard the term, "slop the hogs." The term did not exist with the Yates' modern farm. There was feeding bin, as replacement for the trough, and 50 lb. bags of feed, which replaced the slop. He and Billy made three trips, with a sack each trip, from the barn to the bins in the field, where the feed was deposited into the bins. The hogs had no problems lifting the flaps, at the base of the contraption, and helping themselves.

It was well he had taken the time for the probing conversation. Had they met later on, according to the original plan, he would have found Billy with urgent reason to get to Berrydale; they would not have had the chance for the talk, which revealed Billy's exact position. "Yesterday man, wow! I never seen anything like it. Like I told ya, people were waitin. As soon as I got there I sold four. Even if I wanted to, I didn't have time to go into the stuff, cause after seein' how fat the dimes were, and I told um like you said, 'three for a quarter,' two of them came back and bought quarters, and that's the way it went. In an hour and a half, I was dry man. When I got down ta the last four, I kept one for myself, and wham!!! The other three went; just lack that." Soame did not expect the flow through the small community to be as fast. Billy explained, "what they really want is reefer, and this is how this whole thing got started. It's been a long time around here, and throughout the territory, since people have had any money. We're gonna be doin' better than most, cause we go the late harvest and the exchange is boomin', practically beggin' for wheat. I sold out of the reefer I had, two weeks ago. I told um, but they kept comin' for some thing ta get high on. That's when I started sellin' my personal, cause it was sooo good, I doubled the price on it, and wham!!! It was gone too, just like that."

"That's how it started with the Cat and Jenny. Last week I went Saturday without anything. People were in from all over, for the dynamite smoke. I came home and told them. They had the stuff, and I told um the price I charged. I asked to sell it for um, but the Cat wants ta get smart and go, sell her own. Naturally, Jenny wanted to follow her. So I could make some money, I put Cat on my coke, while they rolled their joints. Hay man, last Sunday afternoon, Cat's first time in Berrydale in a year and a half, she and Jen sold every piece of reefer they had. I sold out of coke. Only their coke was left. I had already put B-1 with it Saturday night, and you know how it went form there."

"Yea, what I want to know is, with the activity still, why didn't you call me, or drive to Smath, and let me know?"

"Shit!! You said not ta sell it! The Cat and Jen were scared ta death. How was I ta tell ya? What was I ta tall ya? Ya been real good ta us Soame. Ya, don't know it but it's a miracle; you! Made a miracle happen. My paw don't like nobody. I mean, beside you helping us out of debt and all, Paw really has a likeness for ya. He use ta run half the guys away that came here ta see the Cat. Jenny wasn't suppose ta start courting, till school starts this year. You do not know what it means for ya to be invited here, by my paw, ta court my sisters. If little Thad and them, would na told me, without me seein it, I wouldn't believe it."

"he's that strict, ha?"

"Shiiit, the other one's he allowed, they knew he didn't like um, and they wouldn't stay long, cause they knew he didn't like um, we're the Yates Soame!"

"I can dig it; now check this out." Billy then heard what type of package he had prepared. In the package, is a sample for you. You are about to start making some real money, according to what you say. Don't go against what I've told you. Some of the people you sell to, are going to buy quarters, break them down, and add cut to them, and start selling also. Don't worry about them as competitors. Sell them as much as they want; you are their only source. Billy, do not become you best customer. Now that you are making money with the product, I will only give you a sample of what you will be handling. Some of your customers will come to you short, if they only have $5.00, you sell them half the package, add a dollar with it, and you've got a half a package for a dollar. Do not let your merchandise go on credit, it's the worst thing you can do, to lose a customer." Billy stopped and looked at him inquisitively. "I will not go into total depth with the explanation, I'll let you find out for yourself this way: wait, until you have established regular clientele. When one of your regulars then, come to you for credit, extend it to just that one. See how long it takes from that point ,for that person to come back to you with the money owed, and buy another piece . I'll tell you in advance what will happen. You lose not only the $10.00 package, but also not only could you have sold the package to someone else, that person will spend money with the competition, three or four times, before they come back to you, if ever they come back. With that, you are intelligent enough to figure out, in setting up and conducting a business of this means of cash, it is not a good principal to credit; regardless of the circumstances…take only cash money. Thieves will bring you stolen goods, in exchange for your product. Billy, um telling you, no matter how good it looks, or how bad you may want , or even have need for it, take only cash money for the coke you get from me."

It was then it came back to Billy, the seriousness involved in Soame, when talking about cocaine and money. The day before he asked him for a small amount of money, after having given him portions twenty times as much. Soame caught him in the spell of concentration on seriousness; they gazed into each others eyes! "Cocaine is cash money. Any city or town you go in, in American, cocaine is a faster conversion, than calling, and having money sent by Western Union. You are about to begin making more money than you have ever dreamed of; it will be fast, and women will trample over others to get to you. I know what you are about to experience. Concentrate on making the money; do as I instruct you, and you will become rich. Experiment in your own way, and you will be out of business. Like the bad sale, I give only one set up; You are in the midst of that. Yesterday and today is your set up. Only you can put yourself out of business. I've told you how to operate."

They had emptied the last two sacks of feed in the third bin. Little Thad had long since, checked the water flow from the windmill. Knowing they were deeply embedded in conversation, he went through the pasture, toward the house, hopped the fence and ran across the large yard, around the garden, to the house. Walking back to close the barn, he delivered more to Billy. "This may turn out to be the most important thing I'll tell you. Let's both hope it doesn't happen, but remember, if you get arrested, and you inform on me, with both of us in jail, there may not be anyone to get us out. Whereas, if you get arrested and keep your mouth shut, within twenty-four hours, I will have you out of any jail in this state, unless you have committed murder, with the charge of possession and, or, sales."

"You have never been arrested before, if it happens, do not panic. Do not get boisterous to your friends who may see you, and shout out Soame will get me out. Bla, bla, bla. Keep my name out of your mouth. This is your shit when you take it; if you're man enough to handle it, be man enough to claim it! To arrest you, the police must read you your rights. Billy, once your rights are read to you period, you have nothing to say to them, nothing. At the police station, they may harass, threaten, or intimidate you, and if anyone lays a hand, unlawfully, on you, get the number from their badge, or the name from their ID tag, that must be worn as a part of the uniform. You must be given a call. Your safest call for me, is your call home and having the message relayed, without using my actual name; there may be a wire on the phone you use. For sure, if you are asked for the number so they can dial it for you, call home. Should you call me, and I do not answer, ask for Fred Smith; who ever answers will know then. Tell them who you are and where you are, immediately. At that point they will hang up."

"Now listen, when the phone hangs up, do not get excited, panic, or become frustrated, and try to call again. You will have done all I've instructed you to do. I expect you to do that in that manner, and I want you to know now, within two hours, after you place that call, that one call, either a bondsman or a lawyer will be at that jail. Keep your mouth shut, even in the cell. You are a fairly rough dude. You can last at least a day in any county or city jail in America. Play cards, tell jokes, relax, and sleep. I will get you out of jail, before you spend a day. Do you understand what I have told you?" They were closing the doors to the barn.

"Why yea, but you make it sound kind of rough, is it really like that?"

"That's the reason I'm taking this time." They had walked to the tractor shed. The rear of the Furgerson was partially out. Soame stopped and sat on the cross bar of the tractor, which had been left midway the height of the back tires. "Check this out dude...the police have designed methods, that have been proven to make you spill your guts on me, your family, and everyone else. It's called interrogation. The most commonly used is, one tries to be rough, and frighten you while his buddy seemingly wants to be your friend. The first time in jail victim panics with fright, spilling his source to the friendly fellow. There are several other tactics, techniques, and methods seen on TV, have nothin' ta say. When I get the phone call, use judgment as ta call home or you. Deliver the information, Fred Smith, or without using your name at home. Then I wait."

"Believe me, they might show you a photograph of a sale you made. They might even have and show you a package you sold, you might be confronted by someone you know you sold to, who comes in and says, 'He's the one who sold it to me.' They may shake chairs, throw cups against the wall, filled with water or coffee. They have all types of boo tactics to make you scared, so you will talk. Of all the things they do, they know their jobs is their livelihood. They cannot harm a hair on your head, without jeopardizing the jobs they have, and subjecting the city or county to suit. You are an American citizen. It's your constitutional right to not answer any question asked, and be allowed a phone call. Do not be harassed, intimidated, or friendly coaxed into talking; not even wise cracks about knowing your rights." "

"I've got a question?"

"What is it"

"Suppose there ant no phone, or they don't let me use it?"

"Have you ever spent a night anywhere but home?"

"No, but Paw says if I want ta get a place of my own, then I can."

"I'll know Billy, just sit tight and keep your mouth closed. Should they insist on harassing you, state 'I am invoking or using my right to be questioned in the presence of my lawyer.' From that point, you notice and remember their names. They may ask who your lawyer is. Then you ask for the phone call. You will have thrown a scare into them. That is the absolute most they can legally do. They have their methods. As an American citizen you have the constitutional law on your side. In the Unites States of America, there is not other higher authority. Do you have anymore question?"

"Man am I glad you told me that. I can handle it Soame, if it happens. I never woulda known that, thanks."

Walking towards the house Soame told him about the motel operation and mentioned Cathy and Jenny working evenings and weekends. They walked to the Jeep. Billy was given two joins of Panama reefer, his sample, and his package. Giving him the package, Soame told him, "try your sample before I leave. Tell me if it's right or not. You'll work the package if it's right. It's worth $1,000, with 100 dimes. You'll owe me six. After you've checked your sample, and if it's right, give me some money on the six." They had a mild conversation to the house, arriving, at the porch, Cathy and Jenny came out, in new clothes. Billy teased them and went inside.

When Billy returned from the inside of the house, he had on a change of clothes, and was biting into a sandwich. The truck was parked next to an older model station wagon, to Billy's left, off about twenty yards from the porch, at the edge of the yard, between the yard and the blackberry patch. He had been inside nearly twenty-five minutes. The threesome was at the Jeep. Purple, gray, and flamingo, closed in highlighting colors on the skies, projecting mid dusk, with illumination of the house, when he stepped form the porch.

Soame was sitting on the fender. He had wiped his shoes, and had also taken his sweater off, and shook dust and feed particles form it. To protect his hat, each time he carried a sack, he cocked it to the opposite side of his head. A sister stood, leaning against the fender, on each side of him. They had been smoking gold reefer and doing Soame's personal "girl" with him. Each had been given a quarter and two joints of red smoke. Billy was off the porch, before the screen door slammed calling twenty yards directly in front of him, "I'm on my way out, I'll stop by, let me get the truck." He then veered to his left, hopped over an aster patch, leaving the white, purple, and yellow colors behind, he approached the pink and white flowers of the bitterroots with long strides. The bed was in his path. There was no grass in the yard scattered with flowerbeds. He had to back the truck out and exit the driveway, past the jeep.

The idea about working at the motel had already been presented to the sisters, who were lost in a float, on a cloud, with delighted realistic thoughts of more new clothes than they'd ever before had, at one time, in their lives. They had not done coke since the previous evening. The grass they had finished that morning. Though he was comfortable and at ease in their presence, Soame wanted to get home. "it's right man, there is a one on it."

"Good shot, I'll see you Wednesday evening unless you call. I'm at the motel, but I've call forwarding from the house. Let's see what heppens."

"Right, later Soame. I guess you two are gonna milk those cows in the mornin', after sleepin' in them new clothes all night, ha?"

"William Thadeous Yates we got others sides these, ta work and sleep in, and just don't you start worrin' bout us!!!" Jenny passed him the bag she relayed from her brother. She and Soame were fanning dust, while "the cat" was still screaming. Soame looked into the bag, tossed it over the windshield, into the driver's seat, and eased down.

Except for the two with him, strolling to the house, and their participation in the Berrydale scene, it had all gone according to his estimation. They had been told not to tell their parents about the prospect of the job. The pay scale was not mentioned. They were all content with the happiness they shared between them. At the top of the steps Cathy kissed him, without reservation, and with deep sensitivity and sensuousness. When the lengthy kiss was over, Jenny had her back to the wall of the house, standing between the screen door, and the front window. She called to him

Arriving at the motel, the jeep was parked in front of the only entrance into the office and registration desk, for patrons. Smitty gave Soame the requested connection to Neil's room. Neil was asked to the lobby, from the guest phone.

He then asked for an outside connection, and had the Blanchard number dialed. The question imposed on Soame's mind was, why hadn't he parcel service delivery been made on Elm Street, at his home that day, during the same trip? He wanted to check and find if the deliveries had been made to Cindy and Janet. Cindy answered the call. "Oh Soame, thanks for returning the call, how are you?"

" I guess I'm fine, I've had a pretty rushed day. I'm about to clear my outside doings, before I attempt toward relaxing. I'm at the motel, I didn't know you called, are you alright?"

"Sure, and you are a true darling, but it wasn't me who called, we persuaded my father to do it, after he came in. All afternoon, I though you'd call. You said last night you would have a busy morning, but the jacket and coat came today; mother's absolutely ecstatic Soame, and you're almost much too far beyond my belief in a man, other than my father, being sooo good to me, but that's not all." There was a pause. She thought maybe he would interrupt, but wasn't disappointed when he didn't. "Words seem a way too lacking, as a means of relaying thanks, and this is the first time in my life, I've ever been trapped in this awkward situation, I've got to see you. I want you to be with me, when I give you the news. When can you come?"

"Well, well, that sounds pretty important. You can't be pregnant."

"Oh Soame, please, don't make fun of me. Mother's standing here drooling with anxiety to speak with you; hold on." Following a brief pause this time, Janet's whispering voice came over the phone. "You mother fucker, you raunchy mother fucker, Soame how could you do this? I have never been so impressed with anyone. I am ladened and totally overbeared with happiness, in trying to convey thanks, and I find myself shameless with appreciation." The voice had risen to standard tone, through her continuous talk. "Evidently you can talk or can't you?" Neil then entered through the glass door. He had been seen in his approach, through the glass fronted structure. "Yes and no, um in the lobby of the motel. Hold on a second or two, will ya?"

"Sure!" A paper bag, folded small, with a rubber band containing the flap, was then passed to Neil. "That should hold you for a while, I'll see you in the morning."

"Thanks Hudson, I'll see you then. I'll be in the breezeway at 10:00."

"Hay yea, well even though you think of my gift as being sleazy and somewhat risqué, I cheerfully except your verbal expression of gratitude. Whatever warmth, happiness, and joy it brings you, I feel comforted in extending it."

"You're really too much, thanks, I really treasure it. Say by the way, was that Neil Jefferies I heard you speaking with?"

"Yea, ya know him?"

"Oh brother, he was a real pain at one time, and sight I desperately dreaded to see, with every measure I took, in carefully trying to avoid him. For almost two years, he pestered me and did everything he could to get into my drawers. I've never gone out with him, or anything of the sort, but his wife had their second child, he saw me at the hospital the day the baby came, and began hounding me from that point on. He became totally untolerable with his persistence. Rather than tell Tom, he was one of the main reasons I quit the job. So you're not going to be able to make it tomorrow, ha?"

"I didn't say that, you simply heard your flower of passion say we've got a meeting at ten. Judging from Cindy's excitement, I'd be low rated, and thought of as a slapdash gone forever, if I failed to make it."

"You've really put my baby where I wanted her to be, with physical maturity and mental attitude and complacency; I am forever grateful to you for that. She talked about my anxiousness, she's been pushing, nudging, and reaching for this receiver since two seconds after I got it. So we're on for tomorrow ha?"

"Yea, if the farm house in the afternoon doesn't present a problem for you."

"Just tell her what time, here she l—"

"How about, so I won't encounter the same problem as Jefferies, don't wear any panties."

"What!!! Alright, just you remember, you asked for it. Thanks again."

"So we'll be together again tomorrow?"

"Unless you want to declare this an emergency, and meet me shortly, or later tonight."

"I guess I can wait, and don't worry, you'll be glad to hear the news."

"Now that you've put it that way, I wonder if I'll be able to sleep through my wondering."

"Why are you at the motel? Is it the idea you said you're working on?"

"I'll tell you about it tomorrow. Let's say 2:30 at the farm house. I'm tied up in the morning, and I don't know how the early afternoon is going to break."

"Last night was really grand. Thanks again for taking me out. The catalog doesn't have the charms, and the bracelet won't be big enough to make notation of all the events we're encountering."

"We'll think of something. A step at a time, oh! And Janet's been asked not to wear panties tomorrow. What do you have in mind."

"So that's what the commotion was about. Do you have anything else to say Soame?"

"You haven't answered my question."

"We'll be there then, good night."

"Sleep tight Cindy."

At the table that late afternoon, during the course of their meal, the fact that DD would be keeping account of outgoing activity with the product, and incoming cash, resulting form distribution, was presented to Camille. Soame did this, with hopes of the spunky accountant being interested in the project, to the point of helping DD construct a method, using coded symbolisms to record the transactions. In fact, it was his projected suggestion, which she found immediately comprehendible, and carried on with further elaboration. When the meal was finished, DD was taken back to the basement, where Camille went through a section of her stored goods, and within five minutes, presented DD with a slightly used ledger. With the notations already in the book, and Camille's careful explanations, DD had no problem in grasping what was to be done, and how to go about doing. Soame left them on the living room couch, using the coffee table, involved in the exercise.

He'd parked the jeep in its regular spot, next to the Seville, and walked across the parking lot. Before stepping on the corridor walk, he heard the amplification of the stereo. Soame then used the walk to the breezeway to go upstairs, and enter form the bedroom. He knew where he would find DD and Camille. His calculation was not wrong. FiFi advised them of his approach, before the key slid into the door lock. She whined, and stood attentively toward the door. Camille was laying toward the foot of the bed, watching TV and on occasion nonchalantly prating with DD. Fully reclined in the lay-z-boy, DD knew it could only be him, who'd attracted the dog's attention. Knowing Soame had the tub removed, the two women had a bubble bath before leaving the house, and were comfortable in their alluring attire.

The foot rest portion of the chair folded, as he stepped in the door. "Darl—Suarme where have you been? What on earth have you been doing? She had taken two strides toward him, and abruptly stopped and asked, in almost suspended horrification. There was a big smile on his face, in entering. He was triumphantly happy. DD's reaction momentarily bewildered him. Soame looked over at Camille, on the half pulled covers, who looked also as if she was uncertain it was him she was widely gazing at. It hit him, "Oh, um a farmer, didn't ya know that?" He sated whimsically. This started Camille laughing. "You're no such thing, look at yourself Suarme! What have you been doing?"

"Don't look at me, look at the money I've got." He said extending the bag to her. "You've always had money; besides how much money can you carry in such a small bag? How could you do this to yourself, come, come." Camille had become hysterical with laugher. Her eyes were streaming tears, while she laid, rolled and tired to clap her hands and missed.

"You don't know what this means, what is it represents." She was pinching the elbow of his sweater, leading him to the shower. "I know only that you need to sho—oh Suarme, what is that odor?" It wasn't funny to Camille anymore either; she also asked, "What is that!?" Clamping two fingers, daintily on her nose, "poo" and shooing him away, with the other.

"DD, will you look at he money I have in her—stop pullin' me! Look will you please!?" He stopped with his insistence and jabbed the bag toward her, "Suarme do not touch me with that filthy bag. I will look in the shower." He was almost in front of the door, standing sideways. DD had walked around, and out of his path, placing him between her and the open door, she shoved. He stumbled into the bathroom conversion crying out, "Oh Shit!" Camille hollered out "that's exactly what it is, look under his shoes." He slammed the door.

A minute and a half later, Soame came out of the shower room, dressed only in his underwear. In one hand he held the Stacyes, extended from his body, waist high. DD had opened the divider and was between the section waiting for the approaching Chairly, who cold not hear her summon for a roll of paper towels and ammonia, which was all they had as cleaning materials. In his other hand there was a wad of bills, in a mangled cluster, clutched in his fist. Camille had moved to the far side of the bed, and was comfortable in the love seat. He had to look back, over his shoulder to see DD.

"Hay you two, I didn't mean to bring this in here on you like that, I didn't know about it. Gee, I didn't know I had tracked the floor up too."

"I will clean it up. Take the boots outside Suarme."

"Well, what do ya think um doin, just tell me that ha?" There was no reply to him, she was looking the other way talking to Chairly. He stood waiting for DD to turn back to him. "Soame please, it's such a horrible smell," pleaded Camille.

"Suarme, what are you doing, you come in here with all that mess on your feet, and you will not go out with it?"

"Well, if you two will wait a minute, and I'm positive a little shit ant gonna hurt you to smell it, I want to tell you about the first money we've made, after all this time, and the thousands invested. Now count this money, and put it in the book." He flung it at her, and went to the door. "It's from Billy Yates. A payment on $600.00 he owes, for the product we made up today." He said, looking at her, Camille, and the scattered bills. Camille had seen the entire picture, with the initial presentation of the bag, and guessed what the money was for. DD then understood why he had been so happy when he entered the door.

The money received the day before was from given and personal product. The express purposed of the packets they made that day, was for marketing. There was a preliminary, but this was his true beginning.

After scraping the chicken droplets, cow manure and hog droppings form the bottom of his boots, caked between the soul and heel, ten minutes later, he returned to the room. The boots were left outside, by the door. Chairly had been sent back to the kitchen for a plastic linter, for the depositing of the $125.00 H.I.S., brown, dust and debris filled sweater. With that, and also into the plastic bag went the $50.00 Brooks Brothers shirt, and the soiled Levies, and socks. DD was at the dresser, cleaning the $275.00 Stetson with her hair brush. Chairly was coming out of the shower room, with the tied bag. She had not beenseen by him until then, since he'd been there; he froze. After several seconds, Chairly had walked to the divider. "Stop!! Right there." Looking at DD, pointing vividly with pokes of his index finger, toward Chairly, he asked "what is that all about?" DD merely slightly shrugged her shoulders, glanced at him, and continued rolling and brushing the hat saying, "Maybe you should ask her."

It was his clothes, and the description of himself as a farmer, that had earlier struck a humorous note and chord with Camille. Wherein she was the only real parent in the household, she was the one to answer Soame, "Oh, please let me explain: After you left the house, DD and I had a bubble bath. We were in the tub, maybe for a half hour. About twenty minutes ago, us good white folks have listened to how you 'kicked her ass,' and you are the only man in the whole wide world who could do it in such a fashion, that's been done on instant replay, and characterized, demonstrated, and acted out over fifty times between the three of them. In the other room you will find two other identical marks of brutality, us 'good white folks' were fortunate in not having to witness you inflict or something to that effect, wasn't it DD?" She dropped both the brush and hat on the dresser, walked to the bed, and sat with her elbows on her knees, with her palms resting her chin. Shaking her head, she replied, "I do not know, with these two, I do not know at times."

"What are you going to do with that bag?"

"I don kno."

"Bring it here." He took the bag from Chairly. "I got changing clothes here?"

DD replied, "We have two drawers apiece. Yours are the two large ones. On the hangers you will find, with our clothes, two pairs of jeans, three pairs of dress pants, and four shirts. There are shoes and boots over there also." Soame placed the bag outside with the boots, walked back past Chairly, and before entering the shower room, DD said to him, "Give me you underclothes Suarme."

"Come get um."

Chairly had long since shampooed and conditioned the waves out of her hair. Using a relaxer, she simply combed it back and wore it in a pony tail or loose, looking boyish. She was confident in the appearance of her face, with the application of makeup, and truly felt a gorgeous hairdo, wasn't really necessary as a beauty attraction. She was not wrong. She was growing into her natural attractiveness. The properly applied makeup only boosted her beauty without giving her an artificial composition. When Soame saw her with the bag, she had on a pair of alligator flats, baggy fitting stain pants, a football jersey with the 00 inscription, her hair was combed back, and under the baseball cap, which she had turned sideways, the straight, combed hair as not tied. It was her common appearance to shine, sparkle, and glitter, with arrayed jewelry. It surprised him to see the made up, black eye. He avoided the big ambushing surprise, which would have left him startled and "stumped," when he did not enter from the kitchen: upon seeing him come up the stairs, the three pranksters were to present the black eyes to him, and run crying to the glass partition, "He beat me, Soame is beatin me, help us he's beating us." DD was to then lock the glass division. Camille wanted no part of it. DD felt Margrett's idea would "serve him right!"

The best part of the idea in their opinion, was in knowing his temperament. He would never break the glass or lock. To get into the bedroom, he would have to retrace, back and down through the kitchen. While en route, he was to have been criticized, harassed, intimidated and ridiculed, for physically chastising the "innocent" Chairly. Her pretence was to have been sound asleep; it was also a part of the humor Camille enjoyed, knowing he had tricked the tricksters. After all, who else did they have to play with? The question in his mind was, why didn't Cathy and Jenny advise him of the remaining dust and seed particles in his clothes, on his face, and in his hair?

Following the shower, DD brought him a heaping bowl of ice cream. He ate it and fell asleep; for three hours he rested. It was past 11:30 when Soame asked DD if she would dance for him. She had brought clothes over especially to do so. She needed the bedroom to make ready. It was then he saw the recorder she purchased, for the first time. After freshing himself, he went to this desk. It was the first time he worked from it. On the other side of the room, Chairly, Margrett, and Beverly were watching blue movies, with volume only from the stereo. They had long ago discovered the long couch to be a convertible. However, except for their shoes, they were fully dressed, on top of the covers they had made up. Again, unknowingly, he had outflanked them. Their embarrassment from failing to pull their caper off, wounded their prides, and mocked their consciences. They would not use the shower. Not knowing their planned endeavor, but being aware of their fake black eyes, he ignored them.

At the desk he wrote an entire page, using sentences with words he knew Chairly massacred, in her speech. It was Camille who came out, and discontinued the videos. The sofa was folded, the recliner was positioned for the person to whom the entertainment was dedicated to, and Margrett and Chairly brought in the love seat. DD selected the ones she would use, from all the records they had at the house, and those they found in reserve there at the office,.

Except for the rotating multi-colored light behind the bar counter, all the others were extinguished, for the introduction made by Camille. She came in and sat on the love seat. Soame had seen and noticed the dress she wore before, but never realized it was, the show piece it was. He had criticized her for losing weight. He did not realize, when they met, she had not worked regularly for a while. The weight she lost, while they were together, was the weight she had picked up, over a year and a half. Even with the lights out, they all could tell, she looked as if she had been poured into the gown. The best seamstress in the state, could not have fitted the extravagant material more perfectly. With it she had on long gloves, her diamonds, and her hair had been rearranged to her commonly used French roll; in the back and to the side. Everyone there knew she looked grandly superb. Even she displayed confidence in that fact, through her poise.

None of the others knew about what was about to take place, when Camille ordered the entertainment center off. He was rereading the page, making final corrections, when the bed was being folded. Soame, in his pj's, robe, and slippers, went to the bar, poured a half glass of vodka, over cubes, and when it had chilled, with the added orange soda, gulped it. He lit a joint, and by the time everything was situated, with Camille having a stool near the entertainment center, Chairly and Beverly on the couch, and Margrett comfortable on a bean bag, she came in and was seated. He did a huge one. "And now for your viewing consumption, and Soame's personal entertainment, dedicated to him from his first lady, to the last and only man in her life, for Soame, Miss Dubanee!!!

The adjustable lamp, on the pole, behind the entertainment center had been centered to where she would stand. *"Love TKO",* by Teddy Pendergrass, eased up with volume, while DD eased into the light with exotic movements of entrancing romanticism. He did the other huge one. The beat of the record was captivating, with the display of her moves. *"Girls Just Want to Have Fun,"* by Cindy Lauper gave her a chance to strut, and demonstrate some of the moves she'd taught "Mizz Fine," but they knew she only danced for one person. Her attention was never diverted from him. Other than looking down, with sweeping lashes, that took her concentrated looks and casual glances to various parts of his body, and stares into Soame's eyes, her direct vision included nothing else. It was during the second record, she removed one of her gloves. The gown was full length, with a slit on its left side that ran up, almost to the top of her thigh. Several times Chairly cleared her throat, coughed, and did movements, attempting to aver the artist's attention; there was no deterring. The initial mood of the presentation had been somewhat melancholy. The second record differed the pace. The tune *"That's Life,"* by Frank Sinatra, resumed the melodramatic style of the exotic display and movements of her body, with the upkeyed tempo from the first record, and a subtle receding from the loveliness of the second tune. The Sinatra record was a well blended and selected rendition, focusing tempo between the two. At the end of the record, she had on no gloves. They had been tossed to the lap of the person in the recliner.

At the close of the fade of the record, DD received the first applause after she had begun, when Camille announced a five minute intermission. During the opening phase of the interval, the common became the peculiar, and focused in on, as the outlandish attempt at disruptive intrusion, the act presented; it was a blatant display: Fifi was laying between Chairly and Beverly on the sofa. Margrett had dragged a bean bag form the stairway area, and sat to Soame's right, off to the center of the two walls; this somewhat encircled DD's performance. Between records, Margrett lit her pipe, Soame sniffed, and all along Chairly "tooted," as well as at those times. The coffee table had been completely taken out of the picture, and removed behind Soame and Margrett, toward the bedroom. The love seat was toward the entertainment center, in the corner. No one noticed Camille bring in the pipe and table lighter. The items, with a "rock" were place on a shelf, behind the bar counter, before the video and stereo went off.

When the intermission was announced and during the applause, DD gracefully went to the corner of the bar. Camille preceded her there, and was behind the counter. With her back to the audience, who were involved in their interests, the stored items were passed to her. Lighting her pipe, the flame attracted Chairly. "Uuuuh, I wont sum," she hastened to her feet, and in her second stride to DD, Margrett yelled, "leave her alone, here, have some of this." Chairly looked over to her, sucked her teeth at Margrett, threw her head in the air, and in the next two strides, stopped in front of Camille, who had stepped form behind the bar, and stood with her hands on her hips. "Don't you dare!!!" She said with a very serious growl. The dejected Chairly still would not recognize Margrett's invitation, but did not violate, to trespass against the warning. She turned about, went back to the couch, and began stroking Fifi. When Beverly leaned over and inquired, "why'd you do that?" She merely shrugged her shoulders, and slightly motioned her head implying, "I do not know."

DD never relinquished her back to them, nor did she turn her head, when all the verbal utterances through the still and quiet room, were heard by them all. She knew that Soame had viewed the entire scene, and heard all that was said, and would be casually looking at them all, in the aftermath. She was correct with her thinking. After she had taken two more "hits," she looked at Camille, who had just deposited the remainder of a joint in an ash tray. They smiled at each other; DD nodded, and Camille went back to the entertainment center. "And now, Soame's office, is proud to present, for your viewing and Soame's personal pleasure, the second half of the presentation of…Miss Dubanee!!!"

The Nitty Gritty Dirt Band music crescendoed, with the tune *"Mr. Bo Jangles,"* there was applause, and Beverly cheered. She was marvelously captivating, and inspiring to the young minds and hearts in the room. Her visual concentration had not changed. Because of the music, the event that had taken place, and the overall fact that she was so tied emotionally and physically to the gratefully presentive person before them, water formed in Camille's eyes.

During his entrancing, Soame got lost in his thoughts of who else in the world, of the hundreds upon hundreds of burlesque dancers he's seen worldwide, which of them couldn've duplicated the moves presented in front of him. Some were quite general, but the majority he'd not seen before. With heels, she glided across the floor on the ball of her feet, in phases doing somewhat a soft shoe, but the spirally movements of her body, with the luring invitation of her hands and arms, confused the vision as to which part of her to watch; she never snagged in the plush carpet.

Noticing the suspended far away look in his eyes, she stopped directly in front of him, with spread legs. Vulgarity was out of context with the display of her presentation, but the two full revolutions of her hips, with "hunches" between and ending the mid body circles, commanded his strict attention, and swayed all their interests to the indifference in style. They had all before, seen her dance with vulgarness. The injection was so ruthlessly out of place, and done with so much force and impact, it shocked them all with amazement. Beverly threw her hands to her mouth, and unconsciously cried out "uuuh." Chairly jumped and gazed with stretched eyes. Margrett's head snapped with a twisting jerk; her elbow slipped form her knee, and she had to plant the opposite hand on the carpet, to restabilize herself. When Soame's concentrative stare found the direct path once again, to her eyes, he lowered his view to her midsection movements, and following the last ranging hunch, he looked back into the blazing concentration, that saw only him. As if she had stumbled and fallen, Camille vehemently cried out "Oh my Lord, DD!!" In his reflective thoughts, Soame realized, if she could've found her way, DD would had easily "made it" at any top club in America as a dancer. In Berlesque, she would have ranked as a queen. The record was fading; she turned her back to him, and with refined skill, lowered the zipper in the center portion of the gown.

"She's got Betty Davis Eyes" by Kim Kanres allowed DD to give a full demonstration of parade burlesque. Using the slit in the dress, and its unfolded top, she strolled with twining movements, in and out, circling his immediate front. Her nipples and their encirclements were capped with a glittering substance, but her full breasts were not exposed. One arm held the top of the gown, under the low portions of her breasts. The other hand exposed portions of her leg and thigh, when her feet were parallel. It was most enticing; especially when she bent over, and in his face lowered the top, and while shaking her shoulders, allowed the glands to juggle loosely, in front of his eyes. The hassock was next to the recliner.

Standing erect, still holding the top under her breast, flapping the slit, rotating and swerving her hips, DD indicated with the pointing of the tip of her shoe, "here darling, place it here." The record was fading; she brought one of the stools, also closer to his sight.

DD had gotten Camille's attention while placing the stool, and asked her to hold the last recording. She then seated herself on the love seat, and it was there Camille removed the pins from her hair, allowing it to fall loosely past her shoulders. The pole lamp was focused to her, seated with her head bowed appearing to be sleepy, when the music resumed. To the tune of *"Gypsy Woman,"* by Jerry Butler and the Impressions, DD rose in her stocking feet, doing a graceful spin. After turning twice, placing herself directly in front of Soame, they all became fascinated; she did it. Of them, only he had see her do it before. Even if it could have been captured in slow motion, it would have been only more spellbinding: while turning, she released the top portion of the garment. In the pivotal stops in front of him, she beckoned his strict attention with her hands and arm gestures, in presenting her waist. Standing in place, DD tantalized him, with the swirling, twirling, movements of her hands and hips, she presented "The Dubanee Special." She caught the bust portion of the gown, before it touched the carpet. After bringing it back, to her pubic regions, she "hoochechooed" in a way so sensuous, the other women applauded. Stepping out of the gown, she laid it across his lap, and form that point, with her dancing, she used the hassock and stool as aids for her visual posing shots. The three piece ensemble she was clad in, featured a pair of thong bikinis. At the beginning of the fade of the records, DD was standing spread legged, with her back to him, in front of the foot stool. Butterfly style, she bent forward. Using one hand to brace on the hassock, she used the other to pull the silk strip to the side. Over her shoulder, she was looking back at him "Suarmmeee" she softly called, releasing the material, and as the music closed, the silk had been wind and grined back into place.

DD strolled with vivaciousness to the love seat. Soame rose with applause and "bravos," placing the gown on the back of the chair, disrobing. Walking to her he said, "I regret only that I do not have at least a dozen long stemmed roses for you, you were more than grand, and beyond regal. It is the best I have ever seen anywhere." Placing his robe over her shoulders, he continued, "You have truly earned the contents of both my slide and my clip." She kissed him with enthralling passion. When that kiss was over, he smacked her lips once again. It as nothing new to them, seeing the couple kiss. All of them had kissed and been kissed; even so, they stood around watching, waiting to offer congratulations to DD. Camille had tears in her eyes. "Free drinks for everyone" he called out. "Big deal" replied Margrett. Everyone laughed to the bar. "I have a wine you will love" he told her, taking position behind the counter, Fifi had been lifted to the top of.

Twenty minutes later the talks had simmered, and found Beverly for the second time, having been refused to participate in "any" drinking activity, including the sweet black cherry wine. She smoked reefer openly and sneaked, while often doing powder with Chairly, but really had no inclination to drink. She had sat at the bar, without dampened feelings, enjoying soda, and appreciating the high from the grass she smoked. Both DD and Camille told Soame about information they had forgotten to pass on to him: He had purchased just over 3,300 acres of land from Tom; he had also leased the same amount. In the original agreement, "Bottumland" was the referred term to prime soil. Soame had also extended a cash loan to Tom. A certain amount of prime land was to both be sold and leased. The official papers, redone and notarized by Jack Stillman, which were still being reviewed in the package by Roland Burtrume, clearly showed the entire 2,500 acre plot at the Hodges place being leased to Soame. Camille had a copy of all the papers being reviewed by Burtrume, at the office. She duplicated, from them, a sheet showing the notarized entente signed by Soame and Tom. This paper also depicted the stipulation, wherein if the loan had not been paid in five years—to the date—the leased land would become Soame's, in lieu of payment, by forfeiture. This did not bring the vision of owning the land in the future, as a prospect to Soame. However, he was happy about the fact, through the co-op, he was actually farming the land, already green with winter wheat. Once he explained this to them, Camille responded, "you really are a farmer."

"There was a phone call for you also darlinggg."

"I know, I found out earlier. I'll tell you about it later. Right now, before it's too late, I've got to get dressed and go to the house. I've got work to do."

"Suarme, what! At this hour in the morning? It's almost 2:00"

"Well, my idea is toward putting together 150 dimes and 50 quarters. I can't afford to have Billy run out, without a reup."

"That means putting my scale into operation, I will go to." That started the break up from the bar. "That means I'll have the bed to myself for a while, it would really be good if this was tomorrow night, we don't have to be at the new place until 9:30 Wednesday." Camille told them, walking toward the bedroom.

Beverly and Chairly were unfolding the sofa, Margrett was dragging the bean bag back into place. Soame looked at the two at the sofa, while getting DD's gown and gloves, "how about you two cleaning the bar." He then thought about the letter and recorder. Circling toward the desk, he gathered the shoes and told Margrett, "You want to get dressed and come with us? I want you to learn how to do something."

Chapter 6

NEIL and Soame had been talking in the breezeway at least ten minutes, when Beauford drove up. Upon their initial encounter, with a shake of hands and greetings, Soame extended to him a three finger "lid" of Panama Red, after finding out he smoked. The day before, Beauford had given him almost the equivalent in gold, and according to Neil, the presumption expressed by Beauford was, "Soame will probably give ya some of that to, and if he doesn't, that'll tide ya over for a while; it's some really good stuff. I've had it for a week and can't smoke no more in a half a one." Soame didn't tell him the distinction between the two grades. Their qualities spoke for each, if they were to be separated.

Their opening conversation was about school. As a parent and head of a household, Neil was quite concerned about the opening of school, with September less than two weeks away. It was almost a certainty, if there was to be a town and school, it would be at least two weeks late opening for the scarcity of teachers factor alone. Many teachers had moved from the county, some had already been commuting from other counties, and a few as far away as North and South Dakotas, which both state lines were within a seventy mile distance. Busing was scant in mentioning, and the state issue involvement was presented. Then it was brought to light by Neil, the town had actually been written off, to the benefit of particular politicians, but the subject was changed, before Soame could probe.

"Sure, I've already told you it's a workable idea, and explained some of the problems I'm confronted with to the sheriff, but it's my baby, and it's not only my plan, it's also my most concentrated desire to make it work, if this town can pull the appropriations to support itself, while I try. Even with the foundry, from the ground, I'll be starting from scratch. Boxes are wood products. My idea is the wood that goes into today's modern homes, throughout America." Neil injected, "we've got a lot of that around here and throughout the state; wood should be the least of your problems."

Beauford then walked up, and after greetings were exchanged, "I was telling Neil about my idea of the implantation of the colonial style furnishings, using the mini furniture concept, and he's mentioned the abundance of wood here in Montana. I've looked into what's available here, and the best this state has suited for my purpose is cedars. Even at that, the read cedar, I'll have to import from southern Alabama and northwest Florida." This statement took both the other men by surprise. They looked at each other, and back at him and his motion. Both knew and recognized a firm delivery, and through to it's conclusion, there would be a precise explanation, with the fifth largest state in the union being a quarter covered with forests. Soame went on.

"Mind you now, the idea being expressed here pertains to the best woods used in modern day furnishings. The major manufacturing markets are in North Carolina, Connecticut, and parts of northern Florida. In this state, a large percentage of the wood in the forests is not available, because it's on national reserve. That which is available is predominantly related to the pine family. My ideas and plans do not include the manufacture of pine boxes." He sternly looked into both their eyes, as emphasis on the point, without stopping. Beauford was the only one of them wearing shades.

"Though it may be expensive, and almost next to impossible to do, I'll get some red wood from California. That'll be like getting wood out of one of the national forests, here in Montana." They each gave a gruffing chuckle, in verification of one of the points earlier stressed. I'll only use top quality woods such as mahogany from Iowa; black walnut, hickory, red cedar and pecan, I can get from the state lines of Alabama and Florida. Georgia is also an available spot for those woods, but from here, it's a greater freighting expense. Cedar is the less expensive, and a very soft wood. Compared to the redwood from California, it has a resemblance, especially under a polyethylene finish, which is the process I plan to use. The beauty of the two woods, presented in such a manner is incomparable. However, the red wood form California, and the other hard woods I've mentioned, speak for themselves as lasting quality products."

"Here's where I am in getting of the ground, even with the working space I've leased. It's easy to say, 'sit up a factory,' but I cannot produce boxes without wood. To set up for production, I've got to have men go into woods and forests, bring out logs, and from there the logs have to be carried out to roads, and loaded on trucks. The logs are transported to mills from there, to be stripped and cut into boards. The boards, in various sizes have to be transported here, from that point and handled as a shop product. I haven't mentioned treatments, curing processes, and the time involved, which are additional cost involved in the procedure of getting set up."

"Sure, the federal government may be willing to grant a half million dollars to this area, for industrial expansion. We all know the need and what the money will be used for. While the people of the area work and earn a living from the industry who provides?" Beauford then removed his hand from his chin, which with his other arm folded, he'd been holding pyramid style. Then place both hands on his belt. "Soame, can ya do it? Now yesterday ya told me about the half million in salaries and equipment, you'd have ta use ta lift this off the ground, over a years time. You've phrased it so simply, we understand very well. The question still is, can you do it?"

Soame looked at him, smiled, looked away, took a step away from them, and in reapproaching looked at Neil with a smile. Then after easing the freshly cleaned Stetson back on his forehead replied, "Um tryin to figure a way to tell you this. In fact, that's how we got into the discussion before you arrived. Twice before I've tried at this idea, and it'll work this time because of the concentrated area, availability of the skilled men I'm keeping on hand, and your interest and help. Let me ask you this: you guys ever have a favorite western star, or watch many cowboy movies?" It was Neil who responded "Sure, we all did as kids, that's what basically made us the men we are today; the images we saw on the screen. I still get into a good western on occasion, when a good one comes on TV." Beauford, after nodding his head in consent to Neil's acknowledgment, gave a really serious look into Soame's brown eyes asking, "Why do ya ask a question like that? Cowboys don't make jewelry boxes." Neil laughed, and in seeing the seriousness involved in the confrontation, cleared his throat and sniffled. "Well Beauford, that's exactly why we're here today, and the express reason as to why I stated, 'Your interest and help.' No they didn't make jewelry boxes, but in particular every western movie, where there was a town atmosphere, you saw cowboys hanging out in saloons. In the saloon, there was money, liquor and women. For the total success of this project, that's the type of atmosphere we're in the process of establishing." The two local men looked at each other in wonder.

"The people here don't have money to spend, and because of there being no money in circulation, the town's becoming a ghost town." He saw Neil's eyes light up, and gestured his hearing the matter out." Men from other towns and states will be flocking here to spend money, on products they're interested in. They'll do that because they can get what they want, in better quality, and at a better deal than they can anywhere within a thousand miles of this town. It'll be like the end of a cattle drive for some. This is how cities like Kansas, Cheyenne, Wichita, and Abilene got started. That's how you'll make money Neil, they'll have to eat."

"Looking at Beauford he said, "fast food service is the now thing. You don't need to bring in, or allow a fast food service chain. Like since the beginning of capitalism on the western front, in the movies, whenever there is money in circulation, and being rapidly exchanged in an area, you're gonna find women around, getting part of the action. Prostitution is the oldest profession on the face of the earth. An attempt at trying to look over it, with what's being set up, is like trying to overlook nature."

Beauford then spoke, "I am far and way out in front of ya with this one. I wondered when you would get around to it, and what type approach ya'd use; what your idea on the matter will be like…I'll tell ya this muhch, and I know this about the situation: one way will cause us nothing but headaches, and will eventually get us all into trouble. There's another way, which might work, but it'll take the right person who knows what they're doing, and even at that beign conservative is almost an understatement."

It was the exact indirect precise commitment Soame wanted to hear him make, and responded, "first of all, I want no prostitution as part of this motel." He saw surprise in both their faces. "My idea is to carrel it in one specific location, off the main drag, and not allow it any place else. In other words, a house." He could tell the idea disillusioned what either of them had in mind, and continued. "As it stands, I haven't worked out the finer points in detail yet, because I do not have the personnel. I am not a pimp; I will not allow any woman of my household to have anything to do with the matter, except Camille. She keeps books on all of my involvements. Other than that, it's my plan to locate and import beauties for the purpose."

Beauford looked away from him, scratched and rubbed the side of his jaw. Looked back at Soame, took his hat off, and with the other hand scratched his head, while walking toward the eastern end of the breezeway. He walked to the midway point in the hall, and turned back. "Soame, we've got ta be right on the line with this, and if it's mishandled, it could very well blow the entire operation."

"That's exactly what I'm telling you. I'm stretched out in quite a few areas right now. Everything is formulating toward prospective success. With my expenditures, one idea is basically operative either with, or in support of the other. The jewelry box factory is the primary interest to us all. It is an expensive project, that will pay in return, far beyond it's investments. These ideas are in support of that main project. Let's put this undeveloped matter at rest, for the present time. Give me ten days to clear and put into force one or two of my other projects, and with them in motion, I can then concentrate on this matter, and give you a full measured plan. In answer to your prior question, if I can do it? Everything I've got and have invested in, even the preliminary stages of the ground work involved in getting Neil started, is geared to the development and success of that factory. I appreciate again, your interest and support, we will succeed."

"That's all I really want ta hear Soame. Whenever ya need me, I'll be there." Beauford told him with a hard hand shake. He, while still holding Soame's hand, looked over at Neil saying, "In the meantime, no one else is ta know about any of this."

"Right Sonny." The sheriff had released the hand he was holding, and did a full turn to Neil, with his profile to Soame's view. He looked at the other local man with timid embarassment; his lips moved between a frown and a smile, exposing his dimple. Turning back to Soame, there was a wide grin on his face. Neil walked up to his side. They were like two little boys, as an impression, when Beauford gave Neil a nudge and chuckled with his grinning saying, "That's my name Soame. Has been sicne I was a kid, Beauford 'Sonny' Allison, that's me." Neil added, "Just you wait until election time, the posters read 'Sonny' Allison." Soame smiled, thinking of "unks," and the picture of the childhood frineds presented. He asked Neil, "How long do you plan on holding the rooms? I told Smitty you might be here until the end of the week. Pete Thompson is inside, he's the forman of a construction crew I have in opeation. We should get together with him, before you leave, and come up with a plan for the building you'll be working from." Beauford stepped from the walk onto the pavement, looking to the side saying, "I'll see ya'll later, I've been away form my radio almost forty-five minutes, ya'll have a good day."

He assured Neil there was no rush in him leaving the motel. After giving him his home number, they made plans to get together with Pete at close of the week, and devise a sketch, projecting their combined conceptions, as to how the structure should look. DD and Margrett remained at the house. When all the "bagging" was done, Soame and DD stayed up, talking, looking at videos and making love. She prepared breadkfast for them, for the first time in a long while. After calling Camille, and arranging to drive her to work form the motel, he drove her car, waited in the lot. The late model Plymoth drove roughly. It skipped, the brakes were faulty, and for some time, he had been asking her about getting new tires. In route to the office, he mentioned the needed repairs and asked when she'd changed the oil last. The door sitcker showed a three year old date. "I only dirve it to work. It runs fine to me; I'm not talking it out of town, so it serves its purpose and I'm satisfied with it." Parking at the office he asked, "what were you going to do about the car if you had to move Camille?"

"Well, I didn't have to move, and now both me and this car are fine…. she won't be in until after 9:00, you coming in for a while?" He knew what the invitiation meant. In accepting, he found it to be turbulently boisterous, with unrulyness. He was inside the office almost an hour.

While talking with Neil near the breezeway, after the sheriff drove off, the two men started walking toward the front of the building. Midway the front portion of the building, Soame heard the scratching of Fifi's paws on the walk. He turned, saw the dog, and bided good day to Neil. Chairly and Beverly were rounding the breezeway corner. "Hay Pooch, and just where are you two going?"

"I thot da furst thang ya sae in da monin is?"

"Oh yea, well gooood morning, now wh—"

"Good monring Soame, my sister called about thirty minutes ago, and the clothes we had an early delivery on, arrived; we saw Beauford's car leave, and came on this side like you told us, because of the carpenters. We're on our way to the house."

"Have you had breakfast?"

"We don haveta eat no brekfast! Sides, we can eat, whin we git dare."

"I'll bet you know, just about everything to know, in your whole big world, don't you?"

"Chile com on, he don wanna do nothin but mess wid us. Thank he so smort." Fifi was sitting at his feet "see ya later Soame" Beverly waved follwing Chairly. "Com on hea gurl, foe he try da git smort agin. Here Fifi, come, come."

"Arff arff"

"You two be careful with yourselves."

"We will Soame, don't worry." Chairly was silent, but slung her hips, looked back and gave a "bye bye" wave.

He went to the room behind the office, called the Blanchard house, took ten minutes in explaining not being able to make the afternoon date; a trip to Rapid City was his reason. It was a beautiful day, already the temperature had climbed to 63 degrees. Soame drove the jeep to the office, had a brief conversation with Mrs. Tillman. Asked for Camille's keys, and drove her car to Rapid City.

The meeting uplifted his lifted spirits. He would have enjoyed being with someone, but chose to spend the time alone. DD and Camille separately, was too much of an experience to make the encounter with Janet and Cindy later, and he knew better than to over exert himself and, or disappoint either of them. What he told Beauford was exact. He knew what he basically wanted to do, but did not know how he would go about doing it. Such was the presentation to the sheriff. Soame knew what he wanted to tell him; he nevertheless, being forward with the presentation of the idea of prostitution, had not been easy. Once again he had put himself somewhat "on the spot." Beauford once again prevailed, with the carry through of his prior commitment. Inside and throughout, Soame felt rejuvenated. The drive alone, cherishing his private thoughts, added to his vivacious feeligns of personal accomplishment.

His first stop after entering the city was at a car wash. While being pulled through the automatic service, he began comprising his list, for replacement accessories he would drive by an auto parts store and inexpensively pruchase wiper baldes, interior lamp cover, brake peddle cover, a leather cover for the steering wheel and a few other noticeable items he looked for, with that particular interest. After thoroughly vacuuming the interior, he raised the hood. Checking the radiator cap, he found it to be rusted, the rubber lining was hard and brittle. It was added to the list as a replacement.

Sight seeing, he found his way to an auto parts center. After purchasing the items, including new floor mats, Soame asked for directions to the nearest Goodyear service center .There, he had the Plymouth analyzed on a diagnostic computer, and requested a tune up according to the results. There was also to be an oil change, and a set of all weather tires. Mrs. Tillman was the most respected woman in the town he lived in, for some time he had known that .The former school principal retired from the school system, and after a period of mourning, began handling operations at her late husband's realty agency. A month or so prior to his individual trip to Rapid City, in her talks of the noteworthiness of her employer, Camille said, "If she was a man, she would have long ago been mayor." That morning in the office he asked Camille if she'd ever gotten stuck daring the winter. "I'd call the office, she'd send the jeep you drive, over to either pull me out, or simply give me a lift. People have always been happy to do anythhing for her. I don't know of anything she can't have done in this town, with a simple phone call." Before leaving the car for the repairs and adjustments, he added a pair of winter treads, with the complete brake job that was to be done.

It would be at least an hour and a half before the car went up on the rack, to be greased and lubed. He called a cab and visited an Army surplus center. Pete and a couple of his other employees for a while, had been teasing him about the "fancy" boots and shoes he wore, and the approach of winter. Even though their remarks were in a teasing fashion, he knew and distinguished the warnings extended to him. Soame knew what cold was really all about; once during a military training procedure, he was sneakily dropped into Siberia in the heart of winter. In the store, he selected two pairs of fur lined, insolated boots, two pile caps, and glove shells. The gloves he then had to buy would be a size too large. He had confidence in the fact, with a wool skull cap over a pile cap, his head would be warm, during a winter in Montana.

The cab driver had gladly accepted the $100.00 bill, for the two hour hire. Their next stop was to the "best ladies boutique" in city, according to the driver. It was in a plaza. The Thursday before, in spending time at the farm house with Cindy and Janet, he learned of her application acceptance at both Oregon State, and the University of Wisconsin. The day Soame and Tom went to town, from home she sent the two applications, with cash through their mail box. To his summation, judging from what Janet said the night before, the big news Cindy wanted to break to him, was her accepted admission into the other Oregon school. The one she favored above the others. Her size was 5; he purchased ten pairs. Five regular styled and five thong bikini panties. They were in an assortment of colors. With them he also purchased two top and bottom sets of sheer sleeping wear, with two matching robes; one long and the other short. He saw a sleeping shirt he liked, which probably could have been bought anywhere, but he chose it for her. The picture on the shirt front reminded him of her personality. The giraffe could not be distinguished as being old or young; it's pleasing, bright eyed look, enabled the thought of it being cuddly. Soame and Cindy, with Cindy and Soame was the design he wanted monogrammed on the panties and shirt. During the thirty minutes it took for the lettering, the driver browsed with him, in a nearby bookstore.

The first book he selected was a biography. Throughout the days of Hollywood, there has been but one "Garbo." From the silent screen era, through the transition into the "talkies," Gretta Garbo left her name with the movies she made, as an everlasting symbol of grace, achievement, struggle, and triumph to the Hollywood and world. In a course called cinema, Soame had studied them all. Long before he took the course, and that day saw the book by Alexander Walker, "Garbo" of them all was his favorite. Instantly he thought of "Mizz Fine" and the probable impression the book would make.

Soame bought for DD "The Egyptian" by Mika Waltari, "Oliver Wiswell," by Kennith Roberts was chosen for Camille, and before leaving he purchased two books for Cindy: "The Count of Monte Cristo" by Alexander Dumas and "Fountainhead" by Ann Rand. Except for the "Garbo" book, he had read them all, and knew the individualistic pleasure each book would bring the person it was chosen for.

At the boutique, the person who'd done the monogramming encountered a minor problem, but completed the beautifully done work regardless. Soame was left with the option to purchase, and displayed no hesitancy in responding, "That's fine, in fact, it's excellent, and would you wrap them also." There was no difficulty in placing both names on the bikini panties, but there was only room for one, to be positioned on the thongs. His name, in contrasting color, with a small heart was what she exhibited, in the material he saw. After selecting a card, he left the shop and went two doors to optical store. Soame spent ten minutes in choosing a pair of replacement glasses for Janet. The gift wrapping had been completed at the boutique, when he returned. With a $10.00 tip, he drew smiles when he extended the shades to be wrapped also.

In route back to the service center, they passed a pawn shop. On a notion, he had the driver turn back and stop. He really went in to see if there was a selection of old records and albums available. When he was told there were none, he looked around and saw the "special of the week." The 35 mm camera looked new. The carrying case and flash equipment came with it. Soame recognized the $450.00 value as a real deal, at $150.00; he bought it. At the service center he tipped the "cabbie" a ten spot, went in, paid his tab, checked the trunk for the winter tire, and was on his way. He'd seen the nearby floral shop while riding in the cab. The dozen long stemmed roses he did not have the night before, he obtained. Driving into town, he'd passed a Buick dealership displaying banners, balloons, streamers, and big signs at various points of the lot, reading "September clearance, NOW!!!" Soame stopped on the opposite side of the road, walked across the thoroughfare, and onto the lot. He looked from car to car, with no particular interest. In less than ten minutes, a salesperson approached him. All the cars in the lot he' been walking about, were new. The two talked less than five minutes. A row away four cars down, the salesperson pointed to a particular car. Elaboration took place for another minute; a handshake was exchanged, with the presentation of a business card. Soame walked away and drove home.

Camille usually didn't leave the office until 4:30. She was still there when he arrived. In presenting her key and the book for her, he also explained the selected book for Beverly. The idea really impressed her, and when she saw the full page size pictures of the famed actress, while fanning through the pages, the idea manifested with brilliance. He asked where the others were, and found out everyone else was at home. DD's book was then given to her, and asked also to be presented. It was 4:19, Mrs. Tillman had gone for the day. Except for the early morning breakfast, he had not eaten. The sensitive kiss Camille gave him, had a very strong invitation, and though he wanted to accept, Soame was working, and his day was not finished; she understood. Because of how and where he parked it, she had not seen the car. He removed the remaining items to the Jeep and drove to the motel.

After parking in front of the "accounting" room, all the packages were removed from the Jeep, and taken into the room, except for the roses. Cindy answered his call to the Blanchard home. "Hello," "How are you Kitten, what's happening?"

"You're what's happening Mr. Hudson, how was your day in Rapid City?"

"That depends on how well your day went Miss Blanchard, on the Blanchard Farm."

"Days around here are sort of routine. I've got some exciting news to tell you darling."

"Well, that's an excitement within itself. Has it gotten more exciting since last night?" With a slight giggle she replied, "Wellll, I don't know."

"What color panties do you have on?"

"Soame! That's gross over the phone."

"Why? Do you think your line is tapped, and panty sniffing agents might hear this?" Laughingly, she took the mouth piece away from her face, and chuckling, said, "I don't believe this; Soame please!"

"Please what?"

"Alright they're pink, and you're the only panty agent I know of."

"Pink's a pretty color, and I'll guess they're beautiful in your jeans." It was a low volume, cuddly voice, responding "you guessed rii-iight."

"SO! What are you going to wear tomorrow morning at 10:00?"

"You mean, you're going to be there, then?"

"You guessed ri-iight….now, what are you going to be wearing?"

"What would you like?"

"I've already told you."

"Well, why don't you wait and see."
"I'll see you then."
"We'll be there."
"Sleep tight."

With the roses,the moves took him through the dining room door, leaving the flowers on the table, from there upstairs. He'd just poured a drink, when the phone chimed. "Worldwide, Soame."

"Soame, how are you I've called, looked downstairs and saw your Jeep, knocked on your door, and you seemed to have disappeared until now."

"Neil, how's it going?"

"Recognized my voice ha, I'm surprised."

"Well, it's sort of catchy Neil, what's going on?"

"I came up with something that might be of interest to you, I've been thinking about it since I left you this morning, can you meet me in the breezeway for a few minutes?"

"Sure, how about now?"

"I'm on my way." Neil's rooms were upstairs, opposite Soame's bedroom. With a drink in his hand, he simply went out the bedroom door, and saw Neil approaching the breezeway, from the north end of the building.

"My wife and two of my kids are in the room, two of the rooms we have adjoin, and I'll tell you…at times, kids in this town have a better grape vine than we do. Anything you do is hot news around here, right now." He captured Soame by surprise, in his attempts to avoid modesty. "Yea, alright Neil, so what's happening?" They had walked to the center of the upstairs breezeway.

"There's a guy that used to hang around the bar all the time. I've had it closed almost a year and a half, but he's still around lives out in an old farm house, a couple of miles east of town. Soame, he's a discard and a drunk, but he knows more about wood than any man I know of, including the carpenters around there. I took interest in what you had to say this mor—"

"Boss, is that you up there with Neil? Hay Neil how ya doin?" It was Pete, they both heard him walking to, and turning into the passageway. "I've got these papers you said to have signed and completed. "Yea Pete, how does it look."

"Pete, I'm fine, how about yourself?" The two men were descending the stairs; all three came into view of each other. "I'm doing a lot betterin I was doin the last time we saw each other, it's getting where I can stretch my legs out under my table now and then." Neil patted him on the shoulder, in the exchanged of handshakes. Pete looked at Soame passing him the mentioned forms saying, "I came over to glance at the last of the detailing. Tim says it's all done; the place is ready accordin ta him. It's looks pretty good, I'll come by first thing in the mornin, go through everything, and let you know later on, at the big house."

"Do you know anything about bar-b-q grills Pete?"

"Indoor or outdoor?"

"Indoor."

"Well, the drafts important in both, but with an indoor grill, ya want ta be sure all your smoke goes up and out the chimney. Jake's one of the best bricklayers I've seen anywhere. From there it depends on how big the place is to be, and if it's commercial, how many ya plan ta seat, the size of your counter and so forth. You plan on puttin up a stand?"

"Yea, what we have in mind is to put Neil here into operation, on the opposite end of his café there. I figure we can work on it, and the fence together, with the fence being up by the close of next week."

"You said the lumber will be here next Tuesday, right?"

"Right, and I've got a much bigger job in mind, that should lead us right into the foundry, if it all works our right…I'll tell ya what Pete…run the bar-b-q stand idea through your mind, to accommodate seating arrangements for 12-15 people, wouldn't you say Neil?"

"Sounds about right, in fact it's almost precisely what I have in mind to, you see Pete, what we're trying to get our ideas together on, is a bar-b-q fast food service. That lot is 50 x 30, I see it with a counter sitting three or four people, and the remainder of the seating accommodations for two rectangular type tables in front, behind a picture window, and another table of the same type, on the side, back, wall. With each table seating four people, and a register on the counter, I'd say the inside should give us what we want, with still a lot of parking space for the come and go carryouts."

Pete appeared to be enthused about the idea. The foreman looked from Neil to Soame. "How about thinking it over, as to what style building to put up. In the morning, meet me at the house. We'll run the idea across to Jake, before the decorators get there. Maybe they can give us some ideas also. Friday morning the four of us will meet here at 10:00, we'll inspect this place, then Pete and Jake will put together a draft on paper. How's that with you Neil?"

"I like your planning. My lights were turned on at home today. It's been a long time since I've had my family away from the house. I'll still be here then, if it's alright with you."

"I've told you about that before, as long as you like. So I'll see you in the morning Pete."

"You'll have a good evening; I'm sure we'll have no problems puttin the bar-b-q barn together." Soame and Neil snapped heads, toward each other. Pete walked away, with a wide grin on his face.

"Soame, you got thirty or forty-five minutes? I was telling you about "Neb." Your delivery on wood was really interesting this morning. All day long, I've thought about what you said, and introducing you to a guy, who knows more about timber, wood processing and anything else you might have in mind, to ask or talk about, concerning wood. I'd like to take you out to where he's living, and have you talk with him. I've always thought of him as an interesting fellow; everyone else sees him as a drunk and a bum. I'll be good if we could carry along a bottle of liquor, wine, or whatever you might have to drink."

PART IV

Chapter 7

THERE was no porch furniture, but the house looked a lot better than some of the houses Soame had seen during his travels, in and around town. The place had a deserted look. No one could have guessed someone lived in the house. On the way to the place, in the Jeep, Neil told Soame more about "Neb," and his dog Butch: "That dog of his would wait on the sidewalk in front of the bar, from sundown until sunup, if it took 'ol Neb that long to get a drink. Throughout the day, they'd spend their time rustling through garbage bins, searching through trash cans, and scrounging about here and there, hunting food for Butch." When they drove into the yard, he was saying, "I think they do a little trapping nowadays, and occasionally my brother and the grocer gives them scraps and leftovers. A drink of liquor or wine is pretty hard for the old timer to get these days. Stepping out of the Jeep, Neil called for the panhandler.

"Soame, this is Neb; Neb meet Soame Hudson. He's the person in town, who is turning the old foundry into a factory. I thought I'd bring him by to meet you. You've always talked about wood. Soame here, is going to be using a lot of it. I thought you two might want to talk on the subject of the common interest you have. As Neil talked, the two other men exchanged handshakes. "I'm pleased to meet you, Neil told me also you like the taste of spirits, at times. We brought along something for you to wet your whistle," he said extending the quart of rum to bearded, long haired, shabby looking man, standing on the porch, without shoes.

The visitors were standing on the grown. In accepting the bottle, Neb extended them the invitation to make themselves comfortable on the porch. He took the bottle inside, for glasses, leaving the door wide open. A direct look through the house displayed no furniture. Shortly, he returned with three glasses, and a tall shaggy dog at his side. Butch looked to be part Irish Setter, with a goldish red coat. Neil said, "Hi Butch, hay old feller." The dog gave several wags of his tail, and went to the corner of the porch, where he laid down, with attention toward them. Neil and Soame's feet were on the ground, with their seating positions turned toward Neb. When he offered a drink to Neil, the response was, "Now you know I never touch the stuff. It hasn't been that long since we've seen each other; I haven't changed. Soame told him, "Sure, I'll help you christen your bottle, but just a little. I haven't had lunch or dinner."

Charles Alfred Lynch came down and sat with them. He was an arborist with 104 hours toward an undergraduate degree in forestry, at North Carolina State University. Before receiving his degree, his parents were killed in an automobile accident. At the close of his junior year, during the following summer, he took a position with a furniture manufacturing company near Charleston. He examined and purchased timber for the company, before the logs underwent the milling process, and was converted into planks and boards, which the company was contracted to receive. A year and a half following his employment, he had gotten married. During his four year marriage, he and his wife had a two and a half year old son. His wife and child drowned as a result of a boating accident while they were on a picnic with friends. At the time he was out of town working. He then moved to Connecticut, where he'd had a job offer more than a year prior to the accident. The job description and performance was basically the same, except he did not have to go into forests and examine precut timber. However, he purchased the logs preceding the milling conversion.

At a logging camp, while examining for a prominent disease in the area, he witnessed an accident take place, which shattered his mental, physical, and emotional stability: he saw a flume give way above six men who were instantly crushed to death. He and others watched helplessly, unable to provide aid or assistance. Eight years prior to that day, meeting Soame, he took a job in Fargo, North Dakota, as a salesman at a lumber yard, with a logging firm. He was about to get engaged again, when a careless smoker allowed a cigarette butt to ignite stored chemicals. The fire raged and spread before it could be brought under control. The accident resulted in the entire yard being burning to the ground. Smath was as far as he made it, from the last woman he loved. According to the events that plagued his adult life in succession, he felt he would eventually lose her also, with the life style he had adapted, his consensus was, he was avoiding the tragedy.

Beneath the unkept beard and hair on Neb's head, which showed a tarnish of gray, Soame saw an individual whose face was hardened with events of his past. He had mixed views about Neb, who totaled out in Soame's opinion to be a coward, with a welcome sign and open invitation to the bottle which had been given. He had seen and heard of them in many walks of life: in the military, the suppose to be a soldier, who's trained to destroy the enemy, and becomes frightened and cringes with the exploding sounds of a grenade. The surgeon who, through involved training, completes his course of study, and finds out he cannot tolerate the sight, or rubberized touch of blood. In every major city there is a "break corner." Men of the same caliber and description as Neb, rather than seek regular employment with skill, training and trades they are versed at, stand on the "corner" waiting for a "break." In place of earning a salary at the close of a week, for the exertion of their experience in practicing their skill or trade, they jump cars and trucks in the early hours of the morning, to do anything all day, to be paid minimum wage, for that day's work. These men like Neb are afraid of something. That something inside them affect their way of thinking toward standards, and allows them to except a part of nothing, for a larger part of something. That same flavor of a male will lay in a city, county, or state jail cell for the convenience off "three meals and a cot." Day after day with and to his fellow inmates, he will brag on what he's done, how much he's got on the outside, and how smart, or ridiculous he's been to commit either the petty, or hideous crime he's been sentenced for. In many cases, it's his taste to go no further than the meals he's selected to be satisfied with, and the comfort in living arrangements he's found. Cowardness is an inborn trait, or self satisfaction. Psychologist will term the trait and satisfaction as being unstabilized; are they wrong for not simply terming the person as a coward? Neurologists will "front" the satisfaction, or trait with a term referring to a disorder. Are they themselves, cowards for not openly admitting cowardness, or are they the succeeding strivers toward and for the money?

Soame did not care about Neb's cowardly way, in going through life; he saw through it, and saw the person of keen wit, with a commonly practiced method of "baby doll" or "lolly pop," asking for a chance. Just as Neil said, in his contemptible way of dismantling himself in the bar, begging for drinks. The retribution he self administered the day after day, plundering in filth and discards of others. Neil did not have to tell Soame, nor did Neb have to state his hours of credited schooling. Two minutes after he'd gotten into his delivery, seeking pity, Soame and anyone else who knew and could recognize formally trained character, would have no problem in seeing the toil that had gone into producing the under surface scholar. He chose to defile himself in the presence of unlearned men. He'd deliberately become a degenerate and was placed in living in such a perversed manner of masochism. Neb was a freak, who thrived in the degradation he created for himself. He beseeched the slimy condition, and the scorn from lesser, who were supposed to see him as a member of the higher echelon. He could have been any one else, it would not have mattered. In the very same token, he could have been anything else, and Soame would have walked away leaving Lynch with the remaining contents of the liquor bottle forever. He was a tree specialist, and through Soame's designed plan, in Smath, the finished process for some trees, would be their conversion into jewelry boxes, and some other finely finished products.

Neb told how he and Butch got together in Bismark, and panhandled their way through Rapid City to the town. The puppy looked to be less than six months old, when they found each other at a truck stop. He was the only thing remaining, the drifter had not given up during his adult life. He gave an idea of his worthwhile, staring into Soame's eyes talking directly on the subject he knew Soame wanted to hear a display of his knowledge on, wood. He gave the loacation and types of timber, aging and curing processes, types of grain, and facts Soame had never considered, concerning both hard and soft woods. He was asked if he'd like to possibly make a home of the deserted farm, and clean himself up, and if in doing so he'd consider putting himself back into the mainstream with employment. A positive smile with a seemingly positive attitude brought a $50.00 cash gift, and advice from his future employer, to "be around in the morning, I'll send some supplies for you and Butch. We'll see how it goes from there." The mention of the dog's name brought slaps on the wooden porch floor. The animal had risen to his feet, and stood at his master's side, when Soame and Neil rode away.

Two days prior, Billy had given Soame a wad of bills. During the ride back to town, Soame instructed Neil, "would you take a look in that glove box, and you'll find some cash, count out a hundred dollars. Are you busy in the morning?"

"No, I've told you. This is the first vacation I've had in six years. The last one was a three day weekend visit with my sister. I'm really enjoying myself." Neil spoke with a big smile on his face, almost laughing. "Eating at the restaurant, and with the time I'm spending with you, it's the most I'm doing right now, which amounts to having a ball!" With that he gave a hardy laugh, "Say Soame, I've never had coke or weed so good, and Sonny and I've been smoking grass since we were teenagers. You're about to set up a monopoly, covering a huge range, with the coke; you know that don't you?" Soame looked over to him, "we'll see what happens. You know the area much better than I do. I've got a pretty big overhead, putting machinery, tools, and the purchasing goes on and on."

"Yea, I know you're right there, but shit, if you can supply them, dealers will be coming to you for ounces and pounds at time."

"Maybe so, but the most in quantity to be purchased from that booth is a gram; they can buy a hundred, a thousand grams, or whatever, but the largest piece will be a gram, and the price will be set on the single gram basis, only."

"That's really smart, in fact, it's amazingly unique."

"Not really, it's is simply because of the area. In fact, you see the principal behind the idea, because you've worked a bar. You sell liquor by the shot, rather than by the bottle. Where I'm from, this method is quite basic and common with small time street hustlers, it's called 'Grinding.'"

"That money you have there. I'd appreciate it if you'd fill your car with gas, stop by a store and get Neb two pairs of jeans, three khaki shirts"—"Hold on a minute. I got into the habit of carrying pen and pad, working the bar; right now I'm sort of glad I kept it…shirts, go on." "Underwear, socks, and a pair of work" boots, and get him a baseball cap and a belt too will ya? A hundred bucks ant too much, but with the prices in this town, it'll go a long way. I've got an account at the hardware store. How bout stopping by, and tell Phil I said to let you have that Western Flyer, the old styled one, with the fat wheels, and put it on my bill. Then I'd like for you to go by—get a pair of scissors too, from the hardware, will ya?"

"Scissors, and you were saying go by?"

"The grocery store, get soap, deodorant, aftershave, and a bag of disposable razors for him, a case of canned dog food, and a 50lb. Bag of dried dog food for Butch. Tell your brother I don't care if it's breakfast and dinner, or lunch and dinner, however Neb wants to do it, but two meals a day. You got any cased liquor left?"

"Sure, I've got about fifteen cases, they're assorted sizes and brands."

Neil was looking questionably at Soame and asked, "Now let me get this straight. The things on this list are for Neb. You are getting them for him, because you, wherein you can hire him, not as a shop worker, but in some type of high up position, and you're going to hire him as a drunk Soame?"

"Not really, you've seen and heard it Neil, but you only saw the picture he presented, and haven't thought about what he didn't say. For example if something, and we hope nothing does, but if something happened to you, and you only had one kid who was in college, and he or she inherited all you possessed and cash from your insurances, what would be the first thing you think you'd hope your descendant would do?"

"Soame, I thought about that also, and the fact that he went on through school for the remainder of that year, is what drew my attention to why didn't he finish." Exactly, and from there on, each tragedy encountered by him, nor that one, was his fault. Yet he ran, and the last thing, the fire which supposedly depressed him into the state he's in. hell, it wasn't the Coeurd' Alenes or the Yacolt burn, and even in the camp he was in, he didn't mention anyone being hurt as a result of the fire, he was in no way balmed for it, but he ran again. Though he's lost his parents and family, even those times he ran, after gaining everything else."

"No, I don't want him to be a drunkard. I simply don't believe he has the courage to drink. Like all the other things, in having what he wanted, I think he'll run away from the bottle. Sell me two cases of liquor Neil, fifths or quarts, and let's find out."

"That's amazing, I never would've thought of it that way. You sound as if you may not like him personally Soame."

"I won't give you my personal feelings toward him. They really don't matter, not even to me. I think he might be capable of doing a job for me; for that service, if he can perform, I will pay him a salary. I'll let nothing I know of, in my control, detour, impede, or stop the progress toward the success of the jewelry box factory." He glanced over, and Neil seemed to be staring forward in a trance. "Neil, I have no personal feelings for men. Check this out, Ed lives further out on this road, a mile or two past the place Neb's in. He has a truck."

"I know Ed Bryant, good man you've got with you there Soame."

"Glad to hear your opinion. Tell Lynch, tomorrow after Ed's off from work, I'll be sending bedroom, sitting furniture, and a TV. I'll take you by the room where we have stored the furniture from the rooms that have been renovated, and you can take him some lamps and a mirror. Tomorrow Camille will make arrangements to have the lights turned on, and for other little items like toothbrush and paste, shampoo and conditioner, nail clipper and emory boards, comb and brush, take out another $10.00, oh! Don't forget the q-tips, and let's see how Charles Lynch turns out. Pass me the change will ya?"

At the motel, in getting permission from Smitty to "discard" the stored items, the owner came out to assist them. They were taken to another room which held items he had stored during the years. Soame chose only a radio, of the unclaimed articles. After finding it in proper working order, thanking and parting company with Smitty, the pair then went to Soame's storage place. Neil saw the practical use for two sets of curtains, a small table, pictures, and an ample supply of linen towels, pictures to hang, and a couple of pillows, with blankets and spreads. His idea was in taking the items to Neb first thing, and return with him, to fit the clothing and footwear. Consenting to the idea, Neil was shown the door being left unlocked for his return entry, and the two men stepped out on the porch.

"Soame, there's one remaining thought that sort of nags me about this. You've brought to light the fact about Neb's running away."

"What is it dude? Um hungry, and trying to get home to dinner."

"In this sense, here also you seem to be supplying him with what he needs, and if he works out, in time he'll no doubt get what he wants. Doesn't that set up the same type scenario?" Looking and speaking to Neil in a direct and positive way, he replied, "After the factory is set up and gets underway, even I can be replaced Neil…now if you're superstitious, the insurance I have will replace everything else. I'm not related to him. However, you may be a far distant cousin or rel—hold on a second, where're you goin' Neil?" Neil had given Soame a serious stare, indicated "no" with his head, turned his back, and while walking off, gave Soame the "Hell no, get away from here with that absurdity" sign, with the hand wave, and in answering, slightly turned, looking back, "I'll get those things out, take them to him in the morning, and tell him what you asked me to, and bring him into town. You're one heck of a guy. I'm really glad to be working with you Soame, I'll see you later." It had been the humor of the day for Soame. Twilight had sat in over the surroundings.

"Hello," "What's for dinner?"

"Darling, rest afterwards; you need to come home, have your food and rest Suarme. You are driving yourself really hard."

"Oh, well now that may be just a fact I will consider."

"I got the book, thank you, I'm sure I will enjoy reading about our culture you used to talk about."

"Yea well, it does well in that way, and in another it offsets the known fact with distortion. The Egyptians were a black race of people. I've told you before, the people who are now predominant in Egypt are descendants form the first Creoles, who were offspring of slave Europeans. They were imported into Africa, and after being bred, the original Creole was treated as an outcast, accepted by neither the black masters, or the enslaved caucasoids. Through time they had no choice but to unite. The now Egypt is a demonstration of power of the two races. The story in the book also shows the Jew as a prominent member of the society, during that period, which is a joke beyond the description of a farce. Remember, as members of the Caucasian family, they were also slaves and that sect were being slaughtered at one period, because the prophesied rumor predicted one of them to be born a leader. There Moses 'the greatest con man of all times' came about, and after being found, was raised in a black household, which afforded him the education, as an avenue toward his exploits. The author of the story depicts the Jew as a rich land owner with flourishing enterprises, owning horses, being carried from place to place in carriages, on the shoulders of Negroes. Believe this, during the times when that story was supposed to have taken place, any and every Jew in Egypt was doing and would have done, any and everything they could do to get out of there.

The absolute and proving fact about it, is in what is expected in the Christian world, as the Ten Commandments. According to what Moses is to have said, 'Out of the land of Egypt, from the house of bondage.' When I read the book, I looked over those purposeful insurrections by its writer. I will have to aid you through it, for it's worthwhile, in relation to us, and a true reflection of Egypt."

"Suarme, I thought you implied you are hungry."

"I am and are you going to read me a bed time story from your new book, when I have eaten?"

"I have something better in mind. No one has eaten, we are waiting for you. Come eat, and I will show you something from the pages of the book I already know by hart."

"Um on my way."

Following the presentation of the roses, the dinner was enjoyed by them all. Because she still had her monthly sickness, and at times experienced cramps, Margaret was not in accord with the bright and cheery atmosphere at the table. Camille seemed somewhat disturbed, and toward the end of the meal, Margaret excused herself to lay down, and Soame inquired to Camille, "Are you alright? Is there something wrong?"

"With the car and all! This should be a very happy day for me. Until just before I left the office, it was. I've got something to tell you, let's wait until we leave the table."

DD knew of the mistake Camille made. Camille knew parts of the chastisements DD and Chairly received the previous day. This did not phase her, in that direction; her concern was toward the possibility of a setback, in Soame's planning. Chairly and Beverly displayed the new items from Denver and proceeded to clear the table, to wash the dishes. The majority of the goods delivered by the parcel service were for Richard, who would not join them until after the move. Soame thought of the leather cushioning, which had not been wrapped around the steering wheel. The wipers and mats had been installed. There was also the new interior lamp cover. According to Camille's praises and thanks, it was like driving a new car. Earlier, when she arrived home from work, she took DD for a ride. The both were invited outside, for their company, during the remaining installations. While lacing the leather she told him, "today I received a phone application for the butler and maid positions. It took my attention to the calendar, where I noticed the date. The other ad was to have started yesterday, the 22nd. I misread the calendar, and to each newspaper, I requested the ad to begin on the 29th, which is the coming Monday. It was a mistake I made, that'll cause a weeks delay in the publication of the ads, in all five papers. I'm so terribly sorry Soame, I really am."

"Well, they say whatever happnes, happens for the best. I believe, if it happens, and it's not according to plan, a person with perseverance will salvage, and make the best of the situation." This did not stop stringing and wrapping the vinal cord. DD was comfortably laying across the back seat, with the door open, snuggled in the black fur of his matching Harbormaster. She playfully added, "I do not think that is fair Suarme. Aren't you going to have her do some 'I'm so terribly sorry Suarme's? I will at least count them for her."

"It was a mistake. I really cannot fault her for a mis"—"Oh, but I will gladly do some, I've heard how they are done."

"Oh yea, well Miss Instigator in the back seat still owes me more than Gold."

"I do not! It is 427 from this morning."

"So, well now, if you did some, you would also have to add that little tidy finish you put on the end there…how does it go, I really am." He had done a prankly imitation of her. The two women bust into laughter, during his seldom comical gesturing, and mood. "Alright, alright, I'll add that also and do 50, how's that sound?"

"You!" He turned and pointed to DD. "Vodka and reffer for us. Bring the coke and close that door."

Chapter 8

"It won't work boss, I understand how you feel about the idea, and if there was a safe possibility of doing it, I'd say yea maybe, but I won't tell ya wrong, ya been good to all of us…Soame that idea will not work."

Up to that point Soame thought he was "on a roll." His ideas were falling into shape, within the force, the way they were being used as practical measures. It was the first time he'd expressed his planned mechanics, involved in the conversion of the house he lived in, into a two story club and "house." He and Pete had been told by the other, as they came in for work, about the meeting in front of the fireplace they could dip their heads and walk into. It's hearth measure 45' from the foyer entrance. The other carpenters were practically all drinking coffee with the conversations they were having. They were not in ear shot range of the talks going on at the fireplace.

There was no response from Soame. Pete knew he awaited the explanation, as to why not? "First of all, your first floor wall structure is not built to support a second floor, and if we took the roof off, removed the rafters, gutted the entire interior walls ta making bearing walls, we still couldn't give enough support beneath the floor to take on the added floor, walls, rafters and roof, with twenty people, two showers, and four toilets. It would collapse. I haven't mentioned your ten beds and other lounge furniture, including the big screen. Soame, it all has to come down and be rebuilt, if the basement floor and walls can support it, even then…the Swede built the place, let's call him over, and see what he says about it. Want me to call him?" It had been a real setback in thought and concentration. He really liked the spot. Though there were other houses, some already two story, his idea was concentrated to that spot. Wearily he replied to Pete, "Yea, sounds like the thing to do from here."

…"The Swede," Yohan's Father's Grandfather migrated from Sweden to Massachusetts. During the initial phase of the Civil War, within a week after the surrender of Fort Sumter, Massachusetts sent the first of its newly formed regiments to Washington. The first Yohan was a member of that 6th Massachusetts group, formed as a militia. In route to Washington, to change trains in Baltimore, the volunteer fighting military group marched through the city, and encountered a mob of furiously enraged secessionist civilians. Brickbats and paving stones were thrown, pistols were fired, and Yohan with other soldiers fired their muskets. Both civilians and militiamen were killed. On that day, Yohan killed the only man he would kill during the Civil War.

Through the investigation of the incident, Yohan was discovered to be a blacksmith, by civilian trade. As a blacksmith, he was assigned to a unit along the Potomac. There he saw the change of command three times, with Generals of the Union Army. As a non fighting soldier in the North's best kept and most powerful army, Yohan was liveryman for McClellan, Hooker and under General Meade, he was made sergeant. He was then selected by Secretary of War Stanton, in a company of other carefully chosen soldiers to accompany and escort Smath, to the Eastern Montana area. At that time, only the Eastern sector of Montana was a state, through the Louisiana Purchase of 1803. Yohan was transferred with his group, shortly after the discovery of gold on Grasshopper Creek.

It was the incident in Baltimore on April 19th, 1861 with the 6th Massachusetts, which caused President Lincoln to see the severity of the loss of Maryland to the South. He then put into force every possible means, and secured the state in the Union. In 1865, after the close of the war, the first Yohan became a civilian, and prospected for gold, in a nearby mining community, he found a sweetheart. After their marriage, Yohan brought his wife out of the wilderness, to the area he'd been in during the last phase of his military service. In the area of the foundry, which had not yet been named Smath, he purchased and cleared land, while also working as a blacksmith. Yohan's first son was also named Yohan. The land was inherited and extended by his son, who was also taught the trade of shaping metals. His eldest son, whose name was also Yohan, farmed and also practiced the same trade. His son farmed, but the automobile was becoming a prominent means of transportation. Though he was also taught to forge, he also had an interest in building. This last Yohan had ventured to Wisconsin as a ripening adolescent, and developed his building in becoming a general contractor.

When Yohan's father became ill during the sixties, Yohan was married, and had four children. He brought his family home, to the rural area of Smath, and cared for his parents. He saw both their demise. As a farmer, he had seen both good and bad times in the area, upon Soame's arrival. As a contractor, he'd worked in and out of town, general and sub contracting; he also worked in other states. As the third largest farmer in the area, Yohan was also a member of the town counsel. He was the senior carpenter of Soame's construction crew. Expecting the pik – paid in kind – payments prior to the farming year, Yohan's fileds were unplanted, except for the 750 acres of barley, and 500 acres of sugar beats, three of his five sons farmed. By contracting during the parlous times, he was stabilized as the most secure farmer in the area. He was between contracting jobs, when Soame came to town, and asked about carpenters. The pay wasn't much, but considering the expense involved in transportation, and with his sons, plus the possibility of the development of an idea which had prospect toward breathing life back into the town, he worked with Soame. Beauford had also been a worthy influence toward his signing up and staying on. Yohan was also the building and construction inspector for the county.

At that phase of operation, Soame had gotton to know all the men that worked for him. He did not concern himself with their personal lives, but had an interest in their backgrounds, with the skills they applied under his employ. All of the carpenters respected Yohan, not only fort the reasons stated, but also because he was a gentle and caring type person, in a burly body. The majority of the Yohan descendants stood more than 6'3"tall, and weighted an average between 260-290 pounds; this one was not an exception. In choosing "Pete" Thompson as foreman, Soame did not know the background facts he later learned about "the Swede." Never the less, Pete knew the type boxes Soame had in mind, and had made them in more styles than Soame had seen or heard of. It was essential to keep Pete, if possible, for that reason alone. As time progressed he noticed his employees, and their responses to the supervision directed to them. It was a vital element in the work production, and his observance of them. He had noticed Yohan in comparison to Pete. Pete won "hands down," because he had innate leadership quality. Instead of driving or pushing with his position, Pete would instantaneously jump out front, with the demonstrative technique, projecting "follow me," in showing how it was done. All of the men were experienced in their trade. Still, it takes a certain type of man to work other men, through pleasing and grumbling times. Soame had never considered being dissatisfied on the fact he'd given the job of supervision to Pete, since the day he made him foreman.

… When Pete called "the Swede" over, Soame glanced his watch, it was 7:57. During Yohan's approach, Pete counted his men. "Everybody's here Soame."

"Tell them to just stay relaxed for the next ten or fifteen minutes, I want to talk to them." The foreman stepped away form the huge brickolator fireplace, as Yohan walked up. Greetings were exchanged, and in four minutes, Soame had explained what he wanted to do with the house, the contractor built, and what

Pete said about them not being able to do it. Pete was rejoining them with a cup of coffee, when Yohan began his reply.

"Yah, he tells you right. Wid dat many toilets aund rooms, what is your idea, a cot house or something?"

"Exactly, a whore house."

"You are a lucky man Soaume. You see, with your idea it is impossible, ut when I built der house, because it is near der irrigation canal, aund der soil is sandy in dat area, under your basement floor you have footers 16' deep aund 12' wide. Der basement floor is poured slab. Der county wanted a quiet spot for der doctor. He was from back east. Der only way, was aun offer wid der living quarters. Eighty years ago, dis was not a deserted town. Dat is der quietest spot in town, maybe you find dat out ha?"

He asked with a broad smile. Soame returned the smile with a consenting nod. Both men before him knew their employer was very seriously interested in what remained to be said about the positive way of completing the idea, if it could be done.

"Because of der melting snow in der spring, der creeks rush aund aut times overflow. Dis causes der canal to overflow aut times, but der waters have never gone beyond der shade tree in your yard. Dat is why I left it dare, like a marker. So dare would be no seepage in der basement, der walls are 12" thick, aund I poured dem not wid rebar, but wid railroad tracks. Der railroad repair crew had left dim out near the bins. Der county stored dim, I used dim. Day are 4' apard aund welded wid cross beams. Der wall will hold."

"Your oak floor con be taken out in sections aund reused. Der rafters con be used again also. Der outside aund interior boards aund paneling, we will have to see. Der beams under der floor have to be replaced wid 4 X 10's, splitting a thurd of each section wid cross beams to support der joists. Dat on top of I beams, aund we take her up according to your plan, with bearing walls, supported with a bonded reinforcement walls, a quarter der distance, front aund back, on both sides. For der toilets we replace der septic tank wid commercial tanks, aund wid der materials, you have what you want in three weeks to a mondth. Wid dis experienced crew, dat will take in everything."

Though the permits and construction sights in the county were inspected by Yohan, the elm street project would be the first outside job, the crew would have in town. Though Yohan had not built the mansion per se, the mid west contracting firm that did, used his license, and employed him as a sub, in erecting the gorgeously grand house. He was instrumental in navigating the decorators, DD, and Camille, into areas with the feasibility of their ideas of change. To that time, that house was the last building put up in the town.

Soame knew a state inspector had not been seen in the area in years. When he inquired about the possibility of one appearing on the scene, on Elm Street, "the Swede" responded, "Dat you should not worry about, but after der place is open, people a hundred miles away will know. Den, if someone asks… you build it."

"Alright fine, I've got an industrial electrician coming in next week, to analize the foundry and start setting up. With his consent, would you mind if he does the wiring on Elm Street?"

"It will be the best, if he does. You could not get a better job."

"Thanks Yohan; Pete, I think Yohansen here will be your floor forman, when we move into the factory." A wide grin came over the Swede's face, as he extended his hand. Not understanding, Pete appeared to be worried. Soame told them, "Let's call the meeting to order." It was 8:17.

"I am very proud of each of you, and what all of you have done so far, together as a group. We started a while back, with the idea in mind of a jewelry box factory. This is our third project, involved in the campaign toward that goal, which now appears to be imminent. With all of you working here, this should be a short task. I will not be here today, when the declorators present their formal plans. I'd like for each of you individually, and all of you as the group, pay strict attention to what is said, and that to be shown in the plans, as renovations for the section each of you will be working in. Before they leave, each of you will review the overall plans. Nothing is automatic. Do not assume anything."

"Any questions you have now, and those you may arrive at after hearing the decorators, and seeing their plans, direct your question not to Pete or Yohansen, but to the decorators. The two ladies who will be living in this house, after the job is completed, will also be present. Ask them anything you may have in mind, pertaining to the completing of this project. Pete, it is your responsibility to assemble everyone in this room, and allow a session for questions and answers. Do not confuse that with your responsibility as individuals or a group, asking any questions you please, while you tour with them. Are there any questions you'd like to ask me."

It was Ed who asked, "How far off are we from going into and setting up the foundry?"

"Good question, I'm getting to that, sit tight. By the way, I'd like to see you after we adjourn. Anyone else?"

"Alright, according to Pete, and if they don't bring in anything really new, or if DD and Camille don't have additions they failed to tell me about last night, this job will be done Monday, Tuesday at the very latest. From here we have two other jobs, which you will work in separate crews. In front of the restaurant, on the opposite end of the lot, we will put up a fast service barbeque restaurant. The big job at hand is the dismantling of the house I live in on Elm, and rebuilding it into a two floor structure. Jake and Yohan will head the two crews. Pete will be with a man on the fence, separating the motel from the parking lot."

"I'm sure you have seen and know about the five men working around the foundry. Yohan, this may sound as if it slows your projected thought toward completion, but not only is it the best I can do right now, this idea may round off with the same effect you expressed as a schedule, with more men toward the middle of the Elm Street job. The fence will take two or three days. Pete and his helper will then join Jake. That job should take ten days to two weeks. When it's completed, everyone then joins you on Elm Street."

"Gentlemen, and Ed, in answer to your question; from that point, willing the almighty, we move into the foundry, converting it into the jewelry box factory." The men applauded and cheered. "Now here's what's happening in the mean time, starting with your $20.00 a week raises, beginning this week; Pete you get $5.00 on top of that." The men were dumbfounded, looking at each other, when Tim broke out with applause and a shrilly whistle. He was then joined by other clapping, whistles, grins, and other varying sounds, including words of thanks.

"I've mentioned the five men. Today they, as temporary help, will be done outside, and when the decorators leave, Pete will move them inside the building, as a clean up detail. Their job should be done next week. Three of them will join Yohan; the other two, Pete will assign to Jake. We have industrial planners, engineers, and an electrician coming in next week also, to plan and design our set up. I'm pleased to announce your crew forman in remaining in his senior supervisory position as shop forman, and as floor forman, you will have Yohan Yohansen" Applause and cheers erupted. "For each of you, who will be section formans, if there are no questions, this meeting is concluded."

He had caught them by surprise, once again. Following the momentary spell of dismay, the question was voiced to his attention, "Soame, do you mean we all will be formans?"

"Jerry, just as soon as we step into the building."

The camera he purchased the day before, had been left in the pool area bar, where he called to the foreman from , when Pete reported to work earlier that morning. Two of the mentioned five men were already on the pay roll as temporary help. They had been doing horticultural functions there, around the house. With those chores temporarly completed, Soame choose two other applicants, and sent the four of them to do the outside work at the foundry. One of the men had a tractor with a "bush hog." He was paid extra for the use of his equipment, in cutting the two and a half acres surrounding the building. There was a another applicant, who had been persistent in stopping by the office. Camille had promised him, "When he does mention hiring someone, I'll be sure and mention you." She did, and the next morning Pete stopped by, informed him of the temporary job, and brought him to work; he had no phone. A hedge row separated the mansion's estate, from the acreage of the foundry. The original owner of the house, with all probability, did not invision the possibility of the foundry being reopened. Soame had the workers shape the overgrown hedge row into a shoulder high hedge. With the well manicured lawn, the sprouting gardens, trees around the house and industrial building all shaped and trimmed, and the separating hedge, the area really looked as if new life had been pumped back into it. Since dawn that morning he had been inspecting, and found himself pleased with the development of the exteriors.

He tipped Ed $10.00 at the conclusion of their short talk, and asked everyone to remain in the living room. Pete accompanied him to the pool bar. "This will show up on your pay check beginning next week, until all these outside jobs are done. You'll be burning gas and it'll be a bit of wear and tear on your car, but you've got to keep each of these jobs in operation at once, and I want you to keep a close eye on those guys in that building there after you let them in today." He had given him $15.00.

Every brick mason can not build a brickolator fire place. Only masters of the trade, through years of experience, can put together an efficient brickolator. To contstruct a fireplace of that type, the size of the fireplace in the house, a mason with bricks, had to be one of the best. For that reason Yohan recommended Jake to the builder of the house. Because Jake was also a farmer who'd lived in the area, behind his father and grandfather, and refused to move when times were hard, Soame was able to afford him with the construction crew.

Jake had his trowel, and in different standing and kneeling positions, posed proudly. He and Yohan were the only two who had worked in originally constructing the hosue; they took pictures together. Soame did it mainly for their benefit, knowing the grand masterpiece otherwise would only be accountable to Jake, in his memory. Then in front of the fireplace and staggerd on the steps, Soame took pictures of them all.

Mrs. Tillman was not a nosy person. Since entering town, primarily all of Soame's business affairs were conducted from, through, and often in her office. The carpenters no longer lined up on Friday afternoons and filed through her office, but basically that was the only deviation from the pattern he'd established since he'd been there. She was a separate entity, but in that way a part of him, with pride in seeing him grow. With their greeting exchanges, and at times short casual conversations, the two were quite fond of each other in an easy sense. She admired his enthusiasm, and silently cheered him on, with each new project he undertook. Soame had no idea of the openness between Mildred Tillman and Camille Johnson. They were employer and employee, coworkers, and best friends. Long before Soame came to town, they were deeply embedded in all phases of their platonic relationship. They were, with each other, natural gossipers. They talked about anything and anybody, everything and everyone. With respect toward each other, Mrs. Tillman never relayed Soame's bedroom affairs to Beauford. Likewise, Soame nor DD knew what it was like to be sexually involved with the sheriff. Soame respected Mrs. Tillman because of her reserved mannerism in presenting herself. He also liked and admired her conservative outlook, and the display of quality in her taste. She had assurance with her character, and did not flaunt a make believe air of distinction.

The previous day, upon entering the office, and greeting her, in passing her glass partitioned area, to get to the back and Camille's desk, Mrs. Tillman called his attention for an audience. "Young man, you should have your temporary help fill out work slips, as you did with your regular employees. This will insure their compensation, should anything happen to them, while they work for your company." Giving him a copy of one of the forms, she went on to say, "I've been here for quite a while, and heard about a lot to go on around that old foundry. You're moving men on the inside soon, and there is a substantial amount of old equipment and excess wrought iron and other metals in there." He was standing in front of her desk; during her pause, she looked sternly at him, over her half moon shaped bifocal glasses and continued, "Sooner or later you're going to have those men, or someone move that material around and out of there, to provide you with ample working space. That will present a danger to both you and your company; for that express reason there is insurance Soame."

The extra men were hired as "temporary, full time employees. To insure them the policy would cost $159.00 per quarter. He called over the partition to Camille, and had her draft a check per Mrs. Tillman's instructions for insurance, and gave her the amount. The office owner and director then extended four other forms, identical to the one he had, instructing him "You should not allow either of them inside that building, until they've signed these forms. We have their addresses and social security numbers on file."

Excepting the papers Soame responded, "Mrs. Tillman um pretty busy rightnow could you call or have Camille call the motel, tell Smitty to relay word to Pete, and have him stop by here for these papers... will you instruct him for me Mrs. Tillman?"

"I most certainly will, and thank you for your attention and patronage toward this."

"You're welcome mam, is there anything else?"

"Yes, by the way." She answered, and remained looking at him in a direct matter of fact way. "There is young man, are you an Indian?"

He was caught off guard, but quickly responded, "No mam."

"Well then it's, I am, when you state your being in a hurry; I am."

"Yes mam, I am, am I excused mam?"

"Please have a good day Soame."

The following morning, after the meeting with the carpenters, Soame went directly to the real estate office. Because Camille would be accompanying DD to the meeting with the decorators and carpenters, Mrs. Tillman opened the office; giving Camille the morning off. She was very strict about the office being opened at 8:00, even though at times in the afternoon, she closed early. Soame had never seen her hair having gone without attention. That morning, it was freshly done. The gray blouse she had on, had a white flumed ruffling chiffon center for buttons, and flared at its long sleeved ends with the same white material. The chiffon split, in the flume at the V collar, a piece traced around each side of the neck. The cat eyed shaped glasses, had small rhinestones compressing each corner. They were held around her neck by a silver, rope styled chain, as a decorative item, when not being looked through or over. Mrs. Tillman's gray streaked hair set her gloriously ablaze with exquisiteness. She flamed her adornment of fine jewelry. The overall radiance was casted with the smile of the plush woman in her mid 50's, to Soame, in her greeting. During the reciprocation, he presented the signed papers. In examining each sheet, she invited him to be seated. Completing the examination she said, "Good, these men are now insured through my carrier."

She presented a lovely smile, and Soame was off to the business at hand. "Mrs. Tillman, I have a notation here for Camille to attach an insureance form with each application passed out, and anyone who's called should be requested to fill one out, if they are among the applicants we already have, they should undergo this procedure, before reporting to work."

"That's a sound idea, and if you'll except my using term, it's quite nifty."

"The word's practical enough, mam… speaking of terms, I have a young lady in my family, whom I'd like to employ your attention toward. She's from Louisiana, and has a more black illiterate connotation with her speech, than she has a southern accent. It's amazing, she reads perfectly well for her age, and speaks, so I 'm told, almost flawless French. I'm at the point of getting her a tutor, and I'm asking your advice and consideration toward the idea."

"That is very wise in your consideration toward Chairly, whom I met yesterday. She and Beverly were by yesterday morning. I noticed her and what little she had to say. She's strikingly mod, very butch, and from what I saw, extremely intelligent and grown up. She'd rebel Soame, but that's not the problem or the reason I will not except toward the tutorial. It's classic, and a problem instructors have been confronted with, since there have been instructors for children, and members of her age group. It is the most basic problem in any school system in the world; it deals with discipline. You know what she needs; you know very well, how to see to and administer her need toward speaking properly, and yet you want to send her to me. She's bright enough to learn, and you are sharp enough to aid her. Don't you have the time, with the concern you have?"

"That's an amazing aspect involved in the problem. She reads words, as they are placed in the books. I've had her read to me aloud, and it's inconceivable, after listening to her read, she would talk so roughly incorrect. Two days ago I purchased a recorder to dictate into, have her repeat and listen to what she records. I have not tried the method, but beyond it, if it fails, I only have alternative ideas toward a tutor. I will not take more time than that, for that, toward her."

"She admires you. Perhaps it'll work. You know her far better than I do. To get to her, in delivering the message of her verbally projecting what I teach, for her to learn, I would have to tear down the wall of resentment she would set up between us. To me, it would be no obstacle I haven't encountered a thousand times before. At the end they are grateful. They hardly ever look back and realize the discontent, headaches, and frustrations involved toward them attaining that point of happiness. You are a qualified man, why didn't you teach?"

"For that reason, and this one, I've been in pursuit of long before coming here; the jewelry box factory is my quest."

"Then my advice to you now, with her as a part of your goal, is your doing or aiding her in a continued constructive manner. It will only gain you admiration from her as her guardian, instructor, or however you place in her life, young man."

Seeing the advice had already been calculatively assumed by him, she injected a change of subject into his nonchalant reaction. "I've asked you to be seated, to talk with you about your ad."

"Oh, you know about it to?"

"I most certainly do, I've call two of the applicants back, didn't Camille tell you, I wanted to hear if they at least sounded professional?"

"She did, and I confused the ad you are referring to, with the veteran's ad. Pardon me, please go on Mrs. Tillman."

"That's quite alright, would you care for a cup of coffee?"

"No thank you, I drink it only during spells. I'd be happy to get you a cup, if you'd like."

"No, no, you're probably in a hurry with a set schedule; I'll tell you this, so you can be on your way." With that she did a dainty primp, and began expressing her concern.

"House servants are particularly important in your home, because of your valuables. Their work is a focal point toward their employment, but as live in domestics, with their efficiency, you must also be assured of their trust-worthiness. I have a friend in Concord, New Hampshire, whom I haven't seen in over a decade. In fact, my late husband and I vacationed there, and through the years we've exchanged cards during holiday season and so forth. It's been three years since I've spoken to her by phone." Her reflections seemed to have carried her off into a drift of subtle reminiscence. Reapproaching the meaning within the text, she went on "She operates a reputable, if not the most recognized placement and referral agency in that area. I've thought of giving her a call, and inquiring about the possibility of her helping you find the butler and upper story maid your ad has been placed for."

"Of the four DD's spoken to, two mentioned decent references, but the people for whom they worked, now have to be checked on for at least substantial creditability. Camille has basically encountered the same problem. None of them have a refined history with their butlership, which is the exclusive factor I've instructed them to inquire regarding. I'd appreciate very much your assistance in that way, if you would, and I thank you for the offer."

"Well, as I've said I haven't spoken with her in years; its no problem at all. Besides I'm happy to see you prosper, and I have an interest towards Camille's personal comfort and stability. She's the only help I have. A more pleasant home atmosphere, creates a better mental composition, for a more productive work environment. Your expansions are filling voids in this office so far, with productivity." She had a cheery smile, further projecting her glow, and continued. "We'll just have to work, while waiting to see what the future brings, and hope to escalate with our works, while we're waiting. If you have no further questions young man."

"I've got some notations I'd like to leave on the desk, in the event I'm not able to call her before late this afternoon."

"Go right ahead, and I'll have her let you know how my call turned out." She told him, as he left the area, placing a weight on the paper he'd left on Camille's desk. "Thank you again Mrs. Tillman," he said placing his hat and tipping it. Hers was the only partitioned section in the office. It occupied the quarter section of the back wall, in the front of interior. Crafted from wood, waist high, ran it's perimeter, with hazed galss, to the shoulders. He passed her open door, exiting. "Thank you, and you have a nice day Soame."

Chapter 9

THE ad read: Vietnam veterans attention!! Are you down and out? Have you forgotten how it feels to be needed and depended on? Here's a chance to earn top pay in security, and re-explore the advantages of being worthwhile. Send resumé, etc. The P.O. Box number in Smath was included in the listing. When it was initially sent to newspapers, to be ran simultaneously in major cities in the country, the phone had not been installed in Soame's office. The weeks delay allowed him to arrange for the adjustment, by adding the phone number. The line was added to the office phone, with call forwarding to the realty office, and both lines were also forwarded to Elm Street after four, and on request.

His notation to Camille that day, was in making the adjustment in the ad. He had already discussed the rental of the farm house and property for Lynch. That night she was instructed to rent the thirty acres for six months, after being informed of the "more than likely" possibility of the owner gladly welcoming a $50.00 a month proposal. Each dwelling in the rural areas, had it's own supply of water, supplied through an electric pump. When the electricity was turned on, it not only enabled the lighting, but also activated the water supply. Soame reconsidered the matter, and had no other apparent reason for renting the property, other than Lynch. His notation also included a change in arrangements for the property rental. He did not know how "Neb" would work out. The liquor could have a retrospective result to his applied diagnosis. The well versed person with trees, could very well go on a binge. He instructed Camille to, "Rent the place for a month, with an option toward a year's lease, renewable at the end of the six month period."

Leaving the realty office, and all other business concerns behind, Soame's plans, for the remainder of the morning and early afternoon, were toward fun, sex, and relaxation. After stopping by the accounting room at the motel, for the packages he'd purchased the previous day, he was happily on his way to the farm house. At 9:50 the jeep stopped in rounding the curve, at the edge of the forest, turning in on the road leading to the house. The stop served it's purpose well. In his attempt to think ahead of them, if they had preceeded him with their arrival. His original thought was in removing his pants. Doing so he saw the tracks, left by the El Camino. It was his place. A place away from other places. He had been there during various times during the day, and knew, with the quiet of the woods, and the stillness of the forest, a car motor could be heard in it's approach, at least two miles away. At night, a headlight beam traced through the dark, and it's penetration through the woods, could be seen as much as five miles, from the porch.

In the 60 degree temperature, Soame had on his car coat. Noticing the tracks he knew Cindy and Janet were there. The Blanchards were the only quests he'd invited to his remotely secluded spot. There was no doubt in his mind of Janet complying with his desires toward her "non" dress, though Cindy appeared to be uncalculatively finicky regarding the matter. The camera was ready with a fresh roll of film. Not only did he remove his trousers, when he drove into the yard, he did not have on undershorts. Noticing the tire prints leading off to the barn, the barn door being closed, and ther bing no vehicle in sight, other than his, he realized their attempt at non harmful mischief. His attention toward the tracks could not be noticed. Casually taking the gifts out of the jeep, with the camera case slung over he shoulder, the only thing out of place about him was, with his boots, hat, and buttoned coat, over his sweater, there were no pants. Both women knew where the key was, for the accessibility toward one of the cachings. Laying the packages on the porch, he found the key in place, and proceeded, and after opening the screen door, the main door swung away from him, "Surprise, surprise!!" It should not have been, according to his expectations, but it was. The actual and real surprise found, caught, and suspended Soame, in dazzled fascination. In a more powerful way than he had taken time to foresee, he was trapped totally stretched out between substance and reality, with the overwhelming summation, he had never before seen his woman, and her mother with their faces on, with make up. He became shocked into a spellbinding trance of splendid loveliness and beauty.

"Soame, Soame are you alright? Soame!" Cindy waved her hand in front of the face, with only eyes shifting from one to the other.

He was marveled by the marvelousness before him. "He's alright baby, nothing can really happen to this one, watch. Take a look at this, Mr. Hypnotized." Janet stepping back, and opened her coat. No other part of his body moved, in coordination with his eyes, except his mouth; a big grin came over his face. Until that point, except for the coats, it was almost impossible to distinguish which of the two women was herself. He had honestly been perceptive of ambush, and after Cindy had spoken, found himself slightly embarrassed, having considered the two have exchanged coats, for the ultimate deceptive prank. "You two have done it again, and this time it's going to take a heck of a lot of convincing, to prove to me, you aren't twins, masquerading as mother and daughter." He took a step over the door facing.

"Bull shit! Mother fucker," Janet stated to him, turning her back, flaring her coat, and in stride toward the bar she added, "I'm still her mother Soame, and that's the maturity you instilled in the remaining cherry you had two months ago." In the store, the coats did not look as extraordinarily imposing with appearance, as they did on the two women in the room. The two fur items were chosen from a company of six, demonstrated on mannequins, comprising the decorative display, advertising the sale, in the quality recognized store. The contrasting involved, excelled from degree to the other extreme, in variation. Yet, each served it's particular purpose in being unique; an unmatched item of exquisiteness. The black on Janet, the white on Cindy; the full length sable; the ermine jacket. Before Janet turned her back, flaunted her head upward with pride, and strolled to the bar, and after stepping back, she stepped back out of the door way, and displayed her nudity, beneath the coat. Both of her fists clutched fur, snuggling the collar under her chin, when she greeted him. Cindy stood then with both hands in a pocket. His eyes had not drifted downward, to see the pink panties, she held the jacket for him to see, as the only material under it.

"You've got a lot of nerve, feeding us those sugar coated fairy tales about two ounces, and ten-thousand bucks in that place in the basement. Tom took the last of my stuff this mrning, to the fields over near Hammond. Say, what do you have on under that coat? Frisk him baby, let's see what we find."

He and Cindy looked into eachothers eyes and found their commons. As Janet babbled, he casted his view to what she openly presented him once again. This time he did not miss it. "Good morning you two extravagantly ravishing beautiful portraits of magnificent loveliness."

"Nothin doing buster! Give me that camera. Come on, unbutton him. Let's see what's doin."

She had been standing with an elbow propped on the bar, her high heeled matching fur slipper on a round of one of the stools. Soame, in his verbal greeting, extended a thumb under the strap, to unsling the camera from his shoulder. After her first instruction to Cindy, Janet began moving toward them, reaching for the camera as she neared. "Is this the surprise I drove out here for?" he asked, as Cindy undid the last of the two buttons.

"Is it alive?" Janet asked.

"I'm going to school."

"Well you told me that last week."

Where's the switch to this thing, you're first, again!" Janet told him, attaching the flash, looking for the shutter trip. He was limp.

Cindy's arms flew around his neck, and she kissed him with impusive feelings that were staggereing, activating his locking her into a reciprocative embrace. The flash went off, and Cindy felt the limpness move away. Janet took his hat, and seconds later there was another flash. "Your kiss really improving, you know that?"

"I thought you couldn't tell the difference, smart ass! Look!! It's alive!" She flashed the semi-hard erection, between the couple.

"It's the University of Portland, I've been excepted."

"Goo-" she smothered him with another kiss, and grinded against the hard, Cindy knew she had promoted and felt totally comfortable with.

Practically everything about the camera was automatic. It also had an automatic tiemr, but he did not have a tri-pod. "Take his coat off baby, and let's have some real fun with him and this thing."

There were four rolls of film in the bag, including the one in the camera. "I've got some thigns on the porch for the both of you."

"What you've got is a hard on, and I want it on film; so when in time, the feature "flash" changes; well have these to remember, remember?"

The rear hall and bedroom heaters were set at a low blue flame, to take the chill off the air. The hall window and one of the windows in the bedroom, as well as the side window in the living room, was also partially opened by Cindy, while Janet lit the heaters, upon their arrival. A soft breeze out side, circulated the warmed air, with the draft. Just as he wore it in his pants, the hard meat slanted to the right. IT was kept at it's full measure, because of the instructions Janet directed to Cindy, in holding it in various ways, "To get a comparison in size to your hand." After complementing them, on the superb manner in which they enhanced the excellent, delicate, and rare beauty of the furs, Soame then told them of the film, mail order, development center, in Silver Springs, Maryland. His plans were to send the rolls, and request triplicate reproductions, allowing each of them prints. Janet had already flashed more than seven exposures. He then complemented them on their beauty once again; Janet interrupted, "Crap! Soame, we're the same bitches you made two moths ago. Here baby, you take some, we want to remember we had hard core action with our features, during these days." He had been moved around in different places in the living room. Extending the camera to Cindy, she also began disrobing. After placing her wear on the sofa, Janet shifted him to the totally remodeled fireplace, which had never been used. The grate and accessory metal frame container, held the poker, tongs, shovel, and broom. The bellows sat in front of the fresh hearth, between the displayed utensils. They were shining, with sparkling newness. An interior chair sat in the nook. More than half the roll was shot, before he was able to retrieve the packages from the porch.

Cindy had the entertainment center in operation, when he re-entered the living room. The musical introductory pad to the foreigner record "*I Want to Know What Love is*," had just begun. "Alright, with what you have for your Oregon experience already, including the camera, this also is for you."

After passing three beautifully wrapped boxes to Cindy, Soame turned to Janet, who had seated herself on the couch, comfortably in the coat. "Because I'm going ta fuck you into unconsciousness today! This is for your throughout recovery period of nostalgia, before and after."

"I don't believe you."

Knowing he was very serious excepting the small package, her voice quailed, "Are you serious Soame? Thanks."

There was another package in his hand; Cindy was exploding with happiness, and displaying it a bright eyed grin. She'd open the box containing the night shirt first. On his way to the bar, he was intercepted, and greeted with a strong hug around the waist and a lavish kiss.

He was pouring the second four finger drink, when Janet took a seat at the bar, wearing the ostentatiously fashionable sunglasses. "I've never known you as a palaverer, yet you flatter me with your intended deception, why?"

"Here, have a drink."

"Mother! Look at these!"

The sleeping lingerie excited her. He took it for granted she had cotton and warm fabric styled pj's, but Soame looked within the scope of renowned reputation of the school. Students of class and sophistication, from aristocratic backgrounds would be in attendance. Cindy not only had to do well in her studies, in creating, excepting, and coping with her environment, for mental concentration and congeniality, she had to get along at least decently well, with others. Her personality would not allow her to be considered snobbish, or in anyway be referred to as being prude. In retrospect, being in close quarters, residing in a domiciled atmosphere, with other young women who'd developed those characteristics over the years, some through natural traits, could put Cindy at a disadvantage in small ways, to be looked down upon. Naturally there would be a percentage of the ones, who weren't as well bred, as they would pretend. These would be the most annoying, in that way, of flaunting an over wheening zealousness of pretense, toward aristocracy. Knowing of their middle and sub middle class standing in reality, they search for flaws in others of complexes, in an attempt to build their esteem. Girls parade their lingerie sometimes as a mark and, or brand of distinction. He felt truly, if the fine materials accomplished nothing else, they would aid her self confidence, whenever and wherever they were displayed, noticed or simply slept in; that was his overall thought behind the presentation of the gift.

The second 45 to be heard from the turntable, was a record by the Hollies," *The Air That I Breath, And To Love You*." During the preceeding record he turned the volume up. It was before either of them had taken a drink. In turning from the behind the bar entertainment center, Cindy did not hear the toast her mother made phrasing it almost as a commitment, "We will be with you always Soame." They were drinking black label scotch. In joining them, Cindy brought the two opened boxes to the bar, and placed them in front of Janet, while thanking Soame with a sensitive smile displaying sincerity. The unopen box was on the foot stool. She opened the packages while sitting in the cushioned chair, in the corner. It matched the sofa, and with the floor lamp, it was in comfortable position between the front and side windows. "Have you had breakfast?" Janet asked him.

"Around six, I had a couple of pieces of toast with butter, jelly, and a cup of hot tea."

"I took steaks out of the freezer, that's about all you have here."

The records were changing when Cindy joined them; her drink had been poured. She was able to hear his response. "Well there's a dozen eggs that's been in there for a week or so, preserves in the basement, have you forgotten? And there is also a bag of self rising flour. Can you make biscuits without milk?"

"I can, I told her that's what the menu would be, when I found the flour."

"Saaay, this is some realy fine stuff Soame," Janet told him, holding up a top piece to a set.

"Aren't you two warm in those coats? How about each of you putting on a top; let me see if you do as much for these pieces, as you do to the coats."

Following words of appraising compliments toward the furs they took off, with recollections of the shock incurred in receiving them, and on and on thanks and kisses, he asked in a relaxable way, "Sooo, when is registration?"

He was nude behind the bar, and had done half of his drink. "Didn't I tell you?... no I didn't," she said in complete surprise, pulling the top over her head.

"Oh pardon me. It-"

"That's alright I understand the excitement, excuse me, Janet, before you take that seat again, there's something for you in my right coat pocket."

They were in the middle of an Al Stewart record. Janet told him at the beginning of *Time Passages*, it was her dedication to Cindy, and wanted her to look forward to, and go through her college exploration, with the frame of mind, implicated in the song.

On the way to the coat, which was on a wall rack, Janet flared the top, in her turns, modeling it. The rack was on the front bedroom wall, beyond the coffee table and couch. The door would have concealed the rack, had it been open. Seeing Janet model the piece, with her black fur-like heels, Cindy went as far as in front of the coffee table, in her bare feet, demonstrating an inexperienced display, with a true effort in a show of faith. She seemed to spring on the plush carpeting. Stephanie Mills *"Sweet Sensation"*

began playing during their paired, runaway return to the bar. "I didn't mean to be rude, you started telling me about the date."

He had lit a joint. "The first week next month for regular registration, which begans on the first. There's a $50.00 late fee after the first week, until the 15th. From that point the academic dean has to approve a registration of specified reasons."

He looked at Janet, they smiled at each other, and looked back at Cindy, who seemed as if she was about to bust out in a giggle. "What'd you have for breakfast?"

"Sausage and scrambled eggs, on toast."

He dropped another cube in his and Janet's glass. After refreshing the two drinks, he added more ginerale chaser, while telling Janet "Two of those are for your stash. You put them there before you leave; so you will be positive. The other three, you can share with Tom." He looked at Cindy. "Are you ready for your first drink of scotch?"

"With you, the first and duration of anything."

The player had gone silent, in the middle of a change. He proposed a toast, and the three of them clicked glasses, "To us." " *Some days are like diamonds, some days are like gold,*" by John Denver, poured through the speakers.

Twenty minutes later, Dieon Warmick's *"Don't Make Me Over,"* was playing in the background of their fun and relaxed conversation. They had talked on variational subjects. Cindy had opened and discovered a surprise she had never before seen or heard of. The thong panties also caught Janet off guard. Soame finished his drank, and smoked a half joint of the reffer, and had began "tooting." Janet told him how she had gone through four hours preparing to meet him, and waiting anxiously, doing hits from Cindy's coke. This was while Cindy was outside, cutting primroses. Sitting in the chair, opening the two gifts, she had discovered something missing. Between the chair and the door, there was a round top Louie V type table. It sat in front of the curtained window, without a scarf, but it held a vase in it's center. When she inquired to her beau, concerning the use of artificial decoration, he merely shrugged his shoulders, replying "Who has time, or interest toward such a thing lady?"

Excusing herself from the bar, Cindy went into the kitchen, and in her pink panties and new nighty, passed back by them with a smile. The flowers she brought in were primarily yellow, but there were other variations of colors, in the clustered leaves. They complimented her. She completed her drink, with the diluted cubes, and during the newly engaged conversation, she asked for a refill. After placing cubes in her glass, Soame filled it with ginger ale. With a big smile, he told her, "Wait another fifteen or twenty minutes." He then leaned over and gently kissed her lips, and asked her, "Want a puff or tow of this, or a toot? We're going to be here all day," and explained "Scotch is a much heavier drink than Vodka; be mellow and relax."

Soame opened the gift he'd withheld. In presenting the Dumas book to Cindy, with his casual smile he said, "You'll like this. Who knows, perhaps one day we'll own a yacht."

"Is that what they story is about, boating? I haven't had an interest in yachts before, thanks."

"I thought it would aid your interests, during a portion of the week before your trip. I have something planned for you to do next week; I will tell you later, what it is. You'll have to read the book, to find out what the story of adventure is all about."

"I won't attempt to deceive you. Both of these are intended for Cindy. However, I feel, in this indirect way with your presence, it's fitting and app-"

"Cut the bullshit Soame! You want me to read th- Ann Rand!!" Janet grasped the book with a slight jerk, during his both physical and verbal presentation. Because it was still in the paper during the delivering to Cindy, Janet could not see the title, or the name of the person who wrote the book. "I've tried to read her before. There was so much talk about 'atlas hur-"

"Shrugged; Atlas Shrugged," he injected. "Anyway, I couldn't get into it, after reading nearly half the book."

The phonograph snapped off. The last of that set of 45's had played. Thorugh the aftermath of silence Cindy told him, "You're right, there's a refined difference that comes to life, with the weed. I remember what you told me before about knowing when satisfaction is obtained. This is real smooth intoxicating pleasure."

"That's cool, relax, take it easy; hold on, let me get this straight with Mizz Fast Fingers, who wants ta know everything."

"I didn't say or imply that I know everything, Mr. Smart Ass, but I will ask you, why would you buy her a book by such an accredited writer as Dumas, and throw haze into the focus, with this!?"

"Will you tell me, how can you give an opinion on that book, and you haven't read it?"

"Because not only were the girls talking about it at the hospital, I saw the national best seller listings and ratings, and the other one showed up, for a month each time I read the ratings. I also remember it vividly, because I didn't borrow the copy the girls were circulating around the hospital; I drove to Rapid City and purchased a copy. To enlighten you further on my opinion, which is concrete and invincible, Mr. Knowledgeable, good lovin, industrial, benevolent merchant… no writer can make such a turn about in their style of writing. This book we haven't even heard of Soame; I know what she likes, and she simply won't get into it."

Cindy reached over the counter, and with the ginger ale she brought to her disposal, poured it over her remaining ice cubes. Noticing her with the bottle, Soame indicated with a shrug, he had been laxed in noticing her needs. She waved and fanned the ridiculous gesture off. It was in the midst of Janet's compiled description of him.

"I'll tell ya what, since you're so set in your opinion, I'll make a proposition with you."

"Let's hear it."

"You read a third of that book, and if you don't like it, and tell me so, I'll buy you any diamond item of your choice, watch, bracelet, necklace, whatever. On the other hand, if you complete the book and thoroughly enjoy it, as I say both of you will, within a week after she's left for school, you meet me here, drink a half quart of scotch with me, and give me head for five hours, slow head."

"You're on buster! And I'll tell you now, I want a necklace to wear with my coat."

"Bet, and um gonna get a tri-pod, to set up the video."

Cindy then asked him, "How do you know about the name of the other book?"

"I tried to read it to; my opinion is the same as her's. I read more than half of it. I guss different people have varied tastes in reading, which substantiates the reason for the listings and ratings."

"What! Do you mean to tell me… Soame, this is the ultimate in ill-mitigative subtleness."

"What it is, is a bet, and a bet is a bet, my dear. You've witnessed the bet, is it a bet, my dearest?"

Cindy did not reply to him. She looked away from his eyes, and into her mother's stare. He scrutinized the both of them, and their looks confronting each other's gaze. Soame saw something between them he had never seen before. The closest estimation he could make a comparison to, was their first encounter, with Janet achieving an erogenous zone climax. The comparison was, to her look afterward, and her look to Cindy, in explaining what had happened. He could not be sure of his interpretation of what he saw in Cindy's eyes either. It revolved in the perplexity of choice, and the outwardly acknowledgement of having been chosen; through this had always been a commonly understood factor, within the triangular affair. She knew neither would expect her to voice an opinion against either; knowing she was not independent of either. Between them he did see maturity. The ripeness flourished, in distinguishing them. They were what they appeared to be. There was clam within and between them. However, one of them was married. This was also a commonly understood factor between them all. He liked what he saw; they boosted his pride, lifted his inward feelings of accomplishment, and carried his esteem with exultation. The spell was brief, simultaneously. Most of all he found no contempt. What he did find, he treasured, and knew it was very real. Janet said to him, "It was an agreement, deary."

"You have yet to read the book, and give me your opinion Janet."

During his time behind the counter, Soame selected an album, from a host of albums they had also brought, and were stacked on the far side Cindy. He had examined the record and placed it on top of the entertainment center. When he began clearing the turntable, Janet started with the preparations of fitting her works; Cindy took a swig of the ginger ale and did a hit of his coke. After the adjustments, Soame put the Fleetwood Mack album on, and chose a particular cut, *"Where the Rainbows End."*

That was the preliminary to their last morning, and afternoon together, as a trio, for years to come. The three of them were filled with expectancy when they encountered each other, on a schedule. During the entire rendezvous, neither of them encountered dissatisfaction, nor was there disappointment. The delmonicoes were wrapped in pairs; two packages had been taken out, and for lunch fitted the conclusive opionated menu. They had never before dined together. The delicious meal they shared, set the mood for the interesting talks they enjoyed. Each of their meetings accelerated and surpassed each previous one. This one was superb to any other of their times together. It lasted until 6:10 that early evening. Soame was primed both mentally as well as physically, for the togetherness. Since the rescheduling, all of his moves were planned and geared, toward the deliverance of satisfaction to the two women. On a whim, that morning, obliviousness was a sexual demarcating point of attainability, described to Janet. Throughout the day their moods fluctuated, excelling to and ebbing after, the release of their passions. The most listened to of them all from the records in the house, was the first record played of the day, by Foreigner.

Had he not mentioned it, and cued her guard, and if he had been persistently undulating throughout the right moves, into various positions, he may have done it. Toward the close of their day together, the experienced pair copulated, for the last time. During that encounter at various times, the windows had been raised and lowered; both bedroom windows had been raised and lowered frequently. Each knew the other's moves, to the extent of almost calculating with certainty, what response would take place, if the harmony was not disrupted, with their continuous drives. He never laid heavily on her, and did not inhibit her motility. She slung and twitched to his rotations and pushes, for almost an hour and forty-five minutes. They intercoursed in ways both of them had not done in years. After three previous ejaculations, the three of them knew Soame would have stamina to pursue any course he chose. Janet knew she had given him great gratification, in accepting one of his eruptions, deep in the back of her throat. Too, she knew also, with the liberty he allowed her, in changing positions and moving as she desired, they galloped copulating in thrills with harmonious strides of ecstatic fulfillment, to the pleasure and triumph of satisfying each other. When it was over, they all knew the experience would be remembered with glorious nostalgia and there would be another time.

Because the tub had been removed, and the shower was installed according to his designs, there was ample room for the three of them, in the sliding door, glass encasement. It was an invigorating highlight of the overall experience. Each roll of film contained thirty-five exposures. Three of the rolls were used. "Because I care for you, and the concentrative thought you've projected, concerning our feature changes, in the future."

She was sincere, but long before then he had noticed more than care, in her eyes. While making the statement, Janet was clearing the bar counter. She gave him nearly a dozen, vividly explicit, some of them close up, nude, sex, shots. All of them knew though they were outrageous, thirty years from that day, each of them would view the experience and shots with pride, and classify them as "personal."

Pictures were taken in and playfully, outdoors. The only shots taken at the barn, were with the door open, at the close of their meeting. Cindy and Janet stood and sat, in front of and on, the tailgate; with and without their furs. The last shot was taken, capturing them standing side by side, waving. That day Soame also received a gift; the records brought over were especially selected for him. The present soared his emotional and complete mental state of being.

Chapter 10

SOAME had been at the Yates' home almost a half hour, when he and the two sisters heard the sound of both tractors turning in. Though the International was much larger, it operated more quietly than the Ferguson. The three of them were sitting in the jeep; the sisters brought the variational difference to Soame's attention. Thad had turned in and re-accelerated. Cathy directed his listening attention, "Now watch, Billy's gonna wait until he gets right at the corner, throw the throttle up, slide with the brakes, come off and hit the one wheel brakes, that'll throw him in the turn, and before he straightens up, he'll have that tractor wide open again."

Jenny added, "You'll hear little Thad holler, if ya listen close."

Cathy told him, "He tanks it's the funniest thang. Last year Billy slung him off. Good thing no plows were behind; here they come."

The throttle engine revved "woo-a," was heard in a faint off distant cry, and the full throttle sound resumed. The evening colors of dusk, were commencing their invasion of the firmament. "Paw's gonna hafta help um feed up. I already told ya, they're runnin late."

"Wait a minute! Since Billy's always doin this Evil Kaneivl dare devil styled driving, why is he always running last?"

He looked at both of them; one shrugged fully, the other slightly hunched her shoulders, and looked away. Jenny looked back at him and replied, "Sometimes he just stays in the field longer, cause he knows he can't keep up anyhow.' The International then came into sight. A gray stream of smoke, stood the exhaust stack cover straight up.

"Take this in the house for Billy, when he comes in. Come back out when I'm through talking with him. I've got to talk with your dad right now, I'll help um feed."

He'd already given them four joints a piece. It was Red reffer, with some of his personal coke. The two women had already received a severe warning. The three of them climbed out of the jeep. Soame went toward the barn; Cathy and Jenny proceeded to the house.

Thad had a 50 lb. Bag of feed on each shoulder, when Billy and little Thad met them in the barn door. "Little Thad, you look after the sheep, me and Soame'll have this done in a minute or two. Billy you handle the rest."

Soame judged the fact, with the three sacks, they would only have to make two trips. It would give him more time to talk with Thad. He greeted the younger Yates, "dapping" his free hand. Two were entering, as the other pair exited.

The Yates were jubilant with anticipation of further triumph with the crops, yet to be harvested. Thad gave Soame a precise figure, on the number of trucks loaded from the Hodges field. A third of the haul had been topped with Thad's wheat, when the harvest was completed for Soame, and they started in Thad's field. The prices were still rising, as had been anticipated. It was almost mechanical, the way Thad dropped the sacks, slit one, laid it partially over and into the bin, slit the other, and tugged on the ends of the first one, emptying it. He worked with full concentrated vigor, while talking to Soame, who stood with a sack on his shoulder. Hogs stepped on his boots, and bumped about this legs. He was interested in what Thad had to say. "Take your bag ta the other bin, and leave it. I'll be done with this in a jiff, we'll talk on the way to the barn."

After they finished feeding the hogs and the farm talk, walking toward the house, Soame presented the direct fact involved with the operation of the motel. When he mentioned the function of the capitol, and it's necessity, as a means to funnel finance into the operational set up, development, and maintenance of the factory, Thad stopped, and was looking at him inquisitively. "Money from the co-op will be a good and sound profit for me Thad, but I'm confronted with at least a quarter of a million dollar overhead, within the next four months, and that's just to get set up. I'll lay money out of my pocket, but I've got to have a source of reimbursement, and supply toward development and maintaining the set up. It may be a couple of years before I can even show a small profit with the factory. On the other hand the attempt may very well collapse on me. The loss would be a catastrophe. I've got to insure a definite means to replace my investment. It's my responsibility toward my security, and this is the only other way I know how to generate a compensable cash flow."

"Soame I don't think I've ever talked with anyone as business minded as you."

"I don't know about that, but what I'm asking you is about Cathy and Jenny working at the motel in the evenings and on weekends. I've discussed and explained the idea to Beau-"

"Sonny was out ta the field yesterday morning. That's the reason we didn't finish harvestin and loadin you out till almost eleven. I shut my harvester down, and after thirty minutes, tried ta put Billy on it, and talk with'm while coutin and loadin the trucks. When he said it was private, I figured it was pretty important. It took him a half hour ta tell me how much good the factory will do, when everybody around here mite near knows that. What I didn't know, is the grant's gonna be approved, accordin ta what he says Jack Stillman says. So it was good news and worthwhile after all. Then he told me Soame. He's already said ya might ask me."

The conversation had been direct, since their greeting. Soame had no idea Beauford had been forerunner with the news. "Ya know Sonny thinks a lot of ya, which I do also. I guess that's why we spent better'n a hour and a half talkin about this this yesterday. Haven't seen'm for about eight months before then. People around here do mite near as they please, but I've known Sonny all our lives, and you're the first outsider I'v seen'im not only speak kindly of, but he's gone out of his way ta help ya. The factory is important ta all of us Soame, but I think he just likes ya as a person. Of course I know ya well enough ta have my own opinion, but I thought I'd let ya know, as a compliment."

"Now back ta the girls… Caty is almost old enough ta- you boys go on ta the house. We're talkin about somethin private. Tell ya ma I'll be along in a while." Billy and his brother had walked up. They were a considerable distance away, and if they heard his first few words, Thad's voice would fade, with their forward progress. "Soame we're tryin to raise these children right; all of them. No matter how you look at it, if Cathy's allowed, Jennifer will want ta follow her. Neither one is out of school, and I know they're part time jobs, but like I told Sonny, I'll present it ta Darlíne, and if she says no, I want ya ta understand that's the entire end of it, right there. I'm really glad you stood up and asked, instead of sendin them. It makes a lot of difference. I was waitin ta see what you'd say, before I discussed the entire matter with my wife."

Soame reasoned, there was another involvement not sitting too well, when Thad stated "overall matter." He wanted to make a proposal, but Thad continued, "That phone in the house has rung more in the past two weeks, than it has in the last five years. People call at 3 and 4 in the mornin. Now I told ya, I wouldn't pry inta your and Billy's concern, and judgin from what's been said about the motel between you'n Sonny, it's sorta plain ta all of us, what's goin on. Soame, I don't run my house like that. Darlíne's goin ta have the phone number changed Friday. Naturally you'll have the new number, but whatever Billy's doin with ya, if his mother says so, when I talk with her about the motel, he may be doin it from his own place. He's of age now ta be out on his own, and if he has ta get calls at that hour, I'd rather he have the freedom of his own place ta do as he chooses. You started ta say somethin."

Soame was more embarrassed than anything, with the circumstance leading to the disturbance of the Yates household. Evaluating everything Thad said, it dawned on Soame, when he didn't sound negative, he didn't say either of them couldn't work, nor did he show resentment toward the idea, except for the phone.

"Thad about the phone-"

"Don't worry about the phone. Excuse me for cutting ya off, but he's my son, livin in my house. I've got the phone under control, as of Friday."

"Alright, here's what I was about to say, we'll have our second meeting Sunday, the co-op. Since you'll be in town at the motel, let me show you the layout, and the arrangements I've made to insure safety. I'd like to show and explain it to you, before you and Mrs. Yates come to a decision."

"That's my exact line of thinkin. In fact, that's what I told Sonny. Mind you, what I said about any decision she makes regarding this matter. I provide for us all, and do the best I can around here, but those girls, and that little boy, well… I'll wait until this weekend, ta mention it ta her, and Sunday night after I've seen the place, I'll talk ta her in detail about it, we'll just have ta wait and see what she says. I'm bout ta go in and talk ta that boy of mine now, about the phone. I thought I'd wait and see what you had ta say, after yesterday." They walked toward the house, talking about farming.

Darkness had began infiltrating the atmosphere. At the porch, Soame asked Thad for the use of his phone. Mrs. Yates and little Thad were waiting for Thad to have supper. Cathy and Jenny were in the living room also. "We missed it again Soame, and I'm gettin better all the while."

"Harvesting doesn't allow you too much time for practice, does it?"

"Saturday I killed a rabbit."

"Hay! Bringing food in with it; now that is getting good. Don't worry, we've got time, I'll see how well you shoot soon."

"Thadeous, you washed up?"

"We're waitin on you paw."

He was trailing his father throgh the house toward the kitchen. "Soame, with these two critters sittin around waitin, even if you were hungry, they'd probably spoil your appetite, if you looked across the table at those homely faces."

"Ah, ma."

"Ma please."

She jokingly embarrassed them. The only phone in the house was in the living room.

Margaret answered the phone at home. When he spoke with DD, he could not say directly, when he'd be home. He spoke in an evasive way. "I will keep your dinner warm; we will go on and eat then."

It was cool outside. Each of the sisters sat on a side of him, on the couch, talking, watching TV, while they waitied for Billy. It was twenty minutes before he walked out, in a change of clothes, looking refreshed, with a big smile on his face. He had a paper bag in his hand. "What it is man?"

"Yo, so how's it going?"

"Let's step out here on the porch, I've got something for ya."

When Soame motioned to rise, so did the sisters, on both sides of him. "You two must be his body guards, or somethin."

His sisters had their faces made, and were dressed in new clothes. "Did pistols come with those outfits?"

"It ain't no business of yours what we do, or what we wear, William Yates!" When Cathy finished yelling, Billy was already on the porch.

"Hay man, wow! I've got twenty-seven left. There's a guy from across the rier, over in Volborg, he bought thirty and says he wants to buy me out, when he comes over the next time. He works in Miles City, and I think he's handling it there. I saw the package you brought; some are larger."

Soame took the bag containing the money, and gave Billy the half gram sample. Billy was asked to go inside, test his sample, and bring back an accurate count on his package. Long before, Soame had discovered the heater being one of the best features of the jeep. The motor warmed while idling, and began putting out heat. The three were comfortable, relaxed in their talks, snorting and smoking, when Billy returned. He liked the sample and gave Soame the right count. The bag contained $500.00. The calculations were made, carrying the balance added to the new debt. The quarters were explained, as being identified by the size and fold. Billy mentioned him having to get back in the house. When Soame inquired as to why, he explained, "My pa says, every time the phone rings, when I'm at home, no matter what time it is, I've to ta answer it. I've got to sleep on the couch until Friday, and the people callin for whatever I've been handling over the phone, I've got ta tell them not to call back. It's a breeze man; I can handle it, no problem."

Soame gave him ten joints of the "Red" reffer, and said "I'll have a tab sheet for you, when we see each other the next time. I'll explain what it is, and how we will keep notations on our transactions, if that fellow buys you out, give me a call." Twenty minutes later he was on his way home. He had a date the following day at 2:00, with the sisters.

He had been away from home since dawn. With just as much drive, determination, and fortitude with faith in himself he could do it, with the smoothness and tact Jackie Robinson used, each time he succeeded in stealing home plate. Soame had a desire to get into the house, and be excepted by pleased and smiling faces. His dirty boots were left outside on the porch, with his "fog" over the railing. He knew DD would be waiting for him in the living room, with everyone else gathered around. Except for Camille, it was as he anticipated: entertaining the door, extracting the money from the bag, he had a grin on his face when she began moving toward him. Purposely he had not cleaned his sweater. "Not again Suarme, no."

"Ha, count this, and put it in the book."

"All day you did not come to the house, we were there, all of us, until two. Then Camille had to go to work."

"Work? Did you say work?"

DD knew from that point, it would be useless to continue with anything toward a chastisement. Knowing his character, seeing the money and knowing he was pleased in having it, she sighed into a frustrated womanly pose, with her arms folded across her breast. He had given her all she'd ever dreamed of, and was thankful for what he had produced for himself. She would not attempt, nor would DD allow anyone to take the gratefulness, he'd filled himself up with, self derived pleasure.

"All day, and still there is more work. Chairly, get the foil and scissors. Take Bev to the basement, and show her how to cut two-hundred dime squares from foil and waxed paper. Margaret, you show them how to make up seventy-five quarter squares."

"Suarme, will you get out of those clothes, now!" She snapped, unfolding her arms.

"Do not take them into my bedroom."

Fifi "arffed," and as he started to undress, DD took the money, and everyone else began moving. DD sent Margaret for a plastic liner. As he began shedding his sweater, pants, and undershirt, DD collected the items with a pout, disposing them into the plastic bag, being held by Margaret. Then walked down the hall.

In the bedroom, Camille was comfortably relaxed on stacked pillows. An ashtray on the nightstand held the remainder of a joint of reffer she lit that morning, and had been trying all day to finish. She was reading her Kennith Roberts book. "Well hello, how was your day?"

"That depends, how was yours Camille?"

"Come here, the indication will be in the kiss I have for you."

She was sitting in a reclined position, with her back against the pillows; they were leaned against the headboard. Approaching her, Soame gave her the number of trucks, including the parcel, that completed the hodges filed harvest. "Perhaps that will enhance the succulence."

DD stepping through the bedroom doorway. She turned right into the bathroom saying, "Don't sit on the bed Suarme."

Following his shower, he dressed for bed, and in his robe had dinner. He filled the ladies at the table with him, in on all the latest farming news, and was informed of other agricultural developments, from the newspaper reports, and those earlier broadcasted on TV. He ployed in such a way, not because of a guilty conscience, but because he had consideration toward DD's feelings. It had been a very exciting day for her. Camille was also boiling with aroused feelings through the accomplishment, and anticipation was highlighted. He had made all the preparations, which still had to be physically constructed, beyond the forms presented to them during the day. He was finishing his meal when DD went for the ledger. Camille began telling him about the exciting day they had. After the entries had been logged, and the money put away, DD began giving her version of the rewarding day, at their new home.

The descriptions of exciting times extended to the basement, with Camille joining them merely for observation. He weighted up a quarter pound of cocaine, and put a full one on it. While doing so, he discovered DD being wise in handling the furnishing arrangements for their new home. The furniture was ordered, with some pieces to be tailored. She and Camille selected from picture pamphlets and catalogs; sizes, colors, styles, and materials. Other than the drapes, which the decorators would make and the kitchen and her bathroom, every other order was put on hold. This was explained as being a decision resulting from the conversation they had the previous weekend in the basement. With the longevity of their stay being uncertain, DD concluded, "I thought it was the best thing to do, in using what we have, until we are sure the community will last around us."

It was also brought out, during the question and answer period, Pete and two other carpenters, who had worked for a furniture manufacturer, offered to make the platform king size bed she wanted. Of course the materials would have to be purchased, including the canopy. The sketch she preferred was taken from the pamphlet, and given to her by the decorator. DD liked the drawers in the queen size illustration; everyone in the basement laughed, when she commented, "I will use them to store my money in." She then puckered friskily, for the smacking kiss Soame delivered.

Shortly after they began weighing and wrapping, Camille received a smack from both of them, and went upstairs "to read and retire for the evening." After the dimes and quarter packages were done, as a package for Billy, Beverly, and Chairly then went upstairs. Margaret joined them, only to bring DD's pipe back. He made the sample gram package, which was a quarter less potent than the actual package. The remainder of the half pound was folded into half and gram packets, in preparation for the window. To ensure potency, those packets were placed in a wide mouth gallon jug. When the lid was twisted on, it became air tight. Soame then made love with the two women in his company. It was much easier than the love making sessions during the previous day, because the two women with him in Margaret's bed, also loved each other as lovers.

Near noon, DD woke him to answer an urgent phone call from Pete, who was at the hospital. An emergency had been experienced at the foundry with one of the temporary workers. Soame had rented a flat bed truck with boarded sides, and the driver included in the package hauled scrap metal and old equipment, to a junk yard in Rapid City. The material was sold, to be transfered and molted to ore. He would make a considerable worthwhile profit, through the sales. At the hospital, Pete explained the mishap with an oblique indication, toward it being purposely done, for him to see. He was walking through a bay, into the foundry. Carelessly, the worker was "supposed" to have slipped. One of his legs was pinned, crushed, and at the hospital, it was also proven to be broken. Pete had no comment in response to the statement Soame made concerning "A million dollar wound."

Dr. Hue Wuynn facilitated as the county doctor. He came from Vietnam as a refugee. In his homeland, Dr. Wuynn was a licensed physician. He had been in America sine 1980, but in order to be recognized in any state in the United

States, as a practicing doctor of medicine, he had to attend an American school of medicine, for a short stipulated period, to be licensed by the state he'd work in. His license would be achieved through that state's medical board, following the stateside schooling. He had not gone to school in America. Never the less, he was the only physician in town, and worked as the county doctor. It was the first opportunity each had the chance to meet each other. The doctor explained the simple fracture to Soame, displaying the injury on an X-ray screen. There was no trauma, the patient was under sedation, and a cast had been applied to his lower leg. With all probability, the worker would be kept for two or three hours, and relased during mid afternoon. Soame did not visit the patient.

Camille had gone home for lunch, by the time he had chance to call her. Soame went by the hardware, and on his way to his office, visited the deli section of the grocery store. He enjoyed his brunch. It was quiet and relaxed, with easy listening music filtering through the speakers of the sound system. During and after his meal, there were several calls made. One of them was to the car salesman in Rapid City; he'd seen and spoken to him at the beginning of the week. Soame negotiated a deal on the cash purchase of a new automobile. The cash reduction made it a pleasing day to Carl Willises' car lot. Leaving the office, he stopped by the realty, delivering the paperwork. Camille already had the general news, he filled her in on the details of the accident. He then spent five minutes across the way with Willis. Soame was then on is way to spend time with the two sisters. They had to be back home by 5:00, to milk the cows.

Friday morning with Camille's departure for work, he roused everyone else in the house. They were told to prepare themselves, and make breakfast, "We're all going to the motel for the remainder of the day." When Fifi brushed against his leg, Soame scooped her up, told them he'd be right back, and with the dog, he grabbed his briefcase, and went out the front door.

The rooms leased in the northern front section of the motel had almost duplicated renovations, to the office, bedroom, kitchen, and dining room facilities, in the southern portion of the building. There was no lavish partitionment, separating the upstairs east and west rooms. A regular size door opened from either side, as entry into a narrow zig zagging hall. In lieu of the office, there was a spacious lounge, with a single bed, reclining chair, bean bags, two floor lamps, a cushion chair, a small table, and with the radio, there was a regular motel TV. The bathroom in the lounge had been removed. The bathroom across the hall in the accounting room could be used for toilet needs, or the one downstairs in the bedroom. The two remained the original standard motel bathrooms.

The upstairs adjoining room, on the east side, remained the original motel bedroom also. It featured a false door and a plexoglass picture-window. These two feautures were also additions with the lounge, across the hall, and accounting room down stairs. The hall had sharp turns; these were results of extensions of bathrooms it lead behind. The bathroom in each upstairs room, in the northern sector, had not been changed. A light bulb every thirty feet in the hall, provided ample lighting, from the ceiling. The brick walled hallway, lead to a downstairs room, on the farmost eastern side of the building. The room was divided in half with a brick wall, containing a solid oak door, with a latch slam lock. Through the door was the window for "Service," where the transactions were to be made. A straight, railed stairway, made the divided room accessible, from the hall.

In appearance the set up for "Service" was similar to that used in walk up, or drive through bank teller and fast food service windows. The 2" mirrored plexoglass held a 7" tubular container. The open mouth of the cylinder revolved from in, to out, and was controlled from inside the room by a lever. The lever carried the contents of the tubing out of the room, and in retrospect, brought whatever deposited into the mouth inside. When the window was not in operation, a specially designed aluminum fitting plate, was used to cover the mirrored service window, which was recessed 4" from the outside wall of the breezeway. The divided room had a block and brick enforced bonded wall, separating it from the room it butted. A technician from the phone company was paid to install the light switch styled silent alarm. It was located shoulder high, on the right side of the door facing, in the service room. With the straight stairway also displaying a sturdy hand rail, leading up to the hall, that, constituted the designed set up, as the renovated idea to sell cocaine from the motel.

They had seen the designing and construction of the house they would live in, two days prior to the day Soame took them to the motel. They had also seen and spent time in the office suite, in the southern end of the motel. That Friday morning, arriving at the motel, Soame took them through the northern set up's only entrance, the accounting room. He had been explaining every function and feature of each room, for more than twenty minutes, on that end of the building. DD was there basically for observation. In the accounting room, the purpose of the long conference styled table and chairs, was explained to be used in totaling up before and after the window. During that course of explanations, Chairly made "wise cracks." Twice Soame asked her to refrain from the annoyances. The third time he said to DD, "You've taught her how to speak and understand French. It's important to them and me, they understand what's to be put into operation here. I've invested considerable time and money, to protect them and their lives, while they work from this building. There is a risk involved with this operation. I can not get through to Chairly, it seems, in English, and I speak it fluently. She's your guest and your friend. Tell her… listen, everyone except Chairly, go upstairs, through the door in the back wall, to the room across the hall, and wait for me. I'll be there shortly. DD take Fifi with you."

There was nothing to question. The three women left him and Chairly along. "Close both doors behind you," he instructed Margaret, who was last to go up the stairs. In the Seville was the briefcase, which contained the recorder and the sheet of paper he'd been waiting for the right time to present.

"Soame wh-"

"No, no, don't say anything now. Just sit down and be quiet; I'll be right back." He exited the room.

When he returned, in his hand was the briefcase. Placing it on the table in front of Chairly, he said while opening it, "You've got a problem. Its getting to be a serious problem not only for you, but it's also having an effect on all of us. It's your adolescence and maturity fighting each other. You recognize the problem, and deep inside, you want to help yourself, but you evidently can't. You do not have enough self discipline within you. I'm not angry Chairly, because I understand." He was examining the recorder, as he spoke. "It's my responsibility to apprise. Do you know what that word means?"

"It mean ta put a prize on somthin."

"The two words are similar in sound, but that word is a-p-p-r-a-i-s-e, and you are correct with it's meaning. The word I stated is a-p-p-r-i-s-e. It means to call your attention to. To inform you of and, or to enable you to learn."

"You want to be mature, and eventually you will. Deep inside, you do not want to let your primary youth go, and it's truly good you do realize the value of being young, but Chairly your childhood days are over. You are experiencing the sexual life, and other aspects of life, as a mature woman. You are handicapping yourself with the misuse of the language you speak, in an effort to hold on to your childhood, while other aspects of your mind develop with your body and emotions. Do you understand what I have said?"

"Sorta."

"Well now, you see? That's the fact I'm pointing out to you. I know how smart you are. I know also, you know exactly what I said and its meaning. You understood completely, but your childish reactions motivated you to reject it, and pretend you did not. That's also the problem you have with words. You know the correct words to use, in their proper conjunction with verbs, but you want to hold on to something that's phasing out of your life. Where you're from, your childhood, and we will always be black, so I can't kick about words like ant, ya, and um, which I at times purposely, as expressions of our mutually shared pride, in being identified as being black."

"I've done something that should help you, with your language problem. Now, you talk only to be heard, and gain attention to the handicap you're afflictively burdening yourself with. Who knows? Perhaps someday you will mature into a beautiful woman with a gorgeous figure. My intent is for you not to have the affliction, and to precede in helping you, do without the handicap. I will aid you Chairly, toward the preparation of being listened to and admired, because of your proper speech."

"On this recorder is my voice, reading what's on this sheet of paper." He did not give the paper to her, because of the possibility of the writing distracting what was being said to her. "I've written and pronounced words you improperly use, and verbs you fail to conjugate in their proper context."

"You've demonstrated something I detest. You do not want to learn, which is bad in itself. You've attempted to disturb and intefear with the progress of others and their efforts to comprehend. That will not be tolerated with the time, money, and effort I've put into each of you, and that which I'm trying to accomplish. You hear what's recorded; compare it to what's written, and on the blank portions of the tape, practice reading and listening to yourself. Do it until you have come as close as you can to what I've recorded. Do not erase my recording. Chairly, there is a solution to your problem. I'll go as far as it takes in helping you. For example, you'll be left here for the remainder of the morning. When I bring your lunch, if I'm not satisfied with what you have on the tape, you will sped the afternoon here, trying."

"I've got an idea bout how far you will go, to have your way, but check this out; if by this evening you haven't satisfied me with what I expect of you as accomplishment, I will take you out to the farm house, where you will remain until school starts. Then, I will have the chairman of the school board, have you begin your studies in the 7th grade, as a remedial alternative. You seem to want to heckle and disturb others with your childishness. As a 7th grader, you can get all the attention you want. It goes further than that Chairly. You may be a mentally disturbed; the overall extensiveness of this effort in helping you, may produce that conclusive result. Should you fail to progress with the enhancement of your speech on that junior high level, there are means to probe further, to find out if you are unbalanced to the point of derangement. Chairly, hear me, and understand me well. Should these methods, after they've been exhausted, show as an attempt, you will have almost proven my failure with you. I will not except failure. To prove that point to you, I will have you casted into an asylum."

The impact of what he said rained on her. They knew each other, and each knew the other would have their way. To what point, was the factor. She was still in mental astonishment when Soame continued. "You may do well with the recorder today and join us, with the fool hearted thinking I will not notice every word you speak, from that point on. I will be listening for subject and verb agreement, usage of proper words and correctness in your grammar, period. I promise you, I will not tell you this again. Step by step, I will demonstrate my sincerity toward your care, my interest in your future well being, and the compulsion I now have toward your speech improvement. You will become a lady who speaks well, projecting pride and dignity with your blackness. Again I tell you Chairly, I will not fail, with my care and concern for you, toward meeting that goal."

There was a brief passage of time, in their looking into each others eyes. He resumed, "You have an alternative. There's the door. You may leave, and all you have on and in your bag, you may have in parting. Once you've made that decision, without recording what's written on that sheet of paper, to my satisfaction, do or say to change your abandonment. I will not allow DD to except you again into our house, or in anyway provide for you. Should you decide to leave, I'd appreciate your at least saying good bye to her. Without her, you would not be here; she's been extremely good to you. Are there any questions?"

"Why didn't you tell us Wess was from Luzanna?" He was taken by surprise. During the pause, it took his reflective thoughts toward having been told by DD, the Yerby book had been passed on to Chairly. The only Wess he'd ever known of, was the story's main character. "It took a moment or two for me to compose and center my thoughts. The setting in that particular book does open, and the majority of the scenes described by Yerby takes place in Lou-isi-ana, Chairly. Remember the day we met, and mispronounced your name?"

She indicated "Yes" with the nod of her head.

"Well in the same association you used the verbal demonstration of the word chair; that's how important it is for you to practice speaking correctly, because anyother way is wrong." There was an intrim of silence.

"Anyway, 'Ingraham's Crest' is the plantation setting in southern America, but the actual story begins in Africa, with a preceeding book called 'The Dioman.' It's strange DD did not mention that fact to me."

"I noticed it an das why I axed. You real smort Soame."

"Not really, I'm simply older than you are, and I've got a lot more experience in other areas you haven't been exposed to. I think you are very smart, and I want to help you see and present your intelligence outwardly in a different manner. I see quite a bit of goodness in you. I am attempting to bring it out, in you presenting yourself with ladylike qualities, which will excel you far beyond your natural womanhood. Anything else you want to ask?"

"I'll do it."

"Good, we'll be back after while."

He was half way up the steps when she called "Soame."

He stopped and turned. Doing so Soame saw the glossy, water filled eyes, looking at him. "Yes."

"Um a good woman fa ya, an I jes got ta kno dis. Do you luv me?"

"Chairly, I love only myself." He completed the turn, and descended the stairs, walking back to the spot he stood before.

"It may sound strange to you, but I know a lot about love. It has good as well as bad spots in my life. Time and time again, I have given love to different women; each time, as a result, I've found that the love I have can only be intrusted to me. I will not use it as a tool to hurt myself. Chairly, there's a lot more to life than love. Something may happen to me today, tomorrow, next week, or a year from now. I want you to be able to take care of yourself, your mind, because your heart will mislead you. Your mind will take you places, where your body should only be admired. I want to cultivate your mind, and help you project from your mouth what you feel, the way you feel about it, and why you feel the way you do, so hover hears you, will know an intelligent person is expressing herself. Love is a natural feeling. I care very much for you Chairly, but first of all you must care enough to improve yourself, in this way. I am spending time and money with you, I can't do it all. Do your part; then let's talk about love." With that, he walked away.

Chapter 11

THE room beneath the one he joined the women in, belonged to Smitty. The original design of the manager's room, allowed 5 ½' more space than any other double occupancy room in the building. The room next to the manger's residence was rented as a "single," with a single bed. Smitty hadn't rented it, since owning the motel. When Soame presented the idea of completely removing the wall and bathroom, allowing him and his wife more space, with the addition of a breakfast counter, it was a dream come true. Smitty had lived in a four bedroom home, before moving into the town.

Soame's idea went beyond the leasing agreement. He was happy to extend the favor to Smitty, for an exchange agreement, to allow hall space behind each room upstairs, in that section of the building. Smitty did not smoke marijuana; his wife did. Both of them did coke, though it had been years. In finalizing the arrangements, Soame gave the owner of the motel a half pound of grass and two ounces of coke, with a one on each. It had been a month since Smitty said to him, "With the cash you've invested in this place, and this, you could've bought the entire motel. I'm sure you know what you're doing. I'm with you, whatever you want to do." Shelves, a closet and other purposeful additions enhanced the enlargement.

"Where's Chairly?" Beverly asked, when he joined them.

"She's still in the accounting room. You'll see her on your way out. She's busy trying to improve her speech. Let's hope she completes what she's been assigned to do. "He looked at DD in finishing his say, "I'm about to put her out." Giving his view back to Beverly, he went on, "If she joins us later, before dark, you help her with her grammar. It'll be important to her, not starting school here, in the 7th grade." Soame then went on with the explanation and functions of each room.

The hallway was 3' wide, at all points. This was the maximum allowance, from each upstairs room, in that section of the building. Every rear wall, in each room, had been gutted, to install the hall. Each bathroom remained untouched, which created the zig zag. Under the extra thick carpet were two layers of padding. Soame explained how important it was, for them to walk through the hall, without touching or bumping the walls. When he brought detection, guns, and robbery into the picture, they listened with strict attention. He felt they would have more insight toward his strictness with Chairly, when he made them aware of the risk factor. "We only live once. Each of you know how desperate people around here are for money. Two weeks ago I told you, you'd be handling a lot of it. It'll be more than you have ever imagined passing through your hands. One mistake, can be the prelude toward actions, which may later threaten your lives. That mistake will only occur if you allow it. I will show you how not to make that mistake." He lead them to the hallway they passed through, entering the room.

"I will walk to the other end; a minute later, DD you will be called, then Beverly, and Margaret you will be last. Walk in the center of the hall, take your time at the turns, and anything you have on that may jangle, fasten it, tuck it in, or take it off." He stepped away. After she'd been called, DD joined him, and left him in the hall, at the top of the stairs. As she had done in the room they left from, she turned on the air conditioner. The single unit device had been reinstalled and constructed in the center of the room, with –ducts-channeling apparatuses to pass equal distributions of air into the divided room. The sisters then joined her. They had gotten the impression the hall was to have been a rigorous exercise. As it turned out, walking the hall was a simple thing to do. The room they entered contained only two chairs and a table. The stairway and the bathroom were the only other components of the enclosure. It all had been explained to them. He pulled the curtain and indicated the sealed door as a physical demonstration. They were then shown the service room door latch; he had the only key to the lock, which was automatic when the door closed. A simple turn of the knob from the inside, released the lock and latch. An exact door and lock were at the top of the stairs; that lock had to be opened by a key from both sides. The key Saome had, opened both doors.

They would work from the window in pairs. There were two swivel, half back, stools at the window. Should difficulty, in anyway, be encountered at the window, the "shout down" was to be enforced. That was the drill Soame proceeded with. DD took a seat in the entry room, and observed the procedure. The sisters were relaxed, after having the process explained to them. Margaret was into her daintiness, and Beverly was as "fly" as ever. During the initial thirty minutes, they both thought of it as being fun and games. As they began to get the true hang of the situation, and the total gist of the "shout down," Soame became stern in directing them away from the window, after telling them their lives could one day depend on their capabilities to effectively carry through on a "shout down" procedure.

The process involved a four step detailed sequence: leaving the window, flipping the switch, slamming the door, and up the stairs. The drilling instilled in their minds, the money at the window became valueless, if the procedure was activated. It was to be dropped and, or left immediately. The purpose of the turning seat, was in allowing them comfort and convenience of movement. Leaving the window, with a turn toward the door, opening out, flipping the shoulder high switch, next to the door facing; slamming the door, and up the stairs, was the routine they drilled. The door was oak; they went up the stairs hastily. That was the extent of the procedure Soame carried them through that morning. Both women worked up a mild sweat.

The aluminum fitting was not taken from the window during their practice "shout downs." Not only did the pair have to psysically execute the plan, verbally each had to explain, "I'm sitting at the window, a customer pulls a gun, I know no bullet can penetrate the plexoglass, I respond without hesitation, dropping or leaving the cash, turning in my seat, etc." At 11:15 DD was sent to take Fifi for a walk, check on Chairly and wait with Chairly for Camille's lunch break. Chairly's perdickerment was explained to her. She was told "talk with her, if you want to help her. Do as much as you can, but you will have to leave her alone, to do what she's been assigned."

She was directed to use the phone in the accounting room, to coordinate Camille's lunch break, to allow them a means to bring back lunch, from the deli for all of them. Soame, Margaret, and Beverly were to meet them in the dining room of the suite at 12:15. After giving her the key, he proceeded with the instructions on a canister, or smoking device being placed in the window cylinder. It would be reacted to as regular shout down. They talked themselves from the window: "If I am at the window, and a smoke or gas device is placed, etc." The last instructions were warnings in watching who steps before them and noticing strictly, what's being placed in the mouth of the tube. They left for lunch.

Margaret and Beverly preceded him to the suite. Soame spent time listening to what Chailry had on the recorder, while she had lunch. When she was done, he heard her verbal presentation. She read almost without flaw. It was a duplicate to what was on the recorder. The errors came about with words such as that, this, and don't. The word and was also one of the primary words on the paper.

Chairly was proud of what she had done, and he shared the exhibited pride with her, in hearing the progress she had made in both forms. Never the less, it was her expected reading norm. Soame had an inward deep fear of her being resistant and falling below par. Her production and response displayed acceptance to the idea; this he could work with, and with the constant help from the others, he felt confident she would pull through, with the expected improvement, in time.

His delivery at that point, was in coaxing her to put into action, the use of the words in her general conversation. Soame then took the time and instructed her through demonstrations of rolling her tongue, and sliding its' tip from behind the teeth, to produce the T in this, and that. He had done this before in Wyoming, and at one point she had been improving quite well. The words were recorded, with both of them displaying correct pronunciation. Leaving her he said, "Have you noticed I haven't called you kid in a while? I've stopped; not only because you stated it's not your name, the word seems not to fit anymore. Technically it never did, and in the way I used it, you've outgrown the description. Check this out Chairly; I don't expect you to change in one day, what you have been incorrectly practicing all your life. I've gone through all of this before with you, but this is the first time you've had the chance to listen to yourself. You can do it. I would not ask you to do something you were ill fitted, or could not do. Do it Chairly, and do it right." He walked to the door and out.

Camille had interesting news from the office. Sixteen men showed up, to replace the injured worker. Most of them had previously applied. The majority were still waiting on the office step's, and standing around on Willises car lot. She was directed to give them insurance forms and examine the applications for carpentry skills and experience. They were to report back Monday afternoon, to be assigned to one of the three job sights, Tuesday morning. Stillman had been called to Helena. Plans were being proposed to activate the school system, which was never a threat of becoming inoperative, except it's being ran from an adjoining county. The salaries were paid through the county by the state. The county maintained and operated the schools, with it's financial support. The chairman and two other school board members, made the trip to the capitol earlier that day. The meetings were the last through Monday, possibly as late as Tuesday, according to the relay from Mrs. Tillman.

Elrus McMaulin, the male realator who worked part time at the office, and was a school teacher, had been in that morning. His summer vacation was spent in southern California, where he also upgraded the rank of his teaching certificate, with summer courses. According to Camille, "He had the most gorgeous tan" she had ever seen. The news completed the meal, after which they had drinks and refreshments upstairs, and it was back to work for everyone; Camille preferred walking the block and a half.

When DD mentioned taking Chairly a drink, and waved the partial quart bottle of Blue Label, Soame responded, "With all the shit she's got in her purse, what does she need a drink for? That's probably the problem with her; you give her any and everything she wants." Knowing he was equally as guilty, he lead the way downstairs, neither consenting or objecting.

After leaving the bottle, DD was the last one up the stairs, from the accounting room. When they were all in the room across from the lounge, Soame closed the door saying, "Alright out of your clothes." When the three women looked at him with surprise, he stated once again, "Come on, get out of your clothes. I might even get some pussy."

"But Suarme, why else would we take off our clothes?"

Beverly giggled and Margaret was flushed with embarrassment. "The hallway, we're about to go through the procedures in the hall. In case you haven't noticed, it's not air-conditioned."

Margaret then asked, "So we don't have to get completely nude?"

"If you want me to see it, you can."

She gave him a look of contempt, and eased her look from his stare. He undressed with them down to his boxers, and when they only had on panties and bras, Soame told Margaret, "Let me see it." She lowered the front of her bikinis. Casually he said, "I only see some hairs," and took three steps to her. DD then sat on the bed, relaxed. He placed his hand in her twat and began massaging. "Come on Soame, you don't really want to do this, not now."

He brought five record albums with him from his office. They were suppose to simulate them carrying a tray, each would be using, going to and coming from the window. Soame took them to the hall, and explained the hall light switch, located next to the door paneling, in the lounge. Each of them saw how the hallway became completely blackened, with it's use. Beverly was requested to remove her glasses. The two of them wore the censored lenses everywhere, all the time, except in bed. They had gone to the extent of mail ordering changeable pairs, from an optical display section they noticed in one of DD's magazines. She and Chairly thought it would be impressive at school, to have a change of glasses.

The switch in that spot was Pete's idea, as a last safety precaution, if someone invaded the scheme, through the window, and somehow got past the two oak doors, and pursued the workers. The light switch extinguished all the lights in the hall; this enabled the bathroom extensions to be used as an advantage. The chasing culprit would be trapped in the dark, bumping his way, allowing the workers the chance to exit the building. "Getting out of the building safely, is the primary functional purpose of the shout down." He then took them to the opposite end of the hall, leaving the lounge and room doors open. There was no fan to push the air through the brick passageway. DD was wearing "sling shots," she lead the way carrying the albums, with Soame behind her, grabbing a rub or a feel, at each turn.

The women knew the most difficult portion of the day was over. There was a red light at the end of the hall; they had seen it before until Soame brought the light switch, to the left of the door fcing, to their attention, neither of them had noticed it. The switch controlled the red light. "In the event of a shout down, after you've come up the stairs, slam this door; if you think of it, throw this switch. It controls only this red light. It's in preparation for that impossibility, here's another door, with a slam lock, just as strong. This door stays open all the time, except in the event of a shout down. That aspect may vary, I'll let you know later. This door being open, serves two purposes: it allows cool air and light into the hall, and it is added protection against the impossible. It is impossible for anyone to knock, kick, or push this door down, from the steps. Once it's closed, and if you remember, flip this switch. This is another precautionary measure. You know what's in this hallway, the intruder doesn't. You flip this switch, turn that light out, and watch what happens." He closed the door, and doused the light. They saw the shadowy glow from the next light around the corner. "Remember, by doing this, he will walk into darkness, because his eyes will have to make the adjustment. Now do you see the purpose of the switch at the other end?" There were no questions. He opened the door, they descended into the room below.

After explaining the purpose of the records, he demonstrated carrying the "tray" up the stairs. It was simple; Margaret and Beverly did it only twice. There was an outside and a wall railing. All of them were right handed. The tray was to be carried in their right hand. "Use the rail to be absolutely sure of sturdiness." He then demonstrated how the tray was to be carried through the passageway with both hands, and took the sisters back to the open door, at the top of the stairs. The albums were then given to Margaret. "Walk from this end to the next, without touching the walls. Stay in the center of the corridor and come back." She went to the first corner, and he stopped her. Taking Beverly with him, he approach Margaret, directed her through the turn, with the "tray" tucked next to her abdomen. Soame then followed her to the end. She did well, it was not a difficult assignment. Beverly executed carrying the records back. They each went through the procedure twice.

In the divided room, he asked them, "Have you noticed anything, that's not in this room, found in the other rooms?"

Beverly answered, "There's no phone, no radio, or TV."

"You're right. Those are intentional non fixtures. At the window, later, after you have gotten thoroughly accustomed to the actual routine, we'll add radio music. The idea here is work, and it involves your full concentration toward who approaches the window, and what they deposit into the canister. In pairs you will be assigned to shifts. One will leave the other alone at the window, only when she uses the bathroom. I'll have security when we get underway. Your responsibility toward yourselves, in the event of an irregularity, is to throw the switch, in the other room, and get out of there according to plan. Security will handle the rest, to be done. You control what you take in the window with the lever. Your only outside contact, in the event of something goes wrong, is with security. You must be able to remember to throw the switch. Now! Lets take the shout down procedure all the way through, slamming the door upstairs, and turning the light off."

"Oh no, Soame, we've got it."

"Yea, I know. I want to feel assuredly positive, you will not let it get away from you. We're not practicing for something that's going to happen tomorrow or next week. However, if it happens next month, next year, or a year or two after then, I want this lasting impressionable reaction, to be spontaneous reflex at that time, as if it happens two hours from now. Um not gonna loose your pussies, because of my lack of persistency, yielding to your trifling whims."

Beverly exclaimed, "That's gross and dogmatic Soame."

"Good you know how to use such expressions of your opinion. I've never learned the particularization involved, with such meaningful aim toward an arrived objective. Now twitch them pussies in the room, and let's see how this goes from bottom to top." They went to the window, Beverly pushed the lever, he had deposited money in the cylinder, when she pulled it down the money rotated back to them, Margaret was extracting it, when he yelled "Shout Down!" He drilled them together and one at a time, for thirty minutes

After that phase, he held their attention once again, in the stairway portion of the room. Soame threw a towel on the rug. "Margaret, if you were carrying your tray along the hall, and you dropped that, how would you pick it up?"

She attempted to answer; he interrupted by asking her to, "Get the record albums and demonstrate."

When she did, Beverly was then asked to execute her version, as to how she thought it was to be done. Both of them held the "Tray" with one hand aided with the knee, and removed the towel, with the other hand. Soame demonstrated sitting the albums completely down on the floor, next to the fallen object, placing the object on the tray, with accessibility of both hands on the object and tray. This alleviated the possible tilting of the tray, which was the focal point. At the window, he pointed out four large wing nuts, used to hold the outside shield into place. "DD you take them through picking up an object, with the tray in the hall, and going up the stairs with the tray. I'm going to stop by the accounting room, and go outside. Leave this door open, I will tap on the covering four times; remove the wing nuts."

Soame existed in a world of tranquility. He moved about in it freely, from day to day, through the hours of the day, in total peace and harmony, with that which he came in contact with. Two days prior, he'd expressed success with the jewelry box factory, as being his quest, to Mrs. Tillman. In part, that was true. None the less, long before discovering the town he lived in, Soame became aware of the fact, the most ambitious goal he had during his adulthood, had been accomplished. In actuality, he was a millionaire. The factory remained as a motivational secondary achievement, in boosting his personal pride, while exuberantly floating his inward esteem. Though his immediate personal cash flow was sliding from low, to exhaust, he had capitol for business operations, in escrow. This depending upon his expenditures. Along with having a definite reserve, he had an income. Anyone in the proximity of his realm, could easily distinguish his flamboyantly alive attitude. Each of his constituents was giving him an independent excelling lift, which raised his motivational spirits, and aspired his desire to procede with commitment.

His enthusiasm was accentually enhanced, in receiving the money he'd gotten from Billy. Each time, he became more enthusiastically inclined. It was proof of his idea and hopes of generating a cash flow. He only trusted that which was real. The plans were his sure enough, but they were promises, and even though his, they remained unmaterialized. The wheat from the fields to the storage bins, were in essence potential ideas for cash. Though the amount from Billy may have been considered trivial to others, it was a positive view of something tangible. He produced it, through the efforts, and that was the true worthwhile evidence he brought out of himself, and the real love he knew he had.

Being in the building with him, the women saw deeper into what they had been noticing all along. Each of them knew his nature as he knew their's. He was endowed with a compulsively zealous sex drive, which was relentless toward the satisfaction of the women he was intimately involved with. It is a scientific fact: food and sex are man's most impelling urges to gratify; their order exchange visa versa, depending upon the individual. Obtaining the cash and reserve almost at the same time with DD, well rounded his hopes toward an enjoyable pleasant life style. Just as immediate, thereafter came Chairly. It was during their stay at the hunting lodge, after the triangular involvement, and his discovery of DD's bisexuality, DD brought Chiarly's sexual extreme aggressiveness to his attention. He had noticed signs, and seen Chairly's responses all along, but had not mentioned nymphomania to DD. In their initial group contact with the Johsons, ostentatiousness was not a part of their sexual encounters. Through ingenuity, luck, or fate, Soame derived at the exact perfection comprehensible, in achieving and surrounding himself in a sexual utopia. Camille's sexual drive was almost as dauntless as Chairly's. As an adult, through experience, she was partly able to restrain herself toward her ungovernable impulses. Her affair and sisterhood with DD, enabled her to completely unleash the uninhibitory sexual release of herself. The two women always felt comfortable with each other, and the ways they shared the bedroom and their lives with Soame.

It wasn't long after they'd been living as one household, and after he inquired, Camille confided in him the rumopr she'd heard several times, and the fact she thought her youngest daughter was a lesbian. Beverly's choice did not matter to either of them. Margaret lived in a world of gratitude and defiance. She was pleased and thankful she was no longer poor, and at times gave her body in exchange for items she could not afford otherwise; this included marijuana, which she had a mental addiction for. She did however, become addicted to the pipe, physically. This was done through continuous use with DD. She had experienced smoking "crack" from a can more than several times, prior to meeting DD. The occasions were rare and far in between, because of it's unavailability in the area. The substance was a sure winner for boys who could find it, for the enticingly favorable Margaret. Being tall, with a slim, shapely body, and a petit waist, added with her blossomy bosom, brought radiance to her attractive face; though glamorous prevailed as an undertoned description of her, it was in no way an understatement. Her reputation enfolded having a "smoking head" and a "snapping coochie."

Early during the previous school year, one of Margaret's teachers got wind of her exploits and became the exploiter. He did not have the local connections for the grass, and because of the scarcity of powder or "rocks," he drove back and forth to Billings, each month on pay day. Her attractiveness would win any average man's attention. She'd learn to use her pleasing body to gain his heart, and earn his favors. Within the teacher-student relationship, because of the privacy that had to be maintained and kept, the other young boys she continued to date, were not detoured. She had done well in providing for herself, until people began moving away; then came summer, and her teacher was gone.

That day, during lunch at the motel, when Camille mentioned McMaulin's visit to the office, except for DD, it appeared no one else noticed Margaret's keen interest in the topic. Margaret had long before then, told DD about "The guy in my mother's office." Camille did not mention his asking about Margaret. What none of them did not know was, Elrus had carefully budgeted and scrapped up enough money, to purchase two ounces of prime marijuana, and "crack," amounting to two grams. He did this while in southern California. He'd calculated, being economical in stretching what he had, in small distributions to Margaret, until the close of the year holidays. What he didn't know, partially centered around the fact, at that time, Margaret was smoking two grams, and at times more, a day. She had found love with DD, and cherished her fantasy of love for and from Soame.

It was Margaret who addicted herself to the pipe. Thinking cocaine was still scarce in the area, she attempted two feats, resulting in frivolousness. Initially she attempted to out smoke DD. It took at least two weeks for her to realize the unquestionable absurdity. At that point she attempted to exhaust their supply, by smoking around the clock until it was all gone. DD saw the ridiculousness involved, after staying up with her twice. She then gave Margaret one of the pipes, and left her to her folly. A week later she smoked "rezz," and with that, none of the locals could compete. It can not be produced from a can. Within the household she lived, Margaret was far beyond any other local person's imaginative reach. The coke was part of it; there was another aspect which held her mind, body, existence and her heart, in complete and total ravishing rapture. Margaret's love for DD was unrelinquishing. It was with the excessive depth, buldging to go beyond commitment, if elasticity would yield to the eternal existence she sought. In the most delicate way, she loved the other woman, Dominique Dubanee was the first woman she had ever had an affair with. DD's love for Soame was not a fantasy.

Realizing her self submission to the pipe, Margaret willingly submitted herself to DD. Submissively, she did it with docility. It began with the presentation of herself in the master bedroom during the day, when DD was there alone. The pipe and it's essentials would be on the table or night stand; she'd imply "I want to smoke."

"It is there, you are welcome, smoke if you want."

"Make me DD; make me smoke it. I want you to."

One morning soon afer, she caught DD by surprise. They were smoking, she told DD, "I want to make up your bed."

"Sure, you may."

"Make me, I want to be made to do these things, in pleasing you."

This persuasive, permissive promiscuity became entangled, and weaved itself into their sexual participations, establishing their indulgences in the tone of another level. They readily excepted the enhancement to their delights with each other, with boardored acts of masochism and sadistic gratifications. There were times when their pleasures were taken beyond the border, and it did not off center their hightened joys. Margaret may have had a well rounded guess, but she was never told, DD had been a prostitute. Throughout her life DD had never had direct power over anyone. She in fact, had been domineered. Even with Chairly, DD had to use tact with her approach, on some issues, because of her inexperienced position. As she and Margaret plunged deeper into their relationship, DD discovered new liberty, in a way she subconscientiously craved.

In that way Margaret eased her way into DD's favor. This had been gradually seen and noticed by them all. A smoldering undeveloped trifling became further lifted, between the three. Chairly had no grounds; through the nights at times, even with all their doors closed, she could be heard, as Beverly brought her to low, satisfying, pulsating, whimpers. The gained closeness in the relationship was hardly overlooked by Camille, who had a man with whom she discussed practically everything. Soame would never over look, or neglect anything within his power, when it came to the women of his household. Though he never implied with demeanor, neither of them had ever been loved and, or treated better and cared for, by anyother man they had before known. When Camille presented the issue during one of their private discussions, he responded, "Yea, I know; what do you want ta do about it?" After acknowledging her speechlessness, he suggested "Let's see how it turns out, we've got to get along. We're going to continue to live together Camille. Say listen, can you take another half hour off?" They had been there an hour and a half, during her lunch break, christening the bed in the office suite.

Soame got the full and in depth meaning of their relationship, the night after DD had danced, and he left the motel with the two of them, to make packets. None of the women ever knew where the money or the coke was stored. He moved parts of both, at various times, until the farmhouse was complete. Each time he went into each stash, he would move it's remainder to his house, and barn location. Still he did not move it all to the area; in the event someone found a cache, they would have that portion only. With the coke he was most particular, of the two. The heroin, he kept away from the coke and the money. After storing it in the loft of an abandoned house, he had not been back to it. The better than six kilos, was worth five times the value of the other two combined. That night, after leaving the motel he took them home. Either of them would tell him openly, if he didn't know, the other's periods was on, if she didn't let him know directly. It was the second day of Margaret's menstruation; she knew he knew it was on. After entering the house, she excused herself from their company, to attend her personal hygienical needs. She rejoined them in the back portion of the basement. There, on the table, Margaret saw a portion of a "key" and one which was fully wrapped. Until meeting the couple in her presence, Margaret had not before seen more than a half gram of powder, at once. Every dime rock she had ever seen, was used for her enticement, which she later shared, or in meetings with the teacher, she smoked it alone. After he cut and measured the substance, Margaret's responsibility was to fold the product into the squares she and DD had made.

Like a scientist hard at work, he made his measurement; then the rocks were crushed and he did the over and over sifting. It was late, he was tired and knew, though it was exciting to the couple sharing the pipe, they wanted to get to bed also. They'd enjoyed basic and general conversations and laughs, when abruptly he heard "Get out of your clothes."

It was an outstanding fact about Soame and the women in his household, in his audience and company with all of them, he never interfered in their doings, with and toward each other. There had been more than a few arguments, which they had gotten accustomed to, but never physical fights. He ignored them, sometimes to the point of closing, or having the door closed, but he never settled their spates. None the less, he was usually drenched with explanations after the verbal lashings. It was common for Soame to encounter, or be in the presence of DD and Margaret during both their physical and verbal entwining. He either observed, or pretended to ignore them. All the women in the family knew it was an impetuous arousal for him. In the basement, he simply moved along with his mixing.

When Margaret disrobed, DD stated, in a matter of fact way "Put on your sweater, I do not want you to catch a cold."

He could not help but notice, it was said in such a way, it was beyond the way he would tell any of them to do something. In Camille's presence this was noticed, but quite more reserved. His summarization was, DD wanted him to witness them, perhaps they both did, to gather his responses to the harshness Margaret had on only her sandals, and underthings, with the sweater. "Sit so we can look at you." to do this she had to sit on the table.

They were done with the squares long before he finished the mixing. The two women kissed and fondled each other, passing the pipe and exchanging a peppermint ball from one mouth to the other, with sniggles and giggles, calling his attention to their playfulness and petting. After he completed the mixing, Margaret was shown how to place the paper n the foil and fold. He was almost an expert at scooping from the plate on the paper, Margaret then folded. When they were done, he made up the sample; in doing so he heard "Take your sweater off, and get on that table." He was waiting to hear it, and it came "Show him your sling."

"I'll see it later, goodnight."

The two of them made grams from the remainder of the open key, DD progressed with her apologies, and before they went upstairs, she cleaned the scales.

…All afternoon at the motel, Soame attempted the sterness he'd demonstrated that morning. With his attempt he accomplished a continual hard, which could not be quelled without either one, or all of their aid. He and Beverly basically only had admiration for each other; the two were more like friends, who saw each other coming and going, with the exchange of greetings, usually with cheerfulness. They understood each other and there was no pretense involved in their non-intimate relationship. In his boxers, he could not hide his projecting tool. In their undies, they knew why he maintained the erection. When his and Beverly's eyes caught each other's, she merely looked away with a smile. She was a young likeness of her mother. Camille told them Margaret inherited her father's basic structure and features. She was a naturally feminine woman, with her attractiveness. Anything she did was done with fastidiousness. A person not knowing her, could easily gain the impression, she was overbearing with her femininity.

That morning, after a few tries, he'd noticed her daintiness, in holding and turning the door knob, and said "Margaret, the nice little door knobwill not bite you, please turn the knob as if your life depended on you getting out of this room."

It always gave her pleasure to smirk and turn her nose and, or entire head up at him. Two tries later, because of her natural superfluous style, he yelled, "Margaret! Turn the knob! And open the God dam door will ya!?"

When she did, and after they'd completed the carrythrough to the top of the stairs, DD said to him, "Suarme please."

"Well we're trying ta do a shout down procedure. Do you think you can show her how it's done, without her entreatingly primping her way through this operation?"

"But darling, she's like that."

DD then really superfluously primped, fluttering her extravagant lashes, touching and toying with her hair, holding her head to one side saying, "And besides, we do not know these big words you use; what's a lady to do?"

The sisters applauded and laughed through their cheers. With a sour face he rebutted "Yea, yea, yea."

He had lost five pounds since the day he met DD. He no longer jogged or did calisthenics, but as a sexual participator for exercise, he did marvelous work, in keeping his body in shape. Because Soame left home in a heavy turtle neck sweater, beneath it he had on a sleeveless undershirt. It fitted him tightly. His upper torso was permeated with sleek, well formed muscles, that did not buldge, until the ripples were seen across his abdomen, even through his undershirt. His shorts were somewhat baggy in the waist, and loosly covered his hips, projecting the studded wedge and the agility of the swiveling mid section. His biggest fault with women; Soame never tried to out think them. His opinion was, he couldn't. Women had nothing to do, but think; they thought all the time. With all his considerations toward the women in his life, unless they obviously presented what they wanted him to see, and if his natural instincts did not motivate his attentions or inclinations toward it, he did not notice it. Every woman he'd ever known, had never known a bigger, more robust pussy hound.

The women in the motel with him, knew these characteristical, if not distinguishing facts about the only man in their lives. They knew his depth composit, on as a person, in an immediate perspective, far better than he did. He only paid attention to the generality; they viewed and analized the specifics of his mechanisms. Though he was aroused by them, he had no motivational insights toward the thought of the excitement he was generating throughout there bodies, which were tingly, with readiness for him. The erection extending half way down his thigh, taking up the slack in the silk boxers, became a formative instigation, for the enticement of their womanishly displayed antics. They could not help but notice it. At times they could not keep their eyes off it. Beverly moistened her lips often, with an ostentative smile. He had initiated it by reaching into Margaret's crotch, fidgeting her clit, with fiddling strokes. Anytime in the presence of Soame she became afflicted in ways, similar to milquetoast. His stimulations beckoned her collapsing weakness; Margaret placed her head on his shoulder, reminding him of what she'd told him, about having sex in front of her younger sister: "I will make love with you anytime and anyplace, but I will always prefer, never to make love in the presence of my sister." In the passageway, not only did he feel and massage DD's swirving, loosly slinging hips, he toyed with the silk between her cheeks. It was fun for him, until he got to the work scene.

Soame's mind existed as an inner-sanctum of complacency. The tranquil environment he'd established for himself enabled the smugness. Had Captain Ahab conquered the white whale, he would have found such personal satisfaction. The Great Waldo Pepper would have found the zenith, had he been able to carry through on the loop, conquering centripetal force. In true reality, if it had not rained, the night before the brilliant cannoneer Napoleon Bonaparte engaged in his last battle, the general could have maneuvered his artillery, and annihilated Wilmington; thus finding mortal peace within himself, through the triumphant conquest… too, the illusive fact remained with Soame, and how long it would last, was the question, he could not shout out. Would he walk the streets penniless, and die as a pauper, like Christopher Columbus did in Europe, following his accredited discovery? Would he die as a penniless drunk, like the general who won the biggest war ever fought on American soil, and went on to become the 17th president of the United States? Soame knew there would be no statues raised in his honor, and if his overall plan was carried out through completion, a score of years after the factory produced the first jewelry box, less than fifty people in the town would remember his name.

He was living faster than he'd ever lived before. Doing it with the experience and maturity he had developed through the previous years. Soame found it incredible to have developed and live with such comfort and ease, in such a small town. The woman in his household had never before been capable of the possible thought of flexible fixed ideas, leading to the lifestyle they were most certainly enjoying, and if he succeeded in carrying through, a better one, on a higher level, was imminent. Those in the room wanted to relieve his hard, ensuing the pleasures involved. He pretended to ignore their invitational gesturing, with attempts at concentrating on the work at hand. "16 additional men, with a house to tear down, rebuilding it into a club. A barbeque stand to put up, and cleaning up a foundry. Extensions of the payroll; with the raises, quadrupling it. Equipment and materials, with the income generated from the sale of the foundry scraps and equipment; how long will the money in escrow last now?"

They had been in the room, back and forth through the hall, up and down the stairs, for an hour and a half. In the hall, Margaret had sashayed earlier, to the first turn and stopped, squared the turn holding the stack of records with one arm, looked to the side at him, and gave a perky wave, with the twinkling of her fingers. Like a bunny rabbit, she then scooted with a hop forward. Illusively, her attempt was to allure him around the corner, away from the presence of her sister. Soame had something on his mind he wanted to relay to her, and it wasn't having sex in the hallway. Like a big time director on a Hollywood set, he yelled "No, no, no! Come on Beverly, I want to show you this also."

At the end of the hall Beverly called through the open door to Chairly, who replied, "Tell my ole man I sade I wanna see him."

Soame did not say anything, but indicated for the exchange of the records, and it was Beverly's turn to try. "Bebly didn you hea me gurl?"

Margaret yelled, "Tell him yourself, he's right here!" he looked in to her gleaming eyes, she smirked, tossing her head up, in looking away.

What Chairly considered an invitation, brought her up the stairs. "Soame is you up hea? Hia you got me down hea reading this stuff an you won't even com to hea hia um doin?"

They were face to face in the doorway. "What are you doing up these stairs?"

She was looking around him, at the other two. " Whach yall doin wid ya close off?"

"I thought you're supposed to be down stairs, bettering your speech."

"I talk good a nuff ta kno what I see. What yall doin beb?"

"Chairly, get down the stairs."

"Soame whin you commin to lisen to what I did already?"

When he did not answer, she grumbled her way back, while they proceeded, with Beverly in the lead. Margaret began grabbing feels, until he put her in front of him. That was worse; she lagged, spoiling his view and concentration on Beverly, and at the first bump into Margaret, she grinned her complete lower dorsal onto him. He pushed her along, though she booted over, and wobbled enticingly, in the bikinis. Soame made it to the end of the hall, with both of them.

The room was saturated with the smell of marijuana. They all had also been doing continuous hits of powder. During a break, Margaret went over to take a hit from DD's pipe. Her back was to Soame, DD whispered something to her, she shook her fannie at him, and lowered her panties to expose the lower curvature of her cheeks. "Alright, that's enough, back to work. I see I can't be nice to you all. Can't you see, it's important that you learn this?"

Demonstrating the lift of the fallen object and the tray, from the floor, his shorts rose up his thigh, nearly half of his hard meat was exposed. DD said "Uh la la."

In attempts to lure him in every way they could, at that point they blatantly gestured to him, with enticements, without physically touching the erection on their minds. Finally, DD turned her back to him, and with her left hand, pulled the pin from her hair; it sprung to a flop, and dangled past her shoulders. At the same time, with her right hand, using her index finger, she guided the silk thong from between her cheeks, and pulled it to the side. When she looked over her shoulder, into the eyes transfixed on her, she was ushered to the window, and received the instructions to wait for the rapping. Soame left them.

When Beverly went up the hall alone, upon returning she delivered Chairly's message. Twice Chairly yelled down the hall for him. During the course of the afternoon, his mind reflected back to something she'd said one night in the bedroom, explaining she was the best bitch he had, other than DD. He had also given careful consideration, in an effort toward concentrated thought regarding the situation at the close of lunch that day; DD asked to take her liquor. That reflection drew flashes of guilt. He had allowed her to go on with the deformation in her speech. They were all his responsibility, and it was his position to have been more interested in the correction, long before that day at the motel. It was true, it could not be totally rectified in one day, but he had a more positive start again, and this time he would carry through with aiding her. Most impressive to him, were the words she used correctly in the doorway.

Just as compelling with lingering thought, was the song he heard the day before, for the first time. The lyrics and music were gripping, and soul binding. Over and over the record played. At the motel, over and over his mind reflected to: "I got to read between the lines, in case I need it when I'm older; I got no where left to hide, looks like love is finally over. Now this mountain I must climb, feels like the world's upon my shoulders." That's the way he played it, over and over in his mind, as an evasive tactic to combat the persuasiveness of the women in the room, mainly DD and Margaret. He had been a bachelor for a long time. Single men were scarce. A large percentage of black men were exterminated during the Vietnam War. The majority of those left in Soame's age group, who remained unmarried, were warehoused away in prisons, and some waisting their lives as junkies. Not overlooking a percentage of those survivors classed as gay, leaving a small percentage of a small percent. As a heterosexual, black, American, male, Soame Hudson stood as a very rare commodity. Being the true stud he survived as, he roamed in a domain of prominent uniqueness. Having a degree with a formal education, and being rich, classed him in a percentage so few, the people who knew of his existence, and had knowledge of these facts about him, marveled at the fact, he was real.

Under normal conditions, no real man could resist DD. Especially with her being out of her clothes, down to a sheer silk bra and a matching strip, she had to constantly replace over her vulva, as she explained, "Well you know the lips are big, so I have to do this." She gave him another demonstration, with a slight flex in her knees. "To keep this tiny thing in place, you see?" Each time she had done it, he could not help but to notice, and got around to asking "Why do you persist, on doing that?"

The long black hairs almost completely covered the material in her lower front. Her round bouncy cheeks lost the silk, as it lead from the top of her upper buttocks. He had never before attempted the slightest resistance for her; there was never before a reason. His reason presented an abnormality, motivating a resistance temporarily, toward the woman he felt the almost certainty, he was falling in love with.

Even though she was younger Chairly was becoming the domineering prevalence in the affair, between her and DD. The encounters between Chairly and Soame were in ways, somewhat trivial compared to the tongue lashings she and DD gave each other. The conduct did not start after meeting the Johnson's. Soame had long before then told DD, Chairly was her charge. He saw the relationship muster, and bloom into maturity. At the cabin they had run ins almost daily. DD had a casual way of handling her. Never having had younger brothers or sisters, and hardly any playmates, she attempted Soame's approach, without having his experience. In total, DD did not fail as a friend. As her lover Chairly gained leverage. With her strong will, keen insight, perseverance, and inate love making qualities, she began getting her way with DD, in all aspects. Verbally they fought like cats, in every house they lived in. Names were called, doors were slammed, and Fifi seemed to always be caught in a whirl, when during the times, both called almost at once. She never shunned her true mistress. That fact would always aggravate Chairly into either a stupor, or excel her tantrum. The times she remained away after their initial encounter, Chialry could be declared the victor, in the verbal spat. It was the times she reignited the relinquished discourse; each time in every way, she lost.

The brandish display of tempestuousness toward the siren woman, in the immediate rematch, every time brought Chairly the indignity of careless, clumsy, defeat. DD had been almost unrealistically fortunate in not having been slashed or stabbed in the streets of New Orleans, throughout her previous existence there. She had encountered the roughest street women on Bourbon and Canal Streets. The boyish style Chairly later developed with Beverly, was less than petty to DD. She had seen, known, and encountered true dikes, who not only pimped both men and women, but also in public places were respected as having casted their gender in the opposite direction. Being fully dressed and excepted as men, wearing loafers they used only men's facilities, without reluctance. It was nothing for DD to allow Chairly the mental uplift, in thinking she had won an argument. In fact, it was less than nothing, because she truly cared for her only female friend and lover. However, the lady of both houses they'd lived in would only sacrifice so much, to heighten the younger, inexperienced woman's morale. Once, at the cabin, in a furious flash of anger, DD pushed her. Chairly quailed, and Soame saw it was right judgment on DD's part, in proving to Chairly it wasn't a fluke occurrence, with the same direct challenge, while lashing her verbally, DD shoved her into her room, and ordered her not to come out for the remainder of the afternoon. That night Chairly used the bathroom; other than that, she did as she had been told.

The most apparent disheartening circumstance for Chairly, came about when she'd argue with DD, and Fifi would growl, yipe, and snapp at her. This she seem to barely be capable of handling. Inwardly, it tore her to pieces. Each time she would seek the solitude of her room, and boo hoo cry. The incidents also over rode the occasion on Elm Street, when DD slapped her. Soame was not at home during the day it happened. As Chairly, she illusioned being Soame, DD, or the "Boy Cherry." She was very dutiful toward any assignment given to her, but always wanted to handle what she did at her pace and leisure. Chairly detested being told what to do, and liked very much, issuing the instructions to others. Beverly never argued with her; she either did it, if it was right to do, or ignored Chairly. Always after an initial exchange of words, Margaret would "run" to DD. The majority of the times, Camille pretended Chairly did not exist. The one fact about her was, Chairly was the internal life of the house. From sonorous music, videos, scampering about with Fifi, lolly gagging in the kitchen, cleaning and instructing, Chailry kept things going.

It was very good and positively to her best interest she contained herself physically, and did not strike back at DD. Not only would she have lost her fight, Soame would have definitely put her out, after either witnessing or hearing about it. It would have been immediate, without explanation, and DD nor would anyone else would've had opposing influence against the decision. All of them knew there was to be "No physical fighting, ever; under no circumstance will there be an excuse." It was as nonreproachable as other laws they all knew, could not be violated. They all knew also, DD would not be surpassed or replaced. She was not their biological mother or sister. Except for Beverly, she was their lover. She was a friend to all of them. Soame remained silent in their affairs, for those reasons He could not tell them how to love each other; nor could he guide them through a friendship. They had structured harmony within the household understanding. Camille was satisfied and pleased, with coexistence of the two families, as one.

She did not hear him, then she saw him stepping on the third round of steps. Chairly sprung to her feet, "What took you so long? I been callin an I sent fa you to , Soame um ready."

"Yea I know, get out cha clothes."

Verbally responding with the unbuttoning of the silk shirt, in a downcast way she told him, "I don learned all that, an um usin it to, but you don't cae. Soame why you hab me do all this, an you don evin lov me?"

She held the chair, placing the toe on the heel of one of the loafers, in taking it off. "Turn on the recorder."

Chairly happily did as she'd been instructed, and continued to undress. The rendition would have lasted seven minutes. Beneath her designer baggy pants, she had on expensive flashy under garments. He instructed her to remove the garder belt and stockings. When it was done Soame turned off the recorder, saying to Chairly, "Sit down. You owe me 140 apologies from Monday, give me 10." He had not dressed, she reached into the fly of his boxers, extracted the instrument, and began with fellation.

After completing the number with her verbal delivery, he told her to position herself with a stance over the table. "I do all this, an you kan evin sae to me you luv me."

She had extended her hands on the top of the table, toward it's center, and was bent over for entry. Lowering her panties he said, "Spread your legs bitch, whatch you mean, you don't wanna gimmie no pussy?"

"You my man Soame, I got no right."

"I told you I wanted you to be able to read what's on that paper, to help improve your speech, is that what I told you?"

"Thas what you sade."

"Well I also said I wanted to do it to help you, somehow you missed that part, but I want you ta get your mind right, with the bullshit that's commin out a yo mouth! Get that paper, get on over like you were, and start reading." He massaged and entered her.

Placing the paper in front of her as a pretense, she began reciting. He soon realized the feigned act of her part, through the movement of her head. She became instantly involved with their copulatory actions, and always, assisted with every manageable rhythmic move she could produce. Repeating the words, while shaking her head wildly, she tossed her body whipping slings of rotational rivets, pulsating drives, hunches, and swirls. Within two minutes she'd stopped the recitation, and began talking sexually to him; it was the beginning of her first orgasm. Within ten minutes she was commencing with her third eruption. He pulled himself out of her. "No, no, pleeze no, um a do it Soame I swea, anythin, don stop, pleeze."

Of all that which she wasn't, Chairly was everything Soame expected her to be. She met his expectations of her, to the letter. He had known many men who did not have the courage she had. She was arrogant with pride, self willed, adjustable to any situation he'd ever placed her in, highly intelligent, blossoming into beauty, and most important, respectful. It amazed him to see her approach the boardring point in a situation, tilt, as if she would go beyond the illegal point of demarcation, totter on the fringe, and retreat back into safety. She was that daringly courageous, without foolishness. Chairly always displayed an interest to find out what they other side was like. Her most favorable impression on Soame, was her disinterest in the pipe. He knew when DD started her to smoking; it lasted two days. On her own Chairly sustained her composition as a refrainer. She was rough and feminine, and would wear a dress for him, as quickly as she would put on pants for DD and Beverly. He was her only male friend and lover. She placed no one she'd ever known or knew, higher than her realistic thoughts of Soame. This was basically always the unspoken understood catalyst, motivating friction between her and DD. The three of them totally understood each other. She'd earned a place in his life, and kept a spot near his heart. With him, only she shared a culture none of the other others could claim; of their immaterial possessions, it ranked highest of all.

"You gon do it thar? Ant no KY jelly. Let me call Beb."

"You don't need her, you know what to do."

"Ooooh lawdy." She'd been sodomized before, but neither of the times had she done it without DD stimulating her with cunnilingus. It was an extremely delicate and precise, erotic art. Soame directed Chairly into her gratification, and through her own judgment, she masturbated and stayed the height of their ejaculation, until she felt the swell of his knot. It was done with meticulousness, they climaxed together. Chairly was greatly satisfied; she flopped on the table. After easing out of her, Soame went toward the shower calling her. When he'd taken a few steps, and did not hear her reply, he turned slightly and looked back at her. Sleepy eyed, she was looking over her shoulder at him. "Um commin, it was toooo good Soame."

After retaining her explosion, when she did erupt she drained, with the most intense and longest lasting orgasm she'd ever had. The young woman had become exhaustingly weak as a result. It was far better than the three of them participating, because of her regulating herself. He left her sprawled on the able top. After adjusting the water temperature in the bathroom, he went back and assisted her to the shower. The intensity of the overly sustained explosion and geyser type continued eruption, freed her thought in accomplishment and exploration of sex. It was barely audible, but in leaving her on the table, after he took one step, she said "I luv you Soame, thas why you my man."

It was their first shower together, ever. Soame had never before seen Chailry so lively and pleasingly humorous. They splashed suds, tickeld each other, and playfully fondled one another's body. The two washed each other's back and genitals. With the loveliness, Chailry was also tenderly inviting, with her intimate inducing. Soame became aroused, but knew there was another purpose, which was the principle reason for them being at the motel. She did not want to understand, and pleaded with him while he dried himself. "No, I've told you I have something else to do."

"Well gimmie my money thin."

"You'd better get your ass outa here."

"You don busted it all up Soame, gimmie my money."

"Do I look like I've got some money on me, get dressed."

Putting on his shorts, he sent her upstairs for his pants, sweater, and tennis. Soame was pulling his sweater over, when Chairly reached for her garder belt. He had already directed her to the front, downstairs room, to join the others. "You don't need that. Why do you wear it and stockings, with pants, any how?"

"Cause das da-"

"Alright now, keep talking that jive, and find yourself in 7th grade, in a week or so."

"School won opin that soon. This is the way ladies dress. Cause day neva kno whin thea man might com callin. Gimmie my money Soame."

"A true lady never asks her man for money, because she knows he knows what his responsibility is toward her needs."

"Well you sho act lack you tryin to get outta hea dout meetin yo sponsobility. Soame I need my money. I shooda got it foe I took off my close, lack DD sade; den I would na had this problem."

"Stop talking that ho talk to me; you wanna be a ho?"

"You sade I don haf ta be, long as I live unda yo roof."

"Well, then what's the problem?"

"The problim is I don habe my money, gimmie my money Soame."

"Tell your ole man ta come get it." He walked out, and closed the door.

Chapter 12

SOAME went down the corridor to the breezeway, up the stairs, and to the security room. The room's biggest renovated feature entailed a miniature picture window. The mirrored plexoglass window allowed a clear view across the hall and railing, to the two convex mirrors in the upper extremities of both ends of the breezeway. The curved mirrors allowed visual monitoring of any and all parts of the breezeway's activities.

A single bed replaced the original double bed set up. The window was constructed into the farmost corner of the northern wall. Next to it, on the back wall, was an intercom panel. A 1 ½' counter extended from the wall, under the window, and intersected the back wall, under the panel. In the room was a chair under the counter, and a red flood lamp above the picture window. The interior fixtures included another flood lamp between the door and the room's regular picture window; it was green. Also in the room was a blue flood lamp on the southern wall, near the bathroom entrance. The renovated atmosphere also contained a regular office desk, away from the counter, along the northern wall, but not in the corner. On the desk was a telephone with three lines. Only the motel line ran through the motel's switchboard. Security had it's private line, and the company line had it's set up, with a line in the security room. With the addition of a floor lamp, everything else in the security room was standard, and the original motel design, with a fresh paintjob.

Entering the room, he noticed the flood lights. The switch in the room downstairs had not been turned off. The primary function of the security room, centered around the protection of the people in that room, while they were at the window at work. Soame left the door open, walked over and turned on the air conditioner. The only control switch for the flood lights was down stairs, in the room at the service window. The flood lights was the silent alarm. The 400 watt lamps created heat in the room. He looked at the counter, and carried a button to "on," in the panel. The systems were basically simple for their practical purpose. The intercom, with a radio, featured a volume control knob, regulating tone for the buttons, "talk" and "monitor." The installing technician was to have allowed the radio to be played with the monitoring. He told Pete his mistake in not doing so. When the information was relayed to Soame, it was then decided to operate the monitor without the radio, until the women at the window became accustomed through experience, with their responsibilities. It was the first time Soame had been in the room, after the installation of the systems. The brief observation allowed him to plan a correction toward the monitor and radio. The radio would have only been aired, if it was on. His immediate thoughts were toward a light at the window, indicating them being monitored. To that point, the technician's mistake had been a beneficial one. Soame was casual in his observations, and with pride he seated himself at the counter. He had pride in his accomplishments at the motel, but a huge percentage of his pride came from his feelings toward the women downstairs, and the one at the realty office. Those who worked with him that day boosted his pride in accomplishment. He was proud of them, all of them; they worked well, they were a team that had never worked together before. He was very satisfied with what they all did. He took a joint from a pack of menthols, and placed the vile and straw in front of him.

The button he activated was the monitor. It was evident the door dividing the room downstairs was still open. Within a minute after he "keyed" in on them, Chailry came down the stairs. Soame turned the volume up. It seemed the others were pleased to have her join them, except for the silence from Margaret. Finally, when she did speak, it was a question. "He's been gone for more than forty-five minutes, what have you two been doing?"

"Chille, my ole man took me round the worl! He trabels honny, you ought ta try it sometime, all yall."

There were laughs, and for twenty minutes he smoked, snorted, and eavesdropped on their prat talks and elaborations on the window, stairs, and hall. Three times Chairly was taken to the window. Twice the flood lights went out, and directly back on. Twice the door was closed; once for better than five minutes. During that time, with the extent of the volume, he could barely hear them.

Soame had never before heard DD's imitation of him, before that day. It turned out to be the highlight and conclusion of his listening in: as they often did, DD chatted with Chairly in French, though Margaret and Beverly were beginners with a rapid growing interest, they understood enough to get the gist of what was being said. This was more than Soame cared about learning, or really paid attention to, until he heard DD attempt a harsh crimpy sound. He then heard Margaret's name with the remainder of the quotation in English, exactly as he'd said it, telling Margaret to open the talk button to "on," saying "Hardy ha, ha, ha. It's really good to know you all are having so much fun, during your first day at work; this is called orientation."

"Soame, whea sa neva you is, I wont my money!"

"Suarme, where are you?"

"I'm upstairs in the security room. It's the first room upstairs, toward the parking lot, on the way to the office. The speaker is there over the window for a particular reason. The reason is the voice amplifier, there in the center of the window. Maragaret and Beverly, can you hear me also?"

"Hi Soame,"

"We hear ya."

"Good, now can both of you also see the three inch circle, with screen and strips of metal in it?"

"We see it."

"Alright now lis- will one of you hit the switch and tur- great thanks. That switch is controlled only from that room. Sometime later I'll bring you up here, and let you see what exactly it is you will be in collaboration with from this room. Right now I want you to know about this monitoring device. It picks up all the sounds from the room there. This talk switch over rides yours, in the small panel, opposite the alarm switch. When it is not on, to get the attention of a security personal member, who will be on duty in this room any time the window is in service, you move your talk button to on, and say what you've called for. Does everyone understand that?"

Beverly replied, "When we want security we press the button and talk, or turn the light switch on." There were giggles, and he distinctly heard DD clear her throat.

"You're right and wrong Bev. The alarm switch is as indicated, an alarm. The people or person in this room, will have gone through a drill, and received instructions on what to do, in reacting to the alarm, don't play Chicken Little, alright?"

"Got it Soame."

"I'll be down in a min-"

The doorway shadowed. It was Pete. "Well hello stranger."

"Pete, how are you?"

"I'm fine, as long as I keep makin these pay days. I stopped by the office ta drop those checks off for the scrap metal; they totaled a bit more than $4,600.00 Mrs. Johnson said she needed them before four. I found out you were here. I just gave the drafts to Neil. He likes the barn style idea, and says he'll look at um with you over the weekend. I've gotta get back and knock the crews off, they want ta get paid." Both men looked at their watches, it was 3:40.

"Does everything check out with you here?"

"It seems to be fine; I haven't had time for a thorough check. We'll take an hour next week, when both of us are here. So far, it looks pretty good; I'm pleased. You all haven't disappointed me yet. I don't think you will. Do you know if the wood's been delivered? Phil said he'd have it here late this afternoon, or first thing Monday morning."

"I saw it; it's here and so is the sand: Neil said it came about an hour ago."

"Good, then the bricks and cement will be on schedule first thing Monday."

"Neil's excited as stepped on fire ants, but… we've got some pretty big pieces in the foundry. And ta avoid the possibility of what happened yesterday, takin place again, can I get a tow motor in there, we're gonna put three more men in there Tuesday, give you three with the fence, and put ten on the barn with Jake. Tuesday, we want him out of the house, if you all aren't finished. I want you and him on this fence and barn; get this area out of the way. When Yohansen starts on Elm Street, your fence should be done."

"Your crew joins Yohansen; by then Jake should have the foundation and corners laid, perhaps a course or two up, with the added man power. He, a couple of masons and helpers and finish the job from there. That'll throw all the other men on Elm; snatch as many men then, as you can out of the foundry. With the lift and the added men – have um send another truck and driver when you call Pete. I want that foundry finished, so the planners and that electrician can get right at what they come to do. That house has got to come down, and the club should go up, before anybody really knows what's going on, you've got the man power, can you handle it?"

"Which one of those lines boss?"

"It's Soame Pete, Soame. The middle line is the company line."

Pete was on the phone five minutes, making the arrangements for expedient efficiency in clearing the foundry. During the time, Soame used the bathroom. He had walked out, and was standing at the counter, about to sit, when Pete finished ordering. "It's all done. They only have a dumper available; it's a sixteen yarder with tandem axles. The 'Toe Mo' with the trailer will come with it."

"Sounds good. Now listen, when you go by to pick your check up–"

Soame made a swift move to the phone, called Camille, and instructed

Camille to give Pete the applications of the men who appeared at the office that morning. The AM factor was injected because throughout the day, a total of 24 men had been to the office. She'd already told him how busy the phone had been. In mentioning the 16 had already been marked "hire," she told Soame how Pete was swamped by stragglers, with pleas. Pete had gotten to be a big man in town. In the area, all the people knew practically everyone else.

The insurance forms would be turned in Monday. Pete was instructed to take the applications home, and during the weekend arrange for site placement of the new men, according to their qualifications. Excpeting the task he asked, "Say is that pot over there? I thought I smelled a trace of it, when I stepped in. Must be pretty good; wasn't too much smell to it."

"Yea, want some?"

"I'd sure appreciate it. Haven't had any good herb since I left the south."

"Here, take a couple joints. Monday I'll give you an ounce or two; keep it to yourself. Anything else you'll have to get from the window downstairs. Um gonna open it a week from Sunday."

"Hay thanks boss. I'll take care everything; have a good weekend and I'll see ya then Soame."

"You to, later Pete."

His original intent was not to leave the "key" open. The decision was impromptu. Rather than be discourteous to the women, he allowed them to listen in, hoping they wouldn't reveal themselves. He was pleased they didn't. Far more than that fact they had a chance to hear and visualize his projection toward a male, however, allowing them to eavesdrop, and the encounter with Pete was merely something to have happen, by chance, and done not to influence them one way or the other. Never the less, it was most impressive. Neither of them had before seen or heard him discuss business.

Even though she was not there, Camille's view was more broad, and she saw with more depth and perspective, his accomplishments toward the immediate goals and the overall idea. It had been the busiest day ever at the office. She was bubbling with pride. Not only did Camille have the checks Pete told him about, Mrs. Tillman relayed the news through her from the placement agency in New Hampshire. It would be a welcomed surprise for them all.

In twelve minutes, Soame unraveled their sensitivities, putting them in gear and in touch with their responsibility toward the overall operation. "You all still there?"

"We're here, and even heard the flushing of the toilet. Suarme, do you think it is such a good idea to have this room so carefully monitored? Girls like to talk you know."

"It'll only be for a week or so. When everyone becomes familiar with the operations involved, I'll have a red light installed, to indicate when the monitor is in operation."

"We goa get paid for dis? And I wont my money from today!"

"I told you to send your ole man for it. Listen, I'm shutting this down, and coming to the window. Bev, I want you to get dressed, call your mother from the phone in the accounting room, and tell her you coming home to help her with dinner. Take Fifi with you, it's about time for her walk. DD you're going to have to take Chairly through the drills. I'll be down in a minute."

There was a bolt near each end of the square shield, over the window. The round head of each bolt had an exact fitting into a 1/16" indentation in the aluminum, and extended through the wall of the building, into the booth. Four large wings nuts unfastened the concealment. One by one the nuts were unscrewed, from the inside. He held the plate in position while extracting the last 10" bolt. After leaning the shield against the wall, placing the bolts next to it, Soame raised to the mirrored window, just above is waist, reflecting his upper torso. The round activator was just below his mouth. "Can you hear me in here?"

"Yea, we hea you cheapskate, put my money in da tube, ar ya don git nothing outa dis winda, ar frum eny a us."

He took his clip from his pocket, and extracted three hundred dollar bills, plainly for them to see. They had a downward view, and in revolving the mouth of the cylinder to him, they saw Soame mistakably drop one of the bills. He stooped to pick it up, and when he rose they saw him carry the three bills to the mouth of the tube. Chairly pulled the leaver down, and the mouth of the canister revealed a burning cigarette. "Chille dis a shut down, I knoed he was gonna do somthin lack dat. Com on DD, wees spose ta go don we?"

That was all he heard. Fifteen seconds later, there was still no sound. In a normal tone he said, "I didn't hear the door slam." Another interval later, there was still no sound. Soame leaned to the mirror, placed both hands to shade his eyes, from the sides of his face, in an attempt to peer through the mirror. "Boo!!" the four of them shouted, really catching him off guard. Beverly stayed to see what the outside would look like. It was after seven, when the remaining four arrived home. During dinner the family received news from Camille, a butler was available with the best of credentials, and statements of recommendation. The Concord agency also had an excellent maid with prestigious recommendations, and the two came only as a pair. She had given consent to "secure them by all means," and left instructions to be forwarded, that the arrangements for their travel would be made no later than by noon Monday. Following the meal, Soame went directly to bed.

Saturday, between intercoursing sessions with Camille, he slept all day. At 6:00 that evening, Soame was at the Yates farm, in the Seville. Within an hour he saw the pride in Billy's face, in having more cash money at once, than he'd ever before seen in his life. All of his quarters had been sold; there were only sixteen dimes left. The majority of it had been sold to one person. "Man this guy's got at thing about tryin ta buy me out. Each time he asks 'How much you got left?' I'd tell him, as long as you got the cash, I got the snow." The next night he'd meet me at 9:00 at the turn in, and wham!"

"Yea, well how long you been knowin this dude?"

"Ahhh, don't even worry about it Soame. He's bought grass from me for three years. He works at the hydro plant in Miles City. Last year I drove to his place a couple of times, cause times were hard, and I sold him ounces of weed. He's always been a good customer cause he hustles it off."

Because they were still harvesting, Billy hadn't been to Berrydale. He paid Soame $1,500.00 and received the largest package he'd gotten, to that point. Billy was shown how to keep the tab Soame made, on his account. "Berrydale swings on the weekends man. I got people waitin for me."

Soame gave him the news about the window, and instructed him it would be open, "Next Sunday at 7:00 AM, until 1:00 the next morning. Everyday, from then on, it'll be open from 7-1, and on Friday and Saturday, nights, it'll be open around the clock, if your parents allow Cathy and Jenny to work. It won't hurt you, because I'll make our dimes and quarters just a little bigger; you spread the word." Without a bath, Billy was on his way to the small community, which housed two "jukes" and a small restaurant. Soame drove more than sixty miles with Cathy and Jenny, to enjoy a drive in movie.

Sunday he slept until 10:00, when he was awakened through arousement, administered by Camille. She insisted he remain in bed, which he did, and she served him breakfast at 11:30. DD took the others for an afternoon ride, and except for the use of the bathroom, the dozen during a manicure, and had intermittent sleeps between love making sessions with Camille. At 4:30 they all had an enjoyable dinner, and the co-op meeting was at 5:00.

There were nine candidates to join the farming organization. They included two of Yohansen's sons, and three men who were working with Thad, plus two who were working with Tom. Billy presided and did a very good job of explaining the functional purpose of the cooperative. He had read the guideline book on parliamentary procedure, and in carrying through the course of the meeting, they were directed to "new business." It could not be decided who had been waiting to verbally engage the other in conflicting confrontation, but Thad and Tom had their chance, and the inevitable showdown was enabled.

The issue presented was crop rotation. The two men met each others challenge with significant meaningful input on rotating crops. All of the men in the room were wheat farmers, except Soame who owned and farmed more land than the others. Rotating crops in wheat fields are clover, corn, oats, timothy, and soybeans. Subs cops in Montana are barley, hay, potatoes, and sugar beats. Tom favored barley, if the rotational plan was to go into effect the following season, but "it is ridiculous and almost insane to grow anything but wheat, with the prices so favorable at the exchange!"

"Building the soil, through the productive growth of other crops, enables a better wheat crop ta sell at the exchange. There's a season for all things; we grow wheat, and winter wheat. By rotating we get better wheat or better winter wheat, plus the price of the crop we use for rotation."

Bickering between the area's two top land cultivators lasted more than forty minutes. They wrangled with tension, back and forth on the subject of rotation, presenting ideas about barley in conjunction with, and being opposed to corn, soybeans, and oats. Other members added their input. It was both an agriculture and a history lesson for Soame. He learned that barley's history dated back as far as the history of civilized man, with a beginning in Egypt. It is Montana's second largest farming crop; the state is third in America with it's production, and the U.S. ranks second to the Soviets, in the world market with the crops out put. Because it grows best in cool climates, Tom preferred it over corn, oats, soybeans, sugar beats, and potatoes. Soame added the word hectar to his vocabulary, as the Yohansen used it as a description of their land holdings. The none farming land owning member also discovered the value of 53,767 worms that are essential in each acre of farm land. He pieced together words he had previously been exposed to such as tillers, crown, tubers, spikelets, and fallow, with coherence to the issue, involved in the heated debate.

Occasionally Billy sounded the gavel requesting order. Three farmers were not present, which would have comprised all the farmers in the county. The largest acreage owned by an individual was 720 acres, of the smaller farmers at the meeting, proportions varied to 140 acres. Rotation effected the small farmers because of the lesser price the sub crop would pay. Though they had made money the previous season, they were still heavily in debt. None of them had cleared their mortgages. When Tom brought the focal point to narrowness, and beamed in on the small farmer, they can't afford to rotate this coming season, because," etc. Thad became furious. "Of all the gall and contemptuous neve you have the audacity to attempt ta mention consideration for the small farmers!" Billy rapped the gavel repeatedly. Three other men moved in the path of the two men, who'd began stepping toward each other, from opposite ends of the table. The sergeant at arms, brushed past men and plowed over a chair in his path, in the crowded room. Above the yelling of the two restrained men, and the grumbles and mumbles of the other members, a voice was heard motioning for a recess. Half of the men at once second the remedy toward confusion. The door was immediately opened, after Billy announced, "this meeting will stand in recess for the next fifteen minutes," and struck his gavel. Men poured out of the room.

Soame ushered Tom out of the door, with him saying, "confound it!!! How dare he talk to me that way!" A few paces toward the breezeway Tom inquired, "You've been telling and inviting me to the office you have here; well I'd sure like to use it during this spell, in privacy." While he manipulated the key from his ring, directing Tom to the dining room entrance, he concluded, "at the close fo the meeting, I want you to wait for me at the real estate office; it's urgent and extremely important. I'll be tied up here for a little while, but I will be directly there." That seemed to both cool and excite Tom." I'll be there."

"That bar is upstairs."

"Thanks old buddy." That implication, toward their friendship, excited Soame.

His reentry into the room, through the open door, put him face to face with Billy. "I was just coming out to see ya. I've got somethin in the wagon for ya. Man what a brawl ha?"

"That's as close as any of us want to come to getting out of hand. You handled it really well. Let's take care of that, when the meetings over; I've got to talk with your dad about something right now."

"Sure thing man. Um gonna smoke a roach I got, and do a toot."

Billy had been moderating from the head of the table, opposite the door. As secretary, Tom had been seated first in position from the chairman. With Soame on the opposite end, nearest the door, Thad purposely sat away from the secretary, first in position from Soame. In total, eight people had been seated at the conference table. Chairs had been brought in to accommodate the other candidates, who had been expected and joined. Thad was at the end of the table where Billy had been presiding. He was flanked by three other farmers; two of them Soame had met for the first time that evening. Soame's approach and presence was acknowledged with an invitation into the conversation. "I've listened to you and Tom very carefully, as I'm sure everyone else has. I'm sure we all agree, that is one of the purposes of this organization and this meeting…but Thad, and if you gentlemen won't think rude of me, I'd like to call your attention to something upstairs I want to show you during the break, and"—Thad motioned the interruption with his hand. " I saw your back when you left out, and when I saw you talkin with that boy of mine, I said we might have some business to discuss, when I saw you walkin this way. Think we got time?" Will you all excuse us?" Soame had made a move to the steps. Thad tugged on the chain holding his pocket watch, while trailing him; they had eleven minutes.

They went through the lounge, without explanation. Soame hit the hall switch, in opening the door, and stepping across the narrow hall opening and entering the room, he began explaining, in his turn to Thad. The winter months, in the event Cathy and Jenny became stranded from home due to snow, was the focal point and brief definition of the room. He explained the lounge while striding and turning down the hall. Descending the steps Soame began explaining the divided room. Thad was shown the slam lock, with the indication to the one at the top of the stairs, and the entire operation of the booth was explained the demonstrated. On the way back up the hall Soame explained the "last resort security precaution." Leaving Thad in the hall, he entered the lounge hit the switch, and five seconds later, Thad was entering the lounge form the blackened hall. They were in the lounge nearly two minutes, when Billy called up, "Paw, we're about ready ta start."

In calling the resumption of the order, the president of the organization, as presiding chairman, respectfully acknowledged both men and their positions toward the issue holding the floor, and reminded them of the "respect we expect from ya both toward yaselvs, each other, and not only us, but also this meeting and our purpose here, to plan and function as a group…Mr. Blanchard, I acknowledge you havin the floor, before the interruption and our recess; if you care ta continue, this chair allows you that chance."

Soame looked at Thad. Pride poured out from within him in all directions. He looked back at Soame, and with the eye contact, he gave a slight quaint smile, a hardly noticeable shrug of his shoulders, and turned back toward the direction which Tom was rising to a stand. Tom's delivery was on point and direct. All of them were heavily mortgaged. As wheat farmers they were prepared to raise wheat crops. Barley could also be planted, cultivated, and harvested with the same equipment, which they'd been using all their lives. He gave a brief history of the lands and farming development, from the days of it's early settlement, with Caucasians, who grew barley. The majority of the farmers in the room lasted as survivors not only because they farmed, but they also owned clay loams. These rich tracts of naturally fertile land, feed into that sector of Montana, as extensions form the Dakotas. He concluded "ecology is fine, toward the preservation and future use of the land we live on, and soil we work to earn our living. There is a time for all things. We can not eat the word ecology. You can not water sugar beats, hay and potatoes with the word ecology, and it costs to irrigate. The rich land we farm has been here, and two years from now, when we've better lifted ourselves from the debt we're bogged in, it'll be here for the proposed rotational plan. In the meantime, we grow wheat and barley, and feed our families."

Except for three, every other man in the room became a mutterer, as Tom took his seat. The utterances rumbled through the atmosphere, and were hushed with the sound of the gavel. "Ah, Paw….would you like to say something?"

"Mr. Chairman, in view of the fact we all are attemptin ta get our winter crops planted, and there are meetings scheduled between now and next spring, which'll enable us to further evaluate the use of the rotational plan I'm proposin, I motion we leave the issue for now, to be continued at another time, and get on with the next in order for new business." The motion was seconded without opposition

During the following hour and half, the nine men who'd been given applications made their submissions, and in doing so, and stating their concern toward the organization, became full-fledged members of the co-op. Seven of them needed assistance to get a winter crop of wheat in the grown. One of the men managed to save his farm, but to afford the expense of caring and providing for his family, he lost a valuable piece of equipment, which had also been mortgaged. It wasn't the bank, but the mortgage he'd acquired came through the federal supplemental assistance program. Without the spring-tooth harrow that had been confiscated, he could not prepare his land for planting. "I'm not ashamed ta tell ya, I gathered my crop, and like mite near everyone else, I rushed it ta the exchange. I paid on my note and was left with a choice. I could starve my family, and plant for the winter with hope, or put food on the table and make it ta this meetin the Swede told me about. Me and my family is fine so far; I go the same hope in this co-op, as I would have had in that harrow I lost."

There was no initiation or neophyte standing toward the brotherhood. The organization was not fraternal, but there was a fellowship with a shake of hands with each member, in acceptance. Except for the Yohansens, every new member came to the cooperative for support. Except for their word of good faith, they could not offer collateral. Because all the farmers knew each other, Thad motioned for each new member to receive attestation from a standing member in his support; it was second and the procedure was carried through. A financial report was then requested by the president. $15,000.00 had been deposited to set up an account at the local bank, for the organization. Tom rattled off expenses that whittled at the finance in escrow, for twenty minutes, equipment rental, fuel, seed, repairs, and labor. Six of the men in the room were on salary, working as laborers with either Tom or Thad. In finalizing the report, the secretary gave a figure amounting to less than $3,000.00 remaining in the account.

The money had served it's intended purpose well. Soame and Thad had wheat stored, to be shipped to the exchange. Thad was still harvesting, with a crop of sugar beats to finish off his harvest. Tom had planted wheat and potatoes. The other small farmers had began the preparation of the fields, to plant winter wheat. Nonetheless, with all the indications toward future prosperity, there was less than $3,000.00 to be divided between seven men, who were as desperate as the men in the previous meeting, in setting up the organization; all but one.

When the floor was open to suggestions, some of the men looked toward the opposite end of the table, from the president, who recognized the raised hand. "Mr. Moderator, I motion a proposal." It was the sergeant at arms, the most supportive member, and organizer of the group. Every one looked in his direction, as he stood and spoke. "We've all heard both the circumstance of our newly excepted members, and our financial position. It is hardly imaginable for the moneys we have left, to be held in reserved support of our immediate needs, including the continuation of salaries, and be used in the support of the dire need, expressed by the members taken into our fellowship. My proposal is in having the seven men submit an itemized list of costs to you Mr. President, by the close of daylight, Wednesday. This list can be given to you by phone, but must have, in total comparison to the signed statement you must have, your records should reflect 'an anonymous' loan to this organization, in support of its members, for the fulfillment of it's purpose. I say to you new, fellow members; there will be no excepted excuse offered as reason, as to your not meeting the obligation to yourselves, in not having the mentioned list to the chairman before you, by sundown Wednesday. Should that be done by phone, at sundown Saturday, if the written list is not in the hands of the president or the vice president, the verbal communication becomes invalid, and that person failing to do so is then disqualified for this proposed support."

"Mr. Chairman, I motion this proposal be carried as 'unfinished business,' and in future meetings we arrive at a means of securing reimbursement, after the payment of their mortgages, moneys then due this co-op, supporting them as an active member." Thad immediately seconded all two proposals and the motion. Finding no opposition, Billy sounded the gavel to adjourn. "Wait up a minute there Billy, I've got to get this all in." It was Tom, writing feverishly, recording his minutes. When he was almost done he directed a question to Soame, "Soame would you care to disclose the amount of the loan at this time?"

"Mr. Chairman, may I have the floor reopened, to present a late motion at this time?"

"The Chair recognizes Soame Hudson, and his request. The floor is now therefore open to hear his motion."

"I motion a recorder be afforded for the secretary." Tom hastily seconded, and brought laughter throughout the room. "10,000.00 Tom."

Following the meeting, and while the room cleared, Soame made a brief call to Neil, and arranged to see him first thing the following morning. After securing the accounting room Thad and Billy went with him to the security room. Thad was impressed with the provisions, and spoke favorably toward the idea of the study lounge for homework, as well as congratulating Soame for having the insight for the coming winter. "We do get stranded often, between December and late February." Billy was watching and listening with $2,500.00. He could not put the cash he was carrying in his pockets; he had it in a brown paper bag.

Had he been to Berrydale, he would have sold out, according to his calculations. As president, Billy could not miss the meeting. "Also, I like the idea of them havin jobs. As good as the crops look, with the unbelievable price the exchange is offerin, we'll need the added income. Times are changin, and I really don't mind them workin…Soame even though you're carryin us through a crisis, it's goin ta boil down ta what I told ya before. We'll just have ta see what Darlíne says."

Tom and Soame drove out to the Blanchard farm. During the return trip, Tom mentioned his insurance policy. "So what's your life insurance policy got to do with it?"

"Well, you see that's as close as I ever want to come to using it."

"Come on dude! You're not suicidal, and I know that for a fa"—"No silly! I was going to use it for a loan. My parents had one since I was a kid. I continued to pay the premium after they passed. It's the one thing I did not disturb. The cash loan value would have bailed us out of here, with transportation. I know Willis was in a strain too; I could have gotten this, or a good deal on something else, for little or nothing. Where, I'm not sure, but Janet can get a job anywhere. I would've use the money to set us up, and with the three of us working, Cindy would have gone to school next semester, if it had to be at a nearby junior college."

"I didn't know that about insurance policies."

"Only life insurance Soame, and don't ever try it, but you'll never need the loan."

"Hold on, why never try it?"

"Because once you borrow the money, the policy becomes worthless, unless you pay it back. 90% of the people who borrow their policies die, before the policy is arranged to pay dividends. My loan wouldn't have in no way matched what you've done for her. It's far beyond my conception, with anticipation on getting her into school. I'm so happy I can shout! I can hardly wait until tomorrow." The Irish sitter between them, licked Tom's face.

It was almost 11:00 when he arrived home. A kilogram of cocaine contains 1,000 grams. That night, the six of them made up 500 dimes, and 500 quarters. Camille went to bed at 4:00. Except for four ounces, Soame had put a one on the "key." The others were still making halves, when Camille left for work, at 7:50. It was another step within the beginning of the beginning. The initial ten days of Soame's arrival into the town, and the last ten days to that point, were most important for him. Those time periods set into the establishment of his projections. His structural development was all gathered, and about to be launched toward the substantial progress and accomplishments he envisioned. The arrival was from the sunny skies of Florida, to the big sky country in Montana, he motioned for a better placement in society.

-30-

Printed in the USA/Agawam, MA
October 5, 2010

554458.001